HUMAN RESOURCE MANAGEMENT IN SPORT AND RECREATION

Third Edition

HUMAN RESOURCE MANAGEMENT IN SPORT AND RECREATION

Third Edition

Packianathan Chelladurai, PhD
Troy University

Shannon Kerwin, PhD
Brock University

HUMAN
KINETICS

Library of Congress Cataloging-in-Publication Data

Names: Chelladurai, P., author. | Kerwin, Shannon, 1981- author.
Title: Human resource management in sport and recreation / Packianathan
    Chelladurai, Shannon Kerwin.
Description: Third edition. | Champaign, IL : Human Kinetics, [2017] |
    Includes bibliographical references and index.
Identifiers: LCCN 2016034635 | ISBN 9781492535850 (print) | ISBN 9781492548225 (e-book)
Subjects: LCSH: Sports administration. | Personnel management.
Classification: LCC GV713 .C5 2017 | DDC 796.06/9--dc23 LC record available at https://lccn.loc.gov/2016034635

ISBN: 978-1-4925-3585-0 (print)

The web addresses cited in this text were current as of January 2017, unless otherwise noted.

Senior Acquisitions Editor: Myles Schrag
Acquisitions Editor: Bridget Melton
Developmental Editor: Katherine Mauer
Senior Managing Editor: Carly S. O'Connor
Managing Editor: Ann Lan Seaman
Copyeditor: Tom Tiller
Indexer: Nan N. Badgett
Permissions Manager: Dalene Reeder
Graphic Designer: Julie L. Denzer
Cover Designer: Keith Blomberg
Senior Art Manager: Kelly Hendren
Illustrations: © Human Kinetics, unless otherwise noted
Printer: Sheridan Books

Printed in the United States of America   10 9 8 7 6 5 4 3 2 1

The paper in this book is certified under a sustainable forestry program.

Human Kinetics
Website: www.HumanKinetics.com

United States: Human Kinetics
P.O. Box 5076
Champaign, IL 61825-5076
800-747-4457
e-mail: info@hkusa.com

Canada: Human Kinetics
475 Devonshire Road Unit 100
Windsor, ON N8Y 2L5
800-465-7301 (in Canada only)
e-mail: info@hkcanada.com

Europe: Human Kinetics
107 Bradford Road
Stanningley
Leeds LS28 6AT, United Kingdom
+44 (0) 113 255 5665
e-mail: hk@hkeurope.com

E6873

To my friend, philosopher, and guide, Ponnu Chelladurai, who makes me tick.

—Packianathan Chelladurai

To Tom, Rachel, and Cameron—you inspire me in every way.

—Shannon Kerwin

Contents

Preface   xi
Acknowledgments   xiii

PART I

Human Resources in Sport and Recreation   1

1 Significance of Human Resources   3

Service Operations 7 • Sport and Recreation Services 12 • Paid and Volunteer Workers 15 • Clients as Human Resources 16 • A Model of Human Resource Management 17 • Chapter Pursuits 18

2 Volunteers and Volunteerism   21

The Need for Volunteerism 22 • Voluntary Organizations 29 • People Who Volunteer 32 • Why People Volunteer 34 • Altruism and Volunteerism 36 • Role of the Sport or Recreation Manager 39 • Chapter Pursuits 40

3 Professionals and Professionalism   43

Original Definition of a Profession 44 • Process of Professionalization 46 • Semiprofessions, Mimic Professions, and Deprofessionalization 48 • Professional Status of Sport Management 51 • Professionalism and Volunteerism 55 • Role of the Sport or Recreation Manager 58 • Chapter Pursuits 59

4 Clients as Human Resources   61

Customer as Input, Throughput, and Output 62 • Customer Participation in Sport and Recreation Services 63 • Client Motives for Participation 65 • Role of the Sport or Recreation Manager 69 • Chapter Pursuits 71

PART II

Individual Differences in Human Resources   73

5 Abilities   77

Issues in the Study of Ability 78 • Cognitive Abilities 79 • Emotional Intelligence 82 • Role of the Sport or Recreation Manager 85 • Chapter Pursuits 88

6 Personality   89

Determinants of Personality 90 • Type Theories 92 • Trait Theories 93 • Personality and Organizational Behavior 96 • Role of the Sport or Recreation Manager 105 • Chapter Pursuits 106

7 Values   **107**

Values, Beliefs, Attitudes, and Norms 108 • Sources of Values 110 • Terminal
and Instrumental Values 110 • Hierarchy of Values 112 • Value Types 112 •
Functions of Values 113 • Values in Organizations 116 • National Values
and Sport 121 • Role of the Sport or Recreation Manager 122 • Chapter
Pursuits 123

8 Motivation   **125**

A Model of Motivation 127 • Other Theories of Motivation 132 • Motivation
as Personal Investment 139 • Role of the Sport or Recreation Manager 142 •
Chapter Pursuits 143

PART III   Human Resource Practices   **145**

9 Organizational Justice   **147**

Distributive Justice 149 • Procedural Justice 158 • Interactional Justice 159 •
Role of the Sport or Recreation Manager 161 • Chapter Pursuits 163

10 Job Design   **165**

Job Design Strategies 165 • Task Attributes 169 • Motivational Properties
of Tasks 174 • Implementing Task Attributes 177 • Task Attributes and
Individual Differences 179 • Other Approaches to Job Design 180 • Task
Dependence, Coordination, and Variability 182 • Role of the Sport
or Recreation Manager 186 • Chapter Pursuits 188

11 Staffing and Career Considerations   **189**

Purposes of Staffing 190 • Focus of Staffing 190 • Matching People and Jobs
195 • Psychological Contract 204 • Career Considerations 206 • Mentoring
210 • Role of the Sport or Recreation Manager 214 • Chapter Pursuits 215

12 Leadership   **217**

Leader Behavior 218 • Multidimensional Model of Leadership 221 •
Transformational, Transactional, Servant, and Authentic Leadership 229 •
Leadership and Decision Making 235 • Role of the Sport or Recreation
Manager 239 • Chapter Pursuits 241

13 Performance Appraisal   **243**

Purposes of Performance Appraisal 243 • What Should Be Evaluated 246 •
When to Conduct Performance Appraisal 255 • Who Should Do the Appraisal
256 • Errors in Rating 256 • Role of the Sport or Recreation Manager 262 •
Chapter Pursuits 263

14 Reward Systems   **265**

Purposes of Reward Systems 265 • Types of Rewards 267 • Bases of Rewards
273 • Reward Systems and Member Preferences 276 • Role of the Sport
or Recreation Manager 277 • Chapter Pursuits 279

15 Internal Marketing   281

Forms of Marketing 283 • Process Versus People Orientation in Internal
Marketing 285 • Marketing Principles in Internal Operations 288 • Functions
of Internal Marketing 292 • Issues in Internal Marketing 296 • Role of the Sport
or Recreation Manager 296 • Chapter Pursuits 298

PART IV   Attitudinal Outcomes   299

16 Satisfaction   301

Theories of Job Satisfaction 303 • Satisfaction With Volunteer Work 309 •
Participant Satisfaction 312 • Measurement of Satisfaction 316 • Role of the
Sport or Recreation Manager 320 • Chapter Pursuits 321

17 Commitment   323

Multidimensionality of Organizational Commitment 325 • Occupational
Commitment 330 • Development and Effects of Organizational Commitment
332 • Correlates of Organizational Commitment 335 • Role of the Sport
or Recreation Manager 338 • Chapter Pursuits 339

Conclusion: The Future of Human Resource Management in Sport and Recreation—
   Guiding Themes   341
Appendix   355
References   357
Index   383
About the Authors   391

Preface

Sport organizations and their managers are concerned with a variety of issues relating to their operations. Of these issues, the management of human resources takes center stage for several reasons. First, as emphasized in total quality management, the source of all quality is the human resource engaged in producing goods and services. This view holds particularly true for services in which production and consumption occur at the interface of clients and employees, who are human resources of the organization. Because most sport organizations produce services, the management of human resources is a critical concern of sport managers. Therefore, in order to be an effective sport manager, one must understand the dynamics of human resources and their management.

Collectively, we have been teaching management of human resources in sport and recreation for more than four decades. In our earlier years, we assigned a set of readings for the courses due to the lack of a comprehensive text covering the subject. Because these readings were drawn from disparate sources (e.g., texts and journal articles from the diverse fields of business administration, sport psychology, and sport sociology), they did not present a coherent picture of the concepts studied or the relevance of these concepts in the field of sport and recreation management. In this book, therefore, we endeavor to present a clear and concise treatise on the critical aspects of the management of human resources in sport and recreation organizations. We also synthesize views regarding the role of the sport or recreation manager in managing human resources.

The theme of the book is to bring into focus the three divergent groups who constitute the human resources in sport and recreation organizations—paid professional workers, volunteer workers, and clients—and to match managerial processes with individual differences in the three types of human resources. We have limited our selection and treatment of variables involving individual differences and organizational processes to those that impinge on individual motivation and performance in the context of sport and recreation organizations.

This book is organized into four main parts, which are followed by a conclusion identifying important themes throughout the text. Part I outlines both the unique and the common characteristics of the three sets of human resources: volunteer workers, paid professional workers, and clients. Chapter 1 describes consumer, professional, and human services and emphasizes the importance of volunteer workers and clients as human resources. It also provides a model of human resource management to highlight the organization of the book. In chapter 2, we discuss volunteerism, volunteers, and volunteer organizations and explain the concepts of altruism and volunteer incentives. Chapter 3 describes the attributes of professions and professionals and emphasizes that the concept of professionalism is applicable to any occupation, irrespective of its status as a profession. Chapter 4 emphasizes clients and customers as one set of human resources because their involvement is necessary for the production of sport services.

Part II focuses on differences between people and how they affect behavior in sport organizations. In chapter 5, we describe the nature of cognitive abilities and their relevance to sport and recreation management. Chapter 6 covers personality traits and their effects on behavior in sport and recreation organizations. In chapter 7, we discuss the nature of personal values and their influence on attitudes and behaviors, and chapter 8 focuses on processes of individual motivation and their implications.

In part III, we describe organizational processes in the management of human resources. Chapter 9 addresses the components of organizational justice: distributive, procedural, and interactional justice. In chapter 10, we describe job attributes and their effects on motivation, as well as the concept of job enrichment and methods of coordination between jobs. Chapter 11 addresses job analysis, job description, and job specification as preliminary steps in recruitment, hiring, and training. This chapter also discusses the concept of a career from the perspectives of both the individual and the organization. Chapter 12 focuses on the importance of the leadership provided by sport managers and describes relevant theories of leadership. Chapter 13 covers the purposes and processes of evaluating individual performance and the pitfalls associated with performance appraisal. In chapter 14, we discuss the types and bases of reward systems that can be instituted in sport and recreation organizations. Chapter 15 addresses internal marketing as a management strategy for improving both the production and the marketing of an organization's products.

Part IV covers two significant outcomes expected of human resource practices: satisfaction and commitment. Chapter 16 describes theories of satisfaction and discusses components of satisfaction among paid and volunteer workers as well as clients. Chapter 17 addresses the importance of commitment to both the organization and the occupation. Finally, in the book's conclusion, we synthesize the information presented in the various chapters and present a set of founding and guiding themes.

Each chapter begins with a list of its learning objectives to help readers organize the information presented therein. To solidify understanding, periodic short reviews summarize the material covered up to that point in a given chapter. In addition, a recurring "Viewpoint" element highlights key statements from scholars and experts related to the topic at hand. Some of these statements present viewpoints opposed to one that is stressed in the text, thus facilitating healthy discussion. Other sidebars highlight important topics and applications in the field. New for this edition are sidebars—titled "Diversity Management of Human Resources" and "Technology in Human Resource Management"— that provide further connection to practice for sport managers as they confront issues in the workplace.

The chapters each also include a new section, titled "Role of the Sport or Recreation Manager," that further connects theory and practice. In addition, each chapter features a case study that allows students to apply concepts to a real-world scenario. Each case study is accompanied by tasks that prompt critical thinking and discussion.

Learning aids presented at the end of each chapter include a chapter summary, a list of key terms that readers can use to review their understanding of the chapter's content, and questions under the headings "Understand" and "Interact." In a classroom setting, discussion of these questions can help students understand the chapter's content. Such discussion also permits the teacher to present other perspectives on the topic.

Also new for this third edition are an instructor guide and an image bank to help instructors use this text to greatest effect. These materials are provided free to course adopters. Instructors can access these materials at www.HumanKinetics.com/Human ResourceManagementInSportAndRecreation.

The most obvious audience for this text comprises students in sport and recreation management, which encompasses physical education, athletics, campus recreation, and community recreation. In addition, teachers of coaching courses may also find most of the book's content relevant to their courses. These management areas face the same, or similar, contingencies and involve working with the same three types of human resources. All readers will find the content of the book to be straightforward, and teachers will benefit from the flexibility to choose or emphasize specific chapters and introduce their own material to supplement the book.

Finally, the content and organization of this book are born out of insights and experiences from four decades of teaching the subject. The content distilled here reflects training in both physical education and management science, coupled with feedback from a large number of undergraduate and graduate students. Obviously, the theories presented, the references cited, and the positions taken are a reflection of our own preferences and experiences. This orientation provides the opportunity for teachers to bring up views and theories that run counter to those expressed in this text. That kind of discourse is vital for the advancement of the field.

available at
HumanKinetics.com

Acknowledgments

The publication of this text is the culmination of long and arduous work sprinkled with moments of joy as well as frustration. These efforts, and their success, have been reinforced by several individuals and institutions who have been instrumental to our growth and development.

Remarks from Dr. Packianathan Chelladurai:

I am forever indebted to Earle Zeigler and Garth Paton for introducing me to the field of sport management, expressing confidence in my abilities, and providing continued support for all of my academic efforts. I am also grateful to Bert Carron, who taught me the "ropes" of research.

The University of Western Ontario, The Ohio State University, and now Troy University have provided the institutional base and support to facilitate my academic endeavors.

My family has provided the motivation and support for all of my efforts. Ponnu, Ruban, Karen, Chandran, Sally, Jason, Daniel, Shane, Andrew, and Michelle are constant sources of energy and excitement. I hope that this book will make them proud of me.

Remarks from Dr. Shannon Kerwin:

I would not be here without the support and guidance of one incredible man: Dr. Packianathan Chelladurai. One fateful lunch at NASSM 2015 brought us together and began the journey to this new edition of Chella's life's work. I am honored and privileged that he brought me along for the ride. I have learned more than I can express in words, and I will never forget the opportunity that Chella has provided for me. Thank you for believing in me, Chella.

Since I entered the world of academia, many mentors have provided unconditional support for my passion for research and teaching. Drs. Alison Doherty, Joanne MacClean, Lucie Thibault, and Lisa Kikulis have affected my career, and my world, in multiple ways. I owe any of my successes to their guidance.

I could not have completed the edits of this textbook without the unwavering support of my love, my life, Tom. You make it possible to have the world I have always wanted, and I am forever indebted to you for the role you play in making my work life easier. My family (Rachel and Cameron) are my world. I would not change a thing. Thank you.

HUMAN RESOURCES IN SPORT AND RECREATION

Definitions of *organization* and *management* (Robbins, Coulter, Leach, and Kilfoil 2012) generally include the three distinct elements of (1) specific goals to be achieved with (2) limited resources by coordinating the efforts of (3) people. Of these three, the people component is the most perplexing, problematic, and demanding of managerial attention. Indeed, many authors contend that, for a manager to be effective, he or she must be a good manager of the people who make up the organization and make everything work (e.g., Bach and Edwards 2013).

People can also be seen as the most important element in the management of organizations because it affects the other two elements. That is, it is the people of an organization—in the form of various constituencies (e.g., managers, employees, and clients or customers)—who argue about, discuss, and influence decisions about the organization's goals and its distribution of available resources in pursuing these goals.

From another perspective, it is people who make money and materials meaningful as resources and turn them into wealth. For instance, a stadium becomes a resource only when athletes perform in the stadium and spectators flock to it to see a contest. Even the most modern electronic scoreboard becomes a resource only when knowledgeable technicians are available to operate it and people are present to watch it. These two examples show that a material resource is a resource only when people with the know-how (e.g., athletes, technicians) use it to serve the needs of other people (spectators).

Concern for human resource management is driven by three imperatives (Chelladurai 1995a). The first imperative is profitability. Profit-oriented organizations can enhance productivity and thus their profitability by instituting effective human resource practices to enable their human resources to function optimally. The second driving force consists of changes in the values and awareness of the workforce and the customer base. More specifically, this imperative is constituted by an organization's altered conceptions of good human resource practices, its expectations for enhancing these processes, and their influence on important organizational outcomes. Third, as an agency of society, an organization is beholden to society, which includes the human resources of the organization. Thus, when an organization institutes effective human resource practices to enhance quality of life for its human resources, it also contributes to society as a whole. Thus we might refer to this third force as the imperative of social responsibility.

Chapter 1 begins the main text by introducing the particular importance of human resources for sport and recreation organizations. The process of managing human resources should begin with insight into the broad categories of human resources that the organization addresses. On the basis of this logic, the following chapters 2 through 4 are each devoted to describing one of these three forms of human resources: volunteers, paid professionals, and clients. Chapter 2 describes voluntary organizations and volunteer motivation. Chapter 3 describes the nature of professions and the concept of professionalism, then addresses the considerable similarity between the processes of professionalism and those of volunteerism. Chapter 4 discusses clients of sport operations with particular focus on their motivation for participating.

CHAPTER 1

Significance of Human Resources

LEARNING OBJECTIVES

After reading this chapter, you will be able to

- define and describe human resources and human resource management in sport and recreation;
- describe a service and its unique attributes;
- describe transfer of ownership;
- distinguish between consumer and human services;
- distinguish between egalitarian, elite, and entertainment sport; and
- explain the importance of clients as human resources.

An organization can function effectively only if it has at its disposal the necessary resources. The resource-based view of organizations (Barney 1991, 1995) posits that an organization's resources can confer competitive advantage if they are valuable (i.e., contribute to achievement of organizational goals), rare (i.e., are not available in abundance), imperfectly imitable (i.e., cannot be reproduced by other organizations), and hardly substitutable (i.e., cannot be replaced by another form of resource). The resources of an organization can be categorized as either physical capital, such as facilities, equipment, and geographic location; human capital, such as the expertise and experience of managers and employees; organizational capital, such as the organization's history, tradition, and culture; or financial capital, such as reserves, debt, and surplus revenue (Barney 1991, 1995).

Though it is trite to say that human resources differ considerably from material resources, it remains useful to look at the unique characteristics of human resources that affect managerial practices. Management of human resources holds greater importance than management of other resources and requires a totally different type of attention. The organization must recruit human resources individually, and each targeted individual has the option not to participate in the organization. In addition, the return on any investment in human resources is unpredictable; that is, one cannot be certain of how any individual will perform in the organizational context (Killian 1976).

Thus, it is not surprising that the field of study known as human resource management (HRM) has gained increasing significance. Textbooks and scholarly journals in this field have been and continue to be published, and almost every school of business administration addresses it in at least one specialized course. Here, we adopt the definition of HRM as involving "all management decisions related to policies and practices that together shape the employment relationship and are aimed at achieving individual, organizational, and societal goals" (Bach and Edwards 2013, p. 19). Moreover, "human resource management constitutes a distinctive approach to employment management which seeks to achieve competitive advantage by strategically deploying a highly committed and capable workforce by means of an integrated array of cultural, structural, and personnel techniques" (Storey 2007, p. 5). These definitions emphasize that organizations can be effective if they engage in appropriate techniques and practices to create a committed and capable workforce.

The management of human resources has been placed in a central position in general management

VIEWPOINT

The emergence of the "knowledge-based economy" (KBE) began in the mid-1990s and has taken shape throughout the early 21st century (Godin 2006). The KBE is based on the free flow of information and the use of technology and innovation to create a competitive advantage. As noted by Godin, the KBE highlights two points: First, knowledge is one of the most important resources that an organization can have; second, the application of information and communication technology is the driver of the new economy. This prevalence of knowledge and information flow via technology can be seen in the promotion of organizational values via social media outlets. For example, the Canadian Olympic Committee (COC) can now use Twitter as a means to share its values of competition and strength with internal staff members and volunteers, as well as external members and clients. As a result, the reach of these messages is far greater now than ever before in promoting the COC's organizational values and connecting it with both internal and external stakeholders.

mainly due to the pressures created by slumping employee productivity and growing international competition. However, this approach is rather narrow, both because it focuses on productivity and profit for the organization and because it views employees as cost. In contrast, theorists emphasize that in order to realize long-term benefits for all concerned—that is, organization, employees, and society—organizations would do well to consider their employees as capital and attempt to enhance their growth and potential, which in turn will contribute to performance and productivity (Beer and Spector 1985; Odiorne 1984).

Legge (1995) characterized these two perspectives—employees as cost and employees as capital—as the "hard" and "soft" models, respectively, of human resource management. The hard model views employees much as it views land and capital—as factors of production. The soft model, on the other hand, treats "employees as valued assets, [as] a source of competitive advantage through their commitment, adaptability and high quality of skills, performance, and so on" (Legge, p. 35). Alternatively, Legge refers to the two approaches as utilitarian instrumentalism and developmental humanism, respectively. The hard or instrumental approach cannot be dismissed easily; however, given the fundamental role of people within the human resource management process, this text takes the orientation of the soft or developmental approach.

The emphasis on human resources as capital is much more pronounced in the case of service organizations because

- their products are intangible,
- customer involvement is necessary for the production of services, and
- the production and the consumption of a service occur simultaneously.

Theorists and practitioners note that service quality resides ultimately in service providers, which are referred to in this text as human resources (B. Becker and Gerhart 1996; Bitner 1990; Chelladurai 1995b; Parasuraman, Zeithaml, and Berry 1990; B. Schneider and Bowen 1995). Because service providers are in contact with both the clients and the organizations that they represent, they project the image of the organization (B. Schneider and Bowen 1995). Thus, it is critical to emphasize the management of human resources in sport and recreation.

Based on the preceding commentary, this text focuses on **human capital**, and the discussion deals with recruiting personnel and managing them effectively so as to enable them to be both valuable for the organization and hard for other organizations to imitate or substitute for. In other words, by mastering the complexities of the value-creation process for human resources, an organization can create a source of competitive advantage that is rare, inimitable, and nonsubstitutable (Bowen and Ostroff 2004). Readers of this text will recognize that these processes are well practiced by intercollegiate athletics departments. These departments spend inordinate amounts of money and effort to hire the best coaches, recruit outstanding athletic talent, and groom that talent into winning teams. Every sport organization can institute similar human resource practices to achieve competitive advantage through its human capital.

The emphasis on human resource management is driven first by the financial imperatives of business enterprises. At the same time, there is a growing realization that all innovations in production technologies and processes rely fundamentally on people, who implement the policies and procedures of the organization. Managers expect any attention paid to human resource management to yield greater returns through greater worker productivity and commitment to the organization. A careful reading of the literature on total quality management shows that the human resources at a manager's disposal serve as the ultimate source of both quality and profit (Chelladurai 1995b; Goetsch and Davis 1997).

Although financial and quality concerns probably serve as the immediate catalysts of change in an organization, they constitute a transitory force. That is, such concerns may recede in good economic times, and as a result, any related emphasis placed on human resource management may also fade. However, two other forces, both rather permanent, are also active here. The first force is the increasing sophistication of both employees and consumers. As they become more educated and informed, they form changing perceptions of what constitutes good HRM practice and develop higher expectations for such practices. In terms of cumulative effects, this altering of values—and the increase in modern worker–client awareness, alertness, and influence—have refocused management attention to human resources.

The second and more permanent force relates to the fact that organizations are agencies of society at large and are sustained by society. Almost all adults in a given society work in an organization, and every organization bears a social responsibility to attend to the welfare of its workers and enhance their quality of life (Chelladurai 2015). Thus, management of human resources merits extreme care not only from the economic, efficiency, and quality perspectives but also from the perspective of social responsibility.

As more people recognize the significance of human resource management, researchers have suggested that it should be considered as part of strategic management, particularly in the service industry (Grönroos 2007; B. Schneider and Bowen 1995). Strategic management involves identifying goals for an organization, delineating its market, and specifying necessary processes to achieve its goals. In essence, then, strategic management defines the business that an organization is undertaking and the market in which it serves. From this perspective, one's consideration of human resource management practices must resonate both with an organization's business and with its market. Therefore, we need to account for the unique features of the sport industry and their ramifications for managing human resources.

All of us know intuitively that industries (e.g., farming, banking, mining, tourism) differ considerably in their products, the types of employees who produce them, and how they are managed. Consider, for example, your own university. It produces knowledge (thus the emphasis on research) and propagates that new knowledge in the form of presentations, publications, and, more important, teaching. As you know, these two primary functions (i.e., producing and propagating knowledge) are carried out by the university's primary employees—that is, researchers and teachers. You are also aware that another set of employees makes the system run: administrators, financial experts, human resource managers, physical plant personnel, caretakers, and so on. In addition, you may know that different human resource practices are applied to these two sets of university employees.

Likewise, sport organizations differ in what they produce, who they hire to produce their products, and the employment practices they use. Based on this perspective, this chapter

- clarifies the nature of the sport industry in terms of its products,
- identifies the types of human resources used in sport and recreation, and
- specifies a model for managing human resources in sport and recreation.

The nature of any industry is defined by the products that it produces; for instance, contrast

DIVERSITY MANAGEMENT OF HUMAN RESOURCES

Successful management of human resources depends on *strategic* management of the people who develop, maintain, and sustain organizational functioning. In light of growing population diversity, we must ensure that our HRM practices proactively value and manage diversity to better serve both internal and external stakeholders. With that need in mind, we provide here an integrative framework for managing diversity (Chelladurai 2014) that is applied in subsequent chapters.

In sum, the first necessary condition for managing diversity is to *value* it, such that awareness, acknowledgment, and acceptance of diversity are filtered into all HRM policies and procedures. Managing diversity should also involve two distinct strategies—accommodation and activation—whose implementation can vary based on a given group's task type. Accommodation involves "permitting and facilitating the symbolic expression of behavioral preferences of diverse individuals" (Chelladurai 2014, p. 349), whereas activation is the "process of deliberately bringing divergent perspectives to bear on a task or project" (p. 350). The condition of *actualization* occurs when the process of valuing and managing diverse people, perspectives, and outcomes enables the group or organization to reach its full potential (Chelladurai 2014).

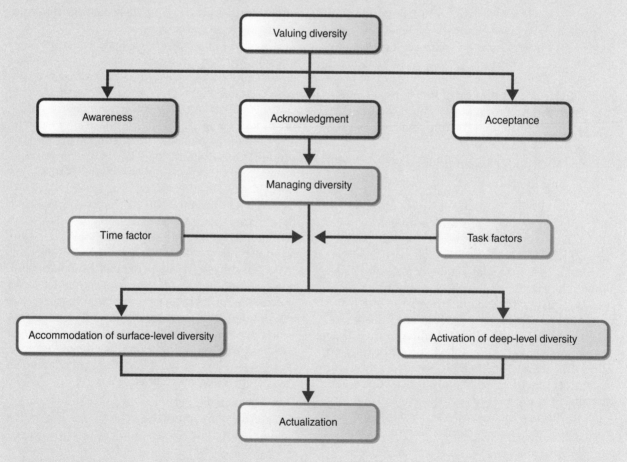

The integrative framework for managing diversity.

Reprinted, by permission, from P. Chelladurai, 2014, *Managing organizations for sport and physical activity: A systems perspective*, 4th. ed. (Scottsdale, AZ: Holcomb Hathaway Publishers). © P. Chelladurai.

VIEWPOINT

The following statement by Simons (2011) emphasizes the importance of human resources:

Human resource management is the strategic approach to the management of an organization's most valuable asset—the people who work for that organization and who, individually and collectively, contribute to the achievement of the objectives of the business. Simply put, human resource management means employing people, training them, developing their talents, and utilizing, maintaining and compensating them for their services as appropriate to the requirements of the organization. (p. 8)

educational institutions with the agriculture industry or the automobile industry. In other words, the nature of a product carries implications for human resource management because the nature of the people (and their attributes) attracted to a given industry, or needed in that industry, varies with the industry type. In the context of this book, sport and recreation organizations produce services rather than goods. Therefore, let us now look into the nature of services in contrast to goods.

SERVICE OPERATIONS

Many authors have documented the distinction between service-producing organizations and goods-producing organizations, as well as the concomitant differences in managerial practices (Grönroos 1990; C.H. Lovelock 2001; Mills and Margulies 1980; Sasser, Olsen, and Wyckoff 1978). J. Fitzsimmons and Fitzsimmons (2011) defined a **service** as "a time perishable, intangible experience performed for a customer acting in the role of a co-producer" (p. 4). In contrast, a good is a tangible physical object or product; it can be created now and used later, whereas a service is created and used simultaneously (Sasser et al. 1978).

It is true that some goods can be involved in the production of services. For example, the expensive testing equipment used by an exercise physiologist facilitates his or her services of fitness assessment and exercise prescription. Similarly, the service of renting a tennis court requires the existence of the facility, and of course the services that a retailer offers in assembling and displaying sporting goods necessarily involve the goods themselves. As a result, the price that one pays for a basketball includes both the ball manufacturer's cost and profit for the good itself and the cost and profit of the retailer's services. Thus, to some degree, many service transactions also involve the facilitation of goods or facilities. However, our discussion here focuses on the service component because of its greater relevance to the management of human resources.

Characteristics of Service

Many writers have emphasized four basic characteristics of a service: intangibility, perishability, heterogeneity, and simultaneity (C.H. Lovelock 2001; Sasser et al. 1978; Schmenner 1995). Let us briefly examine each characteristic posited by this view.

- *Intangibility:* The notion of intangibility arises because the client or customer cannot judge the quality of the product before obtaining it. This reality can be seen in the example of consuming a live sporting event. As Sasser et al. (1978) pointed out, the customer experience at a live sporting event (i.e., the service) remains intangible because the sensual and psychological benefits (i.e., feelings, such as comfort, status, and a sense of well-being) that customers derive vary by the individual.

- *Perishability:* A service cannot be stored for future use. For example, a fitness consultant cannot produce his or her services without customers being present and store them for use at some future time when customers arrive. In contrast, a manufacturer can produce fitness equipment and inventory it for future sales.

- *Heterogeneity:* Services are likely to be heterogeneous (variable) because of multiple influences. For one thing, as noted earlier, the intangible nature of a service derives in part from customers' varying perceptions of it. Thus two clients may hold different perceptions of the quality of the same service provided by the same employee (e.g., the service provided by a fitness instructor) due to variations in their individual psyches. Furthermore, the same client may perceive a service differently at two different points in time due to changes in his or her mood or frame of mind. Shifting to the employees' view, the two fitness instructors may provide different levels of service quality due to differences in their levels of experience and expertise or their leadership styles. Similarly, the same instructor may provide different levels of service quality at different times for any number of reasons. Thus both clients and instructors are subject to changes that can affect the quality of the service offered.

• *Simultaneity:* Because a service is perishable and cannot be stored, it must be consumed as it is produced. Furthermore, because the production and consumption of a service are simultaneous, great importance is attached to the interface between the employee (the producer of the service) and the client (the consumer of the service). In contrast, a product, such as a tennis racket, is produced at one point in time and sold to a customer at another point in time. Thus, no interface occurs between the producer and the consumer of the good.

The traditional view just outlined—that a service is distinguished from a good by the four attributes of intangibility, perishability, heterogeneity, and simultaneity (i.e., inseparability of production and consumption)—has been questioned by C. Lovelock and Gummesson (2004). These authors noted that when customers order either a good or a service (e.g., an exercise machine or the repair of a machine) online or by telephone, they cannot touch that good or service, feel it, or test it before purchase. That is, the concept of intangibility then extends to both the good and the service in question. By the same token, some services can be verified before purchase. For example, one may go to a few golf courses and assess the layout, parking facilities, locker room, barrooms, and other amenities. The service provided at the golf course lies in the rental of its facility and equipment; thus that service is not intangible. In addition, if a service (e.g., the towel service) is mechanized (as when one puts a dollar into a slot and a clean towel drops onto a tray), the concept of heterogeneity or variability does not apply to that service.

As for inseparability, C. Lovelock and Gummesson (2004) pointed out several separable services in which the customer or client is not involved at all. For example, if you contract out the maintenance of the lawn at your facility, you as the customer are separated from the service provided by the lawn care firm. The same is true if you leave your tennis racket at a pro shop to be restrung or your sport clothes at a laundry facility. As for perishability,

Lovelock and Gummesson noted that when a factory is shut down due to a power failure, it loses the capacity to produce goods at that time. Thus, the concept of perishability can apply to both goods and services and is therefore not a good criterion for distinguishing a service from a good.

C. Lovelock and Gummesson (2004) suggested that the one criterion that reliably distinguishes a good from a service is the notion of transfer of ownership. For example, when a good (e.g., pair of hockey skates) is exchanged in a sporting goods store, ownership of the product is transferred to the buyer. Contrast this situation with the case of paying court fees in order to play tennis. One does not buy the tennis court, and there is no transfer of ownership. Or consider the sharpening of skates. One leaves the skates with a technician, who sharpens the skates for a fee; again, there is no transfer of ownership, either of the skates or of the technician's skills. Insofar as ownership is not transferred, then, a service constitutes "a form of rental or access in which customers obtain benefits by gaining the right to use a physical object, to hire the labor and expertise of personnel, or to obtain access to facilities or networks" (p. 34).

Within this nonownership framework, C. Lovelock and Gummesson (2004) identified five broad categories of service.

1. *Rented-goods services:* The customer pays a fee to use a physical good for a set time (e.g., renting a golf cart).

2. *Place and space rentals:* The customer pays a fee to use a specified place or space in a location (e.g., a seat in an arena for a basketball game or a spot in a parking lot).

3. *Labor and expertise rentals:* The client simply rents the labor or expertise of another person or firm to carry out certain activities (e.g., hiring an accountant, lawyer, or fitness specialist).

4. *Physical-facility access services:* The customer gets access to a facility and the exhibits therein (e.g., a Hall of Fame or the Rogers Centre in Toronto).

5. *Network access and usage:* The customer livestreams an event (e.g., boxing match) to a smartphone. Though access to some streamed content is free, access to viewing a live event is not.

We have argued (Chelladurai 2005) that while C. Lovelock and Gummesson's (2004) transfer of ownership marks the dividing line between a good and a service, the traditional four attributes do not lose their potency, because most services do differ from most goods in these attributes. Furthermore, services themselves may differ in the degree to which they are characterized by each of the four attributes. Therefore, it is appropriate to conceive both of a dividing line between goods and services marked by Lovelock and Gummesson's transfer-of-ownership criterion *and* of four continuums representing the four attributes on which various sport services may be located (Chelladurai 2005).

This framework is illustrated in figure 1.1, where goods and services are separated by the criterion of transfer of ownership. That is, if ownership is transferred, then the product is a good, as is the case when you buy a tennis racket. If, on the other hand, you rent the use of a tennis court by paying a court fee, there is no transfer of ownership of the court; therefore, the product offered by the organization is a service. By the same token, if you take tennis lessons, the tennis pro does not lose ownership of his or her knowledge and expertise; therefore, the tennis lesson is also a service. More specifically, the rental of the tennis court and the tennis lesson are labeled, respectively, as a consumer service and a human service. Distinctions between types of service are elaborated in the following sections. For the moment, figure 1.1 shows that the presence of the four attributes of a service can be either low or high based on the type of service (consumer or human).

Services offered as products provide experiences that are intangible, perishable, and variable both over time and across different service providers. A service can be differentiated from a good by the lack of transfer of ownership of the product. Because services are produced and consumed simultaneously, the interface between the service employee and the client constitutes a critical element for the organization.

Professional Versus Consumer Services

The interface between an employee and a client or customer is critical to service operations; in fact, what transpires in the **employee–client interface** defines the nature of the service. More specifically, the extent to which a service is complex and tailored to the needs of individual clients—and the extent to which knowledge and expertise are involved—have been used as critical criteria for classifying the service as either professional or consumer (Sasser et al. 1978).

Professional services are "individualized for each customer and delivered by a relatively

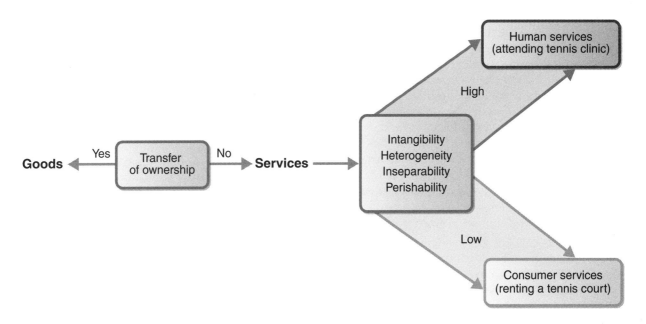

FIGURE 1.1 Transfer of ownership and service attributes.

Adapted from P. Chelladurai, 2005, *Managing organizations for sport and physical activity*, 2nd ed. (Scottsdale, AZ: Holcomb Hathaway), 28. © P. Chelladurai.

high-skill workforce" (Sasser et al. 1978, p. 400). For example, schools, colleges, and universities offer professional services to their clients when they hire expert coaches to train their athletes. Another example would be a fitness consulting firm that employs highly trained exercise physiologists. The services provided by such organizations are based largely on their employees' knowledge and expertise. Such services are also nonstandardized in the sense that they are determined by the needs of each customer. Thus, the professional employees must be allowed considerable freedom in their operations, and their managers must recognize that traditional bureaucratic control mechanisms are neither relevant nor adequate.

In contrast, **consumer services** have been defined as including "a limited range of services delivered by a relatively low-skill workforce to a large aggregate market" (Sasser et al. 1978, p. 400). For instance, a city recreation department builds and operates an arena for use by all of the city's citizens. The basic service provided here is the use of the arena and the scheduling of various activities in it. More specifically, a reservations clerk working in the arena serves a large number of people in the community, and his or her operations are limited to simple acts such as checking whether the applicants are entitled to reserve the arena and entering the date and time of such reservations. Thus, the clerk's operations are largely standardized and routinized.

These differing characteristics of professional and consumer service employees call for different approaches to making decisions, organizing work, and motivating employees. In this vein, Mills and Margulies' (1980) scheme identifies seven variables associated with the employee–customer interface that differ among service organizations.

1. *Information:* Services differ in the extent and type of information processed during their delivery. For example, a professional coach in a tennis club processes many bits of information for training and instructing players, but a reservations clerk needs to know only the client's preferred schedule and whether he or she is entitled to reserve a court.

2. *Decisions:* Services can also be distinguished on the basis of the relative complexity of decisions made during the employee–customer interface. For example, a reservations clerk's decisions are relatively simple, whereas a tennis professional's decisions are more complex.

3. *Time:* Because professional services require more information processing and more complex

decision making, they take more time than do consumer services. For instance, a tennis professional spends more time with players than a reservations clerk spends with clients.

4. *Problem:* Another important distinction between the two operations lies in the extent to which the client is aware of the problem and its solution. In reserving a tennis court, the client knows exactly what he or she wants and informs the reservations clerk accordingly. In the case of tennis lessons, however, the coach knows more than the client does about the client's weaknesses and the possible remedies.

5. *Transferability:* Forms of service are also distinguished by the ease with which employees can be replaced. Because consumer services involve simple and routine decisions, it is relatively easy to train a newcomer or replace a current employee. On the other hand, replacing a professional employee is more difficult and more disruptive of current service levels.

6. *Power:* In our ongoing example, the professional coach is presumed to possess more knowledge and expertise than the clients do and to be more aware of their problems than they are. These features bestow on the coach a power over his or her clients, whereas this is not the case with the reservations clerk. To emphasize the point, the power held by the professional service provider stems from the greater knowledge and expertise that he or she possesses relative to the client. That is, the client depends on the professional to solve problems. By the same token, an organization that specializes in knowledge-based services depends on its own professional employees. For example, a university athletics department depends on coaches to recruit outstanding athletes and mold them into winning teams. To that extent, a coach holds some power over the athletics department.

7. *Attachment:* Because of the close association between the employee (e.g., coach) and the client in a professional service operation, the employee is likely to be more attached to his or her clients (e.g., athletes) than to the employing organization. In contrast, a consumer service employee (e.g., reservations clerk) is likely to be more attached to the organization than to its clients.

Mills and Margulies (1980) pointed out that these seven variables "are closely interrelated to each other and are linked to the need for information, [which is] the raw material of service organizations" (p. 262). The distinctions between consumer and professional services are based largely on the amount of information exchanged between the service employee and the customer and on the extent to which the employee must possess expertise and knowledge in order to solve the customer's problem. Table 1.1 summarizes the differences between a consumer service and a professional service as suggested by Sasser et al. (1978) and Mills and Margulies.

Human Services

As we have discussed, sport and recreation organizations provide both consumer and professional services; within this division, professional services themselves comprise two major types. For instance, lawyers, architects, accountants, and stockbrokers all provide complex professional services to their clients or customers. Professional services are also provided by teachers, guidance counselors, physicians, and clergy. However, these two sets of services can be distinguished from each other. Specifically, in the first set, professionals apply knowledge and guidelines regarding something in which clients are interested (e.g., a legal issue, a building, or an investment), whereas professionals in the second set transform the clients themselves (e.g., educating a child, guiding a student, treating a patient, or enhancing a person's spiritual life).

In this latter set, which is referred to as **human services** (as distinct from nonhuman professional services), the "input of raw material . . . [consists of] human beings with specific attributes, and . . . [the] production output . . . [consists of] persons processed or changed in a predetermined manner"; in addition, the "general mandate is that of 'service,' that is, to maintain and improve the general well-being and functioning of people" (Hasenfeld and English 1974, p. 1). These features characterize many of the services provided by sport and recreation organizations. More specifically, many of these organizations cultivate a healthy lifestyle among their clients; educate them about the benefits of physical activity; change their attitude toward physical activity and recreation programs; and provide opportunities for health, fitness, or skill enhancement, as well as overall fun and enjoyment.

 Human services are distinct from other forms of service because their inputs and outputs consist of clients. In other words, these services are concerned with processing and classifying people, preventing or delaying decline in the welfare of people, and altering specific attributes of people (e.g., health, skills, and knowledge).

TABLE 1.1   Consumer Service Versus Professional Service

DIMENSIONS	CONSUMER SERVICE (E.G., RETAILING OF SPORTING GOODS)	PROFESSIONAL SERVICE (E.G., FITNESS CONSULTING)
Information base	Weak	Strong
Decision type	Simple	Complex
Interface duration	Brief	Lengthy
Client's knowledge	High	Low
Type of product	Standard with low knowledge or skill	Nonstandard with high knowledge or skill
Substitutability of employees	High	Low
Perceived power of employee	Low	High
Type of employee	Unskilled operators	Professionally trained, self-motivated individuals
Type of organizational structure	Rigid hierarchy, standard procedures, strict control	Unstructured hierarchy, loose control

Reprinted from P. Chelladurai, 1985, *Sport management: Macro perspective* (London, ON: Sports Dynamics Publishers), 39. By permission of author. Based on Mills and Margulies 1990; Sasser, Olsen, and Wyckoff 1978.

The nature of human services in sport and recreation organizations can be further elaborated by the following three-level classification of such services (Hasenfeld 1983).

1. *People-processing function:* This function involves testing or screening people and designating them as belonging to a particular class based on a classification scheme. Typically, the resulting information or labeling is used by another human service agency, such as a juvenile court, credit-rating bureau, or medical testing and diagnosing unit. For example, guidance counselors act as people processors when they test individuals on specific aptitude or attitude scales. This function is also performed by fitness-testing laboratories when they rate customers on a scale of relative fitness. Another example is found in the testing of athletes for drugs.

2. *People-sustaining function:* Human service organizations may also perform the function of sustaining people—that is, preventing or delaying a decline in clients' welfare or status. For example, this function is the major role played by welfare departments, nursing homes, and chronic wards in hospitals.

3. *People-changing function:* This function is most characteristic of sport and recreation organizations, which are typically engaged in changing people in terms of one or more of their biophysical, psychological, or social attributes. For example, degree programs in physical education change their clients into more knowledgeable persons in the field; fitness programs make people fitter and healthier; recreation programs make their clients more relaxed and energized; and coaching programs make their clients better performers.

In summary, organizations operating in sport, physical activity, and recreation provide services. Furthermore, though some of these organizations provide consumer services, most of them provide professional services. Sport and recreation organizations are also distinguished by the fact that some of them are engaged primarily in *human* services—that is, in people processing, people sustaining, or people changing. Figure 1.2 illustrates the three types of service and their interrelationships.

SPORT AND RECREATION SERVICES

The various services offered in sport and recreation can be collapsed into three broad categories labeled as the following manifestations of sport—egalitarian sport, elite sport, and entertainment sport (Chelladurai 2012; see figure 1.3).

Egalitarian Sport

Also referred to as mass sport or participant sport, egalitarian sport is fundamentally a gregarious activity that is done at least in part for pleasure. It includes everyone, irrespective of ability. The services offered in this segment include **consumer pleasure services**, in which customers participate in physical activity for the sheer pleasure of participation, and **consumer health services**, in which they participate in order to improve their health. Specific services offered include scheduling reservations of facilities or equipment as requested by clients, as well as organizing and conducting tournaments to enhance pleasure in physical activity. Prime examples of this type of service include youth sports, bowling alleys, and fitness clubs.

As noted earlier, some clients may seek guidance and instruction to engage in physical activity for health reasons. Services offered toward this end of the spectrum are referred to as **human sustenance** or **human curative services**. They entail organizing and conducting exercise and fitness programs on a regular basis under the guidance and supervision of expert leaders for the benefit either of healthy clients (sustenance) or clients who are considered deficient in fitness, health, or physical appearance (curative services). Examples in this group include exercise-based cardiac rehabilitation, relaxation and stress reduction, and weight-loss programs.

Elite Sport

In elite sport, individuals pursue excellence in a given sport. Excellence implies that one is among the best in a given class or competitive level—e.g., middle or junior high school, high school, collegiate,

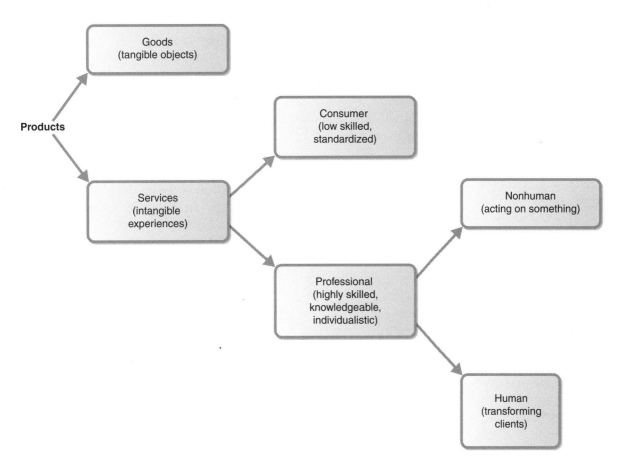

FIGURE 1.2 Classification of organizational products.

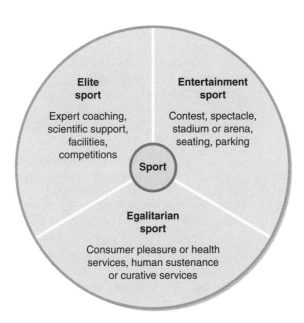

FIGURE 1.3 Manifestations of sport and the associated services.

Adapted, by permission, from P. Chelladurai, 2012, Leadership and manifestations of sport. In *The handbook of sport and performance psychology,* edited by S. Murphy (New York: Oxford University Press), 328-342.

or professional level. Elite sport is restricted to persons of high ability with a determination to excel in the activity; it is characterized by high dedication, huge sacrifices, and extraordinary effort over a long period of time. Thus, in contrast to egalitarian sport, elite sport is a serious business requiring a great deal of planning for deliberate practice and progressively challenging competitions. As such, it involves an exclusionary process wherein those who do not meet the standards are eliminated at successive levels, thus leaving only the best at the top. Relevant services include expert coaching, support services provided by specialists (e.g., psychology, sports medicine), provision of practice and competition facilities, arrangement of competitive schedules, and transportation.

Entertainment Sport

The third segment of the sport industry is entertainment sport, which, fundamentally, is an offshoot of the pursuit of excellence. The entertainment value of a particular sport is determined by its popularity in a given community, region, or nation. For example, although football holds the highest entertainment value in North America, cricket has the most entertainment value in India, Pakistan, and Sri Lanka.

Sport leagues (e.g., NFL, NBA, NHL) have capitalized on the entertainment value of their respective sports and organized competitions involved selected teams of high-caliber athletes. The related services include, for example, the contest itself (including the quality of the home and opposing teams and the rivalry between them); stadium access, including ease of parking; aesthetics and cleanliness of the facility, including seating comfort; scoreboard quality and signage; fan control; food service; and pregame, halftime, and postgame entertainment (Byon, Zhang, and Baker 2013; Wakefield, Blodgett, and Sloan 1996).

The differences between the three segments can be summarized by saying that egalitarian sport involves playing just to have fun, whereas elite sport is more akin to farming, in which effort goes into plowing, seeding, watering, and waiting for a long time in order to reap the harvest (Chelladurai 2012). Entertainment sport, in turn, might be likened to hunting, which involves animals "brought up" by nature (with no effort by the hunter) and *then* hunted to be served as food. In a similar manner, professional sport enterprises are not known for developing their own players but for spending large amounts of money to buy players developed by others and parade their excellence as entertainment.

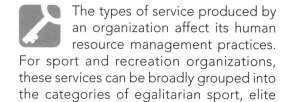 The types of service produced by an organization affect its human resource management practices. For sport and recreation organizations, these services can be broadly grouped into the categories of egalitarian sport, elite sport, and entertainment sport.

Another distinction that can be made among sport and recreation organizations is whether they belong to the public (i.e., government) sector or the private sector. The fundamental distinction here lies in the fact that public organizations derive their funding through taxation of the public, whereas private organizations get their funding through contributions from customers, private donors, or investors. For example, both a private golf club and a city recreation organization funded by city taxes can offer consumer-pleasure services at a golf course.

Of course, sport and recreation organizations can also differ in size. For example, some universities are larger than others, and their athletics and recreational-sport departments also vary in size; the same is true of city recreation departments. In the broader picture, some sport governing bodies are larger than others based on the popularity of their sport and participant membership. Such variations can impose demands and constraints on the management of human resources, and these factors are discussed later in the book.

We have used the terms *sport* and *recreation* to modify *organization* (i.e., "sport organization" and "recreation organization") because some confusion exists regarding the use of the word *sport* to cover both sport and recreation. For instance, the constitution of the North American Society for Sport Management (NASSM) defines the sport management field as "the theoretical and applied aspects of management theory and practice specially related to *sport, exercise, dance,* and *play* [emphasis added] as these enterprises are pursued by all sectors of the population" (NASSM, 2016, para 1). Because this definition covers all of the services described earlier, it is legitimate to refer to all of these services as sport services and to refer to all organizations providing them as sport organizations. However, some distinctions are made by scholars across North America between sport and recreation in that the term *sport* is used to refer to elite sport (e.g., intercollegiate and professional sport) and the term *recreation* is used to refer to other forms of participant sport (e.g., university or city recreational sport). Because this text covers the management of human resources in organizations providing all forms of the services described, we have used both terms—*sport* and *recreation*—to refer both to the services and to the organizations that provide them.

PAID AND VOLUNTEER WORKERS

Having defined and described the types of products provided by sport and recreation organizations, we need now to examine the types of human resources used in sport and recreation in order to facilitate our understanding of managing them. The workers in the sport and recreation industry can be classified as either human service workers or consumer service workers. Members of both sets are remunerated for their work in some material form (usually salary or wages), and organizations and their managers can use such monetary rewards as mechanisms for controlling employee behavior. For example, salary or wages can be used to help recruit an employee; they can also be increased based on work done, experience, or cost of living indexes in order to foster continued employee participation. In addition, incentives (e.g., merit pay, bonuses) can be used to enhance employee motivation.

Such practices are not relevant, however, in the case of a **volunteer**, who is

> an individual engaging in behavior that is not bio-socially determined (e.g., eating, sleeping), nor economically necessitated (e.g., paid work, house work, home repair), nor sociopolitically compelled (e.g., paying one's taxes, clothing oneself before appearing in public), but rather that is essentially (primarily) motivated by the expectation of psychic benefits of some kind. (D.H. Smith 1981, pp. 22-23)

Because volunteers' participation is not based on material rewards, such rewards cannot be used as incentives for volunteers. Therefore, different approaches must be used when managing this set of human resources (i.e., recruiting them and, more important, retaining them) in sport and recreation organizations. The incentives relevant to volunteerism are discussed in chapter 2.

Many sport and recreation organizations depend on volunteers for carrying out their operations. For example, volunteers organize many of the youth leagues in various sports and coach the teams; furthermore, volunteers have founded or managed

several sport governing bodies. However, the most common type of volunteer participation comes in the form of the frontline workers who deliver services, whether they are consumer or human services. Indeed, it is inconceivable that sport and recreation could exist without the services of volunteers. Thus, volunteers constitute a valuable set of human resources without the cost of the material rewards provided to paid employees.

Of course, a sport or recreation organization can include both volunteer and **paid professional workers** (professionals and professionalism are discussed in detail in chapter 3). These two sets of workers bring different attitudes, beliefs, and biases. They also differ in their knowledge and expertise and in the rewards that they seek through participation in organizational activities. This mixed composition can create a different kind of problem—namely, conflict between the two groups.

For instance, Kerwin, Doherty, and Harman (2011) suggested that one persistent problem in nonprofit organizations in Canada involves conflict between paid staff members and volunteer boards of directors. Their findings suggest that these disagreements often hinge on power struggles that go unmanaged and become personal. Such conflicts can emanate from perceived expertise on the part of paid professional workers and perceived altruism on the part of volunteers. Inglis (1997) noted tension between volunteers and professionals that resulted from "differing opinions among the professional staff and board volunteers as to the degree of technical expertise, policy development, or advice that constituted an appropriate relationship" (p. 161). Similarly, Amis and Slack (1996) pointed out that conflict between volunteer board members and professional staff in volunteer sport organizations in Canada may be attributed to a struggle for control:

> Despite efforts by [the Canadian] government to make the process of decision making in these organizations "more businesslike" by standardizing procedures and placing operational decisions in the hands of professional staff, many volunteers resisted this type of change… The culture of informal control is thus retained as volunteers see any efforts to increase standardization as a possible erosion of their power base. (p. 83)

The potential for such conflicts poses a threat and a challenge to the management of human resources. The essential point to remember is that both paid employees and volunteer workers are found on the

---

TECHNOLOGY IN HUMAN RESOURCE MANAGEMENT

Social medial platforms are designed for social and business networking (e.g., Facebook, Google Plus, LinkedIn) and microblogging (e.g., Twitter, Tumblr). The pervasive use of social media makes it directly relevant to multiple human resource management functions, such as recruiting and hiring, internal communication, and performance evaluation. As of 2012, as noted by Qualman (2012), 55 percent of Americans aged 45 to 54 years had a profile on a social networking site. Moreover, the only demographic group that fell below expected participation in social networks consisted of those 55 years or older, but even 30 percent of this group had joined the social networking world. Among social media platforms related to business in North America, Qualman (2011) noted that the highest adoption rates were found for Facebook (75 percent of market share), Twitter (20 percent of market share), and LinkedIn (10 percent of market share). In terms of sheer numbers, in 2016, there were 1.7 billion worldwide registered Facebook accounts, 500 million registered Instagram accounts, and 313 million registered Twitter accounts ("Leading Social Networks" 2016). Clearly, social media have become staples in the lives of individuals across the globe.

---

staff of most sport and recreation organizations. Equally important is the fact that both of these types of workers can provide a consumer service, a human service, or both (see table 1.2).

TABLE 1.2   Types of Workers and Servers

	PAID	VOLUNTEER
CONSUMER SERVICE WORKERS	Locker room attendant	Gymnasium supervisor
HUMAN SERVICE WORKERS	Exercise leader	High school coach

Sport and recreation organizations rely heavily on volunteer contributions. Although the economic value of volunteer participation in sport and recreation is quite significant, sport and recreation managers must also capitalize on the social benefits (e.g., sense of community, social engagement with others) of volunteer involvement.

CLIENTS AS HUMAN RESOURCES

The two types of human resources just discussed (i.e., volunteer and paid workers) are not the end of the story. There is also another type, which is unique to the service sector and is characteristic of sport and recreation: clients. Because sport and recreation organizations produce services, particularly human services, their clients or customers constitute both the input and the output of organizational processes.

A more elaborate description of clients is provided in chapter 3; for now, the importance of **clients as human resources** is highlighted by the simultaneity of production and consumption. As noted earlier, because a service must be consumed as it is produced, the interface between the employee (producer) and the customer (consumer) is critical. This simultaneity brings customers into the organizational domain as one set of human resources. In fact, Mills and Morris (1986) suggested that customers should be considered partial employees of the organization:

> Clients or customers of service organizations are indispensable to the production activities of these organizations. . . . [I]n complex services where customer performance is crucial to

service production, boundaries of the service organization have to be expanded to incorporate the consumers as temporary members or participants. (p. 726)

Inclusion of the client in the process of service production can be seen as a cost-saving effort on the part of the organization. This view is largely valid in the case of profit-oriented organizations, such as commercial banks or grocery stores, which may require the customer to perform certain activities traditionally carried out by a service employee (e.g., filling in deposit slips or bagging one's own groceries). However, such a limited utilitarian view of customer involvement is inappropriate in the case of sport and recreation organizations, which provide human services—more specifically, people-processing, people-sustaining, and people-changing services. These types of services cannot be completed without the client's active participation in the production process.

Thus, management of human resources entails specific processes to entice clients to be active and to comply with directions. Client participation in sport and recreation service operations affects management in two ways. The first effect involves the obvious face-to-face interactions between service employees and clients. The second effect involves the need for—and difficulty of—securing clients' compliance with the requirements for producing the service.

We need to view our clients as human resources because they must be involved actively in the production of our services. From this perspective, clients are part of the organization; they are in fact partial employees.

A MODEL OF HUMAN RESOURCE MANAGEMENT

The foregoing classification of human resources—paid professional workers, volunteers, and clients or customers—in sport and recreation organizations takes only the first step in managing those human resources. A more comprehensive approach also addresses

- the individual differences between the three broad categories of human resources;
- the managerial processes appropriate for each category of human resources for recruiting, retaining, and facilitating the growth and development of human assets; and
- the fundamental outcomes of organizational efforts towards managing the three broad categories of human resources.

The three types of human assets (i.e., resources) listed in box 1 of figure 1.4 are described in chapters 2 to 4 in part I of this book. Though such a classification of human resources is useful in many ways, it overlooks the individual differences between people within each category. Certainly, managers must be attuned to the three broad classes of human resources, but they must also be cognizant of individual differences. Hence, individual differences in abilities, personality, values, and motivation (box 2 of figure 1.4) are discussed in chapters 5 through 8, respectively, in part II of the book. As already implied and as shown in figure 1.4, such individual differences, along with the differences between the three types of human resources, inform and influence the choice and implementation of HRM practices. Part III of the book elaborates on the specific HRM practices of organizational justice (chapter 9), job design (chapter 10), staffing and career considerations (chapter 11), leadership (chapter 12), performance appraisal (chapter 13), reward systems (chapter 14), and internal marketing (chapter 15).

The productivity of individuals, groups, and the organization as a whole can be enhanced if management strives to secure commitment and collaborative effort by both workers and clients to achieve organizational goals. This commitment and effort constitute a significant outcome in the model (box 4 of figure 1.4). A second, and equally important, concern involves employee satisfaction (box 4). In other words, management should ensure not only that workers and clients grow in their competence and performance capabilities but also that they have opportunities to meet their personal needs (e.g., personal development, need for achievement). Meeting these needs enhances their satisfaction with their involvement in organizational activities. Part IV covers the attitudinal outcomes, shown in box 4 of figure 1.4, of job satisfaction (chapter 16) and organizational commitment (chapter 17). The model posits that these two attitudinal outcomes depend on the extent to which HRM practices are geared

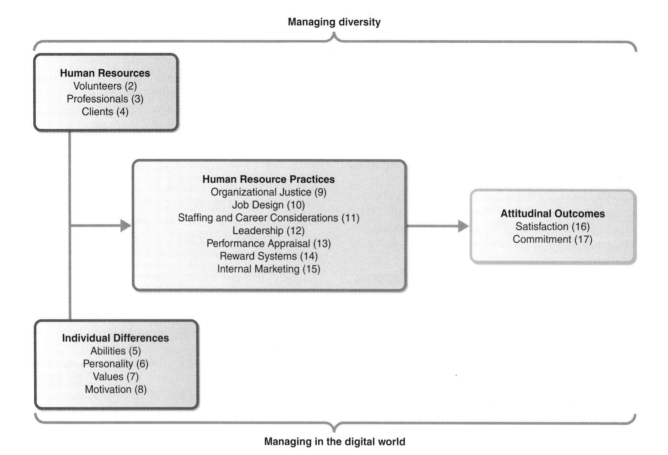

FIGURE 1.4 A model of human resource management.

to the needs and preferences defined by subgroup and individual-difference factors.

Along the way, each chapter highlights the influence of technology on HRM practices in sport and recreation, as well as the importance of managing diversity when managing our human resources.

We also outline the role of sport and recreation managers in fostering positive outcomes in an organization's human resources. Each chapter concludes with a case study that allows readers to apply their new human resource management knowledge.

CHAPTER PURSUITS

SUMMARY

We must keep sight of the fact that organizational policies and procedures are implemented by people, who thus help the organization achieve its goals. Therefore, management of human resources is as critical as any other process of management. More specifically, an organization's facilities and equipment serve as resources only when they are used by people. In addition, because sport and recreation organizations are concerned largely with

the production of services, this chapter provides detailed description of the concept of a service and its attributes.

The chapter also emphasizes the distinctions between consumer, professional, and human services. In addition, the broad category of human services can be subdivided into people-processing, people-sustaining, and people-changing services. The services typically provided by sport and recreation organizations can also be classified by the type of sport activity—egalitarian sport, elite sport, or entertainment sport. Because services in sport and recreation require physical involvement by clients—that is, our services cannot be produced without clients' participation—clients constitute one set of human resources, which needs managing. In addition, because some sport and recreation organizations rely heavily on volunteer workers, volunteers constitute another category of human resources in the field. Of course, the needs of paid workers, particularly professional workers, must also be addressed in the management practices applied to human resources.

Finally, the framework presented in this chapter suggests that human resource management practices of organizational justice, job design, staffing, leadership, performance evaluation, reward systems, and internal marketing should address the concerns of the three types of human resources (i.e., volunteers, professionals, and clients) and should be consonant with selected individual-difference variables (i.e., abilities, personality traits, values, and motivation). Effective human resource management practices should result in satisfaction among volunteer and paid workers and in their commitment to the organization. Effective practices also enhance clients' adherence to the use of services within sport and recreation and their commitment to the organization.

KEY TERMS

clients as human resources 16
consumer health services 12
consumer pleasure services 12
consumer services 10
employee–client interface 9
human capital 4
human curative services 12
human services 11
human sustenance services 12
paid professional worker 15
professional services 9
service 7
volunteer 15

UNDERSTAND

1. Compare the employee–client interface in sport and recreation organizations with such interfaces in other service organizations (e.g., a bank).

2. This chapter proposes three kinds of human resources at the disposal of sport and recreation organizations. What is the relative importance of these types of human resources in different kinds of sport and recreation organizations?

INTERACT

1. In your experience as a volunteer or a paid worker, have you seen any conflict between volunteers and paid staff? If not, reflect on a conflict you have experienced or seen in your everyday life. Discuss the reasons and solutions for such conflicts.

2. Human services may involve processing people, sustaining people, or changing people. Discuss the extent to which these three forms of human services are provided by various examples of sport and recreation organizations (e.g., Buffalo Bills, Florida Gators, local parks and recreation organization).

CHAPTER

2

Volunteers and Volunteerism

As noted in chapter 1, volunteers constitute an important set of human resources for many sport and recreation organizations. For example, volunteers run youth sport leagues in small cities and towns and serve as managers, coordinators, registration clerks, coaches, referees, and locker room attendants. Volunteers are also recruited by charitable organizations, such as the Young Men's Christian Association (YMCA), to manage their ongoing sport and recreation programs. The Special Olympics is a great success not only because of the great leadership that its administrators provide but also because of thousands of volunteers who contribute their time, energy, and effort. Volunteers also serve on the governing boards of national sport organizations, and many university athletics departments capitalize on the services of volunteer ushers on game days.

These are just a few examples of how volunteers serve in sport and recreation. As Stephens (1991) noted in his study of several volunteers, two underlying dimensions exist for volunteering: leadership and nurturance. Leadership is reflected in the tendency of some volunteers to hold offices and manage organizations, whereas nurturance is reflected in the inclination to serve those in need on

a one-on-one basis. In more practical terms, some volunteers in sport may be interested in serving as leaders and managers of organizations or programs. Inglis (1997) referred to volunteers on the boards of directors of sport governing bodies in Canada as "policy volunteers" because they are involved in setting policy, which is a leadership function. In contrast, some sport and recreation volunteers prefer to be involved directly with clients—for example, as coaches, teachers, or counselors. These individuals are referred to as "service volunteers."

Irrespective of the specific roles played by volunteers, it is critical that a sport or recreation organization effectively manage its volunteers and their contributions. The specific managerial concerns and practices associated with volunteering are identified and discussed in subsequent chapters. This chapter addresses

- the history of volunteerism;
- the economic and noneconomic significance of volunteer action, with special reference to volunteers in sport and recreation;
- the types of volunteer organizations;
- the demographics of volunteers;

- the motivation and incentives for volunteering; and
- altruism as related to volunteerism.

THE NEED FOR VOLUNTEERISM

North American societies are distinguished in part by the enormous contributions that volunteer workers make to national economies and social welfare (Moyer 1985). Historically, the tradition of **volunteerism** and community service in the United States began with the early settlers from Europe (Ellis and Noyes 1990). They found that their survival depended on their banding together and helping each other in various affairs, such as settlement defense, resource procurement, and construction of individual houses and common facilities. As Mason (1984) stated,

> It was a new kind of society: a culture of cooperation. It was a culture comprised of people who believed in self-help, in hard work, and in voluntarily going out of their way to reach out and help those whose need required their strength. In bustling coastal cities and on the isolated frontier, they had to cooperate voluntarily in order to survive. As they moved beyond survival and into prosperity, they held on to their ethic of cooperative voluntary action. (p. 1)

The significance of joining associations for the common good began to diminish as governments took over several functions of these voluntary associations through various social programs. Since this government intervention, however, voluntary action has surged upward because of several sets of factors. First, since the 1970s, many citizens have believed that neither big governments nor big businesses act in the best interests of the common person and therefore that concerted pressure must be brought to bear on them. Such pressure can be generated only if people band together in action groups (Carter 1983). These views resulted in the birth of associations, such as the consumer groups that are sometimes referred to as "third-sector" organizations (Etzioni 1973; Levitt 1973).

The second factor stems from government budgetary actions that funnel fewer and fewer dollars to the social programs that governments usurped from the associations in the first place. In the United States, beginning with the presidency of Ronald Reagan, a constant push to trim "big" government has led to reductions in the support provided to social programs. Recognizing the need for these programs, leaders in both Canada and the United States have begun to emphasize the role of voluntary action. For instance, Pierre Elliott Trudeau (cited in Morrison 1986), while prime minister of Canada, made this suggestion:

> The not-for-profit and voluntary sectors of our societies could be made to flourish. . . . Their decline has been inevitably reflected in the growth of government and commercial services. It has resulted in a loss of a sense of community. Surely we need this sector. We need to develop alternate styles of work and leisure and we need to demonstrate that there are other ways of doing the community's work. On a broad second front we must give encouragement and sustenance to these efforts. (p. 17)

In the United States, leaders have expressed similar, often more emphatic, views. For instance, President George H.W. Bush's theme of "a thousand points of light" advocated self-help and volunteerism. This theme was reiterated by President Bill Clinton in April 1997 when he organized the Presidents' Summit for America's Future, where he joined former presidents Bush, Jimmy Carter, and Gerald Ford—as well as former First Lady Nancy Reagan and former Secretary of State Colin Powell—in calling people to service and citizenship. Clinton stated, "The era of big government may be over, but the era of big challenges in our country is not. And so we need an era of big citizenship. That is why we are here" ("Clinton Urges Service" 1997).

In the same tradition, President George W. Bush created the USA Freedom Corps to, in his words, "continue the momentum generated by the countless acts of kindness we saw after the attacks of September the 11th, 2001. I asked every person in America to commit 4,000 hours over a lifetime—or about 100 hours a year—to serving neighbors in need. The response was immediate and enthusiastic, and has remained strong. Over 75,000 service organizations now work with USA Freedom Corps, and a growing percentage of Americans have answered the call to service" (Bush 2003).

Efforts in support of volunteer services may be found at the state and local government levels. As noted earlier, departments of recreation or sport in many cities rely heavily on volunteers to run their programs (e.g., youth soccer leagues, men's and women's softball leagues).

In the United States, the importance of volunteering in national life has been stressed by successive presidents. Here is what President Barack Obama said in proclaiming National Volunteer Week in 2014.

Presidential Proclamation—National Volunteer Week, 2014

NATIONAL VOLUNTEER WEEK, 2014
BY THE PRESIDENT OF THE UNITED STATES OF AMERICA
A PROCLAMATION

Through countless acts of kindness, generosity, and service, Americans recognize that we are all bound together—that we move this country forward by giving of ourselves to others and caring for those around us. Every day, Americans carry forward the tradition of service embedded in our character as a people. And as we celebrate National Volunteer Week, we embrace our shared responsibility to one another and recommit to the task of building a more perfect Union.

By performing acts of service, we can shape a Nation big enough and bold enough to accommodate the hopes of all our people. Across our country, volunteers open doors of opportunity, pave avenues of success, fortify their communities, and lay the foundation for tomorrow's growth and prosperity. They are often equipped with few resources and gain little recognition, yet because of their service, our country is a better and a stronger force for good.

My Administration is dedicated to engaging Americans through service. Through the Corporation for National and Community Service, we administer programs like AmeriCorps and Senior Corps, and we have designed innovative initiatives such as School Turnaround AmeriCorps and VetSuccess Ameri-Corps. In giving their time and talent, our volunteers can learn new skills and focus their vision, energy, and passion on projects ranging from improving disaster relief . . . [to] delivering better education . . . [to] assisting returning veterans and military families. And by establishing the Task Force on Expanding National Service, we are creating new opportunities to support our communities through service.

The American experience stands apart because our triumph is found in the example of our people. With unity of purpose and unmatched resolve, we confront our shared challenges as one people and emerge stronger than before. We saw this spirit in action when, in the wake of a devastating mudslide in Washington State, Americans stepped in to provide food, shelter, and support to survivors. We saw it last year when a tornado struck Moore, Oklahoma, and volunteers came together to rebuild homes, schools, and hospitals—because we are a Nation that stands with our fellow citizens as long as it takes. As we renew our commitment to each other during National Volunteer Week, I encourage you to visit www.Serve.gov to learn more about service opportunities in your area.

NOW, THEREFORE, I, BARACK OBAMA, President of the United States of America, by virtue of the authority vested in me by the Constitution and the laws of the United States, do hereby proclaim April 6 through April 12, 2014, as National Volunteer Week. I call upon all Americans to observe this week by volunteering in service projects across our country and pledging to make service a part of their daily lives.

IN WITNESS WHEREOF, I have hereunto set my hand this fourth day of April, in the year of our Lord two thousand fourteen, and of the Independence of the United States of America the two hundred and thirty-eighth.

BARACK OBAMA

Reprinted from The White House Office of the Press Secretary, 2014, *Presidential proclamation--National volunteer week, 2017*. Available: https://www.whitehouse.gov/the-press-office/2014/04/04/presidential-proclamation-national-volunteer-week-2014

Volunteerism is also invested with importance on a global scale. For example, in his 2015 election platform, UK Prime Minister David Cameron announced that he was committed to providing workers with three days of paid volunteering leave each year (Gosden 2015). The move was intended to provide a foundation for economic security in the future. Furthermore, under the umbrella of UK government leadership, the Volunteering England organization provides resources to community volunteers. As stated on its website, the organization merged with the National Council for Voluntary Organizations in 2013 and strives to support, enable, and celebrate volunteerism in all its forms. In discussing his role as chief executive for Volunteering England, Justin Davis Smith noted, "It takes time and money to effectively manage and support volunteers, and they themselves require training and development. . . . If volunteering is going to be an even more prominent feature of our society, attracting and retaining those volunteers is of paramount importance" (Volunteering England 2015).

The significance of volunteering also derives from past and ongoing changes in the workplace. In the past, technological innovation was expected to influence the volunteer sector in developed countries in two ways (S. Smith 1986). First, it was expected to give a large segment of society more spare time thanks to shorter working days, weeks,

and years. That time would need to be spent effectively in the pursuit of health and happiness, and volunteering would be one avenue through which individuals could seek personal growth and comfort through enhanced personal connections. Therefore, more human resources would be available for the voluntary sector. Unfortunately, this promise of more free time as a function of technological innovation has not been fulfilled. To the contrary, the combination of technological innovation and fierce international competition has caused many business and industrial organizations to downsize their workforce and pay the remaining workers less money.

This practice, in turn, has led many employees to work longer hours and at more than one job. Therefore, we are relying on young people to fill the gap in volunteerism that has been left by an older population that has less time and energy to volunteer. To this point, the National Council of Nonprofits (Chandler 2015) reported that in 2014, more than 62 million Americans volunteered. However, in one troubling trend, the Council reported that young people were very focused on career development and did not view nonprofit work as a viable career option; therefore, they devoted less time to volunteering. In addition, much of the volunteering they did perform took the form of mandatory high school service learning and therefore was not freely

---

LONDON OLYMPICS VOLUNTEERS

Following the 2012 Olympic Games and Paralympic Games in London, Prime Minister David Cameron made a concerted effort to thank the volunteers and allow them to share in the events' success. As part of this effort, he sent a thank-you letter to the thousands of volunteers who contributed to the Games. In the letter, he wrote the following:

> To see tens of thousands of people giving up their time to support London 2012 has been truly inspiring. . . . You have not just helped make London 2012 happen, but through the welcome and spirit you have shown, you have put a smile on the nation's face . . . [and] have been an essential ingredient in a remarkable summer that millions of people across the country have shared and will remember for a lifetime. You have sent an incredible message about the warmth, friendliness, and can-do spirit of the United Kingdom around the world. Quite simply, the Games couldn't have happened without you. (Prime Minister's Office 2012)

As noted by Cameron (Prime Minister's Office 2012), the Games attracted more than a quarter-million volunteers, 10 percent of whom volunteered on the days of the actual events and more than 10 percent of whom signed up for future volunteering. The Games inspired many people to volunteer for the first time and, it is hoped, will catalyze many to continue giving their time to make a difference in the community.

chosen. These trends imply that sport and recreation organizations that depend on volunteers must work harder at recruiting and retaining volunteers—especially young adults, who of course constitute the future of the volunteer workforce.

According to S. Smith (1986), the second expectation regarding technological innovation was that the demand for human services would grow and that neither the private sector nor the public sector could meet all of the increased demand. Therefore, greater pressure would be placed on the voluntary sector to provide these services. This point was also stressed by Clinton (1997) in the 1997 Presidents' Summit for America's Future as part of its call for citizens to help youth at risk.

The foregoing review indicates that the need for voluntary action will continue to grow. Indeed, volunteering will act as a strong determinant of how well a society can handle itself and ensure the welfare of its members. Thus, management of volunteers needs as much emphasis as management of paid workers.

> The recent emphasis on voluntary action has been brought about by recognition that such action is needed in order to advocate for social change, make up for the decreasing governmental financial support provided to social programs, provide personal growth opportunities for people with increased leisure time, and respond to increasing need for human services.

Economic Significance of Volunteers

National economies generally consist of the products of businesses and government agencies. However, as Beamish (1985) pointed out,

> the economy is much larger and far more pervasive than the work world of wage labor, capital, and public bureaucracies or corporations; a highly significant and ever-present part of the economy is the production and distribution of resources based upon private, *nonremunerated* work. (p. 218, emphasis added)

Let us consider the nonremunerated work to which Beamish referred. A research report from the Corporation for National and Community Service (2013) showed that 63 million Americans, or 25 percent of the adult population, contributed nearly 8 billion hours of volunteer service during 2013. Furthermore, the Bureau of Labor Statistics, as indexed by Independent Sector (2015), estimated that volunteer labor was worth just over $23 per hour in the United States, yielding a total dollar value of $173 billion for volunteer time.

Though it is unclear how many people volunteered specifically for sport and recreation in the United States, the reported rate in various recent years was 19 percent of all volunteers in Canada (DePratto 2014), 39 percent in Australia (Australian Bureau of Statistics 2010), and 53 percent in the UK (Institute for Volunteering Research 2015). Some years earlier, Tedrick and Henderson (1989) estimated that 21 percent of Americans who

---

TEAM IDENTIFICATION AND VOLUNTEERING

Some sport organizations struggle to recruit and retain volunteers, whereas others have the luxury of many individuals clamoring to volunteer. For instance, applicants to volunteer at The Ohio State University football games have waited as long as four years to serve as ushers (Fiely 2006). In addition, they pay up to $50 for their uniforms, and some fly in from far-off places to be at the games.

In volunteering this way, these individuals couple their love of Buckeye football with service to the university and community. Granted, they get to see every game and enjoy the prestige of helping to manage such a prominent event. But their eagerness to usher, at considerable cost to themselves, also expresses their identification with Buckeye football, their devotion to the university, and their desire to serve the community. This dedication is evidenced in the fact that since the 9/11 terror attacks, much more is required of ushers. For example, they must follow guidelines that are more formalized, undergo preseason training, and receive training in disability services and terrorism prevention.

volunteered did so in sport and recreation. On the basis of these figures, we can safely surmise that roughly 20 percent of all volunteers in the United States are involved in sport and recreation and that the economic value of their contributions amounts to about 20 percent of the total dollars just mentioned, or slightly over $34 billion. The enormity of this amount is highlighted further when compared with the total worth of the U.S. sport industry, which was about $190 billion in 2005 (Milano and Chelladurai 2011).

The need for and the significance of voluntary action are nowhere more pronounced than in sport and recreation. In fact, sport services at the amateur level are organized and delivered largely by a vast network of volunteers and voluntary associations

RESEARCH ON VOLUNTEERING

The importance of volunteers in sport organizations is highlighted by the number of studies carried out on various aspects of volunteer involvement in sport. In order to show the range of topics investigated, this section outlines a number of studies published in the *Journal of Sport Management*.

Focusing on volunteers at the executive level, Doherty and Carron (2003) found that volunteer executives expressed higher cohesion (e.g., coming together as a working group) regarding the task at hand than regarding social aspects (e.g., social gatherings). They also found that task cohesion was predictive of the volunteer executives' level of effort and intent to continue with the committee and that both task and social cohesion predicted member satisfaction and perceived effectiveness of the committee. In a study of executive committees of Canadian sport organizations, Doherty, Patterson, and Van Bussel (2004) found that the norms surrounding committee functioning were quite strong in terms of both social and task interactions. In another study of volunteer executive-committee members in Canadian sport organizations, Hamm-Kerwin and Doherty (2010) found that conflict between volunteers was negatively related to both committee decision quality and individual satisfaction with and commitment to the organization.

Other studies have taken up a wide variety of subjects. For example, Malloy and Agarwal (2001) studied perceptions of ethical climate in a Canadian provincial sport organization and found that internal strategies of control and conformity did not exert much influence on members' perceptions of the ethical climate. In a theoretical paper, Kikulis (2000) discussed continuity and change in the governance of Canadian national sport organizations. The paper highlighted the institutionalization of volunteer boards, the reinstitutionalization of volunteer control, and the semi-institutionalization of paid executive roles as explanations for changes in governance and decision making in national sport organizations. In a different part of the world, Colyer (2000) studied the organizational culture of a few sport associations in Western Australia on the basis of the competing values approach. The results showed the existence of subcultures defined by tensions between volunteers and employees.

Cuskelly, McIntyre, and Boag (1998) found that organizational commitment among volunteers in community-based sport organizations was predicted by age group, occupation, years of organizational membership, and time spent on administration. They also found a strong positive relationship between committee functioning and organizational commitment. Harman and Doherty (2014) interviewed 22 volunteer coaches and found that volunteer coach behavior was influenced by both transactional and relational expectations of their sport clubs; results differed by level of play and coaching tenure. Addressing decision making, Auld and Godbey (1998) studied Canadian national sport organizations and found that

(Government of Canada 1992; B.D. McPherson 1975; Slack 1985; Tedrick and Henderson 1989). Volunteer involvement in sport and recreation takes many forms. For example, in many national sport governing bodies in both the United States and Canada, the governing boards consist of volunteers who help make policy for their organizations. Volunteers also head state-level (or provincial-level) organizations and sustain activities at the grassroots level of all sports. In addition, as noted earlier, volunteers help with many projects initiated and run by government agencies and for-profit enterprises.

Taking a step back, three caveats must be noted in relation to the calculations presented earlier. First, the survey respondents self-reported the information on which the estimated volunteering rates are

influence in decision making was not mutual between volunteers and professionals and that each group exerted greater influence in specific areas of decision making.

Inglis (1997) studied the executive directors, volunteer presidents, and volunteer board members of provincial sport organizations in Ontario, Canada, and found that gender and position influenced survey ratings or perceptions on the roles of the board relating to mission, planning, the executive director, and community relations. Amis and Slack (1996), in a study of the size and structure of a set of voluntary sport organizations, found that the unique features of these sport organizations and the presence of conflict between volunteers and professionals for control did not permit a consistent relationship between the sizes and structures of the associations. Farrell, Johnston, and Twynam (1998) surveyed 300 volunteers in the Canadian Women's Curling Championship of 1996 and found that their motivations could be categorized as hinging on purposiveness, solidarity, external traditions, and commitments. The authors also found that volunteer satisfaction was differentially associated with particular attributes of the event organization and competition facility.

There has been a trend toward voluntary giving of time in sport-for-development organizations. Welty Peachey, Bruening, Lyras, Cohen, and Cunningham (2015) found that volunteers at a large, multinational sport-for-development event developed social capital through relationship building, learning, and enhanced motivation to work for social change and reciprocity. Along similar lines, in a study of volunteers at the 2010 Nordic Skiing World Cup, Skirstad and Hanstad (2013) found that a major reason for women to volunteer was to improve their social capital and to get involved in useful networks. These authors point to a distinction between traditional volunteers, who are for the most part males and members of sport clubs, and a modern volunteer culture defined by younger females.

In studying the transition of individuals from the role of playing sport to that of volunteering, Cuskelly and O'Brien (2013) found that in such transitions, individuals were interested in extending their connections to sport and their involvement in it. Volunteering also provided a means of continuing the relationships built during one's playing career and enhancing one's sense of belonging. Schlesinger, Egli, and Nagel (2013) investigated the factors that impelled individuals to continue or terminate their volunteering in sport clubs. Their results showed that more workers who felt satisfied intended to continue their volunteering and that a volunteer's orientation toward collective solidarity influenced his or her tendency to continue volunteering. Even more important, orientation toward group solidarity exerted stronger influence than did volunteer job satisfaction. Accordingly, the researchers suggested that "the promotion of obligations of solidarity and reciprocity, a cooperative club atmosphere, and the emotional and social attachment of club members need to be central elements for effectively managing volunteers and retaining them in sports clubs" (p. 48).

based. Second, time spent volunteering may not equate to work done. Third, the calculation of the dollar value of volunteer labor was based entirely on minimum hourly wages, but some volunteer work may be worth more (in economic terms) than other volunteer work.

Noneconomic Significance of Volunteers

Apart from their economic significance, volunteers also bring intangible and nonquantifiable assets to the situation. As Tedrick and Henderson (1989) suggested, clients perceive that volunteers are more credible, legitimate, and sincere because of their free service in an activity of their liking. Because they are free from considerations of financial benefit to themselves, they can be objective and critical in their evaluation of organizational processes. Such unbridled and constructive feedback helps keep the organization on the right track.

In another advantage as compared with full-time paid employees, volunteers hold greater control over the pressures associated with performing a service. Because they choose the type of service that they perform, and the times during which they do so, they can tailor their volunteering to be consistent with their tolerance level for stress and pressure. This tailoring proves beneficial both to the volunteers and to their clients, as better service results from the flexibility in time. Furthermore, organizations can expect volunteers to try out new and innovative approaches to delivering their services

because they are less concerned with organizational constraints or reprisals.

From a broader perspective, volunteers can serve the public relations and fundraising functions effectively and unobtrusively because they are drawn from the community in which the organization operates. In addition, as noted by Kerwin, Warner, Walker, and Stevens (2015), volunteering for small-scale sport events can increase volunteers' sense of community. This increase, in turn, provides many benefits, both individual (e.g., increased well-being) and societal (e.g., increased civic engagement). These social benefits are just as important as, if not more than, the economic value of volunteers' contributions to the organization because they have a long term impact on those who volunteer. Therefore, managers of sport and recreation organizations should make every effort to capitalize on the availability of volunteers and their enormous tangible and intangible contributions.

Volunteering is a significant economic activity in terms of the time and energy contributed and the expertise provided by volunteers. Equally important is the noneconomic or social significance of volunteering. Specifically, volunteers provide a source of credibility and legitimacy for their organizations, provide objective and constructive evaluation of organizational processes, and admirably fulfill public relations functions.

DIVERSITY MANAGEMENT IN HUMAN RESOURCES

The pool of volunteers brought into a voluntary organization to serve as board members can influence the organization's ability to value diversity, which constitutes the first stage in Chelladurai's (2014) integrative framework for managing diversity. Acceptance of diversity starts with surface-level diversity, wherein a board president must strategically recruit diverse members for the board and acknowledge the value of diverse opinions and ideas. To begin with, the composition of the board can be diversified through intentional processes of recruitment and selection (or election). Next, the organization should actively embed acceptance and acknowledgment of the benefits associated with deep-level diversity (e.g., differences in value, opinions, and expressions) in all HRM practices (e.g., recruitment, training, orientation, and performance evaluation of board members).

VOLUNTARY ORGANIZATIONS

The foregoing discussion addresses volunteer action in general; however, this action takes place in various organizational contexts, for various purposes, and with various motives. Therefore, it is useful to consider the basic types of volunteer organizations. Sills (1972) defined a voluntary organization as

> an organized group of persons (1) that is formed in order to further some common interest of its members; (2) in which membership is voluntary in the sense that it is neither mandatory nor acquired through birth; and (3) that exists independently of the state. (p. 363)

Sills' definition is similar to Knoke's (1986) definition of an association: "a formally organized named group, most of whose members—whether persons or organizations—are not financially recompensed for their participation" (p. 2).

These definitions are broad enough to include a variety of organizations, ranging from local sport clubs to nationally organized groups, that promote the interests of a group of persons or organizations (e.g., the NCAA) or a particular ideology (e.g., the National Association for Girls and Women in Sport). Because these voluntary associations also differ among themselves, they can be subdivided into specific categories. Though several classification schemes exist, the one proposed by Palisi and Jacobson (1977) best fits our purposes. These authors based their scheme on earlier efforts by C.W. Gordon and Babchuk (1959) and Warriner and Prather (1965). Their scheme consists of five classes of voluntary organizations: **instrumental–productive for members**, **instrumental–productive for others**, **expressive–pleasure in performance**, **expressive–sociability**, and **expressive–ideological** (see figure 2.1).

- *Instrumental–productive for members:* Some volunteer organizations have been created and are maintained for the benefit of their members. Examples include labor unions formed to ensure the rights, privileges, and benefits of their members (i.e., the workers), including various players associations (e.g., NFL Players Association) and referees guilds (e.g., World Umpires Association). This class of volunteer organization is instrumental in enhancing the welfare of its members.

- *Instrumental–productive for others:* Instrumental–productive volunteer organizations (e.g., Humane Society, American Red Cross, Goodwill Industries) exist primarily to produce goods or services for the benefit of the community or for one of its deprived segments. Their critical activities are intended to change or improve something or someone outside of the group's membership, and

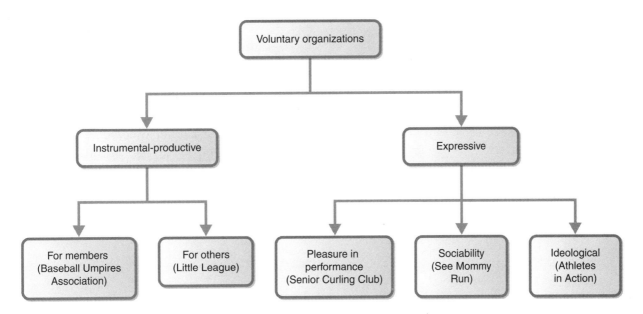

FIGURE 2.1 Palisi and Jacobson's typology of voluntary organizations.

such activities do not create specific benefits for the membership itself. Some charitable organizations, such as Rotary Clubs, are engaged in providing sport and recreation services for youth in the community. In contrast, the major purpose of a national sport governing body (e.g., Basketball Canada, which has a volunteer-based board of directors), is to govern and regulate its own activities for the benefit of participants in the sport.

• *Expressive–pleasure in performance:* These organizations offer activities in which their members can participate exclusively. The activities of such organizations (e.g., square dancing, bowling, curling) can enable pleasure in performance itself without any intention of producing goods or services. Examples include intramural co-ed volleyball teams and community bowling leagues. Such associations are usually formed around activities governed by rules provided by an external agency, such as a national association or a professional group (e.g., American Bowling Congress, Curling Canada).

• *Expressive–sociability:* Some volunteer organizations focus on satisfying their members' social needs through various activities (e.g., happy hour club, birthday club). For example, in Canada and the United States, there has been a surge of "mommy and me" playgroups where mothers and other caregivers get together with children and organize fun activities (e.g., arts and crafts). Such groups (e.g., Niagara Mommy and Me Playgroup) often use online platforms that enable moms and other caregivers to connect and make plans to get their children together.

• *Expressive–ideological:* When an organization's activities are carried out to evoke and reaffirm a valued belief system (e.g., Communion in the Christian church), the association performs a symbolic function. Such associations are formed on the basis of a sacred belief or doctrine symbolized by standardized or ritualized activities. Examples include churches and some lodges.

The general classification scheme for voluntary organizations holds some specific relevance for sport and recreation organizations. For example, many sport clubs (e.g., intramural teams) provide members with the pleasure of participation in physical activity. Many others (e.g., recreational soccer or volleyball clubs) also serve the social function. The production function is exhibited by service clubs such as the Lions, Kiwanis, and Knights of Columbus when they organize sport teams and competitions for youngsters in their communities.

In fact, some organizations (e.g., Little League Baseball and Softball) are exclusively production oriented; adults manage these organizations and carry out their activities for the benefit of youth (thus they are instrumental–productive for others).

It is more difficult to think of sport and recreation organizations organized around the symbolic function. However, one might argue that this category includes, for example, groups of bodybuilders or joggers who do their activity with a religious fervor and create routines and symbolic rituals of their own. In another example, Athletes in Action uses sport as a means to propagate Christian ideology.

The contrast between volunteer associations that focus on benefits for members and those that focus on benefits for others carries implications for management. For instance, it affects recruiting practices. Organizations that are instrumental–productive for members recruit volunteer *members*, whereas organizations that are instrumental–productive for others recruit volunteer *workers*. Obviously, recruiting a member is not as difficult as recruiting an unpaid worker; this issue is discussed in greater detail in chapter 11.

Volunteer organizations can be distinguished on the basis of instrumentality (whether they are formed to create benefits for members or for external target groups) and expressiveness (whether they offer opportunities for members to engage in specific forms of activity, to satisfy social needs, or to express an ideological perspective). Each type of volunteer organization imposes certain demands and constraints on management.

Volunteer organizations also differ in their degree of accessibility and their capacity to confer status (C.W. Gordon and Babchuk 1959). An organization may be so open that persons with different social, economic, and demographic backgrounds can become members or participate in programs. For instance, the YMCA sets no membership criteria and allows everybody in the community to participate in its programs. On the other hand, some organizations restrict membership to specified classes of people who possess certain valued attributes. For example, a club comprising former athletes of a particular university restricts its membership on the basis of achievement. Similarly, some clubs restrict membership based on sex, which once was

VOLUNTEERING AND SERIOUS LEISURE

Most sport and recreation agencies depend heavily on volunteers to plan and implement their programs, especially for mass participation. Even as these volunteers provide recreational opportunities for others, their volunteer activities often also form part of their own leisure experiences. For a subset of these individuals, their volunteering can best be described as "serious leisure." When asked to introduce themselves, these volunteers are quite likely to identify their volunteer role in addition to, or instead of, their profession or place of employment. Serious leisure has been defined as "the steady pursuit of an amateur, hobbyist, or career volunteer activity that captivates its participants with its complexity and many challenges. It is profound, long-lasting, and invariably based on substantial skills, knowledge, or experience, if not a combination of these three. It also requires perseverance to a greater or lesser degree" (R.A. Stebbins 2001, p. 54).

Thus, although volunteering is a leisure-time activity for all sport volunteers, it constitutes serious leisure for those who spend considerable time and effort to become more proficient in their volunteer jobs. For instance, a volunteer may become the president of the local, regional, or state sport association. In that position, he or she strives to learn all about the sport and how to run the organization. To this person, serving as volunteer president involves serious leisure. Those who are involved in serious leisure tend to persevere in the chosen activity despite hardships; treat their involvement in the activity as a second career; extend their effort, knowledge, or skills to the activity; gain a sense of self-actualization, accomplishment, and self-renewal; be part of a social world with its own culture; and identify strongly with their volunteer activities (R.A. Stebbins 2001).

Sport and recreation managers must recognize the differences between those who volunteer in the mode of serious leisure and those who volunteer in the mode of what R.A. Stebbins (2001) refers to as casual leisure. Serious-leisure volunteers seek highly engaging and challenging assignments and are willing to learn. In order to meet the specific needs and preferences of these volunteers, managers must tailor their recruiting, retention, and recognition strategies. In a study by Misener, Doherty, and Hamm-Kerwin (2010), older adult volunteers in sport (65 years and older) engaged in volunteering characterized as serious leisure because they were involved substantially (e.g., put in hours similar to those of a part-time or even full-time job), strongly identified with the activity (e.g., considered their volunteering as part of their identity), and demonstrated a need to persevere through difficult times (e.g., stayed engaged despite hardship). As a result, the researchers concluded that managers need to recognize negative experiences of serious-leisure volunteers and proactively manage them in order to prevent attrition as an outcome of burnout and dissatisfaction.

On a different note, Gibson, Willming, and Holdnak (2002) took issue with Stebbins' (1982) statement that "sitting at a football game," or spectating, does not constitute serious leisure. As implied by the title of their article, "We're Gators . . . Not Just Gator Fans," they posit that serious leisure is indeed entailed in being a diehard fan. Their study of selected fans of the University of Florida football team showed that these fans were characterized by the same attributes of serious leisure suggested by Stebbins. Specifically, they persevered with the team through the unsuccessful years (i.e., they were not "fair-weather friends"); were involved with the team for a long time; invested significant effort and money in the activity; gained personal benefits of social interaction, sense of belonging, self-enrichment, and recreation; took part in a unique social world with its own subculture; and identified very strongly with the team.

an ascription that assumed men held higher status than women. However, more recently, restrictive memberships based on factors such as sex and race have been successfully challenged in courts and are becoming obsolete.

Volunteer organizations also differ in their capacity to bestow prestige on their members. That is, belonging to certain associations (e.g., the New York Athletic Club) may confer a desired status on a member even without regard to the organization's activities or the member's participation in them. Organizations may also confer status and prestige due to the inherent worth of their programs or the significance attached to those activities by the community. For instance, consider the various sport governing bodies. Members of these organizations enjoy a degree of status and prestige because they are engaged in developing elite athletes in their respective sports. However, because some sports are more popular than others, enjoying greater fan and media support, members of the organizations associated with those sports enjoy even greater status and prestige.

PEOPLE WHO VOLUNTEER

The preceding description of volunteer organizations provides a framework for analyzing and prescribing managerial activities. However, we must also gain some understanding of the people who compose volunteer organizations. After all, those who manage or carry out the activities of an organization exert considerable influence on its character and its operational procedures. Furthermore, volunteering need not be confined to volunteer organizations. Indeed, it is becoming increasingly common for other forms of organizations, including governmental ones, to use the services of volunteers. Therefore, the discussion of volunteers and volunteering should not be confined to volunteer organizations. We need to understand the dynamics of volunteering with reference to various organizational contexts.

Volunteer Demographics

One enduring line of research in this regard focuses on the social correlates of joining voluntary associations. More specifically, cross-sectional surveys have studied volunteer background variables, such as age, sex, education, income, marital status, and race. For example, table 2.1 lists the rates of volunteering

in 2010 in Canada and 2007 in the United Kingdom among groups defined by sex, employment status, and age; the data for Canada also include average educational and income levels. In the United States, for the year ending in September 2014, the Bureau of Labor Statistics reported volunteering rates of 27 percent for whites, 20 percent for blacks, 18 percent for Asians, and 16 percent for Hispanics. During the same period, the rate was about 20 percent for married people, people never married, and people of other marital status (U.S. Department of Labor 2016).

One potential benefit of this line of research is that it might identify groups whose members are likely to volunteer. Unfortunately, however, the research results have not provided a clear *pattern* of relationships between background variables and rates of volunteering. That is, although several studies have shown a relationship between selected variables and volunteering, such relationships have not been shown to be significant when considered simultaneously. Thus, continued research is needed to properly identify variables that would allow sport and recreation managers to group volunteers in an effort to predict future volunteering.

Traditionally, women volunteered more than men presumably because they had more leisure time. However, abundance of leisure time can no longer be advanced as a reason for this differential rate of volunteering because most women are in the workforce and an increasing number of women are single parents. As of 2007, women (64 percent) continued to volunteer at a higher rate than men (54 percent) in the United Kingdom (see table 2.1).

Another gender-related aspect of volunteering was highlighted by J.M. McPherson and Smith-Lovin (1986), who reported considerable gender segregation in voluntary organizations. Their results showed that almost 50 percent of the memberships in the voluntary organizations that they surveyed consisted exclusively of women and 20 percent consisted exclusively of men. They also reported that the instrumental organizations were the most heterogeneous and that expressive groups were the most likely to be homogeneous. It is not clear whether such differences exist in sport and recreation organizations today. Although gender-based segregation could exist among sport teams because of the rules surrounding a sport, cross-gender participation is becoming increasingly popular. In the future, sport and recreation organizations could be nudged further toward heterogeneous membership by the continuing evolution of views on gender-based roles, as well as recent court rulings.

TABLE 2.1 Rates of Volunteering by Sex, Education, Age Group, and Income

GROUPS	VOLUNTEER RATE (%) IN CANADA (2010)	VOLUNTEER RATE (%) IN UK (2007)
Sex		
Male[†]	46	54
Female	48[*]	64[*]
Employment status		
Employed[†]	50	62
Unemployed	34[*]	57[*]
Not in labor force	44[*]	55[*]
Education		
Less than high school[†] diploma	37	NA
Graduated high school	43[*]	NA
Some postsecondary	54[*]	NA
Postsecondary diploma or certificate	45[*]	NA
University or college graduate degree	58[*]	NA
Age group (years)		
15-24[†]	58	57
25-34	46[*]	57[*]
35-44	54[*]	64[*]
45-54	45[*]	58[*]
55-64	41[*]	64[*]
65-74	40[*]	NA
75 or more	31[*]	NA
Income ($)		
Less than 20,000[†]	33	NA
20,000-39,999	36[*]	NA
40,000-59,999	42[*]	NA
60,000-79,999	51[*]	NA
80,000-99,999	51[*]	NA
100,000-119,999	54[*]	NA
120,000 or more	58[*]	NA

[†]Reference group for which percentages are based

[*]Statistically significant difference ($\alpha = 0.05$) from reference group

Based on Statistic Canada 2015. Available: www.statcan.gc.ca/pub/11-008-x/2012001/t/11638/tbl02-eng.htm; N. Low et al., 2007, *Helping Out: A national survey of volunteering and charitable giving* (National Centre for Social Research and Institute for Volunteering Research). Available: http://www.ivr.org.uk/images/stories/Institute-of-Volunteering-Research/Migrated-Resources/Documents/H/OTS_Helping_Out.pdf.

VIEWPOINT

Noting a decline in volunteer participation in sport in Australia, Cuskelly (2004) suggested that volunteer labor in sport can be bolstered by increasing recruitment efforts, increasing the workload of current volunteers, or retaining current volunteers for longer periods of time.

Another avenue to focus on in volunteer participation in sport and recreation is the recruitment of previous athletes to volunteer. Specifically, Cuskelly (2004) proposes the transition-extension hypothesis to explain the fact that a large number of players turn to volunteering in sport once their playing days are over. Cuskelly (2004) uses continuity theory (Atchley 1989) to discuss the transition-extension hypothesis, which postulates that "adults are drawn by the weight of their past experience to use continuity as a primary adaptive strategy for dealing with changes associated with normal aging" (Atchley 1989, p. 183, as cited in Cuskelly). On the basis of this perspective, Cuskelly argues as follows:

> The transition from a playing to a volunteer role in sport can lead to a heightened sense of engagement. During or after the transition from playing sport, volunteers acting out of self-interest, altruism, or feelings of social pressure sometimes increase their knowledge and commitment to a sporting activity or a particular sport organization. (p. 71)

Corporate Employee Volunteering

One modern trend is for business and industrial enterprises to help the community by giving their employees time off to volunteer in community-oriented programs (Ilsley 1990; Sagawa and Segal 2000; Steckel and Simons 1992; Tedrick and Henderson 1989). These businesses may facilitate employee volunteering for specific organizations as part of their initiatives toward corporate social responsibility. In one study conducted in Canada, Ayer (2009) found that 43 percent of businesses in the study supported or encouraged volunteering by their employees; the percentage was nearly twice as high (82 percent) among businesses with annual profits of more than $25 million.

The effects of employee volunteering on job performance have been examined only in limited research. For instance, Rodell (2013) addressed volunteering and work as two separate domains of activity and advanced two hypotheses about them: congruence and compensation. The *congruence* hypothesis envisages that employees volunteer because "meaningfulness in their jobs has whetted their appetite for volunteering." The *compensation* hypothesis proposes that employees volunteer "only to make up for the lack of meaningfulness in their jobs" (p. 1277) Rodell's research showed "a positive trend between meaningful job experiences and volunteering" (i.e., support for the congruence hypothesis) and "a positive indirect relationship between volunteering and job performance through job absorption" (p. 1287), where job absorption is linked to focusing a great deal on the job or work that a volunteer takes on.

Taking note of the fact that volunteering by employees does elevate their productivity, businesses should encourage their employees to volunteer. Business that do so will benefit in two respects. First, enhanced employee productivity will help their bottom line (i.e., profits); second, they will gain recognition for being socially responsible.

WHY PEOPLE VOLUNTEER

Although it is useful to identify types of people who are likely to volunteer, it is equally necessary to understand *why* people volunteer. That is, the psychological and motivational patterns of volunteers matter as much as do their socioeconomic backgrounds. In fact, one could argue that the question of why people volunteer is even more critical than the question of who volunteers. Specifically, answering the question of why someone volunteers can provide information as to the needs of the volunteers, how needs can be served, and thus how to retain volunteers for future events and programs.

People differ in many respects—for example, attitudes, beliefs, and personality. All of these factors underlie a person's motivation to engage and persevere in an activity; therefore, they bear on the

Although volunteering rates differ somewhat according to gender, race, age, education, and income, it is unclear whether any of these demographic characteristics is related to volunteering for a particular organization or program in sport or recreation. Regardless, sport and recreation managers may ask business and industrial enterprises to give their employees time off for volunteering, with the expectation of a positive response from their employees.

management of human resources. These individual differences are operative in any context—for example in the family, in friendship groups, and in organizational settings—regardless of whether the individuals are paid or volunteer workers. Concerns relating to individual differences are addressed in detail in chapters 5 through 8. However, one fundamental question needs to be addressed at this stage: Why do people volunteer? That is, why do people choose to act out their beliefs, attitudes, and personality in volunteer activity? What do individuals seek through their participation in voluntary work?

This question may be fundamentally answered with Knoke and Prensky's (1984) three-mode incentive scheme for understanding volunteer participation. The three modes are as follows:

- Utilitarian
- Affective
- Normative

Utilitarian Incentives

By definition, voluntary action precludes direct payment of salary or material benefits to volunteers (reimbursement of expenses incurred on behalf of the organization is not considered a utilitarian benefit for our purposes). However, it is conceivable that individuals may gain some benefits indirectly from their volunteering experience. For example, a sport or recreation management student might volunteer to help organize and conduct a Special Olympics event. In the process, the student would gain valuable experience in event management as well as understanding of the philosophy and ideals of the Special Olympics. At the same time, a parent of a participant might also volunteer to help with the event and, in the process, help his or her own child.

In these two examples, the same event provides two very different bases for volunteer incentives: experience and caring for one's child.

Such varied utilitarian benefits may provide the motivating force for many people who volunteer. Therefore, sport and recreation managers need to recognize that different incentives may motivate different individuals to volunteer for any given project. According to Vaillancourt and Payette (1986), these **utilitarian incentives** can be explained by two models from economic theory: the household production model and the human capital model.

Household production comprises domestic chores and child-rearing and child-minding activities, and people may volunteer as an extension of their child-rearing and child-minding activities (Vaillancourt and Payette 1986). For example, a parent may volunteer to coach a youth soccer team of which his or her child is a member. Such volunteering is based on utilitarian incentives associated with child-rearing and child-minding. The value of these benefits to a household increases with the number of children in the household. Therefore, it is not surprising that one of the more frequently cited reasons for volunteering in youth sport programs is that one's own children participate in those programs. However, these benefits can accrue only if several households cooperate in volunteering to provide the overall set of necessary services. That is, several other children need to bring their parents to the playground to coach other teams, referee games, or serve in other roles.

Human capital consists of knowledge and skill that act as determinants of wages or salaries. Individuals generally try to improve their human capital through education and work in order to increase their monetary rewards. Yet human capital can also be enhanced through volunteering. That is, individuals may learn as many new skills and gain as much new knowledge through volunteer work as through paid work. Such opportunities are more welcome to people who are excluded from regular paid work, such as those who are unemployed, too young or too old to work, or taking time off to rear their children. Reasons cited for volunteering in this vein include developing knowledge of sport and recreation and skill in teaching, leadership, and administration (e.g., Henderson 1981; Mitchelson and Slack 1983; Tedrick and Henderson 1989).

Affective Incentives

The affective incentives are a function of interpersonal relationships that result in fellowship, friendship, prestige, and similar outcomes. Thus these incentives play a greater role in the three forms of expressive organizations (see figure 2.1), particularly those that emphasize the sociability function. More broadly, because all organizations are composed of people, these outcomes are theoretically possible in various types of organizations. However, the degree to which they accrue to an individual volunteer may be affected by the particular composition of an organization's membership and the purposes and processes adopted by the organization. Again, these social incentives have been cited as reasons for volunteering in sport and recreation (e.g., Henderson 1981; Mitchelson and Slack 1983; Tedrick and Henderson 1989).

Normative Incentives

Volunteer organizations may pursue the goal of helping others by enhancing their happiness, health, and welfare. Individuals may share these organizational goals and join these organizations because of their genuine concern for the welfare of others. Normative incentives hinge on the satisfactions derived from doing something good as reflected in the organization's purpose. This particular set of incentives is most relevant to organizations categorized as instrumental–productive for others or as expressive–ideological (see figure 2.1).

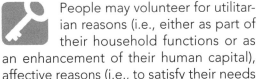 People may volunteer for utilitarian reasons (i.e., either as part of their household functions or as an enhancement of their human capital), affective reasons (i.e., to satisfy their needs for friendship, fellowship, and status), or normative reasons (i.e., the need to do something good).

Another framework of volunteer motivation was provided by Clary and associates (1998). In their study of volunteers' motivations, they found that the act of volunteering serves six key functions, and they developed a survey scale referred to as the Volunteer Functions Inventory. Here are the six functions, each given with a sample survey item.

Values: Volunteering provides opportunities for individuals to express their values related to altruistic and humanitarian concerns for others. Sample survey item: I feel compassion toward people in need.

TECHNOLOGY IN HUMAN RESOURCE MANAGEMENT

Managers can use social media technology strategically to determine incentives that are meaningful to volunteers. For example, following individuals on Twitter who represent a potential pool of volunteers for an event or program can help a manager track the discussions held by these individuals and prompt conversations regarding their needs. With Twitter, once you "tag" an individual in a tweet, you can communicate with all other individuals in that person's social network. The first step for a manager is to connect with volunteers; the next step is to create strategic messages that allow for information sharing regarding the needs of the potential volunteers.

Understanding: Volunteering facilitates new learning and provides opportunities to exercise personal knowledge, skills, and abilities that may not be used elsewhere. Sample survey item: I can learn how to deal with a variety of people.

Social function: Volunteering allows for social gathering with friends and participation in activities favored by significant others. Sample survey item: People I know share an interest in community service.

Career-related benefits: Volunteering may foster benefits related to one's career. Sample survey item: I can make new contacts that might help my business or career.

Protective function: Volunteering serves to reduce feelings of guilt over being more fortunate than others and to address personal problems. Sample survey item: Volunteering is a good escape from my own troubles.

Enhancement: Volunteering strengthens one's ego in positive ways. Sample survey item: Volunteering increases my self-esteem.

Note the similarities between the classifications of volunteer organizations and the types of volunteer incentives (or motives). For instance, the expressive–sociability function of a volunteer organization is consistent with the affective incentives. Similarly, the expressive–ideological function subsumes the normative incentives. The distinction between the two schemes lies in the fact that one focuses on the organizational perspective and the other on the individual perspective.

VIEWPOINT

Volunteering, as conceived of here, is a planned act that differs from spontaneously providing help. In precise terms, Rodell (2013) defined volunteering as "giving time or skills during a planned activity for a volunteer group or organization" (p. 1274), such as a charitable or nonprofit group. Rodell highlights three key elements of this definition: volunteering is (a) an active involvement, as distinct from, say, giving a monetary donation; (b) it is a planned (proactive) activity, as distinct from a spontaneous (reactive) act, as in the case of an emergency; and (c) it occurs in the context of a volunteer or charitable organization.

ALTRUISM AND VOLUNTEERISM

The preceding sections largely clarify the incentives and motives for volunteering. However, the discussion becomes more complex, and even perplexing, if we also consider the notion of **altruism**—selfless concern for others—in volunteering. Therefore, clear understanding of this issue is critical to effective management of volunteers in sport and recreation organizations.

Altruism is the reason cited most often for volunteering; indeed, it is often embedded in definitions of career (longitudinal) volunteerism (Stebbins 2015). Yet the traditional view that altruism underlies volunteering is debated by scholars and practitioners alike. For example, D.H. Smith (1981) pointed out that debates about the relationship between altruism and volunteerism tend to be muddled by differing definitions, that the "arguments tend to be endless," and that "heat tends to far exceed light in these debates" (p. 21). In his view, altruism is

> an aspect of human motivation that is present to the degree that the individual derives intrinsic satisfaction or psychic rewards from attempting to optimize the intrinsic satisfaction of one or more other persons without the conscious expectation of participating in an exchange relationship whereby those "others" would be obligated to make similar/related satisfaction optimization efforts in return. (p. 23)

This definition envisages two kinds of outcomes emanating from the same action: egoistic outcomes (i.e., one's intrinsic satisfaction or psychic rewards) and altruistic outcomes (i.e., satisfaction and rewards experienced by others). D.H. Smith (1981) further suggested that absolute altruism is not a necessary condition for volunteerism and that concern for some kind of personal reward underlies all volunteering:

> The essence of volunteerism is not altruism, but rather the contribution of services, goods, or money to help accomplish some desired end, without substantial coercion or remuneration. It is the voluntariness and nonremunerated character of volunteerism that is distinctive. . . . Volunteers are not angelic humanitarians in any sense. They are human beings, engaging in unpaid, uncoerced activities for various kinds of tangible and intangible incentives, with psychic or intangible incentives being especially important. Nor are volunteer organizations paragons of organizational virtue in any sense. Some do very positive things for the general welfare; others are harmful, and selfish in the extreme. (p. 33)

VIEWPOINT

Psychologists have studied the mechanism behind "helping" behavior (Batson 1991; Cialdini et al. 1987; Dovidio 1995). One view, the egoistic view, holds that people help others only to relieve their own stress or to improve their own moods (Cialdini et al.). In another view, the altruistic view, people can also be motivated to help in order to improve the welfare of others without reference to personal stress or mood (Batson; Dovidio). Most of the research in this ongoing egoism–altruism debate addresses helping in a single incident involving some form of emergency. However, when extended, these concepts suggest that volunteering in sport and recreation can also be either egoistically or altruistically based.

In contrast, other authors hold that "altruism is a central, and potentially the central, impetus for volunteer activity" (Flashman and Quick 1985, p. 156). As stated by H.B. Miller (1982),

> Altruism does exist. Obviously it is sometimes hopelessly entangled with, and sometimes swamped by, other sorts of motives. There is not as much of it as many of us would wish; but it does exist, and it isn't even particularly rare. . . . Most of us fairly frequently, and probably almost all of us sometimes, act for the good of others. (p. 50)

In this way, Miller acknowledges that an altruistic involvement in volunteering might yield psychic benefits to the participant while arguing that such personal rewards do not negate the original altruistic motives.

This discussion leads us to the conclusion that altruistic motivation can operate concurrently with self-rewards or self-reinforcements. That is, volunteer motivation can be simultaneously other oriented and self-oriented. This view is analogous to the distinction that Sills (1972) made between the satisfaction derived from the purposes of the organization (other orientation) and the activities themselves (self-orientation).

As an illustration, consider two sport associations (one for soccer, the other for tennis) that espouse the same altruistic goal of enriching the lives of youth. Assume that this altruistic goal attracts you and that you want to help local youth by joining one of the two associations. Suppose also that the two associations choose different sets of activities to achieve the specified goal; adopt different organizational structures and processes; and recruit different sets of volunteers with different personal dispositions, abilities, and skills. Faced with this set of conditions, you are likely to base your choice of one association over the other on your preference regarding the activities, organizational processes, and people of the two associations. That is, you are likely to choose based on self-orientation even though your original reason for volunteering was

the altruistic purpose of helping youth, which is the goal of both associations. These relationships are illustrated in figure 2.2.

From a different perspective, it may be that one's initial entry into volunteering is indeed altruistic but that continued participation depends on the satisfaction of individual needs (M. Phillips 1982; Wolensky 1980). For instance, Henderson (1981, 1985) subscribed to the notion of simultaneous other orientation and self-orientation in volunteering. Specifically, the author suggested that volunteering might serve as a form of leisure for some participants; in this case, leisure participation, which is personally oriented, could be coupled with altruistic intentions of helping others.

Yet another perspective holds that in certain ways self-orientation may be necessary for carrying out other-oriented activities. In this vein, Flashman and Quick (1985) introduced the notion of self-care (i.e., ensuring one's physical, mental, and spiritual well-being) as opposed to self-neglect (i.e., disregarding one's basic needs). Of course, altruism is based on a degree of selflessness as opposed to selfishness, but Flashman and Quick argued that selflessness and self-care act as mutually reinforcing components of altruism:

> Intelligent self-care enables an individual to be at his or her best, to function at a high level of well-being. When an individual is functioning at a high level of well-being, he or she is in an optimal position to be aware of and contribute to the welfare of others. Similarly, as a person intelligently and selflessly contributes to the well-being of others, that person tends to enhance his or her own well-being in that he or she feels a sense of satisfaction and others tend to care for him or her. (p. 159)

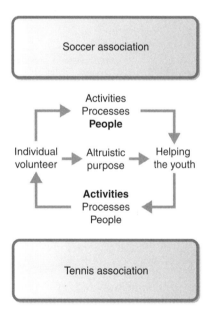

FIGURE 2.2   Organizational purpose and activities can serve as sources of attraction. Here, one group has fascinating people, whereas the other's strength lies in its activities. Which association would you choose to join?

 The essence of altruism, defined as "unselfish concern for the welfare of others," is not minimized merely because a person gains some benefit (e.g., increase in skills and experience) as a by-product of volunteering. In fact, a volunteer's personal growth ensures better service to clients.

VOLUNTEERS AS PARTIAL CLIENTS

Though it is useful to consider the differences between managing and motivating volunteers (unpaid workers) and paid workers, we may also consider volunteers as partial clients of the organization. Even in conventional organizations that use only paid employees, the idea of treating employees as customers has been staunchly promoted by emergent approaches to internal marketing (see chapter 15). But the focus of internal marketing is to enhance workers' productivity and therefore organizational performance. In contrast, our interest in conceiving volunteers as partial clients lies in satisfying the needs and preferences of the volunteers.

By definition, volunteers do not seek financial remuneration; instead, they come to an organization to satisfy personal needs and motivations. Thus they are clients of the organization, albeit of a different kind than usual. From this perspective, the organization should provide a setting and appropriate avenues for the satisfaction of volunteers' needs. Indeed, the experiences of volunteers in the organization—and their reactions to those experiences—constitute critical outcomes for the organization.

ROLE OF THE SPORT OR RECREATION MANAGER

Volunteers are essential to the delivery of sport around the globe. In the United Kingdom, Australia, New Zealand, and Canada, volunteers provide the person power that fuels the club-based sport system. In the United States, volunteers help support and deliver intercollegiate sport events (e.g., NCAA national championships). They also help in the hosting of international mega events (e.g., Pan American Games, Olympics, Women's World Cup). Given this importance of volunteer contributions, the role of sport and recreation mangers is to understand what motivates volunteers to give their time and to stay involved. More specifically, a manager must recognize that volunteers may give their time for utilitarian, affective, or normative reasons (which are not mutually exclusive) and that those motives must be served and may evolve over the course of a volunteer's experience. As noted by Welty Peachey, Bruening, Lyras, Cohen, and Cunningham (2015), when sport volunteers are satisfied that their motives have been fulfilled, they continue to donate their time.

When designing volunteer recruitment strategies, managers should understand the context from which their volunteers are drawn. One way to gain this understanding is to conduct a quick survey asking what the population looks for in a volunteer opportunity; these aspects can then be targeted in the volunteer recruitment marketing plan. For instance, the survey might show that the majority of individuals look for opportunities to learn new skills that are useful in their career or in life as a whole (these are utilitarian incentives). In this case, volunteer recruitment material could outline the skills that volunteers would develop from their experience with a club or event. In another example, a manager might learn that a given volunteer population prefers face-to-face communication rather than the use of social media; therefore, this pool of volunteers might best be drawn in by a town hall meeting.

Whatever the particulars, sport and recreation managers must be acutely aware of what does and what does not motivate their population of volunteers. In addition, if a manager recruits volunteers on the basis of utilitarian incentives, then the experience must include opportunities for volunteers to meet these needs.

Case Study

Volunteer Recruitment Strategies

You are the volunteer coordinator for the 2018 U.S. Women's Open Golf Championship hosted by the USGA. As you prepare your volunteer recruitment plan, you realize that you are desperately in need of volunteers for the transportation committee. You decide to conduct a quick survey using items from the Volunteer Functions Inventory to determine what the community members near the course look for in a volunteer role. Your goal, of course, is to find out what will lead them to volunteer for your event.

You send out 1,500 surveys to local residents and receive 550 responses. The results overwhelmingly suggest that community members want their volunteer experiences to include social gatherings that allow time with friends and participation in activities favored by their significant others. They view sport as a meaningful avenue for social interaction and would be eager to volunteer if social interaction were promoted as part of the experience. The survey results also suggest that some members of this group value career-related development opportunities. Specifically, young adults are looking to use their volunteer experience to develop business connections that will help them either obtain a job or move along on their current career path.

With this information in hand, you decide to construct a tailored marketing plan for recruiting transportation volunteers that highlights the social and career-related benefits of this volunteer opportunity.

Case Study Tasks

1. Do a web search to learn about the roles and responsibilities of transportation volunteers at major sporting events (including the U.S. Women's Open).

2. Develop a volunteer recruitment plan for the transportation volunteers at your event based on the case study. This plan must include the message that you will deliver and the marketing plan that you will use to promote the social and career-related benefits that are important to your potential volunteers. You must *sell* the transportation volunteer role and create a plan to ensure that community members sign up to volunteer for the transportation committee.

CHAPTER PURSUITS

SUMMARY

This chapter discusses types of volunteer organizations, types of people who volunteer, and reasons for which people volunteer. Classification schemes for voluntary organizations, particularly that of Palisi and Jacobson (1977), clarify the organizational purposes of various associations. These purposes provide the basis for all organizational activities and processes and therefore must be understood by all members of an organization, whether they are managers or frontline workers.

The literature addressing the types of people who volunteer does not show a consistent pattern and therefore does not provide much help to practicing managers. In more practical terms, the literature does not provide organizations with a clear indication of what groups, as defined by various socioeconomic factors, tend to volunteer their time most often. Therefore, recruiters of volunteers must conduct their own research about potential volunteer groups in order to determine what motivates them to contribute their time and energy.

The literature addressing reasons for volunteering (i.e., volunteer motivation) is more promising and thus more helpful to managers. This literature shows that self-orientation can act as a significant motivational factor for volunteering and does not minimize serving others (if the purpose of the organization is to serve others). The literature also shows that a volunteer's self-orientation may be reflected in various ways: indirect utilitarian benefits (i.e., household production, enhancement of human capital, or both); solidary (social) benefits of participation; and satisfaction derived from doing something good for others. We can add to this list the sheer satisfaction of doing something well. These satisfactions are intrinsic to the activity and are not typically realized during the event but rather after completing it (e.g., recognition from family or peers). On the basis of this information, managers may find the following guideline useful:

> The clear implication . . . is that volunteer organizations should never depend solely on appeals to altruism and other purposive incentives. . . . Material and solidary incentives, appropriate to the particular volunteer group or program, should be provided as the major elements of the reward system if volunteerism is to be maximized. (D.H. Smith 1981, pp. 31-32)

KEY TERMS

altruism 36

expressive–ideological 29

expressive–pleasure in performance 29

expressive–sociability 29

household production 35

instrumental–productive for members 29

instrumental–productive for others 29

utilitarian incentive 35

volunteerism 22

UNDERSTAND

1. Compare your own motives for volunteering with the motives discussed in the chapter. Are your motives different from those of others who have volunteered with you?

2. Consider the organization for which you volunteered most recently. How would you describe that organization in terms of the types of volunteer organizations discussed in this chapter?

INTERACT

1. Many students volunteer in sport organizations. Although most of them enjoy their volunteering, some have had negative experiences. Discuss possible reasons for negative experiences and strategies that you might use as a sport or recreation manager to address these negative experiences.

2. Discuss with your classmates the role of altruism and self-interest in your volunteering and in that of others.

CHAPTER

3

Professionals and Professionalism

As noted in chapter 1, most sport and recreation organizations include both volunteer and paid workers, and it can be challenging to manage these two groups because they have divergent orientations. More specifically, the professionals who form one subgroup of paid workers need to be managed in a particular way. Who are the professionals in sport and recreation? Some of them, of course, are the managers who are paid to manage other people. Other examples include intercollegiate athletics directors and their marketing directors. In addition, the NCAA and the professional leagues in various sports hire managers with extensive professional qualifications; they also hire lawyers to handle their legal matters. Similarly, many sport teams (collegiate as well as professional) hire coaches, athletic trainers, and other medical professionals.

As suggested by this range of examples, the concept of professionalization is applicable to any discipline or practical field in sport and physical activity. Moreover, there has been a shift toward classifying an increasing number of occupations by professionalized standards. For instance, there is talk of professionalism in mountain tourism (Cousquer and Beames 2013), exercise physiology (Boone 2012), and coaching (G.A. Kerr and Stirling 2015); as a result, certification is increasingly required in order to access a career in various segments of sport and recreation. For example, coach certification is becoming a requirement for many recreational sport clubs, as well as high-performance sport teams.

In order to know how to manage professional workers effectively, we must understand the distinctions between professional workers and nonprofessional workers. To that end, this chapter reviews the concepts of a professional and of professionalism. It also highlights the extent to which sport management itself can be considered a profession. More important, it shows that professionalism and volunteerism are largely consonant with each other.

ORIGINAL DEFINITION OF A PROFESSION

The most common attributes of a profession include

- a systematic body of knowledge,
- professional authority,
- community sanction, and
- a code of ethics. (Goode 1969; J.A. Jackson 1970; Ulrich 1997)

VIEWPOINT

In advocating the professionalization of exercise physiology, Boone (2012) noted six basic characteristics of a profession: "(1) It is intellectual with responsible standards of education and practice with high personal responsibility; (2) it is based on systematic, theoretical views and ideas that are readily researched and published; (3) it has a relationship with professional colleagues regulated by a code of ethics; (4) it has a formal professional association supporting a professional philosophy and culture; (5) it is organized internally to promote its members; and (6) it is recognized legally by a certification board staffed by professional members" (p. 4).

By basing the practice of a profession on a systematic **body of knowledge**, the practitioners of a given occupation make a conscious effort to

- generate more knowledge by carrying out research, as well as compiling and distilling the experiences of successful members;
- transmit the specialized knowledge to new entrants; and
- develop the special skills and competencies of members through a prolonged and arduous period of training.

Training in the specialized body of knowledge consists of both intellectual and practical experiences. As a result, the status of established professions is associated largely with the number of years of training required for entry into a given profession. In other words, length of training serves as a surrogate measure of the quantity and quality of the knowledge to be absorbed.

The members of a profession hold **professional authority** to decide what, how, and when a service should be provided to a client. This authority stems from, and is limited to, the professional's knowledge base. More specifically, the extent of one's professional authority is determined by the knowledge *differential* between oneself (as the professional) and the client (Mills and Margulies 1980; Sasser, Olsen, and Wyckoff 1978). Of course, in order for professional authority to exist, the client must first recognize and accept this knowledge differential. More broadly, the authority of a profession as a whole also relates to the extent to which it can claim a monopoly over relevant knowledge.

In order to operate, a profession must receive **community sanction** (i.e., sanction from society through its various levels of government) to control the training of candidates and the admittance of members to its field of practice, to monitor and evaluate the activities of its members, and to reward members for good performance and punish them for deviations from the technical and ethical standards established by the profession. In general, control over the profession is vested in a national association of the profession's members. For example, the American Medical Association (AMA) and the Canadian Medical Association (CMA) regulate the activities of the medical profession and its members in their respective countries. Furthermore, the respective governments restrain nonmembers from engaging in the activities of the profession, thereby creating a monopoly for these organizations. For instance, no one can practice medicine in the United States without being a member of the AMA.

To enhance its legitimation, a profession formulates a set of ideologies that include its mission and values. Generally speaking, professions tend to emphasize the values of service, impartiality, and rationality. Indeed, Goode (1969) claimed that the ideal of service is critical to the concept of a profession and to professionalism. To maintain a service orientation, a profession prescribes a **regulative code of ethics,** which sets standards of behavior for members in professional practice.

As shown by even a cursory analysis, these four criteria—systematic body of knowledge, professional authority, community sanction, and a code of ethics—are *not* met by a large number of occupations. The two occupations that have been recognized as true professions are the medical and legal professions. Other occupations can be placed at different points along a continuum ranging from craft to full profession. For example, Etzioni (1969) designated teaching, nursing, and selected other occupations as semiprofessions for several reasons:

> Their training is shorter, their status is less legitimated[,] ...there is less of a specialized body of knowledge, and they have less autonomy from supervision or societal control than "the" [e.g., legal and medical] professions. (p. v)

Please note that the preceding discussion is foundational in terms of the definition of occupations; however, it provides a very narrow definition of a profession, is relatively dated, and fails to acknowledge emerging fields that are regulated but may not have official sanction from the community. For example, the Ohio Department of Education requires that "individuals who will direct, supervise, or coach a student activity program that involves athletics, routine or regular physical activity, or activities with health and safety considerations" obtain a permit issued by its Office of Educator Licensure ("Coaching Permits" 2016).

 An occupation constitutes a profession when its services are based on an extensive body of knowledge, the knowledge differential between the service provider and the client is large enough, the community recognizes the importance of the occupation and gives its approval for the occupation to monitor and control itself, and the occupation institutes a strict code of ethics.

NASSM'S ETHICAL CREED

With guidance from the eminent scholar-philosopher Dr. Earle F. Zeigler, the North American Society for Sport Management (NASSM) drew up a set of standards for ethical behavior in sport management (Zeigler 1989, p. 4). The following excerpts derive from the version modified and accepted in June 1992:

> Members of the North American Society for Sport Management are scholars and practitioners within a broad profession, who honor the preservation of and protection of fundamental human rights. We are committed to a high level of professional practice and service. Our professional conduct shall be based on the application of sound management theory developed through a broadly based humanities and social scientific body of knowledge about the role of developmental physical activity in sport, exercise, and related expressive activities in the lives of all people. Such professional knowledge and service shall be made available to clients of all ages and conditions, whether such people are classified as accelerated, normal, or special insofar as their status or condition is concerned.

> As NASSM members pursuing our subdisciplinary and professional service, we will make every effort to protect the welfare of those who seek our assistance. We will use our professional skills only for purposes which are consistent with the values, norms, and laws of our respective countries. Although we, as professional practitioners, demand for ourselves maximum freedom of inquiry and communication consistent with societal values, we fully understand that such freedom requires us to be responsible, competent, and objective in the application of our skills. We should always show concern for the best interests of our clients, our colleagues, and the public at large.

> The NASSM also maintains a code of ethics that contains principles covering the conduct of sport managers; ethical obligations to students and clients; and ethical responsibility to employers, colleagues, and society. These principles are presented in the appendix of this book.

PROCESS OF PROFESSIONALIZATION

Forsyth and Danisiewicz (1985) proposed a model of **professionalization** that depicts the process through which the members of an occupation strive to make it into a true profession. The model, shown in figure 3.1, includes both the nature of the service provided by an occupation and the occupation's efforts to project its image. As Forsyth and Danisiewicz noted,

> The nature of the service-task performed by the occupation predisposes that service-task to the profession phenomenon if it is *essential* (of serious importance to clients), *exclusive* (the occupational practitioners have a monopoly on the service-task), and *complex* (the service-task is not routine and typically involves the individual and discretionary application of a specialized body of knowledge). (p. 62, emphasis added)

The following sections detail the process of professionalization by describing the concepts of **essentiality**, **exclusivity**, and **complexity**. As indi-

cated in figure 3.1, these three elements are critical if an occupation is to attain professional status.

Essentiality

Some services are deemed more essential than others. The professional rights and privileges referred to earlier are sanctioned only if an occupation addresses recognized social concerns and problems of living (J.A. Jackson 1970). According to Forsyth and Danisiewicz (1985), a society's essential needs can be identified and hierarchized, and occupations can then be rated higher or lower in essentiality based on which needs or problems they address. For instance, occupations that address life-and-death problems are considered more essential than are leisure services.

The same kind of logic can be applied to individual members of a given occupation. For example, in the teaching occupation, society accords greater status to teachers of certain subjects because those subjects are deemed more essential than others. As another example, people may consider the services of an exercise physiologist in a fitness club to be more essential than the services of the receptionist because the exercise physiologist assesses one's

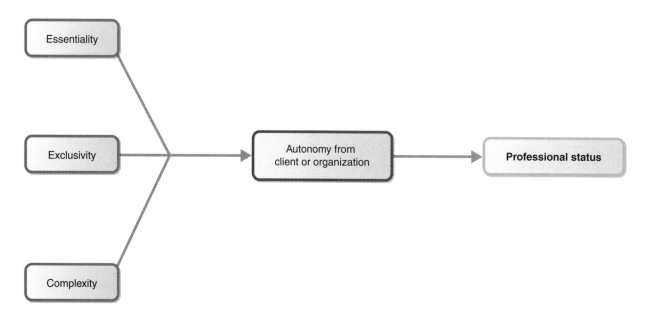

FIGURE 3.1 Model of professionalization.
Based on Forsyth and Danisiewicz 1985.

PROFESSIONAL STATUS VERSUS TYPE OF SPORT SERVICES

Chapter 1 describes the various sport and recreation services. How do these services—and the people who provide them—rate in terms of professional status? As indicated in our discussion here, consumer services (i.e., consumer pleasure and consumer health services) generally hold lower professional status than do human services (i.e., human excellence, human sustenance, and human curative services). In particular, human curative services, and the people who provide them, hold high professional status because they address life and quality of life.

This sort of professional status differs from economic significance. Consider the coaching ranks in NCAA Division I sport. Coaches of all sports perform a human service insofar as they help athletes achieve excellence; therefore, they are all rated equally in terms of professional status. Yet administrators, media, and the public tend to accord greater status to coaches of football and basketball teams, both because those sports are more popular than others and because they generate more revenue. Our focus in this chapter is on professional status.

---

fitness and prescribes exercises to improve it. Similarly, some people may consider a sport psychologist's services to be more essential to an athletic team than the services of the team manager. In general, the contrasts between human services and consumer services discussed in chapter 1 suggest that society views human services as more essential than consumer services.

Exclusivity

The exclusiveness of a service hinges on the occupation's monopoly over its services. Such a monopoly can arise because people who are not members of the occupation lack knowledge or special skills needed to perform the services. An occupation can legally forbid nonmembers from providing specific services only if it can prove that nobody outside of the occupation possesses the knowledge and competencies necessary to perform such services. For example, being a brain surgeon requires much knowledge and training. As Friedson (1973) noted, professionalization is

a process by which an organized occupation, usually but not always by virtue of making a claim to special esoteric competence and to concern for the quality of its work and its benefits to society, obtains the exclusive right to perform a particular kind of work, control

training for and access to it, and control the right of determining and evaluating the way the work is performed. (p. 22)

Exclusivity may involve political maneuvering in competition against other occupations. Historically, in fact, forming associations and engaging in political activity were necessary conditions for occupations to gain professional status (Wilensky 1964).

Complexity

The complexity of a service relates to the variety of techniques required in order to perform the service; it also reflects the fact that services vary depending on the specific client or problem that a service provider addresses. Thus, for example, because the problems that physical therapists face are varied and the treatment of each problem may involve different techniques and pieces of information, their services are more complex than those of a locker room attendant. This notion of complexity underlies the distinction made in chapter 1 between consumer services and professional services, where consumer services are viewed as less complex than professional services. In accordance with this explanation, sport and recreation services can be graded along the dimension of complexity that is outlined within the Continuum of Complexity sidebar.

CONTINUUM OF COMPLEXITY

To illustrate how various jobs in an organization can be graded on the dimension of complexity, let us consider the example of a fitness club. The job of the club's chief accountant is more complex than that of a bookkeeping clerk because the accountant manages the complexities associated with city, state, and federal laws. Similarly, the club's manager has a more complex job than an exercise leader does because the manager addresses larger concerns, such as market trends, personnel decisions, legal issues, and public relations. In the same way, we can place various jobs in a university athletics department at various points on the complexity continuum. For instance, the athletics director manages more complex matters than does a facility manager, whose job in turn is more complex than that of a caretaker. Similarly, the football coach's job is more complex than that of the equipment manager.

Image Building

If an occupation is to attain status as a profession, it must—in addition to possessing the attributes of essentiality, exclusivity, and complexity—engage in image building. Specifically, it must convince society that its services are indeed essential, exclusive, and complex. The ultimate aim of such efforts is for the occupation to gain society's recognition and sanction to control its own activities. Such control is manifested in the power wielded by service providers in the occupation. In turn, the service providers make operational the power of their autonomy from both their clients and their employing organizations.

The community sanctions the professional status of an occupation and allows it to monitor itself only when the services of the occupation are considered complex and essential to the community and when only the members of that occupation—who have been extensively trained—can provide the services. In order to obtain this sanction, an occupation must also engage in image-building activities to convince the community that its services are essential, complex, and exclusive.

Although these attributes enable an occupation to attain the status of a profession, occupations vary in the extent to which they possess the attributes. They also differ in the degree to which they can control the entry of individuals into the occupation and restrict nonmembers from engaging in the occupation's distinctive activities. For instance, anyone in the United States who wants to be an athletic trainer needs to be certified by the Board of Certification (BOC) in connection with the National Athletic Trainers' Association (NATA). However, the occupation of athletic trainers does not enjoy the status accorded to medicine because athletic training only partially meets other requirements to be a profession. For instance, the training period is much longer in medicine than in athletic training. Furthermore, medicine is founded on a much broader base of knowledge than is athletic training. Finally, medical practitioners are permitted to carry out the functions of athletic trainers, whereas athletic trainers are prohibited from performing many of the functions of a medical professional.

In a similar manner, many other occupations in sport and recreation may meet some but not all criteria for being a profession. The designations for such occupations are explained next.

SEMIPROFESSIONS, MIMIC PROFESSIONS, AND DEPROFESSIONALIZATION

Forsyth and Danisiewicz (1985) suggested that society grants occupations varying degrees of professional status, prestige, and power based on both the true nature of the services they provide (i.e., essential, exclusive, complex) and their promotional activities. As noted earlier, the power

PROFESSIONAL ASSOCIATIONS

The status of a profession is reflected in the strength of its professional association. Consider AMA and the North American Society for Sport Management (NASSM). As noted earlier, the medical profession enjoys much higher status than does the sport management profession because it deals with life-and-death matters, which are of greater concern to society. Another reason is that the AMA includes more than 200,000 registered members ("American Medical Association" 2015) whereas the NASSM has about 770 members (Ammon, business office manager, North American Society for Sport Management, personal communication, May 3, 2016).

Although these contrasts differentiate the two professions, they do not decrease the significance of the NASSM to its profession. Each profession relies on its association to help it grow through the sharing of knowledge and support. More specifically, a professional association sets and regulates the norms for the profession, facilitates the diffusion of newly generated knowledge, and tends to unify the thinking and behavior of its members (Knoke 2001).

L. Chen (2004) noted that professional associations are voluntary organizations of a special kind and that they account for two-thirds of all voluntary organizations. Professional associations rely on the members of the occupation to become association members, pay their dues, and attend meetings in order to sustain both the association and the profession itself. Focusing on professional associations in sport, L. Chen (2004) investigated incentives that encourage members of a profession to join its association; he identified the following four types of incentive:

- *Utilitarian:* material rewards or tangible benefits given only to members of the association
- *Solidary:* emotional attachment to the association, occupational affinity, sense of belonging, professional identification, friendships, and social interaction
- *Purposive:* intrinsic satisfaction with the appeal of social norms, occupational standards, political ideology, and value system
- *Informative:* information through the network of members resulting in tangible benefits (e.g., discount programs, new jobs) or intangible benefits (e.g., new knowledge, research data)

The first three incentives are generally applicable to all voluntary organizations; the informative incentives, however, are more germane to professional associations.

held by practitioners is exemplified by the extent to which they are autonomous with reference to both their clients and their employing organizations. For instance, a client's perception of his or her own needs does not guide a medical practitioner as much as it would a salesperson. At the same time, the medical practitioner is likely to be less controlled by his or her organization than is a salesperson. Thus, some occupations (e.g., medicine, law) gain true professional status because their practitioners possess both kinds of autonomy; some other occupations (e.g., education, nursing) can be considered semiprofessions because they enjoy autonomy only from one source—their clients.

In the context of human resource management, when exercise physiologists at a large fitness club prescribe exercise programs for their clients, they are guided by their knowledge of the field and their assessment of each client's fitness. Although the exercise physiologist may consider a client's personal preference for one form of physical activity over another, the client's preferences are not likely to influence the duration, intensity, and frequency of the prescribed exercise program. Thus, the exercise physiologist can be considered autonomous in relation to clients. He or she is *not* likely, however, to experience such autonomy from the organization, insofar as the organization decides his or her employment status and work assignment. Thus, exercise physiology may be considered a **semiprofession**.

From a different perspective, Forsyth and Danisiewicz (1985) referred to those occupations that have claimed professional status but have not been granted it as **mimic professions**. They provided the following description:

> Principles of natural selection may explain the evolution of one animal species to look like another species having some vital advantage. Analogously, mimic professions may have a code of ethics and other trappings of professions, but they have no power. They have taken on the coloration but not the substance of a profession. . . . Thus, there are limitations on the role of image building in the professionalization process. Mimic professions have built an image that exceeds credibility. (pp. 64-65)

Of course, some nonprofessional occupations make no claim to be professional. On the acknowledgment of the notion of semiprofessions and mimic professions, Hasenfeld (1983) classified human service workers as either professional, semiprofessional, or paraprofessional.

> Human service occupations vary in their degree of professionalization; they range from physicians, who enjoy the highest degree of professional power, to social workers, teachers, and nurses (who are classified as *semiprofessionals*), to hospital attendants, eligibility workers, and prison guards (who are classified as *paraprofessionals*). (p. 163, emphasis in original)

For example, consider the medical staff attached to a high-level athletic team. The medical doctors are professionals, whereas the athletic trainers are semiprofessionals. People who assist the doctors and athletic trainers in carrying equipment or injured athletes are paraprofessionals.

Just as an occupation may strive to gain professional status, counteracting forces may work against those efforts; these counteracting forces deprofessionalize an occupation. Building on work by Haug (1975) and Toren (1975), Lawson (1979) enunciated the bases of **deprofessionalization** as

- increasing education among the citizenry that redefines the professional–client relationship,
- reliance of an occupation on experience or experiential skills and knowledge that the lay public easily masters, and

VIEWPOINT

One of the more long-standing professions requiring certification in North America is that of athletic trainer. In the United States, athletic trainers are certified by the BOC, which was incorporated in 1989 "to provide a certification program for entry-level Athletic Trainers (ATs)" and has been responsible for the certification of ATs since 1969. The BOC establishes and regularly reviews both the standards for the practice of athletic training and the continuing education requirements for ATs. Since 1982, the BOC has been continuously accredited by the National Commission for Certifying Agencies (NCCA), and the BOC has the only accredited certification program for ATs in the U.S. The BOC must undergo review and reaccreditation every 5 years through the NCCA, which is the accreditation body of the Institute for Credentialing Excellence.

From the Board of Certification of the National Trainers' Association, 2015. Available: http://www.bocatc.org/public

- advances in technology that allow work to be done by persons with minimal professional training (e.g., Quicken WillMaker Plus).

In fact, for multiple reasons, even established professions (e.g., medicine, law) are losing some of their power over laypeople. For one thing, some occupations that traditionally provided support services to the professions have gained enough knowledge and competence to claim professional status for themselves. For instance, hospital nurses are sufficiently knowledgeable and competent that they can perform many of the services traditionally provided only by doctors. In addition, the explosion of knowledge in every field has made it impossible for any individual to master all of the knowledge in any given field; as a result, specialists have emerged. This increasing specialization leads to the dispersion of authority and a consequent decrease in professional status. For instance, gone are the days when an athletics director of a Division I undergraduate school could handle all necessary managerial functions and enjoy the resulting high

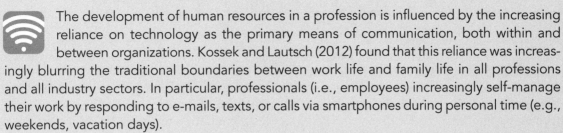

TECHNOLOGY IN HUMAN RESOURCE MANAGEMENT

The development of human resources in a profession is influenced by the increasing reliance on technology as the primary means of communication, both within and between organizations. Kossek and Lautsch (2012) found that this reliance was increasingly blurring the traditional boundaries between work life and family life in all professions and all industry sectors. In particular, professionals (i.e., employees) increasingly self-manage their work by responding to e-mails, texts, or calls via smartphones during personal time (e.g., weekends, vacation days).

Moreover, the use of smartphones, laptops, and other devices has led to increased connectivity between employees and employers. Therefore, managers must realize that new technologies "can turn homes into electronic work cottages, expanding work into family time, and the reverse" (Kossek and Lautsch 2012, p. 153). In response to this new reality, managers should identify employees' preferred ways of coping with work–life conflict and tailor organizational expectations and policies regarding technology-facilitated work (particularly outside of regular work hours) toward these preferences. Furthermore, according to Leonardi, Treem, and Jackson (2010), managers should ask employees what types of technology and technology-related messages are productive and which are distracting or stress inducing. In the end, if technology is not managed constructively, it can cause burnout and stress in professionals as they attempt to navigate work expectations and family expectations simultaneously.

degree of authority. Indeed, specialists in areas such as marketing, public relations, and sport law now tend to know more about their specialties than does a typical athletics director. Therefore, the athletics director shares professional authority with these specialists.

PROFESSIONAL STATUS OF SPORT MANAGEMENT

Although the management of sport services cannot be deemed a profession, this status should not be viewed as diminishing the field's significance. As noted earlier, the concept of a profession itself may be outmoded and may need adjustment as the distinction between an occupation and a profession becomes less clear. Still, the notions inherent in the ideal of a profession should guide all occupational efforts. The emphasis here is on being professional, not on being a profession. That is, an occupation may be characterized by a high degree of professionalism without being a profession in the classical sense. The concepts of professionalism and being a professional hold significance for all human services, including sport services.

Jurkus wrote in 1978 that, for two reasons, even management itself (i.e., management in general) could not yet be deemed a profession. The first reason was that no central professional association governed the activities of all managers. Since that time, some strong associations have emerged, such as the Academy of Management, the North American Society for Sport Management, and the National Intramural-Recreational Sports Association (NIRSA). These associations have formulated codes of ethics for their members. As of yet, however, there is no mechanism (such as disbarment in the legal profession or defrocking in the clerical profession) by which managers, including sport managers, can be forced to abide by a code of ethics. The second factor that restrains management, including sport management, from being deemed a profession is that current knowledge about management is less solid than is the knowledge held in fully recognized professions.

Writing in 1987, Raelin argued that management had made much progress toward being a profession but had yet to become one. In terms of progress, managers are trained in accredited professional schools through prolonged and specialized education; in addition, as in established professions, they enjoy autonomy, at least at the top levels. However, as laid out in Raelin's stance, management continues to lag behind in two significant respects. First, the professional associations in management are not strong enough to police the conduct of their members. Second, although service to society is part of the ethical code of management, managers are typically committed to an organization and its owners; when these two orientations conflict, the orientation toward the common good is not guaranteed to prevail. For instance, an athletics director might be committed to the development of athletes and to equity in athletics, but the preferences and dictates of university authorities may run counter to these professional commitments. Thus, to the extent that the athletics director is beholden to the university, his or her professional commitments may take a backseat.

Raelin's (1987) view was echoed much more recently by Barker (2010), who wrote the following in the *Harvard Business Review*:

Although managers can be formally trained and qualified, and their social status is similar to that of doctors and lawyers, management is not a profession. We rely on professional bodies to define what their members should know and to certify them as fit for practice. But the abilities and learning required to be a good manager don't lend themselves to such oversight—and business education is more about acquiring the skill of integration than about mastering a set body of knowledge. (p. 55)

Within this broad characterization, the status accorded to specialized management fields may vary with the types of products that the field is concerned with and the size of operations. For example, hospital management is accorded higher status than restaurant management because it involves managing services that address life and death. Similarly, industrial management is generally considered more critical to society than is parks management because of its greater economic impact. Therefore, it is appropriate to discuss not just sport management itself but also the status of the services under its jurisdiction.

How do sport and recreation services rate on the dimension of essentiality? Do they address universal social problems or problems of living? From this perspective, how would society view sport and recreation services as compared with occupations such as medicine and law? All three address people, but sport and recreation services

differ from medicine and law in significant ways. First, most people view sport and recreation services as addressing diversionary, leisure-time activities. (Of course, this perspective contrasts with the views of professionals in the field, who hold that sport and recreation services are essential to the quality of life.) Thus, the content of most sport and recreation services tends to be perceived as less serious than the content of medicine (i.e., life and health) and that of law (i.e., justice). Just as dentistry is accorded less status than medicine because life can go on without one's natural teeth, sport and recreation services are accorded much less status than some other occupations because life can go on without leisure activities.

In another way of looking at it, established professions address problems such as disease and disorder, whereas sport and recreation services are concerned largely with growth and learning. Society tends to favor occupations that solve immediate problems and tends to take other occupations for granted. Thus, a physiotherapist is likely to be more highly respected than a playground instructor.

What is the status of sport and recreation services in terms of knowledge and competency? The fact is that they are not likely to gain respect from outsiders for their knowledge base. The field is not focused on clearly defined subject matter and is not founded fully on scientific knowledge. This statement does not deny the great progress that managers have made in generating and synthesizing a body of knowledge unique to our field. However, these advances cannot yet match the status of other established professions.

In order to claim power through knowledge, an occupation must exercise a monopoly over that knowledge; that is, it must develop the attribute of exclusivity (J.A. Jackson 1970). Sport and recreation services face a problem in this regard because their knowledge base is multidisciplinary. For instance, management, including sport management, is founded on the knowledge generated in fields such as psychology and sociology. Consider the case of marketing a sport or recreation service. The notion of market segmentation based on social and economic factors is derived from sociology, but attempts to sell the sport product are based on knowledge of the dynamics of persuasion, which is a research thrust in psychology. To the extent that the knowledge base of management is anchored in other disciplines, those other disciplines are not likely to yield their ownership of that knowledge.

VIEWPOINT

In pointing out the relationships between sport management and sport sociology in regard to leadership in particular, Knoppers (2015) noted the following:

The use of critical sociological perspectives requires researchers to question assumptions and definitions. Such questions should pay attention to both content and context. For example, little is known about how discourses about sport and organizations (sociology) inform the ways [in which] sport management is practiced and is defined. Being a leader in a sport organization may mean taking on values embedded in popular discourses about sport and about corporate life. The constructions of these values inform how problems are defined, which questions are asked about leadership, and how theories about managers and management are constructed. (p. 498)

Thus, Knoppers highlights the fact that sport management and sport sociology are inevitably intertwined and therefore should be critically examined as such.

Insofar as the competencies and skills in sport and recreation services are based more on practical experience than on a body of knowledge (Morford 1972), many outsiders can claim the same expertise on the basis of having been involved in sport and recreation. This is particularly true of sport and recreation for young people. As J.A. Jackson (1970) commented about primary schools, they are where "everyone goes to learn what everyone knows" (p. 5). Along similar lines, Morford noted, "Few of the public are lay physicists or mathematicians. But lay coaches? They are a dime a dozen. Their number is legion, far in excess of those with professional credentials" (p. 90). What Morford refers to, of course, is the common phenomenon of "Monday-morning quarterbacking."

As a result, workers in sport and recreation services generally do not enjoy professional authority as we have defined it. Again, such authority or power is a function of the knowledge differential between the professional and the client. Thus, to the extent that a physician possesses more knowledge than patients do about illnesses and remedies, the physician possesses authority and power. In contrast, in the absence of any extraordinary knowledge, as is the case in sport management, practitioners possess less professional authority.

Sport and recreation services do engage in image-building activities through their national associations. However, the effectiveness of these efforts is limited by societal perceptions of our services (as not essential, exclusive, or complex) and by the lack of a strong and unified voice representing all of our interests.

Given that general management itself cannot claim professional status, the community is unlikely to accord professional status to sport management. Because sport managers work in a newer field of study, they have not built up a body of knowledge that they can call their own. That is, many others outside of sport management can carry out the same activities, albeit with less efficiency and effectiveness. Furthermore, because sport managers are concerned with management of sport and recreation services, their efforts may not be considered essential.

In order to be better equipped to serve the public, sport and recreation managers need to strengthen the following characteristics of **professionalism** as outlined by Morrow and Goetz (1988); they can also facilitate the development of these characteristics in the occupations included in the general field of sport and recreation services.

- Application of skills based on technical knowledge
- Requirements of advanced education and training
- Formal testing of competence and control of admission to the profession
- Existence of professional associations
- Existence of codes of conduct or ethics
- Existence of commitment, calling, or sense of responsibility by members for serving the public (p. 94)

Ideally, on an individual basis, the members of our field would

- use the profession and fellow professionals as a major referent for decision making,
- believe that the profession provides an important service to society,

- support regulation of the profession by its members,
- feel a lifelong sense of calling, and
- believe that individuals should have the right to make decisions in their work without the approval of others. (Morrow and Goetz 1988, p. 94)

 Managers and service providers in sport and recreation should be professional in all of their activities. Being professional involves believing in one's cause and calling, constantly striving to improve one's knowledge and skills, following the guidelines of one's professional associations, and behaving ethically in all situations.

SPECIAL COMPETENCIES

The discussion here compares the professional status of sport management with the status of established professions, such as medicine and law. This discussion does not deny that many occupational categories in sport management require extraordinary knowledge and competencies that are valuable and not easily replicated.

Take the case of the global media team at Wasserman Media Group. The team at Wasserman assists clients with multiplatform distribution, rights negotiations, content acquisition, and commercial strategy (Wasserman Media Group 2016). Due to the lucrative and specialized nature of media acquisitions, agents in the firm's global media division require unique certification and hold prestigious positions in the industry. In another example, the Sport Law and Strategy Group is a firm that operates from Canada to "educate, advise, consult, facilitate, and innovate" (Sport Law and Strategy Group 2015) in order to help sport organizations perform to their highest potential. Many of the consultants in the group possess a law degree or graduate education in management strategy.

However, these special competencies and insights are unique to individuals in these agency-based sport organizations; they are not general characteristics of practitioners in these occupations. For example, to classify these individuals into an occupational category, one must first ask, Is there a body of knowledge in the sport agency consulting context that another consultant can absorb?

DIVERSITY MANAGEMENT OF HUMAN RESOURCES

Valuing diversity must be prioritized in sport management. More specifically, the topic must be addressed in our courses in organizational behavior, human resource management, and organizational theory. Doing so can help us ensure that students are able to embrace the value of diversity (at both the surface and the deep levels) and strategically manage diversity to enhance organizational outcomes and become good citizens of the world. If we train students to be mindful of the benefits of diversity as they develop their human resource management skills, the field will be filled with managers who inherently are aware of, acknowledge, and accept diversity as a necessity for effective organizational functioning.

PROFESSIONALISM AND VOLUNTEERISM

As noted in chapter 1, many sport and recreation organizations employ both paid professional workers and volunteer workers. The challenging task of managing these two sets of workers is addressed in detail in part III. For the moment, let us consider some of the similarities and differences between professionalism and volunteerism.

For starters, the management of workers with a professional orientation can be both challenging and satisfying in and of itself. These workers cherish and seek autonomy, both from their employing organizations and from their managers. Therefore, managing these workers effectively requires creating a climate in which their inclination toward autonomy is not stifled while at the same time facilitating their efforts to serve their clients.

Beyond these challenges, the presence of both professional and volunteer workers in the same organization can create problems for management. Still, even though researchers have documented many conflicts between volunteer and professional workers (Chelladurai 1987; Hinings and Slack 1987; Inglis 1997), careful analysis of the bases of professionalism and volunteerism shows that, at least on a theoretical level, no inherent conflict exists between the two groups. To elaborate on this issue, the following section restates the most salient features of both professionalism and volunteerism.

VIEWPOINT

In considering the challenges faced by part-time coaches (whether paid or unpaid) who integrate their coaching career with their regular employment, Mercier (2000) provided the following suggestions: (a) discussing their involvement in coaching with their employer and emphasizing how coaching and their regular job complement each other; (b) explaining how their success as a coach may reflect positively on the organization; (c) using vacation and leave time effectively by "banking" extra hours of work and covering for others as a quid pro quo; (d) behaving professionally in both roles by adhering to high standards, meeting deadlines, and following through on commitments; and (e) maintaining good relations with co-workers and expressing gratitude for their support.

Merton (1982) summarized the essence of professionalism as consisting of a triad of dominant values: knowing, doing, and helping. In this context, knowing involves developing a body of knowledge unique to the field and training the field's members in that unique body of knowledge. Doing involves skillfully applying theoretical knowledge to the problems of life, and helping involves using the acquired knowledge and skills to assist others.

How do these three processes—knowing, doing, and helping—relate to volunteerism? The analysis of volunteerism presented in chapter 2 shows that volunteers' altruistic motivations (i.e., helping) and their concerns for self-development (i.e., learning) need not be inconsistent with each other and may in fact complement each other. Thus, both professionalism and volunteerism are founded on the notion of learning (i.e., knowing) and acting effectively (i.e., doing) in order to serve (i.e., help) others. In short, both groups strive toward the same ideal (see figure 3.2).

Obviously, however, although both sets of workers move in the same direction, the extent to which they have advanced in that direction often differs. Theoretically, paid professional workers have received more extensive training and therefore possess more knowledge in their chosen field than do volunteers in the same field. Paid professionals are also generally more skilled in performing the required activities. On the other hand, professional actions are relatively less altruistic because they are recompensed formally in tangible ways.

Despite these distinctions, the boundary between professionals and volunteers is blurred by the existence of volunteering professionals and professional volunteers. Volunteering professionals are professionals who volunteer their time and effort toward a particular cause without any remuneration. For example, a medical professional might volunteer to

VIEWPOINT

Cuskelly, Hoye, and Auld (2006) noted that the majority of work in voluntary organizations falls on the volunteer committee (i.e., Board of Directors); in addition,

> as sport has become more professionalized and commercialized, enhanced levels of specialized knowledge and different types of skills are required to manage in this more complex environment. (p. 100)

Sport and recreation volunteers may often be seen as "career volunteers" (Cuskelly et al. 2006), thus blurring the line between professionalism and volunteerism. Moreover, the complexity of sport operations makes professional and highly skilled volunteers increasingly valuable to sport organizations that rely on volunteers.

work in a developing country. In the context of sport and recreation, the coach of a university team might volunteer to coach a team in a local youth league. Such efforts may be as altruistic as a layperson's volunteering.

In contrast, professional volunteers are volunteers who make a profession of volunteering. As Pincus and Hermann-Keeling (1982) noted, they

> give their time . . . and have extensive experience in a field. They make a profession of their volunteering, and are quite different from short-term volunteers. They are committed as deeply or more deeply than many of their paid colleagues. (p. 87)

Because the services of professional volunteers are focused on a particular cause over a period of time, these volunteers develop considerable knowledge and expertise about that particular operation. For instance, a volunteer administrator of a sport club may become as proficient as a paid counterpart, both in the sport and in the management of such clubs.

Thus, on a theoretical basis, the presence of both volunteers and professionals need not be a source of

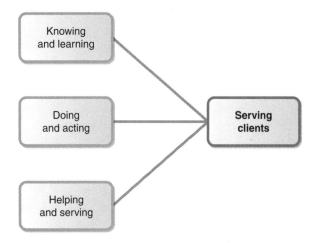

FIGURE 3.2 Triad of values for professionals and volunteers.

concern for managers of human resources in sport and recreation. However, Hasenfeld's (1983) caution about the "dominant professional caste system" may be extrapolated to the professional–volunteer dichotomy:

> In their efforts to gain professional status and recognition, semiprofessionals attempt to delegate downward what they consider dirty work, resulting in the emergence of a paraprofessional cadre of workers such as nurse's aides, teacher aides, social work technicians, and the like. In addition, some evidence suggests that aspiring professionals tend to increase their social distance from the poor and other 'less-desirable' clients. (p. 165)

If such tendencies on the part of professionals and semiprofessionals exist, then volunteers may be allocated all of the so-called dirty work while professionals and semiprofessionals arrogate to themselves the prestigious work. Unfortunately, these differences—which are of degree, not of kind—are sometimes allowed to dominate and create interpersonal conflicts between the two sets of workers. The challenge to management, then, is to highlight the underlying and unifying forces of both volunteerism and professionalism—specifically, service and self-development (Ilsley 1990). As Pincus and Hermann-Keeling (1982) noted,

> The blurring of lines between professional and volunteer can be a healthy, humanizing process—one in which everyone gains something. Professionals, immersed in their own specialties, are exposed to new perspectives and greater spontaneity in working with individuals with other experiences. (p. 94)

At the same time, although the notions of volunteerism and professionalism are theoretically congruent, some characteristics of professionalism negate the central thrust of volunteerism. Ilsley (1990) cautioned that professionalization of volunteer organizations may negatively affect the volunteer experience and noted the following signs of professionalism in a volunteer organization:

- Increased complexity of procedures and division of labor
- Management by hierarchy
- Fixed jurisdictional areas
- Emphasis on accountability and "putting things in writing"
- Elaborate training procedures (for volunteers)

- Appearance of ancillary materials (e.g., journals and newsletters), programs (e.g., workshops and conventions), and organizations (e.g., associations)
- Excessive use of scientific methods (reliance on statistics and jargon)
- Excessive standardization
- Unquestioning acceptance of assumptions

Adapted from Ilsley 1990.

Whereas increasing professionalization of administration is considered necessary and meaningful, such professionalization in a volunteer organization may have negative effects. According to Ilsley (1990), potential negative consequences include overly strict adherence to rules, limited public access to the organization, decreased diversity and innovation, lower levels of volunteer participation in decision making, alienation of volunteers from paid staff, and increased totalitarian tactics and consequent disenchantment among volunteers and clients. As Ilsley stated,

> Managing professionalism in a way that allows organizations to reap its benefits without having the spontaneity and life choked out of them by its rigidifying force is likely to be one of the greatest challenges that volunteer managers [and professional managers as well] will face in the coming years. (p. 89)

Thibault, Slack, and Hinings (1991) found similar rigidifying tendencies among provincial-level sport governing bodies in Canada. These authors found that the introduction of professional staff resulted in greater centralization of decision making, standardization, and specialization. They also noted that the increases in standardization (i.e., formalization) and specialization were more pronounced in organizational subsystems concerned with technical aspects of sport (e.g., coaching, officiating, training of athletes).

 Professionalism and volunteerism have very strong ties in their orientations toward increasing one's knowledge and skills and being dedicated to helping and serving clients. The challenge for management is to harness these common attributes of professional and volunteer workers while minimizing the effects of any divergence in less relevant characteristics.

ROLE OF THE SPORT OR RECREATION MANAGER

Ilsley's (1990) point about the need to manage professionalism holds true today as sport and recreation organizations try to reap the benefits of standardization and consistency while enhancing diversity and innovation. Today's sport system includes organizations with relatively sophisticated management systems and professionalized processes (T. Taylor, Doherty, and McGraw 2008). Furthermore, governing bodies at the provincial, state, and national levels (e.g., US Lacrosse) maintain a growing number of paid staff whose positions replace those once held by volunteers (Auld 1997; Kikulis 2000).

Professionalization brings increased complexity in procedures and division of labor, higher levels of hierarchy among personnel, and elaborate training procedures for volunteers (Ilsley 1990). The responsibility of sport managers is to ensure that this professionalization does not stifle creativity or growth. For example, increases in the complexity of procedures and the division of labor come with an increased need to ensure that roles and chains of communication are clear. In this vein, A. Doherty and Hoye (2011) found that clarity about one's responsibilities as a volunteer board member in a sport organization was the strongest predictor of enhanced performance. Thus, making clear statements about roles and responsibilities in today's increasingly complex organizational structures may be a crucial step in enhancing effectiveness; examples include accurate and up-to-date job and role descriptions.

Furthermore, the use of elaborate training requirements for volunteers can prompt a backlash regarding volunteers' time. In the context of volunteer coaching, Wiersma and Sherman (2005) noted that mandatory training would place an unwanted demand on volunteers. Specifically, their sample of coaches foresaw a possible coaching shortage due to the time demands already made on volunteer coaches and the lack of personnel and monetary resources to implement mandatory education programs. Thus, finding ways to educate coaches or volunteers during their volunteer hours or in condensed, predetermined time slots may be the best way to ensure professionalism through training without unduly burdening volunteers' time.

Case Study

Volunteer Training and Management

In your role as volunteer coordinator for the 2018 U.S. Women's Open Golf Championship, hosted by the United States Golf Association (USGA), you recognize that your volunteer laser operators (for ball position) require specific traits and experiences that make additional training mandatory. Specifically, the USGA (2015) has indicated that individuals in this role will

> assist through the use of computer-operated laser-measuring devices to determine ball position information to record various aspects of player statistics, including but not limited to each ball's location on a hole, drive distance, and distance to hole. This position may require the ability to climb ladders and operate from elevated platforms. Significant training and additional time commitments will apply. Previous experience, familiarity with technology, good eyesight, and strong golf knowledge are preferred.

Thus there is heightened need to train individuals specifically for the laser operator position, which is more professionalized than those in, say, a transportation or admissions position. As a result, special steps must be taken to manage the time requirements of these volunteers in order to calibrate the level of challenge that gives them an enjoyable and rewarding role without overburdening them (thus reducing satisfaction) with excessive training. As a seasoned volunteer coordinator who has worked with the USGA to manage volunteers over the course of several championships, you understand the importance of (a) clearly stating expectations in the job description, (b) clearly outlining responsibilities and time commitment in the orientation, and (c) explicitly describing the training required for the position and why that training is necessary.

Case Study Tasks

1. Research the role of laser operator for this and other golf championships.
2. Create a job description for this role.
3. Put together a clear outline of the responsibilities and time commitment required for the position, as well as an orientation schedule for prospective volunteers.
4. Provide a clear and explicit one-page outline of the training required for prospective volunteers. Within this outline, please explain why extensive training is required and highlight the importance of proper training to the event's success.

CHAPTER PURSUITS

SUMMARY

Occupations can be distinguished according to the extent to which they are based on a systematic body of knowledge, enjoy professional authority in relation to clients, gain the sanction of the community to monitor and control the activities of their members, and institute a code of ethics. The sanction of the community is a function of the extent to which an occupation's services are perceived to be essential to the community, can be provided exclusively by the occupation, and are complex in nature. Professionalization occurs when the members of an occupation strive to gain status as a true profession. Recently, there has been a trend towards deprofessionalization, which removes professional control. The forces of deprofessionalization include increasing levels of education among laypeople, easier mastery of the skills and knowledge required for occupations, and advances in computer and media technology. Sport management and similar occupations cannot claim professional status, but the ideas and the practice of professionalism are more critical than the attainment of professional status itself. Finally, the essential elements of professionalism and volunteerism include similarities and converge in their focus on serving clients.

The challenge for sport and recreation managers is to understand the dynamics of the motivational patterns of volunteers and professionals and to recognize the parallel thrusts in these patterns that bind them together, as well as the divergent forces that may set them apart. These insights help managers harness these two valuable sources for contributions toward organizational survival and growth. These issues are further elaborated in part III.

KEY TERMS

body of knowledge 44

community sanction 44

complexity 46

deprofessionalization... 50

essentiality 46

exclusivity 46

mimic profession 50

professional authority 44

professionalism... 53

professionalization... 46

regulative code of ethics 44

semiprofession 50

UNDERSTAND

1. Focusing only on occupations in sport and recreation, identify those that enjoy greater recognition and status than others. What accounts for these differences in status?
2. The chapter concludes with the idea that professionalism and volunteerism are similar in their orientations toward serving clients. What other similarities exist between professionalism and volunteerism? What attributes set them apart? How might such differences affect the management of these two sets of workers?

INTERACT

1. Considering the occupations with which you are familiar, identify those that rank higher in social status, and discuss the reasons for their higher rank. Do you agree with your classmates' assessments? Why or why not?

2. Many occupations strive to attain professional status. What is the significance of professional status? That is, why should an occupation try to become a profession?

3. Have you come across any friction between professionals and volunteers in a sport organization? If so, describe frictions that you have noticed. What led to them? If not, comment on why professionals and volunteers may get along well in sport organizations.

Clients as Human Resources

───── **LEARNING OBJECTIVES** ─────

After reading this chapter, you will be able to

- explain the significance of viewing clients as one set of human resources in sport and recreation management;
- describe the various motives of individuals who participate in sport and physical activity and classify them into categories based on the pursuit of pleasure, skill, excellence, or health and fitness; and
- understand the broader classification of motives for the programming of sport and recreation services.

The popular terms **quality** and **total quality management** represent an approach to management that focuses on consumers. All gurus of quality management suggest that every operation of an enterprise must be tuned to satisfying or delighting the customer (Goetsch and Davis 1997; Zeithaml, Parasuraman, and Berry 1990). This emphasis on customer (i.e., client) orientation is particularly critical to organizations that provide a service. (Please note that the terms *customer* and *client* are used interchangeably in this text.)

As noted in chapter 1, services are characterized in part by the fact that the production and consumption of a service occur simultaneously. That chapter also notes that customer participation in production may be more critical in some forms of service than in others. In fact, active participation by the client or customer is required for the services provided by most sport and recreation organizations. Even spectators at a sporting event are expected to conform to regulations and expectations regarding seating arrangements and orderly behavior. When spectators abide by these behavioral expectations, they themselves contribute to the quality of the service provided. As a result, sport and recreation organizations must secure compliance and cooperation from their customers or **clients** in order to enable the production of their services and ensure high quality. Therefore, organizations need to include the customers as part of their human resources.

We can distinguish between our clients and the markets—that is, the collections of potential customers—that they represent. Almost every organization attempts to enroll potential customers as actual customers. These efforts are usually labeled as marketing or promotional campaigns or programs. Only when potential customers opt for the products that an organization offers do they become actual customers of that organization. And only then do they constitute part of the organization's human resources. With this caveat in mind, the remainder of this chapter describes

- the role of customers in the production and consumption of a sport or recreation service, from a systems perspective;

- the uniqueness of customer participation in sport and recreation services; and
- customer motives for participation in sport and recreation.

CUSTOMER AS INPUT, THROUGHPUT, AND OUTPUT

As already noted, customers in many of the sport and recreation services act as both the inputs and outputs of the service operations. Hasenfeld (1983) pointed out that this view is particularly pertinent to human service operations, and Lengnick-Hall (1995, 1996) elaborated on this perspective to provide a systems view of customer participation in the production and consumption of a service. In her view, the customer acts simultaneously as a resource, a coproducer, a buyer, a user, and the product. This view of the customer is illustrated in figure 4.1 wherein the three significant customer roles of resource, coproducer, and product are superimposed on the input-throughput-output conceptualization of a system.

Clients form a resource for an organization to the extent that they bring with them their own physical and psychological attributes and provide necessary information. Because human services aim to transform clients in specific ways, each client serves as a resource, as well as the product, of the service enterprise. Also, because clients of most sport and recreation services need to engage in vigorous physical activity in order for the service to be produced and for the client to be transformed, they become

TECHNOLOGY IN HUMAN RESOURCE MANAGEMENT

As sport and recreation managers, we must recognize the value of technology in helping us connect with our clients as human resources. As cited in Leftheriotis and Giannakos (2014), social networking technology (e.g., LinkedIn, Facebook) now enables employees to connect with clients in ways that were unavailable just a few years ago. These platforms allow for instantaneous two-way interaction that fosters question-and-answer sessions and information sharing. In fact, Benson, Morgan, and Filippaios (2014) argue that online social networking has become a cultural norm in the daily lives of individuals worldwide and should be optimized in order to improve organizational capacity through engagement with external human resources (i.e., clients).

coproducers of the service (Chelladurai 1996). From a systems perspective, the customer role of resource as defined by Lengnick-Hall (1996) relates to the input stage, the coproducer role relates to the throughput stage, and the product role relates to the output stage.

Input	Throughput	Output

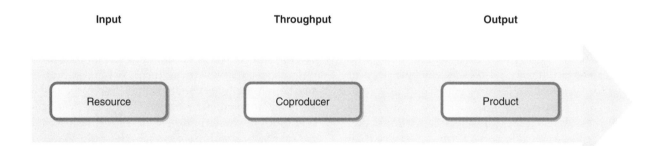

FIGURE 4.1 Customer roles in the input-throughput-output cycle of a system.
Based on Lengnick-Hall 1996

INTRINSIC VERSUS EXTRINSIC

Motivation to participate in sport and physical activity may be described generally as either intrinsic or extrinsic. Within this broad frame, Vallerand (2007) has provided a more elaborate description of intrinsic and extrinsic motivation in sport and physical activity. In this definition, intrinsic motivation involves "performing an activity for itself and the pleasure and satisfaction derived from participation" (p. 60). More specifically, Vallerand described three types of intrinsic motivation: (a) to learn new things associated with a given activity; (b) to accomplish, or at least try to accomplish, something in that activity; and (c) to experience pleasant sensations.

In contrast, extrinsic motivation involves "engaging in an activity as a means to an end and not for its own sake" (Vallerand 2007, p. 60). Vallerand invokes Deci and Ryan (1985) to describe four types of extrinsic motivation. When an individual engages in an activity for rewards, this participation is said to be externally regulated. An individual may also internalize such reasons for taking certain actions, and this type of motivation is referred to as introjected regulation. When an individual engages in an activity on his or her own initiative even though the activity is not pleasant, this participation is referred to as identified regulation. Finally, in integrated regulation, individuals engage in an activity, even though it is not pleasant, because it is consistent with their interests.

CUSTOMER PARTICIPATION IN SPORT AND RECREATION SERVICES

The notion of consumer involvement is generic to the production of many services. For instance, a hair stylist can effectively perform his or her services only if the customer is present in the chair while the service is provided. However, after the customer expresses a personal preference for a specific hairstyle, he or she is involved in the production of the service only in terms of his or her presence in the chair. This type of involvement is referred to as passive participation (or involvement) in the production of the service.

In contrast, the service of an aerobics instructor cannot be completed unless clients engage actively in aerobics; in other words, their active involvement is necessary for the production of the service. Furthermore, in aerobics classes and some other services, the client's active involvement may also be agonistic—that is, the **client's physical exertion** may be uncomfortable. These services—the ones that require active and agonistic involvement by clients—are where you may hear the slogan "no pain, no gain," which reflects the fact that it may be problematic for service providers to get clients to participate in such programs. Hasenfeld (1983) noted this issue with reference to human services in general:

> Patients may refuse to comply with a physician's orders; students may ignore their teachers; and clients may resist discussing their interpersonal problems. The need for client compliance and cooperation is particularly heightened when the method aims at some major changes in the client's behavior, and when it necessitates active client participation and involvement. . . . Consequently, the control of the client and the need to elicit conformity are critical issues in human service organizations and consume much of the efforts of their practitioners. (pp. 122-123)

VIEWPOINT

As noted by Akehurst (2009), user-generated content plays a significant role in shaping the image and "buzz" associated with an organization. For example, a customer of Nike might create a Snapchat story of his or her experience using a new Nike shoe. If that user-generated content goes viral, it has the potential to inform Nike management of reaction to the shoe, persuade other consumers of the potential worth or utility of the shoe, and encourage (or discourage) future sales. Therefore, the increased presence of user-generated content makes the client that much more prevalent as a human resource.

Of course, many clients are unwilling to engage in such agonistic endeavors, and it is not uncommon for clients to drop out of sport or exercise programs. In fact, exercise adherence is a major topic for many researchers (Buckworth and Dishman 2007). On the other hand, countless others do exert themselves willingly in various forms of sport and recreation activity. For example, racquetball players grunt, groan, and endure pain while running around the court to retrieve or "kill" the ball.

This dichotomy between those who persist and those who do not highlights a significant issue for sport and recreation managers—specifically, the relative ease or difficulty of securing client compliance in the production of sport and recreation services. This challenge can be affected by several factors, including the availability of time, the accessibility of facilities, the client's level of fitness and motivation, and the quality of leadership. In addition to addressing the factors they can control or modify (e.g., facilities and leadership), sport and

CUSTOMER LOGIC

The preceding description of our clients and their motives provides insight into managing clients, but there is more to customer management. In their book *Service America in the New Economy*, Albrecht and Zemke (2002) caution us as follows:

> In designing service systems, we need to remember above all else that our logic is not necessarily the same as the customer's logic. As we have seen, the customer has a special perceptual frame of reference that is unique to his or her specific needs in a specific situation. Passing through the cycle of service, the customer sees the service in terms of a total experience, not as an isolated activity or set of activities. (p. 141)

In order to firmly grasp customers' logic, these authors advocate establishing three important ways of "listening" to customers. The first way is *scientific listening*, which involves conducting market research "to figure out (a) whether your organization is doing the right things, (b) whether the right things are being done well, and (c) who among your customers likes what you are doing." The second way is *dramatic listening*, which is intended "to visibly demonstrate to your customers that you really are listening and not simply going through the motions. . . . That is why we say listening is a contact sport—listening without contact, or dramatic connection, is like looking without seeing" (Albrecht and Zemke 2002, p. 82). The third and final mode of listening is *motivational listening*, whereby managers secure the most convincing information through personal experience (i.e., where managers first use the service as a customer then speak to customers as an educated service provider) of the service and the service providers. "Experiencing things directly and personally can make an impact that hours of reading static customer satisfaction reports never can approach" (Albrecht and Zemke, p. 83).

recreation managers should also be purposeful about the programs they offer to clients who differ in ability, fitness, and motivation. More specifically, managers need to design programs to meet the particular needs and motives of their clients. With this need in mind, the following section outlines various motives that lead individuals to participate in sport and recreation.

 All service operations require a certain degree of client involvement in producing their services. In addition, some sport and recreation services are participant oriented and therefore require greater client involvement in terms of intensity and physical exertion.

CLIENT MOTIVES FOR PARTICIPATION

The psychological dynamics in client logics are best understood if one considers **client motives** for participation in physical activity. Therefore, schemes have been developed to classify attitudes toward physical activity and motives for participation in sport. Regarding attitudes, for example, Schutz, Smoll, Carre, and Mosher (1985) carried out several studies to develop psychometrically sound instruments to measure seven dimensions of children's attitudes toward physical activity. Regarding motives, Gill, Gross, and Huddleston (1983)

VIEWPOINT

Whereas some scholars have focused on client motives for participation, others have investigated the functions of sport from a societal perspective. For instance, Bloodworth, McNamee, and Bailey (2012) suggested that sport and physical activity help meet fundamental human needs and that when certain segments of society (e.g., children in some public schools) are denied opportunities to engage in sport and physical activity, or when opportunities are significantly reduced, members of those segments suffer a deficit in well-being.

identified eight factors of motivation for youth sport participation (see table 4.1). Although such classifications have focused on different aspects of sport and physical activity participation—for example, attitudes versus motives—all of them relate to one's reasons for participating in sport and physical activity.

Whereas the schemes just discussed address the attitudes or motivations of participants in youth sport, another proposed scheme applies to all ages (Chelladurai 1992). This four-level classification addresses motives for participation in sport and

TABLE 4.1 Motivations for Participation in Youth Sport

DIMENSION	DESCRIPTION
Achievement and status	To win, feel important, be popular, gain status, do something one does well, or reap rewards
Team	To be part of a team and experience teamwork and team spirit
Fitness	To get exercise and be physically fit
Energy release	To get rid of excess energy, release tension, have something to do, travel, or get out of the house
Skill development	To improve skills, learn new skills, or advance to a higher level
Affiliation	To be with friends and make new friends
Fun	To have fun; to experience action and excitement
Miscellaneous and situational motivations	To be with parents, close friends, or coaches; to use equipment and facilities

Adapted from Gill, Gross, and Huddeston 1983.

physical activity and includes the following components:

• *Pursuit of pleasure:* People may participate in a physical activity because they enjoy the competition, the associated kinesthetic sensations, or both (as in the case of the two racquetball players mentioned earlier). They do not seek any other benefits outside of their participation itself. When clients are energized by such pleasure-seeking or "hedonistic" motives, sport and recreation managers can more easily motivate them and secure their compliance with the organization's rules and regulations.

• *Pursuit of skill:* The desire to acquire physical skills is innate to the human species, and it may impel people to participate in physical activity. That is, individuals may focus on perfecting their skills through continued vigorous physical activity. Services aimed at helping clients fulfill this desire include organized physical activity classes, sport camps and clinics, and lessons from professionals. The participation of people of all ages in these efforts gives evidence of the pervasiveness of the desire to learn skills.

• *Pursuit of excellence:* The pursuit of excellence is broadly defined as the effort to win in a contest against a standard. The standard may be one's own previous performance, someone else's performance, or performance directly against an opponent. Within this general motivation, one may participate in a given form of physical activity in order to excel either in that same activity or in another activity. For example, a client who grimaces and struggles while lifting weights may be training to compete either in a regional weightlifting competition or in a track meet. The intention to prepare for such contests—that is, the motive of excellence—generates a willingness to comply with instructions and guidance from a coach or teacher. This willingness is seen, for example, in athletes who go through uncomfortable exercises while chanting the motto "no pain, no gain!"

• *Pursuit of health and fitness:* Some individuals participate in vigorous physical activity mainly for the health-related benefits, such as fitness, stress reduction, and longevity. The benefits of such participation are extrinsic to the activity itself; that is, they reside outside of the specific physical activity and are derived after prolonged physical activity.

Here, we see the relevance of Hasenfeld's (1983) distinction between individuals who function adequately and those who function below an adequate level. That is, many individuals who are sufficiently

VIEWPOINT

According to Greer and Stewart (1989), attitudes toward or motives for participation do not constitute generalized dispositions of individuals. Their study of 585 fourth- and fifth-grade students found that attitude toward participation varied according to context—specifically, neighborhood play, organized sport, or school recess activity. These authors noted that "winning was more important when playing organized sports than when playing with peers in the neighborhood. . . . The schoolyard context was generally perceived as similar to organized sports in that winning was valued and seen as significantly more important than it was in the neighborhood" (p. 341).

fit and healthy want to maintain that level of fitness and health. Therefore, they continue to participate in physical activity, and their motives may be properly labeled as sustenance motives. Others may participate in physical activity in order to *enhance* fitness and health levels that have been judged inadequate; these motives may be properly labeled as curative.

The preceding description of motives for participation in physical activity assumes that individuals participate of their own volition. However, it is not uncommon for individuals to participate due to necessity or coercion. Consider the case of a basketball coach taking the squad for a 4-mile (6.4-kilometer) run as part of a training program. Some of the players may run with enthusiasm, whereas others may be reluctant. Even though all players recognize the value of enhancing their endurance through such running, their compliance is hard to secure because such benefits are extrinsic to the activity of running.

Although these motives for participation in sport and physical activity are distinct from each other, the activities selected to satisfy any one of them may result in outcomes related to other motives. For example, racquetball players motivated by the pursuit of pleasure may also gain fitness and enhance their performance capabilities. Similarly, people who jog for the sake of fitness may learn to

DIVERSITY MANAGEMENT OF HUMAN RESOURCES

The outcome of actualization—in which an organization reaches its full potential (Chelladurai 2014)—from a diversity management perspective is increasingly important when operating in the client services industry. More specifically, given that participants in sport and recreation have varied motivations for being (and staying) involved, managers must embrace the value of diversity and incorporate these varied participant values into training, orientation, and performance evaluation. For example, a coach who does not value and embrace diversity among participants may not recognize that athletes are motivated in various ways. As a result, the coach may lead his or her players in inappropriate ways. Thus, in order to be effective, the value of diversity must be communicated by management to ensure that specific motives and satisfaction factors are addressed. A narrow-minded homogenous focus on the part of managers and coaches can quickly deter athletes and parents from a sport or recreation organization.

enjoy the kinesthetic sensations and the sense of achievement in jogging farther or faster.

From a managerial perspective, however, it is critical to establish the *primary* purpose for participation in a program of physical activity in order to develop and implement it in a smooth and coordinated fashion. For instance, the key to motivating clients before and during participation varies with the purposes of such participation. In the pursuit of pleasure, the activity itself serves as the reward; therefore, it acts as the motivator for the participants. However, in the pursuit of excellence, skill, or fitness and health, the reward is not immediate; therefore, the sport agency must shoulder more responsibility for motivating the participants.

Motives for participation can be classified broadly into four types: pursuit of pleasure, pursuit of skill, pursuit of excellence, and pursuit of health and fitness. Although these categories are conceptually distinct, active participation in a given sport or physical activity may satisfy more than one of them.

Programming to meet client motives is generally done on a group basis. That is, a sport manager may set up a program to cater to the pursuit of pleasure, of skill, of excellence, or of fitness and health. Consider the programs offered by a typical university recreation department (see table 4.2). Analysis of these programs shows that, without stating it spe-

cifically in their official descriptions, they cater to specific groups of people differentiated on the basis of ability, interest, and motivation. Access requirements vary; more specifically, entry into some programs (e.g., adapted recreational sport) is controlled by the university, whereas others (e.g., sport clubs, wellness programs) are open to all. It is understood here that the department's clients choose specific programs (and activities within programs) to satisfy their personal interests, needs, and motives.

As outlined in chapter 1, the discussion of client motivation is most relevant to **participant services**. However, this form of service is just one of many forms in sport management, and, as described earlier, participant motivation may not be relevant to other forms. For example, one significant component of sport management is the provision of entertainment through sport (i.e., spectator services). Although participation motives may be relevant to the athletes in the sport, and to the manner in which the athletes are coached, they do not apply to the fans, who are also customers. Granted, fans need to be present in order to consume the entertainment, but their presence is removed from the activity itself; that is, their participation is not required for the production of the service itself.

These customers' motivational patterns for consuming spectator services may be quite different from those discussed earlier, whereby consumers are not necessarily active members of the sport product being consumed (e.g., sport fans consuming sport at home via television). In fact, researchers

TABLE 4.2 Sample of Programs Offered in a Typical University Recreation Department

PROGRAM TYPE	DESCRIPTION
Fitness services	Provide fitness equipment and instructions.
Sport services	Make available sport facilities for general use and organize competitions in various sports.
Programs for children	Organize physical activity programs for children of faculty, staff, and students.
Summer camps	Offer educational and physical activity programs for children of various age groups during summer months.
Sport clubs	Facilitate student clubs focused on sport and recreational activities.
Wellness programs	Offer programs to address health-related needs of students, staff, and faculty.
Adventure programs	Offer adventure activities (e.g., offering climbing centers).
Disability sport	Provide activity programs modified to facilitate participation by individuals with disability.

SPECTATORS AS HUMAN RESOURCE

Several attributes can be used to distinguish between the client groups found in sport management, but for any given group to be considered as a human resource it must participate in the production of a service. Both the degree and the type of such participation vary with the diverse services offered by sport and recreation organizations. For instance, active and agonistic participation by clients is required for the production of most of our participant services. In the case of our spectator services, however, the core service we provide is entertainment in the form of excellence in competition; in this case, therefore, the athletes, coaches, and event and facility staff make up our human resources.

How are the spectators involved in the production of the spectator service? For one thing, the 100,000 or so people who go to a stadium to witness a game hold certain expectations about their experiences. For instance, they expect to witness a high-class competition, and they hope that their favorite team wins. They also expect that their entry into and exit from the stadium will be smooth and speedy. And they expect to be able to witness the game without undue interference from other fans. Event organizers are well aware of these expectations, and they draw up plans and execute them most efficiently.

However, all of these plans would be of no avail if spectators did not adhere to the rules of conduct and respect the rights of other spectators. Thus, spectators contribute to the effectiveness of the service by abiding by the rules and following common guidelines for courtesy. Because spectators are generally well behaved in North America, we may not realize the significance of the contributions they make to the orderly and safe conduct of competitions. Of course, many spectators also contribute to the total entertainment package. Their outfits, slogans, singing, dancing, shouting, booing, witty comments, and flag waving all contribute to the spectacle.

In contrast, consider event sponsors. We all realize that many athletic organizations cannot survive without the infusion of huge amounts of money from sponsors. But this contribution is not born out of generosity; rather, it is given in return for access to the markets created by the sport organization and the opportunity to be associated with excellence. In addition, although sponsors help finance the production of our varied services, they do not get involved in the production per se. The same is true of individual donors who provide valuable financial resources to our operations. To the extent that they do not participate in the production process, they remain benefactors of our programs and are not part of our human resources.

have performed considerable study of motivations for consuming sport services, patterns of such consumption, segmentation of sport consumers, fan behavior, and loyalty to teams (e.g., Backman and Crompton 1991; Hansen and Gauthier 1989; Howard and Crompton 1995; Mullin, Hardy, and Sutton 2000; Murrell and Dietz 1992; Wann and Branscombe 1993). Given the connection between consumption patterns and profit, these issues are critical to marketing sport and recreation.

ROLE OF THE SPORT OR RECREATION MANAGER

Sport and recreation managers may not be linked directly to clients in the production of participant services. In the previous three chapters, we describe two sets of workers—volunteer and paid workers—who may be involved in the production of human or consumer services. Because these workers come into direct contact with clients, they must be more attuned than managers are to clients' motives. In contrast, managers are more concerned with motivating the service providers—that is, the paid and volunteer workers.

For example, the director of an intercollegiate athletics department may not be involved directly in training and motivating athletes; those tasks are left to coaches, who are the service providers. Similarly, the manager of a city recreation department may be removed from clients as they consume the department's services. Figure 4.2 illustrates the linkages between sport managers, service providers, and clients.

Because sport managers are linked to clients largely through service providers, and because a manager's greater task is to supervise service providers, it may appear that sport managers do not need to be concerned with client motivation. However, insofar as managers are responsible for developing and managing the organization's programs, they must be aware of the broad classes of their clients' motives. This understanding helps them develop programming that suits clients' motives and effectively manage the service providers who deliver that programming.

In general, sport and recreation programs are instituted to serve a class of clients rather than individual clients. For example, from one perspective, programs can be classified broadly as serving youth, adults in general, or seniors; more specifically, youth programs can be divided into specific units based on age. From another perspective, recreational sport programs are conventionally separated from competitive sport programs. These programming aspects are discussed in part I.

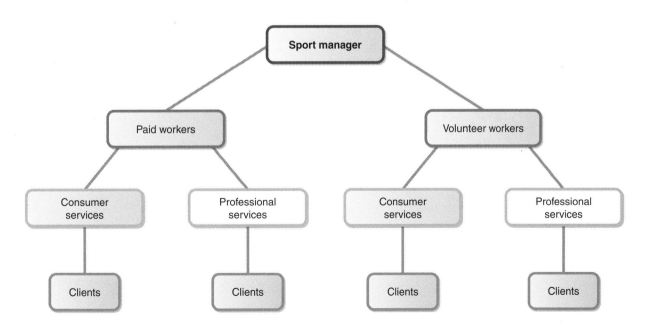

FIGURE 4.2   Linkages between sport managers, workers, and clients.

Case Study

Managing Employee–Participant Relations

The Sport Club Program at Florida State University (FSU) is home to more than 40 student organizations focused on sport and recreation (Florida State University Campus Recreation 2015, Sport clubs). As part of its mission, the program seeks to engage the student community in lifelong wellness, encourage discovery, and help students build character and align their actions with their values (Florida State University Campus Recreation 2015, Our mission & values). Members of the program participate in intramural sport events and leagues; receive discounted rates on training services and wellness testing; and receive unlimited access to the student recreation center. The program's values include integrity, experiential learning, wellness, excellence, innovation, and community. The membership base consists of male and female registered students who typically live on or near the Florida State campus in Tallahassee, Florida.

As the director of campus recreation, it is your job to ensure that your staff members serve your member-clients in a way that is congruent with the program's values. For example, staff members must consult with member-participants in order to spur innovation in the form of new and original opportunities for fun and learning in the club-based system. In 2002, for instance, FSU offered the first collegiate kiteboarding club (Florida State University Campus Recreation 2015, Kiteboard), whose goal was to spread the word and offer the experience of this amazing sport. Although very successful in generating new members for the kiteboarding club, the office staff of the Sport Club Program seems to be somewhat disconnected from the kiteboarding club's member-clients.

More specifically, given the adventure-seeking nature of the kiteboarding club, the staff should be continually looking for new ways to foster creative participation options for the club's members. You want the Sport Club Program to foster continued innovation and support participants' learning through experiences that enhance their personal, academic, and career development. With these goals in mind, you decide that it is time to directly ensure that your newly hired assistant director of intramural sport is communicating constantly with the members of the kiteboarding club. You are taking this step to ensure that the kiteboarding club is properly served with updated and member-focused program policies and procedures.

Case Study Tasks

1. Refer back to the four-level classification of motives for participation in sport and physical activity (Chelladurai 1992). Create a one-day employee training guide for the assistant director of intramural sport to use for training staff that connects the values of the FSU Sport Club Program and what you identify as the key motives of participants who engage in kiteboarding.

2. As part of your training plan, outline strategies for ensuring that the training program helps both staff members and club participants develop meaningfully in personal and academic (or career-related) terms. Specifically, how will the employee training be linked with engaging the motivations of the kiteboarding participants?

CHAPTER PURSUITS

SUMMARY

This chapter discusses the significance of our clients as part of our human resources. Clients are relevant to human resource management in sport and recreation because most of our participant services require clients' vigorous participation. This participation requirement obviously excludes customers receiving spectator services because they do not participate in the production of those services; such production is left to the athletes and their coaches. The critical issue for sport and recreation managers is to differentiate between the various motives for client participation and tailor their programs to satisfy those motives.

One concern for sport and recreation managers involves the relatively high dropout rates among participants in sport and physical activity. These rates carry obvious implications for profit-oriented organizations. If clients do not continue to participate in a given physical activity (e.g., tennis, golf, or fitness classes), the organization faces the uphill task of constantly recruiting new clients. Beyond the for-profit world, educational and community organizations that promote sport and physical activity must also be concerned with encouraging their clients to continue participating in physical activity. Indeed, for them, failure to do so would be tantamount to forsaking their organizational goals.

KEY TERMS

client 61

client motive 65

client's physical exertion 63

participant services 67

pursuit of excellence 66

pursuit of health and fitness 66

pursuit of pleasure 66

pursuit of skill 66

quality 61

total quality management 61

UNDERSTAND

1. Consider your own participation in sport and physical activity, then explain the reasons for your participation. Have these reasons changed from your childhood to the present time?

2. What are some ways—other than those discussed in this chapter—to classify people's motives for participating in sport and physical activity?

INTERACT

1. Discuss the utility of classifying clients' motives into the following four categories: pursuit of pleasure, pursuit of skill, pursuit of excellence, and pursuit of health and fitness. What are the managerial implications of such a classification?

2. Discuss the various motives that might influence participation in each of the programs outlined in table 4.2.

PART

II

INDIVIDUAL DIFFERENCES IN HUMAN RESOURCES

In the previous three chapters, we suggest that the human resources of sport organizations consist of volunteers, professionals, and clients. We also note that these three groups of people differ in their motives for participation in organizational efforts. If we were content with these classifications, then the world would be much simpler and management would be much easier. However, humans differ in an infinite number of ways along multiple dimensions. More specifically, the members *within* each category of human resources (i.e., volunteer, professional, and client) vary considerably among themselves. Therefore, the categories alone do not enable us to fully understand their members or motivate them toward organizational goals.

Indeed, one of the permanent features of organizations and their management is the presence of individual differences between employees. These differences may involve, for example, productivity, ability, desire to achieve strong results, desire to be empowered, preferences for certain leadership styles, style and quality of interpersonal interactions, commitment to the organization, or level of self-esteem (Dubrin 2002). Such differences affect the performance of individuals, groups, and the organization as a whole. Thus, we need

to understand individual differences and their influence on work performance.

Individual-difference variables are the human attributes that set one individual apart from another; they also influence the variability in individual performance within an organization. Although many characteristics can set one person apart from another, our interest here lies in the following factors that relate directly to an individual's performance in an organization:

- Abilities (i.e., cognitive ability)
- Personality
- Needs and values
- Motivation

Our interest in individual differences also stems from the concept of person–task fit. That is, our major concern involves creating a fit between the task assigned to an individual and that person's profile on relevant individual characteristics. Person–task fit begins with purposefully designing and describing a job, specifying the necessary skills and competencies required to perform it, and hiring a person who possesses them. These critical managerial tasks are described in part III, whereas the chapters in this part of the book outline the more salient individual-difference variables.

The concept of person–task fit is critical from the perspectives of both the organization and the individual. The organization can expect greater productivity if its members possess the attributes required by their assigned tasks; meanwhile, the individual member feels more competent, confident, and satisfied.

The psychological literature abounds with lists of individual-difference characteristics. Some of these attributes, such as gender and height, can be accurately measured or determined. Others attributes are conceptually derived and harder to measure; in fact, these attributes are inferred through values registered on other indexes associated with the concept in question. For example, an individual's intelligence is inferred from his or her score on a series of tests that are supposed to measure some aspect of intelligence. Thus, individual-difference variables differ in the extent to which they are tangible or abstract.

In another area of contrast, some attributes may be more stable over time than others. For instance, race is a permanent attribute, but knowledge in a management area is a transient attribute. That is, one's race, of course, does not change in a lifetime; however, knowledge in a management area can change with training and practice. Thus, some individual-difference variables are stable, and others are transient.

Another distinction exists between interindividual and intraindividual differences. For instance, employee A of a fitness club may be proficient at keeping the firm's accounts, whereas employee B may be good at communicating with clients. This difference in skill area between employees A and B is an interindividual difference. From a different perspective, employee A is more proficient at accounting than at communicating; similarly, employee B is better at communicating than at accounting. Within each individual, this difference in proficiency with the two skills is an intraindividual difference. Managers need to be aware of both types of individual difference. Interindividual differences imply that a manager cannot expect all individuals to perform a given task equally well. Intraindividual differences, on the other hand, imply that a given individual cannot be expected to be equally good at all tasks.

As mentioned earlier, myriad differences distinguish one individual from another. Our interests here, however, are restricted to variables that contribute to or constrain performance in organizational contexts. We can facilitate our choice of relevant variables by applying a well-known principle—the notion that performance is a function of ability and motivation. Another significant set of individual-difference variables, which may affect both performance and interpersonal relations in the workplace, includes needs, values, and personality.

While acknowledging that people differ both in their capacity to carry out tasks and in their manner of interacting with others, we must guard against making value judgments about people based on these individual differences. For example, how can anyone decide an individual's worth based on his or her score on the personality dimension of affiliation (i.e., the tendency to make friends and enjoy association with people)? We must remain mindful of the fact that differences are not deficits.

Moreover, we as managers must make the best possible use of differences in order to benefit both our organizations and their members. For instance, although one's performance is a function of one's abilities and motivation, management also bears a responsibility to foster members' abilities, spark their motivation, and channel them into task performance. In fact, poor management practices have been associated with many problems, such as tardiness and lack of productivity among workers.

For our purposes here, ability is the capacity of an individual to carry out the tasks assigned to him or her, and cognitive abilities are the subject of chapter 5. Chapter 6 focuses on personality, which consists of the relatively stable pattern of traits that define the uniqueness of a person. This pattern of traits predisposes the individual to behave in specific ways toward others and toward situations. Chapter 7 discusses values, which are the beliefs that individuals hold about what is right, what is wrong, what ought to be, and what ought not to be. Personal values exert great influence on decision making in organizations. If these values are congruent with organizational goals and processes, the organization can expect greater performance from its employees. On the other hand, if these values conflict with organizational goals, the organization can expect inhibited performance.

In general terms, motivation involves the inner force that drives a person to act in specific ways. The driving force is the individual's desire to fulfill his or her needs. The individual scans his or her environment (i.e., the set of stimuli presented to the individual) and reacts in specific ways in order to satisfy needs. Several theories of motivation are addressed in chapter 8.

CHAPTER 5

Abilities

LEARNING OBJECTIVES

After reading this chapter, you will be able to

- define the concept of cognitive abilities;
- understand inherent capacity (as compared with current capacity), heritability of ability, and generality of ability (as compared with specificity of ability);
- distinguish between ability and skill or competence;
- define emotional intelligence and discuss its role in work performance; and
- identify and explain significant managerial competencies.

In any performance situation, one needs to possess abilities related to the task at hand. We can observe this reality in any number of examples. For instance, certain abilities are required in order to succeed as captain of a basketball team, whereas other abilities are required in order to succeed as a basketball coach. In another example, the leader of a fitness class needs a different set of abilities than does the fitness club's manager. Similarly, specific abilities and skills can set apart the director of a city recreation department from the people who maintain the playing fields and from those who organize and conduct the competitions. In the same way, an athletics director is distinguished from his or her staff members by a particular set of abilities.

In yet another example, the task of a coach requires cognitive abilities to demonstrate sport-specific skills and properly assess the motivational factors affecting his or her athletes. This is particularly true in youth sport, where the coach must be cognitively aware of each athlete's levels of motivation and skill. In this vein, and in reference to a discussion about the functioning of teams, D. McClelland (1996) stated the following:

As would be expected, attention was first turned to such matters as being sure that there is a clear mission for the team, a proper assignment of tasks to different members of the team, good informational and organizational supports for the team, proper resources to work with, etc. All of these things are clearly needed—without them the team couldn't function—yet I kept feeling that you could have all these things like a well-designed Swiss watch—but the team might still not go. Why? Because fundamentally it is people with certain *competencies* that make teams go. (p. 17, emphasis added)

In the final analysis, irrespective of one's position in the organization, every worker needs to possess specific abilities in order to perform effectively in his or her job. Therefore, we must begin by clearly defining and describing the abilities required of the jobs performed in our organizations. Other important steps include identifying people who possess the required abilities and placing them in the right jobs. To help you complete these steps effectively, this chapter first describes abilities in general terms, then outlines cognitive abilities as they relate to organizational contexts.

Abilities constitute an individual's capacity to engage in a host of tasks, behaviors, or activities. In our discussion here, *ability* is used to mean the same thing as *aptitude* (a term used to refer to an innate talent), and these terms (which are used interchangeably) refer to one's innate potential for performance. Another term, *competency*, is also used interchangeably with *ability* and *aptitude*. It is defined as "an identifiable aspect of prospective work behavior attributable to the individual that is expected to contribute positively and/or neg-atively to organizational effectiveness. In short, a competency is future-evaluated work behavior" (Tett, Guterman, Bleier, and Murphy 2000, p. 215). Accordingly, this text focuses on tasks, behaviors, and activities that are relevant to the organizational context. Thus, a person's ability to cook is not of con-cern to an organization unless cooking itself is a task undertaken by the organization (e.g., a restaurant). That is, this chapter focuses on a person's ability to participate in organizational activities and carry out assigned tasks.

Narrowing the focus, the performance of orga-nizational tasks by sport and recreation managers depends on an individual's cognitive abilities. **Cognitive abilities** (i.e., intellectual abilities) include a person's capacity to comprehend what a task entails (i.e., what is to be done, as well as how, where, and why); to understand the relationships between his or her own task, the tasks of others, and organizational goals; and to make good decisions. Of course, the specific cognitive abilities needed vary from job to job.

ISSUES IN THE STUDY OF ABILITY

The study of ability has been beset by controversies involving its definition, measurement, heritability, and generality. Researchers generally accept that ability involves one's potential capacity to carry out specified tasks (e.g., to learn in a school setting or to manage an organization). Measuring this potential, however, has proven difficult (Heneman, Schwab, Fossum, and Dyer 1983). For example, early researchers (e.g., Guilford 1967) defined intelligence as an individual's inherent capacity (i.e., potential) to learn. However, existing tests of intelligence measure only "the individual's *current* capacity—whatever has been learned from whatever source" (Heneman et al. 1983, p. 70).

Regarding the **heritability** issue, one group of theorists (the behaviorists) hold that a person acquires ability not through inherent factors but through experience and learning. An opposing camp (consisting of biological determinists) holds that ability is endowed genetically. According to this latter view, individuals are born with differing abil-ity levels, and these differences are merely accen-tuated by experience (i.e., learning). Most people, however, subscribe to a compromise viewpoint (posited by the interactionists) that sees ability as a function of both biology and environment. Accord-ing to interactionists, environmental influences can compensate, to some extent, for deficiencies in the biological component of ability. That is, practice and training can compensate for the lack of inherited capacity.

Here, it is useful to think of a continuum of abil-ities. At one end lie abilities that cannot be trained easily (e.g., emotional intelligence); at the other end lie abilities that *can* be trained easily (e.g., word fluency). Researchers generally agree that environ-mental influence is likely to be higher in the early stages of one's life than in adulthood (during which time it is minimal). This point carries implications for management. That is, in general, members of an organization are adults; therefore, they are likely to be characterized by (more or less) permanent behavioral traits that define their ability.

ABILITIES VERSUS PERFORMANCE

Although abilities are critical for perfor-mance of a task, they are not the only contributors to performance; indeed, several other factors can contribute to, or detract from, performance. For instance, an individual's motivation to perform well in a task is as critical as are his or her abilities. The individual's performance is also affected by organizational practices, including the provision of opportunities to use his or her abilities, as well as by the organization's processes for evaluat-ing and rewarding performance. Thus, abilities are necessary but not sufficient for effective performance.

Regarding the **generality** or **specificity** of ability, it was once believed that ability was a global factor—that is, that an individual who scored high on one intellectual task would also do so on other tasks. However, researchers modified this view to allow for both a general intellectual factor (a *g* factor) and a number of specific cognitive abilities (*s* factors) (Heneman et al. 1983).

Although we can distinguish between potential ability (i.e., potential capacity) and current ability (i.e., current capacity), any test of ability tends to measure only current ability. It is useful to view abilities as determined by both genetic factors (i.e., nature) and environmental factors (i.e., nurture). The relative influence of each set of factors may vary across different abilities.

Although comprehensive lists of abilities are available, not all of those listed are relevant to all organizational contexts. Rather, some are relevant to some organizational contexts and some specific tasks. With this caveat in mind, consider the cognitive abilities that are relevant to organizational contexts as you read the next section.

COGNITIVE ABILITIES

As noted earlier, a number of specific abilities exist. Conceptualizations differ, however, regarding the type and number of specific abilities, as well as their descriptions. For instance, Guilford (1967) suggested that there are as many as 120 distinct cognitive aptitudes. However, because such a scheme is relatively impossible to apply in a real-world context, most researchers are content with describing the cognitive domain in 10 to 20 dimensions. In fact, Dubrin (2002) holds that the seven competencies shown in table 5.1 constitute an adequate set capable of predicting performance in organizations.

The abilities listed in table 5.1 are fundamental to the execution of any type of task in any context. However, their theoretical origins and the associated jargon do not help the manager to a great extent. Therefore, managers need to look at this issue from the practitioner's point of view. Fortunately, some management scholars have identified several work-related competencies or skills that are more readily comprehensible and useful to practicing managers.

JOB ANALYSIS AND ABILITIES

Sport and recreation managers need to determine what abilities are required for any given job, which requires thoroughly analyzing the job in question. The subject of job analysis is discussed at length in chapter 11. For now, let us note that Caughron, Mumford, and Fleishman (2012) reviewed the Fleishman Job Analysis Survey (F-JAS; Fleishman 1992) and concluded that its behaviorally anchored scales for the cognitive, psychomotor, physical-ability, and sensory-perceptual requirements of jobs and tasks remained valid and applicable in today's North American workplace. The F-JAS has been adapted and applied in a variety of international contexts (e.g., France, Germany, Romania) and through online platforms.

POTENTIAL VERSUS CURRENT CAPACITY

Although the issue of potential versus current capacity is real, it does not necessarily impede the process of hiring people. If a sport or recreation manager can specify the abilities required by a particular job, then the manager can verify whether an applicant for that job currently possesses those abilities. That is, the solution is to match the job's current-ability requirements with the applicant's current capacity. For instance, if a sport management job requires problem-solving skills, then the manager can ask candidates to solve a series of problems that may arise on the job and evaluate their solutions. Of course, a capacity to solve problems can also be indicated by previous experience and success in similar jobs.

TABLE 5.1   Cognitive Abilities

COMPETENCY	DESCRIPTION
Verbal comprehension	Understand the meaning of words and comprehend written and verbal communication.
Word fluency	Find and use words quickly and easily.
Numerical competency	Apply simple concepts measured or expressed with numbers.
Spatial competency	Visualize objects in space and manipulate them mentally, especially in three dimensions.
Memory	Store, retain, and recall symbols, words, numbers, and associations.
Perceptual speed	Quickly and accurately compare visual details, noting similarities and differences, and perform tasks requiring visual perception.
Inductive reasoning	Combine multiple premises to reach a specific conclusion and use it to solve problems and make logical decisions.

Based on Dubrin 2002.

As pointed out at the beginning of this chapter, the relevance of specific abilities or skills varies from management level to lower operating levels. For instance, the skills and competencies that a university requires of the athletics director differ from those that it requires of a facility manager. However, although this perspective is generally valid, lower-level workers (e.g., supervisors of facilities, playing fields, and competitions) are managers in their own right. Indeed, a stadium manager may supervise the work of 20 other workers, who may themselves possess various kinds of requisite skills. As a result,

> Management is best defined not as a limited number of 'top' or 'leading' positions, but as a set of competencies, attitudes, and qualities broadly distributed throughout the organization. Management skills are not the property of the few. Effective local authorities [sport managers] will recognize that many jobs which have not conventionally borne the tag "manager" rely none the less on that bundle of actions—taking charge, securing an outcome, controlling affairs—which amounts to "managing." (Local Government Management Board 1993, p. 8)

From this perspective, several of the managerial abilities and competencies described next may be relevant to successive levels of workers in an organization. As stated in chapter 1, human services strongly involve the control, direction, and motivation of clients in some form of physical activity. In essence, then, human service providers manage, as necessary, the people, the activity in which they engage, and the facilities and equipment. Therefore, several of the **managerial competencies** outlined may be relevant to human service providers, even though they may not be designated as managers. For instance, Ivancevich and Matteson (2002) hold that, when taken as a set, the seven competencies shown in table 5.2 can be used to predict performance in organizations. Some of the skill types listed (e.g., technical, human relations) are more important at lower levels, whereas others (e.g., analytical, conceptual) are more critical at the top level.

In a study of what characterizes intelligent functioning among senior managers, Klemp and McClelland (1986) identified eight general competencies that underlie intelligence (see figure 5.1). They grouped these eight competencies into three broad categories: intellectual, influence, and other. The intellectual competencies relate to gathering, analyzing, and evaluating information; understanding the whole system and its parts and how they interact with each other; and visualizing the alternatives and the implications of selected actions. Although these competencies are critical for managerial effectiveness, they do not by themselves make an intelligent manager.

To the contrary, because a manager's competencies in these areas must be translated into action—and because such actions are typically carried out by subordinate members of the organization—the manager must also be intelligent in influencing members of the organization to carry out specified activities efficiently and effectively. Therefore, the manager needs to possess what Klemp and McClelland (1986) referred to as the "influence competencies." These competencies include the capacity to

TABLE 5.2 Forms of Managerial Skills

SKILL TYPE	DESCRIPTION
Technical	Use practical knowledge, capabilities, and resources to perform specialized tasks.
Analytical	Break down problems to identify key parts and their relationships or interdependencies.
Decision making	Choose from among alternatives. The quality of the choice ultimately determines the manager's effectiveness. A manager's decision-making skill is greatly influenced by his or her analytical skill.
Computer	Efficiently navigate technological and digital media tools to increase a manager's productivity. This skill is essential for managers in the 21st century.
Human relations	Work with, communicate with, and understand others—all of which are essential for managers.
Communication	Communicate effectively through written and oral transmission of common understanding. This type of skill is critical to success in every field but is crucial to managers, who must achieve results through the efforts of others (consider, for example, event managers).
Conceptual	Think holistically, see interrelationships between parts of an organization, and understand how those parts fit together.

Adapted from Ivancevich and Matteson 2002.

exercise power in order to direct members' actions, to participate in and collaborate with groups, and to set a good personal example (which includes only self-confidence).

Curricular requirements for degree programs in sport management have been jointly proposed by the National Association for Sport and Physical Education (NASPE) and the North American Society for Sport Management (NASSM). Careful analysis of these guidelines shows that they are aimed at developing specific skills or competencies in specific areas of sport and recreation management. Skills and competencies have also been the subject of concerted research in sport management (Fielding, Pitts, and Miller 1991; Jamieson 1987). For example, in a survey (Fielding et al.) of 73 sport management academics from 38 universities in the United States and Canada, respondents identified the following competencies as most significant for success in sport management jobs: management (named by 37 percent of respondents), communication (30 percent), math (15 percent), marketing (15 percent), accounting (14 percent), and thinking (12 percent). Some of these skills parallel the functional areas of management—for example, management, marketing, and accounting. Others, such as communication, math, and thinking, are general in nature and transferable across functional areas.

DIVERSITY MANAGEMENT OF HUMAN RESOURCES

 In reference to table 5.2 and figure 5.1, managers vary in terms of the types of skill and the level of each skill or competency they bring to their respective organizations. Strategically managing diversity involves recognizing that diverse skills and abilities are a form of deep-level diversity and that activation of diverse skills and abilities is "the process of deliberately bringing divergent perspectives to bear on a task or project" (Chelladurai 2014, p. 350). From the perspective of human resource management, this process involves actively recruiting and orienting individuals who possess divergent skills and abilities in order to form an employee pool that brings comprehensive, unique, and innovative ideas to the table.

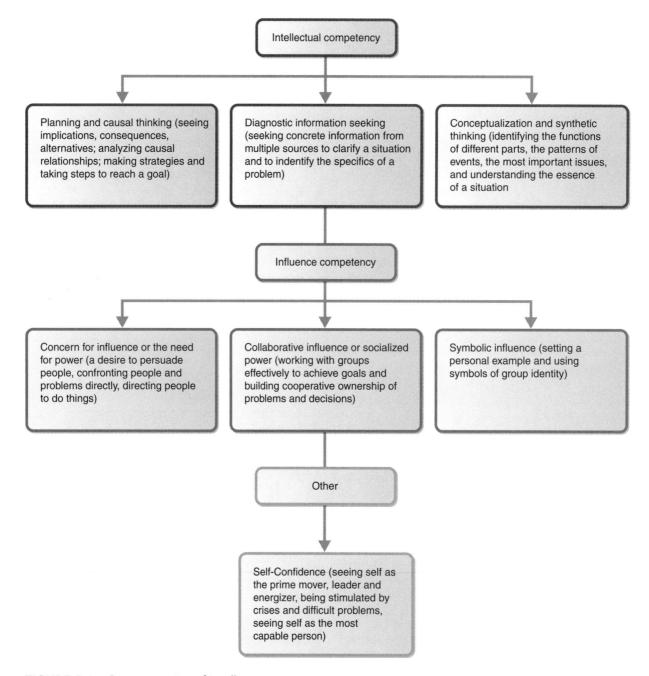

FIGURE 5.1 Competencies of intelligent managers.
Adapted from Klemp and McClelland 1986.

EMOTIONAL INTELLIGENCE

Interest has been growing in the role of emotional intelligence in organizational affairs. In fact, some researchers have suggested that, along with cognitive ability and personality (discussed in chapter 6), emotional intelligence acts as a dominant influence on how members experience and react to organizational life. But what exactly is emotional intelligence?

The label *emotional intelligence* was introduced by Salovey and Mayer (1990) and then defined by Mayer and Salovey (1997) as "the ability to perceive emotions, to access and generate emotions so as to assist thought, to understand emotions and emotional knowledge, and to reflectively regulate emo-

LEADERSHIP QUALITIES

For the purpose of assessing the credibility and prototypicality of effective leaders in sport, Swanson and Kent (2014) provided support for the unique role played by sport-domain factors. As it relates to leadership, credibility involves important attitudes such as trust and confidence, including belief in a leader's "knowledge, intelligence, and sincerity" (Hovland, Janis, and Kelley 1953, p. 20). A prototype, on the other hand, is an "abstract conception of the most representative member or most widely shared features of a given cognitive category" (J.S. Phillips 1984, p. 126). Swanson and Kent (2014) highlighted the influence exerted by sport-domain factors (e.g., sport-specific knowledge, experience, and skill) in people's judgments about the effectiveness of sport leaders. In support of propositions by Todd and Kent (2009), they concluded that complex, industry-specific employee attitudes in sport create perceptions of what is required for a leader to be viewed as successful in sport (Swanson and Kent 2014). Specifically, Swanson and Kent (2014) outlined eight attributes that are important in judging the credibility and prototypicality of sport leaders:

- Functional area of expertise (e.g., sport marketing expertise)
- Sport-domain expertise (i.e., expertise in a specific sport or in sport generally)
- Trust (i.e., trustworthiness and integrity)
- Experience in playing sport (e.g., having played at the competitive level)
- Experience in coaching sport (e.g., having coached at the competitive level)
- Dynamism (i.e., energetic person with aggressive mind-set)
- Functional area of knowledge (e.g., sport marketing know-how)
- Sport-domain knowledge (e.g., knowledge of a specific sport or of sport generally)

tions so as to promote emotional and intellectual growth" (p. 5). It refers to the competence to not only identify and understand emotions but also regulate them in oneself and in others for better interpersonal interactions (Matthews, Zeidner, and Roberts 2002). Thus, emotional intelligence refers to verbal and nonverbal abilities to recognize one's own emotions and those of others, understand them, and employ them in dealing with the demands and pressures of interpersonal situations.

The importance of emotional intelligence was highlighted by Van Rooy and Viswesvaran (2004), who noted that significant instances of emotion and emotional expression have become commonplace at work, particularly in times of downsizing, restructuring, mergers, and outsourcing. As a result, emotionally intelligent persons are likely to succeed even in turbulent times. The challenge is heightened by increasing diversity in the workplace, which can elicit varying forms and expressions of emotion. As Bodtker and Jameson (2001) commented,

Different cultures are more or less expressive in general, are more or less comfortable displaying certain emotions (like anger), and use different behaviors to express particular emotions (crying to indicate anger; smiling to indicate discomfort). Emotionally intelligent persons are likely to be effective in recognizing and understanding these emotions of the diverse workforce and be able to cope with the complexity. By the same token, emotional intelligence is likely to facilitate the performance of work teams characterized by diversity. That is, emotionally intelligent members of the team would be able to understand other team members better and find ways to collaborate with them, and enhance team performance. Because emotional intelligence has been shown to improve performance of individuals and groups, workers and managers need to understand the dynamics of emotions (their own and those of others). (p. 262)

The preceding definitions and description highlight the following four dimensions of emotional intelligence:

• *Identifying emotions:* This is the ability to correctly perceive one's own emotions and those of others. For example, when a sport manager meets with subordinates after an unpleasant encounter with a client, the manager may tend to interact with subordinates in an ineffective way. If, however, the manager is emotionally intelligent, he or she can control or regulate the current emotional mood in order to be effective during the meeting with the subordinates.

• *Using emotions:* This is the ability to use, generate, and assimilate emotions in thinking and action. For example, as mentioned earlier, coaches tend to spark relevant emotions (e.g., loyalty to the university, anger at opponents) in order to arouse players to greater effort and better performance. One classic example is found in Coach Vince Lombardi's famous call to win "one for the Gipper."

• *Understanding emotions:* This is the competence to understand various emotions, how they change, and the interrelations between them. This dimension involves a general understanding of various emotions and their effects on behavior. For example, if one's friend is killed by a drunken driver, the immediate emotion is sorrow, which likely then turns into anger against the driver. If a fellow worker is terminated unjustly, one's immediate emotional reaction may be to pity the person who lost the job, but it could also involve rage and resentment against management. Such understandings are facilitated by emotional intelligence.

• *Managing emotions:* This is the ability to regulate emotion in oneself and in others. Recognizing one's own and others' emotions can be difficult in itself, and managing them is even harder—especially those of others. Even so, managers are often faced with the task of managing the emotions of their employees. Managers who are high in emotional intelligence are likely to succeed at this challenge.

Perlini and Halverson (2006) found that self-awareness, emotional management, stress tolerance, and general mood were significantly higher

TECHNOLOGY IN HUMAN RESOURCE MANAGEMENT

Archer and Davison (2008) noted that employers of new graduates increasingly consider both social skills (particularly communication and teamwork) and personality (e.g., emotional intelligence) to be more important than degree qualifications. For example, because communication in the workplace is more and more closely tied with enhanced adoption of technology in organizations, the ability to use technology to communicate between virtual teams across the globe has become a much-sought ability in human resource candidates.

among National Hockey League (NHL) players than among members of the general population. In their survey analysis of 79 NHL players across 24 teams, the results suggested that emotional intelligence helped predict a player's number of scored points and games played, thus highlighting the cognitive abilities required of athletes in the professional sport setting.

In order to better manage emotions, both in ourselves and in others, we should be familiar with the types of emotion. To this end, the commonly understood positive and negative emotions are presented in table 5.3.

Noting that earlier descriptions of managerial competencies were not complete, Tett and colleagues (2000) developed a more comprehensive list of 53 managerial competencies categorized into 9 classes (table 5.4). In this taxonomy, emotional intelligence is connected to cognitive abilities through the discussion of person orientation as a broader class of competencies. Furthermore, this extensive list demonstrates the wide range of competencies that managers must possess in order to be effective. Human resource managers must ensure that these competencies are available to the organization through the processes of hiring, training, and development. For example, specific competencies can be included in a job description and subsequently assessed during the interview process.

VIEWPOINT

Peters (1987) and Klemp and McClelland (1986) argued that success in both work and everyday life depends not only on conventional academic intelligence but also on "practical intelligence." Peters identified several components of practical intelligence, including

- self-understanding (to understand one's needs and abilities),
- social intelligence (to manage group processes through effective communication),
- body intelligence (to control one's body and manipulate objects),
- spatial intelligence (to get, process, and use information about shapes, sizes, distances, and geometrical relationships),
- verbal intelligence (to employ verbal comprehension, fluency, and vocabulary),
- logical-mathematical intelligence (to think systematically and abstractly), and
- critical thinking (to think creatively, intuitively, and, above all, critically).

TABLE 5.3   Positive and Negative Emotions and Some Associated Feelings

POSITIVE EMOTIONS	ASSOCIATED FEELINGS
Enjoyment	Happiness, delight, euphoria, joy
Pride	Satisfaction, self-esteem, fulfillment
Love	Affection, friendliness, kindness, devotion
Relief	Ease, contentment, release
NEGATIVE EMOTIONS	**ASSOCIATED FEELINGS**
Anger	Fury, animosity, hostility, annoyance
Fear	Apprehension, nervousness, panic
Guilt	Shame, remorse, regret, contrition
Sadness	Sorrow, gloom, despair, self-pity
Envy	Jealousy, suspicion, resentment, spite
Disgust	Contempt, scorn, aversion, revulsion

Data from Draft 2015.

ROLE OF THE SPORT OR RECREATION MANAGER

As business shift from a production (mechanistic) to more humanitarian focus, the levels and types of competencies required of sport and recreation managers have shifted toward the need for emotional awareness. As more and more managers are required to understand their own emotions and the emotions of others, it is increasingly ineffective to focus solely on traditional functions such as strategic planning and goal setting. Sport and recreation managers must now also consider competencies related to emotional intelligence that enable individuals to understand the effect of an emotional response on others. In fact, such competencies are particularly relevant in sport, where the passion of competition is often interwoven with emotion during performance and decision-making processes.

Furthermore, although the complexity of the list presented in table 5.4 demonstrates the breadth of competencies required in management positions, the sport and recreation manager must assess his or her particular context in order to understand which competencies are most salient to achieving organizational goals. In other words, managers must interpret and operationalize (e.g., create accurate and up-to-date job descriptions) the competencies needed in roles, jobs, and occupations. This operationalization of competencies must also reflect the particular sector of the sport and recreation industry in which the manager functions (e.g., club sport, intercollegiate athletics, fitness club, provincial or state associations [Chelladurai 2005]).

The manager's role in operationalizing competencies is to understand the types of managerial competencies needed in a given organization and to recruit or develop these competencies in the organization's human resources. For example, in preparing for the 2015 Women's World Cup, held in Canada, the planning and organizing committee

TABLE 5.4 Comprehensive List of 53 Managerial Competencies

FUNCTION	DESCRIPTION
Traditional	
Problem awareness	Perceives situations that may require action to promote organizational success.
Decision making	Uses good judgment in resolving problems.
Directing	Clearly specifies to subordinates what needs to be done.
Decision delegation	Assigns true decision-making authority to qualified subordinates.
Short-term planning	Prepares the steps needed to complete tasks before action is taken.
Strategic planning	Develops long-term plans to keep the organization aligned with future demands.
Coordinating	Organizes the activities of subordinates and the allocation of resources.
Goal setting	Identifies organizational work-unit objectives and the methods for achieving them.
Monitoring	Compares current work-unit progress with predetermined standards, objectives, and deadlines.
Motivating by authority	Influences subordinates directly by using rewards and punishments.
Motivating by persuasion	Persuades others to achieve excellence for its own sake.
Team building	Identifies and integrates distinct subordinate roles in a spirit of collaboration.
Productivity	Accomplishes goals set by self or others.
Task orientation	
Initiative	Takes preliminary steps to do what needs to be done without direction.
Task focus	Stays on task despite complexity or ambiguity.
Urgency	Responds quickly to pressing organizational demands.
Decisiveness	Does not hesitate in making tough decisions.
Person orientation	
Compassion	Shows genuine concern for the welfare of others.
Cooperation	Seeks to accomplish work goals through collaboration with others.
Sociability	Initiates and energetically maintains friendly interactions with others inside and outside of work.
Politeness	Demonstrates proper manners when dealing with others.
Political astuteness	Takes advantage of political relationships and the distribution of power in pursuing goals.
Assertiveness	States views confidently, directly, and forcefully.
Seeking input	Actively pursues others' contributions to work-related discussion.
Customer focus	Seeks to maintain or enhance customer satisfaction.
Dependability	
Orderliness	Maintains a high degree of organization in the physical work environment.
Rule orientation	Realizes the importance of organizational rules and policies and willingly follows them.
Personal responsibility	Accepts responsibility for own actions, decisions, and directions to subordinates.
Trustworthiness	Maintains confidentiality in dealing with sensitive information about the company, its customers, and its workers.
Timeliness	Shows appreciation for and abides by routine job-related time limits.
Professionalism	Demonstrates the standards of his or her career or occupational group.
Loyalty	Shares the company's goals and values.

FUNCTION	DESCRIPTION
Open-mindedness	
Tolerance	Values judgments different from his or her own.
Adaptability	Readily adapts to new situations and immediate work demands.
Creative thinking	Fosters creative thinking in the organization or work unit.
Cultural appreciation	Appreciates diversity in cultural experiences and beliefs.
Emotional control	
Resilience	Maintains a positive attitude in response to failure.
Stress management	Deals effectively with feelings of job-related stress and their causes.
Communication	
Listening skills	Actively attends to what others are saying.
Oral communication	Expresses thoughts verbally in a clear, pleasant, and straightforward manner.
Public presentation	Is effective and comfortable in presenting material to groups of people.
Written communication	Expresses self clearly and succinctly in writing (e.g., by letter or memo).
Development of self and others	
Developmental goal setting	Collaborates with individual subordinates to establish work objectives for their career advancement.
Performance assessment	Evaluates individual co-workers' performance with respect to their personal developmental objectives.
Developmental feedback	Gives regular, specific, and timely feedback to subordinates in relation to personal goals.
Job enrichment	Gives employees learning opportunities to expand job-related expertise.
Self-development	Seeks out and engages in self-improvement opportunities.
Occupational acumen and concerns	
Technical proficiency	Knows what it takes to do the job.
Organizational awareness	Knows how the organization works as a whole and in terms of individual work units.
Quantity concern	Works to meet or exceed existing organizational quotas.
Quality concern	Works to meet or exceed existing quality standards.
Financial concern	Understands the importance of generating and saving money for the organization.
Safety concern	Emphasizes accident prevention in the workplace.

Adapted, by permission, from R.P. Tett et al., 2000, "Development and content validation of a 'hyperdimensional' taxonomy of managerial competence," *Human Performance* 13(3): 205-251.

recognized in 2013 the need for task-orientation competencies in individuals hired for director-level positions. Therefore, the competencies of initiative, task focus, urgency, and decisiveness were added to the job-posting and interview protocols. In interviews, prospective candidates were given task simulations related to problems that could occur during event preparation. As a result, hiring managers had the chance to rate each candidate on the key competencies. This process enhanced the managers' ability to judge the fit of each candidate with the competencies relevant to the position.

Case Study

Training a Sales Manager With the Orlando Magic

The NBA's Orlando Magic have experienced a drop in attendance due to poor play and lack of star power. The front office is eager to jump-start ticket sales for the next season by promoting the right staff member to the position of season ticket sales manager. Upper management decides that the individual promoted to this role will supervise a team of seven sales staff and report directly to the director of marketing and strategic sales. In this role, the individual will be charged with increasing season ticket sales by 5 percent and ensuring the retention of 85 percent of previous season ticket holders. The role requires a dynamic individual who can motivate junior-level staff members to go above and beyond in order to sell season tickets, even though the product on the court isn't as strong as it once was.

Case Study Tasks

1. Review the list of managerial competencies presented in table 5.4, then describe 10 competencies relevant to the position of manager of season ticket sales.

2. Create a job description for the position that includes the job title, the reporting structure (who reports to the position and to whom the position reports), the position's responsibilities, and key competencies for the position.

CHAPTER PURSUITS

SUMMARY

This chapter describes a short list of cognitive abilities and discusses the issues of inherent capacity (as compared with current capacity), heritability of ability, and generality of ability (as compared with specificity of ability). It also explains the role of emotional intelligence and addresses the competencies associated with effective managers. Not all of the abilities are relevant to all organizations or tasks; therefore, a prudent manager considers them in relation to the contingencies present in his or her own organization.

Schemes for classifying abilities provide the basis for analyzing jobs in terms of what they require, classifying jobs on the basis of similarity of ability requirements, setting performance standards for each set of jobs, hiring new employees who possess the necessary abilities, assessing the abilities of current employees, assigning employees to appropriate jobs, and instituting appropriate training programs to enhance abilities in which they are deficient. In addition, services must be tailored to the ability levels of clients. In some cases, as in recruiting a fitness instructor, the results of an assessment of the fitness instructor's emotional intelligence abilities can be used as primary criteria to judge the job candidate's ability to meet clients' needs. Later chapters deal with the processes of recruiting, hiring, training, assigning individuals to specific jobs, and evaluating their performance.

KEY TERMS

cognitive ability 78
generality 79
heritability 78
managerial competency 80
specificity 79

UNDERSTAND

1. What is your perspective on the role of emotional intelligence in sport and recreation management? How can we best measure emotional intelligence in sport and recreation?

2. In your view, which of the cognitive abilities are important in which of the jobs found in sport and recreation? Please explain your reasoning.

INTERACT

1. Discuss which dimensions of emotional intelligence are most important in managing sport and recreation employees. How might the importance of certain dimensions of emotional intelligence vary across different roles or different organizational sectors?

2. Considering the competencies listed in figure 5.1, discuss the relative importance of each competency in two different managerial positions in sport and recreation.

CHAPTER

6

Personality

LEARNING OBJECTIVES

After reading this chapter, you will be able to

- define and describe the terms *personality* and *trait*,
- explain the genetic and environmental factors in the formation of personality,
- distinguish between personality as a state and as a trait,
- understand Jackson's comprehensive list of personality traits and the "big five" personality domains, and
- identify and describe the personality traits most relevant to organizations and management.

In chapter 5, we note that ability is one of several factors affecting performance, which is also influenced by one's personality, values, and motivation. Because personality predisposes an individual (whether manager or worker) to react in specific ways, understanding the nature of personality facilitates better management. For instance, personality characteristics form part of the basis for making good decisions when selecting individuals, placing them in specific jobs, and promoting them to higher positions. In addition, we can modify methods of supervision and motivation to fit the personalities of individual workers. In order to realize these benefits, we must understand the dynamics of personality in the workplace and how to make the best use of individual differences in personality in order to benefit both the individuals and the organization.

As with many psychological concepts, the definition of personality has been the subject of some confusion and controversy, and the development and description of personality have been addressed by several theories. Our intention here, however, is not to delve into these issues but to discuss

- the modern view of the development and manifestation of personality,
- descriptions of personality, and
- the personality constructs relevant to organizations and their management.

After collating information from 50 definitions, Allport (1937) offered his own definition of **personality**: "the dynamic organization within the individual of those psychophysical systems that determine his [or her] unique adjustments to his [or her] environment" (p. 48). One might expect that after such elaborate analysis and synthesis, researchers would come to a consensus on the concept of personality. Instead, differing views persist today.

VIEWPOINT

Because personality characteristics create the parameters for people's behavior, they give us a framework for predicting behavior. For instance, individuals who are shy, introverted, and uncomfortable in social situations would probably be ill suited as salespeople. Individuals who are submissive and conforming might not be effective as advertising "idea" people. . . . Can we predict which people will be high performers in sales, research, or assembly-line work on the basis of their personality characteristics alone? The answer is NO. But knowledge of an individual's personality can aid in reducing mismatches, which, in turn, can lead to greater job stability and higher job satisfaction. (Robbins 2000, pp. 375)

For example, Tosi, Mero, and Rizzo (2000) defined personality as "the relatively stable organization of all of a person's characteristics" and as "an enduring pattern of attributes that define the uniqueness of a person" (p. 33). According to Luthans (2010), personality relates to the ways in which individuals view themselves and in turn affect others. In this case, personality involves internally and externally measured traits and includes person–situation interaction (Luthans 2010). In the view of Lefton and colleagues (2005), personality is "a pattern of relatively permanent traits, dispositions, or characteristics that give some consistency to people's behaviour" (p. 14). To Schermerhorn, Hunt, and Osborn (2011), personality involves the unique aspects of an individual that directly influence how the individual reacts and interacts with others. Finally, Maddi (2001) defined personality as an established set of traits that are continuous across time and predict convergence and divergence in the psychological behavior (thoughts, feelings, and actions) between individuals.

These definitions suggest that people are both alike (i.e., they have commonalities) and different

(i.e., they have differences). The definitions also refer to personality as stable and as having continuity over time. Much of the remaining debate regarding personality centers on determinants of personality and on the relative influences of personality and situation on behavior.

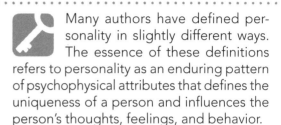

Many authors have defined personality in slightly different ways. The essence of these definitions refers to personality as an enduring pattern of psychophysical attributes that defines the uniqueness of a person and influences the person's thoughts, feelings, and behavior.

DETERMINANTS OF PERSONALITY

The traditional view is that personality is largely determined genetically. However, Mischel (1973) argued that personality traits are learned characteristics and that personality development is both a cognitive and a social learning process—a cognitive process in the sense that individuals consciously process the information they receive, and a social learning process in the sense that people learn from social interactions and their consequences and then reorient themselves to the environment. Bandura's (1986) social cognitive theory (formerly known as social learning theory) also suggests that one's behavior is shaped by cognitive processes that revolve around personal experiences and by perceptions of others' experiences.

The traditional view and the more recent view need not be seen as mutually exclusive. In fact, the growing consensus among psychologists holds that hereditary factors (i.e., **genetic influences**) play a part in the development of personality, which is also modified through one's exposure to culture, family, and referent groups (i.e., **environmental influences**). Examples of environmental influences include the following:

• *Cultural influences:* If personality is a function of the developmental process, then the culture in which a person is reared exerts a significant effect on his or her personality. As a general influence, culture determines the range of experiences and situations to which the individual is exposed and the range of possible values that he or she may hold. All of this bears on the individual's personality. For instance, the values of independence and competitiveness are cherished and rewarded in North American culture, but they are not fostered in Asian cultures. Even so, of course, individuals in a culture do not all develop the same personality traits (or develop them to the same extent).

- *Family and social groups:* In line with arguments for the influence of culture, one's immediate family and social groups also help define one's personality dispositions. Family and social groups interpret and inculcate values and norms derived from the culture. Thus, members closely associated with the individual mediate culture's influence on his or her personality development. Family and social groups also define roles for the individual and the appropriate behaviors for each role (e.g., parent, child, leader, follower). People who perform different roles acquire the tendencies appropriate to their specific roles.

- *Situation:* Apart from the nature-versus-nurture debate over personality, another issue concerns whether an individual's behavior in a given situation is determined by the individual's personality or by the demands of the situation. If one holds the view that personality is inherited, then it is logical to conclude that personality determines behavior. If, on the other hand, one accepts Mischel's (1973) view of personality as a learned characteristic, then one also holds that situational demands determine behavior. However, research and experience support neither of these views. Instead, the interactionist view—that the characteristics of the person and the situation interact with each other in influencing behavior—is gaining acceptance.

This view is consistent with Lewin's (1935) formula B = f(P,E), which suggests that behavior (B) is a function (f) of the person (P) and the environment or situation (E). For example, when a basketball player constantly crashes the board for rebounds, it is supposed that the player possesses an "aggressive personality." According to earlier theories, such a player should be aggressive in all situations, but research has not supported such an assertion. Instead, the basketball player might be submissive in his or her dealings with family or with the coach. What emerges from this example is the notion that the basketball situation calls for aggressive actions and that the player's aggressive personality manifests itself in that situation. However, the family situation does not require such behavior, so the personality lies dormant in that situation. Thus, particular situations constrain an individual's behavior in specific ways.

One view holds that personality is largely determined by genetics—in other words, that it is an inherited characteristic. A contrasting view holds that personality is a learned characteristic and that this learning occurs through personal experiences and perceptions of others' experiences. The most widely accepted perspective is the interactionist model, which holds that personality is determined by both genetic and environmental factors.

The realization that personality manifests itself in some circumstances and not in others has led scholars to distinguish between **personality as a trait and as a state**. A trait is a general predisposition to specific experiences or behaviors, whereas a state is the activation of the trait in specific situations. A good example is found in the distinction between trait anxiety and state anxiety. Some individuals are prone to be more anxious than others, which indicates that they are high on the anxiety trait. However, this implication does not mean that those who score higher on the trait are more anxious than low scorers in all situations. Rather, anxiety manifests itself and sets apart more anxious persons only in situations in which some element of threat, such as an evaluation or comparison by others, is present.

The foregoing analyses carry two implications for students of sport management. First, given the same situation for all members of an organization, members with different personalities tend to behave in different ways. That is, if the situation does not exert a strong influence, then members behave differently based on their personality predispositions. The second implication is that if the situational influences are strong enough, then all members behave according to the dictates of the situation. For example, if a fire starts in the stands, then everyone reacts in the same way—by running for their lives! Hold these implications in mind when reading the next section, which reviews some of the personality traits, particularly those more relevant to the organizational context.

A general disposition to act in a specific way is a personality trait. However, that trait is exhibited only when activated by strong situational cues, and it may lie dormant in the absence of such cues. When situational cues trigger a trait into action, it is a state.

VIEWPOINT

In explaining how to coach or mentor people, Megginson and Clutterbuck (2005) refer to individuals as having separate selves:

Separate selves is a simple but practical tool for helping people understand the complexity of their own thinking and move into concerted action. In recent years, the notion of a single personality for each person has been questioned in the light of contrary evidence. Whatever the truth of that debate, it is clear that people often have a different set of perceptions, responses, and attitudes in different situations. At its simplest, this may be seen in the difference in the voice tone, body posture, and manner of someone on the telephone compared with how they would speak face to face; this is seen at its strongest among generations who grew up without universal personal telephone access, giving the appearance that they have "become a different person." Other examples might be how someone behaves at work versus at home; or being subdued and withdrawn in the company of strangers, yet [being] the life and soul of the party among close friends. (p. 103)

The authors note that these differences are not always obvious to the individual in question. They also suggest that each person should assess different expressions of the self, as in optimistic versus pessimistic, assertive versus passive, adventurous versus cautious, serious versus fun, and private versus public.

TYPE THEORIES

In the 20th century, psychologists commonly referred to types when describing a person in terms of personality. A good example from the field of sport and recreation management can be found in Sheldon's (1954) classification of temperaments derived from body types. Specifically, he held that every individual could be characterized in terms of the following types:

- Mesomorphy (i.e., muscular, strong body type)
- Ectomorphy (i.e., tall, fragile body type)
- Endomorphy (i.e., round, soft body type)

Sheldon posited that all individuals have more or less of each of the three components and that in some people only one of the three is dominant. He also maintained that each body type is associated with a particular temperament: mesomorphy with somatotonia (characterized by aggressiveness, assertiveness, vigor), ectomorphy with cerebrotonia (marked by restraint, sensitivity, introversion), and endomorphy with viscerotonia (indicated by sociability, tolerance, extroversion).

Sheldon developed his theory based on his clinical experiences with his psychiatric patients. The problem, however, is that his measurement of body types and temperaments were not conducted independently. Rather, he, the theory's originator, measured all of the variables relevant to his own theory, and all of the measurements were subjective. Therefore, researchers have not given much credence to his theory linking temperament to body type.

Sheldon's classification of body types—consisting of mesomorphy, endomorphy, and ectomorphy—is based on muscularity and linearity of body structure. Sheldon also classified individuals on the basis of temperament (i.e., personality) into the following categories: somatotonia, cerebrotonia, and viscerotonia. Although the concept of body types is generally accepted, its linkage with personality dispositions has been discounted.

VIEWPOINT

The general preference for physically formidable leaders has been substantiated in research. Noting that several studies have shown that "people tend to prefer male leaders who display cues of health, strength, and height," M.E. Price and Van Vugt (2015) pointed out that this preference could derive from our ancestral past as hunter-gatherers. The authors noted that "the hunter-gatherer activities that require leadership, especially hunting and warfare, generally require athletic ability, physical strength, aggressive formidability, and skill with weapons. . . . As a result, leaders in small-scale societies tend to be physically formidable males" (p. 178).

M.E. Price and Van Vugt (2015) also point out that a mismatch exists between this ancestral need for physically formidable leaders and modern organizational life, which, of course, does not generally entail hunting and fighting for survival. The persistence of this archaic view of leadership perpetuates a sexist conception of effective leadership and highlights body-based discrimination that cannot be tolerated in today's inclusive sport and recreation organizations. Thus, sport and recreation managers must create and maintain a culture of diversity focused on embracing contemporary forms of leader behaviors rather than certain aspects of leader appearance.

TRAIT THEORIES

Trait theories may be considered as forming an extension of type theories. That is, instead of placing individuals into one of a limited number of categories, as type theories do, trait theories describe individuals in terms of several traits. Thus, trait theories acknowledge the complexity of personality and describe it in more elaborate terms than do type theories.

Researchers have identified several hundred traits (Allport and Odbert 1936), and several scholars have tried to distill this multitude into fewer and more meaningful categories. Usually, these attempts have led to the development of scales (or inventories) for measuring the specified personality traits. The best-known of these instruments are Cattell's (1957) Sixteen Personality Factor Questionnaire, Hathaway and McKinley's (1967) Minnesota Multiphasic Personality Inventory, Gough's (1969) California Psychological Inventory, and D.N. Jackson's (1984) Personality Research Form. The traits measured by the Personality Research Form are comprehensive and applicable to any group of subjects. Because they are representative of many other schemes proposed, they are defined in table 6.1 for illustrative purposes.

The 1990s brought a move to describe individuals in terms of what are referred to as the "Big Five" personality domains (Barrick and Mount 1991; Goldberg 1990; McCrae and Costa 1987):

- Surgency and extroversion
- Agreeableness
- Conscientiousness
- Neuroticism and emotional instability
- Openness to experience (closely correlated with intellect)

The purpose of this move toward the Big Five was to group several of the individual traits included in other schemes into meaningful domains. Researchers have found that these five domains, which are outlined in figure 6.1, relate to several forms of behavior in organizations (e.g., Mount and Barrick 1995). For instance, Barrick and Mount (1991) found the personality domain of conscientiousness to be predictive of job-performance measures among professional, police, managerial, sales, and skilled and semiskilled workers. Similarly, the domain of surgency or extroversion was found to be related to performance in jobs requiring social interaction (e.g., managerial and sales). And the domain of conscientiousness seems to be related meaningfully to all job contexts. As Barrick and Mount noted,

This aspect of personality appears to tap traits which are important to the accomplishment of work tasks in all jobs. That is, those individuals who exhibit traits associated with a strong sense of purpose, obligation, and persistence generally perform better than those who do not. (p. 18)

TABLE 6.1 Traits Measured by Jackson's Personality Research Form

SCALE	DESCRIPTION OF HIGH SCORER
Abasement	Shows a high degree of humility, accepts blame and criticism even when not deserved, exposes self to situations in which he or she is in an inferior position, and tends to be self-effacing.
Achievement	Aspires to accomplish difficult tasks, maintains high standards, is willing to work toward distant goals, responds positively to competition, and is willing to put forth effort to attain excellence.
Affiliation	Enjoys being with friends and people in general, accepts people readily, and makes efforts to form friendships and maintain associations with people.
Aggression	Enjoys combat and argument, is easily annoyed, is sometimes willing to hurt people to get his or her way, and may seek to "get even" with people perceived to have harmed him or her.
Autonomy	Tries to break away from restraints, confinements, or restrictions of any kind; enjoys being unattached, free, and not tied to people, places, or obligations; and may be rebellious when faced with restraints.
Change	Likes new and different experiences, dislikes routine and avoids it, may readily change opinions or values in different circumstances, and adapts readily to changes in environment.
Cognitive structure	Does not like ambiguity or uncertainty in information, wants all questions answered completely, and desires to make decisions based on definite knowledge rather than guesses or probabilities.
Defendence	Readily suspects that people mean harm or are against him or her, is ready to defend self at all times, takes offense easily, and does not accept criticism readily.
Dominance	Attempts to control his or her environment and to influence or direct other people, expresses opinions forcefully, and enjoys the role of leader and may assume it spontaneously.
Endurance	Is willing to work long hours, does not give up quickly on a problem, perseveres even in the face of great difficulty, and is patient and unrelenting in work habits.
Exhibition	Wants to be the center of attention, enjoys having an audience, engages in behavior that wins the notice of others, and may enjoy being dramatic or witty.
Harm avoidance	Does not enjoy exciting activities, especially if danger is involved; avoids risk of bodily harm; and seeks to maximize personal safety.
Impulsivity	Tends to act on the "spur of the moment" and without deliberation, gives vent readily to feelings and wishes, speaks freely, and may be volatile in emotional expression.
Nurturance	Gives sympathy and comfort; assists others whenever possible; is interested in caring for children and for people who are disabled or infirm; offers a "helping hand" to those in need; and readily performs favors for others.
Order	Is concerned with keeping personal effects and surroundings neat and organized; dislikes clutter, confusion, and lack of organization; and is interested in developing methods for keeping materials methodically organized.
Play	Does many things "just for fun" and spends much time participating in games, sports, social activities, and other amusements; enjoys jokes and funny stories; and maintains a lighthearted, easygoing attitude toward life.
Sentience	Notices smells, sights, tastes, and the way things feel; remembers these sensations and believes that they are an important part of life; is sensitive to many forms of experience; and may maintain an essentially hedonistic or aesthetic view of life.

SCALE	DESCRIPTION OF HIGH SCORER
Social recognition	Desires to be held in high esteem by acquaintances, is concerned about reputation and what other people think of him or her, and works for approval and recognition from others.
Succorance	Frequently seeks the sympathy, protection, love, advice, and reassurance of other people; may feel insecure or helpless without such support; and confides difficulties readily to a receptive person.
Understanding	Wants to understand many areas of knowledge and values synthesis of ideas, verifiable generalization, and logical thought, particularly when directed at satisfying intellectual curiosity.
Desirability	Describes self in terms judged as desirable and, in response to personality statements, presents favorable picture of self, whether consciously or unconsciously and whether accurately or inaccurately.
Infrequency	Responds in implausible or pseudorandom manner, possibly due to carelessness, and exhibits poor comprehension, passive noncompliance, confusion, or gross deviation.

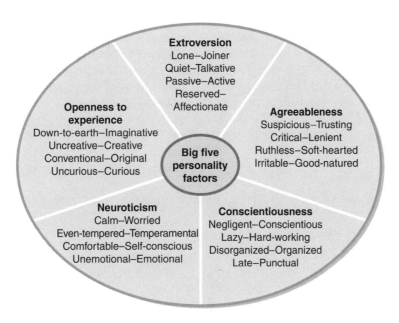

FIGURE 6.1 The Big Five personality domains, with descriptors of low and high scorers.
Adapted from Kelly 1992.

VIEWPOINT

After reviewing the research on the relationship between personality and job performance, Rothstein and Goffin (2006) concluded that personality measures contribute to the prediction of job performance and that the Big Five-factor model of personality has become increasingly popular in personality–performance research. They also noted, however, that "more specific, narrow personality measures continue to demonstrate equal or greater utility for personnel selection" (p. 174).

Researchers have proposed many lists of many personality traits. However, the proposed Big Five personality domains—surgency, agreeableness, conscientiousness, neuroticism, and intellect—may be sufficient to describe a person.

PERSONALITY AND ORGANIZATIONAL BEHAVIOR

The preceding descriptions of personality and its dimensions are general and can be applied in any context. Debate continues, however, about whether broad personality traits are sufficient to predict behavior in the workplace. Although it is generally agreed that broad traits (e.g., the Big Five) are generalizable across situations, some authors argue that more specific traits would be more useful in selecting individuals for specific jobs. For instance, the trait of conscientiousness would predict that an individual would be organized, disciplined, and decisive in any job situation, but it does not say whether the person would be more suitable for a production job or a sales job. Consider two people, Mark and Mary. Both are conscientious, but Mark also has specific traits suited to a job in sport marketing, whereas Mary has specific traits more suited to a job in facility management.

The following sections describe the specific personality traits considered germane to the management of human resources: **authoritarian personality**, **bureaucratic orientation**, **attitude toward authority**, **attitude toward individualism**, **tolerance for ambiguity**, **locus of control**, **positive affectivity**, **negative affectivity**, **service orientation**, **Machiavellianism**, and **problem-solving style**. These traits are generally included in the Big Five personality domains described earlier; some of them overlap with each other.

Authoritarian Personality

The concept of authoritarian personality was advanced by Adorno and colleagues (1950). In their view, a person characterized by this trait respects authority and order. The trait is reflected in the person's adherence to rules and regulations and obedience to superiors' orders, as well as in his or her expectations that others should also adhere to rules and obey orders. Persons with an authoritarian personality believe that some are born to lead and others to follow; they themselves make good followers. They also tend to put events and persons into

---

TECHNOLOGY IN HUMAN RESOURCE MANAGEMENT

Personality tests began to be used as part of the hiring process in the 1940s and 1950s, then largely fell to the wayside in the 1960s and 1970s because of the cost of administering them (L. Weber 2015). However, according to L. Weber, "In 2001, 26 percent of large U.S. employers used pre-hire assessments. By 2013, the number had climbed to 57 percent, reflecting a big change in hiring practices that some economists suspect is making it tougher for people, especially young adults and the long-term unemployed, to get on the payroll."

The recent preference for the use of personality tests for hiring revolve around the current focus on testing for very specific personality traits. For example, statistical modeling and increased computing power have given employers the option to customize their assessment tools to include specific skills and personality traits relevant to a given organization. As a result, assessment can now gauge whether a candidate is a good match for an organization's overall culture, as well as for a particular work team. Of course, sport and recreation managers who use online personality tests should take care to apply them in a fair and equitable manner by making sure that each candidate is assessed in a similar way and a valid scoring process is adopted.

VIEWPOINT

It would be wrong to conclude from this chapter that a manager or work group should try to change or otherwise directly control an employee's personality. Doing so is impossible, and even if it were possible it would be highly unethical. Rather, the challenge for managers and employees is to understand how to measure and examine personality when explaining some aspects of human behavior in work settings (Rothstein and Goffin 2006).

may disrupt organizational change processes and destroy their own health and well-being.

Bureaucratic Orientation

M. Weber (1947) coined the term *bureaucracy* to refer to a form of organization that he considered to be efficient and rational. In his view, an efficient form of an organization possesses the characteristics of specialization and division of labor, hierarchical authority structure (i.e., designation of superiors and subordinates), explicit rules and regulations to govern the activities of both superiors and subordinates, impersonality in managing customers or clients, technical competence as the basis for hiring and promotion of employees, and written documents attesting to the activities and decisions of the members of the organization.

In turn, L.V. Gordon (1970) developed a scale to measure the personality trait that he labeled "bureaucratic orientation" based on the notion that individuals may vary in their level of preference for functioning in a bureaucratic organization. Bureaucratic orientation consists of five subcategories, as shown in figure 6.2.

In summary, bureaucratic orientation refers to a preference for order and for rules and regulations as major ways of managing organizations. People who have this orientation value discipline, compliance with rules, and impersonal relationships. They believe that people who occupy higher positions

categories and to behave consistently toward them based on such categorizations. They are intolerant of uncertainty and weakness.

People who have an authoritarian personality are likely to fit neatly into organizations characterized by a hierarchy of positions and extensive rules and regulations. However, they may find it difficult to address the emerging values of democracy, egalitarianism, and openness in various organizations. Furthermore, their persistence in their innate preferences for a stable and ordered environment

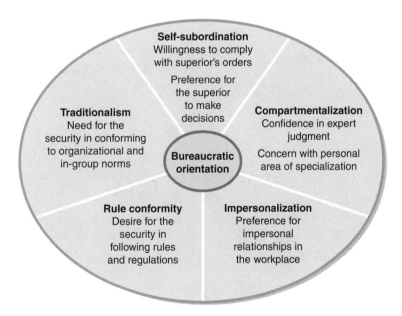

FIGURE 6.2 Subcategories of bureaucratic orientation.
Adapted from Gordon 1970.

have the right to make decisions. They also emphasize organizational loyalty and commitment.

Attitude Toward Authority

Attitude toward authority refers to "an individual's desire for freedom and autonomy as opposed to willingness to be controlled and to be dependent on others for direction" (Morse and Young 1973, p. 312). People who hold a positive attitude toward authority are likely to comply with superiors' orders and to obey rules and regulations. Thus this trait closely resembles Gordon's bureaucratic orientation.

Morse and Young (1973) suggested that the development of this trait is a function of one's experiences with authority relationships in the early years of development:

> The individual faces the autonomy dilemma when he [or she] realizes that he [or she] has the ability to submit to parental demands or withhold the behavior which will please his [or her] parents. If the individual derives pleasure from failure to submit to parental demands, the emerged tendency will be strong desire for autonomy and a need to defy authority figures and restrictions: this is a keystone in the development of the attitude toward authority. (p. 312)

In addition, the support provided by parents and others for the individual's initiatives in using his or her own cognitive abilities and skills fosters the individual's development of a preference for lower levels of control and direction from others.

Attitude Toward Individualism

People differ in the degree to which they prefer to "work alone and be alone as opposed to working or spending time with others" (Morse and Young 1973, p. 311). An individual's position within this range reflects his or her willingness to share responsibilities and duties with others. That is, a person who is oriented toward individualism does not like to be responsible to, or for, others in work performance.

According to Morse and Young (1973), the development of an individual's attitude toward individualism (or group interaction) is a function of his or her experiences involving trust and mistrust, optimism and pessimism, and frugality. If a person's early experiences lead to mistrust and pessimism about the environment and foster a need to be frugal, then that person may well develop a preference to work alone. Such a person relies on his or her own efforts to complete a task and develops internal standards to judge task performance. The individual is also reluctant to share time, effort, or expertise with others. In contrast, a person who has positive experiences that foster trust and optimism may prefer group interaction in the task environment and be willing to share in both the responsibilities and the duties.

ORGANIZATIONAL FACTORS

The three personality traits outlined so far—authoritarian personality, bureaucratic orientation, and attitude toward authority—function similarly in shaping a person's reactions to organizational factors. More specifically, people who have a high level of these traits are likely to feel at home, and to be more productive, in organizational settings marked by a high degree of authority, structure, rules and regulations, and well-defined tasks. For instance, the recreation department of a large metropolitan city is likely to be highly bureaucratized with a number of levels of authority and extensive rules and regulations. Such bureaucratization is necessary to ensure consistent and uniform operations and efficient delivery of services. However, individuals who have a low level of these personality traits may find themselves at odds with organizational requirements for compliance and submission. By the same token, individuals who have a high level of the traits are uncomfortable and less productive in organizations (e.g., a small fitness club) or organizational units that do not have an extensive and rigid authority and rule structure.

People with a high level of the individualism trait are likely to be happy and successful in jobs that require only limited interaction and coordination with other jobs. For example, a tennis professional at a racket club may operate by himself or herself without much dependence on other jobs in the club. Indeed, the club's owner may give the professional considerable freedom to determine his or her own activities.

Tolerance for Ambiguity

A person's level of tolerance for ambiguity reflects his or her "desire [either] for change and new and unusual activities or for a routine, structured existence" (Morse and Young 1973, p. 313). The development of this trait is based largely on the person's acceptance or lack of acceptance, as a child, of his or her parents' values of cleanliness and orderliness.

> Incorporation of this parental value does not just influence physical orderliness but is generalized to all behavior. Thus, attributes are formed regarding orderliness in feelings, ideas, and thoughts. These affect the ability to tolerate ambiguity and confusion and influence desires for a neat and tidy world and punctiliousness. Moreover, submission to parental desires for cleanliness can result in suppression of spontaneity, a doubting of impulses, and the inhibition of creative and novel behavior. (Morse and Young 1973, p. 313)

The implication for management is to place individuals who have a low tolerance for ambiguity in tasks that are well defined and well regulated. For example, the job of a locker room attendant is clearly specified and routinized, so it matches people with lower tolerance for ambiguity. In contrast, the marketing manager of an athletics department faces considerable ambiguity in his or her dealings with potential clients and sponsors. Therefore, this person must possess a high level of tolerance for ambiguity and must be able to enjoy ambiguous tasks.

Locus of Control

Rotter (1966) noted that people differ in the extent to which they attribute personal outcomes to themselves or to external sources. Individuals who believe that events in their life are under their own control and that what happens to them is a function of their own decisions and behaviors are referred

DIVERSITY MANAGEMENT OF HUMAN RESOURCES

As noted in Chelladurai's (2014) integrative framework for managing diversity, the first step toward realizing the benefits of diversity is to create an organizational culture that values diversity. Interestingly, C.C. Chen and Hooijberg (2000) found that attitudes toward corporate diversity programs are negatively related to ambiguity intolerance. Thus, human resource managers need to incorporate ways of measuring ambiguity tolerance during the interview process in order to recruit and hire individuals who embrace the benefits of diversity.

to as internals. In other words, they believe in an internal locus of control. On the other hand, persons who believe in an external locus of control—referred to as externals—attribute what happens to them to luck, fate, or other people.

Research has shown that internals and externals react differently to organizational factors, particularly in regard to decision making (Robbins and Judge 2010). Table 6.2 provides a summary and examples of relevant research findings outlined by Schermerhorn and colleagues (2011). From these findings, we can draw the general conclusion that internals do well in managerial and professional positions involving information processing, initiative, and independent decision making (Robbins and Judge). Examples include sport agent, director of a university athletics department, and chief of a city recreation department. On the other hand, externals do well in positions that require strict adherence to rules, regulations, and directives from superiors (Robbins and Judge).

Positive and Negative Affectivity

Recent years have seen a growing emphasis on affect in organizational life. In fact, Barsade, Brief,

TABLE 6.2   Effects of Locus of Control on Organizational Variables

ORGANIZATIONAL VARIABLE	LOCUS OF CONTROL (COMPARING INTERNALS AND EXTERNALS)	EXAMPLE
Information processing	Externals are satisfied with the amount of information they currently possess, make fewer attempts to acquire new information, and are less efficient at using information.	A ticket sales employee who is in charge of reactivating season ticket holders and possesses an external locus of control would be satisfied with the current list of "those interested" in purchasing season tickets. No attempt would be made to seek new information regarding potential season ticket holders.
Job satisfaction	Internals are generally more satisfied, less alienated, and more rooted; they also exhibit a stronger relationship between job satisfaction and performance.	Fitness trainers who possess an internal locus of control would take it upon themselves to connect with other individuals at the fitness club (e.g., front desk staff) and thus feel less alienated and more satisfied with their job.
Performance	Externals exhibit no change in performance on learning and problem-solving tasks when performance leads to valued rewards because they feel they have no control over the performance–reward relationship.	A finance manager serving on the board of directors of a regional soccer club who possesses an external locus of control would see others as responsible for increasing revenues. Thus, his or her performance would not be influenced by a club's desire to generate more revenue.
Self-control, risk, and anxiety	Internals exhibit more self-control and caution, take fewer risks, and, therefore, are less anxious.	The executive director of a national sport organization who possesses an internal locus of control would exercise caution in allocating funds to athletes and programs.
Motivation, expectancies, and results	Externals have lower work motivation because they see a weaker relationship between what they do and what happens to them, expect that working hard has no connection to good performance, and feel less control over their time.	Staff members working to set up a golf course for a tournament who possess an external locus of control may feel that their ability to set up the course will not change no matter how hard they work.
Response to others	Internals are more independent and tend to rely on their own judgment. They are less susceptible to the influence of others and more likely to accept information on its merit.	When communicating with the media, a public relations manager for the IOC who possesses an internal locus of control would independently judge the motives of media on their own merit.

Adapted from Schermerhorn, Hunt, and Osborn 1997.

IMPLICATIONS FOR MANAGEMENT

The personality traits of attitude toward individualism, tolerance for ambiguity, and locus of control carry direct implications for management. Because these traits point generally to one's preferred ways of acting and doing things, they also suggest the types of job suited for individuals who possess high levels of these traits. For example, people who possess a high level of the individualism trait should be placed in jobs that require less interaction with other jobs (e.g., fitness club accountant). Similarly, those who possess a low level of tolerance for ambiguity and a high level of external locus of control should be placed in jobs that are well defined and well structured (e.g., locker room attendant).

and Spataro (2003) refer to this growing emphasis as "the affective revolution." In their view, almost all reactions by individuals to their experiences in organizations are influenced by their affect. Watson and associates (Watson 2000; Watson and Clark 1984; Watson, Clark, and Tellegen 1988) have explored and expanded on the facets of affect—both positive affectivity and negative affectivity. Positive affectivity refers to the tendency to be active, self-efficacious, interpersonal, and achievement oriented. It "includes temperamental characteristics conducive to joy, excitement, and other states of positive feeling" (Siomkos, Rao, and Narayanan 2001, p. 152). People who have a high level of the positive affectivity trait tend to perceive things in such a way as to experience positive emotional states and a sense of well-being. On the other hand, individuals who have a low level of positive affectivity tend to view things less positively and to have low self-efficacy and a low sense of well-being.

Negative affectivity, on the other hand, refers to an inclination to view things in a way that leads to negative emotional states. In more technical terms, negative affectivity [NA] is "a mood-dispositional dimension that reflects pervasive individual differences in negative emotionality and self-concept. High-NA individuals tend to accentuate the negatives in most situations and are more likely to experience distress than [are] low-NA individuals" (Siomkos et al. 2001, p. 152). Persons who have a high level of the negative affectivity trait generally have a negative orientation toward themselves and their environment, including other people. They view themselves as being in stressful and unpleasant circumstances. They also tend to experience negative feelings over time and across situations. In contrast, individuals who have a *low* level of negative affectivity tend *not* to view their situations as stressful or upsetting. They are also less prone to experience negative emotional states.

This dual nature of affect influences how employees react to organizational phenomena. For example, one employee of a university athletics department may feel and report that the supervisor is indifferent to employees' needs and concerns, whereas another employee who works for the same supervisor may feel that the supervisor is friendly and helpful. Similarly, one client of a fitness club may be critical of the facility and its support staff, whereas another client may be appreciative of the same facility and staff.

After a review of the research on this topic, Barsade and colleagues (2003) reported that trait affects influenced the following factors: group mood; perceptions of job stress and strain; perceptions of job characteristics and job satisfaction;

accuracy in perceiving social interactions, work achievement, and social support; perceptions of fairness, tardiness, early departure, absenteeism, organizational commitment, managerial decision making, and supervisor ratings; and prosocial and helping behaviors. Similarly, state affects have been found to affect one's cognition, social interactions, helping behaviors, persistence, and task success. These effects identified in North America have been replicated in such different international work settings as Australia, China, and the United Arab Emirates. These research findings substantiate Barsade and colleagues' claim that affect has become the dominant trait influencing organizational behavior.

Service Orientation

Unsurprisingly, Hogan, Hogan, and Busch (1984) identified service orientation as another trait relevant to service operations. They define service orientation as "a set of attitudes and behaviors that affect the quality of interaction between . . . the staff of any organization and its customers" (p. 167). People with a high level of service orientation possess the characteristics of good adjustment, social skills, and willingness to follow rules. Service-oriented employees take an interest in their customers and are more courteous to them than are employees who are not service oriented. Furthermore, they try to find ways of satisfying customers' wishes within the boundaries set by the organization. They also make extra efforts to correct any faults in the service provided and to manage any unexpected events in the provision of services.

Baydoun, Rose, and Emperado (2001) conceived of three broader dimensions of customer service orientation as measured by their Customer Service Profile. These dimensions are (a) customer service attitude (intrinsic demeanor and personality that make one a friendly, attentive, and empathetic service provider); (b) customer service aptitude (ability to understand situations faced by customer service employees and to act appropriately); and (c) sales attitude (understanding and abiding by the rules and conventions of selling products).

Sanchez and Fraser's (1996) Customer Service Skills Inventory (CSSI) measures eight dimensions of service orientation (as cited in L.A. Martin and Fraser 2002). These eight dimensions are described in table 6.3.

Service orientation is relevant to all service operations and therefore to most sport and recreation organizations. It focuses on the interface between service employees and customers (e.g., an aerobics instructor and the clients in the class), which in turn

TABLE 6.3   Eight Dimensions of Service Orientation

DIMENSION	DESCRIPTION
Pressure tolerance	Does not lose control in the face of adversity and pressure.
Realistic orientation	Makes realistic appraisals of what is doable and what is not.
Time appraisal	Accomplishes things within time constraints and deadlines.
Independent judgment	Is not afraid of deciding.
Responsiveness	Pays immediate attention to customer problems and concerns.
Sensitivity	Shows flexibility to accommodate others.
Balanced judgment	Does not make extreme or radical decisions.
Precision orientation	Is concerned with precision and details.

greatly influences both customer satisfaction and customer retention. Thus sport and recreation organizations must recruit and hire service employees who are high on this trait. The concept is equally applicable to processes within the organization and to other positions, including managerial positions (L.A. Martin and Fraser 2002). For instance, the manager of a city recreation department may need to interact with community leaders, elected officials, and other city departments. The manager must also interact with immediate subordinates (e.g., playground supervisors, accounting manager) and employees at the tertiary level. Managers can be very effective in these internal interactions if they are high on the dimensions of service orientation shown in table 6.3.

CLIENT INTERACTION

Individuals who interact with clients directly in delivering sport and recreation services need to have a high level of both positive affectivity and service orientation. These traits in a service provider contribute to warm and friendly interpersonal interactions in service encounters. This type of interaction is critical because these encounters can enhance (or detract) both the quality of the service provided and the perceptions of that quality.

Machiavellianism

Christie and Geis (1970) promoted the concept that individuals differ in their tendency to be manipulative in their interactions with others. They referred to this trait as Machiavellianism in reference to Niccolò Machiavelli, the Florentine statesman who wrote *The Prince* in 1513 (Buskirk 1974). The book is a compendium of recommendations to the prince on how to manipulate his subjects (including his immediate subordinates) in order to gain and hold power in ruling his state. Over the years, Machiavelli's writings have been interpreted as advocating deceitfulness, dishonesty, and cunning in manipulating others for personal gain. Reflecting this common use of the term, the Merriam-Webster Dictionary defines Machiavellianism as "the political theory of Machiavelli; *especially* the view that politics is amoral and that any means however unscrupulous can justifiably be used in achieving political power" ("Machiavellianism" 1976).

However, Buskirk (1974) pointed out that such negative evaluation of Machiavellian principles does not do justice to Machiavelli's insightful comments on the art of managing people and institutions:

> Many times Machiavelli says in essence, "if you must do such and such, then here is how you should do it." In such cases, he is not recommending an action—in fact, many times he strongly advises against an action, citing the probable adverse outcomes—but is merely accommodating the ruler in power by advising his conduct in action that is a foregone conclusion. (pp. xii-xiii)

Buskirk (1974) also argued that the merit of Machiavelli's book is reflected in its survival; most of the literary works of his time have perished. More important, Buskirk suggested that "Machiavelli's basic advice is not only applicable to the ruling of a state but is also germane to the problems of managing any organization" (p. xii).

Despite Buskirk's arguments, the term *Machiavellianism* still carries a negative connotation. As a result, individuals who have a high level of this trait (referred to as "high-Machs") tend to be cool and calculating in pursuit of their self-interests. They are likely to form coalitions with relevant others in order to maximize their power and profit, and they may resort to lies, deception, and flattery in exploiting others for personal gain. They also possess high self-esteem and self-confidence. In contrast, sentiments such as sense of loyalty and friendship do not carry much weight with high-Machs, and they may break their promises without much guilt or regret. These tendencies are measured by Christie and Geis' (1970) Mach scale, which contains items similar to those shown in figure 6.3. The higher one scores on the Mach scale, the higher one's Machiavellian tendencies (some of the items are reverse-scored).

Although the preceding description of high-Machs is negative, this orientation does include a positive aspect. That is, high-Machs do well in jobs that require face-to-face interaction and are less governed than others by rules and regulations, thereby permitting improvisation (Robbins and Judge 2010). For example, a marketing director who seeks sponsorships or donations needs to be persuasive, flexible, and innovative. Thus, a person in that position would benefit from the positive aspects of the Machiavellian orientation. The danger, however, is that the negative aspects of cunning and deceit might violate the principles of business and managerial ethics.

Problem-Solving Style

In solving problems, individuals differ in how they go about gathering information, evaluating it, and making decisions (Myers 1987). For example, in gathering information, one person might prefer detailed, well-defined, and concrete pieces of information; another person might prefer looking at the "big picture" and taking on new problems to solve. The first individual is what is referred to as the sensing type, whereas the second person is the intuitive type.

In evaluating information, one person might be concerned about other people and about possible disagreements or conflicts; as a result, this person may tend to conform to others' views and preferences. Such a person is the feeling type. In contrast, another person might base his or her judgments on reason and intellect while excluding emotion as a factor. This person is the thinking type.

The combination of these two dimensions—sensing–intuitive and feeling–thinking—yields four problem-solving styles. Table 6.4 describes

Item	Disagree			Agree	
	A lot	A little	Neutral	A little	A lot
1. The best way to manage people is to tell them what they want to hear.	1	2	3	4	5
2. When you ask someone to do something for you, it is best to give them real reasons for wanting it rather than to give reasons that might carry more weight (reverse scored).	1	2	3	4	5
3. Anyone who completely trusts anyone else is asking for trouble.	1	2	3	4	5
4. It is hard to get ahead without cutting corners here and there.	1	2	3	4	5
5. Honesty is the best policy in all cases (reverse scored).	1	2	3	4	5

FIGURE 6.3 Sample items from the Mach scale (to measure Machiavellianism).

Adapted from *Studies in Machiavellianism*, R. Christie and F. Geiss, pg. 18, copyright 1970, with permission of Elsevier.

TABLE 6.4   Four Styles of Problem Solving

STYLE	DEFINITION	SPORT AND RECREATION EXAMPLES
Sensing–thinking	Decisive, dependable, applied	Sport marketing, facility planning, sport data analytics, website development, direct supervision of interns
Sensing–feeling	Pragmatic, analytical, methodical	Coaching, fitness leadership, personnel administration
Intuitive–thinking	Creative, progressive, perceptive	Sport law, sport and recreation policy development, budgeting
Intuitive–feeling	Charismatic, participative, people oriented	Sport agency, public relations, social media, ticket and merchandise sales

Adapted from Schermerhorn, Hunt, and Osborn 1991.

each of these styles and lists some job areas that fit a particular style, including examples from sport and recreation management.

- *Sensing thinkers:* Sensing thinkers tend to be decisive and to make decisions that are well thought out. They are also persevering, committed, and realistic in their expectations. They prefer clearly specified rules and regulations. One negative characteristic is that they tend to be impatient and judgmental about people. They are preoccupied with data and may conceive of and prepare for too many contingencies.

- *Intuitive thinkers:* Intuitive thinkers take a global or gestalt perspective in analyzing their situation. They are intellectuals and focus on principles and abstract ideas. They tend to plan and design rather than to execute. By the same token, they are impersonal and therefore may engender or encounter interpersonal problems. They may feel restless, and their restlessness may rub off on their associates.

- *Sensing feelers:* Sensing feelers are pragmatic and manage concrete problems effectively. They tend to work within the frame of reality and make the best use of the opportunities that the situation offers. These individuals are oriented toward the present and attend to the demands of the immediate situation. However, they dislike new or abstract ideas, and they may fail to be effective in the absence of rules and regulations.

- *Intuitive feelers:* Intuitive feelers are articulate and tend to communicate their positive feelings to associates. They are capable of seeing things abstractly and managing unstructured and complicated situations. One negative characteristic is that they may make decisions based on their personal likes and dislikes. They may also try to please too many people. Insofar as they understand and appreciate the emotions of others, they tend to become slaves of others' emotions. They constantly seek recognition from others.

Managerial Potential

Researchers have tried to find ways to use personality to predict an individual's potential for success as a manager. These efforts have generally focused on identifying a set of personality traits related to managerial effectiveness. For instance, Gough (1984) advanced the Managerial Potential Scale, which was derived from the California Psychological Inventory mentioned earlier. Gough collated the 34 items in the scale after a series of studies relating the scores on personality variables to managerial effectiveness. Thus, these items do not reflect particular traits but represent what Gough called **managerial potential**. For each of the 34 items, respondents answer either *true* or *false*. High scores (roughly 24 or more) correlate with managerial effectiveness. The scale is

 Several personality traits may be more relevant than others to organizations and their management. These traits include authoritarian personality, bureaucratic orientation, attitude toward authority, attitude toward individualism, tolerance for ambiguity, locus of control, positive affectivity, negative affectivity, service orientation, Machiavellianism, and problem-solving style, and all relate to assessing and measuring managerial potential.

purported to recognize behavioral effectiveness, self-confidence, cognitive clarity, and goal orientation, all of which make managers more effective. Although the notion of managerial potential was advanced in the context of industrial and business organizations, it is equally relevant to the management of sport and recreation organizations.

ROLE OF THE SPORT OR RECREATION MANAGER

Working in the sport and recreation industry typically involves relatively high levels of personal interaction with employees, volunteers, and clients or customers. Therefore, managers must recognize the mix of personality traits, both among co-workers and between managers and subordinates, if the organization is to function effectively and minimize interpersonal conflict. For example, a study conducted by B. Jackson, Dimmock, Gucciardi, and Grove (2011), found that greater dissimilarity between coaches and players in terms of extroversion was associated with reduced commitment and relatedness between coaches and players. Specifically, individuals who were extremely disparate

on the trait of extroversion were uncomfortable with one another's forms of interaction. Thus, consideration of personality "matches" may help avoid dysfunctional relationships in organizations or groups.

Of course, personality clashes are inevitable in sport and recreation organizations. It is unrealistic to expect all employees and volunteers to possess personality traits that mesh perfectly and form uniformly tranquil working relationships. Therefore, it is up to sport and recreation managers to understand where personality conflicts exist and decide on the best conflict management strategy. As noted by Kerwin (2015), simply ignoring personality conflicts can be a very toxic management strategy. In fact, in the case of personality conflict, ignorance can lead to festering problems between individuals that produce negative outcomes not just for the individuals involved but for entire groups. Thus, it may be appropriate to separate individuals with personality conflicts during times when stress is high (e.g., sport event delivery) and personality clashes peak. Once a stressful situation is deflated (e.g., in the post-event wrap-up), the individuals should come back together and work through their personality differences (Kerwin).

Case Study

Personality Clashes in Your Local Soccer Club

As director of your local soccer club, you have taken note of the interaction between the coaches of your U15 rep boys travel team (i.e., competitive travel team that requires tryouts). The assistant coach is an emotional young man who is a fantastic leader for the boys; he is very knowledgeable and always has the best interest of his athletes at heart. However, he tends to go quickly from very excited and happy to very angry and aggressive, especially when he feels that his power or ego is being tested.

The head coach is also very extroverted. Specifically, she is gregarious, sociable, active, and energetic while also managing to keep her emotions in check. When necessary (e.g., during disagreements), she can be very assertive and tends to implicitly demonstrate her power over the assistant coach by dominating the conversation.

At a coaches' meeting, you notice tension between the head coach and the assistant coach. Specifically, during a discussion about parent dis-

putes, the assistant coach is very expressive and angry when addressing some concerns. He nearly yells when recounting an interaction with a parent that he thinks was handled poorly. The head coach is fairly assertive in her response that the issue was handled with care; however, her assertiveness seems to make the assistant coach uncomfortable. The clash lasts only a few minutes, but you quickly realize that you must manage this personality difference or the clash could carry over into the season.

Case Study Tasks

1. Based on the preceding description, outline the key personality traits (see table 6.1) of the head coach and the assistant coach. Defend your choice of traits for each coach.

2. Do some research about conflict management strategies.

3. Discuss, in detail, two conflict management strategies that you could use to help mend the somewhat volatile relationship (i.e.,

the personality conflict) between the head coach and the assistant coach. Describe the strategies, discuss why they are appropriate in this situation, and create a verbal script that you could use when approaching the coaches.

CHAPTER PURSUITS

SUMMARY

This chapter defines personality and describes the factors associated with the formation of personality. Researchers have suggested that an individual's behavior is a function of both his or her personality and the characteristics of the situation in which the behavior occurs. The chapter discusses the trait and type theories, then presents 11 personality traits associated with behavior in organizations—authoritarian personality, bureaucratic orientation, attitude toward authority, attitude toward individualism, tolerance for ambiguity, locus of control, positive affectivity, negative affectivity, service orientation, Machiavellianism, and problem-solving style—and how all of them relate to assessing and measuring managerial potential.

Sport managers need to understand that despite clear-cut goals, policies, and procedures, members of an organization may react and behave differently in part because of differences in their personalities. These differences may also cause variations in members' preferences regarding the ways in which a manager acts toward them. In addition, possession of specific traits is conducive to better performance and satisfaction in specific jobs. However, as Certo (1992) cautioned, "Personality tests can be used advantageously *if* the personality characteristics needed to do well in a particular job are well defined and *if* individuals possessing those characteristics can be pinpointed and selected" (p. 326, emphasis added).

Thus, an organization member's personality is one more of the complex variables that a manager must contend with and manage. Specific ways in which personality traits impinge on managerial practice are addressed in later chapters.

KEY TERMS

attitude toward authority.................................... 96

attitude toward individualism 96

authoritarian personality.................................... 96

bureaucratic orientation 96

environmental influence 90

genetic influence 90

locus of control.. 96

Machiavellianism 96

managerial potential 104

negative affectivity 96

personality... 89

personality as a trait and as a state 91

positive affectivity... 96

problem-solving style 96

service orientation 96

tolerance for ambiguity 96

UNDERSTAND

1. Give examples that illustrate the difference between personality as a trait and as a state.

2. Compare bureaucratic orientation, attitude toward individualism, and tolerance for ambiguity.

INTERACT

1. Discuss a situation in which you had a personality difference with another employee or volunteer. Which personality traits were different? How did the difference affect you during tasks? How did the difference affect you personally? Discuss how this clash of personalities was (or should have been) managed.

2. Which of the various personality traits described in the chapter would help the following individuals be effective in their respective jobs: a tennis professional, a fitness instructor, a facility manager, a ticket office clerk? How so?

CHAPTER

7

Values

LEARNING OBJECTIVES

After reading this chapter, you will be able to

- define and describe values and distinguish them from attitudes and norms,
- distinguish between terminal and instrumental values,
- identify and discuss the sources and functions of values,
- understand how values held by management and members may affect sport organizations,
- define and describe value congruence and management by values, and
- relate the values in sport to societal values.

The preceding chapters describe some of the cognitive abilities and personality traits that people bring to organizations. Some of the characteristics are transient (i.e., trainable), whereas others are more or less permanent. This chapter presents another set of attributes that bear on the management of human resources: the values held by the members of an organization.

The term **value** carries different meanings in different contexts. In general, it refers to the equivalence or worth of a thing or act in terms of money or goods (e.g., the worth of one's athletic talent), something that is desirable (e.g., the value of sport participation), or a belief about what ought to be (e.g., there should be no emphasis on winning in sport). The concern here is with the last meaning, which is explored in detail in this chapter.

Although values are probably the most nebulous area of individual-difference variables, they are, as noted by Yusko and Bellenger (2012), important to address:

Selecting employees who share these work [i.e., organizational] values is critical. This is because identifying candidates who are a

good fit increases the chance that the candidate will support and reinforce the organization's values, priorities, and "way of doing business," such as working long hours as necessary, taking a courageous and ethical stance even when there is an easy way out, or constantly seeking opportunities to innovate and improve the organization's products and services. (p. 184)

It is generally accepted that the performance of individuals, groups, and organizations is a function of (among other things) congruence in the values held by organization members. In part for this reason, the increasing diversity of the workforce in North America is seen as both an opportunity and a threat to organizational performance. It provides opportunity in that different people bring different strengths to the workplace. At the same time, they may also bring different values, which, to the extent that these values diverge from each other, can result in conflict and confusion. Therefore, sport and recreation managers must understand the concept of values and their effect in the workplace.

If you analyze your comfort level in associating with specific individuals or groups, you can recognize that part of your comfort (or discomfort) stems from the degree of congruence (or divergence) between your beliefs and attitudes and those of others. You may have experienced such convergence or divergence of values in your own work life; accordingly, you may have been more satisfied and more motivated in some jobs than in others. If you have felt the effect of values (including beliefs and attitudes) on work, then as a manager you understand the need to communicate your organization's values and goals to employees and to hire people who share those values and goals.

> A value is a belief about what ought to be, what ought not to be, what is right, or what is wrong. Values are relatively enduring traits that influence our thoughts, feelings, and actions.

VALUES, BELIEFS, ATTITUDES, AND NORMS

Several definitions have been put forward for the term *value*, but the following definition by Rokeach (1973) is the one used most often in the context of organizations and management:

> A value is an enduring belief that a specific mode of conduct or end state of existence is personally and socially preferable to an opposite or converse mode of conduct or end-state of existence. A value system is an enduring organization of beliefs concerning preferable modes of conduct or end states of existence along a continuum of relative importance. (p. 5)

Values and Beliefs

Sproull (1984) organized **beliefs** into three broad categories: phenomenological, causal, and normative. Phenomenological beliefs relate to the nature of things or people; for example, a student may believe that the athletics program spends more money on one particular sport than on others. Causal beliefs address causal relationships between observed phenomena; for example, the student may also believe that the athletics program spends as much money as it does on the one sport because of pressures from alumni and media. Finally, normative beliefs refer to one's preferred states of nature or sense of how things ought to be; for instance, the student may believe that the athletics program ought to budget its dollars equitably among all sports.

Rokeach (1973) also posited three kinds of belief: descriptive beliefs (which can be verified as true or false); evaluative beliefs (which involve judgments about something being good or bad); and prescriptive and proscriptive beliefs (which relate to the desirability, or lack thereof, of some means or ends). As defined by Rokeach, values belong to the category of prescriptive and proscriptive beliefs; they also belong to the category of normative beliefs in Sproull's taxonomy (1984). In other words, sets of beliefs about "what ought to be" form the essence of values. Indeed, Goldthwait (1996) noted that "every value-claiming proposition has the idea of ought at its very foundation" (p. 34).

A significant difference exists between values as normative beliefs and the other two forms of belief. Specifically, one can prove both phenomenological and causal beliefs to be either true or false. For instance, by verifying the budget and statement of expenses, one can determine whether the athletics program spends more money on one sport than on another. In contrast, one cannot prove values (i.e., normative beliefs) to be right or wrong.

Values and Attitudes

Another term that is used in conjunction, and often synonymously, with *value* is **attitude**. Rokeach (1973) contrasted values and attitudes as follows:

> An attitude refers to an organization of several beliefs around a specific object or situation. . . . A value, on the other hand, refers to a single belief of a very specific kind. It concerns a desirable mode of behavior or end-state that has transcendental quality to it, guiding actions, attitudes, judgments, and comparisons across specific objects and situations and beyond immediate goals to more ultimate goals. (p. 18)

Figure 7.1 shows the relationships between beliefs, values, and attitudes. Of the three kinds of belief, normative beliefs generate the values held by an individual (the terminal and instrumental values shown in the figure are described later in this chapter). The person's values lead to the formation of attitudes toward specific persons, objects, and events; in turn, these attitudes are reflected in the individual's behavior.

Beliefs

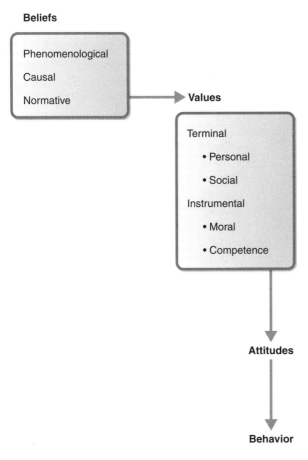

FIGURE 7.1   Rokeach's beliefs and values.

Rokeach (1973) further pointed out that "values occupy a more central position than attitudes within one's personality makeup and cognitive system, and they are therefore determinants of attitudes as well as of behavior" (p. 18). Although a person holds fewer values than attitudes, the number of attitudes a person holds may fluctuate depending on the number of objects and situations to which the person is exposed. In addition, values are held much more deeply and are more enduring than attitudes. Finally, as illustrated in figure 7.2, an attitude toward a target manifests more than one value, and a single value may influence several attitudes.

Values and Norms

According to Rokeach (1973), *value* refers both to end states and to the means for achieving them, whereas **norm** refers only to the means—that is, the modes of behavior. As noted earlier, a value is not limited to a specific situation; a norm, however, specifies a code of conduct in a particular situation. Finally, a value is personal and internal to the individual. In contrast, a norm is a code of conduct reflecting a common understanding among the people involved in a situation; therefore, it is external to the individual. For example, although society values winning in competition, norms control the means to such winning. Consider the case of a coach

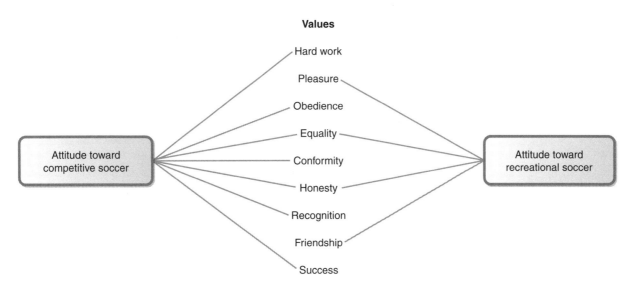

FIGURE 7.2   Hypothetical relationships between values and attitudes toward sports.

VIEWPOINT

Everyone needs to be aware of their own personal values and value systems so that they may deal pragmatically with any situation that may arise. This awareness allows for any marked differences between individuals or between an individual and the demands of the organization to be taken into account before action of any sort is contemplated. Value conflicts often arise at places of work. It is necessary to recognize that this does occur, and to take action to formulate a management style that can accommodate it where necessary and reconcile divergent values. (Pettinger 1997, p. 82)

yelling, screaming, and throwing a chair. Although society tolerates such behaviors to some degree at higher levels of competition, it frowns upon them in youth sport. Indeed, in that setting, the normative expectation is that the coach will be relatively gentle and caring in addressing his or her young charges.

Although the terms *values*, *beliefs*, *attitudes*, and *norms* are closely related, they refer to distinct concepts. In addition, the concept of value is broader in scope and subsumes the other three. Values constitute one set of beliefs (i.e., normative beliefs) that influence a person's attitude toward an entity. Norms, which are the accepted standards of behavior in a given situation, may reflect values shared by a group.

SOURCES OF VALUES

The fact that values are personal to the individual does not mean that values are totally individualistic. To the contrary, from the early stages of life, an individual is bombarded with value statements from various sources (e.g., family, friends, school, church, the media, celebrities, and movie and sport idols); therefore, people tend to share several values with one another. For instance, most North Americans hold generally similar values regarding liberty, freedom, equality, democracy, activism, and optimism. Narrowing the focus to our context here, society generally values the pursuit of excellence in sport.

Of course, despite such convergence of values on some crucial issues, people may also differ on other, equally important issues. Consider, for example, the issue of abortion. North American society's divergent values on abortion are as divisive as its values on freedom of expression are binding. As another example, while most in North America value the pursuit of excellence in sport, we see divergences in the values applied to the issue of resource allocation to various teams. One group of people emphasizes the value of equality and suggests that the athletic budget should be distributed equally, either between men's and women's programs or across all sports. In contrast, another group holds to the value of equity and prefers that the budget be distributed differentially in proportion to certain selected criteria (e.g., spectator appeal or tradition). When different individuals or groups offer differing—and often conflicting—values, the significance that people attach to these values is likely to serve as the deciding factor between one set of values and a competing set.

TERMINAL AND INSTRUMENTAL VALUES

The reference to "mode of conduct or end-state of existence" in Rokeach's (1973) definition of values leads to the classification of values into two broad categories: **terminal values** (which relate to ends desired or goals pursued) and **instrumental values** (which relate to the desirability, or lack thereof, of the means to the desired ends). In other words, instrumental values involve one's personal views about what means should be used to achieve a given terminal value. That is, if two means exist for achieving a terminal value, then an individual may prefer one means over the other because of his or her instrumental values. For instance, many people hold the terminal value of achievement and therefore applaud athletic excellence. Some, however, disapprove of the means of recruiting athletes (Trail 1997); instead, they would prefer simply selecting the best of those who report for tryouts and training

VIEWPOINT

In discussing the significance of values in high-performance organizations, Holbeche (2005) commented as follows:

Work represents the dynamic intersection between social, business, and an individual's personal needs and values. Most people have personal values, even if they never consciously think about them. They only become aware of their values when they feel discomfort or, worse, when they are placed in a position of contravening their own values. All organizations have values, or beliefs which they hold dear, whether or not these values are socially acceptable or evident in written statements. . . . Employees understand what is real about these values, not so much from what is written but from what is put into practice. For example, if an organization claims to value its customers but in practice condones poor customer service, employees are more likely to believe what they experience rather than the words. . . . [I]f the gaps between the "walk" and the "talk" are large, employees are unlikely to trust their organization to look after their interests, or be willing to commit to it emotionally. . . . [I]f individuals' values are very different from those of their organization, they are unlikely to stay long. If the match between individuals' values and those of their organization changes over time, especially if the organization changes direction, employees can feel betrayed and become cynical about change. (pp. 375-376)

them to be excellent. This perspective reflects an instrumental value.

Note the contrast between instrumental values and the norms described earlier. Instrumental values focus on the means to achieve an end, whereas norms are behavioral expectations held by a group of people in a particular context. For example, administrators, coaches, and educators generally subscribe to the norm that athletes should be treated as students first, with dignity and with concern for their academic progress. This normative expectation holds irrespective of whether the school has recruited the athletes or developed them internally, which is a function of instrumental values.

Terminal values can be divided into two kinds: personal (or self-centered) and social (or society-centered) values. For instance, peace of mind is a personal value, whereas world peace is a social value (Rokeach 1973). Similarly, an individual may not value personal achievements in sport but may share the value of national achievements in international sport.

Instrumental values can also be divided into two kinds: moral values and competence values. Moral values focus on the interpersonal aspects of one's mode of behavior; for instance, being honest

and responsible is moral behavior. Failure to abide by this type of value leads to feelings of guilt and shame in most people. Competence values, on the other hand, are focused internally. That is, they relate to one's abilities and capacities to perform adequately in a given context. Thus, one would value being logical and intelligent, and deficiencies in these aspects would lead to feelings of shame. The primary type of value shared by athletes may well be that of competence, and they may be driven by this value when they continuously try to improve their performance.

Rokeach (1973) suggested that an average adult holds about 18 terminal values and from 60 to 70 instrumental values. From this extensive list, Rokeach's values are typically discussed in relation to 18 terminal values and 18 of the more common instrumental values. Specifically, terminal values and instrumental values may also be divided into those which are personal (self-centered) and those which are social (society-centered). These values represent the "focus" of employees as they relate to the desired end state or means to the end of state of work tasks. For example, an employee holding ambition (instrumental, self-centered) as a value will focus on working hard towards his or her own personal goals. Further, an employee holding social recognition (terminal, society-centered) as a value will focus on acknowledgment received from others on completion of the task. The following lists outline examples of Rokeach's terminal and instrumental values, sub-divided into values with a self-centered or society-centered focus:

Instrumental: Self-Centered Values

Ambition (Seeking, Striving)

Capability (Skillful, Competent)

Independence (Autonomous, Individualistic)

Logical (Analytical, Reasonable)

Instrumental: Society-Centered Values

Broadmindedness (Liberal, Nonjudgmental)

Helpfulness (Supportive, Obliging)

Obedience (Compliant, Conforming)

Responsibility (Conscientious, Trustworthy)

Terminal: Self-Centered Values

Exciting life (Stimulating, Energetic)

Accomplishment (Achievement, Impact)

Freedom (Liberty, Autonomy)

Wisdom (Astute insight into life)

Terminal: Society-Centered Values

Peaceful world (Harmonious, Amicable world)

Equality (Fair, Egalitarian)

Social recognition (Acknowledgment by others)

True friendship (Companionship, Relationship with others)

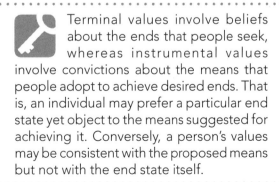 Terminal values involve beliefs about the ends that people seek, whereas instrumental values involve convictions about the means that people adopt to achieve desired ends. That is, an individual may prefer a particular end state yet object to the means suggested for achieving it. Conversely, a person's values may be consistent with the proposed means but not with the end state itself.

HIERARCHY OF VALUES

At any point in life, an individual may hold a number of values; however, not all of these values will carry equal force in any given situation. Rokeach (1973) argues that although people are taught that certain values are absolute and unchanging, they learn through the course of life to make a **hierarchy of values** according to priority or importance.

> When we think about, talk about, or try to teach one of our values to others, we typically do so without remembering the other values, thus regarding them as absolutes. But when one value is actually activated along with others in a given situation, the behavioral outcome will be a result of the relative importance of all the competing values that situation has activated. (p. 6)

In essence, different situations evoke different values held by the same person, and the intensity with which the person upholds those values also varies with the situation. Consider, for example, an individual who holds the values of social recognition, pleasure, and equality. Suppose that the person is exposed to two situations: competitive sport and recreational sport. Conceivably, the value of social recognition would dominate the person's orientation to the competitive situation. That is, he or she might strive to perform better than others and to be recognized for that performance. The situation might also activate the value of equality because the individual prefers that every competitor be treated equally. The value of pleasure, however, may lie dormant in that situation. In contrast, when the same person is exposed to recreational sport, the situation may activate the values of pleasure and equality but not the value of social recognition. The notions of hierarchy of values and situational cues are illustrated in figure 7.3.

The values held by an individual constitute his or her **value system**. These values or beliefs are most likely consistent with each other in content but may vary in intensity. In turn, if an individual's values can vary in their intensity, then it follows that the person can organize them into a hierarchy of values.

VALUE TYPES

As stated previously, a value system is a collection of values that individuals hold, and it also implies a hierarchy among the collection of values. An

Individual's values

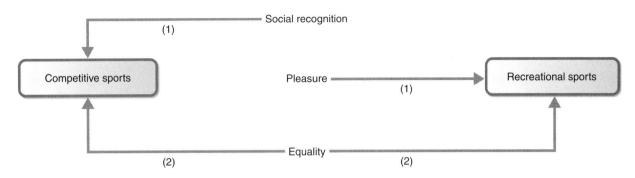

FIGURE 7.3   Hierarchy of values in different contexts.

implicit point is that the values that an individual holds are likely to be complementary, rather than contradictory, to each other. Schwartz (1992) empirically supported this idea and found that analyses of the relationships between 56 values, including Rokeach's (1973) terminal and instrumental values, yielded 10 clusters of values that he referred to as value types. These are (1) *power*, referring to control or dominance over resources and people; (2) *achievement*, meaning personal success through one's competence; (3) *hedonism*, implying personal pleasure and gratification; (4) *stimulation*, represented by excitement, novelty, and challenge; (5) *self-direction*, evidenced by independent thought and action; (6) *universalism*, marked by a concern for the welfare of all and for nature; (7) *benevolence*, referring to enhancing the welfare of the people who are in frequent contact; (8) *tradition*, meaning the respect for and acceptance of traditional customs; (9) *conformity*, which is a concern for not upsetting others or violating norms; and (10) *security*, referring to one's concern for harmony and stability of relationships and society. As shown in figure 7.4, these value types can also be grouped into *individualism* (consisting of *openness to change* and *self-enhancement*) and *collectivism* (composed of *self-transcendence* and *conservation*).

Schwartz (1992) also pointed out that one set of values (i.e., power, achievement, hedonism, stimulation, and self-direction) represents individual interests, whereas another set (benevolence, tradition, and conformity) represents collective interests. The remaining values of universalism and security are mixed in nature. These groupings are indicated on the periphery of figure 7.4.

The implication for management is that persons who hold adjacent value types (e.g., universalism and benevolence, self-direction and stimulation, or achievement and power) are likely to get along well, but people who hold opposite value types (e.g., stimulation and conformity, or universalism and power) are likely to experience conflict over critical issues. Furthermore, individuals who hold the values of achievement and power may be comfortable in organizational settings, such as university athletics, that stress achievement and performance excellence. On the other hand, people who hold the value of universalism may be comfortable in recreation organizations that emphasize greater participation in sport by all segments of the population.

FUNCTIONS OF VALUES

The preceding sections of the chapter allude to how values can guide specific modes of behavior. For instance, Rokeach (1973) outlined values that would enable individuals to choose from a variety of terminal states as well as the means (instruments) for achieving those ends. Similarly, Schwartz (1992) suggested that certain values shape our orientation toward individualism or collectivism. Thus, values play a significant part in our lives through their many functions. Rokeach (1973) grouped the functions that values serve into three broad categories: standards that guide activities, plans for conflict resolution, and motivational functions.

Values as Standards

The function of values as standards that guide activities is exemplified by

- the position one takes on specific social issues (e.g., athletic scholarships),

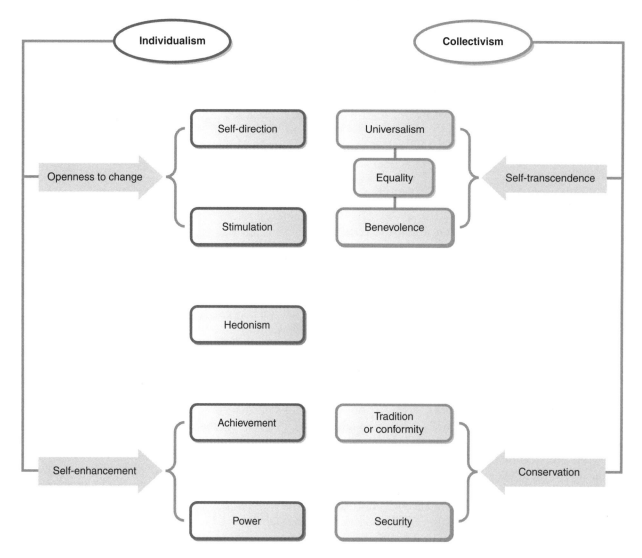

FIGURE 7.4 Schwartz's value types.
Based on Schwartz 1992.

- the tendency to favor a political or religious movement (e.g., Republican or Democratic party),
- the presentation of oneself to others (e.g., choosing to project a high profile or a low profile),
- evaluation of oneself and others,
- judgments about oneself as being moral or competent,
- attempts to persuade and influence others about what beliefs or attitudes are accepted or challenged, and

- rationalization of one's actions that may be unpleasant or unacceptable to others ("an unkind remark made to a friend, for example, may be rationalized as an honest communication" [Rokeach 1973, p. 13]).

In essence, our values set the standards for our behavior. In the context of sport and recreation, for example, we may support drug testing or not; we may appreciate or disapprove of showboating after a touchdown in football; and we may try to influence others' opinions of paying salaries to collegiate athletes. All of these behaviors stem from our value systems; in other words, our values define the standards that guide our actions.

Values in Conflict Resolution and Decision Making

"A value system is a learned organization of principles and rules to help one choose between alternatives, resolve conflicts, and make decisions" (Rokeach 1973, p. 14). As noted earlier, different situations may evoke different values, and a particular situation may activate two contradictory values. For instance, a fitness club might ask a fitness instructor to evaluate a particular decision made by the manager. This situation might activate the values of behaving politely and behaving honestly. Because these two values may call for contradictory behaviors, the choice between the two is based on the relative importance that the individual attaches to each value. In other words, the individual can choose to abide by the value that is higher in the hierarchical system and thereby resolve the conflict and make the appropriate decision. The situation may also elicit other values that affect the instructor's decision to behave in one way or another. For instance, if the instructor's response will affect his or her future with the club, the value of security may impel the person toward behaving politely rather than honestly.

Motivational Functions of Values

Rokeach (1973) argued that "values are in the final analysis the conceptual tools and weapons that we all employ in order to maintain and enhance self-esteem" (p. 14). More specifically, values contribute to this effort by helping us adjust to society, defend against threats to our egos, and test our perceptions and competencies against reality in the process of self-actualizing. Let us now examine each of these contributions in more detail.

• *Adjustive function:* The content of various values (e.g., obedience, civility, responsibility to others, law and order) concerns society as a whole. To the extent that a person holds these values, he or she is well adjusted to societal requirements. This adjustment is especially evident in athletics, in which obedience is valued highly; it is critical, in fact, for all members of a team to be obedient to the coach's specifications in order to enable coordination of the members' activities and performances. Thus, each member needs to hold obedience high in his or her hierarchy of values. As another example, consider the thousands of spectators who move into and out of a stadium in an orderly fashion. This crucial stadium behavior is enabled by the values of civility, responsibility to others, and law and order. Can you imagine the havoc that would result if spectators did not share these values?

• *Ego-defensive function:* When people's needs, feelings, and actions do not conform to social norms and expectations, they can protect their ego by relying on their values to justify their feelings or behavior. Thus, "values represent ready-made concepts provided by our culture to ensure that such justifications can proceed smoothly and effortlessly" (Rokeach 1973, pp. 15-16). When a university football player quits a team and leaves it in disarray, he can justify his action by saying that he values education more than athletics. Society readily accepts and even applauds such justification.

• *Self-actualization function:* The content of some values focuses on personal competence, knowledge, accomplishments, and wisdom. This function is reflected in people's desire to understand their context, as well as the events that occur in it, and to be clear and consistent in their own perceptions and beliefs. To the extent that these values are rated highly by an individual, they cause the individual to strive toward self-actualization—that is, "to become everything that . . . [he or she] is capable of becoming" (Maslow 1943, p. 382). For instance, one's evaluation of personal competence, experiences, and situational requirements determines both one's choice of a specific physical activity and the level of competition at which to participate. This is a step in the process of self-actualization. According to Rokeach (1973), this testing of one's knowledge and competencies—both in relation to one's own values and against reality—is fundamental to self-actualization.

 The values that people hold help them by providing a standard for their actions and their decision making, a basis for maintenance of their self-esteem, a channel for their integration into community and society, and a means for their self-actualization.

VALUES IN ORGANIZATIONS

Values not only bear on our general behavior; they also affect organizational life in particular. Logically, given that values underlie an individual's perceptions and behaviors (Gelfand, Kuhn, and Radhakrishnan 1996; Schwartz 1992), the values held by members of an organization affect the organization's processes. On one hand, if the values of an organization's membership are congruent with each other, this congruence may lead to the development of an organizational culture with positive connotations, member commitment, and productivity (Connor and Becker 1975; Gelfand et al. 1996; Graves 1970; Hughes and Flowers 1975). On the other hand, divergence of values among the membership may lead to conflict and associated dysfunctional effects—and the greater the divergence in values, the greater the negative consequences or behaviors (Chatman 1989; Gelfand et al. 1996; Hamm, MacLean, Kikulis, and Thibault 2008; Meglino, Ravlin, and Adkins 1989, 1992).

Values and Organizational Goals

Personal values affect organizational processes in many ways. The first critical area involves setting organizational goals and choosing courses of action to achieve them. It is unreasonable to expect this process to involve all of the organization's employees and stakeholders; rather, goals are set by senior administrators and other powerful stakeholders. For instance, goals for a city recreation department are set by such people as senior administrators, the elected mayor, and other representatives of the city. Similarly, the goals for a university athletics department are set by the president and the board of governors; this powerful coalition also decides on the courses of action to achieve those goals. The critical point in the present context is that these goal choices are functions of the values shared by the coalition members.

At the same time, in order for the organization to be successful, the selected goals—and the values behind those goals—should be endorsed by most other people involved in the organization (e.g., employees, other stakeholders). Indeed, without such endorsements, the organization's very survival is doubtful. One way to enhance personnel endorsement of values is through management by values. Specifically, Kerwin, MacLean, and Bell-Laroche (2014a) suggest that in order to enhance employee and volunteer buy-in regarding key values, managers should ensure that personnel know the organizational core values, allow them at least some input in defining those values, and highlight the need to embed them in management practices (e.g., recruiting, hiring, and training).

MANAGEMENT BY VALUES

Management by values (MBV) is an increasingly common management philosophy and practice in nonprofit sport organizations. It highlights "the importance of identifying core values . . . at the individual and organizational levels, the centrality of aligning core values with specific objectives, and [the value of] illuminating the leader's personal interest in wanting to manage by values" (Dolan, Garcia, and Richley 2006, p. 28).

For example, a survey study in Canada of 103 individuals in 24 national sport organizations (equivalent to national governing bodies in the United States) found that strategically adopting MBV in practice—that is, using values in recruiting, hiring, and training materials—fully mediated the influence of organizational values on organizational performance (Kerwin, MacLean, and Bell-Laroche 2014b). A follow-up case study of one exemplary organization demonstrated that in order for organizational values to be understood by employees and volunteers and properly executed (i.e., "lived") by these personnel, values must be engrained into everyday policy and practice in human resource management (Kerwin, MacLean, and Bell-Laroche 2014a). Taken together, these studies explicitly demonstrate that organizational values can be strategically managed for the purpose of enhancing organizational performance.

TECHNOLOGY IN HUMAN RESOURCE MANAGEMENT

As noted by L. Wallace, Wilson, and Miloch (2011), social media (e.g., Facebook) can be strategically leveraged to manage a sport or recreation organization's brand—for example, that of an NCAA athletics department. The researchers focused on brand management for clients, but their findings can be transferred readily to the purposes of human resource management. That is, the tools and strategies of social media communication can be used within the organization both to promote the organization's brand and to increase employees' commitment. Specifically, the table shown here provides an overview of the findings related to the use of Facebook as a form of communication, as a mechanism for promoting brand attributes and associations, and as a marketing strategy. The results indicate that NCAA athletics departments that manage brand associations through Facebook are attempting to leverage aspects of commitment and organizational attributes (e.g., prestige of athletic program).

An organization's mission and values must be strategically managed by personnel to foster positive growth and to appeal to stakeholders (both internal and external). Furthermore, the concept of psychological climate becomes increasingly relevant in the conversation as Facebook provides a forum where positive psychological climate can be leveraged to present positive organizational attributes and build an organization's brand. Conversely, if not managed effectively, the platform could communicate the qualities of a negative psychological climate, which can damage an organization's public relations.

These results demonstrate the power of social media and the need to connect proactive human resource management strategies to internal and external communication plans. One way to do so is for sport and recreation managers to be aware of the social media platforms available to them, learn effective applications of these platforms, and train personnel to use and benefit from them.

THE USE OF SOCIAL MEDIA TO MANAGE BRAND ASSOCIATIONS

STRATEGY CATEGORY	BRANDING VARIABLES
Form of communication	Status update, picture, video, link, notes
Brand attributes (based on H.H. Bauer, Stokburger-Sauer, and Exler 2008; Kaynak, Salman, and Tatoglu 2008)	Product: success, star player, head coach, team (members), team performance (team play)
	Nonproduct: management, logo, club colors, stadium, club history and tradition, club culture and values, fans, sponsor or owner, location of team
	Combination: both product and nonproduct factors
Brand association factors (based on S.D. Ross, Russell, and Bang 2008)	Brand mark, rivalry, concessions, stadium, social interaction, commitment, team history, organizational attributes, nonplayer personnel, team characteristics
Marketing	Ticket sales, merchandise, co-branding, sponsorship, event coverage, individual coverage, team coverage, in-game coverage, crisis management

Adapted, by permission, from L. Wallace, J. Wilson, and K. Miloch, 2011, "Sporting facebook: A content analysis of NCAA organizational sport pages and Big 12 conference athletic department pages," *International Journal of Sport Communication* 4(4): 422-444.

DIVERSITY MANAGEMENT OF HUMAN RESOURCES

Management by values is an increasingly relevant way to manage diversity. In practice, strategically adopting MBV means purposefully connecting our human resource management functions (recruiting, hiring, and training) to the organizational values that have been developed and co-created by all organizational stakeholders. With this in mind, adopting diversity as a formal organizational value during the strategic MBV process explicitly links management practice to Chelladurai's (2014) theorization of placing a value on diversity.

Values and Communication

In addition to affecting the choice of goals and the processes for meeting them, values—or, more specifically, value incongruities—also affect communication processes between employees. Generally, the messages received are not identical to those sent; that is, distortions (e.g., additions, deletions, modifications) are always present. A message sender encodes his or her ideas into either verbal or nonverbal symbolic form. The receiver of the message decodes the symbolic form to get the meaning of the message. Errors can be introduced in either the encoding or the decoding phase, and they are accentuated when they involve groups that hold different values (Adler 2002). In more technical terms, Gelfand and colleagues (1996) cited Singer (1987) in suggesting how values might affect perceptions of the stimuli contained in a message:

> Thus, employees who have different values may select different information from the environment and have disparate interpretations of the same encounter. . . . Likewise, in communicative encounters, we assert that the greater the differences in values between the sender and receiver, the greater the chance that they will construe the situation differently and will attach different meanings to the same words and behaviors. (pp. 57-58)

Values and Attributional Confidence

Gelfand and colleagues (1996) pointed to another process whereby value incongruity may affect group functioning. Society tends to attribute people's behavior to particular causes; it also develops an expectation for people to behave in certain ways in response to a given set of stimuli based on experience. "The degree to which people are able to understand and predict how others will behave is referred to as attributional confidence" (Gelfand et al. p. 58). This confidence is crucial in school and in the workplace. In fact, according to these authors, "Employees who share similar values (i.e., have value congruity) may be better able to recognize the behavior patterns of others and have the ability to predict their behavior in future situations (i.e., have greater attributional confidence)" (p. 59).

Values and Leadership

The foregoing line of reasoning can be extended to even the leadership process of coordinating and motivating group members. That is, just as members' personal values affect the communication and attributional processes, they can also affect perceptions of leadership. Perceptions of a leader's efforts to exert influence, and of the reasons for doing so, can vary with the values held by the perceiver. For example, James, Chen, and Cropanzano (1996) found that Taiwanese and U.S. workers not only hold different cultural values but also endorse different leadership ideals. Even within a given cultural context (e.g., U.S. or Canadian), leadership effectiveness is a function of congruence in the values of the leader and the members.

Values of Managers and Employees

Value-based perspectives or conflicts are more pronounced between managers and members than among themselves respectively. Brown (1976) suggested that such manager–member conflicts are rooted in differential exposure to organizational and **management values** (see figure 7.5). That is, whereas society is the basic source of values for all members, involvement at the managerial level of organizations through the years exposes managers to an additional set of values. This difference in experience leads to divergent values and resultant conflicts.

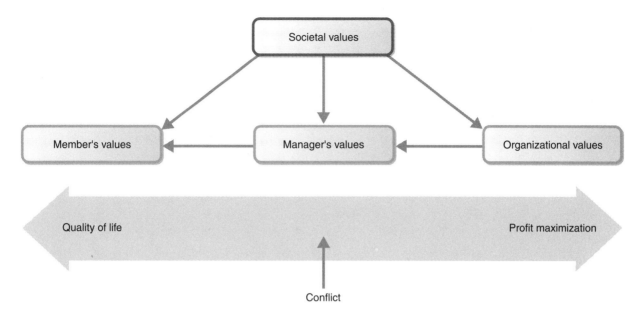

FIGURE 7.5 Genesis of value conflicts between managers and members.

Adapted from M.A. Brown, 1976, "Values–A necessary but neglected ingredient of motivation on the job," *Academy of Management Review* 1(4): 15-23.

To be more specific, the notion of profit maximization is consistent with societal values that promote capitalism and private enterprise (Hay and Gray 1974). Therefore, managers tend to hold that value high in making decisions. Indeed, their background, training, and purpose are geared toward profit maximization which, in turn, enhances organizational prosperity. In this sense, the notion of profit maximization is consistent with societal values. Yet the same society also advances the notion of quality of life for all of its citizens. Different groups may emphasize one or the other of these two values (i.e., profit maximization and quality of life).

For example, the owner and manager of a professional sport franchise (or a fitness club) may emphasize profit maximization, whereas the employees of the organization may promote quality of life. Although both efforts are legitimate in themselves, they lead to the possibility of conflict between management and employees. For instance, management may want to reduce the number of employees in order to reduce cost and maximize profit. The employees, however, may believe that such a move would increase the workload and the associated stress for the remaining employees. In a similar manner, in order to increase profits, the managers of a fitness club may attempt to enroll more members than are reasonable for the facility. On the other hand, the fitness instructors and exercise leaders who provide the services may prioritize

high-quality service and therefore prefer fewer members so that they can provide better service.

Values of Loyalty and Duty

As indicated earlier, congruence between the values held by an organization and the values held by its members facilitates organizational functioning and effectiveness. Congruence of values may arise from three processes. The first process, as pointed out by Wiener (1988), involves identification with the organizational value system on the part of individuals outside of the organization. Such persons may be willing to join the organization, and the organization may recruit them.

The second process involves socializing new members into the organization's value system. The third process, through which organizational members begin to share the organizational value system, involves the values of loyalty and duty. That is, some people may hold the value that "they have a moral obligation to engage in a mode of conduct reflecting loyalty and duty in all social situations in which they have a significant personal involvement" (Wiener 1988, p. 541). Persons who hold these values are likely to accept the organizational value system as one way of expressing loyalty and duty. In addition, certain classes of people, such as athletes and soldiers, are particularly likely to value loyalty and duty. In turn, these values may impel them to

EMPLOYEE VALUES VERSUS ORGANIZATIONAL VALUES

A study of one national sport organization (Hamm et al. 2008) highlighted the importance of understanding the congruence between employee values and organizational values. More specifically, employees in the organization rated equality (as an organizational value) significantly lower than did board members (i.e., representatives of the organization). In this context, equality was measured with a survey scale and represented the notion of management providing an equal opportunity for all employees. Delving deeper into the survey responses, we find that employees commented on the values they felt were congruent (or not) which influenced these perceptions of equality. For a summary of value congruence in this context, see the accompanying table.

These results are particularly relevant given the organizational value of equality and the potential effect of incongruence. First, in sport organizations around the globe, equality is seen as a value of paramount importance. In order to ensure that sport and recreation programs are created in a way that provides equal opportunity to all participants, managers and leaders must promote the value of equality among their employees. Second, any value incongruence creates the potential for a negative effect on operations (B. Adkins and Caldwell 2004; Hood 2003). For example, Hood suggested that perceived incongruence of values regarding equality can lead to a decrease in satisfaction, commitment, and organizational performance, as well as an increase in employee turnover. Indeed, in Hamm et al.'s (2008) study, one participant recognized that her values were not congruent with those of the organization and, following the study, voluntarily left the organization.

Given the relationship between increased turnover and low levels of value congruence (C.L. Adkins, Ravlin, and Meglino 1996; Chatman 1991), it is essential to adopt some form of management by values. In particular, managers must (a) assess their organizational values and strategically communicate them to personnel and (b) understand individual values earlier in an employee's career (through value statements in hiring, training, and orientation) in order to proactively assess the level of congruence with organizational values (Jung and Avolio 2000).

VALUE CONGRUENCE IN A NATIONAL SPORT ORGANIZATION (NSO)

VALUE	DESCRIPTION OF PERCEIVED VALUE CONGRUENCE
Passion for sport	Employees felt that the organization placed a higher value on "passion for sport" than did personnel (noncongruence). Those who did not have a high passion for sport perceived a low value for equality.
Health	Employees valued their personal health but believed that the organization did not value a healthy lifestyle to the same degree (noncongruence). Thus, those who had a high value for personal health saw the context of the organization (e.g., long, grueling hours) as unfair in some cases.
Family	Employees valued their work–life balance; however, participants indicated that the organization did not place the same importance on this value (noncongruence). Thus, those who had a high value for family saw the context of the organization (e.g., long, grueling hours) as unfair in some cases.
Professionalism	Employees believed that sport (and their NSO, in particular) was moving toward a value for professionalism (congruence). Thus, those who had a high value for professionalism regarded the organization's value for professionalism as a means to treat employees equally (e.g., through diversity policies).

Adapted from *Sport Management Review* Vol. 11(2), S. Hamm, J. MacLean, L. Kikulis, and L. Thibault. "Value congruence in a Canadian nonprofit sport organisation: A case study," pgs. 123-147, Copyright 2008, with permission from Elsevier.

accept other values espoused by their respective leaders and organizations.

Values of Work Ethic

At the time of the industrial revolution, German sociologist Max Weber described an emerging set of values that he called the Protestant work ethic (Weber 1958). This ethic involves a belief in hard work, thriftiness, discipline, industriousness, and a desire for independence. As scholars came to realize that this work ethic is prevalent in various cultural and religious contexts, they tended to omit the reference to Protestantism. More recently, Blau and Ryan (1997) developed a scale to measure work ethic that consists of four dimensions: hard work, non-leisure, independence, and asceticism.

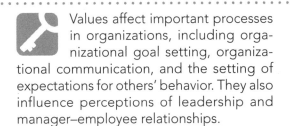 Values affect important processes in organizations, including organizational goal setting, organizational communication, and the setting of expectations for others' behavior. They also influence perceptions of leadership and manager–employee relationships.

NATIONAL VALUES AND SPORT

The growth of the field of sport management is based largely on the popularity of sport in several industrialized nations, particularly the United States and Canada. Several reasons are advanced for the popularity of sport in U.S. society. The more significant reasons are

- sport as a means of entertainment and diversion for alienated masses in an urban and bureaucratic society,

- the influence of the mass media that extensively cover sporting events, and

- an increase in leisure time and a relatively high standard of living (Eitzen and Sage 1986).

According to Eitzen and Sage (1986), the important underlying factor is that sport mirrors society and its values: "In learning the culture (through the socialization process), most Americans have internalized values that predispose them to be interested in the outcome of competitive situations—and competition is the sine qua non of sports" (p. 59). These authors noted that the dominant **American values** are success, competition, hard work, continual striving, deferred gratification, materialism, and external conformity.

To succeed in competition, athletes participate in prolonged and hard training. During periods of training, athletes sacrifice gratification of ordinary pleasures (e.g., partying). Of course, they usually make these sacrifices in the hope of reaping both intrinsic and extrinsic (i.e., material) rewards later. Indeed, modern professional sport is characterized by the excellence of the athletes and the enormity of the monetary rewards they may garner. In seeking these rewards, athletes often exhibit strict acceptance of coaches' authority—that is, conformity. Athletes tend to adhere to the rules that coaches establish even when those rules affect their personal and family life. Along the way, they engage in another hallmark of athletics—constant striving to better their performance; this is true even for those at the top of the rankings. Indeed, society expects athletes to better their own marks. Because all of these characteristics mirror the values of U.S. society, it is not surprising that sport lies at the center of American life.

Although Eitzen and Sage focused exclusively on North American sport, the values they identified also permeate many other societies that are Western, capitalistic, or both. Hence, it is legitimate to extrapolate these values to some other countries.

VIEWPOINT

In examining the role played by national values in the governance of sport organizations, van der Roest, Vermeulen, and van Bottenburg (2015) highlighted a shift toward consumerist sport (e.g., a professionalized, commercial sport sector) in the Netherlands. This shift marks a departure from the nation's traditional national values, which viewed recreation and pleasure as the essential elements of sporting activity. The shift comes in direct response to growing commercialization worldwide but may elicit domestic backlash among citizens accustomed to a sport-for-all mentality.

Outside of North America, scholars in sport sociology have emphasized that sport—more than other activities and spheres of social life (e.g., the arts)—provides a platform for public expression of national values, beliefs, pride, collective unity, and identity (see Topic and Coakley 2010). This distinction may be particularly relevant in places (e.g., South Korea, Ireland) where nation-building efforts use sport as a catalyst to bridge divided cultures (Cho 2009; Cronin 1999; Starc 2005; Tomlinson and Young 2006).

ROLE OF THE SPORT OR RECREATION MANAGER

Values are particularly relevant to nonprofit sport and recreation organizations, for whom profit is not the primary goal of organizational functioning and effectiveness (Kerwin, MacLean, and Bell-Laroche 2014a). For example, US Lacrosse (2013), the governing body of lacrosse in the United States, lays out values on its website that relate to safety, visibility, and coach certification. The purpose of these values is to provide a public document representing the factors that drive the organization. In another example, the International Basketball Federation (FIBA 2015) has outlined its strategic values as promoting and developing basketball in ways that are exciting, smart, progressive, open, responsible, and that which bring people together. The organization defines this list of values as representing the core merits of basketball around the world. As these examples illustrate, in the absence of profit as a key indicator of success, nonprofit and public sport and recreation organizations may strategically use their values to demonstrate the organization's relevance and effectiveness.

In order to benefit from an established and communicated list of organizational values, managers and leaders can use or "live" the values in their daily practice of human resource management (Kerwin, MacLean, and Bell-Laroche 2014b). For example, leaders can work with personnel (both paid staff and volunteer board members) to develop values. If personnel are involved in the process of value development or adjustment, they are more likely to buy in to the values that are established. Once a joint process of value development has been completed, managers must embed the values in the oral and written messages sent both internally (to personnel) and externally (to clients and customers).

Internal communication should also be used to strategically link values to policies and procedures (e.g. recruitment, orientation, training, and evaluation). For instance, returning to the earlier example of US Lacrosse, the value of safety would be a highlight of training and orientation for all personnel. If safety is featured as a focus in formal communication right from the first touch point of an employee or volunteer with the organization, that formal communication and continued emphasis on safety on a relatively frequent basis will trigger an informal or inherent focus on safety as well.

Case Study

Values in a National Governing Body for Sport

You are the executive director of US Soccer, the nonprofit organization that governs youth soccer development and elite-level soccer programs across the United States. Over the past 20 years, the organization has seen tremendous growth in soccer participation; however, a recent debate has arisen about whether to focus on high-performance athlete development or grassroots development. As the organization's leader, you realize that this debate stems from competing values and that you must purposefully determine the organization's values and use the values as a basis for your policies and programs.

In order to establish a clear focus for US Soccer, you must assess the values of your staff and board, as well as current trends in the sport. To begin the process, you decide to critically review your organizational mission and survey your staff and board. You start by reviewing your organizational mission:

> To make soccer, in all its forms, a preeminent sport in the United States and to continue the development of soccer at all recreational and competitive levels. (US Soccer 2015)

A survey of your board indicates that its primary value, as a group, is the success of the national (high-performance) teams. However, board members also realize that youth soccer development is essential to helping young players reach the elite level. Thus, they hold that grassroots development should be the organization's focus. Meanwhile, the paid staff in the office are very vocal about their support for a push to value grassroots development, both to reengage youth in the sport and to maintain a competitive national and international program. The staff are on the front lines, connecting to the organization's programs, and they feel that a reemphasis on youth programming is imperative.

You are pleased with this fact-finding process. You see value congruence between the board and the staff, as well as a direct link of the values to the focus on grassroots development in your mission. Understanding values is the first step; now you must begin creating an explicit list of core organizational values.

Case Study Tasks

1. Create a list of four to six organizational values for US Soccer.
2. Discuss how you would strategically leverage your values through management by values.

CHAPTER PURSUITS

SUMMARY

Earlier chapters identify knowing, doing, and helping as the underlying values of both volunteerism and professionalism. At the same time, differences may exist between these two groups on more specific values. In addition, as Eitzen and Sage (1986) pointed out, racial and ethnic diversity allows for greater differences in the value systems held by subgroups, and the values held are not always consistent with one another (e.g., individualism versus conformity, competition versus cooperation).

It is fashionable to speak of value-free organization science or management. However, if we accept the notion that one's values influence one's perceptions and behaviors, then we must concede that the values held by managers help govern managerial actions. Indeed, according to Barney (1986), "Organizational culture typically is defined as a complex set of values, beliefs, assumptions, and symbols that define the way in which a firm conducts its business" (p. 657). This view—that values and value systems are significant in the analysis of organizations and their management—has been gaining strength (Kerwin, MacLean, and Bell-Laroche 2014a, 2014b).

Just as the values held by managers affect their decisions, the values held by organizational members affect their reactions to those decisions. The value systems of managers set the tone and direction of organizational goals and processes. The influence of values manifests itself in the plans, the organizational structure, the leadership patterns, and the evaluation of individual performance and organizational effectiveness. If employees share the values underlying organizational goals and processes, then they are likely to be more motivated and to execute the plans and decisions that have been made.

Thus, the significance of values in the organizational context should not be minimized. The values held by managers and members need to be somewhat congruent—at least those values that guide organizational processes. For example, one can pursue excellence or pursue pleasure in youth sport. However, the values underlying the pursuit of excellence are success, competition, hard work, delayed gratification, conformity, and obedience—and these values are not consistent with the pursuit of pleasure, in which gratification is immediate and is limited to the sport experience. Thus, if coaches and others who organize and conduct youth sport differ in regard to these values, then conflict is bound to occur. Therefore, it behooves the manager to clarify for all organizational participants the goals of the enterprise and the values underlying those goals. Moreover, in recruiting clients and volunteer and professional workers, the manager should try to ensure that they share those organizational values.

KEY TERMS

American values 121

attitude 108

belief... 108

hierarchy of values.. 112

instrumental value 110

management value.. 118

norm 109

terminal value.. 110

value 107

value system... 112

UNDERSTAND

1. Physical education teachers in high schools teach sports to several classes of students and coach competitive sports. Distinguish between these two situations—teaching and coaching—and identify the specific values that each may evoke.

2. Compare international sport federations and national sport organizations in terms of the dominant values associated with each. For example, can we make value-based distinctions between the International Basketball Federation (FIBA) and Canada Basketball?

INTERACT

1. Identify the terminal and instrumental values that are dominant among your friends and family and explain how those values affect your behavior and decisions. How do they compare with your classmates' values?

2. Discuss the relationships between the values associated with sport and the dominant values in your country. To what extent are these sets of values consistent with each other? Do any of the sport-related values conflict with any of the national values?

Motivation

LEARNING OBJECTIVES

After reading this chapter, you will be able to

- understand the process by which individuals are motivated in an organizational context;
- recognize that motivation leads to desired performance only in the presence of requisite ability and clear role perception;
- distinguish between intrinsic and extrinsic rewards;
- explain the origins of perceived inequity and its effects on motivation; and
- understand motivation as personal investment and explain it in terms of direction, persistence, continuance, intensity, and performance.

The discussion of individual differences in ability, personality, and values in chapters 5 through 7 highlights what people bring to the work organization. The implication is that people who possess differing abilities carry out different tasks with varying levels of effectiveness; similarly, people who have different personalities and hold different values react differently to organizational processes. This chapter, in turn, focuses on the extent to which—and the processes through which—individuals are inclined to work toward the attainment of organizational goals. The inclination to work is generally labeled *motivation*. Individuals differ not only in the strength of their motivation but also in the processes through which they are motivated. Clear understanding of motivational processes in the workplace is critical for effective management. In fact, several managerial practices, such as job enrichment and performance-based pay schemes, have been advanced based on one or more theories of motivation.

This chapter offers several perspectives on work motivation. Its central thrust is to present a comprehensive model of motivation, proposed by Porter and Lawler (1968), that integrates key aspects of other theories of motivation in organizations. The chapter then briefly describes other relevant theories, including Vroom's (1964) expectancy theory, Bandura's (1986, 1997) self-efficacy theory, Maslow's (1943) need hierarchy theory, Herzberg's (1968) motivation–hygiene theory, and Adams' (1963) theory of inequity. The final section of the chapter describes Maehr and Braskamp's (1986) theory of personal investment.

First, let us consider a basic question: What is motivation? Hoy and Miskel (2005) defined it generally as "an internal state that stimulates, directs, and maintains behavior" (p. 157). More specifically, as they quoted from Pinder (1984), work motivation is

a set of energetic forces that originate both within as well as beyond an individual's being to initiate work-related behavior and to determine its form, direction, intensity, and duration. (p. 157)

Hoy and Miskel's (2005) definition applies to behavior in all contexts, but our interest, of course, lies in behavior in organizations. In this context, Robbins (2000) defined motivation as "willingness to exert a persistent and high level of effort toward organizational goals, conditioned by the effort's ability to satisfy some individual need. . . . The key elements . . . are intensity of effort, persistence, direction toward organizational goals, and needs" (p. 407).

These definitions suggest that motivated behavior is directed toward fulfilling a need, motive, or desire. Robbins' (2000) definition also includes the attributes of motivated behavior: intensity, direction, and persistence. Behavior is also influenced by an individual's experience with, and expectations for, the consequences of such behavior.

Several theories of human motivation exist, including some that address human behavior in general and some that address behavior in organizations. Authors have classified the theories of motivation that pertain to organizational behavior into two categories: need-based or **content theories** (Herzberg, Mausner, and Snyderman 1959; Maslow 1943) and **process theories** (Adams 1977; Vroom 1964). Motivational theories based on needs generally hold that when a need is unfulfilled, the individual is aroused and driven to seek sources of **satisfaction** for that need and to act in order to

achieve satisfaction. Need-based theories are also referred to as content theories because they indicate what (i.e., the content that) motivates individuals to engage in specific behaviors.

Theories of motivation come in two classes. Content theories (e.g., Herzberg's [1968], Bandura's [1986, 1997], and Maslow's [1943] theories) address the factors (or content) by which individuals are motivated. In contrast, process theories (e.g., Adams' [1977] and Vroom's [1964] theories), address the process by which individuals choose one behavior over others. Both approaches are relevant to organizational contexts.

Whereas content theories address factors that motivate the worker (i.e., personal factors, such as individual needs, or organizational factors, such as task assignment and rewards), they do not explain how individuals choose one behavior from the several available to them. Process theories, however, address the individual's evaluation and choice of certain courses of action and the ways in which other factors influence the outcomes of such courses of action.

Understanding of these theories provides the manager with a gestalt view of the intricacies and complexities of human motivation, as well as insight into how the theories and their concepts can be applied to specific situations. For instance, if an

TRAITS OF MOTIVATION

Locke (1997) identified the following traits that motivate successful entrepreneurs.

- *Egoistic passion for the work:* Successful businesspeople have a passion for work that would serve their purpose. In Locke's view, making money is virtuous if coupled with love for the work that brings in the money.
- *Commitment to action:* As noted by Locke, successful businesspersons are great thinkers; "thinking, however, is not sufficient if one's goal is to create wealth. One must also act on the basis of one's thinking" (p. 85).
- *Ambition:* Successful businesspeople have great ambition for achievement, responsibility, and expertise.
- *Effort and tenacity:* This trait derives from the others (i.e., passion, commitment to action, and ambition). It is listed separately for emphasis in recognition of the fact that failure does not discourage prime movers; instead, they tend to be tenacious.

employee of an athletics department is not excited about the routine nature of his or her job, the content of the job is in question. Therefore, content theories of motivation (Herzberg 1968; Maslow 1943) may be more relevant in addressing the issue. In contrast, if the same employee complains that he or she received a smaller pay increase than other comparable employees received, the issue is a question of equity. Thus Adams' (1963, 1977) theory of inequity may be more relevant in resolving this issue.

For our purposes here, Porter and Lawler's (1968) model of work motivation is comprehensive enough to include the significant concepts from other content and process theories. We also highlight aspects of five other relevant theories.

A MODEL OF MOTIVATION

The model of motivation proposed by Porter and Lawler (1968) is represented schematically in figure 8.1. In order to facilitate discussion of the model,

we have placed numbers in the boxes in the figure in order to refer to them in the following sections.

Effort

Effort (see figure 8.1, box 3) relates to the motivation behind an individual's expended energy in the work context. That is, the degree of effort expended reflects an individual's motivational state. The level of effort that a person is willing to put forth (or the level of motivation behind it) is a function both of the value that the person attaches to the possible rewards (box 1) and of the person's perception of the probability that making the effort will result in attaining the reward (box 2).

Value of Rewards

Every organization offers some type of reward, such as pay, bonuses, or promotions. In addition to these **extrinsic rewards**, an organization may offer **intrinsic rewards**, such as mastering a challenging task or helping others. It is expected that an individual will desire one or both types of rewards to some extent.

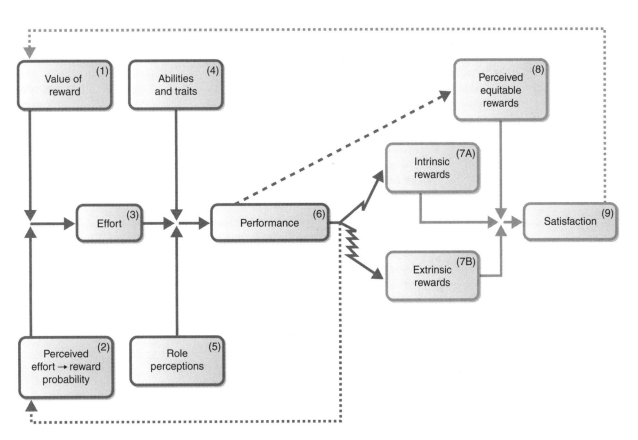

FIGURE 8.1   Porter and Lawler's model of motivation.

Adapted, by permission, from L.W. Porter and E.E. Lawler, 1968, *Managerial attitudes and performance* (Homewood, IL: Richard D. Irwin).

If a person does not value the rewards available in the organization, then he or she may not join it in the first place. On the other hand, the organization can expect people who desire its rewards to join and to work hard to gain those rewards. In figure 8.1, this expectation is implied in the linkage between the value of rewards (box 1) and effort (box 3).

Even so, members may not all place equal value on the rewards offered by an organization, except perhaps in the case of monetary rewards. For example, some members may not value a promotion (in fact, they may reject it) because of the possibility of transfer to a distant location.

Effort–Reward Probability

From a different perspective, a person may believe that his or her own efforts may not lead to the desired rewards. One's estimation of whether effort will lead to desired rewards is composed of two components. The first component relates to the person's belief that his or her effort will lead to performance as the organization expects. If, for example, an employee of an intercollegiate athletics department believes that his or her efforts will result in attaining the sponsorship target that the department has set, that person is likely to put forth much effort in this regard. If, however, the person does not expect to achieve the target despite best efforts, then his or her motivation decreases.

The second component relates to the relationship between performance (i.e., achieving the sponsorship target) and rewards that the person seeks (e.g., salary increase or promotion). Here again, if the person does not see a strong relationship between performance and rewards, then his or her motivation decreases. For example, an employee of a city recreation department may desire a promotion yet fail to put forth best efforts to that end because of a perception that the promotion is based on seniority or that other colleagues are better performers. In contrast, another employee may be convinced that his or her efforts will lead to the desired performance and subsequent promotion and therefore choose to work toward that reward.

In figure 8.1, these relationships are emphasized in the linkage between effort (box 3) and perceived effort–reward probability (box 2). In sum, effort or motivation is maximized when an individual places high value on the rewards available through participation in the organization and its activities *and* when that person also believes that his or her efforts will lead to the desired rewards. The concepts of value of reward and perceived effort–reward

VIEWPOINT

In clearing up the myth that motivation level is simply a characteristic of the individual, Robbins' (2000) view was that not all of us are motivated all the time. There are differences among people in the extent to which they are motivated, and under what circumstances. Therefore, he argues, it is necessary for managers to learn what is important to employees and assign them to the jobs that fit their interests and personality.

probability are similar to the concepts in Vroom's (1964) expectancy model of motivation, described later in this chapter.

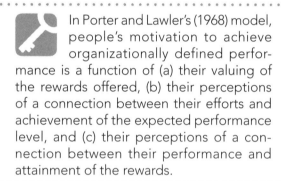

In Porter and Lawler's (1968) model, people's motivation to achieve organizationally defined performance is a function of (a) their valuing of the rewards offered, (b) their perceptions of a connection between their efforts and achievement of the expected performance level, and (c) their perceptions of a connection between their performance and attainment of the rewards.

Performance

Assuming that a person values the rewards offered by the organization and believes that his or her efforts will attain the rewards, the organization can expect the individual to put forth much effort. The organization can also expect that the employee's effort will result in a certain level of performance (figure 8.1, box 6). In this context, the term *performance* refers to what the organization expects of the employee. That is, individuals may have their own standards of performance, but an organization measures performance in terms of criteria such as organizational standards, rules, and expectations.

Abilities and Traits

One of the significant contributions of Porter and Lawler's (1968) model is that it highlights the complexity of the effort–performance relationship. Effort does not always lead directly to good performance. For effective performance to occur, an individual must possess the necessary abilities and traits (figure 8.1, box 4), which were discussed in chapters 5 and 6, respectively. In general, every job requires certain kinds and levels of ability, as well as particular psychological dispositions; people who do not possess those qualities have difficulty performing well in the job. For example, a player who is 1.5 meters (5 feet) tall (which is a trait) cannot adequately perform in the position of a basketball center; nor can a person who is 2.1 meters (7 feet) tall but has no basketball ability. Similarly, a person volunteering to market a sport program can be effective only if he or she possesses the necessary communication and marketing skills. Recall that while traits are enduring and stable characteristics, abilities are transient and trainable qualities.

Role Perception

Another factor that affects the effort–performance relationship is the accuracy of the individual's role perception (see figure 8.1, box 5). Each employee must understand what activities are necessary and how to do them. For example, a university expects a faculty member in sport management to do an adequate job of teaching, research, and community work. A faculty member could also do an outstanding job of coaching various community volleyball clubs, but this would be of minimal value if he or she received low teacher ratings and did little research and writing. The professor's time and effort should be spent in designing courses and preparing lectures and examinations in order to effectively carry out the teaching function. Similarly, the director of a city recreation department needs to engage in several managerial activities, including public relations. However, if the director spends too much time outside of the office participating in civic activities in the name of public relations, his or her performance in other areas will fall short of city administrators' expectations.

Rewards

If an individual possesses the necessary abilities and traits and perceives his or her role correctly, the person is likely to accomplish an acceptable level of performance in terms of organizational expectations. Such a performance results in rewards, which can be categorized as either intrinsic (figure 8.1, box 7A) or extrinsic (box 7B).

Intrinsic Rewards

When a person completes a task, he or she may experience a sense of accomplishment, especially if the task is challenging and meaningful. For example, a new director who is hired to supervise an athletics department riddled with NCAA rule violations and internal conflicts may find the task challenging and, at times, insurmountable. If and when the director brings the department back to order and builds a cohesive and successful unit, he or she may feel a great sense of accomplishment and of having done something good for the athletes, the university, and the community. A volunteer coach may enjoy similar feelings when helping young athletes master the skills of a sport.

In the process, people may also feel a sense of growth to the extent that they have enhanced their own capability to manage challenging tasks. In these cases, other people may compliment them on having done a good job, but the feelings that the individuals derive directly from the experience are truly intrinsic. These feelings are personal to the individual, and others cannot necessarily enhance or diminish the effects of such feelings. In other words, the person administers his or her own reward. These intrinsic rewards relate to the higher-order needs addressed in Maslow's (1943) need hierarchy theory described later in this chapter.

Extrinsic Rewards

In contrast to intrinsic rewards, which are personally derived, extrinsic rewards are administered by external agents (e.g., supervisors). These are tangible rewards known to everyone, such as salary increases, bonuses, and promotions. The problem with extrinsic rewards is that the criteria for distributing them are not always related to performance. For example, an organization might base promotion not on performance but on seniority; alternatively, the organization might set the same salary increase for every employee at a particular level rather than considering individual performance. This latter practice is the case in many government bureaucracies and in organizations where unions have a strong voice.

Note the differences in the lines connecting performance (figure 8.1, box 6) to intrinsic rewards (box 7A) and extrinsic rewards (box 7B). Because intrinsic rewards are derived personally, they should be related more directly to personal performance. However, the job itself should provide the challenge and variety that enable a person to feel good about performance; thus a simple and routine job leaves little room for intrinsic reward. To represent the contingent effect of the job itself on intrinsic rewards in figure 8.1, a semi-jagged line connects performance to intrinsic rewards. On the other hand, to represent how extrinsic rewards are mediated by other considerations unrelated to performance (e.g., favoritism, faulty performance evaluation, seniority-based reward system), a more jagged line links performance and extrinsic rewards.

The distinction between intrinsic and extrinsic rewards is analogous to the distinction that Herzberg and colleagues (1959) made between hygiene factors and motivators in their theory of motivation. Their theory holds that the contents or nature of a job—as well as the opportunities it offers for intrinsic rewards—are more critical in motivating an employee than are salary and other extrinsic factors related to the job. This theory is explained later in this chapter.

Satisfaction

The receipt of rewards generally leads to satisfaction (figure 8.1, box 9). A more detailed discussion of job satisfaction is provided in chapter 16, but for the moment let us note that the relationship between rewards and satisfaction depends on the individual's perception of whether the rewards are equitable (box 8). Adams (1963, 1977) first clarified the dynamics of perceptions of equity in his theory of inequity, which is discussed in more detail later in this chapter.

Equity of Rewards

In general, the notion of equity refers to an individual's perception that rewards are distributed fairly according to previously specified standards on the basis of performance. For example, in the public relations unit of an athletics department, if person A is more effective than person B at managing the media and projecting the desired image of the department, then person A should be rewarded more than person B. If, instead, the director rewards the two equally, then person A may feel the inequity of the rewards, thus decreasing his or her satisfaction with them.

People who believe that they have performed well tend to emphasize performance as a standard for **equity of rewards** rather than the cost–benefit comparisons, as suggested by Adams' (1965, 1977) theory. That is, individuals would like to receive rewards based on their own performance compared to those of others. For example, an NBA player is less concerned about the effort that he exerted to reach the NBA (or exerted during a given season) than about receiving a salary comparable to that of other

---

DIVERSITY MANAGEMENT OF HUMAN RESOURCES

The integrated framework for managing diversity (Chelladurai 2014) uses the term *actualization* to indicate the final step, in which the organization as a whole (including members and groups) attains full potential. To reach full potential, an organization must look to individuals to perform at optimal levels. Optimal performance, in turn, is achieved by engaging the factors that motivate employees to perform, which are highlighted throughout this chapter. More specifically, when valuing diversity, managers in the sport and recreation industry have the opportunity to influence individual motivational factors associated with equity and process, where positive outcomes will develop through the proactive management of diversity.

For instance, Shin, Kim, Le, and Bian (2012) theorized and tested conditions where deep-level team diversity was positively related to the creativity of individual team members. They found that highly creative self-efficacy moderated the association between team diversity and individual creativity such that higher levels of creative self-efficacy led to stronger positive relationships between the two variables. The authors explained this phenomenon by saying that in order to actualize the benefits of a culture of diversity, managers must understand that factors such as self-efficacy influence an individual's motivation, which in turn affects whether or not diversity within teams exerts a positive influence on outcomes.

players who have made similar performance contributions. Thus, the dotted line between performance (figure 8.1, box 6) and perceived equitable rewards (box 8) illustrates the importance of performance in determining the equity of rewards. In contrast, the perceived equity of rewards exerts only a minimal effect on the relationship between satisfaction and *intrinsic* rewards because this relationship is experienced internally.

Feedback Loops

Finally, figure 8.1 shows two feedback loops—one leading from satisfaction back to value of rewards and the other leading from the relationship between performance and rewards back to perceived effort–reward probability. The first feedback loop reflects the fact that the receipt of rewards affects the values attached to those rewards. In the case of an extrinsic reward, such as pay, the value that employees attach to it is likely to decrease as more and more of it is received. Thus, an athlete who receives a high salary

is less likely to emphasize salary increases than an athlete on the low end of the pay scale. This view is consistent with Herzberg's (1987) theory (see p. 109) suggesting that gratification of lower-order needs does not contribute much to motivation. However, Porter and Lawler (1968) acknowledged that the satisfaction derived from intrinsic rewards is likely to lead the individual to value them more. Figure 8.2 shows the differential effects of receipt of intrinsic and extrinsic rewards on the values attached to them.

The second loop in figure 8.1 relates to the employee's perception of the probability that his or her efforts will result in receiving the rewards sought. As noted earlier, this effort–reward probability estimate involves two components. First, there is the issue of whether one's effort will result in performance expected by the organization (box 6). If, for example, a volunteer worker does not reach objectives despite his or her best efforts, then the perceived relationship between his or her efforts and performance is weakened.

The second component relates to the performance–reward relationship. If a volunteer achieves objectives, then his or her sense of "can do" is strengthened. However, although the volunteer enjoys the internal reward of achievement, others may not recognize the performance and may not reward the volunteer with recognition, praise, and gratitude. It is even possible that other volunteers will be praised for similar or lesser achievement.

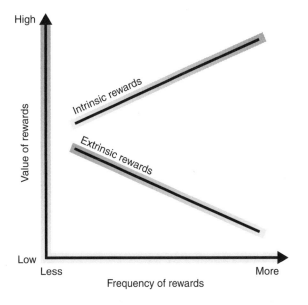

FIGURE 8.2 Value of intrinsic and extrinsic rewards as a function of their receipt.

This lack of a relationship between performance and rewards received from others may negatively influence the volunteer's enthusiasm for the work. Thus, the effort–reward probability estimate combines a person's beliefs about his or her own capacity to perform and the organization's practice of rewarding good performances.

For example, a baseball organization that habitually promotes its managers on the basis of seniority weakens employees' perceptions of the relationships between effort, performance, and promotion. That is, an individual who desires a promotion may not be triggered to work hard, because he or she perceives that the best way to get a promotion is to get old. Thus, as Porter and Lawler (1968) pointed out, organizational practices exert great influence in determining the perceived connection between performance and rewards.

A person's satisfaction with rewards is a function of perceived equity of the rewards relative to one's inputs based on internal standards or external comparisons. Receipt of rewards may reduce the value of extrinsic rewards but increase the value of intrinsic rewards. If organizational rewards are not tied to performance, then one's motivation to perform may decrease.

OTHER THEORIES OF MOTIVATION

Although Porter and Lawler's (1968) model of motivation is comprehensive and provides a good starting point for our understanding of individual motivation in organizations, many other theories of motivation exist. Several of these theories can help us further explore and understand aspects of the motivational system described by Porter and Lawler. This section reviews some of these approaches.

Vroom's Expectancy Model of Motivation

Vroom's model is particularly helpful for understanding two aspects of motivation: reward value and perceived effort–reward probability. The main postulate of Vroom's (1964) expectancy theory is as follows:

> The force on a person (motive) to perform a given act is based on the weighted value (or utility) of all the possible outcomes of the act multiplied by the perceived usefulness of the act in the attainment of these outcomes. Whenever an individual chooses between alternatives that involve certain outcomes, it seems clear that his [or her] behavior is affected not only by his [or her] preferences among outcomes, but also by the degree to which he [or she] believes these outcomes to be probable. (p. 18)

Vroom's expectancy theory incorporates four major variables (or concepts): valence, outcome, expectancy, and instrumentality. The interplay of these variables is illustrated in figure 8.3.

The two sets of outcomes in figure 8.3 are first-level outcome (the performance standards achieved by the employee) and second-level outcome (the rewards for that performance). The organization is mainly concerned with the first-level outcome, whereas the member is largely interested in the second-level outcome.

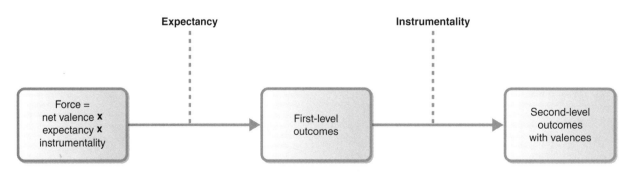

FIGURE 8.3 The interplay of expectancy and instrumentality in Vroom's model.

The probability estimate that effort will lead to the first-level outcome is referred to as **expectancy**. The individual's estimate of the relationship between the first-level outcome and the second-level outcome is referred to as **instrumentality**. In short, expectancy connects individual effort to first-level outcome, and instrumentality links the first- and second-level outcomes. These values may range from +1, where the individual perceives a strong relationship, to 0, where the individual perceives no linkage. In Vroom's expectancy theory, the force (equated here with motivation) with which an individual engages in an activity depends on multiple factors: the valence or attraction of the rewards or incentives offered by the organization, the expectancy that effort results in a certain level of performance, and the instrumentality of such performance for attaining the rewards sought.

An individual's preferences for particular outcomes is referred to as **valence**, which is the same as value of rewards in Porter and Lawler's (1968) model. The valence of an outcome can range from +1, where the outcome is strongly preferred (e.g., promotion), to −1, where the outcome is detested (e.g., transfer to a distant locality). As shown in figure 8.4, this example of concomitant outcomes of a promotion entailing transfer to a different state may elicit both positive and negative valences.

Self-Efficacy Theory of Motivation

The Porter and Lawler (1968) model emphasizes that people's level of motivation is a function of whether they believe that an effort will lead to the expected level of performance and, in turn, that

the level of performance will lead to the desired reward. Similarly, Vroom's (1964) expectancy model includes one's estimates of (a) the probability that effort will lead to the outcomes expected by the organization and (b) the probability that the first-level outcome will lead to the desired personal outcomes. Thus, in both models, the first set of beliefs or estimates relates to a person's abilities or skills for performing the assigned task.

One's estimate of one's personal ability to achieve a given task is labeled *self-efficacy* in Bandura's (1986, 1997) social cognitive theory (also known as social learning theory). Bandura (1986) defined self-efficacy as "people's judgments of their capabilities to organize and execute courses of actions required to attain designated types of performances" (p. 391). In other words, self-efficacy involves the belief that one possesses the needed resources (i.e., physical or mental ability or both) and the capacity to use those resources effectively in performing a given task. That is, self-efficacy relates to what an individual thinks she or he can do.

A person who thinks that he or she can carry out a given task successfully is likely to be motivated toward doing the task. On the other hand, a person who thinks that he or she lacks the wherewithal to carry out the task is unlikely to be motivated to engage in it. If individuals analyze their own preferences for certain tasks and their aversions to some other tasks, two issues emerge. The first issue, obviously, relates to whether the task is attractive and whether the rewards for the activity are desirable. That is, "Do I want to do it?" The second issue involves whether one believes that the task can be carried out. That is, "Can I do it?"

Self-efficacy is task specific. That is, a person may feel quite efficacious at one task (e.g., marathon

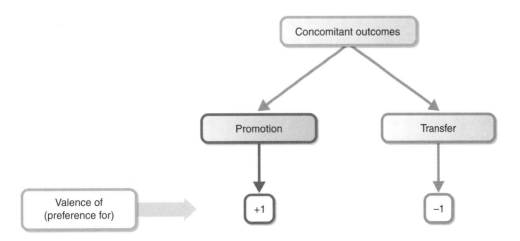

FIGURE 8.4   Differential valence (value of rewards) for concomitant outcomes.

running) but not so efficacious at another task (e.g., pole vaulting). Similarly, a student may feel that he or she will do well in sport marketing but not so well in academic counseling, whereas another student may feel the reverse. In addition, self-efficacy is cultivated through several sources, such as experiences with the task (whether achievements or failures), vicarious experiences of seeing others performing the task, and persuasion from meaningful others.

Scholars in sport have employed the concept of self-efficacy in studying the dynamics of sport participation from various perspectives. For example, one study (Everhart and Chelladurai 1998) investigated gender differences in the role played by self-efficacy in collegiate basketball players' preferences about coaching at the levels of high school, two-year college, Division III, Division II, and Division I. The study found that the genders did not differ in their self-efficacy regarding coaching jobs. More recently, Feltz and colleagues (1999) defined coaching efficacy as "the extent to which coaches believe they have the capacity to affect the learning and performance of their athletes" (p. 765). These authors developed a questionnaire for measuring four dimensions of coaching efficacy, as outlined in table 8.1.

The four-dimensional description of coaching efficacy underscores the notion that efficacy is task specific. For example, some coaches are quite confident about their teaching ability but less so about character building; others may believe in their ability to cultivate character in athletes but feel less confident about coaching during competition. Following the lead of Feltz and colleagues (1999), Kent and Sullivan (2003) found that those who rated higher on coaching self-efficacy were more committed to their respective universities than were those who rated lower on coaching self-efficacy. Sullivan and Kent (2003) showed that two dimensions of coaching efficacy—motivation and teaching efficacy—were correlated with the extent of training and positive feedback provided by the coaches. Similarly, a sport manager may feel efficacious in some managerial duties (e.g., interviewing candidates for a job) but

less confident about performing other duties (e.g., evaluating the performance of subordinates).

Maslow's Need Hierarchy Theory

Maslow's (1943) need hierarchy theory specifies five classes of needs ordered in a hierarchy of prepotency (i.e., power or force). This theory can help us understand the roles played in motivation by perceived effort–reward probability and by different types of rewards. Maslow argued that satisfied needs lose their potency to instigate behavior and that unsatisfied needs provide the only basis for behavior. He argued further that people focus first on meeting their basic needs, then move up the hierarchy of needs. In commenting on the concept of a hierarchy of needs, Maslow (1943) stated the following:

> It is quite true that man [or woman] lives by bread alone—when there is no bread. But what happens to man's [or woman's] desires when there is plenty of bread and when his [or her] belly is chronically filled? At once, other (and "higher") needs emerge, and these, rather than physiological hungers, dominate the organism. And when these in turn are satisfied, again new (and still "higher") needs emerge and so on. This is what we mean by saying that the basic human needs are organized into a hierarchy of relative prepotency. (p. 375)

Maslow proposed five categories of needs in order of importance to the individual: physiological needs, safety and security, love, esteem, and self-actualization (figure 8.5). Physiological needs involve the fundamental and biological requirements of a human being, such as food, shelter, and pain avoidance. From an organizational perspective, the organization must provide the employee with sufficient financial reward (e.g., salary or bonus) to ensure that his or her physiological needs are satisfied. Safety and security needs involve an individual's preference for "a safe, orderly, predictable,

TABLE 8.1 The Four Dimensions of Coaching Efficacy

Game strategy	Belief in one's ability to coach during competition and to lead the athletes to a successful performance
Motivation	Belief in one's ability to influence athletes' psychological skills and states
Teaching technique	Confidence in one's instructional and diagnostic skills
Character building	Belief in one's ability to affect athletes' personal development and positive attitude toward sport

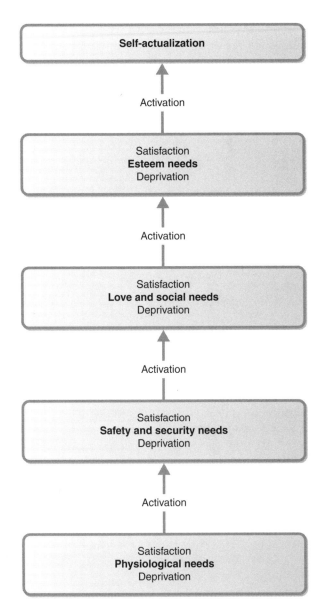

FIGURE 8.5   Maslow's five categories of needs.

of the employee's social needs. Esteem needs are higher-order needs that relate to a person's desire to be recognized by others and to enjoy status among them. According to Maslow (1943), esteem needs include a desire for strength, achievement, adequacy, confidence (i.e., self-esteem), recognition, and respect from others. In an organizational context, esteem needs may be catered to by, for example, the title and status accorded to an individual and the respect that he or she receives from peers. Finally, the need for self-actualization appears at the highest level in Maslow's hierarchy. An individual operating at this level endeavors to reach his or her best potential: "to become everything one is capable of becoming" (Maslow 1943, p. 382).

One important component of Maslow's (1943) theory is often overlooked. Conventionally, unmet need is seen as the driving force of human behavior, and scant attention is given to the effects of need gratification. In Maslow's theory, however,

VIEWPOINT

Despite the common belief that pay is not a great motivational tool, it is very important in practice (Rynes, Gerhart, and Minetter 2004). In the view of Rynes et al., "the broad usefulness of money as well as its many symbolic meanings suggests that, far from being a mere low-order motivator, pay can assist in obtaining virtually any level on Maslow's motivational hierarchy, including social esteem and self-actualization" (p. 385). Their review of research shows that pay tied to performance (e.g., merit pay) is most important to "high academic achievers, high-performing employees, and individuals with high self-efficacy and high needs for achievement . . . just the types of people most employers claim to be looking for!" (p. 386). They also note that the most desirable employees like pay schemes that differentiate individual performance. "Indeed, the average U.S. worker desires individual (rather than team or organization-based) pay-for-performance . . . with high performers desiring it to an even greater extent" (p. 386).

organized world, which he [or she] can count on, and in which unexpected, unmanageable, or other dangerous things do not happen" (Maslow 1943, p. 378). In an organizational context, employees' safety needs take the form of, for example, safe working conditions and precautions against accidents; similarly, security needs in this context are related to job security, health coverage, and retirement schemes.

The third need, love, involves people's desire for friendship and warm interpersonal interaction with others (i.e., being associated with and accepted by others). The satisfaction of social needs in an organization depends on the employee's co-workers, work groups, and supervisors, as well as the intensity

gratification of a need is just as important as deprivation is because gratification releases the organism from one set of needs and activates another set. Figure 8.5 illustrates the process by which deprivation dominates the individual and the gratification of need activates the next-higher need.

Herzberg's Motivation–Hygiene (Two-Factor) Theory

The theory put forth by Herzberg and his associates (Herzberg 1968; Herzberg, Mausner, and Snyderman 1959) began with a study of engineers. Specifically, the researchers asked the engineers to recall the most satisfying event in their work experience and identify the factors that led to it. They also asked the engineers to identify and narrate the most dissatisfying event. Analysis of these responses revealed the following:

> The factors involved in producing job satisfaction (and motivation) are separate and distinct from the factors that lead to job dissatisfaction. Since separate factors need to be considered, depending on whether job satisfaction or job dissatisfaction is being examined, it follows that these two feelings are not opposites of each other. The opposite of job satisfaction is not job dissatisfaction, but no job satisfaction; and, similarly, the opposite of job dissatisfaction is not job satisfaction, but no job dissatisfaction. (Herzberg 1968, p. 56)

The fundamental postulate of the theory is that only higher-order needs affect satisfaction and that lower-order needs are associated with dissatisfaction. As a consequence, the theory is referred to as a two-factor (or dual-factor) theory (Herzberg 1968; Herzberg, Mausner, and Snyderman 1959). This research showed that one set of factors (referred to as satisfiers or motivators) was associated more often with satisfaction than with dissatisfaction. Another set (referred to as dissatisfiers or hygienes) was referred to more often in incidents of dissatisfaction than in incidents of satisfaction. All of the satisfiers or motivators were related to higher-order needs, and the dissatisfiers were associated with lower-order needs.

Herzberg and his colleagues replicated these results in several of their studies (cf. Herzberg 2003). Figure 8.6, which is a composite of the results of various studies, shows the relative-percentage contributions of motivators and hygiene factors to both satisfaction and dissatisfaction. Motivators accounted for only 31 percent of the incidents of dissatisfaction but 81 percent of the incidents of satisfaction. On the other hand, hygiene factors accounted for 69 percent of the incidents of dissatisfaction but only 19 percent of the incidents of satisfaction. These results support Herzberg's idea that different sets of factors are associated with satisfaction and dissatisfaction.

The most important finding of Herzberg's work was that the motivators (or growth factors) were all related to the content of the work itself, whereas the hygiene factors were all related to the context in which the work was carried out. Specifically, the content factors were achievement, recognition for achievement, the work itself, responsibility, and growth or advancement. The contextual factors were company policy and administration, supervision, interpersonal relationships, working conditions, salary, status, and security. The implication of the theory is that management must take steps to eliminate dissatisfaction by improving the hygiene factors—that is, by providing adequate salary and wages, good working conditions, meaningful company policies, and high-quality supervision. However, these hygiene factors alone do not result in motivated or satisfied workers. Therefore, management also must change the content of jobs in order to provide for employees' psychological growth; this issue of changing job content (or job enrichment, as it is called) is discussed in chapter 10.

VIEWPOINT

It may be possible to reduce dissatisfaction among sport and recreation employees by using social media and acknowledging the benefits associated with increased connectivity. For example, J. Price, Farrington, and Hall (2013) found that Twitter, specifically, is opening up new, direct ways to communicate both internally with staff, volunteers, and members and externally with fans. Thus, the power of the "passion" behind sport can be leveraged 24-7 through social media to increase employees' connection with their club or sport organization.

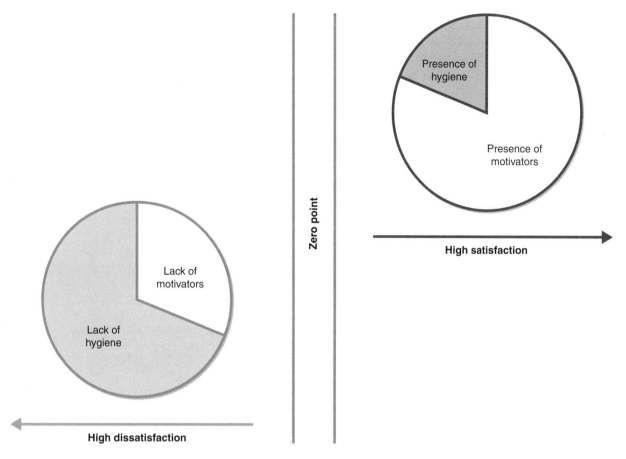

FIGURE 8.6 Relative percentage contributions of motivators and hygiene factors to satisfaction and dissatisfaction in Herzberg's model.

Adapted from F. Herzberg, 2003, "One more time: How do you motivate employees?" *Harvard Business Review* 81(1): 86-96.

Adams' Theory of Inequity

Adams' (1963, 1977) theory of inequity contributes to our understanding of the role played by equity of rewards in motivation. Adams posited that upon receiving a reward, a person compares it with an internalized standard. If the comparison is favorable, then the person experiences satisfaction; if the comparison is unfavorable, however, the person experiences dissatisfaction. For instance, a student may not be content to receive a B grade in a course if that grade is not comparable to what other students receive. Similarly, a merit raise of $1,000 does not provide happiness for a professor if every other professor received $1,001. The important point in both of these examples is that the person's estimation of equity depends not on the absolute amount but on the relative amount.

The individual's internalized standard could consist simply of a comparison between personal effort (i.e., input) and the reward delivered by that effort (i.e., outcome). For example, if a person makes great sacrifices to lose weight but loses only 0.9 kilograms (2 pounds) in six months, the individual experiences a feeling of inequity. This feeling results from a simple comparison of personal cost with personal benefit. In an organizational context, however, the cost–benefit comparison extends to referent others in the organization. That is, an individual compares the personal cost–benefit balance with the cost–benefit ratio of others in the work group. Adams' (1963, 1977) theory is anchored in this comparison to referent others. As he noted (see figure 8.7),

Inequity exists for *Person* whenever he [or she] perceives that the ratio of his [or her] outcomes

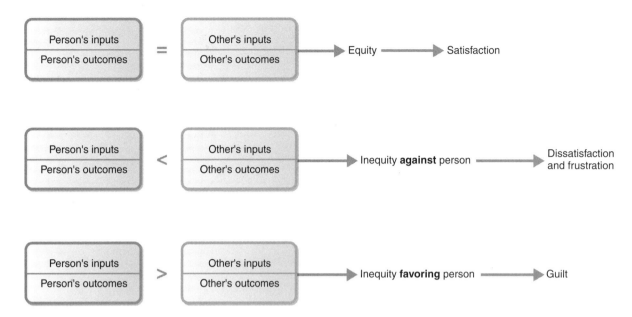

FIGURE 8.7 In Adams' theory, when individuals perceive inputs and outcomes as unequal, the individual experiences either dissatisfaction and frustration or guilt.

to inputs and the ratio of *Other's* outcomes to *Other's* inputs are unequal. (Adams 1977, p. 113, emphasis added)

The Other in Adams' theory could be a subordinate, a supervisor, a co-worker, or an employee in another comparable organization or occupation.

The concept of inputs in Adams' (1963, 1977) theory refers to personal contributions in terms of intelligence, education and training, experience and seniority, personal appearance or attractiveness, health, and effort on the job. Outcomes in an organizational context include pay, seniority and other fringe benefits, working conditions (including status and perquisites), and the psychological or intrinsic rewards of the job.

When a person perceives inequity and feels the tension and discomfort associated with it, he or she may try to restore equity (or reduce inequity) in a number of ways. Specifically, the person may attempt to alter the values of any of the four elements of the inequity formula: personal outcome, personal input, others' outcomes, and others' inputs. The most frequently used strategy is to try to improve one's personal outcome. Thus, an individual is most likely to approach an employer and ask for more pay, greater benefits, and so on. Of course, the person also can reduce the feeling of inequity by reducing personal input through decreased productivity or increased absenteeism.

An individual might also try to reduce inequity by reducing others' outcomes or inputs, but he or she may be constrained from adopting this strategy. Specifically, others' outcomes (e.g., pay, promotion) are most likely determined by superiors; in addition, others are likely to strongly influence their own inputs. More important, a strategy that focuses on others' inputs or outcomes may not be psychologically acceptable to the person in question. For instance, a facility supervisor in an athletics or recreation department is unlikely to ask for a reduction in the rewards of another supervisor; nor is a supervisor likely to sabotage the efforts of another supervisor.

Apart from manipulating personal outcomes and inputs, there are other ways of reducing inequity. For example, Adams (1977) suggested that when individuals experience discomfort with perceived inequity, they may alter their perceptions of their own outcomes and inputs and those of others in a manner that restores perceived equity. They also may change the Other of comparison—that is, the Other with whom they compare themselves. Another possibility is to leave the organization. The significance of Adams' theory lies in the fact that organizational reward systems are considered meaningful and effective only insofar as they create a sense of equity among the organization's members. This notion is elaborated in Porter and Lawler's (1968) model of motivation.

MOTIVATION AS PERSONAL INVESTMENT

An alternative view of individual motivation was provided by Maehr and Braskamp (1986), who suggested that motivation is inferred from the observed behavior of individuals. For example, when we see a young person practicing basketball free throws by himself or herself, we conclude that he or she is motivated (i.e., he or she is making a **personal investment**). This approach can be useful for practicing managers because it explains motivated behavior and, more important, how to identify it.

Behavioral Indicators of Personal Investment

In their model, Porter and Lawler (1968) equated effort with motivation. In their case, effort was the behavior that leads to motivation, which influences performance. Relatedly, it has been stated that observed behaviors can be evaluated on five interrelated dimensions—direction, persistence, continuing motivation, intensity, and performance (Maehr and Braskamp 1986). As you may recall, similar concepts—intensity of effort, persistence, and direction—are included in Robbins' (2000) definition of motivation. However, Maehr and Braskamp's work on observed behavior is more detailed and comprehensive.

- *Direction:* Direction involves the choices that an individual makes among behavioral options. For example, a volunteer coach attends a coaching clinic during the weekend instead of going fishing. Based on this choice of one behavior over another, people infer that he or she is motivated.

- *Persistence:* Persistence involves the amount of time that an individual spends on a particular job or project. For example, basketball players spend much time practicing their shots; based on this persistence, others rate them as highly motivated.

- *Continuing motivation:* Continuing motivation involves the tendency of an individual to return to a task after being away from it for a period of time. For instance, other demands often interrupt the work of a fitness club manager who is developing a strategic plan for the firm. Yet the manager keeps returning to work on the plan. Those who observe this tendency to continue work even after several interruptions infer that the manager is motivated to complete the plan. Thus, continuing motivation involves resumption of an activity after interruptions, which differs from persistence (continuous activity).

- *Intensity:* Intensity consists of the energy expended and the activity level of an individual involved in a task. For example, two coaches of juvenile teams may differ in the level of activity and energy they expend in getting ready for a coaching session even if they spend equal time on the task. Others are likely to believe that the more active person is more motivated. Maehr and Braskamp (1986) cautioned, however, that a difference in activity may be a function of physiological factors; therefore, intensity is not as reliable a measure of motivation as is direction. Activity level can also be influenced by one's traits and abilities. For instance, a more anxious person is likely to be more active in getting ready for a coaching session than a less anxious person. Similarly, one who possesses the required coaching experience and abilities is likely to be less active than one who does not.

- *Performance:* Whenever performance varies, whether between two individuals or within one individual, others tend to ascribe the variations to motivation. This is particularly true when one individual performs differently at different times. Even coaches and media personnel sometimes fall into this fallacy. Whenever a particular athlete performs well, these persons most often attribute the performance to the athlete's dedication and motivation. These attributions also imply that the other athletes were not as motivated as the good performer. However, this view may be far from the truth. Indeed, we must be cautious when making inferences about motivation based on performance. More specifically, managers should not place much confidence in performance as a measure of motivation because performance "is a product of acquired skills, ability, and a combination of the behavioral patterns [intensity, continuing motivation] already reviewed" (Maehr and Braskamp 1986, p. 5). In a team setting, an individual's performance may also be affected by the performances of other team members. Therefore, performance is only a crude measure of motivation and should be used only rarely in this way.

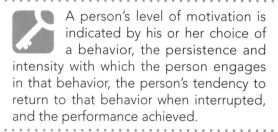

A person's level of motivation is indicated by his or her choice of a behavior, the persistence and intensity with which the person engages in that behavior, the person's tendency to return to that behavior when interrupted, and the performance achieved.

The major thrust of Maehr and Braskamp's (1986) argument is that the discussed behavioral patterns, considered collectively, indicate the extent to which individuals invest themselves in a given activity. Just as people differ in how they invest their money, they also differ in how they invest their personal resources of time, talent, and energy in various activities. This view carries two implications. First, everyone is motivated to do something; that is, people do invest their personal resources in some activities. For example, one fitness instructor may invest the free time available in spending time at a bar with friends, while another may spend that time in the library learning more about fitness and wellness. The former instructor is as motivated to be at the bar as the latter is to be at the library.

> The issue is really not whether a person is motivated but, rather, how, to what ends, and in what ways the person is motivated. The assumption is that all people are motivated to do something; the question is what they are motivated to do. (Maehr and Braskamp 1986, pp. 6-7)

The second implication is that personal investment is a course of action, "a process whereby people take certain available resources—their time, talent, and energy—and distribute them as they choose" (Maehr and Braskamp 1986, p. 7). This concept brings together several behavioral patterns

that reflect a degree of attraction toward something. However, as Maehr and Braskamp noted, "The emphasis is on something . . . done that is observable, objective, and quantifiable" (p. 9).

The advantage of viewing motivation as personal investment is that "one can consider motivation not only as an enduring trait of individuals or groups but as a direct product of the situation in which the person or group is placed. And situations are easier to change than people" (Maehr and Braskamp 1986, p. 8). This is a critical issue for sport and recreation managers. When a manager sees people not investing their personal resources in organizational activities, it is not profitable to label them as unmotivated. Instead, the manager should find out what in the situation causes these members to invest their resources elsewhere and determine how he or she can make the situation more attractive to them. One possibility is to redesign an employee's job to include relatively more autonomy and challenge.

On the basis of this line of reasoning, Maehr and Braskamp (1986) proposed the motivational process shown in figure 8.8. According to the model, external factors (e.g., task design, social norms, and options available to the individual) interact with the individual's personal thoughts, emotions, and preferences to determine the investment of his or her resources in specific activities. The model also suggests that such investment leads to certain out-

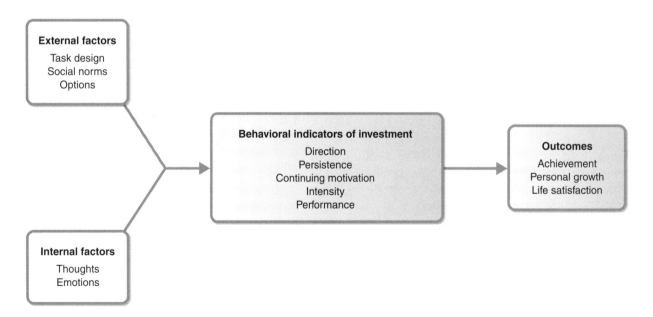

FIGURE 8.8 Model of motivation as personal investment.

Adapted from M.L. Maehr and L.A. Braskamp, 1986, *The motivation factor: A theory of personal investment* (Lexington, MA: Lexington Books), 10. By permission of L.A. Braskamp.

comes (or payoffs) for the person. These outcomes are described in the following section.

Outcomes of Personal Investment

Maehr and Braskamp (1986) suggested that if managers think of motivation as investment, then they also should consider the payoffs or outcomes of such investments. Because individuals invest their personal resources, the outcomes also should be considered from the individuals' perspectives. However, a given outcome may be valued differently by individuals, organizations, and societies. In Maehr and Braskamp's view, the outcomes of any personal investment can be categorized into three broad classes: achievement, personal growth, and life satisfaction and general well-being.

Achievement

Achievement involves "a personal accomplishment—something that is attributed to one's ability and effort. But it is an accomplishment that is not only valued by the person; it also has social significance" (Maehr and Braskamp 1986, p. 13). By this definition, then, a good thing that happens to an individual is not considered to be an achievement if it cannot be attributed to the individual's ability or effort; this would be the case, for example, with winning a lottery. The authors also noted that achievement refers to an outcome that was in doubt. Thus, routine performances, such as a professional basketball player making 60 percent of his or her free throws, are not considered to be achievements.

A more significant criterion holds that the accomplishment must be valued by other people or organizations. For example, a university is not likely to value a professor's expertise and accomplishments in shooting marbles. For that matter, the professor's family may not appreciate such accomplishments either. This does not deny the fact that the professor may value these accomplishments immensely. However, they need to be valued by others if they are to be labeled as achievements. In contrast, the values held by the individual fall under one of the other two categories of personal investment outcomes: personal growth and life satisfaction.

Personal Growth

Personal growth refers to the enhancement of one's ability, skill, or competence. To modify Maehr and Braskamp's (1986) example, consider three sport managers who spend their free time differently. The first manager joins a master's degree program in business administration to further her expertise in management. The second gets involved in ceramics to gain fulfillment from creating things with his hands. The third tries skydiving to face the danger, conquer the challenge, and experience the vertigo. Each case involves the "enhancement of ability . . . but clearly the goal in the first case is achievement, whereas in the other two it is personal growth" (Maehr and Braskamp 1986, p. 14). Although these three people may equally value their respective payoffs, the first payoff—achievement—is more critical in an organizational context because it leads directly to organizational effectiveness.

Life Satisfaction

The final category of outcomes in Maehr and Braskamp's (1986) scheme is that of life satisfaction and general well-being. In their view, although

VIEWPOINT

The theories described in this chapter cannot explain all behavior in an organization. Indeed, in the views of Pinder (2008) and Landy and Becker (1987), they are, in fact, middle-range theories capable of explaining only very specific processes or outcomes. For example, Landy and Becker (1987) suggested that the two-factor theory put forth by Herzberg and colleagues (1959) is more relevant to explaining affective reactions to certain job characteristics or job satisfaction than to other organizational processes or outcomes. Similarly, the equity theory (Adams 1965, 1977) relates perceptions of inequity to negative feelings and dissatisfaction. On the other hand, the expectancy theory (Vroom 1964) can explain choices that individuals make from among several discrete ways of behaving without reference to satisfaction or dissatisfaction. Porter and Lawler's (1968) model of motivation is more comprehensive and tends to integrate the other theories explained in this chapter.

achievement and personal growth are desired and valued outcomes, some personal investments do not lead to either of these outcomes. Such investments may lead, however, to what they refer to as life satisfaction. Consider, for example, a person who has been fishing regularly for the past several years. As this is a leisure time activity for this person, any payoff (e.g., catching a fish) from this investment of time cannot be considered achievement or personal growth. However, the satisfaction that the person receives from such investment may be of great value to the individual and contribute greatly to his or her overall life satisfaction and well-being.

As described by Maehr and Braskamp (1986), the possible outcomes of personal investment in an activity include significant achievement as a result of one's ability and effort; personal growth reflected in the enhancement of one's ability, skill, or competence; and life satisfaction, including the first two outcomes and a sense of well-being.

ROLE OF THE SPORT OR RECREATION MANAGER

As outlined in this chapter, Porter and Lawler's (1968) model of motivation posits that the level of effort that an individual is willing to put forth (or the level of motivation behind it) is a function of both the value that the person attaches to the possible rewards and the person's perceptions of the probability that the effort will result in receiving those rewards. The essential element here is the notion of rewards. Specifically, the sport industry operates through individuals who work as paid staff, volunteers, and interns, and, as we outline in chapter 14, each of these groups is rewarded in certain ways.

For example, a ticket sales employee may be rewarded with an increased commission as a way to extrinsically motivate his or her sales behavior. On the other hand, an event volunteer may be rewarded with a volunteer recognition reception at an event's opening ceremonies to intrinsically motivate hard work over the course of the event. Finally, interns are motivated by the potential extrinsic reward of receiving a strong letter of recommendation from their internship supervisor. Each of these examples operationalizes the model of motivation and highlights the importance for sport and recreation managers of understanding and serving these various motivational factors.

In the model of motivation presented in this chapter, "value of reward" is a key factor in increasing effort (through motivation). No matter the group to be served (i.e., paid staff, volunteers, or interns), sport and recreation managers must assess which rewards are valued by their personnel. This assessment can be tricky because people and groups do not all value the same types of rewards. The key is to conduct fairly frequent audits of personnel in order to understand what rewards are most meaningful to them.

For example, a marketing manager might assume that tickets to an upcoming professional sport competition will serve as a powerful reward to help motivate effort among her staff. However, if a number of her staff are young parents who do not have the time to attend evening professional sport events, then the value of the reward is low and therefore it will exert little effect on motivation and effort. In the case of interns and volunteers, sport and recreation managers sometimes lump these two kinds of personnel into the same category for motivation purposes. However, they may be motivated by very different factors—for example, trying to gain career status (a utilitarian motive) versus serving a cause about which they are passionate (an affective motive). Therefore, rewards offered to members of these two groups need to match their motives in order to ensure maximum effort and effectiveness.

Case Study

Motivating Through Increased Value of Reward

Your company has been contracted by the USGA to perform setup and takedown of signage, ropes, and grand stands for seven championship events.

You are doing so with the help of a sharp group of interns; however, partway through the series of events, you notice a decline in the interns' level of effort and therefore in their performance. Given this decline, you replay in your mind the work done by the interns so far. This review enables you to make the following list of their work done and the rewards they received for doing it:

- For the first championship, setup took a bit longer than normal, but this was easily justified due to it being the first tournament of the season, wherein the interns were getting used to their new roles.
- Takedown of the championship was a breeze. The interns worked hard and put in solid 12-hour workdays.
- There was a two-day break for the interns, and then we moved on to the next championship.
- Hosted a small recognition dinner on the first night of work at the second championship, where the interns were given golf shirts as rewards for their work in the first championship.
- Didn't get a chance to give the interns any feedback, but thought they were doing well and improving as they went.
- The second tournament was somewhat challenging in that a major windstorm destroyed some signage on the course and the interns had to work extra hours for five straight days to ensure that the course was ready for tournament play.
- Takedown of the course was a bit slow.

- Only half a day break and then on to the next championship.
- The interns were given another golf shirt over lunch on the day starting the third championship.

After reviewing the list, you realize that the interns may not feel that the rewards and feedback match the effort they have put forth. Therefore, you decide to come up with a plan to ensure that your interns understand how they are performing and value the rewards you provide them for a job well done.

Case Study Tasks

1. Create a small survey that you would give to your interns to determine the rewards they value.
2. Construct a performance appraisal schedule that takes into account the busy championship season. (For example, would you complete an appraisal after each championship? At the end of the season? And so on.) In accordance with the model of motivation (Porter and Lawler 1968), the appraisal schedule must be linked directly to rewards that you determine to be valuable to your interns.

CHAPTER PURSUITS

SUMMARY

This chapter presents two primary theories of motivation—Porter and Lawler's (1968) expectancy model of motivation and Maehr and Braskamp's (1986) theory of motivation as personal investment. Porter and Lawler's model includes concepts from the theories of Adams (1963, 1977); Herzberg (1968); Herzberg, Mausner, and Snyderman (1959); Maslow (1943); and Vroom (1964)—all of which are also partially described in the chapter. These theories show that sport organizations and their managers can manipulate several factors under their control in order to enhance members' motivation.

All of the theories discussed here refer, either directly or indirectly, to intrinsic rewards; they also suggest that workers derive these rewards directly from performing a job. It is evident, then, that a job and the tasks associated with it can serve as sources of motivation. Therefore, because managers control job design, they can design a job in such a way as to increase its motivating potential (for more on this subject, see chapter 10).

The motivational theories described in this chapter also provide a framework within which managers can analyze and understand members' behaviors and identify ways to reinforce desirable behaviors and modify undesirable ones. For example, the expectancy model of motivation provides the basis for some theories of leadership discussed in chapter 12.

Another significant contributor to motivation in organizations is fairness, both in organizational procedures and in the distribution of organizational rewards. As pointed out by the theories of Porter and Lawler (1968) and Adams (1963), the rewards offered by an organization lose their motivating potential if they are perceived to be inequitable. To make them equitable, some organizations distribute rewards equally among all employees. This practice, however, overlooks the different levels of performance that people may achieve; therefore, it cannot enhance motivation to perform. If rewards are intended to serve as motivators, then they should be tied to performance, which entails accurately assessing individual performance and instituting fair reward systems. These issues are addressed in chapters 13 and 14, respectively.

KEY TERMS

content theories 126

equity of rewards.. 130

expectancy 133

extrinsic reward.. 127

instrumentality.. 133

intrinsic reward 127

motivation 125

personal investment 139

process theories 126

satisfaction... 126

valence 133

UNDERSTAND

1. Consider your current schoolwork or job functions. Do you spend more time and effort on some courses or tasks than on others? Explain what factors contribute to this differential emphasis.

2. What feelings do you have when you complete a course or major job task? What intrinsic and extrinsic factors are associated with those feelings?

INTERACT

1. Think of a paid job you have held with which you were either quite satisfied or quite dissatisfied. What factors contributed to your level of satisfaction or dissatisfaction? During class discussion of these factors and while listening to other students' responses to this question, consider the factors that contribute to your peers' levels of satisfaction or dissatisfaction. Discuss ways in which those factors might be managed.

2. Think of a classmate or co-worker who is highly motivated. Explain why he or she may be so highly motivated. Identify the specific factors that influence your opinion of this person.

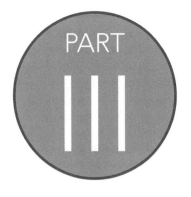

HUMAN RESOURCE PRACTICES

The preceding parts of the book outline the classes of human resources in sport and recreation organizations, as well as the differences between them in terms of individual abilities, personality, values, and motivation. Such individual differences possess functional utility from a societal point of view. Every modern society is characterized by a high degree of division of labor and a multitude of vocational pursuits. Vocations and occupations, in turn, require a diversity of aptitudes, abilities, and temperaments. Fortunately, great variety in these individual-difference variables also characterizes the people in a society.

Even so, an organization can harness the functional utility of individual differences only if it matches these differences with the requirements of its tasks. That is, the performance of the individuals in an organization, and the effectiveness of the organization as a whole, depend largely on the fit between the individuals and their differing characteristics on the one hand and the tasks assigned to them on the other hand. The effective use of human resources also depends on the organizational processes of evaluating and rewarding task performance. Therefore, an organization must assign jobs to individuals that are consistent with their abilities and orientations, influence them to perform their jobs adequately, evalu-

ate their performance on specified criteria, and reward them for effective performance.

As noted earlier, our interest in individual differences stems from the concept of person–task fit. That is, our major concern is with creating a fit between the task assigned to an individual and that person's profile on individual-difference factors. The concept of person–task fit is critical from the perspectives of both the organization and the individual. The organization can expect greater productivity if its members possess the attributes required by the assigned tasks. At the same time, individual members feel competent, confident, and satisfied if their assigned tasks match their attributes.

Human resource management is concerned with creating person–organization fit and motivating people to perform their best in order to help attain organizational goals. In fact, as noted before, creating the person–task fit is itself motivational. Other practices discussed in this part of the book include job design, leadership, performance appraisal, and reward systems. These and other managerial practices are subject to the concept of fairness or organizational justice. The fundamental notion pervading modern North American society is that individuals must be treated fairly and justly in all circumstances. Within an organization, this notion relates to the distribution of rewards to all of the organization's members in a just manner; it also relates to the procedures used to assign members to organizational positions (including promotions) and to evaluate them on their performance fairly and uniformly. Because organizational justice serves as the cornerstone for almost all managerial action, we discuss it at the start of part III, in chapter 9.

In chapter 10, we discuss the nature of jobs in terms of their attributes and motivational properties. The central focus of the chapter is on the job characteristics model, which offers guidelines for increasing the motivating potential of jobs themselves.

One critical managerial concern involves recruiting workers and assigning them to appropriate jobs. In this staffing procedure, the manager must take care to match individual-difference characteristics with characteristics of the task. Chapter 11 presents approaches to assigning jobs to appropriate members of the organization. It also covers procedures for recruitment, selection, and promotion of personnel.

Chapter 12 focuses on leadership and decision making. After recruiting workers and assigning them to specific jobs, management must be concerned with influencing and motivating employees to achieve assigned tasks. That function of leadership is detailed in this chapter. Specifically, the chapter explains theories of leadership and synthesizes them into a more comprehensive model referred to as the multidimensional model of leadership. The chapter also discusses the advantages and disadvantages of participative decision making. This discussion includes a description of various problem situations and specifies, for each, the appropriate level of member participation (ranging from purely autocratic to purely group decision making).

In chapter 13, we discuss the evaluation of individual performance. Such evaluation serves two functions: formative and evaluative. Organization members may see evaluations as tools to foster their individual growth and performance. Evaluations also serve the purposes of the organization in identifying good performances and rewarding them accordingly. Chapter 14 focuses on the various reward systems and their relevance to sport organizations. In chapter 15, we discuss the emerging topic of internal marketing and show how the steps of internal marketing parallel the human resource practices described in this text.

CHAPTER 9

Organizational Justice

LEARNING OBJECTIVES

After reading this chapter, you will be able to

- discuss justice in organizations and the components of distributive, procedural, and interactional justice;
- understand the principles of equity, equality, and need that underlie distributive justice;
- distinguish between various forms of contributions that members or units bring to a distributive situation;
- identify the rules that facilitate procedural justice; and
- understand the notion of interactional justice.

In democratic countries, all interactions between people and organizations are underlain by the notion of fairness. Consider the case of drug use in athletics. The general idea behind both banning drug use and testing for drugs is fairness or justice. That is, the competition should be fair and just to everyone involved, and it is not fair for a person to gain a competitive advantage over others through the use of drugs.

To consider another example, Title IX was promulgated by the U.S. Congress to ensure fair and just distribution of opportunities for athletic participation between genders. In yet another example, the salaries paid to some collegiate football coaches far exceed the salaries paid to university presidents. Both those who oppose this practice and those who support it tend to base their arguments on the notion of fairness or justice. Similarly, affirmative actions are undertaken to correct past unfair practices in admitting students or hiring people. Tax laws are also often justified on the basis of ensuring fair treatment of all citizens; indeed, even when people

disagree about whether tax cuts should be targeted to corporations or needy people, the arguments tend to focus on whether or not a certain approach is fair.

The point of all these examples is that the concepts of fairness and justice permeate our interactions with other people and with organizations, including government agencies. The governments of various countries have instituted laws, rules, and regulations to ensure just and fair practices in all sectors of society, including business and education. For example, some laws are intended to ensure that everyone is treated fairly and justly in the processes of recruiting, interviewing, and hiring—that is, without reference to gender, race, or ethnicity.

Such government regulations are designed from a macro perspective to force and monitor fair practices across all organizations. However, they do not cover all managerial practices *within* an organization or all circumstances surrounding those practices. Thus, though it is necessary for all managers to adhere to government regulations, managers should also realize that they themselves serve as guardians of justice within their organizations. Therefore, sport managers must understand the various perspectives and interpretations of organizational justice so that they can do everything in their power to ensure that their actions are just and fair.

Almost all decisions that managers make affect the people in the organization in one way or another. This is particularly true in the case of human resource management practices: whom we recruit for a position in our organization, whom we hire, how much salary and what benefits we offer, how we interact with new employees, how we evaluate their performances, and how we reward them—all of these managerial actions come under the purview of organizational justice. Hence, we must all be fully aware of what the concept of organizational justice means and how we can make all of our judgments and actions just.

To that end, this chapter introduces the topic of organizational justice before the discussion of other human resource practices in the other chapters in this part of the book. This chapter defines **organizational justice** and discusses three forms it can take—**distributive justice**, **procedural justice**, and **interactional justice**—as well as the interrelationships between them and the principles or rules associated with each form of justice.

The importance of the concept of justice to organizations and their managers can be highlighted from three perspectives—ethical, business, and legal (Greenberg and Colquitt 2013). From the ethical perspective, insofar as society sanctions and supports organizations, the organizations need to abide by the same conceptions and standards of justice adopted by the society in general. This overall view emphasizes that all of an organization's activities should be just and fair, regardless of whether such actions are directed toward employees, customers, or the community at large. That is, although an organization's efforts to maximize profits for the owners are legitimate in themselves, the expectation of justice insists that no one else should be harmed in the process. Thus, for example, society expects organizations not to contribute to air or water pollution and expects customers not to be charged differentially for a good or service based on their gender or race.

The business perspective emphasizes the losses that may accrue to an organization because of its unjust and unfair practices. First, society in general, and customers in particular, may boycott the organization and its products if they perceive that the organization is unjust or unfair. In addition, employees may withhold their effort and cooperation if they perceive injustices in organizational activities directed at the community, at employees as a group, or at themselves as individuals. Such dissatisfaction and alienation can result in lower productivity, for which the organization will suffer.

The third perspective is the legal one. As noted in chapter 3, the distinction between professional and nonprofessional cadres in a given occupation have narrowed as a result of rising education levels in society overall (and in the workforce in particular) and the increased sophistication of training of laypeople. The same line of reasoning can be advanced here with regard to the legal aspect of organizational justice. That is, increasing awareness among customers and employees of what constitutes just practice leads them to expect more justice in the workplace. Furthermore, if society moves toward more litigation, organizations can be confronted with various kinds of lawsuits, and justice in the workplace is fast becoming an arena for such legal actions.

 Managers should be seriously concerned with organizational justice for multiple reasons: because it is morally expected of them as custodians of socially sanctioned enterprises; because organizational justice provides the foundation for good employee relations and customer relations, which ensure organizational effectiveness; and because unjust managerial practices may have legal ramifications.

These notions of justice in the organizational context apply to the community, customers, and employees, but this chapter focuses specifically on organizational justice from the employee perspective. Although almost every organizational activity and managerial decision is subject to the norms of justice, justice-related concerns are more pronounced in areas relating to personnel decisions (e.g., recruitment, placement, performance evaluation, promotion, salary, wage, bonus, and fringe benefits), resource allocation to units, and leadership or supervision.

In each area of organizational activity, organizational justice can be analyzed in terms of the following factors: the outcomes accruing to individuals or units, the decision processes by which outcomes for different parties are determined, and the way in which the outcomes and processes are communicated to individuals or groups. These three analytical approaches are referred to in the following terms:

- Distributive justice (addressing outcomes)
- Procedural justice (addressing decision procedures)
- Interactional justice (addressing the manner in which decisions are communicated)

Figure 9.1 shows that distributive justice is more critical than the other two components in the sense that it addresses the outcomes (e.g., salary, fringe benefits, office space) accruing to individuals. Such outcomes tend to be concrete. On the other hand, procedural justice is concerned with the procedures for determining the distribution of outcomes offered to various individuals and units. This relationship is illustrated by the solid line flowing from procedural justice to distributive justice. Finally, interactional justice addresses outcomes after the fact. That is, it involves explaining outcomes after management has decided them, as well as the procedures whereby they were determined. Thus, dotted lines show its connection to both procedural and distributive justice. These three forms of justice are outlined in greater detail in the rest of the chapter.

DISTRIBUTIVE JUSTICE

The primary focus in discussion and determination of organizational justice has centered on the outcomes experienced by either individuals or groups relative to other individuals or groups—that is, on distributive justice (Colquitt, Greenberg, and Zapata-Phelan 2005). In other words, the major focus has been, and still is, on the distribution of resources to individuals or groups. For example, employees may perceive salary increases for different individuals or groups as either just or unjust; the same is true for budget allotments to different units of a sport organization (e.g., city recreation department) and for the office space allotted to different volunteers.

Although the amount of resources received serves as the immediate catalyst of judgments about justice, arguments on the topic invariably turn to the principles underlying resource distribution. For instance, an employee of a professional sport franchise may be disappointed to receive a $500 raise when he or she expected $1,000. However, these immediate feelings of disappointment and frustration may be relieved if the employee realizes that the allocation was based on fair criteria or principles. For example, if the employee realizes that the franchise suffered a loss in the previous year and

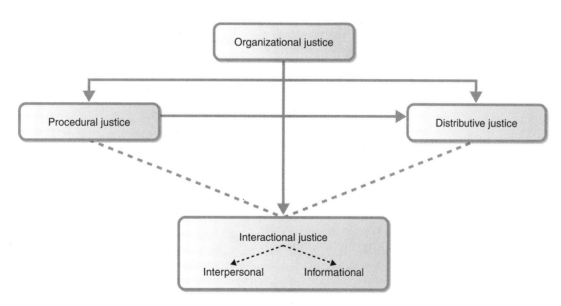

FIGURE 9.1 Relationships between procedural, distributive, and interactional forms of organizational justice.

had to cope by holding back on salary increases for all individuals, then he or she may accept the lower increase. Alternatively, the organization may have based salary increases on relative performance; in this case, if the employee accepts performance as the basis for salary distribution and recognizes that other employees performed better, then he or she may be less disturbed about the increase.

In the first scenario, everybody received an equal amount; in the second, everybody received an amount equitable to his or her performance. That is, the two scenarios involve two different principles of distribution. Three major distributive principles are available:

- Equity
- Equality
- Need

These principles and their subrules are described in table 9.1 and explored in greater detail in the following sections.

Principle of Equity

Chapter 8 presents Adams' theory of inequity, which holds that individuals perceive equity when their rewards or outcomes are comparable to those received by other persons. The chapter also notes that, in evaluating equity, individuals should con-

sider not only the rewards received but also the contributions that other persons make. In essence, the comparison should be based on what one receives relative to his or her own contribution versus what others receive in return for their contributions.

The same line of reasoning applies to the question of justice. That is, the **equity** principle of justice specifies that an organization's resources and rewards should be distributed to individuals or groups on the basis of their contributions to the organization's efforts. Thus, a university coach who compiles a consistent record of winning championships and generates positive publicity, prestige, and donations for the university is likely to be rewarded more than another coach who lags behind in these respects. Similarly, a volunteer who raises funds for a sport organization is likely to be regarded more highly than another volunteer who assists in the organization's routine affairs.

Most employees agree with the principle of equity as a basis for organizational justice—that is, the notion that organizational resources and rewards should be distributed on the basis of the contributions made by individuals or groups. This consensus is quickly shattered, however, when it comes to determining what constitutes "contributions." In the example of coaches, some argue that the quality of coaching, not the win–loss record, should be the major (or even the only) contribution considered by the organization in the distribution of

TABLE 9.1 Distributive Principles and Their Subrules

PRINCIPLE	SUBRULE	DESCRIPTION
Equity	—	Distribution of resources is based on contributions that members make to a group or organization.
	Effort	Members receive rewards on the basis of the amount of effort that they expend on their jobs.
	Ability	Members receive resources on the basis of their relative abilities.
	Performance	Performance (i.e., how well they do in their respective jobs) is the criterion for distribution of resources.
Equality	—	Resources are distributed equally to all members.
	Treatment	Equality is maintained at a particular time of resource distribution.
	Results	Equality is maintained over a period of time and over a number of distribution situations.
	Opportunity	Equality is maintained through ensuring the same opportunity for every individual to receive the resources.
Need	—	Resources are distributed on the basis of the needs of individuals or units.

Adapted from Törnblom and Jonsson 1985.

VIEWPOINT

Jordan, Gillentine, and Hunt (2004) discussed the role of distributive justice. In their study, the authors' discussed coaches as organizational managers; therefore, they proposed studying sport teams in the same manner as other business organizations. More specifically, Jordan et al. described coaching as involving a combination of two justice concepts. The first concept addresses coaches' motivation to act and make just decisions. The second concept addresses coaches' communication of these decisions to athletes in order to ensure that they are perceived as fair. The first concept is directly connected to fairness of outcomes and suggests that distributive justice is prevalent in sport, both on and off the field. This insight may be particularly relevant in the current age of technology, in which players and sport personnel can communicate their perceptions of unfair outcomes instantaneously to the world via social media.

rewards. In the case of a volunteer sport organization that exists to provide a service to the community, it can be argued that the contributions of those who are directly involved in producing that service should be regarded more highly than contributions made behind the scenes.

In discussing the inputs or contributions that organization members may bring to an equity-based distributive situation, Törnblom and Jonsson (1985, 1987) proposed three subrules of equity. According to these authors, a member's contributions may be formulated in terms of

- effort expended by the member,
- innate or achieved ability of the member, or
- performance by the member.

In the sport context, for example, an athletics director may evaluate the frequency and intensity of practice sessions for various teams and use that information as the basis for next year's budget distributions. The athletics director may also look

at the ability levels of the athletes themselves and provide more funds for teams with more athletes of high ability. In addition, he or she may consider the win–loss record of the various teams. Although all of these contributions may be used as the basis for distributing rewards, difficulty arises when different individuals emphasize different contributions in their justice judgments. Thus, most discussions of and disputes over the equity principle of distribution center not on whether contributions should serve as the basis for distribution but on how one's contribution should be defined. This issue is touched on later, in the discussion of procedural justice.

Principle of Equality

Although equity is the distributive principle used most often in organizations, some organizations use the principle of **equality**, according to which organizational resources and rewards should be distributed equally among all who are entitled to them. This distributive principle is widely supported by labor unions. In their bargaining with management over wage increases, they are most likely to emphasize that all workers should be given an equal raise in wages or salary. They can justify the claim of equality for jobs in which all workers perform similar routine tasks. For example, all workers in an assembly line perform similar jobs, and the pace of the machine controls all of them. Under those circumstances, the organization should reward everybody in the assembly line equally. This line of reasoning can be extended to all workers in an industry who are involved in similar jobs. For instance, pay raises in government bureaucracies tend to be equal for members of a particular rank.

From a different perspective, the principle of equality may be justified, and even necessary, under some circumstances. For instance, the principle of equity can be employed meaningfully only if the organization is clear about what contributions are considered in allocating rewards, can isolate each person's contribution from those of others, and can measure those contributions objectively. Consider coaches of university athletic teams. Winning competitions is considered a measure of a coach's contribution to the athletics program; accordingly, the university may reward coaches on the basis of their winning percentages. Some universities, however, prefer to evaluate their coaches on the basis of their contributions to developing leadership and citizenship qualities in their athletes. Although this is a noble contribution, the university cannot easily measure it; therefore, such universities may give equal pay raises to all coaches.

Three subrules of the principle of equality were proposed by Törnblom and Jonsson (1985, 1987). They address the following factors:

- Treatment
- Results
- Opportunity

If one applies the principle of equality of treatment, then every individual or unit receives the same amount of resources. For example, each employee of a fitness club may get the same salary increase as every other comparable employee. By the same token, the organization may allot each unit of the fitness club (e.g., aerobics and weight training) the same amount for operating expenses.

In the principle of results, the organization provides the same results for everyone in the long run, although inequalities may occur in the short run. For example, in applying this principle, the director of a recreation department may give a larger equipment budget to one of three units in one year, to another unit in the next year, and to the third unit in the third year. In this case, inequality occurs in each year, but the overall results are similar at the end of the three-year period; that is, every unit receives a similar amount in the long run.

In the case of equality of opportunity, everyone has the same possibility or chance to receive a certain amount of resources. For example, if a fitness club receives an all-paid invitation for one individual to attend a national convention of fitness leaders, how does the club owner or manager decide which leader gets to go? The principle of treatment does not apply because the trip cannot be divided among the employees; similarly, the principle of results is irrelevant because such a trip will not be available in subsequent years. One meaningful option that the club owner does have is to ask the fitness leaders to draw lots. This option, which gives each leader the same opportunity to win, illustrates equality of opportunity.

Principle of Need

The third significant principle of distributive justice holds that resources and rewards should be distributed according to the **needs** of individuals or units. In an extreme example, an organization might offer to pay increases on the basis of the number of children supported by each employee. The argument here is simple: an employee with more children needs more money with which to support them. In fact, this principle is applied by the income tax codes of many countries, which allow an individual taxpayer to claim additional exemptions for every dependent that he or she supports. Along similar lines, Rawls (1999) outlined a "difference principle," according to which a society's resources should be redistributed in order to improve the relative conditions of people who are disadvantaged. Such redistribution acknowledges and accepts that the conditions of people who are *advantaged* may be worsened.

 Distributive justice can be based on (a) the principle of equity, with resources distributed in proportion to the contributions of members or units; (b) the principle of equality, with every member or unit receiving the same amount, either at a given time or over a period of time, or having equal opportunity to receive the resource; or (c) the principle of need, with resources distributed based on the needs of individuals or units.

In an organizational context, however, personal needs cannot be used indiscriminately as criteria for the distribution of resources. Personal needs may be accommodated through mechanisms such as fringe benefits (e.g., health insurance covering families of varying sizes), but in general the needs of an individual or unit should be perceived from a performance perspective. That is, certain individuals or units may need certain resources for performing their assigned duties. Even though two teams are seen as equally significant enterprises, the distribution of resources (i.e., budgets) is differential because of the varying needs of the two teams. Similarly, the long-distance telephone budget for the marketing department tends to be higher than that for facility management because the employees in the marketing department need to make more long-distance calls to perform their duties.

Applying the Principles of Distributive Justice

In deciding which principle to apply in a particular distributive situation, one must consider the orga-

EQUITY VERSUS EQUALITY

Some authors have debated whether the equity and equality principles (including all of the subrules) are indeed different from each other. One set of authors (e.g., Deutsch 1975) claims that all of the principles are derivatives of the equity rule and that they differ only in the types of contributions considered for determining equity. For example, when someone distributes rewards equally to all members of a unit, this may constitute a use of the equity principle insofar as membership in the unit is itself viewed as the contribution. Consider the uniforms provided to all members of a team. The design and cost of the uniforms are the same for all members, who deserve them simply on the basis of team membership.

Similarly, when resources are distributed on the basis of need, the degree of need (or, conversely, of affluence) is what members bring to the situation (i.e., their contribution). For example, a coach may decide to spend a little more time with first-year athletes because they need such attention. In other words, in this case, the relative abilities and level of experience brought by different players constitute the contributions on which the coach bases his or her allocation of time. Therefore, the differential allocation of time is equitable.

On the other hand, Reis (1986) noted that empirical research supports the distinctions between the equity, equality, and need principles: "Each justice rule predicts specifically how much of what kind of input is to be associated in what way with how much of what kind of outcome" (p. 39). Ultimately, in practical terms, it is better for a practicing manager to disengage himself or herself from these arguments and consider the circumstances under which each distributive principle is most appropriate.

---

nizational values and the type of task in which the members are engaged.

Organizational Values

Meindl (1989) suggested that various organizational values may be subsumed under productivity or solidarity. For its part, productivity, along with profitability, constitutes the central concern in some organizations and in some situations. The question of which values take priority for managers is affected by increases in competition between firms due to the globalizing economy (Thibault 2009). In those circumstances, administrators and workers may opt for distributive justice based on productivity as the contribution. For instance, a sport marketing company may distribute its rewards based on the productivity of individual employees (e.g., signing up new sponsors). This type of distribution is reasonable because the company competes with other such companies for clients; therefore, the company's success depends largely on the productivity of individual employees.

In contrast, interindividual and intergroup friction between members of an organization may cause disruptions in the organization's work flow, which in turn may result in productivity losses. In such cases, the organization's goal may be to create solidarity and goodwill among members or units; therefore, the organization may prefer to distribute rewards on the basis of equality. For instance, a fitness club manager may believe that the club's fitness leaders must collaborate with each other in order to provide clients with high-quality service. Any conflicts among the leaders may translate into disruptions in the club's operation and tarnish the club's image. To address this issue, the club owner may focus on solidarity among the employees and use the principle of equality to promote it; this form of distribution may also be viewed as just by the club's staff members and operational units.

Task Type

Chapter 10 covers the nature of tasks and their attributes and notes that variations in the

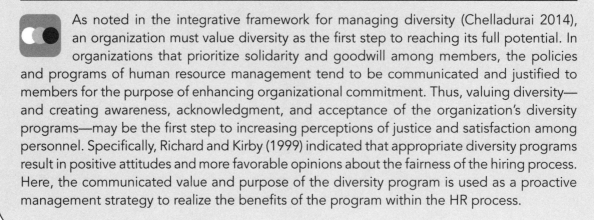

DIVERSITY MANAGEMENT OF HUMAN RESOURCES

As noted in the integrative framework for managing diversity (Chelladurai 2014), an organization must value diversity as the first step to reaching its full potential. In organizations that prioritize solidarity and goodwill among members, the policies and programs of human resource management tend to be communicated and justified to members for the purpose of enhancing organizational commitment. Thus, valuing diversity—and creating awareness, acknowledgment, and acceptance of the organization's diversity programs—may be the first step to increasing perceptions of justice and satisfaction among personnel. Specifically, Richard and Kirby (1999) indicated that appropriate diversity programs result in positive attitudes and more favorable opinions about the fairness of the hiring process. Here, the communicated value and purpose of the diversity program is used as a proactive management strategy to realize the benefits of the program within the HR process.

interdependence of tasks entail different forms of coordination. Such variations among the jobs in an organization also call for different principles of distribution. For instance, a sport marketing firm might employ various marketing experts to take care of business in various regions and might design their tasks to be appropriately independent of each other. In these circumstances, the productivity of individual employees may be used as the basis for distributing rewards; that is, the organization may use the principle of equity). On the other hand, the sport marketing firm might organize its marketing experts into project teams. In this approach, the success of a project is determined by the combined contributions of the members of a given team; therefore, the members of the team share equally in the rewards accruing to the team. In general, administrators tend to prefer the principle of equity based on performance in independent tasks and to lean more toward the principle of equality as the task becomes progressively interdependent.

The term *retribution* has been used to refer to the withdrawal of resources from members or units (Hums and Chelladurai 1994a, 1994b; Törnblom and Jonsson 1985). As an example in the context of human resource management in sport, retributive justice might be used if an employee calls in sick for a shift at the ticket booth during an international hockey championship, then attends the championship as a spectator. Specifically, the organization might assess the penalty of an unexcused absence and withhold sick-day pay for the absence.

Distributive Justice Among Athletic Teams

Researchers have investigated the notion of justice in the context of intercollegiate athletics departments. One study (Hums and Chelladurai 1994b) examined the principles of distributive justice used in allocating resources by male and female coaches and athletics administrators from all three divisions of the NCAA. Briefly, the instrument consisted of a total of 12 scenarios depicting the distribution and withdrawal of money, facilities, and support services. Each scenario was followed by a list of eight rules of distributive justice. The first three of the eight allocation principles listed under each scenario reflected equality: equality of treatment, equality of results, and equality of opportunity. The next four reflected equity based on contributions of productivity, spectator appeal, effort, and ability. The last principle was need.

Seven of these eight factors were suggested as subrules of the principles of equality (i.e., treatment, results, and opportunity), equity (i.e., performance, effort, and ability), and need (see table 9.1). The study's authors (Hums and Chelladurai 1994a) added the principle of spectator appeal because some of the sports attract a large number of spectators whereas others are not as popular. Sports that have greater spectator appeal also draw media attention and coverage. This coverage, in turn, generates a great amount of publicity and prestige for

JUSTICE PRINCIPLES IN WITHDRAWING RESOURCES

Scholars and practitioners alike often overlook the applicability of justice principles to both the situations in which certain resources are available for distribution and the situations in which certain resources need to be withdrawn from members or units. One case in point involves the modern phenomenon of cutbacks. When organizations are constrained to cut back on their expenditures, the principles (whether of equity, equality, or need) that they apply in withdrawing resources take center stage. For example, the Chancellor at UC Berkeley announced that layoffs and cuts in intercollegiate athletics were inevitable as part of sweeping changes needed to balance the institution's overall budget (Asimov 2016).

More generally, universities around the globe are searching for ways to restructure funding, and athletics departments may feel the brunt of budget cuts. Given a need to cut the budget by, say, 5 percent, one athletics department may decide to apply the equality principle and cut each team's budget by the same 5 percent. Another athletics department may apply the equity principle and take out a higher percentage from some teams and a lower percentage from other teams based on their relative contributions to the department's overall objectives. Yet another department may decide *not* to cut the budget of a particular team based on the needs principle because that team needs all of its present budget to operate at all.

the university. Spectator events also bring together students, faculty, and community members who take pride in their team. In addition, these sports generate revenue through ticket sales, sponsorships, and media coverage. Given these extraordinary contributions stemming from spectator appeal, using it as a subrule of contributions is only legitimate.

In each distributive situation, the subjects were asked to rate the justness of each of eight allocation principles and to choose one of the eight principles to implement (see figure 9.2). The results showed that all subgroups (i.e., male and female administrators and coaches) rated equality of treatment, need, and equality of results as the most just and rated the other principles as relatively unjust. The principles rated as most just were also the ones chosen most frequently for implementation.

One caveat: These results suggest only what the subjects thought *should* be the principles applied in different distributive situations; they do not necessarily reflect the principles that decision makers actually use in practice. Consider, for example, spectator appeal. The coaches and administrators in the study (Hums and Chelladurai 1994b) did not endorse this principle in any of the distributive situations. However, the annual budgets of many

university athletics departments allocate more money per capita to some sports than to other sports. This difference between perceptions of what ought to be and what actually happens might also result from other factors, such as pressure from the media and alumni.

Following the work of Hums and Chelladurai (1994a, 1994b), Mahony and Pastore (1998) analyzed the NCAA revenue and expenses reports from 1973 through 1993 and found that more money was provided to sports that generate revenue (e.g., football, men's basketball) than to other sports. The authors concluded that the distribution of resources in NCAA institutions reflected the principle of equity based on the criteria of revenue production and spectator appeal. Echoing the cautionary statements of Hums and Chelladurai (1994b), Mahony and Pastore noted that reasons for differences between the results of the two studies could be that (a) many of the respondents in the Hums and Chelladurai study were middle-level managers and therefore did not wield much power over decision making, (b) the respondents might have interpreted the concept of "need" differently, and (c) the responses might have been influenced by concern for political correctness.

The board of governors has asked the athletic department to trim its budget. How should the budget cuts be shared among teams? Listed below are several options open to athletic departments. Please indicate the extent to which each option is just or unjust by marking the appropriate number on the seven-point scale provided.

	Very unjust						Very just
1. Equal amounts should be withheld from all teams.	1	2	3	4	5	6	7
2. The teams that have received less money in the past should have the least amount cut.	1	2	3	4	5	6	7
3. The teams should be randomly selected to receive cuts.	1	2	3	4	5	6	7
4. The teams that have the best records should have the least amount cut.	1	2	3	4	5	6	7
5. The teams that draw the most spectators should have the least amount cut.	1	2	3	4	5	6	7
6. The teams that work the hardest should have the least amount cut.	1	2	3	4	5	6	7
7. The teams that have the best players should have the least amount cut.	1	2	3	4	5	6	7
8. The teams that need the money the most should have the least amount cut.	1	2	3	4	5	6	7

FIGURE 9.2 Sample case for evaluating distributive justice.

Adapted, by permission, from M.A. Hums and P. Chelladurai, 1994a, "Distributive justice in intercollegiate athletics," *Journal of Sport Management* 8(3): 194-206.

In another study, Mahony, Hums, and Riemer (2002), who employed the same methodology as Hums and Chelladurai (1994b), found that their respondents (athletics directors and athletics board chairs) rated the distribution (or redistribution) of resources based on need as the fairest among all options. Their respondents also indicated that the principle of need was most likely to be used in their respective institutions. Because these results are not consistent with the actual distribution patterns (Mahony and Pastore 1998), Mahony, Hums, and Riemer (2002) concluded, as did Hums and Chelladurai (1994b), that the respondents might have answered in what they perceived to be a socially desirable manner.

The real issue here is how one interprets the term *need*. In the studies by Hums and Chelladurai (1994b) and Mahony, Hums, and Riemer (2002), need as a justice rule refers to the sense of poverty to be alleviated, but the respondents might have interpreted it to mean "requirement." For instance, a football team with a large number of players, expensive equipment, and costly facilities would need more money than a badminton team of four players with less expensive equipment and facilities. From this perspective, if the study respondents interpreted need as a requirement, then their responses would be consistent with the actual distribution of resources in intercollegiate athletics.

Distributive Justice in Community Recreation

The notion of justice is also relevant from the perspective of clients and groups of clients. Consider, for example, the case of community recreation programs offered by local governments. These agencies must consider the justice implications of their decisions in allocating their resources to various programs and localities. This issue was addressed in studies by Wicks and Crompton (1987, 1990),

BENEVOLENCE AND JUSTICE

Trust in leadership is sometimes said to be engendered by leader characteristics of justice (i.e., fairness), benevolence, integrity, and competence. Although the distinctiveness of these four characteristics is generally accepted, confusion could arise regarding justice and benevolence. Livnat (2003) clarifies the difference between these two concepts as follows:

> Benevolence is concerned with someone's welfare. In other words, it is a reaction to someone perceived to be hurting in some way. One exhibiting benevolence would try to help the other out of concern and care for the other. Such concern and care override the reasons for the other's suffering. In contrast, justice is about people getting what is due to them from those from whom it is due [and about] . . . what exactly is due to whom, from whom, and why. (p. 507)

To be more explicit, benevolence is focused on another's needs, whereas justice is concerned with what Livnat (2003) labels as *deserts* (deserved punishment or rewards). When we act out of benevolence and attend to the needs of a person, we are not obliged to consider the needs of others. However, when we consider deserts or what one deserves, we consider the needs, efforts, and history of others in the context. That is, what one deserves is a function of what others deserve. In Livnat's words,

> While benevolence is a purely other-regarding virtue, justice is all-regarding. A benevolent act consists of a sincere attempt to do good for another person, performed out of care for the person whose good the person acting promotes. All the benevolent person has to consider, therefore, is the good of the specific other whom she attempts to help. A just person, in opposition, has to consider not only the good of the specific other person, but also the good of other members of society, including her own, and possibly also considerations of the community as a whole. (p. 508)

Another important difference between justice and benevolence involves the relevance of rationality to the two concepts.

> Justice is about fairness, and the concept of fairness seems to be linked to that of rationality. In order to be fair, we must consider the interests of all the involved individuals in an impartial manner, balancing them in a rational manner. Benevolence, however, is very much about care, and care is a matter of feeling rather than of rationality. While justice revolves around rational sharing, benevolence has to do with emotional caring. On the same grounds, a determination [of] whether we acted justly or not focuses on our actions, while a determination [of] whether we acted benevolently or not focuses on our feelings, motivation, and character. (p. 510)

who assessed the preferences of citizen groups, elected officials, and paid administrators regarding principles used in budgeting for outdoor swimming pools, neighborhood parks, and organized athletic programs. Wicks and Crompton (1987) referred to justice by the term *equity* and used the following definitions:

Equity as equality where resources are distributed equally to every individual or unit of analysis

Equity as need where resources are allocated on the basis of the needs of those who are disadvantaged (i.e., lower socioeconomic level) or where the fewest services now exist

Equity as demand where allocations are based on rates of consumption of services or on strength of claims or advocacy of citizen groups

Equity as market equity where allotments are based on user-fee or tax revenues paid by clients or on contributions to government through general taxation

Equity as efficiency reflecting the least cost of providing a service

The results of these studies (Wicks and Crompton 1987, 1990) showed that the most preferred options were equal allocation to all and allocation to areas where the fewest services existed. In creating neighborhood parks, for example, the residents (i.e., clients) preferred the "leveling-up" option (i.e., distribution of resources to areas where the fewest services existed); for athletics programs, they preferred "fees covering costs." Equally significant, the market equity models (i.e., allocations on the basis of amount of taxes paid) received little support from the residents. These results imply that the three groups of respondents (i.e., citizen groups, elected officials, and paid administrators) share both the egalitarian perspective (derived from the equality principle) and the compensatory perspective (derived from the need principle).

In a follow-up study, Wicks and Crompton (1990) investigated the relationship between perceptions of distributive justice and individual-difference factors, such as age, gender, race, education, and political preference (e.g., liberal or conservative). They found that residents' political preferences generally exerted an effect in most of the allocation situations. Those who were liberal disliked the perspective of market equity (i.e., fees covering costs) and opted for the need perspective (i.e., allocating to disadvantaged people and areas with the fewest existing services). In contrast, those who were conservative preferred allocating resources in accordance with the amount of taxes paid (i.e., market equity). This pattern of preferences mirrors the respective values held by the different groups of people.

PROCEDURAL JUSTICE

Traditionally, as noted earlier, the distribution of rewards and resources has been the primary focus of any discussion of organizational justice. However, another perspective addresses the procedures used to determine outcomes for individuals and groups

VIEWPOINT

Folger and Greenberg (1985) alerted their readers to a distinction between decision control and process control. Decision control involves the extent to which decision makers can control the outcome (i.e., decide on the outcome for each employee), whereas process control involves developing and selecting information and criteria for resolving a dispute. For instance, within process control, the manager of a sport organization may outline the criteria for a performance evaluation of subordinates and outline the information that will be gathered on the performance of individual employees on those criteria.

Process control has changed considerably over the last decade as the rise of social media has increased the amount of informal information disseminated between employees. Specifically, informal communication between employees may influence the development of information for resolving disputes. For example, a manager may provide information to candidates who have applied for jobs to indicate who has received the position. Prior to social media, this information would typically come directly from the hiring manager. However, this process control is reduced if the individual who receives the job posts about his or her excitement via Snapchat and the other candidates see the post. In this scenario, the hiring manager is inadvertently removed from the initial communication of the hiring decision. Human resource managers must recognize this shift in control.

(Folger 1987; Folger and Cropanzano 2001). Procedural justice, as it is called, refers to the degree to which the individuals affected by allocations perceive that the organization is making the allocations according to fair methods and guidelines (Niehoff and Moorman 1993). That is, individuals may perceive the organization's allocation procedures and guidelines to be either fair or unfair. As Folger and Greenberg (1985) noted, then, procedural justice refers to the *means* whereby the organization attains the various ends or content or consequences (i.e., distributive justice).

Earlier conceptions of procedural justice rested on the control (or voice) that an individual has over the relevant processes (Thibaut and Walker 1975). That is, to the extent that an individual wields some control over or provides some input into the procedures used for distributing rewards, he or she is likely to perceive the procedures as fair. Because of the negative connotations of the word *control*, theorists tend to use the word *voice*. In many organizations, individual employees may wield some influence (i.e., voice) in the determination of procedures for allocating resources. However, such participation, or voice, is not a necessary condition for one to perceive procedural justice. For example, even if a citizen did not exercise influence in the writing of tax laws, he or she may consider the laws and the procedures associated with them to be just and may abide by them.

The foregoing description of procedural justice implies that procedures are instrumental to attaining distributive justice, which is the end sought by all participants. That is, procedural justice is only an intermediary stage, whereas distributive justice is the end or bottom line. However, "reactions to a given procedure may also at times reflect an assessment of that procedure as an end-in-itself" (Folger and Greenberg 1985, p. 158). In other words, in perceptions of justice, procedures may be given weight that is equal to, if not greater than, the weight given to outcomes. For example, employees of a university campus recreation department may perceive organizational justice when the criteria for evaluating their performance and the processes of such evaluation are clear and just even though the salary increases they received were less than they expected.

A manager can take steps to ensure procedural justice, and guidelines for doing so have been provided by several authors (Folger and Greenberg 1985; Leventhal 1980). Leventhal suggested that the following six rules underlie procedural justice:

1. Consistency specifies that allocation procedures should be consistent across persons and over time.

2. Bias suppression means that decision makers should prevent personal self-interest or biases in the allocation process.

3. Accuracy means that all allocation decisions must be based on accurate information.

4. Representativeness means that the allocation process is representative of the concerns of all recipients.

5. Ethicality means that allocations must adhere to prevailing ethical and moral standards of the community.

6. Correctability envisages that decision makers may unintentionally violate one or more of the rules and err in making allocations. According to this rule, managers can modify allocation decisions and correct any errors.

 Procedural justice involves the perceived fairness of the procedures used to allocate resources to individuals or units. Individuals tend to perceive procedures as just if they are consistent, free of bias, accurate, representative of all concerned, ethical, and correctable.

INTERACTIONAL JUSTICE

The notion of interactional justice—the third component of organizational justice—addresses both the type and the manner of explanations given for the distribution of outcomes and the procedures used to do so (Bies and Shapiro 1987; Greenberg 1990; Tyler and Bies 1990). The members of an organization generally appreciate any explanation of a decision, even when the decision is not preferred by the individuals or groups in question. However, individuals and groups may evaluate as either just or unjust not only *what* is communicated about outcomes and procedures but also *how* it is communicated.

The first component, the substance of such explanations, is critical to perceptions of interactional justice. If an explanation is meager or faulty, members are unlikely to perceive justice in the process. The second component involves the manner in which the explanation is presented to people. More specifically, the key questions that underlie perceptions of interactional justice include the following: Were respect and concern shown for the individual? Were pleasantness and warmth present in the encounter? To consider an example, both aspects of interactional justice are violated when a coach yells at an athlete or team, "It's my way or the highway!" First, the coach gives no explanation for whatever decision he or she has made. Second, the coach expresses no respect for individuals or the team as a whole.

These two components of interactional justice have been conceptualized and confirmed as two distinct forms of justice, which are referred to as informational justice and interpersonal justice (Colquitt 2001; Colquitt and Greenberg 2003; Greenberg 1993). Informational justice involves the extent to which adequate information is honestly provided to explain the applied procedures and the final

outcomes. Interpersonal justice, on the other hand, involves the extent to which the individual or group is treated with dignity and respect.

Suppose you are a manager in a sport organization and that, due to financial constraints, you are forced to let one of five employees go. Your decision to release a given employee is a distributive issue; that is, you must identify which person among the five will suffer the loss. Your next concern is how to communicate your decision to the person being released. Are you really concerned with the person's plight? Do you respect him or her as a person? Are you willing to help the person find another job? And how do you communicate your genuine feelings and concerns for the individual? These aspects of your interaction with the employee affect interpersonal justice, as do your explanation for the need to release someone and the specific reasons for choosing this particular employee.

Some authors (e.g., Locke 2003) have argued that the concepts of interactional justice and its two subdimensions (i.e., interpersonal and informational justice) are subsumed by the general category of procedural justice. However, it is useful for sport managers to keep these four dimensions of justice distinct. At the same time, they should recognize that distributive justice and procedural justice are the two primary forms of justice from which the dimensions of interpersonal and informational justice emanate. This perspective helps managers identify areas in which they may fail or appear to fail.

VIEWPOINT

Kerwin, Jordan, and Turner (2015) examined the influence of distributive, procedural, interactional, and informational justice on intragroup conflict among paid staff members of regional sport commissions and convention and visitors bureaus. Informational justice is based on the degree of explanation provided to employees regarding two issues: how outcomes are distributed and what procedures are used to make decisions about distribution (Colquitt 2001; Greenberg 1993). Kerwin, Jordan, and Turner's study results suggest that as procedural, interactional, and informational justice increase, intragroup conflict decreases. Thus, the authors suggest that managers in this context of sport tourism organizations ensure that processes for making decisions are clearly articulated to paid staff and that the information is communicated in a respectful and timely manner. If managers exercise care regarding the amount and manner of information sharing, disruptive forms of disagreement may be reduced. Furthermore, if perceptions of justice remain high, the authors state that staff may feel comfortable voicing their opinions, which could result in productive forms of disagreement.

Interactional justice consists partly of the extent to which management gives a clear and correct explanation of the distribution of resources and the procedures used to determine that distribution. This aspect of interactional justice is referred to as informational justice. Another aspect—the way in which management presents such explanations (including warmth and respect for recipients of the information)—is labeled as interpersonal justice. The correction of errors in distribution or procedures is referred to as compensatory justice.

The four forms of justice described here are commonly cited in the literature; in addition, Greenberg (1987) posits compensatory justice as yet another form of justice. This form relates to situations in which either distributive or procedural justice has failed and decision makers try to compensate aggrieved parties for an injustice by rewarding them. As noted earlier, one principle of procedural justice is correctability, whereby managers provide for correcting errors that may occur in the distribution of resources. Such corrections constitute compensatory justice. Thus, affirmative actions and Title IX can be seen as processes by which to advance compensatory justice for injustices endured by minorities and women.

Distributive, procedural, and interactional justice do not occur in insolation. For example, perceptions of unfairness related to process can affect perceptions of unfairness related to outcomes. Figure 9.3 demonstrates the interconnectivity of these and other facets of justice; it also summarizes most of the material presented in this chapter as a set of rules of procedural, interactional, and distributive justice.

ROLE OF THE SPORT OR RECREATION MANAGER

Sport and recreation managers must appreciate the power of perceptions of fairness among paid staff and volunteers. As outlined in the model of motivation in chapter 8, perceptions of fairness regarding rewards are key indicators of motivation and performance. Thus, managers must be actively engaged with their personnel to communicate the substance of their decisions, how the decisions are made, and, most important, information that allows personnel to accurately view the context of decision making. For example, in deciding how to allocate the budget for the upcoming season, an athletics director must provide coaches and administrators with all information that informs the decision-making process, all relevant details of how decisions will be made (i.e., the process by which a final decision will be made), and the opportunity to voice their opinions at any stage of the process in a respectful and open-minded forum.

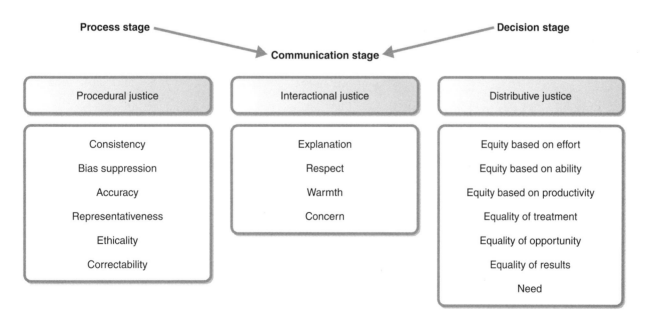

FIGURE 9.3   Guidelines for organizational justice.

PERFORMANCE APPRAISAL SYSTEMS AND PROCEDURAL JUSTICE

The rules of procedural justice are very similar to the attributes of a good performance appraisal system (as discussed in chapter 13). Unsurprisingly, then, substantive overlaps exist between performance appraisal systems and the concept of procedural justice. After all, performance appraisal is a procedure by which the organization assesses the contributions of individual employees in order to make decisions about the allocation of rewards. At the same time, major differences exist between the concepts of performance appraisal and procedural justice. Whereas organizations use performance appraisal to assess only the performances of individuals, they use procedural justice to assess the procedures of both performance appraisal and the distribution of rewards. They also use procedural justice to assess the evaluation of departmental units or groups and the allocation of resources to those units.

For instance, when the director of a city recreation department evaluates the performance of a youth sport program leader or a park or facility manager, the evaluation is properly labeled as a performance appraisal. However, if the director of the city council evaluates the contributions or usefulness of the various sport and recreation programs, or of the facilities, and then determines budget allocations for each, he or she is also addressing distributive issues. The question of whether such budget decisions were based on good information, were consistent, and were free of bias falls within the domain of procedural justice.

When personnel feel that they understand the process and that their opinions are valued, their perceptions of justice increase. This approach is essential in sport and recreation contexts where managers operate with relatively small budgets and where the outputs to be distributed may not be available to every stakeholder group. In this type of situation, distributive injustice may be inevitable; thus, it is crucial to manage perceptions of procedural, informational, and interactional justice.

Case Study

Organizational Justice

According to its mission and mandate, the nonprofit sport organization Hockey Canada (2015a) is

> the national governing body for grassroots hockey in [Canada]. The organization works in conjunction with the 13 provincial branches, the Canadian Hockey League, and Canadian Interuniversity Sport in growing the game at all levels. Hockey Canada oversees the management of programs in Canada from entry-level to high-performance teams and competitions, including world championships and the Olympic Winter Games. Hockey Canada is also Canada's voice within the International Ice Hockey Federation. Hockey Canada has offices in Calgary and Ottawa and operates regional centres in Ontario and Quebec. (n.p.)

Hockey Canada's organizational structure consists of a volunteer board of directors who work in conjunction with a paid CEO and staff members to develop policies, programs, and practices that govern hockey across the country (Hockey Canada 2015b). Within this structure, the board and CEO are responsible for allocating budget dollars to various councils (e.g., minor, female, junior, senior, hockey development) and subcommittees (e.g., governance, audit and finance, risk management, human resources, program standards, and nominating).

As CEO, you have decided to review the policy and practice of budgetary allocation to the organization's five councils. The Minor Council is responsible for all youth-level hockey programs across the country. It ensures that proper policies and procedures are in place at the national level and that they filter down to the provincial and club levels. The Junior Council oversees the governance of junior hockey programs across the country and is seen as a filter system for Olympic-level participation and professional hockey leagues. Among the remaining councils, the Senior Council is responsible for hockey programs associated with more mature hockey participants, the Female Council for all female hockey programming across the country, and the Hockey Development Council for coordinating the various councils and programs in order to ensure that participants are given the opportunity to develop their hockey participation and physical activity throughout life.

The purpose of your review is to determine how motivation and positive climate in the organization are affected by perceptions of distributive and procedural justice regarding budget allocation. For instance, does the Female Council view the dollar amounts of resource allocation to each council group as fair? Does the Junior Council perceive the processes and decisions regarding fund allocation as just? And so on.

To start the process, you begin by looking at the percentage of total Hockey Canada funds that are allocated to high-performance programs (the sector of the organization for which the councils operate). The pot for this year is estimated at $1.5 million, which means that each council would receive $300,000 if the funds were divided equally. As CEO, you are responsible for developing a plan to allocate your budgetary resources among the various council groups and reporting your allocation strategy to the board of directors. In an attempt to improve workers' perceptions of distributive and procedural justice, you review your list of potential resource distribution strategies with an eye toward choosing the best one to ensure perceptions of fairness.

Case Study Tasks

1. Choose one of the three potential distributive principles (see table 9.1) to apply in this case. Then define the relevant content of the principle and explain how it is the best choice for enhancing your workers' perceptions of distributive justice within the organization's council groups.

2. Describe your method for communicating this distribution strategy in order to improve perceptions of procedural justice.

CHAPTER PURSUITS

SUMMARY

This chapter addresses the concept of organizational justice and its components and associated rules. Insofar as the notion of justice pervades all organizational and managerial activities, managerial effectiveness ultimately depends on how well managers respect and implement organizational justice. Thus, organizational justice should be a foundational concern for all managerial practices.

As noted earlier, the principle of equity is dominant in performance-oriented organizations, where managers are justified by the organization in distributing rewards and resources in proportion to member contributions. This view is simplistic, however, because of two fundamental issues, the first of which involves the different contributions made by different members of the organization. Specifically, these different contributions must be ranked in terms of how critical they are for the organization's survival and growth. The second issue relates to how a manager evaluates an individual in terms of the contributions prioritized by the organization—for example, how members of a university event management unit are evaluated and who evaluates them (e.g., superiors, subordinates, visiting teams).

Furthermore, some sport organizations are oriented toward providing services to participants in sport and recreation; examples include city and university recreation departments and youth sport leagues. Here, the principles of equality and need are likely to be more relevant. Even when the application of the principle of equality is straightforward, the question remains of which rule of equality—treatment, results, or opportunity—should be applied in which circumstances. Similarly, if the principle of need is applied, how is need determined, and who makes that decision?

These issues plague management, and effective managers understand them and engage their members in resolving them.

The relevance of organizational justice and its principles is not limited to evaluating the performance of employees and distributing rewards based on such evaluations. To the contrary, the notion of justice impinges on almost all managerial decisions in organizations. For example, managerial decisions also relate to other forms of resources in the organization and how they are distributed to the organization's units. Consider the case of viewing a manager's time at work as a resource. Just like every one of us, an effective manager organizes his or her time and allots the available time to specific activities at scheduled intervals. So far, so good, and the notion of justice does not come into play. However, if the schedule of activities includes interactions with subordinates, the question of how much time is spent with which employee becomes a distributive issue. That is, the way in which managers distribute their time among employees or units is subject to concerns of distributive justice.

In fact, in some cases, the time that a manager spends with an employee can be seen as a reward in itself. Here is a case in point drawn from real life. The coach of a women's soccer team was invited talk to a class in human resource management. The coach was jubilant that morning. The reason? She told the class how happy she was that the former athletics director, Andy Geiger, had attended her practice session the previous evening.

The forms of resources at the disposal of a manager include budget allocations to different departments, office space allocations, allotment of travel money, and other perks. The following chapters focus on job design, staffing, leadership, performance appraisal, and reward systems. Every job in an organization constitutes a resource in itself, and how it is designed to achieve what purpose can be analyzed from a justice perspective. More important, justice evaluations also apply to how the available jobs are distributed and to whom. Justice principles apply as well to the processes of employee performance evaluation and the consequent judgments. Finally, justice and fairness assessments apply to what amounts of rewards are given and to whom.

KEY TERMS

distributive justice... 148

equality... 151

equity.. 150

interactional justice... 148

need 152

organizational justice.. 148

procedural justice 148

UNDERSTAND

1. Consider three or four types of sport organizations. Which of the principles of distributive justice is appropriate to which type of organization? Why?

2. Focusing on your university athletics department, explain the contexts in which you would prefer to apply the principles of equity, equality, and need.

INTERACT

1. Discuss a time during your time in secondary school when you believed that administrators were not just in their distribution of school resources. What principles of organizational justice were violated? How so?

2. Which principle of distribution do you prefer over the others? Why? Is that preference reflective of your value system? How so, or how not?

CHAPTER 10

Job Design

LEARNING OBJECTIVES

After reading this chapter, you will be able to

- distinguish between job simplification, job rotation, and job enlargement;
- understand the concept of job enrichment;
- explain the various attributes of jobs and their motivational properties;
- understand the concepts of interdependence among tasks and the variability of tasks;
- distinguish between standardization, planning, and mutual adjustment as methods of coordinating jobs; and
- select an appropriate method of coordinating tasks based on their interdependence and variability.

It is not uncommon to hear people say the following things about their jobs: "A job is a job is a job." "I love my job." "My job is not a great one, but it pays well." "My job is like any other, but the people I work with are absolutely wonderful." "My job is okay, but my supervisor is intolerable." For some people, a job may be interesting and satisfying, and these jobs may serve as a retreat from the worries and turmoil of the outside world. Others may perceive their job as the penalty they pay for the enjoyment of life outside the workplace.

These different reactions can be found in all kinds of jobs. That is why we have the phrases "white collar woes" and "blue collar blues." At the same time, these reactions highlight the fact that not all jobs are alike. Jobs can differ in their content (which may be, for example, either exciting or tedious) and in their context (e.g., the work group, the leader). Similarly, the rewards of task performance can be either intrinsic (e.g., the job is challenging) or extrinsic (e.g., the job pays well). These concepts

were introduced in chapter 8 in the discussion of Herzberg's (1968) two-factor theory. In this chapter, we elaborate on the nature of a job.

First, we must briefly define the concepts of job design. McShane and Von Glinow (2010) define job design as "the process of assigning tasks to a job, including the interdependencies of those tasks with other jobs" (p. 175). This definition, in turn, implies that a job is a set of tasks performed by a person.

JOB DESIGN STRATEGIES

Theorists and practicing managers have tried to modify job design to increase worker motivation and productivity. This chapter outlines four of the general procedures that have been used: **job simplification**, **job rotation**, **job enlargement**, and **job enrichment**. Because job enrichment is the superior **job design** strategy, it is addressed in more detail.

Job Simplification

Job simplification was initiated in the early part of the 20th century by industrial engineers whose intent was to make each job as simple and specialized as possible in the interest of improving efficiency. These engineers even studied the time taken for each motion in performing a task and tried to simplify those motions. These time–motion studies permitted the engineers to break down tasks into activities and specify in detail how each activity should be carried out. This approach is still found in the assembly-line operations adopted by many manufacturing firms.

In a system of specialized and simplified tasks, employees have little room to vary from specified routines. One potential advantage of job simplification is that of increased economy of operation. This increase is achieved because simplified jobs promote specialization, which, in turn, increases productivity. Another advantage is that simplified jobs can be staffed by low-skilled employees who require little training and are transferable from one job to another. Furthermore, management can easily monitor productivity in these simplified jobs.

On the other hand, several potential reactive outcomes undermine the potential advantages of job simplification. Because job simplification makes a job routine, monotonous, and boring, workers eventually begin to dislike the job; as a result, absenteeism and turnover increase. In addition, even when workers attend work, they may not put forth their best effort, and they may be prone to making mistakes. However, job simplification typically disregards psychological implications such as boredom and isolation.

Rees (1996) remarked that, too often, job design is handled through a Procrustean approach. Procrustes was a legendary figure in Greek mythology who had a special bed and was obsessive about having guests fit into it exactly. In fact, he would take drastic measures to ensure that his guests fit the bed—for example, cutting off their feet if they were too long—but showed little regard for adjusting the bed to match his guests. The moral is that jobs can be designed with little or no thought given to matching a job with an individual. This approach assumes that people can always be found who can be made to fit the job, however badly it may be designed. Although this assumption is not so widely held in modern times, managers must still make a point to assess which employee's abilities, personality, and values (as discussed in chapters 5 through 7) are consistent with simplified jobs.

Job Rotation

In order to counter the negative ramifications of job simplification, researchers have advanced two strategies (Saal and Knight 1995). The first strategy is job rotation—that is, moving workers periodically from one job to another. For example, two workers in a fitness club might alternate each week or month between the job of receiving clients and that of facility and equipment maintenance. Job rotation may have the immediate effect of offering excitement because of the novelty of the different job, location, and work group. Once the novelty wears off, however, workers may still be alienated from their jobs if each of the jobs they move into is simplified, routinized, and boring. Even so, due to the variety involved, rotating into different jobs is more motivational than performing one simplified job.

Job rotation offers another advantage in the form of training the workers: "It allows workers to become more familiar with different tasks and increases the flexibility with which they can be moved from one job to another" (Schermerhorn, Hunt, and Osborn 1997, p. 155). This flexibility is particularly significant when someone is absent (e.g., due to sickness or injury).

Job Enlargement

Another strategy for motivating workers is to enlarge their jobs. That is, instead of being locked into one specialized and routinized job (e.g., filing), a worker is asked to do more things (e.g., data entry, social media monitoring, and phone answering). In the previous example of a fitness club, the two employees may both be involved in facility and equipment maintenance as well as reception work. As in job rotation, job enlargement may have only minimal effect on workers' motivation and satisfaction as long as the added tasks are still simplified. Again, however, the opportunity to do a variety of jobs is better than doing just one simplified task.

Management may undertake job enlargement either in the belief that it will satisfy workers' needs or because the additional work is best assigned to those who do similar work (Saal and Knight 1995). Therein lies a problem. Even when managers undertake job enlargement with the good of workers in mind, workers may perceive it as a management tactic to extract more work from them. One way in which managers can counteract negative perceptions is to clearly articulate the reasons for job enlargement and to explain that the process results in a mix of tasks but not in more work. Furthermore, if the workers themselves are involved in the process of job enlargement, they are likely to better comprehend the rationale for it and accept the decision.

Job Enrichment

Recall that Herzberg's (1968) motivation–hygiene theory proposed that a job's content, rather than its context, best serves an individual's higher-order needs. In addition, the intrinsic rewards of working are derived more from the job itself than from other factors. This theory carries the practical implication that jobs need to be designed in such a way that more of the true motivators (i.e., sources of higher-order need satisfaction) are present in job performance.

According to Herzberg (1968), the issue of job meaninglessness is addressed neither by job rotation nor by job enlargement. From this perspective, these efforts either move a worker into different meaningless jobs or heap more meaningless jobs on the worker. Indeed, Herzberg viewed job rotation as substituting one zero for another and viewed job enlargement as adding one zero to another. Therefore, his concept of job design focuses instead on "vertical loading," or job enrichment. More specifically, figure 10.1 shows Herzberg's six principles for enriching jobs and their connections to the various motivators involved.

As shown in figure 10.1, the purposes of vertical loading are to

- make the worker feel responsible for the job,
- enable the worker to experience achievement and growth in a challenging job, and
- allow the worker to gain recognition (both internal and external) for a job well done.

These purposes can be achieved by allowing workers more authority to decide how they carry out assigned work, making them more responsible for their work, and providing them with fast and accurate feedback. This approach minimizes monitoring and directing by supervisors. Vertical loading of a job also involves assigning more new— and more difficult—jobs to workers. In the earlier example of the fitness club, the two workers might be allowed to decide between themselves how to fulfill the responsibilities of reception and facility and equipment maintenance.

Herzberg (1974) pointed out that an enriched job is characterized by the following features.

- *Direct feedback:* A worker should receive immediate and concrete feedback when his or her work has been evaluated. In some cases, the feedback can be built into the job itself. For example, workers in a professional sport franchise who sell season tickets get their feedback via an electronic survey as they sign up a fan.

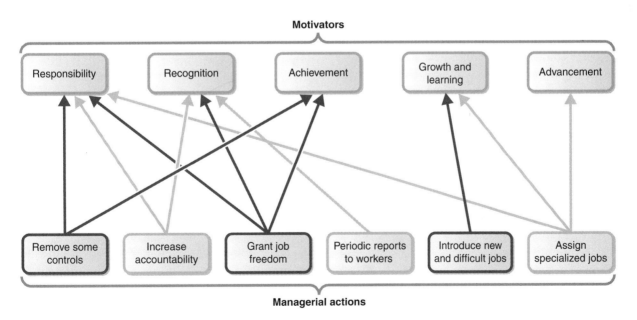

FIGURE 10.1   Principles of vertical loading.
Based on Hersberg 1987.

- *Client relationships:* Herzberg held the view that contact with clients is itself an enriching experience. As noted in chapter 1, sport management is concerned mostly with the production of services, and that process requires client participation. From this perspective, sport management jobs that involve interaction with clients, both in person and through social media, are by definition enriched. Some research (Chang and Chelladurai 2003; Osborn and Stein 2016; Smith 2001) has shown that workers view their interaction with clients as more important or more satisfying (or both) than any other aspect of their job.

- *New learning:* An enriched job provides opportunities for gaining knowledge and learning new ways of doing or managing things. For example, when a student intern in an athletics marketing department is assigned progressively more challenging jobs, the student is enabled to learn more about marketing operations.

- *Control over scheduling:* Job enrichment may also allow workers to schedule their own work. Though not possible in all cases, it can be achieved in most cases through the use of work schedules such as flextime (discussed in chapter 14). For example, this attribute is characteristic of the job of a university professor, whose major responsibilities including performing and publishing research. The university does not say when or where the research should be conducted; rather, professors set their own schedules for research work.

- *Unique expertise:* "In this day of homogenization and assembly line mentality, when everyone is judged on sameness, there exists a countervailing need for some personal uniqueness at work—for providing aspects of the job that the worker can consider as doing [his or her] own thing" (Herzberg 1974, p. 73). It is implied here that the worker will be able to bring personal ability and expertise to bear on the assigned work. For example, younger employees often come into sport and recreation organizations with distinctive abilities in technology and social media, and managers should capitalize on this expertise.

- *Control over resources:* Another feature may be the worker's control over money, material, or people. For example, the secretary of a sport management department may be permitted to handle the budget for supplies as he or she deems fit. Similarly, the marketing assistant in an athletics department may be empowered to manage interns without interference from supervisors.

- *Direct communication authority:* In an enriched job, employees are given the authority to communicate directly with those who use their outputs, or those who provide inputs to the job, or both. For instance, a manager in a city recreation department would be permitted to communicate directly with suppliers of sport equipment and community groups who have a stake in the department's affairs.

- *Personal accountability:* With all of these features built into a job, it stands to reason that the job incumbent is held personally accountable for his or her performance. For instance, a worker in the ticketing department of a professional sport franchise may redesign the way in which he or she carries out the job, including the scheduling of work hours. Such authority is accompanied by accountability for ensuring that the work does not suffer in any way.

Although job simplification ensures uniformity and efficiency of operations, it also makes jobs routine and boring. That boredom may be relieved to some extent by job rotation (i.e., moving employees from job to job) and job enlargement (i.e., assigning different simplified tasks). Job enrichment is a superior method, however, because it allows greater autonomy, responsibility, challenge, and feedback and therefore does more to ensure worker motivation and job involvement.

Hackman and Oldham's (1980) model links task attributes to the motivational aspects of a job. However, such motivational effect depends on how the worker perceives the task; therefore, the worker's perception of job attributes is more critical than the task properties themselves. As a result, two individuals who perform the same task may perceive different levels of attributes in the job and therefore be differentially motivated by it.

For instance, one aerobics instructor may perceive his or her job to be sufficiently autonomous and varied and to involve helping his or her clients get fit. Another aerobics instructor in the same organization may perceive the job to be physically tiring and repetitious because it involves performing the same routines with similar clients in class after class. In another example, one study (Chelladurai, Kuga, and O'Bryant 1999) found that male students in physical education degree programs who had some experience as volunteer coaches perceived

---

SEEKING MEANING IN SIMPLIFIED ROLES

Ferdinand Cheval was a French mail carrier who spent 33 years constructing what he called *Le Palais Idéal* ("the Ideal Palace"). He would pick up curiously shaped stones along his postal route and bring them to the construction site. The resulting palace is wildly intricate and incorporates a fantastic range of artistic and architectural styles. Photos are available online, through Wikipedia and other sources, and video tours are available on YouTube.

If Ferdinand, who was involved in such a routine job, could find a way to exploit his creativity, other workers might also find ways to use their skills and be fulfilled. After all, people work for only about 8 hours per day, which leaves 16 hours for other pursuits. One can argue that it is up to individuals to seek ways to use their skills and find a sense of achievement outside of their jobs. This argument implies that organizations and their managers need not be concerned with job enrichment in order to make work life meaningful for employees. In sport and recreation organizations, however, there are peak times where employees are in the office or on-site at events for 16 hours per day. This reality supports the argument that managers must be concerned with job enrichment that supports fulfillment for employees. Which of these arguments do you agree with? How would you justify your choice?

---

greater variety in the coaching job than did female students. The upshot here is that sport managers must be attuned not only to objective characteristics of jobs but also to workers' perceptions of those jobs. Managers also need to clarify job characteristics for their employees in order to correct any misperceptions about them.

TASK ATTRIBUTES

While the foregoing approaches are grounded in the notion that jobs affect employees, the proponents of these approaches did not effectively articulate the causal relationships between the job, the individual, and the outcome variables. That is, they did not indicate which elements of a task affect which aspects of an individual to produce positive reactions from the worker as well as increased productivity. This topic provides the focus for the remainder of the chapter.

We know that not all jobs in sport and recreation are alike. For instance, a sport lawyer's job differs from that of a public relations officer for a professional sport franchise. The job of a city recreation department director differs from that of a facility manager in the same department. And the job of a ticket clerk in a university athletics department differs from that of the ticketing operations director.

The obvious distinctions between these jobs relate partly to the domains in which they are found (e.g., sport law versus public relations) and partly to their scope of operation (e.g., management of a single facility versus management of an entire department). The jobs can also be distinguished by how variable the tasks associated with them are or how much variety they involve. For example, the employee at the ticket counter experiences less variability and less variety than employees in the other jobs cited. These concepts of variability and variety are just two of several task characteristics, or **task attributes**, that distinguish one job from another. Some of these concepts are alluded to in the discussion of consumer, professional, and human services in chapter 1 (see figure 1.1).

The effects of a task and its attributes have been studied extensively, and researchers report that task attributes affect

- an employee's motivation (Hackman and Lawler 1971; Hackman and Oldham 1980; Herzberg 1968; A.N. Turner and Lawrence 1965);
- an employee's growth, adjustment, and sense of competence (Lorsch and Morse 1974; Morse 1976);
- the effectiveness of leadership style (Fiedler 1967);

- the structure of work units (Van de Ven and Delbecq 1974); and
- the control and integration of work units (Lawrence and Lorsch 1967; Thompson 1967).

This section of the chapter describes task attributes as outlined by various authors (Hackman and Lawler 1971; Hackman and Oldham 1980; Thompson 1967; A.N. Turner and Lawrence 1965) and the processes by which they affect one's motivation. It also addresses how these attributes warrant different forms of control and coordination.

Variety

Skill variety involves "the degree to which a job requires a variety of different activities in carrying out the work . . . [and] the use of a number of different skills and talents of the person" (Hackman and Oldham 1980, p. 78). As the definition implies, variety may relate to the number of tools and controls used by a worker (i.e., object variety) or to a change in work pace, physical location, or physical operation (i.e., motor variety) (A.N. Turner and Lawrence 1965). From this perspective, a fitness club employee who leads an aerobics class, teaches tennis to juniors, and manages the accounting books experiences more variety on the job than someone who performs only one of these tasks. Even within a single sport, one could identify differences in

VIEWPOINT

The notion of a "fulfilling" job is becoming more and more complicated in today's communication- and technology-rich world. As noted by Chesley (2014), increased reliance on technology has resulted in faster-paced work, and increased home-life interruptions have resulted in greater demand to multitask and in higher levels of employee strain and distress. This collection of factors may cause employees to have difficulty in fulfilling out-of-office demands and responsibilities. Even jobs that would otherwise be considered fulfilling are vulnerable to this kind of strain and dissatisfaction if information technology is not handled appropriately.

variety, as is the case with a quarterback and a placekicker in football.

Variability

Variety is closely related to another attribute known as **task variability**. This attribute refers to the frequency of exceptional cases encountered in a job that require different methods or procedures for doing the work (Van de Ven and Delbecq 1974). For example, the jobs of coach and fitness consultant are *variable* to the extent that each client comes with different needs; therefore, the methods and procedures used to help clients are also variable. In contrast, the job of a locker room attendant is less variable because it involves merely assigning lockers and handing out towels to qualified people. Task *variability*, in contrast, relates closely to the extent to which the environment of the task provider is either stable or turbulent. For example, the environment of the fitness consultant is less stable than that of the locker room attendant because the clients' needs and the appropriate services are constantly changing. The consultant's job is also more variable to the extent that new information or technology related to those services becomes available.

Variability is also demonstrated clearly by the difference between tee ball and softball. Batters in tee ball, whose environment is stable and predictable, initiate their own movement and perform a closed skill. Softball batters also exhibit hitting ability; however, the stimulus conditions in their environment are unstable and unpredictable, and their movements are paced by the location and velocity of the ball, as well as the location of other players. In this sense, they are involved in an open skill. The extent of variability in jobs can be indicated by the terms *routine* (i.e., nonvariable) and *nonroutine* (i.e., variable).

Autonomy

Autonomy consists of "the degree to which the job provides substantial freedom, independence, and discretion to the individual in scheduling the work and in determining the procedures to be used in carrying it out" (Hackman and Oldham 1980, p. 79). For example, a basketball coach enjoys considerable autonomy in recruiting players and in choosing training methods and competitive strategies (Chelladurai and Kuga 1996). The marketing director of a university athletics department may enjoy autonomy in terms of making contacts, deciding the manner and substance of communications, and approving final transactions. In contrast, the clerks in the ticket office or the accounting office may lack such autonomy insofar as others specify the tasks they need to do, how they should carry out those tasks, and when they do the tasks (i.e., their hours of work). Even in blue-collar jobs, however, autonomy may be reflected in the worker's freedom to choose which materials and tools to use and what sequence to follow in carrying out various activities (A.N. Turner and Lawrence 1965). For example, a caretaker at a fitness club may enjoy considerable autonomy in carrying out tasks and deciding what materials to use.

Task Identity

Task identity consists of "the degree to which a job requires completion of a 'whole' and identifiable piece of work; that is, doing a job from beginning to end with a visible outcome" (Hackman and Oldham 1980, p. 78). From this perspective, Hackman and Oldham suggested that a social worker who manages all of a client's needs generally finds the job more meaningful than does a worker who manages only one problem. According to this view, a person who evaluates a client's fitness level, prescribes an exercise regimen, and leads and supervises the exercise session perceives the job of rehabilitating the client as his or her own (i.e., experiences high task identity) and therefore finds it more meaningful than does a person who performs only one of the tasks. As another example,

> High task identity would be available to high school coaches. They develop the athletic potential of the few students who report for the team. This development is easily identified and attributed to the coach, who is usually the sole individual responsible for that task. In contrast, classroom teachers cannot easily identify their end product or their personal contributions to that end product. (Chelladurai 1985, pp. 120-121)

Consider clients in various sports. Obviously, people engaged in individual sports (e.g., tennis, wrestling) experience task identity to a greater extent than do those engaged in team sports. Indeed, team sport participants cannot do "a whole piece of work." Some team members may be involved in initiating a task, others may be involved in completing it, and still others may be involved peripherally with pursuit of the group's main objective.

Job Feedback

Job feedback involves "the degree to which carrying out the work activities provides the individual with direct and clear information about the effectiveness of his or her performance" (Hackman and Oldham 1980, p. 80). That is, this type of feedback emanates from performance of the job itself; thus job feedback differs from the feedback provided by other agents, such as a supervisor or client. For example, a sport marketer may experience a "gut feeling" that a presentation he or she just finished went well (or poorly). Facility managers may get positive feedback from athletes and coaches (e.g., on the quality of the field of play) as they ready a facility for a competition. The contrast between feedback from the job and from others is also illustrated when a basketball player gets immediate and positive feedback as a shot goes through the net. These instances of feedback are inherent in the tasks performed (albeit the shooter's coach may point out that the shooting movement was improper or that the shot should not have been attempted in the first place).

Task Significance

The significance of a task reflects

> the degree to which a job has a substantial impact on the lives of other people, whether those people are in the immediate organization or in the world at large. . . . When we know that what we do in our work will affect someone else's happiness, health, or safety, we care about that work more than if the work is largely irrelevant to the lives and well-being of other people. (Hackman and Oldham 1980, p. 79)

For example, an exercise leader's work with cardiac patients is likely to be perceived as more significant than similar work with healthy young adults. Similarly, the job of a coach in youth sport is accorded greater significance than the job of a custodian in charge of the sport facility because the coach exerts a direct influence on the clients and their welfare.

Interaction

A.N. Turner and Lawrence (1965) stipulated two levels of interaction in a job: required and optional. Required interaction is the degree of interaction prescribed to facilitate more efficient operation; this attribute has also been referred to

MOTIVATION IN INTERNSHIP EXPERIENCE

Most students who read this text will be expected to participate in an internship experience as part of their degree program. Internships can be boring if they involve only routine and simplified tasks, but most interns find their internship to be a valuable learning experience. One of our students, Cameron Hughes, wrote the following on this topic.

Throughout my career in the sport management industry, I have worked for various kinds of companies and organizations. The common theme of these positive experiences is that the key to any successful business is positive reinforcement and communication.

Before I had even submitted my first internship application, I was told, "The internship program is about getting your foot in the door and applying the skills you have learned to help a company grow." I was instructed to do research in order to find a company where I would be able to demonstrate my best skills and leave a lasting impact. In order to get the most out of my internship experience, I needed to intern with a company that would keep me actively engaged with relevant tasks.

My internship at Cosmos Sports (a sport marketing firm in Mississauga, Ontario) has been a catalytic factor in helping me sharpen sport management skills that I will use for the rest of my life, regardless of where my career takes me. Through the course of my four-month tenure, each intern in the company was assigned to a specific account or client. My assignment involved working primarily with the University of Toronto to create a strategic business assessment of the Intercollegiate and High Performance Program. As part of this work, I was directly involved in drafting ideas and contributing to the final business plan.

I started my internship at Cosmos Sports ready for anything and everything. I was hired for the position of account executive knowing that I would have a broad range of roles and responsibilities. Because Cosmos engages in all aspects of sport, from

---

as interdependence and as "dealing with others." Consider, for example, the number and types of people with whom an event manager must interact in staging a football game at a large university: city police, university security officials, the media, the athletics director and other superiors, and the personnel in the event department. In other examples, coaches and assistant coaches, as well as exercise physiologists and exercise leaders, must interact with each other in assisting their clients (i.e., athletes and cardiac patients, respectively).

Optional interaction, on the other hand, is not required by the job but takes place at the discretion of the worker. For example, an accounting clerk in an athletics department does not have to interact with others in performing the job. However, the clerk may still have the opportunity to interact with other employees and form friendships at his or her discretion. Similarly, a locker room attendant has the opportunity to discuss the weather or gardening with customers as they exchange their towels.

Strategic Position

Strategic position is determined by the importance of a specific job in terms of the larger group's overall accomplishment (A.N. Turner and Lawrence 1965). The total group's performance may rely heavily on the performance of specific positions. For example, the performance of a baseball pitcher is more crucial to the team's success than is the performance of any other position on the team. The same is true of

consulting to ticketing to branding, I quickly learned that my role encompassed many subjects—report writing, strategic business planning, interpersonal sales, event management, and more. I got to work in all aspects of the sport industry while also sharpening my oral and written communication skills. In fact, as an intern in a busy company, I got to do more than I ever thought I would be able to do. Even as the company guided me, it allowed me to work independently on major projects. Through Cosmos, I have taken part in hiring, client meetings, independent contacts on behalf of the company, and document writing. I have also been welcomed to help out in any area of business where I see fit to contribute.

Another outstanding aspect of the Cosmos Sports internship is the organization's work culture. Cosmos gives credit where it is due and recognizes the hard work and achievements of its employees through an employee-of-the-week program. This approach keeps interns motivated and interested in their work because everyone knows that hard work really pays off. Although there is a hierarchy of employees, no one is perceived to be ahead of anyone in the office. Everyone's ideas are welcomed and encouraged throughout the organization. Similarly, one of the best practices at Cosmos is that everyone answers the phones, regardless of position. Though this was intimidating at the beginning of my tenure, the ability to pick up a phone and be comfortable speaking to whoever is on the other end in a professional and positive manner is a skill that I will take with me wherever I go.

The mentality that "hard work pays off" extends far beyond the day-to-day or even week-to-week aspect of Cosmos. The organization makes a point of hiring internally, from their intern staff on up; in fact, most of the full-time employees started their jobs at Cosmos as interns. This approach promotes hard work and professionalism from the first day and fosters the idea that if a person demonstrates good qualities, then he or she will be rewarded.

a football quarterback and a hockey goalkeeper. In the organizational context, strategic positions are frequently administrative positions; however, some jobs gain a measure of strategic importance simply because they are at the center of activity. For example, the secretary for the general manager of a professional sport team occupies a strategic position to the extent that he or she serves as a conduit for confidential information and as a buffer between the manager and the coaches, athletes, and media.

Risk of Injury

Some jobs (e.g., electrician, welder, construction worker) carry a significant risk of injury. In athletics, contact sports such as football, hockey, and boxing involve greater risk of injury than do other sports. Even in other physical activities, however, the danger of some form of injury is always present; for example, aerobics instructors and their clients are susceptible to injury due to the nature of their activities. Therefore, sport managers are burdened with additional concerns about the safety of their employees and clients. To minimize injury risk in their operations, sport managers must keep pace with technological advances in securing the safety and health of workers and clients. These concerns stem not only from the humanistic perspective (i.e., concern for employees and clients) but also from the legal perspective (i.e., concern for the organization and manager).

RACE AND STRATEGIC POSITION IN AMERICAN FOOTBALL

Over the years, scholars (e.g., DeSensi 1995; Lapchick 1991; Loy and McElvogue 1970) have described and often deplored the practice of "stacking" in professional football. The term *stacking* refers to staffing a team's playing positions differentially by race. Research showed that black players were disproportionately represented in noncentral positions (e.g., corner-back, running back, wide receiver) while white players tended to occupy more central positions (i.e., quarterback, center, lineman, linebacker). Stacking was said to involve the process of excluding African American players from central positions and putting them in noncentral positions (a form of discrimination, according to some authors). Note that *central* in this case refers to positions at the center of the configuration of all players at the time of the snap (i.e., geographic centrality).

Chelladurai (2005) disputed the argument that stacking was a manifestation of discrimination. Citing Chelladurai and Carron (1977), he argued that

> geographical centrality in football does not parallel the functional centrality of the game itself. In football, it is the running backs and wide receivers that are engaged in advancing the ball for a touchdown. Thus, these positions are central to the functions of the offensive unit. Although the quarterback is the most central position both geographically and functionally, all actions initiated by the quarterback have to be completed by one of the geographically noncentral but functionally central positions. The other positions jointly play only a supporting role. Thus, the assertion that there is discrimination against black players in football cannot be sustained by these data. In fact, it can be argued that it is whites who are precluded from the functionally central positions. (p. 409)

In the present context, then, the geographically *noncentral* positions in football are indeed strategically *central* positions.

 Jobs can be differentiated on the basis of specific attributes associated with them. The more significant attributes are variety, variability, autonomy, task identity, job feedback, task significance, interaction, strategic position, and risk of injury. In analyzing jobs, managers must attend to these attributes first, then consider other job factors.

MOTIVATIONAL PROPERTIES OF TASKS

From a practical standpoint, the analysis of tasks and their attributes should lead to

- better description of jobs,
- more effective recruitment of personnel with requisite ability to perform a given job,
- better employee motivation on the job, and
- better coordination of jobs.

Job description and recruitment are covered in chapter 11. Here, we explore the process by which the task itself affects employee motivation (i.e., the **motivational properties** of the task) and how the differences between tasks warrant different forms of mechanisms for **coordination**.

Among studies of the effects of jobs on employee attitudes, satisfaction, and productivity, the work of Hackman and associates (Hackman and Lawler 1971; Hackman and Oldham 1976, 1980) is the most comprehensive and useful for our purposes. Figure 10.2 illustrates their job characteristics model of motivation.

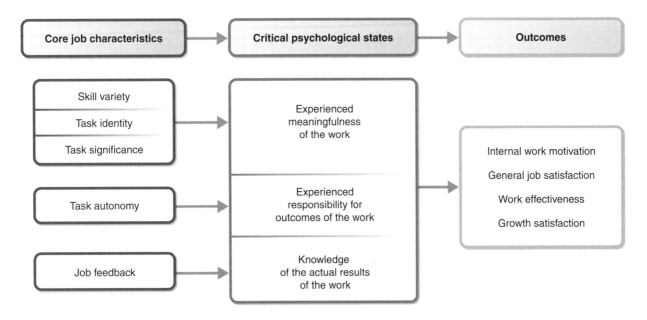

FIGURE 10.2   Hackman and Oldham's job characteristics model of motivation.

From Hackman J.R. Oldham, G.R. WORK REDESIGN © 1980 by Addison-Wesley Publishing Co., Inc. Reprinted by permission of Pearson Education, Inc., Upper Saddle River, NJ.

According to this model, certain job characteristics enhance the **psychological states** of workers: experienced meaningfulness of the work, experienced responsibility, and knowledge of results. In fact, these psychological states represent the intrinsic rewards of performing the job and are therefore instrumental to enhanced internal motivation, job satisfaction, work effectiveness, and personal growth satisfaction. As shown in figure 10.2, Hackman and Oldham's theory supposes that these psychological states can be cultivated by designing jobs to include the significant characteristics (described earlier) of skill variety, task identity, task significance, task autonomy, and job feedback. The authors considered these characteristics to be the core characteristics of a job.

Experienced Meaningfulness and Task Attributes

Experienced meaningfulness in work enhances an individual's motivation, performance, and satisfaction. That is, "the person must experience the work as meaningful, as something that 'counts' in one's system of values" (Hackman and Oldham 1980, p. 73). According to Hackman and Oldham's model, the meaningfulness of a job as the worker experiences it is enhanced by the attributes of skill variety, task identity, and task significance. However, these general relationships are subject to some qualifications. For instance, if skill variety is to be related to job meaningfulness, that variety must both use the member's skills and talents and develop them further.

Regarding task significance, a distinction exists between the significance experienced by an employee personally and the significance attached to a job by other, external agents (Chelladurai 1985). For example, a fitness instructor may perceive his or her job to be significant insofar as it contributes to the fitness and health of clients. However, the lay public, and perhaps even the owners and managers of the club, may believe that the instructor is simply "bouncing around." If external agents attach low significance to the domain, then the fitness instructor may be unable to maintain the personal conviction that the job is significant. This same issue arises when comparing the jobs of coach and physical education teacher. Although the individuals may perceive significance in either or both of these two jobs, the relative significance of the two jobs is likely to be distorted by administrators, the media, and the community. That is, the coaching job is likely to be treated as more significant than the teaching job (Chelladurai and Kuga 1996).

Finally, although each of the three characteristics—skill variety, task identity, and task significance—contributes to the experienced meaningfulness of a task, they need not all be present in order for a job to be meaningful.

For instance, welders working on a large bridge could find their job very meaningful because it contributed to the safety of the bridge, and, consequently, to the safety of the public. Nonetheless, the job would rank very low in terms of skill variety and/or task identity. Similarly, an individual who welds a wrought iron fence might find the task meaningful because all of the work, when finished, would represent a personal accomplishment. (Chelladurai 1985, p. 121)

For another example from the field of sport management, consider the task of individuals who carry an injured athlete off the field. The task itself is devoid of any variety or variability. However, it is highly significant from the perspective of those carrying out the task because their primary concern is the safety and welfare of the athlete.

Experienced Responsibility and Job Autonomy

Internal work motivation can also be enhanced by the perception of personal responsibility—that is, the individual's feeling that he or she is largely responsible for the successful completion of a task.

If personal responsibility is reduced, then internal motivation is likely to be affected negatively.

The only task attribute directly related to experienced responsibility is autonomy. For someone to feel personally responsible and accountable in a job situation, the person must be allowed considerable freedom to decide on processes for carrying out the assigned job. Therefore, to the extent that the job activities are governed by rules and regulations, the person would not feel that he or she is personally responsible for the job. As noted earlier, considerable autonomy is enjoyed by the coach of a sport team; therefore, the individual may feel a strong sense of responsibility for the outcome of his or her coaching.

Knowledge of Results and Job Feedback

Knowledge of results is necessary in order to realize how well a job has been done and to experience feelings of either satisfaction or dissatisfaction. Furthermore, knowledge of results serves to enable an individual to modify one's efforts to match job requirements. This knowledge may also help an individual shape his or her performance aspirations to match job requirements. As noted earlier,

VIEWPOINT

In illustrating the significance of all three psychological states (i.e., experienced meaningfulness of the work, experienced responsibility, and knowledge of results), Hackman and Oldham (1980) cited the example of golfing:

Knowledge of results is direct and immediate; the player hits the ball and sees at once where it goes. . . . Experienced personal responsibility for the outcome also is clear and high, despite the tendency of the golfers sometimes to claim that the slice was due to someone whispering behind the tee. . . . Experienced meaningfulness also is high, despite the fact that the task itself is mostly devoid of cosmic significance. . . . So, in golf, the three psychological states are present, and internal motivation among regular golfers is usually quite high. Indeed, golfers exhibit an intensity of behavior that is rarely seen in the workplace; getting up before dawn to be first on the tee, feeling jubilation or despair all day depending on how well the morning round was played, sometimes even destroying the tools and equipment—not out of boredom or frustration with the work (as is sometimes seen in the industrial setting) but rather from anger at oneself for not playing better. (pp. 74-75)

job feedback must be distinguished from feedback provided by other people (e.g., supervisors). Although both kinds of job feedback can be motivational, the Hackman and Oldham (1980) model emphasizes the feedback mechanisms inherent in the job itself.

In summary, let us review the key features of experienced job meaningfulness, experienced job responsibility, and knowledge of results. Job meaningfulness is enhanced by the job characteristics of skill variety, task identity, and task significance. The perception of responsibility for work outcomes is enhanced by autonomy to decide the manner in which effort is expended. And knowledge of the results of one's work activities is provided by feedback from the job itself. While the preceding attributes affect motivation individually, they also exert more complex joint effects, which, according to Hackman and Oldham (1980), form the motivating potential of a job. These authors even advanced the following formula to assess the motivating potential of a job:

$$MPS = \frac{Skill\ Variety + Task\ Identity + Task\ Significance}{3} \times Autonomy \times Feedback$$

As noted earlier, a task's deficiency in one of the attributes of skill variety, task identity, and task significance can be offset by higher levels of the other two attributes. This effect is reflected in the formula by averaging the effects of the three attributes. In contrast, the effects of autonomy and feedback are multiplicative, meaning that the lower the score on either, the lower the total motivating potential.

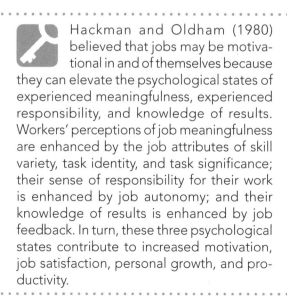

Hackman and Oldham (1980) believed that jobs may be motivational in and of themselves because they can elevate the psychological states of experienced meaningfulness, experienced responsibility, and knowledge of results. Workers' perceptions of job meaningfulness are enhanced by the job attributes of skill variety, task identity, and task significance; their sense of responsibility for their work is enhanced by job autonomy; and their knowledge of results is enhanced by job feedback. In turn, these three psychological states contribute to increased motivation, job satisfaction, personal growth, and productivity.

Outcomes

The outcomes outlined in Hackman and Oldham's (1980) model are

- internal work motivation,
- general job satisfaction,
- work effectiveness, and
- growth satisfaction.

Two of these outcomes are critical to the organization, and the other two are critical to the individual. Work effectiveness, which is a function of high internal work motivation, is necessary for the survival and growth of the organization. However, the individual also needs to be personally satisfied with the work and the context in which it takes place. One's feelings and attitudes toward one's job are referred to generally as job satisfaction, which is covered in detail in chapter 16. In addition to being satisfied with the job, the worker must also feel that his or her experiences in the workplace contribute to personal growth.

IMPLEMENTING TASK ATTRIBUTES

Hackman, Oldham, Janson, and Purdy (1975) advanced five implementing concepts for enriching jobs. Figure 10.3 shows the linkage between these implementing concepts and the five task attributes of Hackman and Oldham's model (shown in figure 10.2).

1. *Combining tasks:* To implement this concept, several pieces of fractionated work are put together to form new and larger modules of work. Thus, instead of several employees putting together a product, such as on an assembly line, each employee may assemble a whole unit. Combining tasks in this manner enhances both task identity and skill variety. For instance, a clerk in a city recreation department may be assigned the task of receiving applications for a youth sport program organized by the department. Another clerk may be assigned the task of scrutinizing these applications and placing them in appropriate categories (e.g., by age or locality). A third clerk may be asked to contact the applicants to let them know the status of their applications. With a view to combining these tasks, the supervisor may ask each individual clerk to handle all three phases of the process for a certain number of applications.

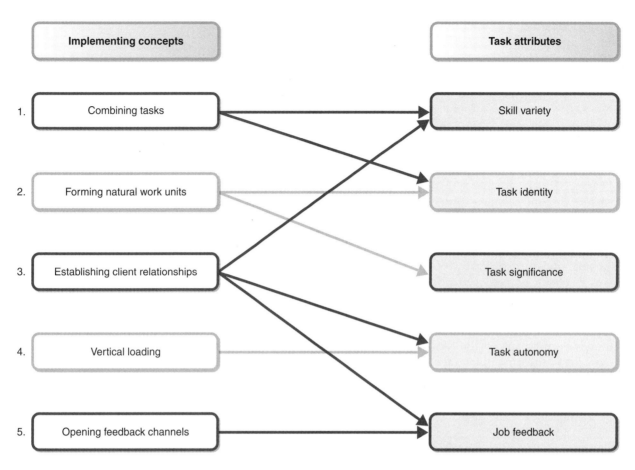

FIGURE 10.3 Implementing concepts and task attributes.
Based on Hackman et al., 1975.

2. *Forming natural work units:* This concept emphasizes the fact that a work unit offers a sense of job ownership—that is, "a sense of continuing responsibility for an identifiable body of work" (Hackman et al. 1975, p. 63). For example, when sport management research colleagues collaborate on a paper, they may use Google Docs to make simultaneous edits on their manuscript. As noted by Hackman et al., this notion of a natural work unit may enhance task identity and task significance.

3. *Establishing client relationships:* Hackman and colleagues (1975) argued that by allowing workers direct contact with their clients, managers can gain three advantages. First, clients' reactions enhance the feedback inherent in a job. Second, skill variety increases because the employee must use interpersonal skills, including communication skills. Third, the worker enjoys greater autonomy because he or she manages the client interactions without direction from external sources.

4. *Vertical loading:* Like Herzberg (1968), Hackman and colleagues (1975) suggested that an employee must be allowed not only to do the job but also to control it. Control depends on the extent of a worker's discretion in performing a task (e.g., choice of methods, scheduling of activities, problem solving, and financial control). The suggestion that an individual must be given more control over his or her own job is a major component of job enrichment (see figure 10.1). Assigning job control to the worker (i.e., vertical loading) contributes to the worker's feelings of autonomy.

5. *Opening feedback channels:* In the view of Hackman and colleagues (1975), management must remove the obstacles that block feedback to the worker. They argue that having quality control performed by another individual or unit at another place and time denies the worker immediate feedback. If, instead, management involves the worker in the quality check, then the worker gets immediate feedback. The results of a performance evaluation should not be merely filed or sent upward to higher-level management; rather, they should be shared immediately with the employee. This practice increases task feedback and lets workers know immediately how well they have performed. In addition, if they have made errors, it is better for them to correct the mistakes immediately than to continue making them.

Managers can increase the motivating potential of a job by combining various jobs in order to create natural work units, allowing employees to make direct contact with clients, increasing workers' control over their jobs, and opening feedback channels. Whether these actions produce the desired effects depends on workers' knowledge and skill level, their need to grow, and their satisfaction with other contextual factors, such as salary and safety.

VIEWPOINT

In an attempt to explain the tendency of school physical education teachers to be more inclined toward coaching than teaching, one study (Chelladurai and Kuga 1996) analyzed the tasks of teaching physical education and coaching a sport. The study examined Hackman and Oldham's (1980) five task attributes, as well as five other attributes that set coaching apart from teaching: group size, homogeneity in members' ability, group acceptance of goals, duration of contact, and member motivation to participate. The researchers suggested that differences in these task attributes may make coaching more amenable to influence by the leader (i.e., coach) and therefore more motivational than teaching.

TASK ATTRIBUTES AND INDIVIDUAL DIFFERENCES

Perhaps the most significant contribution by Hackman and Oldham (1976, 1980) lies in their view of the relationship between job characteristics on the one hand and internal motivation, satisfaction, and performance on the other hand. Specifically, they posited that this relationship depends on the individual's knowledge, skills, growth-need strength (i.e., level of need for personal accomplishment, learning, and growth), and satisfaction with other organizational factors. For example, a job with high motivating potential may still be frustrating to an individual if he or she lacks the required knowledge and skill (i.e., competency) to perform the task. Similarly, a task may lose its motivating potential if the person has low growth-need strength. The third individual-difference factor is the individual's satisfaction with other organizational features, such as pay and job security; great dissatisfaction with such factors may overwhelm a job's potential to motivate the individual.

From an overview perspective, Hackman and Oldham's (1980) job characteristics model extends the content theories referred to in chapter 8 by highlighting the nature of the job and the motivating potential of various job characteristics. It also modifies the content theories by emphasizing the individual differences that can affect an individual's reaction to a job and its characteristics.

Although the job characteristics model is intuitively appealing and conceptually elegant, research results have not yielded consistent support for it (Saal and Knight 1995). In some studies, the distinctions made between the five job attributes do not appear. In some others, the relationships between job attributes, individual differences, and outcome measures do not accord with the specifications of the model. More recently, however, DeVaro, Li, and Brookshire (2007) analyzed representative data from Britain and found support for the predictions of the job characteristics model. In addition, in the context of sport management, Cleave (1993) applied the model to administrators of university athletics, recreational sport, and physical education programs in Canada and Illinois. The results of her study supported most of Hackman and Oldham's (1980) propositions. In a notable exception, the job characteristic of autonomy exerted a direct effect on outcome variables independent of the psychological states.

Theoretical models developed in other fields can provide useful frameworks for understanding phenomena in sport management. However, researchers and others should not simply assume that such models can be transferred directly. To enhance the understanding of the field of sport management, not only must research be based on theoretical models, but these models must be tested within the field. (Cleave 1993, p. 241)

Researchers generally agree that this issue is related more closely to problems in measurement and analyses than to the model itself (Saal and Knight 1995). Despite some of the negative results, the model can serve as a basis for redesigning jobs in sport organizations to match the needs, desires, and skills of both paid and volunteer workers.

Remember that a job is not limited to the five attributes included in Hackman and Oldham's (1980) model. Workers can also be affected by required and optional interactions, risk of injury, and psychomotor aspects of the job. For instance, E.F. Stone and Gueutal (1985) identified three dimensions of jobs that their subjects perceived. The first factor is complexity, which incorporates all five task attributes outlined by Hackman and Oldham (1980). The second factor, serving the public, involves interacting with and serving people outside of the organization. The third factor is physical demand, which refers to the strength and physical activity required in order to perform the task, as well as any entailed hazards to health.

As noted in chapters 2 and 3, a strong sense of service to others characterizes both professional and volunteer workers in sport management; therefore, they experience a great sense of meaningfulness in their jobs. Thus, E.F. Stone and Gueutal's (1985) dimension of serving the public is meaningful in the context of sport management. In addition, many workers in sport management, particularly in participant services, are engaged in physically demanding jobs—for example, coaching and fitness instruction. As is evident, then, Stone and Gueutal's dimension of physical demand also applies to sport management. In the final analysis, both Hackman and Oldham's (1980) job characteristics model and Stone and Gueutal's three-dimensional scheme are applicable to the context of sport and recreation management.

OTHER APPROACHES TO JOB DESIGN

Our discussion of job design has focused largely on the psychological effects of task attributes on employee motivation. However, job design can also be approached from other perspectives, such as those of safety, stress, and health. As noted earlier, although they are not linked directly to worker motivation, attributes such as risk of injury and physical demand are critical. Campion and Thayer (1985) summarized these differing perspectives on job design. Reviewing the perspectives of different disciplines, they isolated four approaches to designing jobs: motivational, mechanistic, biological, and perceptual or motor. These four dimensions, and the expected job outcomes of each approach, are outlined in table 10.1.

APPLYING JOB DESIGN TO VOLUNTEER WORKERS

The job design approaches of job simplification, job rotation, job enlargement, and job enrichment are equally applicable to volunteer and paid workers. The focus in these discussions is on how to make the job itself motivating without reference to whether one is paid for it. For instance, a volunteer association running a soccer league may simplify the task of sending out notices to interested parties by breaking it into simpler units of typing letters, writing addresses on envelopes, and stuffing the envelopes. The association can assign these simplified units to individual volunteers. In contrast, job rotation might mean that volunteers take turns typing, writing, and stuffing. Job enlargement, on the other hand, would involve each volunteer in performing all three tasks. Finally, job enrichment would require managers to assign more difficult and challenging jobs to the volunteers. For example, volunteers who sent out information might also be asked to form teams from individual clients, categorize teams based on specific criteria (e.g., age, skill), or draw up a competition schedule.

TECHNOLOGY IN HUMAN RESOURCE MANAGEMENT

Job design must also consider the role of technology in a job. In particular, sport and recreation managers need to explicitly outline the utility of social media in any given job. From the perspective of human resource management, some workers indicate that they use social networking technology out of habit for nonwork purposes (Giannakos, Chorianopoulos, Giotopoulos, and Vlamos 2012), which may distract them from work-related tasks. This potential distraction emphasizes the need to recognize, harness, and manage the use of technology in sport and recreation organizations. If managed appropriately through job design, this technology can be used to enhance work efficiencies. If unmanaged or poorly managed, however, social media technology (which is a reality for all industries) can act as a distraction and reduce productivity.

TABLE 10.1   Campion and Thayer's Task-Design Approaches and Outcome Clusters

JOB DESIGN APPROACH	JOB OUTCOMES
Motivational • Job enlargement • Job enrichment • Vertical loading	Satisfaction • More intrinsic work motivation • More job involvement • More job satisfaction
Mechanistic • Work simplification • Work routinization • Work specialization	Efficiency • More efficient resource use • Less idle time • Less training time required
Biological • Physical well-being • Seating and tool design • Noise, climate, and stress	Comfort • Increased comfort • Less physical fatigue • Fewer health problems
Perceptual • Information processing • Memory requirements • Visual and auditory skills	Reliability • Improved safety • Increased system reliability • Reduced accident rates

The motivational approach is exemplified by the works of Herzberg (1968) and Hackman and Oldham (1980). It is based largely on the discipline of organizational psychology and emphasizes job enlargement and job enrichment. The mechanistic approach is drawn from classic scientific-management and time–motion studies and from industrial engineering. It advocates work simplification, specialization, and routinization. The biological approach is based on work physiology, biomechanics, and anthropometry; it focuses on the physical well-being of the worker in executing assigned tasks. Finally, the perceptual, or motor, approach is aimed at creating "person–machine fit by attending to people's perceptual/motor capabilities and limitations, thus preventing errors and accidents and reducing boredom and task aversion" (Campion and Thayer 1985, p. 33). The principles of this approach are drawn from experimental psychology.

In addition to outlining the four approaches to task design, Campion and Thayer (1985) isolated four sets of outcomes from among many that organizations seek. They labeled these four outcome groups as satisfaction, efficiency, comfort, and reliability (see table 10.1). Satisfaction involves workers' internal work motivation, involvement in their jobs, and satisfaction with their jobs. Efficiency relates to maximal use of people and machines (i.e., minimal idle time) and less training time for the job. Comfort has to do with physical well-being and includes lack of physical fatigue, lack of back problems, and lack of muscle strain. Reliability involves the safety of the worker in terms of the reliability of the worker–machine system, which is measured by factors such as accident and injury rates. One serious concern in sport management is that of ensuring the safety of both workers and clients. This concern is particularly salient when people engage in risky activities and use machines and tools to deliver services.

Campion and Thayer (1985) noted the logical correspondence between these four sets of outcomes and the four task-design approaches outlined earlier. Their research confirmed that each approach was more highly related to one of the four sets of outcomes than to the other three outcomes. These relationships are shown in table 10.1.

Campion and Thayer's (1985) description of four approaches to job design should not be viewed as merely a theoretical exercise. To the contrary, each of these approaches is relevant to sport and recreation management. The motivational approach suggests that we enrich the jobs found in sport and recreation (e.g., those of clerks and receptionists). Such job enrichment should be considered in conjunction with member potential and preferences. The mechanistic approach to job simplification and routinization may also prove to be beneficial to the extent that resources are better used and work processes are made more efficient (e.g., ticketing operations in an athletics department). In fact, some sport volunteers may prefer such simplified assignments because of their involvement with highly enriched jobs elsewhere.

The importance of attending to the biological and perceptual-motor approaches to job design is illustrated by the fact that some of the recommendations emanating from those approaches are mandated by law. For instance, temperatures in the workplace cannot vary beyond specified limits, and seating and lighting arrangements may also be regulated. Similarly, among athletes, concerns regarding appropriate footwear, helmets, and other protective equipment derive partly from the need for performance improvement and partly from the need for athlete safety. In either case, they fall under the biological and perceptual-motor approaches.

TASK DEPENDENCE, COORDINATION, AND VARIABILITY

The nature of a job affects not only worker motivation but also other managerial aspects. This section addresses the concept of **task dependence** and the methods of coordination.

If an organization is a collection of members who contribute their efforts toward a common goal, then one fundamental task for that organization (or any group) is to coordinate its members' activities. The different contributions of members may be wasted if no mechanism is available to ensure that these contributions are all geared toward attaining organizational objectives. The relative ease or difficulty with which such coordination can be achieved depends on the nature of the tasks—in particular, the extent to which they depend on each other (i.e., the extent of required interaction among the tasks) and the extent to which the tasks are variable (i.e., the extent to which the environment keeps changing and thus requiring adjustments in task goals and procedures).

In discussing the relationship between cohesion and performance in sport, two researchers (Carron and Chelladurai 1981) proposed a classification of sport tasks based on the concept of required interaction. They based their scheme on frameworks that other researchers proposed for organizational tasks (Thompson 1967; A.N. Turner and Lawrence 1965) and that classify sport tasks (Ball 1973; Poulton 1957). Their model proposes that tasks vary in the degree of interdependence required of them and that the type of coordination varies with the degree of interdependence. Although the model was proposed in the context of sport teams, the researchers drew largely from the fields of management and organizational behavior. Therefore, the scheme is readily applicable to organizational tasks. It is explained in greater detail in the following section.

Types of Interdependence

Tasks can be classified as independent, coactively dependent, proactively-reactively dependent, and interactively dependent (Carron and Chelladurai 1981).

Independent Tasks

An independent task can be carried out by one person; it does not require interaction with people performing other tasks. Examples include the tasks of archery, bowling, individual events in track and field, and swimming (Carron and Chelladurai 1981). In these examples, individual performance can be assessed and rewarded. In another example, if two people volunteer to collect donations for the junior soccer league in their respective neighborhoods, their tasks are independent of each other. They need not interact with each other in any way. They go door to door in their own neighborhoods, and the league manager can easily assess their performance (e.g., how much they each collected) and reward them (e.g., with merit badges). The coaches of youth teams in city leagues are also involved in largely independent tasks.

Coactively Dependent Tasks

Coactively dependent tasks depend on a common but external source for initiation or control of their activities. In these tasks, members usually perform more or less similar tasks, and their collective contributions determine the group's success, as in the case of a rowing-eights team or tug-of-war team. In the organizational context, the tennis, swimming, and fitness units of a city recreation department depend on each other only to the extent that they receive their directions and funding from a common source. The nature of this interdependence is best illustrated by their reliance on a common but limited budget. That is, if one unit gets more, another unit gets less. The coaches in a university athletics department are also involved in coactively dependent jobs because their jobs are sufficiently independent of each other yet all depend on a common source for the scheduling of facilities and the distribution of needed resources.

Proactively-Reactively Dependent Tasks

Proactively-reactively dependent tasks are initiated by one member and completed by another. Thus, the first person depends on the second person (to complete the task), and the second person depends on the first person (to begin the task). This category includes all assembly-line tasks. In the context of sport and recreation, it applies, for example, to a four-person track relay team. The first person is proactively dependent on the other three to complete the task, and the last person is reactively dependent on the previous three for initiating the task. In addition, both the second and third runners are reactively dependent on the previous runner and proactively dependent on the next runner.

Proactive-reactive dependence exists wherever a series of tasks is arranged sequentially. For example, the accounting clerk in a recreation department is reactively dependent on employees in other units to submit statements of receipts and expenses before he or she can prepare a master document. By the same token, the director of the department is proactively dependent on the subordinates to carry out his or her policies and directions.

Interactively Dependent Tasks

Interactively dependent tasks require the greatest amount of interaction. In these tasks, members performing various assignments need to interact with each other in order to complete the group task. These tasks tend to be variable; that is, they are open

VIEWPOINT

Before 1800, very few people had a job. Instead, people worked hard raising food or making things at home. They had no regular hours, no job descriptions, no bosses, and no employee benefits. Instead, they put in long hours on shifting clusters of tasks, in a variety of locations, on a schedule set by the sun and the weather and the needs of the day. What we have come to think of as a job was brought about by the Industrial Revolution and the creation of large manufacturing companies. Now, the conditions that created "the job" are disappearing. Specifically, the growth of technology has blurred job descriptions and boundaries, and workers are now expected to work long hours, be emotionally engaged in their jobs, and be constantly available (see Correll, Kelly, O'Connor, and Williams 2014).

to environmental influences. For example, individuals involved in organizing a major sport event (e.g., event managers, facility managers, security officials, media, public relations personnel) are all interactively dependent on one another to carry out their respective assignments and, in turn, the total work.

Methods of Coordination

Managers can coordinate tasks in a number of ways, some of which are more efficient and less costly given a certain type of interdependence among tasks. Carron and Chelladurai (1981) applied Thompson's (1967) three methods of coordination—standardization, planning, and mutual adjustment—to the four types of interdependent tasks outlined earlier.

- **Standardization** involves specifying a set of rules, regulations, and procedures for each task. In essence, such standardization tends to constrain and direct individual actions. As long as the different sets of rules, regulations, and procedures relating to various tasks are consistent with one another, the manager can expect the tasks to be coordinated properly. However, as noted by Thompson (1967), standardization is appropriate only with tasks performed in a stable environment.

DIVERSITY MANAGEMENT OF HUMAN RESOURCES

The role of task interdependence is prominent in Chelladurai's (2014) integrative framework for managing diversity. The framework proposes that the level of task interdependence of a group or unit affects the success of efforts to accommodate diversity and realize its benefits. Specifically, "the effects of diversity can be enhanced in interdependent tasks, where members need to rely on one another to complete their tasks. Interdependent tasks require smooth interaction among group members, who need to communicate, cooperate, and coordinate their efforts (Jehn et al., 1999). Management needs to promote the use of the strengths of such diversity and garner its potential benefits" (Chelladurai 2014, p. 352).

Thus, sport and recreation managers must recognize where task interdependence is high or beneficial and proactively manage a culture of diversity to reap the potential benefits associated with this type of job design. For example, when planning to host a national-level event, sport managers in operations, marketing, athlete development, and promotions must all come together to ensure that the event runs smoothly; thus the work involves high task interdependence. The diversity management framework suggests that these individuals must value diversity and recognize the benefits of embracing unique perspectives in order to produce positive outcomes through their multiple perspectives, experiences, and levels of expertise.

- **Planning** involves establishing goals with individuals and assisting them in scheduling their activities. Thus, the manager gives each member of the group a goal and expects him or her to achieve it within a specified time.

- In some tasks, coordination can be achieved only through **mutual adjustments** by the members involved in the tasks. When tasks are highly variable and complex, any previously established rules, procedures, or plans may be irrelevant. In such circumstances, members need to interact with each other and make necessary adjustments in their goals and activities in order to attain the group's goals.

The final segment of Carron and Chelladurai's (1981) model matches the method of coordination with the type of interdependence inherent in the tasks. Figure 10.4 illustrates the appropriateness of each form of coordination for different types of interdependencies. The solid lines in figure 10.4 indicate the primary mode of coordinating jobs of a particular dependence type. The dotted lines suggest that the mode of coordination in question is also applicable as a supplemental mode of coordination.

Although all forms of coordination may be pertinent to interactively dependent tasks, the predominant form is mutual adjustment. As noted earlier, to the extent that the environmental demands and constraints keep changing, previous standardization and planning becomes obsolete. Therefore, mutual adjustment by members proves to be the most dominant and appropriate mode of coordination in these cases. For proactively-reactively dependent tasks, the most dominant and appropriate coordinative mechanism is coordination by planning. For coactively dependent tasks, the best option is coordination by standardization. And in the case of independent tasks, the need for coordination is minimal and the necessary coordination is achieved by standardization.

Job design efforts should address worker motivation and satisfaction, efficiency, worker comfort, and reliability of the worker–machine system. Mechanisms of coordination include (in order of increasing cost and difficulty) standardization with extensive rules and regulations; the use of planning goals, work schedules, and timelines; and workers' mutual adjustment with one another in carrying out their jobs.

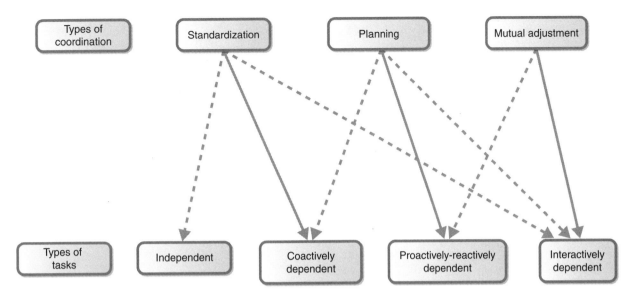

FIGURE 10.4   Types of task dependence and coordination.
Adapted, by permission, from A.V. Carron and P. Chelladurai, 1981, "Cohesiveness as a factor in sport performance," *International Review of Sport Sociology* 16(2): 21-41

INTERDEPENDENCE

Although some jobs are inherently interdependent, management can make some other jobs either more or less interdependent. Consider, for example, several aerobics instructors employed by a university department of recreational sport. The department may permit the instructors to make decisions jointly about their own schedules, the specific groups of clients that they manage, and the locations of their classes. In this scenario, the department has created interdependence among the aerobics instructors, and mutual adjustment among the instructors is relevant as a coordinative mechanism.

On the other hand, the supervisor might schedule the aerobics classes for the instructors in terms of time, location, and client groups. The supervisor might also assign specific instructors to specific classes. This approach minimizes interdependence among the instructors and reduces the need for mutual adjustment as a means of coordination. The choice of one approach over another is a function of both managerial style and member preferences.

The cost of coordination—in terms of effort, time, money, and efficiency—increases as the form of coordination moves from standardization through planning to mutual adjustment. At the same time, the control exerted by top management *diminishes* with the movement away from standardization and toward mutual adjustment. Therefore, both theorists and practicing managers have advocated simplification, fragmentation, and routinization of jobs so that jobs can be coordinated and controlled through standardization or planning.

Task Variability

Just as the extent of interdependence affects the choice of coordinative mechanism, task variability affects the extent of standardization and supervision. Recall that task variability involves the number of exceptional cases encountered in the work that require different methods or procedures for doing the work (Van de Ven and Delbecq 1974). If task requirements change constantly, managers find it more difficult to specify rules and regulations for every contingency that the employee faces. Therefore, managers find it necessary to allow members the discretion to communicate with other members, both horizontally and vertically, and to make appropriate decisions. On the other hand, if the task requirements are stable, then it is more efficient to standardize the tasks (i.e., to specify extensive rules and procedures). In these circumstances, managers can ensure proper control and coordination of activities through proper supervision.

ROLE OF THE SPORT OR RECREATION MANAGER

It is the role of the sport or recreation manager to ensure that job design matches the task and motivation factors of paid staff. For example, in the case of an employee working the line at a sporting goods manufacturing company, job simplification may be the best option for ensuring that the task is done as efficiently as possible. However, human resource managers must determine the motivational factors affecting employees in order to determine whether specific job-design strategies may be beneficial in certain instances. For example, an employee may

---

EXAMPLES OF COORDINATION

Examples of jobs that managers can coordinate through standardization, planning, and mutual adjustment can be drawn from a university athletics department. For instance, the locker room attendants in different locations are involved in independent tasks, but the attendants in one location may be coactively dependent on each other to the extent that their schedules are arranged sequentially. The major form of coordination is standardization, whereby management standardizes the tasks for each attendant by specifying the assigned tasks.

As noted earlier, the coaches in the department are coactively dependent on the athletics director and his or her assistants, both for coordinating their activities and for planning in the form of setting goals for each team, budgeting resources, and scheduling practice sessions and games. The administrators may also set specific guidelines individually for each team or collectively for all teams in regard to recruiting practices, treatment of athletes, and other critical aspects of operation.

The relationships between coaches, facility managers, event managers, and event schedulers best illustrate proactive-reactive dependence. Facility managers and event managers need to know in advance the schedule of events so that they can prepare for them. That is, the individuals who schedule the events should plan in advance and notify the others. If a coach wants specific arrangements for a competition, he or she plans those arrangements in advance and informs the facility and event managers. Thus, planning is the major mode of coordination in proactively-reactively dependent tasks.

In the case of a marketing department, the tasks of the senior marketing executives can best be coordinated through mutual adjustment among those executives. For instance, the athletics director may set the overall target for sponsorship, and the marketing executives then seek sponsors. In the process, they need to adjust to each other in seeking different sponsors and accommodating each other's style of operation. Insofar as they address the idiosyncratic ways of would-be sponsors, and insofar as competition exists for sponsorship money, the marketers' environment is turbulent (i.e., their jobs are variable), and mutual adjustment is the dominant mode of coordination.

possess specific skills in a variety of areas on the manufacturing line of an athletic apparel company. For this employee, job rotation may reduce monotony and ensure that the employee's various skills are used to their full potential, which then reflects the content sources of motivation as outlined in chapter 8.

Furthermore, elements of coordination are particularly relevant when managing staff and volunteers for major international sporting events. In this situation, templates can be used from previously staged events to provide the standardization, planning, and mutual adjustment needed in order to coordinate each committee or planning unit in the event's operational process. Specific guidelines may be provided for each committee, but a communication structure must also be outlined that connects the committees so that decision making in one committee (proactive) can be managed in another (reactive). Without such coordination, the delivery of the event will not reach its full potential.

Case Study

Job Design

As the first appointed director of operations for a new semiprofessional basketball franchise, your front office consists of a group of paid staff members: president and CEO, vice president, coach and general manager, manager of cooperate partnerships and sales, director of operations, and public relations coordinator. As director of operations, you are responsible for seeing that the franchise's daily operations provide the best service to your clients—both athlete members and sport consumers. More specifically, the CEO has tasked you with creating a communication plan for establishing the franchise's image, both in the local community and at the provincial or state level. Given the number of tasks under your operational umbrella, you decide that hiring an intern in digital media and graphic design might help you generate the communication plan.

Before posting the job opening, you need to outline the responsibilities that the job will involve. With laptop in hand, you begin detailing a picture of what the intern's job might look like:

- Create and maintain graphic design content for the franchise's website, flyers and brochures, letterheads, signage, and social media platforms.
- Assist in photo editing for the website and print materials.
- Manage files and archives for safe storage.
- Handle various clerical tasks as assigned.

After posting the job description, you receive a number of applications. You go through a rigorous selection process and end up hiring Lauren, a sharp third-year student completing a bachelor's degree in sport management at a state university. She has experience working with Photoshop and editing photos for a local sport club in her hometown. She is completing the internship for course credit but also wants to obtain an employment position as a graphic design specialist for a professional sport organization after she graduates.

You recognize that Lauren is a self-motivated young woman; however, given that the position will not be paid and that she will have to function on her own when you are on the road, you want to ensure that she continues to be motivated and to perform well over the full course of her internship. Thus, you turn to Lauren's internship job description and reflect on how her job could be designed to serve her higher-order needs and thus maintain her motivation to do well in the internship.

Case Study Tasks

1. Consider the six characteristics of an enriched job (Herzberg 1974) outlined earlier in this chapter (figure 10.1), then create a job design that incorporates relevant characteristics to enhance Lauren's internship and increase her motivation. Describe specifically how each characteristic relates directly to Lauren's internship position with your franchise.

2. Discuss any job design characteristics that may be difficult to adopt in this case; provide an explanation for your response.

CHAPTER PURSUITS

SUMMARY

This chapter presents various approaches to job design, ranging from job simplification to job enrichment. It also presents Hackman and Oldham's (1980) model outlining the motivational properties of jobs. Although sport managers must try to enhance the motivational aspects of a job under their supervision, they must also be aware of the constraints. First, higher-level management may not permit the manager to change the design of jobs under his or her jurisdiction. Second, members of the organization may not have the ability and skill to carry out enriched jobs. Third, members may be content and satisfied with the current level of enrichment in their jobs and may not desire further enrichment. Fourth, the effort and time involved in enriching and coordinating jobs constitute a cost. Sport managers must also be concerned with the internal and external elements of jobs that may be detrimental to the comfort, health, and safety of workers and those surrounding them.

Tasks may also vary in their degree of interdependence; specifically, they can be categorized as independent, coactively dependent, proactively-reactively dependent, or interactively dependent. Coordination among the jobs becomes more difficult with increasing interdependence, and managers must use different types of coordination as appropriate from among the available options, which include standardization, planning, and mutual adjustment.

KEY TERMS

coordination 174

job design... 165

job enlargement... 165

job enrichment 165

job rotation.. 165

job simplification 165

motivational property 174

mutual adjustment.. 184

planning.. 184

psychological state 175

standardization 183

task attribute.. 169

task dependence... 182

task variability 170

UNDERSTAND

1. Bearing in mind Hackman and Oldham's (1980) job characteristics model, describe a job in sport management with high motivating potential and a job with low motivating potential. How does your assessment relate to your own abilities, predispositions, and values?

2. Consider the athletics department of a large university. Which of its units can be coordinated through standardization (i.e., extensive rules and regulations), planning (i.e., goal setting, schedules, timelines), and mutual adjustment (i.e., workers' adjustments to each other in pursuing goals)?

3. The chapter refers to the strategic importance of playing positions in football. Identify the strategically important positions in another sport. Compare those positions with the jobs in work organizations.

INTERACT

1. Chapter 8 asks you to respond to questions related to your motivation. Now consider a job that you enjoyed very much and focus only on the characteristics of the tasks associated with that job. Describe the attributes of the job that were attractive to you and those that you intensely disliked.

2. Consider three jobs that all offer any one of the following: sense of meaningfulness, autonomy in performing the job, or feedback from the job itself. If you could choose one these three jobs, which one would you choose and why?

3. An individual may receive different kinds of feedback from different sources when carrying out a task. What kind of feedback from what source would you prefer? Why?

CHAPTER

11

Staffing and Career Considerations

LEARNING OBJECTIVES

After reading this chapter, you will be able to

- understand the purpose and focus of job analysis, job description, and job specification;
- explain the process of matching people with jobs through recruiting, hiring, and training;
- discuss the concept of psychological contract in terms of individual contributions and organizational inducements;
- explain what a career means from the perspectives of the individual and the organization;
- express insight into career orientation and career anchors; and
- understand the functions, processes, and outcomes of mentoring.

As noted at the beginning of this text, the employees of an organization make the organization's systems work. All of the organization's plans and procedures can be effective only if the organization has the right people to execute them. This is particularly true in the case of service organizations, which include most sport and recreation organizations. Therefore, sport and recreation managers must be purposeful in staffing their organizations. As W. Sullivan (1997) noted, the process of doing so is not an easy one, and it differs from the process of addressing clients, customers, and other external agents. Sullivan also pointed out that typical managers, particularly in small enterprises, spend more waking hours with their employees than with their own families.

Building good staff is like making homemade soup. The people you hire are the ingredients you mix in. High-quality ingredients guarantee a first-rate meal. . . . It is not magical. It takes patience and effort to make it work. The sweat equity invested will reap high dividends. (p. 2)

This chapter outlines the following key steps in the staffing process: staffing needs assessment, job analysis, job description, job specification, recruiting, hiring, and training. The chapter also addresses the concepts of psychological contract and careers and discusses the role of mentoring.

PURPOSES OF STAFFING

The goals of **staffing** can be viewed from two perspectives—technical and citizenship (S.E. Jackson and Schuler 1992). The concern from the technical perspective is to ensure that a person in a job has the right skills to perform that job. Accordingly, the emphasis is on **hiring** the people with the right technical skills and on **training** them further in those skills. From the citizenship perspective (referred to as the control perspective by Jackson and Schuler), the focus is on the predictability and reliability of social interactions to ensure behavior according to organizationally approved norms and values. That is, as Jackson and Schuler noted, the process of staffing should be geared toward ensuring social performance (i.e., citizenship) in addition to job performance (i.e., technical performance).

This view leads to the suggestion that staffing practices need to encompass the requirements of both the job and the organization (B. Schneider and Bowen 1992). That is, these practices should be aimed at the person–*organization* fit instead of the traditional person–job fit. Organizations must attempt to attract people with the requisite personality and ability to participate in and promote the organizational climate for service and, at the same time, to effectively perform the tasks of a particular job. Person–organization fit consists of (a) the fit between one's knowledge, skills, and abilities and the task demands and (b) the fit between overall personality (e.g., needs, interests, and values) and the climate of the organization. In other words, the person must fit both the content and the context of the job. That is, "applicants are hired based upon who they are, not just what they can do" (B. Schneider and Bowen 1992, p. 11).

VIEWPOINT

The staffing problem can be brought into focus for the reader if he or she thinks of a football team or a symphony orchestra, since these are relatively small organizations with clearly identifiable roles. . . . First, there is the problem of attracting the best players. Not all of them want to work for the same organization and, as a result, the pool of individuals applying for work in the organization is likely to be less than ideal. Secondly, there is the problem of selecting the individuals who will develop into the best players. Sometimes, the wrong decisions are made despite a careful analysis of the applicants. In football, for example, players who are not drafted or who are released by teams occasionally end up as stars (such as Johnny Unitas of the Baltimore Colts). Finally, there is the problem of developing the individual players so that when a job opening appears (either because of personnel changes or [because] a new job has been created), someone will be available to fill it. (Nadler, Hackman, and Lawler 1979, pp. 41-42)

The purposes of staffing procedures are twofold. The first concern is with creating a fit between the individual's skills and the job requirements. This technical aspect of staffing is intended to ensure that individuals are capable of performing their assigned tasks. The second concern involves matching individual orientations with organizational goals, values, and culture. The point of this citizenship aspect is to ensure that individuals fit into the culture and climate of the organization.

FOCUS OF STAFFING

The foregoing discussion indicates clearly that the focus of staffing is twofold. First, the organization's jobs are brought under scrutiny in order to determine the number and types of jobs to be filled. In other words, this focus centers on the content of the job. The second focus centers on people to ensure that appropriate members are hired. The process of creating a match between the task and the individual requires attending to the concept of task and that of task characteristics (discussed in chapter 10) and individual differences in abilities, personality, and values (discussed in chapters 5 through 7).

Focus on Jobs

Every job exists only to contribute to the attainment of organizational goals. That is, every job is one piece of a puzzle that makes up the total effort to achieve the expected outcomes. Thus, the manager must ensure that the nature of each job and its requirements fit nicely into the total picture. More specifically, the focus on jobs in staffing involves

- assessing staffing needs,
- analyzing the job, and
- describing the job.

Staffing Needs Assessment

The first step, of course, is to determine how many jobs are vacant and need to be filled. This analysis takes into account the immediate necessity to fill a job and the short- and long-range requirements. Staffing requirements can be influenced by factors such as organizational plans to expand (or contract) and projected retirements for the near future. For instance, the manager of a large fitness club needs to determine how many fitness instructors, facility and equipment personnel, secretaries, and accounting clerks are needed. Such an estimation is based on the number and types of current employees, the prospects of some of them leaving (e.g., retiring or moving to other locations or jobs), and any plans to expand or reduce organizational activities. After

deciding on the staffing requirements, the manager next analyzes the job itself, which leads to job description and job specification.

Job Analysis

As the label implies, **job analysis** involves studying the job and the various tasks associated with it. It involves collecting information about the job's operations, responsibilities, working conditions, and other such critical elements. Job analysis can be carried out in several ways. First, if the proposed job is a new creation, the manager may need to list all of the operations that he or she perceives to be essential for job performance. This conceptually developed list may have to be modified through subsequent experiences. In addition, the manager may decide to observe and analyze a similar job in another organization and generate a list of activities associated with that job.

If such a job is already in place, then job analysis can be facilitated by observing that job as it is being carried out now. The manager can also collect the necessary information by interviewing the employee who is carrying out the job or that employee's supervisor. Another approach is to ask the employee to respond to a job analysis questionnaire. Finally, the manager can ask current employees who perform that job to keep a daily log of all activities and the time needed for each. The major items included in job analysis are presented in table 11.1.

TABLE 11.1 Critical Elements in a Job Analysis

ELEMENT	DESCRIPTION
Job identification	Job title, department or division, and titles of supervisors
Job summary	Brief description of job, including purpose and activities
Duties	Primary duties classified as technical, clerical, or professional; major duties and proportions of time involved; other duties and their time involvement
Responsibility	Extent of responsibility over use and care of equipment and tools, personal safety and safety of others, and performance of others
Human characteristics	Extent to which certain human characteristics are required, including physical attributes such as vision, eye–hand coordination, strength, height, initiative, ingenuity, judgment, writing, education, experience, and training
Working conditions	Description of the physical conditions (usual or unusual) in which the job is to be carried out and any unusual psychological demands
Health and safety features	Description of health or safety hazards and of any special training or equipment needed
Performance standards	Description of how performance on the job is to be measured and of the identifiable factors that contribute to successful performance

VIEWPOINT

Saal and Knight (1995) classified the approaches to job analysis into the following categories: job oriented, worker oriented, and trait oriented. The job-oriented approach focuses on the job outcomes or results and the factors that facilitate those outcomes. In essence, this approach establishes the reasons that a job exists. It addresses, for example, the tasks that a locker room attendant (or receptionist or tennis instructor) is expected to accomplish (i.e., the outcome) and how these accomplishments contribute to the overall objective. The worker-oriented approach centers on the behaviors and activities of workers in performing their jobs. For example, what behaviors and activities of the locker room attendant would lead to the outcomes expected of that job? One would expect the attendant to be organized and methodical in issuing, retrieving, and storing the equipment (e.g., balls, rackets, towels). The attendant also needs to be courteous and pleasant to clients.

Finally, as its name implies, the trait-oriented approach emphasizes the traits that contribute to job performance. For instance, the need for the attendant to be courteous and pleasant may be tied to the personality trait of service orientation (discussed in chapter 6). Saal and Knight (1995) note that the trait-oriented approach, which is the least-known approach, calls for more complex procedures because a single trait may contribute to performance in more than one activity. By the same token, more than one trait may facilitate performance in any given activity. More important, these authors alert us to the "unpleasant possibility that an emphasis on human characteristics can degenerate into destructive and illegal group stereotypes based on race, sex, age, and other demographic variables" (p. 62).

The information gathered from a job analysis is used to generate a **job description**. In addition, job analysis provides information about the kinds of abilities, talents, education, and experience required to perform the job adequately. This information informs the job specification.

Job Description

A job description "describes the duties and responsibilities of the job holder" (Entrekin and Scott-Ladd 2014, p. 131). More specifically, it outlines the particular duties, activities, and responsibilities involved in that job. Typically, a job description includes the job title, as well as information about the immediate supervisor, the number and types of positions that the incumbent supervises, and specific activities of the job. Figure 11.1 provides an example of a job description for an executive director of a local sport and recreation club.

When developing a job description, the manager must make it concise and clear. The description must broadly define the scope of the job in terms of both the nature of the work and its relationships with other jobs. It should also specifically indicate the

complexity of the job, the skill required to manage it, and the worker's responsibility for each phase of the work.

Focus on People

After one assesses the need for specific jobs and analyzes and describes each of those jobs, the focus shifts to the type of person who would best fit the job. This focus is reflected in what is referred to as job specification. Whereas a job description outlines what needs to be done within a job, **job specification** outlines the human qualities needed to carry out the job. Werther, Davis, Schwind, Das, and Miner (1985) distinguished between job description and job specification as follows:

> A *job description* defines what the job does; it is a profile of the job. A job specification describes what the job demands of employees who do it and the human factors that are required. It is a profile of human characteristics needed by the job. These requirements include experience, training, education, physical demands, and mental demands. (p. 121, emphasis in original)

EXECUTIVE DIRECTOR JOB DESCRIPTION AND POSTING

Application deadline: August 22, 20XX

Anticipated start date: September 29, 20XX

Position: OCUA executive director

Type of position: full-time

Job Description

The Ottawa Carleton Ultimate Association (OCUA) is a thriving organization built on a strong sense of community among its members, from youth to adult recreational and competitive players. OCUA strives to ensure that, from cradle to grave, Ultimate players enjoy their sporting experience. Founded in 1986, this not-for-profit organization is among the largest Ultimate leagues in the world. OCUA relies strongly on effective management of volunteers and strategic leadership in order to continue to be a leader in the Ultimate sporting community.

The association's executive director needs to be a successful, results-oriented project manager able to work at the grassroots level and implement concrete plans that further the mandate of the association. The executive director will be leading a small but dedicated team of employees, as well as working with volunteers and partners, to deliver programs to youth, junior, and adult players. Essential skills for the executive director also include continuing to build on the mandate for strong financial sustainability and forging strategic alliances in the public sector, the private sector, and the broader sport community. Serving as the association's chief executive officer, the executive director will make independent operating decisions within policy guidelines set by the association's elected board of directors.

Responsibilities

The OCUA executive director oversees two main areas of responsibility: (1) administration and operations and (2) strategic relationships.

Qualifications

The successful candidate will possess the following mandatory qualifications:
- University or college degree or equivalent experience
- Minimum of three to five years of sport management experience
- Financial analysis capabilities, including skills for creating and managing a budget, basic bookkeeping skills, and/or audit experience
- Strong analytical and problem-solving skills
- Customer-service-driven approach to business
- Demonstrated team-building and leadership skills
- Excellent project management and organizational skills
- Ability to work independently
- Strong verbal and written communication skills and instincts
- High level of comfort with office computing and Internet technologies
- Ability to adapt to a flexible work schedule, including evenings and weekends

The following assets are considered desirable:
- Experience in working with OCUA as a league or program volunteer
- Experience in developing and executing a marketing vision, as well as strategies and operating plans
- Ability to communicate effectively, both verbally and in writing, in both official languages

How to Apply

To apply for this position, please e-mail your resume and cover letter to the attention of the Hiring Committee, OCUA Board of Directors. OCUA will accept applications between August 11th, 20XX and August 22nd, 20XX.

FIGURE 11.1 Sample job description for an executive director of a community-based Ultimate club.

Reprinted, by permission, from Ottawa Carleton Ultimate Association. Available: http://www.ocua.ca/ExecutiveDirectorPosting

CONTINGENT WORKERS

A common trend in staffing is the use of the contingent workforce, which includes both "contract employees and part-time workers who perform short-term and moderate-length assignments for companies that do not directly employ them" (J.R. Gordon 2002, p. 14). The use of contingent workers or part-time workers is becoming common in several industries (Brewster, Mayne, and Tregaskis 1997; Pitts 1998; J.K. Rogers 1995). According to a recent report from the Organization for Economic Cooperation and Development (OECD; 2013a) the part-time employment rate was 19 percent of the total workforce in Canada and 25 percent in the United Kingdom. Short-term hires are used during athletic seasons by many sport organizations, such as intercollegiate athletics departments and professional sport franchises. For example, a golf course in Scotland is likely to hire groundskeepers on a part-time basis for the summer months only, because their services are not required during the winter months.

The reasons for this trend are threefold (Chang and Chelladurai 2003). The first reason is industry based—specifically, a shift in the economy from a manufacturing focus to a service industry focus, where part-time employment is higher (OECD 2013b). The second set of reasons stems from individual differences in job preferences. Many people prefer part-time work because it allows them the flexibility and autonomy to balance their family and work obligations. Some people may also be attracted by the challenge and freedom of freelancing, which allows them to grow and develop in the profession without committing to a career in an organizational setting (Chang and Chelladurai; Heiligers and Hingstman 2000).

The third set of reasons is based on organizational imperatives. That is, organizations may hire part-time employees in an effort to reduce costs (Buchmueller 1999; Epstein, Seron, Oglensky, and Saute 2014; Gornick and Jacobs 1996; Lee 1996; Uzzi and Barsness 1998); more specifically, this practice allows organizations to meet staffing needs at minimal costs (Epstein et al.). The cost reduction occurs because part-time workers are typically paid less than full-time workers (Cappelli 1995; Epstein et al.; Gornick and Jacobs), are not paid benefits (Buchmueller), and are not in line for promotions (Cappelli and Keller 2013). This shift has spawned organizations such as private employment services and employee leasing firms to facilitate part-time employment (Cappelli and Keller 2013).

Although the cost-saving benefit of part-time employment is immediate, sport managers must also be concerned with nonmonetary costs of part-time employment. Some studies in the business and industrial sector have shown that part-time employees were neither as committed nor as productive as full-time workers and that they were less satisfied with their work or with their career (e.g., H.E. Miller and Terborg 1979; C.E. Ross and Wright 1998; Sinclair, Martin, and Michel 1999; Steffy and Jones 1990; Van Dyne and Ang 1998). One study of part-time and full-time workers in Korean sport organizations (Chang and Chelladurai 2003) found that full-time workers scored significantly higher on affective commitment and organizational citizenship behavior, which are conducive to effective performance. Similarly, Epstein et al. (2014) cautioned that human resource managers should assess the effectiveness of part-time employment because it may result in low levels of productivity, commitment, and competence.

For instance, a job specification for a marketing director may not mention anything about physical characteristics; instead, it may emphasize conceptual and human skills, including the ability to persuade prospective donors and customers.

MATCHING PEOPLE AND JOBS

So far, this discussion has emphasized analysis of the types and number of jobs to be filled, the activities and responsibilities of a specific job, and the human characteristics required by a job. The next set of steps addresses finding the right people to join the organization and training them to perform the appropriate jobs. These managerial tasks are referred to as recruiting, hiring, and training.

Recruiting

Recruiting is the process of gathering a pool of capable applicants and encouraging them to apply for a position. This process is similar to the way one goes about buying a car, a suit, or a computer. Take the case of buying a car. After deciding on the type of car we want, we visit more than one car dealer to ensure that we have a selection of that particular type of car from which to choose. In a similar manner, an organization in search of employees must reach out to many different types of sources of future employees.

The most obvious way of recruiting applicants is to advertise the position in several online platforms (e.g., e-mail lists, job-search websites, social media sites such as LinkedIn) and online publications (e.g., newspapers and magazines). Research (e.g., DiMicco et al. 2008; Skeels and Grudin 2009) provides examples where social media technology is used strategically for the purpose of recruiting personnel, connecting with current customers, and watching one's competitors or tracking one's market. In terms of recruiting personnel, employers can communicate with potential candidates from across the world and track the experiences, networks, and communication patterns of a larger pool of potential candidates. However, this idea of a larger pool of candidates can also be a drawback in the sense that the manager must sift through many applicants, some of whom may be totally unqualified.

Another option is campus recruiting. In fact, because universities and colleges are the best source

VIEWPOINT

The social networking platform LinkedIn provides employers with the opportunity to review the skills, knowledge, and experiences of a very large pool of potential applicants. With approximately 100,000,000 registered users (Qualman 2011), LinkedIn can be strategically leveraged to help sport and recreation managers view candidates' experience and track the size and quality of their social networks. Given the value of a wide social network for any human service employee, it is invaluable for a human resource manager to be able to assess these qualities when recruiting and selecting personnel.

of young professionals, campus recruiting may prove to be the best avenue if an organization is seeking professionals at the entry level. The advantage of campus recruiting is that the recruiter gets to meet with several potential candidates and make a preliminary assessment of them. The manager can then contact the more impressive candidates later and encourage them to submit applications. The drawback is that the recruiter may have to interact with several students who may not be interested in the job or the organization.

In addition, managers can encourage current employees to approach qualified friends and relatives to apply for positions. This process is known as employee referral. Because an employee knows the organization, its goals, and its processes, he or she may have a good grasp of who will fit into the organization well and carry out the job effectively. Thus, this process is likely to produce strong candidates. Furthermore, because the image of the employee who sponsors a candidate is at stake, the employee will probably recommend only strong candidates. The drawback of this process is that employees are likely to recommend only people who are similar to themselves. Thus, employee referral may result in homologous reproduction (i.e., a state in which only similar people are employed). In other words, the process may restrict diversity in terms of sex, race, ethnicity, and other demographic characteristics.

RECRUITING OLDER VOLUNTEERS

Kouri (1990) noted "two transition points in older adulthood when individuals are apt to seek rewarding, meaningful ways to structure time and channel their skills and energies. These are times when individuals are likely to be receptive to invitations for volunteer commitments. The first transition point is retirement; the second occurs around age 75" (pp. 65-66).

Kouri (1990) suggested that recruiters may profit from participating in retirement planning programs and company-sponsored gatherings of retired employees to explain volunteer opportunities. Sport and recreation managers can adopt this strategy and approach preretirees and retirees with brochures about the organization, its goals and volunteer opportunities, and job descriptions. They can also visit residences for senior citizens and advertise the opportunities for volunteering in the organization's programs. In addition, Kouri points out several incorrect assumptions that people make about older persons. These assumptions include the notion that older persons necessarily want to do the same work that they did before retirement, that all older persons have difficulty with hearing or vision,

that they will not change, that they want only minimal responsibility, and that they will always come forward to help on their own.

In a study conducted by Hamm-Kerwin, Misener, and Doherty (2009), older adults who acted as sport volunteers were found to have large social networks drawn from a past enriched with involvement in sport as participants and a history of volunteering. The 20 volunteers in their sample reported becoming involved in sport volunteering as an opportunity to use their skills, form and maintain social connections, and stay active. Regarding retention, the volunteers identified quality of health, awareness of volunteer opportunities, and spousal employment status as factors influencing their capacity to volunteer. When interview participants were asked what a sport organization could do to make sport volunteering more attractive to older adults, Misener, Doherty, and Hamm-Kerwin's (2010) research highlighted the need for multiple modes of communication, enhanced coordination among various roles (e.g., volunteer board members and paid staff) in the organization, and job sharing to reduce fatigue in volunteer roles.

While the foregoing approaches are aimed at recruiting qualified candidates from outside the organization, the possibility also exists that some current employees may qualify for an advertised position. An internal search is cost-effective because the manager or recruiter knows the potential candidates and their performances well; thus he or she has no need for further assessment of the individuals. Furthermore, a focus on internal candidates is motivational in the sense that every employee can aspire to higher positions. If the jobs are at higher levels, current employees may prove to be quite suitable and valuable; indeed, ignoring them may be disadvantageous to the organization and unfair to the employees. However, if the jobs are at the entry

level, current employees may be overqualified, and in that case the number of potential candidates would be limited. An internal search may also restrict diversity in the workplace.

Managers can also approach their counterparts in other organizations to ask qualified candidates to apply for the position. The essential point is that the organization must make every effort to reach out to qualified prospects for a job.

Hiring

Hiring is the process of selecting a person from the pool of qualified applicants gathered during the recruiting process. Because the manager has

PROCEDURAL JUSTICE

In chapter 9, we saw that the notion of justice pervades every managerial activity. The justice issues associated with the staffing function are mostly procedural; hence, procedural justice is the most relevant type for personnel selection systems. In accordance with this view, Gilliland (1993) proposed a model of justice for selection systems that included 10 procedural justice rules. On the basis of this work, T.N. Bauer and colleagues (2001) developed a scale to measure applicants' perceptions of the fairness of selection procedures. Their 39-item Selection Procedural Justice Scale (SPJS) measures 11 dimensions of procedural justice.

These 11 factors are grouped into two broader categories—structure dimensions and social dimensions, each of which includes five dimensions—as well as an additional dimension relating to the tests conducted during the selection procedures. Structure factors include justice issues related to the specifics of the selection procedures, such as the actual selection, the content of any tests, and the timing of feedback. The social category relates to communication with and treatment of applicants. These 11 dimensions and their descriptions are provided in table 11.2. Sport managers can use these statements as a checklist to help ensure that their hiring practices are just and fair.

TABLE 11.2 Subscales of the Selection Procedural Justice Scale (SPJS)

Structure dimensions

Job-relatedness/predictive	The selection process employed was related to the job in the sense that those who did well in the selection process would be expected to do well in the job.
Information known	The applicant knew in advance about the selection process and its content and format.
Chance to perform	The applicant could show his or her skills and abilities through the selection process and had the opportunity to demonstrate potential.
Reconsideration opportunity	The applicant had the opportunity to review and discuss the selection process results.
Feedback	The applicant knew and was satisfied with the timing of the feedback.

Social dimensions

Consistency	The selection process was administered to all applicants, and no distinctions were made between the applicants when the selection process was administered.
Openness	The applicant received honest and open treatment and candid responses from selection process administrators.
Treatment	The applicant was treated politely and with respect.
Two-way communication	The applicant received good communication and was able to ask questions and express concerns.
Propriety of questions	There was no prejudice in the questions asked, and questions were not personal or private.

Additional dimension

Job-relatedness/content	The content of the selection process was clearly related to the job in question.

analyzed and described the job and has specified the appropriate human factors, selecting suitable candidates may seem like an easy task, particularly if the application form has been well designed to elicit the most relevant and critical information. In reality, however, the process is much more complicated than it appears on paper.

The major reason for this complexity, as noted earlier, is the need to forge a fit between the individual and the job as well as a fit between the individual and the organization. The process of obtaining this fit is aided by the job analysis, job description, job specification, and advertisements. However, they do not capture the essence of individual–organization fit, which encompasses personal needs, attitudes, values of the individual, and values and culture of the organization. Therefore, organizations and their managers commonly resort to other procedures to select a person who fits the organizational context. These procedures include checking biographical background, considering reference letters, conducting interviews, and using personal judgment.

The problem here is that these latter social dimension processes may elicit personal biases in hiring people; therefore, the manager must take care to make these processes free of discriminatory practices. In fact, federal and state governments make many provisions that govern the employment practices of organizations; table 11.3 provides examples of the U.S. statues and regulations governing hiring practices. Managers should also ensure that they are familiar with legislation in other countries that affect their human resource management practices.

Although these are legal requirements that organizations must follow implicitly, they also highlight the need for managers to be generally on guard in order to prevent any personal biases from surfacing in the hiring process. For instance, managers must be wary of asking unwarranted and irrelevant questions of job candidates. Some questions that may appear to be innocuous can be damaging to both the individual and the organization; examples are included in table 11.4. The point is that selection of a candidate must be based on criteria that are relevant to the job and to organizational requirements; other attributes of the candidate must be made absolutely irrelevant to the selection process.

Another danger during the recruiting and hiring processes is that the individual, the organization, or both may be untruthful about what is being offered to the other. For instance, prospective candidates may project themselves as more capable than they really are and suggest that they can perform tasks (e.g., computer analysis, which they may know

DIVERSITY MANAGEMENT OF HUMAN RESOURCES

The integrative framework for managing diversity (Chelladurai 2014) highlights the fact that diversity management begins with hiring and maintaining personnel who value diversity. Thus, it is imperative to hire individuals who demonstrate awareness, acknowledgment, and acceptance of diversity during the interview process. It also means that diversity management should be reflected in job descriptions, which, as noted earlier, serve as the first point of communication between an employer and potential employees.

To help us understand the importance of job descriptions in relation to diversity management, we can turn to Cunningham (2008), who discussed the organizational dynamics of diversity. Specifically, Cunningham noted that the relationship between macro-level pressures to adopt diversity management strategies and micro-level commitment to diversity initiatives can be moderated by systematic integration, which involves assimilating diversity efforts into the broader organizational landscape. In the case of the hiring process, integration can begin with the job description, where any description should include the value of diversity that each candidate must demonstrate if he or she is chosen to work in the organization. The hiring process can then include specific questions or scenarios that the candidate must work through in order to demonstrate awareness and acceptance of the benefits offered by a diverse workforce.

TABLE 11.3   Selected U.S. Government Regulations for Staffing Procedures

LAW OR EXECUTIVE ORDER	PURPOSE OR INTENT
Equal Pay Act (1963)	Forbids sex-based discrimination in rates of pay for men and women working in the same or similar jobs.
Age Discrimination in Employment Act (1967)	Forbids discrimination against individuals between 40 and 70 years of age.
Title VII, Civil Rights Act (1972)	Forbids discrimination based on race, sex, color, religion, or national origin.
Rehabilitation Act, as amended (1973)	Forbids discrimination against persons with disability and requires affirmative action to provide employment opportunity for persons with disability.
Vietnam Era Veterans Readjustment Assistance Act (1974)	Forbids discrimination in hiring against disabled veterans with a 30 percent or more disability rating; veterans discharged or released for a service-connected disability; and veterans on active duty between August 5, 1964, and May 7, 1975.
Equal Employment Opportunity Commission Guidelines (1978)	Created by the 1964 Civil Rights Act, this commission investigates and eliminates employment discrimination against certain groups of individuals (e.g., women, African Americans, Asian Americans, Hispanic Americans, and Native Americans).
Pregnancy Discrimination Act (1978)	Requires pregnancy to be treated as any other medical condition with regard to fringe benefits and leave policies.
Immigration Reform and Control Act (1986)	Prohibits hiring of illegal aliens.
Americans With Disabilities Act (1990)	Provides for increased access to services and jobs for persons with disability.
Older Workers Benefit Protection Act (1990)	Provides protection for employees who are more than 40 years of age regarding fringe benefits and gives employees time to consider an early retirement offer.
Civil Rights Act (1991)	Allows women, persons with disability, and persons of religious minority to have a jury trial and to sue for punitive damages if they can prove intentional hiring or workplace discrimination.

nothing about) that are required in the organization. On the other hand, the manager may portray the organization as different from what it really is. For instance, the manager of a professional sport club may proclaim that the organization recognizes performance and that all salary and merit increments are based only on performance. In actuality, the club may emphasize seniority or may promote the owner's nephew or niece. False claims on the part of either the individual or the organization carry negative consequences (see figure 11.2).

Recruiting is the process of attracting prospective employees through advertisements, campus recruiting, employee referrals, and searching within the organization. Hiring is the process of selecting a person to fit both the job and the organization based on job-related criteria and conformance to government regulations.

TABLE 11.4   Examples of Irrelevant Hiring Questions per U.S. Legislation

INQUIRIES BEFORE HIRING	LAWFUL	UNLAWFUL*
Name	Name	Inquiry about any title that indicates race, color, religion, sex, national origin, disability, age, or ancestry
Address	Inquiry about place of residence and length at current address	Inquiry about any foreign addresses that would indicate national origin
Age	Inquiry limited to confirming that the applicant meets a minimum age requirement that may be established by law	Requiring a birth certificate or baptismal record before hiring Any inquiry that would reveal the date of high school graduation Any inquiry that would reveal whether the applicant is at least 40 years of age
Birthplace, national origin, or ancestry	—	Any inquiry about place of birth Any inquiry about place of birth of parents, grandparents, or spouse Any other inquiry about national origin or ancestry
Race or color	—	Any inquiry that would discriminate against someone based on race or color Any inquiry made of members of one race or color but not of others
Sex	—	Any inquiry that would discriminate against someone based on sex Any inquiry made of members of one sex but not of the other
Height and weight	Inquiry about the ability to perform	Considering height or weight as an actual job requirement without showing that no employee with an ineligible height or weight could do the work
Religion or creed	—	Any inquiry that would indicate or identify religious denomination or custom Telling the applicant the employer's religious identity or preference Requesting a clergyperson's recommendation or reference
Disability	Any inquiry necessary to determine the applicant's ability to substantially perform a specific job without significant hazard	Any inquiry about past or current medical conditions not related to the position for which the person has applied Any inquiry about workers' compensation or similar claims
Citizenship	Inquiry about whether the applicant is a U.S. citizen Inquiry about whether a noncitizen applicant intends to become a U.S. citizen Inquiry about whether the applicant's U.S. residence is legal Inquiry about whether the applicant's spouse is a U.S. citizen Requiring proof of citizenship after hiring Any other requirements mandated by the Immigration Reform and Control Act of 1986, as amended	Inquiry about whether the applicant is a native-born or naturalized U.S. citizen Requiring proof of citizenship before hiring Inquiry about whether the applicant's spouse or parents are native-born or naturalized U.S. citizens

INQUIRIES BEFORE HIRING	LAWFUL	UNLAWFUL*
Photograph	Requiring photograph after hiring	Requiring photograph before hiring for identification
Arrests and convictions	Inquiry about conviction of specific crimes related to qualifications for the job for which the person has applied	Any general inquiry about arrest, convictions, or time spent in jail
Education	Inquiry about the nature and extent of academic, professional, or vocational training Inquiry about language skills, such as reading and writing of foreign languages (if job related)	Any inquiry that would reveal the nationality or religious affiliation of a school Inquiry about what the applicant's mother tongue is or how foreign language ability was acquired
Relatives	Inquiry about name, relationship, and address of person to be notified in case of emergency	Any inquiry about a relative that would be unlawful if made about the applicant
Organizations	Inquiry about membership in professional organizations and offices held, excluding any organization that has a name or character indicating the race, color, religion, sex, national origin, disability, age, or ancestry of its members	Inquiry about every club and organization where membership is held
Military service	Inquiry about service in U.S. armed forces when such service is a qualification for the job Requiring military discharge certificate after hiring	Inquiry about military service in armed service of any country except the United States Requesting military service records Inquiry about type of discharge
Work schedule	Inquiry about willingness or ability to work required work schedule	Inquiry about willingness or ability to work any particular religious holidays
Miscellaneous	Any inquiry required to reveal qualifications for the job for which the person has applied	Any inquiry that is intended to reveal personal information of the applicant that is unrelated to the qualifications within the job description
References	General personal and work references that do not reveal the race, color, religion, sex, national origin, disability, age, or ancestry of the applicant	Requesting references specifically from clergy or any other persons who might reflect race, color, religion, sex, national origin, disability, age, or ancestry of applicant

*Unless bona fide occupation qualification is certified in advance by the Ohio Civil Rights Commission.

Training

With regard to training, Grönroos (1990) stated that human resource management should focus on "developing a holistic view of the service organization; developing skills concerning how various tasks are to be performed; and developing communication and service skills" (p. 253). Similarly, B. Schneider and Bowen (1992) suggested that a training program should develop both technical job skills and interpersonal or customer relationship skills. The program should also facilitate assimilation of the cultural values and norms of the organization. In essence, then, training programs are designed to further the fit between the individual and the organization.

Another useful scheme in the development of training programs is that of Humphrey and Ashforth (1994), who pointed out that two types of knowledge structures are necessary for effective service encounters: script and categorical. A script knowledge structure addresses a service worker's expectation for a series of coherently organized events in a successful service encounter and for

Organization		Applicant: False pretenses	Applicant: Truthful claims
Organization	Realistic claims	Burden on organization	Ideal fit
Organization	Exaggerated claims	Deserve each other	Frustration Turnover

FIGURE 11.2 Effects of false claims by an organization or applicant.

TRAINING SERVICE EMPLOYEES

C.L. Martin (1990) outlined one way of training service employees. In studying the employee–customer interface in bowling centers, he identified several employee behaviors that influence customer relations. The positive behaviors included greeting customers sincerely, thanking customers when they pay, encouraging customers to visit again, thanking customers for reporting problems, and making a positive comment about customers' performance. Negative behaviors included preoccupation with noncustomer tasks when the customer approaches the employee (whether to obtain a lane, to pay for bowling, or to order food or a beverage). Other negative behaviors included smoking or chewing gum during the customer interface.

C.L. Martin (1990) also found that bowling center employees generally failed to practice good customer relations behaviors. On the basis of his findings, he proposed the following steps to train employees in customer relations behavior. These steps are relevant to all sport organizations.

- Provide a customer relations manual for each employee. The manual should cover a wide range of examples of customer encounters. These encounters vary from one type of sport service to another.
- Ask employees to conduct mystery-shopper audits in which they take the role of a customer at another service firm. This experience should yield insights for the employee into good and bad customer relations behaviors.
- Meet with employees periodically to clarify and expand the contents of the manual. Employees themselves may provide additional cues for good customer relations. Such discussions can also cover the complaints and compliments that have been received from customers.
- Let new employees serve alongside senior employees for a set training period before working on their own.

alternative courses of action available for every event. In contrast, a categorical knowledge structure involves an understanding of the different types of clients, their specific needs and wants, and personal characteristics. This type of knowledge results in the development of client profiles. As Humphrey and Ashforth pointed out,

> Agents must have both categorical and script knowledge. Categorical knowledge helps them understand customers, whereas scripts help them understand the service options available to meet customers' varying needs. (p. 176)

In the context of sport and recreation management, training related to categorical knowledge emphasizes the distinctions between various classes of customers (e.g., youth, women, older persons) and their motives for participation (e.g., pleasure, excellence, health). Training related to script knowledge, on the other hand, focuses on the technical skills needed to provide the service (e.g., techniques and strategies of coaching) and the various stages of providing that service (e.g., progressive training regimen during practice sessions).

Training is the process of cultivating job-related skills, interpersonal skills, and organizational values in newly hired employees. Such training helps the employee adequately perform the technical aspects of the job, interact effectively with different classes of customers, and learn the organization's culture.

Decruitment

The majority of discussion in this chapter focuses on recruiting suitable candidates for existing jobs. The other side of the coin is what managers can do when they find out that their organization is overstaffed. Organizations may be forced to reduce their workforce due to technological advances, foreign competition, or dwindling markets for a given product. Robbins (1997) referred to this process as decruitment: "Decruitment is not a pleasant task for any manager to perform. But, as many organizations are forced to shrink the size of their workforce or restructure their skill composition, decruitment is becoming an increasingly important part of human resource management" (p. 283).

Thus this predicament may be faced by sport and recreation managers. For instance, city recreation departments, university athletics departments, and other such organizations may have to decruit employees when confronted with reductions in the budgets allotted to them. Similarly, profit-oriented firms, such as fitness clubs, may have to decruit if their customer base shrinks, which of course can occur for any number of reasons.

How can managers go about the process of decruiting? Robbins (1997) identified the following options:

- Firing (i.e., permanent termination for cause)
- Layoffs (i.e., temporary or permanent termination due to need to reduce staff)
- Attrition (i.e., not filling positions that fall vacant due to voluntary resignation or normal retirement)
- Transfers (i.e., moving employees laterally or downward)
- External loans (i.e., loaning employees' services to other organizations)
- Reduced work weeks (i.e., reducing the work hours each week or letting employees share their work hours)
- Early retirement (i.e., using incentives to encourage employees to retire early)

Of these options, firing (i.e., termination) is actually a severe form of punishing an employee for a violation (e.g., drinking on the job or frequently being late to work). Because of firing's dramatic effects on the employee, his or her family, and even the manager who orders the firing, such an action should be taken only after careful deliberation. Although some violations (e.g., vandalism, drinking on the job) can be cause for immediate dismissal, some others (e.g., tardiness, absenteeism) may legally require three warnings (Mondy and Noe 1993).

Continued poor performance may itself be a cause for firing, but a sport manager needs to document this poor performance based on the job description and data about the employee's performance. Therefore, a clear job description is crucial to making informed decisions about firing and to defending against any subsequent legal troubles. In addition, all employees should be given a list of violations that may justify termination; it is also helpful to encourage supervisors and co-workers to monitor and warn against such violations.

PSYCHOLOGICAL CONTRACT

When an individual joins an organization, the organization and the individual make a written formal agreement. The formal contract is constituted by such documents as the job description, employment contract, policies regarding salary scales, and procedures for merit assessment and promotion. Another critical component of employment is the **psychological contract**. This contract addresses the implicit expectations between the organization and its members. The elements of the psychological contract include those of the formal contract as well as additional informal and implied elements, such as the privileges and obligations of the person and the organization.

Public and Real Psychological Contract

Tosi, Mero, and Rizzo (2000) conceived of two boundaries of the psychological contract: the public and the real. The public boundary includes "activities [employees] want others, especially their superiors, to believe are the elements of the psychological contract" (p. 423). This boundary tends to consist of the minimal set of activities defined by the formal contract. For example, the public boundary of the psychological contract for a fitness consultant is defined by providing clients with fitness assessment and exercise prescriptions. The fitness consultant may also expect that he or she will undertake such activities between 8 a.m. and 5 p.m. on weekdays. These elements constitute the job description.

However, the psychological contract's real boundary—that is, its true limits—may include, for example, an organizational expectation that the fitness consultant will work overtime and during weekends and will also conduct a few exercise classes. Furthermore, the organization (in the form of the managers who run it) expects the consultant not just to put in the time but to put forth his or her best effort. Meanwhile, the consultant, while complying with these expectations, has his or her own expectation of how the organization will reciprocate in terms of extra remuneration, benefits, and privileges.

For another example, consider the situation in which a branch of the ticketing operation of a professional sport club is closed down and the employees in that branch are laid off. Even if the club has followed all existing rules and procedures for such retrenchment of employees, people may still have held the expectation that the organization would not undertake such procedures and would do its best to retain all employees. Thus, the released workers are not likely to question the basic causes of such closures but may still lament the breaking of the psychological contract. Most often, such psychological expectations relate to one's needs, values, and attitudes.

VIEWPOINT

In hiring employees, the organization seeks individuals who will be fully engaged in the organization and in the jobs assigned to them. According to Castellano (2014), such a full engagement is facilitated when

- jobs are characterized by skill variety, task identity, task significance, autonomy, and feedback;
- clarity exists regarding the role of the individual and the fit between the person and the role;
- positive interactions occur among co-workers, thus fostering a sense of belonging, cohesion, and rapport;
- management is trustworthy and provides clear expectations, feedback, and recognition;
- leadership clearly communicates the organization's vision, is open to suggestions, and encourages passion and independent thinking; and
- the organization treats employees fairly, which elicits reciprocal action from employees in the form of citizenship behaviors. (pp. 162-163)

Individual Contributions and Organizational Inducements

From a different perspective, the psychological contract appears as a system of individual contributions and organizational inducements (Schermerhorn, Hunt, and Osborn 1997). A psychological contract can exist and be meaningful only if the member's contributions hold some worth for the organization and if the member values the inducements offered by the organization. That is, the exchange of values between the organization and the member must be balanced and equitable.

The notion of a psychological contract is more critical to organizations that have volunteer workers than to others. In the case of volunteers, the material inducements of a formal contract (e.g., wages or salary) are not relevant, but the other elements of the psychological contract can attract and hold them. The psychological contract includes elements such as the opportunity to express one's altruistic and helping tendencies through specified activities of the organization. Another critical element is the opportunity to engage in activities that make use of the one's valued abilities. In a study of 22 volunteer coaches in team sports, Harman and Doherty (2014) found that the coaches expected their sport club to provide both transactional support (e.g., sufficient resources to perform coaching duties) and relational support (e.g., support during parent–coach conflicts). The study highlighted the importance of understanding volunteer expectations in terms of their voluntary role in the organization.

Chapter 2 presents the utilitarian, affective, and normative incentives that motivate volunteers. An organization that addresses these incentives in personnel policies affecting volunteers is likely to succeed in recruiting and retaining volunteers. However, to the extent that imbalance exists between a volunteer's contributions and the organization's inducements, the psychological contract between the two parties is tenuous; in such cases, neither the volunteer's commitment to the organization nor his or her maximal efforts can be ensured.

 The psychological contract between member and organization involves the unwritten understanding that the member will contribute to the organization over and beyond the formal contract and, in return, the organization will extend its varied inducements (e.g., rewards).

THE VOLUNTEER–JOB FIT

One obvious but important difference between paid employees and volunteer workers lies in the fact that, by definition, paid employees are motivated to a large extent by the pay they receive, whereas pay cannot be used as a motivational tool with volunteers. As noted in chapter 2, volunteers are likely to be motivated by the organization's goals, the context (i.e., people and processes) in which they work, and the tasks they perform. Therefore, the underlying theme of this chapter—creating the person–job fit—should be extended to volunteers. To do so, managers can take several steps (Kouri 1990); in the context of sport and recreation management, these steps should address the following critical concerns:

- The skills that the volunteer wants to use rather than those that the organization wants used
- The level of responsibility that the volunteer wants
- The type of people with whom the volunteer wants to work
- The volunteer's expectations for the job

These concerns reflect the incentives for volunteer motivation. The manager can best achieve volunteer–job fit if the volunteers themselves are involved in designing the job and if the organization is flexible in creating jobs that volunteers want.

CAREER CONSIDERATIONS

Staffing procedures, including the analysis of jobs and their descriptions, carry long-term implications for individuals as well. Most people spend nearly half of their adult life (roughly, the years between age 25 and age 65) in various jobs in different organizational contexts. To put in another way, jobs form one of the central elements of one's life. If you asked your parents to describe their lives, their descriptions would probably revolve around the jobs they have held in different places at different times. By the same token, if you were asked about your future life, you might well describe it in terms of the jobs you hope to hold. This notion of a succession of jobs is referred to as a **career**. Because most of the readers of this text are likely to embark on a career, the topic needs some detailed discussion. It is useful to discuss the concept of career from both the individual's perspective and the organization's perspective.

Individual Careers

According to Tosi, Mero, and Rizzo (2000), "A career is more than just the job or sequence of jobs a person holds over time. A career is the individually perceived sequence of attitudes and behaviors associated with work-related experiences and activities over a person's life" (p. 91). Thus, a career includes one's preparation for a job or jobs, the actual jobs held during one's lifetime, and one's movement from job to job. The concept also includes one's work-related attitudes, values, and beliefs, as well as the extent to which one's self-identity is related to work (Tosi, Mero, and Rizzo). Apart from the fact that the term *career* connotes a person's objective movement along a path of jobs (which may be either orderly and sequential or discontinuous), the concept of career also implies a fit (a) between what the individual does in a job and his or her abilities, skills, and talents and (b) between the organizational context or environment in which the person performs that job and the person's needs and preferences.

The concept of person–task fit leads naturally to the notion of person–occupation fit. For instance, on the basis of personal needs and aptitudes, an individual may identify more closely with marketing as an occupation than with teaching or coaching. Whereas person–task fit involves the congruence of personal needs and values with a specific job (e.g., marketing director in a recreational or competitive sport setting), person–occupation fit involves the fit between the person and the occupation (e.g., marketing or coaching), irrespective of the specific job. Occupational identity is critical to one's overall personal identity. In fact, in some cases, occupational identity may be the essence of one's overall identity; for example, so-called "workaholics" identify with their work so much that there is no room for any other identity.

Career Orientation

As early as 1909, Frank Parsons wrote:

> In the wise choice of a vocation there are three broad factors: (1) a clear understanding of yourself, your aptitudes, abilities, interests, ambitions, resources, limitations and their causes; (2) a knowledge of the requirements and conditions of success, advantages and disadvantages, compensation, opportunities, and prospects in different lines of work; (3) true reasoning on the relations of these two groups of facts. (p. 5)

To expand on this statement, an individual's **career orientation** is described and defined jointly by the person's individual's needs, values, goals, and preferences; his or her expectations from a career; and his or her estimation of personal talents, skills, expertise, and experiences related to particular jobs. Thus career orientation involves a person's preferences for specific kinds of jobs in specific occupational categories.

Career Anchors

Along similar lines, Schein (1978) viewed people as developing a sense of their own competencies, talents, needs, and values based on their early work experiences. Each individual learns over a period of work experiences that he or she prefers certain work roles over others. These preferred work roles are anchored in one's talents, needs, motives, attitudes, and values. The specific patterns of skills, needs, and values are called **career anchors**, and they keep the person moored within a specific domain of occupation. That is, people tend to gravitate toward jobs and occupations that satisfy their needs, use their skills and competencies, and reflect their values.

Schein's (1978) extensive research identified five distinct types of career anchors (see table 11.5). Career anchors evolve over a period of time; that is, work experiences in the next few years can modify what seems to be a career anchor at the moment.

VIEWPOINT

London (1991) suggested that career motivation (or orientation) consists of career resilience (i.e., capacity to manage career barriers), career insight (i.e., understanding of personal career goals and capacities and work environments), and career identity (i.e., how one defines oneself in relation to work). London suggested that organizations can support career resilience by providing employees with feedback and positive reinforcement, creating opportunities for achievement, and encouraging group and collaborative work. Organizations can enhance career insight by encouraging employees to set career goals, providing information relevant to career goals, and giving performance feedback. And they can help employees build career identity by encouraging professional growth and work involvement through challenging jobs, providing leadership opportunities, and rewarding good performance with recognition or bonuses.

some athletics administrators may seek greater fulfillment in contributing to the growth and welfare of the athletes, whereas others may be more attuned to the accomplishments of teams (e.g., win–loss records). These two kinds of directors have different career anchors or career orientations.

Similarly, some physical education teachers in high schools also serve as coaches. Some teacher-coaches expend large amounts of time and energy in coaching at the expense of teaching. While acknowledging the several external factors that cause such people to focus more on coaching, Chelladurai and Kuga (1996) argued that the nature of coaching as a job, as well as an individual's innate talents and tendencies, can also influence him or her to focus more on coaching than on teaching. This view parallels Schein's (1978) notion of career anchors.

Career Stages

Hall (1976) proposed that individuals go through four career stages covering the period from adolescence to retirement: exploration, establishment, advancement and maintenance, and late career. In the exploration stage (which usually occurs between the ages of 16 and 28), a person explores various occupations or roles, develops needed skills and competencies, and establishes a social network of peers and superiors. Forums for exploring occupations include such activities as summer jobs, volunteer work, and internships. In the establishment stage (usually between ages 22 and 42), the person specializes and gains expertise in a particular area of activity or organizational contribution and develops a clear and focused career plan.

In the advancement and maintenance stage (usually between ages 32 and 55), the individual focuses on progressing within the organization

People may learn that they possess talents they have yet to use or that their basic needs and values are likely to be more satisfied in another line of work. Even within one line of work, certain aspects of a job may be more fulfilling than others. For instance,

TABLE 11.5 Schein's Types of Career Anchors

ANCHOR	DESCRIPTION
Technical or functional	Preference for technical or functional content of a job, such as accounting or ticketing operations
Managerial competence	Preference for managerial positions; belief that one possesses the ability to analyze problems, manage people, and manage one's own emotions
Creativity	Preference for occupations that satisfy the need to create something (e.g., sport product, marketing process, sport agency) and to place one's name on it
Autonomy and independence	Preference for lines of work that permit people to be on their own, i.e., independent of others (e.g., sport agent, fitness consultant)
Security	Preference for long-term job security and a stable future with good income, including retirement benefits

and achieving career goals. The person may also take on the role of mentor to junior members of the organization. Finally, in the late career stage (usually from age 55 to retirement), the individual's value to the organization is based on his or her breadth of knowledge and experience; therefore, mentoring may continue to be a significant contribution. The person may also develop an interest in nonwork endeavors.

The overlaps between the various career stages derive from individual differences; that is, some individuals move from one stage to another at a different time than others do. Despite these differences, people are expected by North American society to follow sequentially the given pattern of moving from one stage to another.

Organizational Career Systems

The foregoing discussion focuses on the career orientation and development of the individual. Organizations also have (or should have) strategies regarding the careers within their domain. In reference to such strategies, Sonnenfeld and Peiperl (1988) used the term *career systems* to describe the "collections of policies, priorities, and actions that organizations use to manage the flow of their members into, through, and out of the organizations over time." These authors argued that because different organizations are characterized by different goals and technologies—and because they face different environmental contingencies—they are also likely to set different strategic priorities. These priorities are reflected in the career systems they institute.

Sonnenfeld and Peiperl (1988) proposed that the various career systems can be grouped into four categories based on two dimensions. The two dimensions are, "first, the movement into and out of the firm, the supply flow, and, second, the movement across job assignments and through promotions within the firm, the assignment flow" (pp. 589-590).

Supply flow is determined by the "openness of the career system to the external labor market at other than entry levels" (Sonnenfeld and Peiperl 1988, p. 590). For example, some organizations (e.g., parks and recreation departments) recruit employees at the entry level but rely on their own members to fill higher-level positions. In some other cases, the organization recruits outsiders to fill even higher-level positions. For instance, a university may hire an athletics director from outside the ranks of its own athletics department. The latter type of organization is likely to experience a greater proportion of employee turnover because local employees

may exit to other organizations in order to obtain better positions.

Assignment flow refers to the criteria by which managers assign or promote individuals within an organization. Sonnenfeld and Peiperl (1988) suggested that an organization may use the criterion of individual performance, which favors the star performer, or the criterion of contribution to the group, which favors the solid contributor.

On the basis of these two dimensions, Sonnenfeld and Peiperl (1988) proposed four kinds of career systems, each with its own unique way of maintaining membership. Figure 11.3 depicts these four systems, which are labeled as team, academy, club, and fortress.

In brief, organizations that resemble baseball teams favor individual performers; that is, individuals are recruited, assigned, and promoted to various positions within the organization and are recognized and rewarded on the basis of their performance. For example, faculties and departments in a university resemble baseball teams to the extent that the university recruits and rewards professors on the basis of their performance through such means as the granting of tenure and pay raises. Similarly, the hiring of coaches in a large athletics department is based on individual performance. Although the emphasis on individual performance reflects the assignment flow, the tendency of such organizations to go outside of their own ranks to

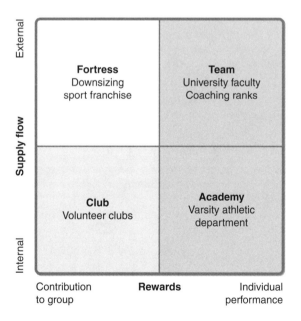

FIGURE 11.3 Sonnenfeld and Peiperl's four career systems.
Adapted from Sonnerfeld and Peiperl 1988.

VIEWPOINT

Thoughts about careers take on a special relevance in the new workplace. We live and work in a time when the implications of constant change pressure us continually to review and reassess our career progress. In particular, businesses are becoming smaller . . . and employing fewer people, and new, more flexible and adaptable forms are replacing the traditional organizational "pyramid." Accordingly, multifunctional understanding is increasingly important as organizations emphasize lateral coordination. . . . In general, the nature of "work" is changing; future work will require continuous learning and will be less bound by the "9 to 5" traditions. (Schermerhorn, Hunt, and Osborn 1991, p. 113)

These authors suggested that an individual must take responsibility for his or her own career instead of continuing the traditional reliance on an organization. To do so, one should build a portfolio of skills and continuously develop it in order to keep pace with the changing workplace. In today's technology-focused workforce, the sentiments of Schermerhorn et al. (1991) are more pertinent than ever. Increasing reliance on mobile phones and social media have made many employees accessible 24 hours a day, 7 days a week. In many areas of the sport and recreation industry, careers are multifaceted, and employees are expected to understand operations, marketing, sales, and public relations while adapting to flexible and ever-evolving work schedules. These changes have increased the demands on employees to the point where career development opportunities are becoming paramount to employee motivation and commitment.

In the sport and recreation context, where employees wear multiple "hats" at any given time, managers must give employees opportunities to develop their skills based on job requirements. For example, if technological advances (e.g., computer programming and analytics) are required for an employee to be effective in his or her role, then a manager may offer to cover the cost of sending the employee to a training workshop in order to develop these career skills. This career support and development results in increased motivation and commitment.

The essential thrust of Sonnenfeld and Peiperl's (1988) argument is that a particular career system may be functional in certain types of organizations or units. In addition, an organization may adopt different systems at different times based on particular circumstances. Ultimately, the choice of one system over the others is determined both by the particular circumstances at the time and, of course, the preferences of top-level decision makers.

For instance, a university athletics department may adopt the baseball team model in the case of hiring coaches. That is, the department may offer good salaries and benefits to outstanding coaches in order to recruit them. The department then recognizes and rewards them as long as they perform well. However, if a coach (or his or her team) fails to perform, the department is likely to replace the coach with a newly recruited star performer. At another time, the department may be satisfied with promoting the assistant coach to the position of head coach. From a different perspective, the directorate of the athletics program (i.e., the director and assistant directors) may resemble an academy that recruits members when they are young, trains them in various positions, and promotes the better performers to higher positions.

hire qualified candidates indicates the external supply flow.

Like the organizations that resemble baseball teams, the academy-type organizations use individual performance as the basis for promotion and rewards (i.e., they use the assignment flow). However, these academies are closed to outside markets (i.e., to the external supply flow). They would rather rely on developing their own members' knowledge, skills, and commitment. For example, in some circumstances, universities and athletics departments rely on internal candidates for filling positions. In such cases, they resemble the academy as portrayed by Sonnenfeld and Peiperl (1988).

The organizations labeled as clubs, like those labeled as academies, are closed to external labor markets. Unlike the academies, however, clubs use *group* contribution as the criterion for assignments and promotions. This criterion is often reflected in the use of seniority as the basis for promotions.

The fourth type, the fortress, was described by Sonnenfeld and Peiperl (1988) as "an institution under siege." In this case, organizational survival is deemed more critical than are the members and their welfare. Although the fortress is open to external labor markets, it does not exhibit any commitment to individual employees or their performances. The more critical concern is whether the group or unit is performing well. For example, many firms in the business and industrial sector have attempted to survive by laying off a large number of their members or by replacing their senior staff (i.e., the highly paid staff) with new recruits. In a similar manner, when faced with declining membership, a fitness club may fire or lay off several of its employees.

· ·

One's career consists both of one's movement from one job to another over a lifetime and of the accompanying experiences. In managing the careers of their employees, organizations rely on either an internal or an external source for higher-level positions and may use either one's individual performance or one's contribution to the group as the criterion for promotions.

· ·

MENTORING

In addition to training, managers can use the process of mentoring to groom members of an organization for advancement in their careers. At the same time,

VIEWPOINT

Despite the notion that individuals are responsible for their own careers—and irrespective of an organization's own career systems—in order to enhance employee commitment and engagement, the organization and its managers must endeavor to support employees' career development. According to Robbins (1997), critical aspects of such support include the following actions:

- Communicate the organization's goals and future strategies so that interested employees can plan and prepare to participate in the company's future.
- Provide employees with opportunities for more interesting and challenging work experiences.
- Offer financial assistance (e.g., tuition reimbursement) to help employees keep current in their fields.
- Offer employees paid time off for additional training elsewhere.

young people who enter an organization must be aware of and capitalize on the opportunities for mentoring relationships, which can be critical to career advancement.

On the basis of the literature on mentoring, Weaver and Chelladurai (1999, 2002) defined mentoring as "a process in which a more experienced person serves as a role model, and provides guidance and support to a developing novice, and sponsors that novice in his/her career progress" (Weaver and Chelladurai 1999, p. 24). Weaver and Chelladurai (1999, 2002) also provided a schematic representation of mentoring in organizations (see figure 11.4). A brief description of the model is presented in the following sections.

Let us begin by addressing what a **mentor** actually does. From a study of 15 executives, Kram (1983) identified two distinct sets of mentoring functions—career and psychosocial—which are described in table 11.6. Career functions enhance career advancement by increasing the **protégé's** skills and abilities, exposing the protégé to challenging tasks and influential superiors, and sponsoring

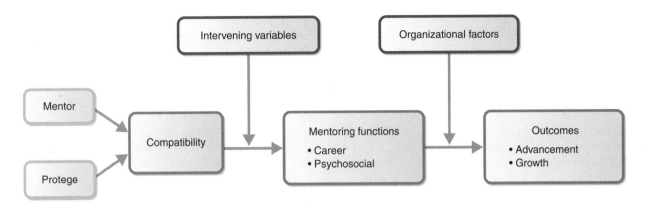

FIGURE 11.4 A model of mentoring in organizations.

Adapted, by permission, from M.A. Weaver and P. Chelladurai, 1999, "A mentoring model for management in sport and physical education," *Quest* 51: 24-38.

TABLE 11.6 Functions of Mentoring

CAREER FUNCTION	DESCRIPTION
Sponsorship	The mentor highlights the protégé's potential and nominates him or her for advantageous transfers and promotions.
Exposure and visibility	The mentor provides the protégé with opportunities to work with key people and decision makers who influence the protégé's progress.
Coaching and feedback	The mentor teaches the protégé about the organization's culture, values, and strategies and identifies strengths and weaknesses in the protégé's performance.
Developmental assignments	The mentor assigns challenging work to help the protégé develop key skills and knowledge that are crucial to advancement.
Protection	The mentor shields the protégé from making serious mistakes and from individuals who may hold an antagonistic view of the protégé.
PSYCHOSOCIAL FUNCTION	**DESCRIPTION**
Role modeling	The mentor models a set of attitudes, values, and behaviors for the protégé to imitate.
Acceptance and confirmation	The mentor confirms and expresses confidence in the protégé's abilities and talent and provides encouragement.
Counseling	The mentor counsels the protégé regarding personal concerns and anxieties.
Friendship	The mentor engages in friendly social interactions, which relieve the pressures of work.

Adapted from Kram 1985.

the protégé for advancement in the organization (Kram 1985). In the psychosocial functions, the mentor facilitates the growth and development of the protégé by acting as a role model, accepting and confirming his or her abilities and talents, and providing counsel and friendship. These psychosocial functions enhance the protégé's sense of competence, identity, and managerial effectiveness.

Outcomes of Mentoring

Successful mentoring should result in significant outcomes for all three parties to the arrangement: the protégé, the mentor, and the organization.

- *Outcomes for the protégé:* The protégé gains two kinds of outcomes from successful mentoring: advancement and growth (Hunt and Michael

1983; Zey 1985). These two outcomes parallel the two kinds of mentoring functions. As just noted, the mentor sponsors and coaches the protégé and exposes him or her to top-level decision makers and high-profile assignments. Therefore, the protégé is more likely than a nonprotégé to be noticed, recognized, and rewarded. As a result, the protégé may enjoy greater career success in terms of salary, bonuses, promotion, status, and power and may also experience greater job satisfaction (Fagenson 1989; Riley and Wrench 1985). The psychosocial functions of mentoring (i.e., role modeling, acceptance and confirmation, counseling, and friendship) facilitate the growth of the protégé in terms of competence, identity, and effectiveness (Kram 1985).

- *Outcomes for the mentor:* Mentors themselves benefit in several ways. First, the rejuvenating challenge of guiding a young protégé and the intrinsic satisfaction derived from the mentoring process may not be available in the tasks associated with the mentor's regular work (Hunt and Michael 1983; Kram 1985; Levinson 1978). The process also furthers the mentor's sense of competence and confidence in his or her own abilities (Noe 1988; Zey 1984). From a different perspective, mentoring brings several extrinsic rewards. The mentor gains in status and esteem from peers and superiors (Jennings 1967; Kram 1980); in addition, because the mentor is training the protégé to take over his or her responsibilities, continued promotion of the mentor is made possible (Jennings). Furthermore, the mentor gains the network of the protégé as a base of technical support, respect, power, and influence throughout the organization (Jennings; Kram 1980). Finally, the protégé may help the mentor engage in new projects that enhance the mentor's reputation as an achiever and star maker (Newby and Heide 1992).

- *Outcomes for the organization:* The major advantage accruing to the organization is the identification and grooming of good candidates with managerial potential for promotion to higher and more responsible positions. A protégé is likely to be more satisfied and committed to the organization and is likely to stay with that organization (Hunt and Michael 1983; Kram 1980). In sum, mentoring reduces the need to hire individuals from the outside. Because of these advantages, many organizations have instituted formal mentoring programs (Zey 1985).

The preceding description of mentoring emphasizes the higher position of the mentor and the power and status associated with that position. However, although the conception of mentors as holding positions of relative power is commonplace in organizations, it does not preclude the possibility that senior co-workers can fulfill many of the mentoring functions. Thus, a five-year assistant to the marketing director in an athletics department can and usually will help a newly hired assistant by teaching the technical and interpersonal aspects of the job, the interrelationships between the job and the various units of the department, and the overall value system of the organization. It is also not uncommon for such a veteran to serve as a spokesperson for the newcomer. These are career functions indeed. By the same token, the veteran can also provide support by being a role model, accepting the newcomer for who he or she is, counseling the newcomer, and offering friendship. These are the psychosocial functions.

Thus, being a mentor is not restricted to senior executives. Even lower-level workers who have gained expertise through experience, and who are inclined to help novices, can serve as effective mentors. Being aware of this opportunity, sport managers should encourage such mentoring relationships among workers.

Mentor–Protégé Compatibility

Although the process of mentoring (whether self-selected by the protégé or mentor or officially arranged) is useful in many respects, it is highly dependent on the compatibility of the mentor's characteristics and those of the protégé (i.e., **mentor–protégé compatibility**). Typically, the mentor is older and more experienced than the novice and possesses the knowledge and expertise to guide the novice (Burke 1984; Levinson 1978). Because of this seniority, the mentor usually ranks high in the organizational hierarchy and has cultivated an effective network inside and outside the organization (Hill, Bahniuk, and Dobos 1989; Hunt and Michael 1983). In addition, mentors should feel a high need for influencing others, including protégés (Weaver and Chelladurai 1999, 2002). Other characteristics of mentors that attract protégés include knowledge of operations and a positive attitude and open mind (Gaskill 1991).

Like mentors, protégés are characterized by a high need for power, and this need is addressed by association with high-level executives who possess real power. Kanter (1977) referred to this effect as "reflected power." Other personal characteristics that mark a successful protégé include assertiveness, open-mindedness, and flexibility (Kram 1985; Noe 1988; Ragins and Cotton 1991; Scandura and Ragins 1993). Potential protégés also need to have strong faith in and appreciation for a mentoring relationship; in contrast, some individuals may believe that their own abilities and talents will suffice to carry them forward in their careers (Noe). Protégés also gain increased potential for advancement; in fact, this benefit is a basic assumption in the mentoring process. That is, when considering individuals for participation in the mentoring process, organizations usually select only those they believe are potential managers (Ragins 1989).

The sex of the protégé may also have some bearing on the mentoring process, for two reasons. First, more men are found in the upper echelons of management, and therefore they form the larger pool of potential mentors (Hancock and Hums 2015). Researchers report that "women hold fewer than five percent of senior executive jobs in corporate America" (Schermerhorn, Hunt, and Osborn 1997, p. 3). Researchers have found similar statistics regarding low representation of women in the administrative and coaching ranks in sport (Hancock and Hums 2015).

Second, research shows that women tend to be relatively more passive in seeking a mentoring relationship (Fitt and Newton 1981; Hancock and Hums 2015). This tendency may be due to a lack of faith in mentoring. As compared with men, women may tend to minimize the effects of the mentoring process, particularly with regard to their advancement in the organization, and may rely more on hard work for advancement (Hilliard 1990; Nieva and Gutek 1981; Noe 1988). In addition, as compared with men, women tend to prefer more of the psychosocial functions from their mentors and less of the career functions (Burke 1984).

In sum, the notion of mentor–protégé compatibility includes mutual adjustments in interpersonal relationships between the two parties and a sharing of interests and goals associated with the desired outcomes of mentoring.

In a mentoring relationship, a senior expert offers guidance to help a protégé (i.e., a novice) grow; the mentor also sponsors the novice for promotion and career advancement. The success of a mentoring relationship is based on compatibility between the mentor and the protégé, including such aspects as age; the willingness, relative ability, and expertise of the mentor; and the flexibility of the protégé.

Intervening Variables

Even when a mentor and protégé are compatible, certain barriers can arise that hinder the emergence of a mentoring relationship. These barriers include fear of sexual connotations, fear of tokenism, and lack of networking opportunities (Gilbert and Rossman 1992; Hilliard 1990; Kram 1985; Shapiro and Farrow 1988).

In regard to sexual connotations, the close association between a mentor and protégé may be uncomfortable in the case of cross-sex mentoring. Either party in the relationship may be concerned about appearing sexually motivated. Even more significant is the fear that others may perceive the mentoring relationship as sexually oriented. Such fears and inhibitions may act as a barrier to successful mentoring. Similarly, a woman or a person from a minority group may perceive the advances and concerns of a would-be mentor as gestures of tokenism (i.e., the tendency to hold concern for one individual as a concern for a group to which the individual belongs). Tokenism may also be perceived by individuals outside of the mentoring relationship.

Another barrier to forming effective mentoring relationships is a lack of opportunity to network with probable mentors. This barrier is particularly operative in the case of women and minorities. To the extent that fewer women and minorities are present in higher ranks, the opportunity for networking is minimized because protégés from minority groups find it hard to locate mentors of similar sex or background who will identify with the barriers and challenges they may face in the workplace. Furthermore, cultural and sexual differences (e.g., not working on certain days due to either religious practice or home-life commitments) may hinder interactions between mentors and protégés.

Organizational factors may also inhibit the advancement or career outcomes expected from a mentoring relationship. In fact, the organization, its policies, and the politics therein largely determine career outcomes such as promotion, advancement, and increased salary. In some organizations, such policies may emphasize seniority rather than performance; in addition, powerful officials in the organization may favor candidates other than the protégé. Organizational factors exert less influence on growth outcomes because these outcomes are administered within the dyad of the mentoring relationship and by the mentoring process itself. In other words, the extent to which the protégé grows (in terms of knowledge, abilities, and performance accomplishments) and gains a sense of achievement and fulfillment lies within the domain of the mentor and the protégé.

Mentoring in Peer Relationships

The discussion so far has dealt with relationships between a senior and a junior in an organization. But the elements and benefits of the mentoring process can also apply to other relationships, either within or outside of the organization. This possibility was the thrust of work done by Pastore (2003), who was inspired by the writings of Kram (1988) and Higgins and Kram (2001). According to these authors, peers can engage in the process of mentoring each other; that is, each can act as a mentor and a protégé of the other. The peers can exchange information, strategize regarding their careers, and provide feedback about each other's job performance. These activities reflect the career functions in a traditional senior–junior mentoring relationship. Peers can also confirm each other's status and strengths, provide emotional support to each other, and offer friendship. These benefits reflect the psychosocial functions of a senior mentor described earlier.

Although the mentoring functions are similar in senior–junior relationships and peer relationships, peer mentoring offers certain advantages (Pastore 2003). These advantages include a more intimate relationship that lasts longer and is characterized by

mutuality. In a traditional mentoring relationship, the mentor is a senior who holds a higher rank and is the dispenser in the mentoring process. In contrast, the parties in a peer relationship serve each other reciprocally. In addition, the mentor in a peer mentoring relationship is more readily available than is a mentor in the conventional mentoring arrangement.

Given these benefits of mentoring within peer relationships, Pastore (2003) advocated extending the process outside of conventional organizational contexts—for example, through membership in professional organizations such as the North American Society for Sport Management. She also urged students to serve as mutual mentors to each other. In fact, many readers may recognize that they have been involved in such relationships when serving as mentors to one another, though without a formal title or arrangement. In other words, they may now recognize that they are already mentors in their own right.

ROLE OF THE SPORT OR RECREATION MANAGER

Today's sport and recreation consumers are savvy and knowledgeable about the products they purchase and services they experience. In this demanding setting, the processes of hiring, training, and retaining the "right" people for the organization serve as strategic tools that can be leveraged to create a competitive advantage. Thus, sport and recreation managers must be acutely aware of their organization's mission and vision in order to ensure that job descriptions, hiring processes, and career development are aligned with the organization's goals and objectives.

To this end, a strategic planning process may be appropriate every five to ten years. Specifically, managers assess job descriptions and career development opportunities for their employees to ensure continuing alignment with broader organizational priorities. This process can include a systematic review of what the organization stands for (e.g., mission, vision, and values) and how employees fit into the larger picture of organizational functioning. These steps help managers ensure that "who we are" matches "what we are," which constitutes an important step toward achieving organizational effectiveness. For example, if a national sport organization wishes to diversify its athlete membership, the executive director must first look to its mission, vision, and values in order to ensure that diversity is valued in both internal and external communications.

Systematic integration of the value of diversity must begin with job descriptions and hiring processes that include a commitment to recruiting, maintaining, and developing a diverse set of individuals who value diversity. In addition, the performance appraisal process (covered in chapter 13) must address an employee's acceptance and awareness of—and ability to harness—the benefits of diversity among personnel, clients, consumers, and other relevant parties. Within this example,

the strategic mandate of an organization (to focus on increased diversity in the athlete membership pool) is effectively connected to internal human resource management processes. Specifically, to effectively encourage diversity among membership, a systematic review of internal personnel must show a diverse staff population. Effective staffing, in line with organizational objectives around diversity, can lead to long term achievement of organizational goals.

Case Study

Psychological Contracts and Management by Values

Michael is a former soccer player who decides that it is time to give back to the sport he loves. Through a web search, he locates a local soccer club in need of volunteer coaches. The club's mission statement states, "Our club is dedicated to creating a fun and safe learning environment where players, coaches, and parents cooperate to ensure that individuals are able to play, develop, and mature through the game of soccer." Having grown up playing soccer with a club that focused more on high-performance development than on grassroots development, Michael is intrigued by the values associated with this mission statement. He decides to put in an application to be the coach of the U10 boys' team; he notes that the position comes with a stipend covering the cost of travel and any needed equipment.

Three weeks later, after the coach screening check and an interview with the club's executive director, Michael is ready to start his first practice with his new team. He finds it a little odd that he was not involved in an orientation for the coaching position and that relatively no training was provided; however, he is confident in his knowledge of the game of soccer and his ability to teach soccer skills to his eager group of young boys.

Unfortunately, Michael's enthusiasm is quickly squashed when two parents aggressively approach him after the first practice to ask about their children's potential playing time in the upcoming game. Michael suggests that in order to serve the club's mission, with its focus on development, he is committed to equal playing time for all players. The parents are quite unhappy with this response and continue to badger him. Given his lack of training and orientation, Michael is unsure both of how to handle the situation and of the resources that the club may have available to help him. He is quickly realizing that the stipend attached to the coaching position may not be worth the hassle of dealing with these parents on his own.

Case Study Tasks

1. Given this chapter's discussion of psychological contracts, which types of expectations (e.g., relational, transactional) were violated in this case? Explain your response.

2. Given the tenets of management by values (MBV) outlined in chapter 7 (including values in hiring, training, and orienting personnel), how could the club's executive director fulfill the organization's transactional and relational psychological contract with Michael in order to help ensure that his expectations are met?

CHAPTER PURSUITS

SUMMARY

This chapter presents the purposes of staffing and the steps involved in it. The preliminary steps include assessing the types and number of jobs that need to be filled, analyzing the tasks associated

with a specific job, describing the job in terms of requirements and responsibilities, and specifying the human characteristics required to perform effectively in the job. The manager must then recruit a large number of candidates for the position; identify and hire the best candidate for the job; and train the selected individual in the tasks associated with the job, in interpersonal skills, and in organizational values and norms.

In addition, the chapter outlines the concept and the significance of the psychological contract in contrast to the formal contract. It also addresses the association between staffing procedures and career considerations from the perspective of the individual as well as that of the organization. Finally, it discusses the benefits of mentoring that accrue to the protégé, the mentor, and the organization and relates these benefits to career progress.

KEY TERMS

career 206

career anchor 206

career orientation 206

hiring 190

job analysis 191

job description 192

job specification 192

mentor 210

mentor–protégé compatibility 212

protégé 210

psychological contract 204

recruiting 195

staffing 190

training 190

UNDERSTAND

1. One way to recognize one's career anchor is to recall one's work experiences and reactions to those experiences. Consider the following experiences and your reactions (positive, negative, or both) to them. Relate these work experiences and reactions to your own perceived talents, needs, and values. A composite of all of these experiences and feelings would suggest which of the five career anchors is more important to you.

   - Why did you choose your major area of concentration in high school and your major in college? How did you feel about these areas?

   - What were your expectations of, and experiences in, your first job?

   - How often have you changed jobs and why?

   - What do you expect to do after graduation? What are your expectations for the next 10 years?

2. You have been mentored by your parents and teachers and perhaps by siblings. Compare these mentoring relationships.

INTERACT

1. The following list presents a set of jobs in sport management. Assume that you are offered all of these jobs and that the remuneration for them is more or less equal. Rank the jobs in order of your preference. Explain your preferences in terms of the attraction of the jobs or organizations, your own estimates of how well you would do in each job, and the match between you and the job.

   - Director of a large YMCA sport and recreation program

   - Director of a metropolitan city recreation department

   - Executive director of a national sport governing body

   - Manager of a sporting goods store

   - Manager of a stadium or arena

   - Marketing manager for a professional team

   - General manager for a professional team

2. Job opportunities for sport management students can be found in professional sport franchises, intercollegiate athletics departments, high school athletics departments, city recreation departments, and private profit-oriented clubs (e.g., fitness clubs, golf courses). Where would you like to get a job when you graduate? Explain your reasons.

3. The concept of psychological contract is applicable to any form of relationship. Consider your relationship as a student with your academic department, then discuss the elements of psychological contract between you and the department.

CHAPTER 12

Leadership

---LEARNING OBJECTIVES---

After reading this chapter, you will be able to

- define leadership and describe forms of leader behavior;
- explain the multidimensional model of leadership, its components, and the relationships between these components;
- distinguish between transactional leadership and transformational leadership;
- define charismatic leadership;
- explain the advantages and disadvantages of member participation in decision making;
- understand the varying degrees of participation by members; and
- identify the critical attributes of a problem situation that determine the appropriate level of participation by members.

One of the key processes in the management of human resources is leadership. The leadership provided by an immediate supervisor and top-level administrators helps employees understand roles, performance expectations, and their relationships to organizational goals and reward systems. In addition, good leadership enhances employees' personal growth and development, motivation, performance, and job satisfaction. Therefore, managers need to have a clear understanding of the dynamics of leadership in organizations.

This chapter begins with a definition of leadership in the organizational context, then presents a multidimensional model that synthesizes various approaches to leadership. We also explain transformational leadership and describe the critical differences between transformational and transactional leadership. The chapter concludes with a section

on decision making. More specifically, the last section outlines the advantages and disadvantages of engaging members in decision making and the various methods of doing so. We also discuss the circumstances in which management should involve members in decision making. Understanding these various approaches to leadership and decision making can help managers analyze the specific circumstances they face and choose the appropriate leader behaviors or decision styles.

All of the definitions of **leadership** imply three significant elements:

1. Leadership is a behavioral process.
2. Leadership is interpersonal.
3. Leadership is aimed at influencing and motivating members toward group or organizational goals.

VIEWPOINT

The following excerpts are drawn from Drucker's (1992) book *Managing for the Future*. Drucker, one of the most renowned management scholars, emphasizes the great amount of work required in order to properly assess leadership theory. Although he focuses on top-level managers, his pronouncements are equally valid at lower levels.

> *Leadership does matter, of course. But, alas, it is something different from what is now touted under this label. It has little to do with "leadership qualities" and even less to do with "charisma." It is mundane, unromantic, and boring. Its essence is performance. (p. 119)*

> *What then is leadership if it is not charisma and it is not a set of personality traits? The first thing to say about it is that it is work—something stressed again and again by the most charismatic leaders. (p. 120)*

> *The foundation of effective leadership is thinking through the organization's mission, defining it and establishing it, clearly and visibly. The leader sets the goals, sets the priorities, and sets and maintains the standards. (p. 121)*

For instance, Daft (2015) noted that leadership "is an influence relationship among leaders and followers who intend real changes and outcomes that reflect shared purposes" (p. 5). Similarly, Tosi and Mero (2003) defined leadership as "a form of organizationally based problem solving that attempts to achieve organizational goals by influencing the action of others" (p. 248). Hitt, Black, and Porter (2005) define *organizational leadership* as "an interpersonal process involving attempts to **influence** other people in attaining some goal. This definition, therefore, emphasizes leadership as a social influence process" (p. 350).

Yukl and Van Fleet (1992) provided a more elaborate definition:

> Leadership is a process that includes influencing the task objectives and strategies of a group or organization, influencing people in the organization to implement the strategies and achieve the objectives, influencing group maintenance and identification, and influencing the culture of organizations. (p. 149)

In this definition, leadership includes shaping organizational objectives (i.e., setting new objectives or altering old ones) and maintaining the group and organizational culture. The definition also implies that effective leaders initiate and implement change when they set a vision of the future and when they persuade and inspire members to embrace the change and try to reach the new vision. Thus, leadership pervades not only at the individual level but also at the group and organizational levels.

If, as noted, leadership is a behavioral process, then the focus is on what the leader does rather than on what the leader is. Therefore, managers must understand the various descriptions of leader behavior and their utility.

 All definitions of leadership emphasize that it is a behavioral process aimed at influencing members to work toward achieving the group's goals. Thus, the focus is on what the leader does rather than on what the leader is. A critical purpose of leadership is to enhance members' productivity and satisfaction.

LEADER BEHAVIOR

Scholars from Ohio State University and the University of Michigan were the first to describe and categorize the various forms of leader behaviors in industry and business. After considerable research over a period of time, the scholars from each of these universities proposed two broad categories of leader behaviors. Specifically, the Ohio State writers proposed consideration and initiating structure (Halpin and Winer 1957), and the Michigan authors proposed employee-oriented leadership and production-oriented leadership (D. Katz, Maccoby, and Morse 1950; D. Katz, Macoby, Gurin, and Floor 1951).

WHAT DOES A LEADER LOOK LIKE?

As discussed in chapter 6, past studies have demonstrated that society in general prefers male leaders with formidable health, strength, and height. M.E. Price and Van Vugt (2015) pointed out that this preference for tall and strong males in leadership positions could be derived from our ancestral past of hunter-gatherers. They also pointed out that a mismatch exists between this ancestral need for physically formidable leaders and modern organizational life, which of course does not generally require hunting or fighting. The question of what a leader looks like, and perhaps more importantly, what a good leader looks like, has transformed from discussing physical attributes to understanding the personal and task related development a leader can foster.

Eagly and Carli (2007) pointed out that conceptual and emotional intelligence are traits that result in effective leadership. In their summary of literature on leadership, general intelligence was determined to be equal among men and women, whereas the traits of emotional intelligence, empathy, and compassion were more prevalent in women. Women also seem to regard ethics at a higher level than men and to be less accepting than men of "unscrupulous" tactics (p. 46). This shift from focusing on the physically formidable to the intellectually adept leader has caused a shift in conceptions of who can be an effective leader.

In the Ohio State scheme, consideration behavior reflects a leader's concern for members' well-being and for warm and friendly relations within the group. Initiating structure, on the other hand, is behavior that clarifies the roles of both the leader and the members for effective performance of the group's tasks. Similarly, the Michigan scholars defined employee orientation as the leader's concern with the human relations aspect of the job and production orientation as the leader's concern with the job and productivity.

A later attempt at synthesizing these efforts resulted in a four-dimensional description of leader behavior with the following key components: support, interaction facilitation, goal emphasis, and work facilitation. Support behaviors aim at enhancing members' feelings of personal worth and importance. Interaction facilitation behaviors foster close and mutually satisfying relationships within the group. Goal emphasis behaviors focus on the group's goals and their attainment. And work facilitation behaviors promote goal attainment by coordinating group activities and providing technical guidance (J.C. Taylor and Bowers 1972).

One of the criticisms of earlier attempts at describing leader behaviors was that just two or four dimensions cannot adequately describe these behaviors. Another concern was that these earlier schemes confounded the extent to which the leader was participative with other forms of leader behavior. For instance, the Ohio State authors' initiating structure included autocratic means of making decisions, whereas consideration included participative behaviors by the leader.

Researchers have suggested that the style of decision making (participative or autocratic) should be separated from the substance of decisions (e.g., Chelladurai and Turner 2006). For instance, the director of a recreation department may make a decision by himself or herself to install air conditioning in the workplace (i.e., reflecting an autocratic decision style), yet that decision is meant to enhance the comfort and welfare of the employees (i.e., consideration behavior). In contrast, another director may engage his or her employees in identifying and implementing ways to improve the performance of the group (i.e., a participative decision style reflecting initiating structure). In other words, a leader's concerns with task achievement or employee welfare should be treated as independent of the extent to which the leader involves the members in making decisions. The issue of the appropriateness of autocratic and democratic decision making is discussed later in this chapter.

Given these concerns, later attempts at describing leader behavior included more categories of leadership behaviors (House and Mitchell 1974; Stogdill 1963; Yukl and Van Fleet 1992). For instance, Yukl's (2002) Managerial Practices Survey contains 11 behavior categories that can be grouped into those focused on the organization itself and those focused on the employees. As shown in the following text, seven of the eleven categories are focused on employees.

Organizational Focus

- *Networking:* Developing and maintaining contracts
- *Planning and organizing:* Setting objectives and strategies and allocating resources to chosen activities
- *Problem solving:* Identifying, analyzing, and solving problems
- *Monitoring operations and environment:* Gathering information on the progress and quality of the work and scanning for threats and opportunities in the environment

Employee Focus

- *Supporting:* Acting friendly and showing sympathy
- *Managing conflict:* Resolving conflicts and fostering teamwork
- *Motivating:* Generating enthusiasm for work and commitment to task objectives
- *Recognizing and rewarding:* Recognizing effective performance and providing suitable rewards

- *Consulting and delegating:* Consulting with members, incorporating their ideas, and allowing member discretion in carrying out activities
- *Informing:* Informing members about decisions, plans, and activities and providing written materials and documents
- *Clarifying rules and objectives:* Assigning tasks and communicating job responsibilities, task objectives, deadlines, and performance expectations

Based on Yukl 2002.

In the context of sport and coaching, we can identify five dimensions of leader behavior in sport situations (Chelladurai and Saleh 1980): training and instruction, social support, positive feedback, democratic behavior, and autocratic behavior. These five dimensions are described in table 12.1. Training and instruction on the one hand and positive feedback on the other hand are related, respectively, to the process of task accomplishment and the degree of task accomplishment. Social support is concerned with the social needs of members, both individually and collectively. Democratic behavior and autocratic behavior concern the degree to which the leader allows members to participate in decision making.

While the description of leader behaviors is necessary, it is not sufficient in itself to grant us a full understanding of the dynamics of leadership and its effects. The critical concern here is whether the various forms of leader behavior described would be appropriate in all circumstances or whether their effectiveness depends on characteristics of the indi-

TABLE 12.1 Dimensions of Leader Behavior in Sport

DIMENSION	DESCRIPTION
Training and instruction	Coaching behavior aimed at improving the athletes' performance by emphasizing and facilitating hard and strenuous training; instructing them in the skills, techniques, and tactics of the sport; clarifying the relationships between members; and structuring and coordinating the members' activities
Social support	Coaching behavior characterized by a concern for the welfare of individual athletes, positive group atmosphere, and warm interpersonal relations with members
Positive feedback	Coaching behavior that reinforces an athlete by recognizing and rewarding good performance
Democratic behavior	Coaching behavior that allows participation by athletes in decisions pertaining to group goals, practice methods, and game tactics and strategies
Autocratic behavior	Coaching behavior that involves independent decision making and stresses personal authority

Based on Chelladurai and Saleh 1980.

viduals involved or of the situation. Because leadership involves situations or organizational contexts in which both the leader and members are embedded, researchers have advanced several theories to suggest that certain forms of behaviors are appropriate in certain situations. The following section outlines a synthesis of the various situational approaches to leadership.

 Several descriptive schemes have been proposed for leader behavior in organizations and sport teams. The categories of leader behaviors focus on both substantive issues and the extent to which the leader allows members to decide on those issues.

MULTIDIMENSIONAL MODEL OF LEADERSHIP

The multidimensional model of leadership (Chelladurai 1978, 1993a) is an attempt to synthesize and reconcile existing theories of leadership. A schematic illustration of the model is presented in figure 12.1.

Essentially, the model focuses on three states of leader behavior—required, preferred, and actual. It classifies the antecedent variables that determine these leader behaviors into situational characteristics, member characteristics, and leader characteristics. The consequences (i.e., outcome variables) in the model are group performance and satisfaction.

Required Leader Behavior

Stewart (1982) suggested that in any organizational context, the manager or leader faces certain demands and constraints that the organization imposes on the position. Demands are activities expected of leaders in a given situation that they must carry out in order to be accepted by the group or organization. Constraints set the limits within which the leader can act; in other words, the leader is prohibited from acting in the domain beyond the boundaries set by the constraints. According to Stewart, the area between the demands and the constraints represents the choices available to the leader.

Situational Characteristics and Required Behavior

What situational elements (i.e., demands and constraints) exert strong influence on leader behavior? Osborn and Hunt (1975) referred to these **situational characteristics** as *macro variables*, which include, for example, the size of a group, its technology, and its formal structure. In addition to these variables, the multidimensional model includes the group task,

---

TRAITS OF ATTITUDE TOWARD EMPLOYEES

Many sport and recreation personnel will branch out and start their own entrepreneurial ventures. For example, an individual who starts his own local sport delivery program (e.g., softball for adults) will be responsible for managing the employees within the program. One set of traits of successful entrepreneurs as identified by Locke (1997) relates to the leader's attitude toward employees:

- *Respect for ability:* Any business leader must have followers, but successful ones pick the best followers and, more important, respect the abilities of their subordinates. This respect for ability is reflected in the leader's willingness to let subordinates question and debate issues within the broader vision set by the leader.
- *Commitment to justice:* "Business heroes are not only great admirers and judges of ability, they are typically generous about rewarding it" (p. 89). Locke conceives of a "success-triad" in which managers "(1) hire extremely talented, motivated people; (2) demand and expect extraordinarily high performance from them while giving them high responsibility; and (3) reward them generously for success" (p. 90).

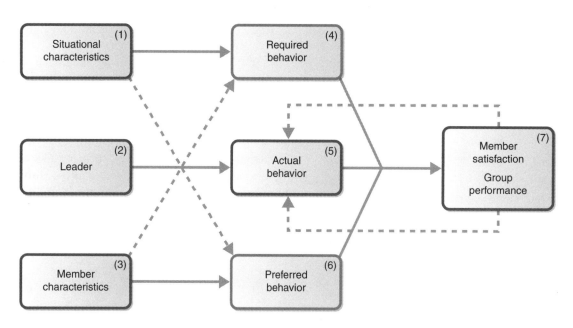

FIGURE 12.1 The multidimensional model of leadership.

Reprinted, by permission, from P. Chelladurai, 2007, Leadership in sports. In *Handbook of sport psychology*, 3rd ed., edited by G. Tenenbaum & R.C. Eklund (Hoboken, NJ: John Wiley & Sons), 113-135.

the organizational goals, the norms of a particular social setting, and the nature of the group as other situational characteristics that influence and control leader behavior.

Because the construct of leadership refers to a group, it is necessary to study leader behavior in terms of the group's tasks, processes, and performance. For example, in a university department of sport or recreation management, multiple units (or groups) may be involved in the performance of various tasks (e.g., undergraduate or graduate programs in marketing or organizational behavior). Similarly, for each athletic team in a university, the group task becomes a part of the situation.

Organizational goals also affect the total group, including the leader. For instance, the relative emphases placed on quality and quantity in a production firm affect both the manager's and the employees' behavior. In athletics, the differing goal orientations of professional and educational athletics lead to different behavioral expectations for the coaches and athletes in these two domains of athletics.

Another set of situational factors that impinge on leadership consists of the norms and codes of conduct that are prevalent (or emerging) in a given social setting. Contrast, for instance, the social norms surrounding a coach with those surrounding a manager of a city recreation department. The social norms of the athletics setting may permit a coach to

yell and scream at players, but such behaviors are proscribed in the case of the recreation manager.

Member Characteristics and Required Behavior

It has been argued that the nature of a group as a whole influences which segment of leader behavior is required in a given situation (Chelladurai 1993a). For example, differential demands are imposed on a leader by differences in orientation between volunteers and professionals (see chapters 2 and 3). One obvious difference between volunteers and paid professional employees is that one group is paid for their work and the other is not. To the extent that the supervisor exerts some control over such remuneration to the worker, the supervisor also possesses the influence to motivate him or her. In the case of volunteers, however, the leader must use other means of influencing members.

From a different perspective, a leader's behaviors also vary across different volunteer groups—for example, youth, adults, and seniors. (The concern here is with the nature of a group as a whole, not with individual differences within a group.) For example, House (1971) referred to perceived ability as an **individual-difference variable**, and groups have differences in actual or perceived ability just as individuals do. For instance, athletes at the NCAA Division I level are presumed to have higher ability

ROLE OF LEADERSHIP IN SPORT

To facilitate greater understanding of the role of leadership in sport, Chelladurai (1981) presented a modified version of the Porter and Lawler (1968) model of motivation (see chapter 8, figure 8.1). He also discussed the relevance of the various dimensions of coaching behavior to the motivational process, as shown in the figure here. Specifically, the effort–performance relationship (from box 2 to box 3 in the figure) is moderated by the member's ability (box 6) and by the accuracy of the perception of his or her role (box 7). In addition, the reward–satisfaction relationship (from box 4 to box 5) is influenced by the member's perception of the equity of the rewards (box 8).

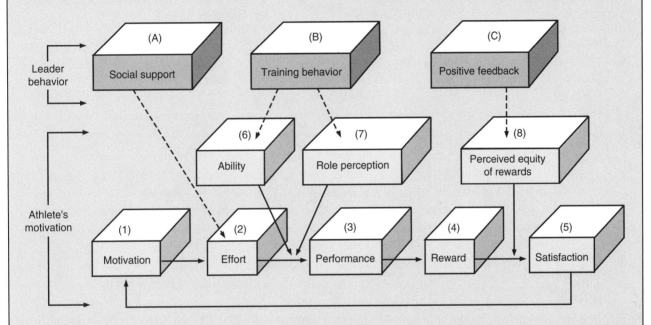

This motivation–performance–satisfaction sequence makes it easier to identify the points at which the coach can profitably intervene in order to enhance the individual's motivational state. The coach's social support behavior (box A) makes the effort phase enjoyable and frees it from interpersonal friction. On the other hand, training and instruction behavior (box B) develops the member's ability and clarifies role expectations. Thus, training and instruction behavior strengthens the relationship between effort and performance, and democratic behavior increases the clarity of the member's role and his or her feelings of involvement in decisions. Finally, positive feedback behavior (box C) ensures the equitable distribution of a coach's personal rewards (i.e., equal rewards for equal performance) and leads to a sense of equity and justice among members.

than those in Division III. Similarly, youth recreation leaders behave somewhat differently from leaders who work with senior citizens. Thus, when ability or maturity is viewed at the group level, it affects how the leader should behave in a given context—that is, the **required leader behavior**.

Preferred Leader Behavior

The preferences held by members for specific leader behaviors—**preferred leader behavior**—stem both from situational characteristics and from characteristics of the members themselves.

Situational Characteristics and Preferred Behavior

House's path–goal theory of leadership (House 1971; House and Dessler 1974), which is discussed in the sidebar, suggests that the effect of the task (particularly, its characteristics of interdependence and variability) acts as an immediate determinant of member preferences. For example, a maintenance worker in an athletics department who is engaged in independent and routine tasks is not likely to prefer higher levels of guidance from the supervisor. In contrast, marketing assistants who are involved collaboratively in the design and promotion of a new sport program may prefer more scrutiny and feedback from their marketing director. Such constraints and demands can be placed on a leader by various situational characteristics, including unit size, technology, organizational goals, and norms.

The same situational characteristics also influence member preferences for specific forms of leader behavior (Bass 1985; House 1971; Yukl 1998; Yukl and Van Fleet 1992). For instance, the preferences of an employee for interpersonal interactions with the athletics director (i.e., social support) would be lower in a large Division I institution than in a small Division III institution because the opportunities for such interactions would be less in larger athletic departments. For example, a larger Division I athletic department would have several associate directors who may act as "middle persons" when assessing the communication process of the department.

HOUSE'S PATH–GOAL THEORY

The main proposition of House's (1971) path–goal theory of leadership is that the motivational function of the leader consists of four elements: increasing personal payoffs to subordinates for achieving their work goals, making the path to these payoffs easier to travel by clarifying it, reducing roadblocks and pitfalls, and increasing the opportunities for personal satisfaction en route. The theory focuses on members' personal goals, their perceptions of organizational goals, and the most effective paths for achieving both personal and organizational goals goals. That is, the theory attempts to specify how leadership should clarify the path by which members can obtain desired goals and rewards.

The path–goal theory views the leader's function as a supplemental one. That is, leadership serves as an immediate source of rewards and satisfaction or as an instrument to future rewards and satisfaction. It also supplements the motivation provided by organizational factors (e.g., goal clarity, procedural precision, and guidance and support from the group).

Another proposition of the path–goal theory is that the motivational effect of leadership is a function of the situation, which comprises the members and the environmental pressures and demands. Members' preferences for, and reactions to, specific forms of leader behavior are affected by their personalities and their perceptions of their ability. Leader behavior should also be varied according to the nature of the task—that is, the extent to which tasks are routine or variable and the extent to which they are interdependent and inherently satisfying. In the sport context, athletes in interdependent sports (e.g., team sports) and athletes in those sports where the environment is constantly changing (e.g., basketball) prefer more training and instruction than do athletes in independent sports and those sports where the environment is stable and predictable (e.g., track and field) (Chelladurai and Carron 1982).

In overview, the path–goal theory places greater emphasis on members, their ability, and their personal dispositions than on other factors affecting leadership. It also views leadership as a process by which members' personal goals are aligned with organizational goals; therefore, achieving organizational goals leads to satisfaction of personal goals.

DIVERSITY MANAGEMENT OF HUMAN RESOURCES

Task complexity and task interdependence play important roles in the process of accommodating and activating diversity (Chelladurai 2014). Indeed, these moderating factors are essential to understanding the situational characteristics associated with effective leadership of a diverse workforce. Specifically, the more complex and interdependent a task is, the more need arises for leaders to strategically manage individuals toward realizing the benefits of diversity.

For example, during the two weeks leading into preparation for hosting a major international competition, the leaders of the local organizing committee must strategically acknowledge, accept, and coordinate diverse personalities, levels of expertise, and previous experience among staff and volunteers. Doing so is crucial in order to ensure that each event management element (e.g., operations, marketing, athlete services, spectator services) realizes the benefits of the diversity brought to the table both by the various work groups and by individuals. This can be a complex process requiring situational leadership to coordinate human resources toward success.

Member Characteristics and Preferred Behavior

Members' preferences for particular leader behaviors are also influenced by individual-difference factors (which are discussed at length in part II). For example, the path–goal theory highlights the effect of task-relevant ability (House 1971; House and Dessler 1974). Consider two new employees, A and B, in the ticketing department of a university athletics department. Employee A perceives that she possesses sufficient ability to carry out the assigned tasks and therefore may not prefer much guidance and training. On the other hand, employee B believes that he does *not* possess the understanding or the ability to perform the tasks and therefore prefers that the supervisor spend more time clarifying the procedures and coaching him.

Members' preferences regarding leader behaviors are also influenced by a number of personality traits, such as need for affiliation and need for achievement. For example, suppose that employees A and B in the preceding example differ in their need for affiliation. The employee who has a greater need for affiliation may prefer the supervisor to interact more often at the social level in order to satisfy, at least to some extent, that need. Employees A and B may also differ in their need to achieve at moderately challenging tasks and to seek feedback (D.C. McClelland 1961). In this case, the employee with the higher need to achieve may prefer that the director provide opportunities for challenge, responsibility, and feedback (House and Dessler 1974).

In addition, Lorsch and Morse (1974) and Morse (1976) suggested that an individual's attitude toward authority affects his or her reactions toward different types of supervision. Those whose respect for authority is high are more compliant with a leader's authority than are those whose respect for authority is low. Thus, a director of marketing in an athletics department needs to vary the extent and manner of exercising his or her authority across members based on their attitudes toward authority.

Another influential factor is cognitive complexity, which involves the ways in which individuals process information and their capacity to manage pieces of information. Researchers expect this capacity to determine, in part, an individual's preference regarding structuring behavior from the leader (Wynne and Hunsaker 1975). For instance, the marketing director may have to spend more time with subordinates who have a low level of cognitive complexity in order to explain each of several aspects of a marketing project and the interrelationships between them.

Actual Leader Behavior

The third, and obviously the most central, state of leader behavior is actual behavior. As noted earlier, two of the determinants of actual leader behavior are the requirements of the situation and the preferences of members. Osborn and Hunt (1975) divided actual leader behavior into adaptive behaviors (i.e., adaptations to situational requirements) and reactive behaviors (i.e., reactions to member preferences). These two forms of leader behavior are also a function of a leader's personal characteristics, particularly personality and ability.

Personality and Actual Behavior

The leader's personality is the central focus of Fiedler's (1967) contingency model of leadership, which is summarized in the sidebar. According

---

FIEDLER'S CONTINGENCY MODEL OF LEADERSHIP

In Fiedler's (1954, 1967, 1973) view, leadership effectiveness is contingent on the fit between the leader's style and situational favorableness. The leader's style (e.g., task orientation versus employee or relations orientation) is a relatively stable personality characteristic. Fiedler measured this personality trait using the least-preferred-co-worker scale, in which subjects are asked to recall an individual with whom they could work least well and to rate that person on 16 to 20 bipolar items, as in the following example:

| Unpleasant | 1 | 2 | 3 | 4 | 5 | 6 | 7 | 8 | Pleasant |

Those who score high on the scale—that is, those who evaluate the least preferred co-worker more favorably—are relations-oriented leaders, whereas low scorers are task-oriented leaders.

According to Fiedler (1967), a situation may be more or less favorable to the leader with respect to the exercise of influence over subordinates. The favorableness of the situation is determined by

- leader–member relations (i.e., the extent of friendship with and respect from the members),
- the task structure (i.e., the clarity of task goals and processes), and
- the power position of the leader (i.e., authority and control over rewards and punishments).

Fiedler's (1967) research showed that in situations with very high or very low favorableness, task-oriented leaders (i.e., low scorers on the least-preferred-co-worker scale) were more effective. In moderately favorable situations, on the other hand, relations-oriented leaders (i.e., high scorers on the least-preferred-co-worker scale) were more effective. These contingent relationships between leader style and situational favorableness are illustrated in the figure.

The lower part of the figure shows the continuum of situational favorableness beginning with the most favorable situation, in which leader–member relations are good, the task is structured, and the leader's power position is strong. The other end of the continuum shows the least favorable situation, in which leader–member relations are poor, the task is unstructured, and the leader's power position is weak. In between are situations of varying favorableness to the exercise of influence, depending on the configuration of the levels of leader–member relations, the task structure, and the leader's position power.

The most important implication of Fiedler's (1967, 1973) theory is that any leadership style can be effective if it is matched with the situation and its favorableness. In addition, because leadership style is a stable personality characteristic, it is easier to change the situation than to change leadership style. That is, the organization can change the situation by altering

- the composition of the group to create better leader–member relations (e.g., reassigning the manager or some employees of a sport facility to another facility),
- the task structure by varying the extent of rules and procedures in the task situation (e.g., letting the manager decide how to manage the facility instead of requiring him or her to follow strict rules and procedures), or

to Fiedler, leaders can be characterized as either task oriented or relations oriented. As the label indicates, the primary motive of task-oriented leaders is task accomplishment; therefore, they tend to behave in a relatively more directing and autocratic manner in order to accomplish the task at hand. Relations-oriented leaders, on the other hand, are motivated by concern for positive group atmosphere, so they are likely to be more participative and less directive.

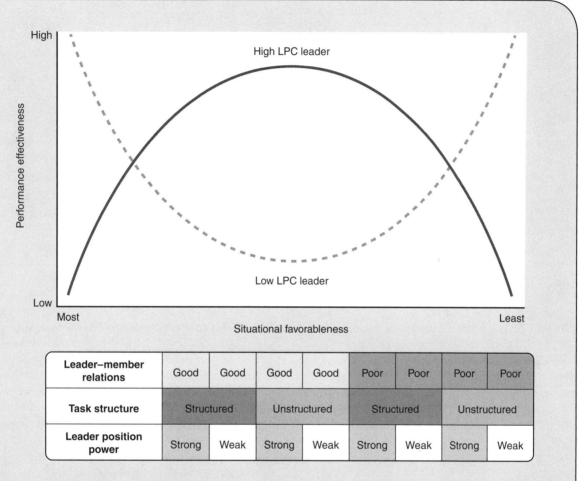

Leader–member relations	Good	Good	Good	Good	Poor	Poor	Poor	Poor
Task structure	Structured		Unstructured		Structured		Unstructured	
Leader position power	Strong	Weak	Strong	Weak	Strong	Weak	Strong	Weak

Adapted, by permission, from F.E. Fiedler, 1967, *A theory of leadership effectiveness* (New York: McGraw-Hill Companies). Copyright F.E. Fiedler.

- the power (or authority) of the leader (e.g., giving the facility manager the responsibility of evaluating employees and recommending merit raises).

The situation of coaching may be relatively more favorable to the leader than are other contexts in sport (e.g., teaching sport) (Chelladurai 1985). Because athletes participate voluntarily and choose the activity and the team, both the coach and the athletes share the organizational goal of pursuit of excellence. In addition, because all members of the organization clearly understand and accept the processes for achieving that goal, a great degree of **congruence** exists between the leader, the member, and the situation. Because the situation is favorable for the coach in relation to exercising influence, an autocratic coach can be very effective. This view is consistent with the finding that coaches do tend to be generally autocratic and task oriented in their leadership style (Hendry 1968, 1969; Ogilvie and Tutko 1966).

MCCLELLAND AND BURNHAM'S THEORY OF MANAGERIAL MOTIVATION

D.C. McClelland and Burnham (1976) suggested that "the manager's job seems to call more for someone who can influence people than for someone who does things better on his own. In motivational terms, then, we might expect the successful manager to have a greater 'need for power' than 'need to achieve'" (p. 101). The need for power reflects "a desire to have impact, to be strong and influential" (p. 103). In addition, "the good manager's power is not oriented toward personal aggrandizement but toward the institution which he or she serves. . . . This is the 'socialized' face of power as distinguished from the concern for personal power" (p. 103).

According to these authors, the need for affiliation, which refers to an individual's desire to be liked and accepted by a group, is the least important need for successful management. In fact, it could even be detrimental to the extent that it leads to compromise on various rules in order to satisfy individual needs. In sum, "oddly enough, the good manager in a large company does not have a high need for achievement . . . although there must be plenty of that motive somewhere in his [or her] organization. . . . The top managers have a high need for power and an interest in influencing others, both greater than their interest in being liked by people" (D.C. McClelland and Burnham 1976, p. 109).

McClelland and his associates (D.C. McClelland 1961, 1975; D.C. McClelland and Burnham 1976; D.C. McClelland and Winter 1969) have isolated the needs for power, achievement, and affiliations as the most significant needs in the organizational context, particularly for leaders or managers. These authors' theory of managerial motivation is summarized in the sidebar. Essentially, they noted that managers with differing levels of these needs behaved differently toward their subordinates. Specifically, they found that managers who had a high level of need for power (moderated by their concern for the group and its productivity), a moderate level of need for achievement, and even lower levels of need for affiliation were more effective than those with a low level of the need for power and a relatively higher level of the other two needs.

Ability and Actual Behavior

The **ability** of the leader is made up of two components, one more specific and the other broader. The more specific component involves the leader's knowledge and expertise concerning various aspects of the group task and the processes necessary to attain the group's goals. This component has been referred to as technical skill (R.L. Katz 1972). This specific ability varies with different leadership positions. For example, in a city recreation department, it involves knowledge of the local govern-

ment's complex rules and regulations that apply to the department's activities. The second component of ability involves the leader's capacity to conceptualize the organization as a whole, analyze the complexities of a problem, and persuade subordinates about the efficiency of a particular approach. According to R.L. Katz (1972), this component consists of conceptual ability, which is transferable across situations.

When a leader possesses technical ability related to specific tasks and processes, he or she should be more confident in giving specific directions to members about how to carry out the tasks. In the absence of such skills, the leader may rely on senior members to provide guidance and coaching to other members. Similarly, when a leader possesses conceptual ability, he or she can explain more easily the relationships of specific actions to a gestalt (i.e., a global picture of what is being sought). Leaders who do not possess conceptual ability may refrain from attempting to explain actions in the context of the total picture or may be ineffective in their explanations.

Performance and Satisfaction

The consequences included in the multidimensional model are **performance** and satisfaction (see figure 12.1). Both of these consequences are influenced by the degree to which the three states of leader behavior are congruent (i.e., the actual behavior is consistent with both the preferred and required behaviors). Thus, any of the states of leader behavior could act as a limiting factor.

For example, in some bureaucratic organizations, outdated and dysfunctional rules and regulations may be in force and managers may enforce them. However, these policies may be intensely disliked by employees, which would reduce both performance and satisfaction. Say, for instance, that employees in a city or university recreation department spend considerable time and effort in interacting with clients. Even so, policy requires employees to punch a clock or keep a daily log of their activities, and the organization expects the manager to enforce this rule. Such a bureaucratic requirement does not relate meaningfully to the quality of the work performed. Therefore, employees are likely to feel dissatisfied and may begin to work merely to satisfy the rule (i.e., to meet only the minimal requirement). Similarly, if actual leader behavior deviates from the requirements of the organization for the leader or from the preferences of members, the deviation would detrimentally affect performance and satisfaction.

Feedback

In the multidimensional model, the leader is assumed to be flexible and capable of altering his or her behavior according to changing conditions. This perspective is consistent with the position taken by several scholars and researchers (e.g., Bass 1985; House 1971; Yukl 2002). If a leader finds that his or her behavior has not resulted in increased group performance, the leader is likely to alter the actual behavior to enhance productivity. For example, the manager of a fitness club may spend more time and effort in motivating the club's employees. By the same token, leaders who find that their group is not cohesive and integrated may begin emphasizing aspects of behavior that foster warm interpersonal relations within the group. Similarly, a leader who perceives low satisfaction among members may alter his or her behavior to enhance

member satisfaction. The effects of the leader's perceptions of performance and satisfaction on actual leader behavior are indicated as feedback loops (or dotted lines) in figure 12.1.

TRANSFORMATIONAL, TRANSACTIONAL, SERVANT, AND AUTHENTIC LEADERSHIP

In recent years, the transformation of organizations has raised great concern. In the face of increased pressure to innovate via technology, as well as growing ethical concerns in sport (e.g., bribery scandals, rules violations), leaders are making frantic efforts to change the structure and processes of all forms of organizations. Such efforts are referred to by various terms, including *downsizing, rightsizing, reengineering, restructuring,* and *refocusing.* Any restructuring or repositioning of an organization requires strong leadership in the top positions and effective communication processes.

Those who guide their organizations to transform into innovative and profitable enterprises are referred to as transformational leaders. The study of these leaders and of transformational leadership has intensified in the last two decades as technology has drastically altered the ways in which we implement and communicate about change. For example, the ways in which a leader can communicate with followers about the purposes and mechanisms for change has taken on new forms with the rise of social media (e.g., Twitter, Snapchat). With these platforms, leaders can connect with employees and engage them in change 24-7.

Several authors have suggested that most theories of leadership view the leader as transacting with his or her members (Bass 1990; Conger and Kanungo 1998; House and Podsakoff 1994). Such transactions involve the leader's provision of resources, including the leader's approval and support, in return for the members' efforts toward attaining organizational goals. Transactional leadership is based on the assumption that the environment of the work group is somewhat stable and that both the leader and the members are satisfied with the work group's purposes and processes. In this view, the members of the group have a stable set of needs and desires, and they are aware of the elements of transaction between themselves and the leader that would satisfy those needs and desires.

The multidimensional model posits that group performance and member satisfaction are related to the degree of congruence between leader behavior required by the situation, leader behavior preferred by the members, and actual leader behavior.

VIEWPOINT

S. Kerr and Jermier (1978) listed a number of factors that might serve as substitutes for leadership in the motivation of employees. These factors include members' characteristics (i.e., their professional orientation and affiliation), the nature of their task and the work group, and the organizational structure (including the policies and procedures). Indeed, members who are highly trained may not need much guidance from the leader; in addition, members may receive needed guidance from professional associations and peer groups. The work group may also provide the needed social support when personal or organizational problems arise. This support is particularly relevant given the growing use of social media (e.g., Twitter, Snapchat, Instagram), which enable employees to receive virtual support from colleagues and friends. Organizational policies and procedures may clearly specify what employee should do, as well as how and under what circumstances (as is the case in bureaucracies), thus making the leader's instrumental behavior redundant. S. Kerr and Jermier stressed that when numerous substitutes for leadership exist, a manager's attempts to influence members must be minimal; otherwise, leadership attempts may be viewed as interference.

In the multidimensional model, the leader operates within the confines of situational requirements. At the same time, the leader is expected to exercise discretionary influence to motivate members; such influence may take the form of rewards or punishments. The leader distributes rewards (or punishments) in exchange for member compliance with (or resistance to) the leader's directions or requests. In this scenario, leadership is strictly a transactional process. That is, the leader offers something to the members in exchange for their efforts toward organizational goals. For instance, the owner of a sport marketing company may be content with the business as it stands and with its management. The manager, in turn, operates as a leader in the transactional mode. That is, the manager may reward his or her employees in the form of a bonus in proportion to the amount of business each employee brings in. This type of leadership, with the creed "You do this, you get that," is transactional in nature.

Transactional leadership is just a type of leadership; the term carries no moral tones. Specifically, the exercise of a leader's discretionary influence entails the leader's setting challenging goals for the members, helping them achieve those goals by enhancing their abilities, and supporting them in their efforts (House 1971). In the example of the manager of a sport marketing company, the manager may guide and coach employees in their efforts to get business, set progressively challenging goals for them, and provide necessary support for their efforts. However, the process is still transactional to the extent that the leader acknowledges and accepts situational demands.

In contrast, transformational leadership is defined as "the process of influencing major changes in the attitudes and assumptions of organization members (organizational culture) and building commitment for major changes in the organization's objectives and strategies" (Yukl and Van Fleet 1992, p. 174). According to this definition, the transformation occurs at three levels:

1. Changes in organizational objectives and strategies
2. Member commitment to the new set of goals and strategies
3. Changes in the assumptions and attitudes of members

In a similar vein, Bennis (1997) noted that effective leaders of groups do the following four things: provide direction for members and signify to them the importance of what they do; generate trust within the group, including the leader; make resolute but sometimes risky decisions; and stimulate hope among the members that their efforts will succeed.

The basis for transformational leadership is general discontent with the status quo, and transformational leaders are concerned with creating a new vision and order for the organization. In the process of changing the total organization, a transformational leader articulates the vision, convinces members of the vision's viability, and expresses confidence in their capacity to achieve the vision. Transformational leadership involves meeting members' higher-order needs, which elevates their level of effort beyond expectations (Bass 1985; Conger and Kanungo 1998). It also involves empowering members to engage in innovative and creative ways to achieve the articulated vision. Again, transformational leadership envisions an alternative to the status quo, and the terms *transformational* and *visionary* are used interchangeably to describe this form of leadership.

The contrasts between transactional and transformational leadership are shown in table 12.2. As the table indicates, transactional leadership influences the cognition and abilities of the member, as well as the exchanges between the member and the leader. Such exchanges reduce turnover and absence rates and increase member satisfaction and expected performance. Transformational leadership, on the other hand, affects members' emotions, values, goals, needs, and self-esteem. These influences raise the aspirations of members, who put forth greater effort in order to achieve levels of performance beyond expectations. Note that these outcomes are also associated with higher job satisfaction and lower turnover and absence rates.

More recently, Rafferty and Griffin (2004) have developed a scale to measure five dimensions of transformational leadership, which are described in table 12.3. In the example of the manager of a sport marketing company, the manager may believe that the business could be much better, given the capacities of the members and the available opportunities in the market. That is, instead of merely operating within existing constraints (i.e., situational factors) and being confined to small-scale operations in a few sports, the manager may see opportunities to expand, not only in the magnitude of each project but also in the breadth of sport operations covered. This vision, of course, needs to be crystallized through a comprehensive analysis of present

TABLE 12.2   Differences Between Transactional and Transformational Leadership

LEADERSHIP TYPE	FACTORS AFFECTED	OUTCOMES
Transactional	Cognition Abilities Exchanges	Lower turnover and absence rates Increased satisfaction Increased performance expectations
Transformational	Emotions Values, goals, and needs Self-esteem	Higher aspirations Greater efforts Performance beyond expectations or call of duty Lower turnover and absence rates Increased satisfaction

Adapted from Bass 1985.

TABLE 12.3   Dimensions of Transformational Leadership

DIMENSION	DESCRIPTION
Vision	Based on organizational values, the leader presents an idealized vision of the future.
Inspirational communication	The leader expresses a positive and encouraging perspective on the organization in order to motivate members and build their confidence.
Supportive leadership	The leader shows concern for members and their individual needs.
Intellectual stimulation	The leader facilitates members' comprehension of problems and efforts to solve them in new ways.
Personal recognition	The leader acknowledges and praises the achievement of specified goals.

Adapted from Rafferty and Griffin 2004.

operations, market conditions, and the human and material resources available.

The next step is to articulate for members both this vision and their place in it. The purpose here is to arouse members' self-esteem and need for achievement. In addition, the manager may work to create a can-do attitude and conviction in members. Equally important is the notion of encouraging and permitting members to be creative in their approach to marketing, both in general and in their own projects, rather than confining themselves to traditional methods. Finally, the manager may express his or her confidence in members' ability and determination to achieve the vision.

Such a leadership orientation is likely to raise the aspirations of the members and nudge them to devote greater effort toward identifying and defining projects to secure new clients and fulfill their needs. As a result, members are likely to perform at a higher level than would be expected from a transactional perspective. In sum, the effect of such transformational leadership is that members develop a psychological stake in their work.

Transformational Leadership and the Multidimensional Model

In terms of the multidimensional model (Chelladurai 1978, 1993a), a transformational leader attempts to alter the situational characteristics (i.e., goals and strategies) and the beliefs and attitudes of members, including lower-level leaders or managers. In other words, instead of accepting the situational and member characteristics as a given, transformational leaders believe that those givens are alterable and act accordingly. Thus, the behaviors and the effects of transformational leadership can be superimposed onto the multidimensional model, as shown in figure 12.2.

Many descriptions of transformational leadership imply that such leadership begins with the chief executive officer of an organization and then filters down to lower levels through the empowerment of successive levels of subordinates. For example, Kevin Frey, CEO of Right to Play International, is part of a global team that uses the transformative power of play to educate and empower children facing adversity. His background in e-learning and development has allowed him to communicate effectively in underdeveloped areas of the world through the common language of sport and education. He could not have helped the Right to Play organization touch so many people worldwide without his dedicated regional directors across the globe and their effective use of technology to connect the organization's vision to employee practice. On a larger scale, renowned transformational leaders such as Mahatma Gandhi of India and Nelson Mandela of South Africa could not have achieved what they did without active cooperation from their immediate followers.

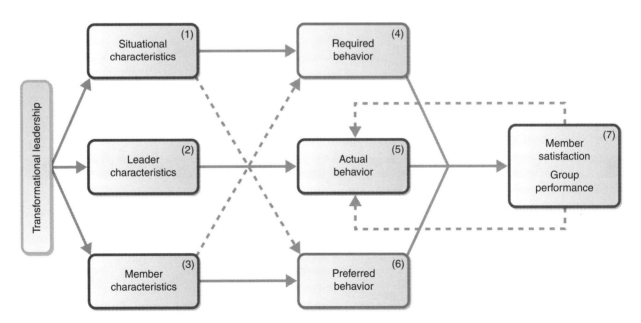

FIGURE 12.2 The modified multidimensional model of leadership.

Reprinted, by permission, from P. Chelladurai, 2007, Leadership in sports. In *Handbook of sport psychology*, 3rd ed., edited by G. Tenenbaum & R.C. Eklund (Hoboken, NJ: John Wiley), 113-135.

In the context of sport and recreation, the current elevated image and status (and, of course, profitability) of the National Basketball Association are largely attributed to the transformational leadership provided by former Commissioner David Stern, who served the league from 1984 to 2014. Although he was eminently successful as a transformational leader, the achievement must also be credited in part to other individuals (e.g. team owners) who bought into his vision and worked to achieve it. Similarly, Donna Lopiano, CEO of the Women's Sports Foundation from 1992 to 2007, has transformed the women's movement in sport and helped spearhead the current focus on gender equity in sport. On a global level, Juan Antonio Samaranch, former president of the International Olympic Committee (IOC), transformed the outlook and orientation of IOC members toward making the committee and the quadrennial Olympic Games a reservoir of revenue potential. In the process, he enlisted the business and media communities to generate enough revenue to sustain the Olympic movement and support athletic endeavor in developing countries.

However, the notion of transformational leadership need not be confined to large organizations with several levels of hierarchical structure. It can also be applied to smaller organizations with fewer levels of management and fewer members. A typical example is that of a coach who transforms a team from a perennial "doormat" into a winning team. Such a coach begins by articulating discontent with the current image of the team, sharing a vision in which the team performs in a winning fashion, and convincing the members that the vision is attainable and that they have the abilities to be that winning team. The only difference between the transformational leadership of the coach and that of a corporate CEO is that the coach does not have to address several layers of managers. Instead, he or she interacts with the members directly.

In the context of sport organizations, Weese (1995, 1996) found that the directors of campus recreation in the universities of the Big Ten and Mid-American Conferences varied in the extent to which they exhibited transformational leadership. Although Weese did not find a significant relationship between transformational leadership and organizational effectiveness as perceived by student participants in campus recreation, he did report a telling finding in that transformational leaders were able to cultivate an organizational culture (i.e., the system of values and beliefs) that, in turn, was positively associated with organizational effectiveness. The point is that the major contribution of transformational leadership is to change the values, beliefs, and aspirations of members (Weese 1995, 1996).

VIEWPOINT

In its work of examining transformation in the sport and recreation industry, the Women's Sports Foundation houses many strong leaders who work toward activating change. One prime example is Sandra "Sandy" Vivas, who not only acts as a member of the foundation's board of trustees but also serves as CEO and president of AthleticLink.com. She is an ongoing advocate for awareness of and compliance with the Title IX gender-equity policy at all levels of education and has made it her life's work to ensure that every young woman in the United States has the opportunity to attain the emotional, physical, and health benefits of sport experience (Women's Sports Foundation 2013). In these efforts, Vivas works to transform the vision of her followers for the betterment of the organizational mission.

Similarly, A.J. Doherty and Danylchuk (1996) found that the coaches of university sport teams in Canada perceived that their athletics administrators exhibited a considerable amount of transformational leadership. This leadership was associated positively with coaches' perceptions of leadership effectiveness, their satisfaction with the leadership they received, and their extra effort to achieve organizational goals. In a later study of the same data, A.J. Doherty (1997) found that female and younger athletics administrators in Canadian university athletics exhibited more transformational leadership than did their male and older counterparts. This research showed that women can be as effective as men in leadership positions and that both male and female subordinates are appreciative of such leadership. Furthermore, Doherty speculated that the changing values and beliefs of younger administrators could be the source of their transformational leadership.

Transformational and Charismatic Leadership

The term *charismatic leadership* is often used in conjunction with *transformational leadership*. Although the two terms have been used synonymously in some contexts, it is useful to consider them as distinct concepts. According to Yukl and Van Fleet (1992), charismatic leadership involves

> the follower perception that a leader possesses a divinely inspired gift and is somehow unique and larger than life. . . . [T]hey [followers] also idolize or worship the leader as a superhuman hero or spiritual figure. . . . Thus, with charismatic leadership the focus is on an individual leader rather than on a leadership process that may be shared among multiple leaders. (p. 174)

In this view, charisma is something attributed to leaders that enables them to transform a group or organization. Thus, charisma involves both a set of laudable attributes associated with the leader and a set of beliefs held by members about the leader. From this perspective, charisma constitutes a personal resource that leaders can exploit to transform organizations and their members. Again, charisma is an attributional phenomenon; that is, it comprises the attributions that followers make regarding the leader's extraordinary abilities. Such strong, positive attributions serve as the source of power that facilitates greater acceptance of the leader's pronouncements and the willingness to abide by his or her dictates and directions. For example, charisma has been exhibited by renowned coaches such as Phil Jackson and Tony Dungy. Similarly, Donna Lopiano, to whom we referred earlier, wields considerable influence because of her charisma and the judicious manner in which she uses it.

As noted earlier, transformational leaders tend to empower their subordinates. This idea of empowering leadership was the focus of a study by Arnold, Arad, Rhoades, and Drasgow (2000). They developed an instrument named the Empowering Leadership Questionnaire (ELQ) that measures five dimensions of leadership focused on empowering subordinates (see table 12.4).

Servant Leadership

A servant leader strives to ensure that followers' highest-priority needs are served and identifies his or her prime motivation for leadership as the desire to serve (Greenleaf 1977). Russell and Stone (2002) summarized Greenleaf's work into nine functional attributes of servant leaders:

1. Vision: possessing an ideal and unique image of the future
2. Honesty: conveying truth in the content of one's message
3. Integrity: conveying consistency in the delivery of one's message
4. Trust: engaging followers to rely on one's integrity, character, honesty, and actions
5. Service: managing the property, affairs, or ideas of another
6. Modeling: providing a visible example of proper behavior
7. Pioneering: initiating the development of an idea or project
8. Appreciating others: explicitly and visibly valuing and encouraging followers
9. Empowerment: entrusting others with power

As noted by A.G. Stone, Russell, and Patterson (2004), the main difference between a transformational leader and a servant leader is the choice of one's prime focus for leading. Specifically, whereas

TABLE 12.4 Dimensions of Empowering Leadership

DIMENSION	DESCRIPTION
Leading by example	Setting high standards for one's own behavior, working hard to maintain those standards, and setting an example of good behavior
Participative decision making	Encouraging and listening to the group's ideas and suggestions and giving members a chance to voice their concerns
Coaching	Helping members improve their performance, encouraging members to share ideas and work together, and supporting group members
Informing	Explaining the organization's goals, policies, rules, and decisions and how the group fits into the organization
Showing concern and interacting with the team	Caring about members' personal problems and well-being, treating members as equals, and getting along well with members

transformational leaders focus on change for the betterment of the organization, a servant leader focuses on change for the betterment of followers.

Recent reviews of leadership literature suggest a call for greater understanding of servant leadership in the sport context (Welty Peachey, Damon, Zhou, and Burton 2015). Sport and recreation may provide a unique context for servant leaders to flourish because many leaders (e.g., coaches, administrators, volunteer board members) become involved in sport in order to enrich the lives of athletes (i.e., followers). Given this shift in focus to servant leadership and the potential benefits of fostering servant leaders in the sport context, Welty Peachey, Damon, Zhou and Burton (2015) supported Yammarino's (2013) definition of leadership in their conceptual model of leadership in sport management:

> Leadership is a multilevel (person, dyad, group, collective) leader–follower interaction process that occurs in a particular situation (context) where a leader (e.g., superior, supervisor) and followers (e.g., subordinates, direct reports) share a purpose (vision, mission) and jointly accomplish things (e.g., goals, objectives, tasks) willingly (e.g., without coercion). (p. 150)

In this definition, the focus on the follower's active role in the leadership process supports the growing presence of servant leadership in the field of sport and recreation management.

Authentic Leadership

Luthans and Avolio (2003) first defined authentic leadership as "a process that draws from both positive psychological capacities and a highly developed organizational context, which results in both greater self-awareness and self-regulated positive behaviors on the part of leaders and associates, [thus] fostering positive self-development" (p. 243). Similar to that of servant leadership, this definition acknowledges the roles of both leaders and followers in the leadership process. To elaborate this definition, Shamir and Eilam (2005) outlined four distinct attributes of authentic leaders:

1. The self-concept of the individual is largely defined by his or her role as a leader.
2. The individual has a high level of clarity regarding self-concept and self-resolution (e.g., looking internally to the self to solve problems).

3. The individual's goals are self-concordant.
4. The individual's behavior is self-expressive.

Each of these attributes most be present in a leader in order for the positive moral benefits of authentic leadership to emerge.

In the definition of authentic leadership outlined by Luthans and Avolio (2003), authentic leaders possess positive moral perspectives characterized by high ethical standards that are said to influence decision making and behavior. This perspective on leadership associated with ethical behavior may be particularly relevant in the current climate of sport and recreation, where ethics and the morality of one's behavior are scrutinized constantly on a global scale. (For examples of [un]ethical behavior, consider the IOC and FIFA.) Thus, as described by Burton and Welty Peachey (2014), it is worth considering the role of this style of leadership in decision making and prosocial behavior in sport and recreation.

 Transactional leadership implies satisfaction with the status quo, whereas transformational leadership is aimed at changing existing goals and processes and inciting followers to accept and implement the changes. Charismatic leadership refers to perceptions of members that the leader possesses extraordinary gifts and talents. Finally, servant and authentic leadership reflect an extension of transformational leadership, wherein the leader is focused on change that specifically benefits his or her followers and wherein the self-concept of the leader brings forth ethical behavior.

LEADERSHIP AND DECISION MAKING

All leaders are engaged in making decisions about critical issues, such as the group's goals and objectives, the appropriate means of achieving those goals, and the distribution of duties and responsibilities to members of the group. These decisions can be viewed as a cognitive process and as a social process.

Decision Making as a Cognitive Process

In viewing decision making as a cognitive process, the emphasis is placed on the rationality of decisions. That is, the concern lies in evaluating the available alternatives and selecting the best one to achieve a desired end. Leaders can arrive at rational decisions only after defining the problem clearly, identifying relevant constraints, generating possible and plausible alternatives, evaluating and ranking the alternatives according to selected criteria, and selecting the best alternative in terms of those criteria.

In this view, decision making depends crucially on generating and evaluating alternatives. Thus, the process focuses on making objective and optimal use of available information. Because more information is available in a group than in an individual, the leader is well advised to include members in the cognitive process of decision making. Such group involvement is beneficial both in defining the problem and in identifying alternate solutions. The next section addresses the extent to which the group can be involved in decision making and under what conditions.

Decision Making as a Social Process

Member involvement in decision making is a major concern in human resource management; therefore, this section focuses in some detail on the social process of decision making. This process depends both on the degree to which members of a group are allowed to participate in decision making and on the degree of influence they exert on the decision. Thus, the social process of decision making may range from strictly autocratic decision making by the manager to varying degrees of participation by members—for example, consultation with one or a few members, consultation with all members, group decision making, and delegation. These variations have been referred to as the decision styles of the leader (Chelladurai and Haggerty 1978).

Some leaders are described as autocratic and others as participative. One obvious explanation is that the personality of such individuals predisposes them to be either autocratic or participative. A different perspective holds that instead of viewing individuals as autocratic or participative, we need to view the *situation* as calling for an autocratic or participative style of decision making (Vroom and Yetton 1973). In this view, being autocratic is neither evil nor immoral in itself.

For instance, when a parent decides autocratically that a preschooler should go to bed, the parent is genuinely concerned about the welfare of the child and is regarded as making an optimal decision, albeit autocratically. On the other hand, the parent would probably permit a teenager to engage in discussions and participate in decisions regarding the choice of a university to attend. The difference between the preschooler and the teenager in their capacity to participate meaningfully in decisions calls for different social processes of decision making. From the perspective of human resource management, a manager must be aware of the benefits and drawbacks of participative decision making and of the appropriate degree of participation under varying circumstances.

Advantages of Participative Decision Making

The benefits of allowing members to participate in decision making can be summarized as follows:

- Higher rationality of decisions
- Better understanding of the decisions
- Ownership by members of the decisions
- Better execution of the decisions

As noted earlier, the rationality of a decision is improved if more members participate in the decision because a group possesses more information and insight than an individual does. This wider and deeper base of information and expertise helps the manager clarify the problem and identify and evaluate possible solutions to it. Even more important, participative decisions enable the members to comprehend more clearly the problem and its solution. In addition, when members participate in decision making, they believe that the decision is theirs and develop a sense of ownership over it. Finally, when members understand and feel ownership of the decision, they are more likely to execute the decision efficiently and effectively.

From the individual perspective, participation in decision making makes a member more knowledgeable and more capable of analyzing problems and their attributes and of evaluating several available options. These experiences are critical to one's personal growth and development, which is one significant aim of human resource management. Furthermore, such feelings of growth and development, as well as a sense of ownership in decisions, are likely to enhance the individual's total job experience and job satisfaction.

Disadvantages of Participative Decision Making

Managers must also be aware of some of the drawbacks of participative decisions. The obvious problem is that participative decisions take time. For example, basketball coaches do not engage in participative decisions during time-outs because they are not long enough for discussion and participation. In addition, in some situations, the leader may have more information than the group as a whole. In such a case, participative decisions would be simply a "pooling of ignorance" (Chelladurai 1985) and might not lead to higher-quality decisions. Another significant factor that affects the effectiveness of participative decisions is the extent to which the group is integrated. If a group is not well integrated and is marked by conflicts, the leader should be very careful in engaging that group in participative decisions.

Advantages of Autocratic Decision Making

The disadvantages of participative decision making point to some advantages of autocratic decision making. More specifically, the autocratic style is appropriate when the leader and the group do not have the time to engage in participative decision making. In addition, autocratic decision making may be advantageous when the group is split into fractious cliques. However, the autocratic style is functional only to the extent that members understand and accept the decisions made by the leader. In the absence of such understanding and accep-

tance, members are not likely to execute the decisions effectively.

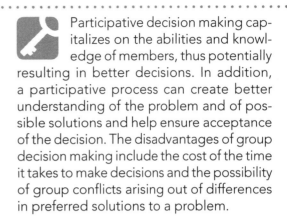

Participative decision making capitalizes on the abilities and knowledge of members, thus potentially resulting in better decisions. In addition, a participative process can create better understanding of the problem and of possible solutions and help ensure acceptance of the decision. The disadvantages of group decision making include the cost of the time it takes to make decisions and the possibility of group conflicts arising out of differences in preferred solutions to a problem.

Decision Styles

Participation in decision making may take several forms. For instance, Vroom and his colleagues identified five procedures for involving members in decision making (Vroom and Jago 1978, 1988; Vroom and Yetton 1973); these procedures are described in figure 12.3. These varying degrees of participation have been referred to as decision styles (Chelladurai 1993b; Chelladurai and Arnott 1985; Chelladurai and Haggerty 1978; Chelladurai, Haggerty, and Baxter 1989; Chelladurai and Quek 1995).

Only the last procedure (GII) shown in figure 12.3 is truly participative; that is, in this procedure, the members actually make the decision. In all of the other situations, the leader makes the decision by himself or herself; however, the degree to which the leader allows members to influence the decision increases from a purely autocratic procedure (AI) to consultation with the total group (CII).

Members' influence in decisions

Autocratic I (AI)	Autocratic II (AII)	Consultative I (CI)	Consultative II (CII)	Group II (GII)
Leader makes the decision based on available information	Leader seeks information from a few and then makes the decision	Leader consults with a few members and then makes the decision	Leader consults with all members and then makes the decision	Leader shares the problem and lets the group make the decision

Low ←———————————————————————————→ High

FIGURE 12.3 Decision styles and their descriptions.
Adapted from Vroom and Yetton 1973.

Problem Attributes

The question now is which decision style is appropriate under what conditions. According to Vroom and Jago (1988), every decision situation can be described in terms of 12 attributes. Basically, these attributes relate to the leader, the members, and the problem itself. A leader may or may not have all of the necessary information to make the decision (i.e., leader information). Because information is critical to making a rational decision, leaders may vary the decision style based on the information available to them.

Another leader attribute is degree of influence over subordinates, which must be great enough that members will be committed to the decision should the leader make it autocratically (i.e., commitment probability). If leaders believe that members will accept and commit to their decision in a given situation, then they can be relatively autocratic. Furthermore, leaders may be motivated either to minimize the time taken (time motivation) or to maximize member development (development motivation). When leaders prefer to minimize the time required for making decisions, they tend toward more autocratic decision styles, including consultative styles. On the other hand, if a leader is more concerned with developmental aspects of decision making, he or she should employ more participative styles.

The member-related attributes are goal congruence (i.e., whether members share the organizational goals), subordinate conflict (i.e., whether members are likely to be in conflict over the solutions), and subordinate information (i.e., whether members have the information to make a good decision). When members do not share the organizational goals, they may not contribute to effective decision making. If members are in conflict with each other, they may not participate in decision making with an open mind. Finally, if members do not have the necessary information, they cannot make the decision any more rationally than the leader can.

The four attributes of the problem situation are quality requirement (i.e., does the problem in question require a high-quality decision?), commitment requirement (i.e., is member commitment required in order to execute the decision?), problem structure (i.e., is the problem simple and structured, or is it complex?), and time constraint (i.e., should the decision be made quickly?). A final attribute is geographical dispersion of the members, which can make it expensive to assemble them for participative decision making.

If a high-quality decision must be made, it may be advantageous to involve the members in decision making. Similarly, if member commitment is critical for the execution of the decision, the leader should get the members to participate so that they will understand and accept the decision as their own. In some instances, the problem may be as simple as deciding whether to buy a water cooler for the office. In this case, resorting to a group decision is meaningless and time consuming. The influence of the problem attributes on the extent of member participation is shown in table 12.5.

TABLE 12.5 Problem Attributes and Their Effects on Member Participation

PROBLEM ATTRIBUTE	SUBORDINATE PARTICIPATION IF PROBLEM ATTRIBUTE IS HIGH
Quality requirement	High
Commitment requirement	High
Leader information	Low
Problem structure	Low
Commitment probability	Low
Goal congruence	High
Subordinate conflict	Low
Subordinate information	High
Time constraint	Low
Geographical dispersion	Low
Time motivation	Low
Development motivation	High

Adapted from Vroom and Jago 1988.

A mix of varying levels of the stated attributes characterizes every problem situation (i.e., decision situation). Thus the leader or manager needs to make an objective assessment of these attributes in order to choose the decision style appropriate to the situation. Although participative decision making is preferable in many situations, the manager needs to ensure that a participative style is functional in the given circumstances. As Vroom and Yetton (1973) pointed out, "The quality of the decision is dependent not only on the information and expertise of those participating in it, but also on their disposition to use their information in the service of the goal stated in the problem" (p. 29).

A consistent finding from research into the model proposed by Vroom and his associates (Vroom and Jago 1978, 1988; Vroom and Yetton 1973) is that situational attributes exerted about four times as much influence on managers' choices of decision styles as did individual-difference (i.e., personal) factors. A similar trend was found in the athletic context (Chelladurai and Arnott 1985). For example, as compared with individual differences between players, problem attributes exerted much greater influence on the preferences of basketball players for a particular decision style used by their coaches in a given situation.

In overview, sport and recreation managers need to analyze a problem situation in terms of the given attributes and select an appropriate decision style for that situation. Such a logical and rational approach maximizes the effectiveness of participative decision making and minimizes the importance of a manager's personal characteristics, including personality, as determinants of decision-style choices.

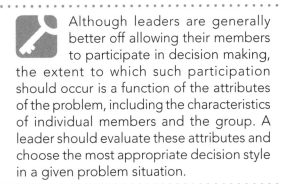 Although leaders are generally better off allowing their members to participate in decision making, the extent to which such participation should occur is a function of the attributes of the problem, including the characteristics of individual members and the group. A leader should evaluate these attributes and choose the most appropriate decision style in a given problem situation.

ROLE OF THE SPORT OR RECREATION MANAGER

As stated earlier, the way in which a leader leads may be influenced by the task of the group, the organizational goals, the norms of a particular social setting, and the nature of the group. Thus, any leader in the sport and recreation industry must recognize the context in which he or she is leading. For example, the coach of a collegiate women's soccer team must know that leading during the off-season may take a different form than leading in the high-pressure environment of the season itself.

VIEWPOINT

We must be careful not to confound the decision style that a person adopts in a given situation with the mannerisms and idiosyncrasies of that person (Chelladurai 1993b). For instance, consider a football coach who presents his playbook for the season to the quarterback with the apparently menacing comment, "This is your bible. You better master it." In contrast, another coach may present his playbook with a smile and the comment, "Here's the playbook I drew up during the summer. You may get a kick out of reading it." The obvious difference in their mannerisms should not be allowed to mask the fact that both coaches autocratically decided the plays.

In addition, we should not be misguided by "window dressing" (Chelladurai 1993b). That is, a person may project himself or herself as democratic by letting members make decisions in trivial matters. For instance, the director of a recreation department may let the group decide what type of water cooler to purchase and where to locate it in the office. However, the director may make decisions autocratically about more critical matters, such as sport programming and scheduling. Thus, the director creates only a facade of democratic leadership.

An effective leader must recognize that leadership behaviors may change and evolve based on the context or situation in which he or she is leading. The leader must also recognize that the nature of the task may influence which type of leader behavior (i.e., task versus relational) is most appropriate to help followers meet their goals. The leader must be acutely aware of the goals of the group and shape the group's norms in order to help them meet their goals. As suggested by the model put forth by Welty Peachey, Damon, Zhou, and Burton (2015), if followers are engaged in the leadership process (e.g., goal setting and accomplishment), this relationship between leaders and followers will lead to positive group and individual outcomes.

It is the responsibility of the leader to know the context, understand the types of behaviors that are effective in a given situation, and proactively manage his or her relationship with followers. For example, a coach may realize that running sprint drills during the off-season requires a more task-based leadership focus. In contrast, conducting player evaluations in-season may require a mix of task-based and relational leadership behaviors; specifically, player affect (e.g., satisfaction and commitment) may be high and relationship management may be essential to player satisfaction and performance.

Case Study

Evaluating Leadership Style

Sir Alex Ferguson, former manager of the Manchester United Football Club (the most famous soccer team in the world), offered eight key recommendations for a leadership blueprint. The following excerpt is the fourth recommendation in his list:

> Never, ever cede control. If the day came that the manager of Manchester United was controlled by the players—if the players decided how the training should be, what days they should have off, what the discipline should be and what the tactics should be—then Manchester United would not be the Manchester United we know. I wasn't going to allow anyone to be stronger than I was. Your personality has to be bigger than theirs. There are occasions when you have to ask yourself whether certain players are affecting the dressing-room atmosphere, the performance of the team, and your control of the players and staff. If they are, you have to cut the cord. There is absolutely no

other way. It doesn't matter if the person is the best player in the world. Some English clubs have changed managers so many times that it creates power for the players in the dressing room. That is very dangerous. If the coach has no control, he will not last. ("Manchester United" 2013)

Case Study Tasks

1. What are your reactions to Ferguson's perspective on absolute control of his team and his authoritarian style? Discuss the relevance of this approach to various organizational settings in sport (e.g., campus recreation department, fitness club, youth sport).

2. Fiedler found that task-oriented leaders were successful in situations most favorable to the leader. Summarize Fiedler's notion of situational favorableness of coaching at the professional level. Critically review how Ferguson's authoritarian style would fit into the Welty Peachey, Damon, Zhou, and Burton (2015) model of leadership.

CHAPTER PURSUITS

SUMMARY

This chapter focuses on the multidimensional model of leadership (Chelladurai 1978, 1993a). The model synthesizes leadership theories such as House's path–goal theory and Fiedler's contingency model. The multidimensional model posits that situational characteristics, member characteristics, and leader characteristics lead to three states of leader behavior: required, preferred, and actual. One portion of actual leader behavior reflects the leader's adaptation to the demands and constraints imposed by situational characteristics. The other portion of actual leader behavior is a function of the leader's reactions to members' preferences. The model also proposes that the degree of congruence between the three states of leader behavior determines the extent to which members feel satisfied and perform effectively, both as individuals and as a group. The chapter also contrasts transactional leadership and its effects with transformational leadership and its effects.

Finally, the chapter notes that participative decision making—that is, engaging members in the process of making decisions—has both advantages and disadvantages. The degree to which a leader should allow members to participate in making decisions is a function of the attributes of the situation. These attributes include characteristics of the members, the group, and the problem itself. Analyzing the various configurations of these attributes (or their absence) leads to appropriate decision styles.

KEY TERMS

ability 228

congruence 227

individual-difference variable 222

influence 218

leadership 217

performance 228

preferred leader behavior 223

required leader behavior 223

situational characteristic 221

UNDERSTAND

1. Define leadership and explain its significance in managing human resources.
2. Describe the advantages and disadvantages of participative decision making. Explain the circumstances in which a participative style of decision making may not be tenable.

INTERACT

1. Think of a good leader with whom you are familiar. Describe him or her in terms of specific leader behaviors that impress you.
   - Which of the leader behaviors were influenced by situational requirements and which were influenced by member characteristics?
   - Would you have preferred to have this leader alter any of his or her leader behaviors? Why or why not?
   - Would you consider this leader to be transformational? Why or why not?
   - Can this leader be described as charismatic? Explain.
   - Compare your list with those of your classmates.
2. Would you label the leader you chose in question 1 as participative or autocratic? Explain. If this leader used various decision styles, was he or she good at choosing styles that were appropriate to different situations? Give examples.

Performance Appraisal

Performance appraisal is an important managerial process that directly affects member motivation and performance. It also serves as the basis for critical managerial decisions, such as training, retaining, promoting, and rewarding employees. Therefore, it must be carried out periodically. Because performance appraisal exerts a direct effect on members' psychological and motivational states, it must be conducted fairly and must be based on valid criteria.

Sport and recreation managers need to understand the ways in which performance appraisal can help the organization. This chapter elaborates on the two major purposes of **performance appraisal**: administrative and developmental. The **administrative purpose** focuses on evaluating members on a comparative basis in order to inform administrative decisions about issues such as salary increases and promotions. The **developmental purpose** is geared toward helping members develop their skills and capabilities.

Every job is characterized by both core and peripheral elements. For a performance appraisal to be effective, it must address all of a job's core components. With this fact in mind, this chapter examines what should be evaluated. It also discuss two other issues that need to be addressed in perfor-

mance appraisals—when to conduct performance appraisals and who should conduct them.

Both the administrative and the developmental purposes of performance appraisal require that it distinguish between employees' performances and that the process be free of bias. The latter part of this chapter addresses ways in which these two requirements are sometimes violated due to common errors in the appraisal process.

PURPOSES OF PERFORMANCE APPRAISAL

One enduring human characteristic is the desire to know how well one is doing on the task at hand. The first question a child asks after drawing a figure may well be, "How is this, Mommy?" At school, when students submit an assignment, they want to know as soon as possible how well they did on it.

Similarly, an employee of an athletics department is eager to know how well he or she performed on an assigned task (e.g., preparing a quarterly report). The employee's concern is twofold. First, the employee is genuinely concerned with the quality of the work done. Does the department director think that the completed work is as good as the employee thinks it is? Has the director identified and complimented the employee for the good elements of the work, pointed out technical and conceptual errors in it, and made any suggestions for improvement in subsequent assignments? Second, the employee is concerned with how the work evaluation may affect the prospect of merit raises and promotions. The employee may also be concerned with comparisons of this evaluation with evaluations for other assignments or with evaluations of other employees on similar assignments.

The athletics director in this situation carries a twofold responsibility. The first responsibility is developmental; that is, the director's feedback is aimed at developing the employee and at improving the employee's ability to conceive, organize, and articulate thoughts in a coherent manner. The second responsibility is to evaluate the employee's performance in relation to that of others in the department for the purposes of personnel decisions, such as merit raises or promotions. In other words, the director needs to ensure that the evaluation is commensurate with the intellectual effort and energy that went into the work and that it is equitable as compared with evaluations of other employees and their effort and energy. Thus the concept of equity of rewards is operative here (for more, see chapter 8).

These two thrusts constitute the essence of performance appraisal in the context of organizations and their management. Defined technically, performance appraisal involves "a formal structured system for measuring, evaluating, and influencing an employee's job-related attributes, behaviors, and outcomes, including absenteeism" (Schuler and Jackson 1996, p. 344). The two operative words in this definition are *evaluating* and *influencing*, which refer to the two main objectives of performance appraisal.

That is, in part, evaluating serves the organizational purpose of comparing an individual's performance with a set of standards or with performances by comparable others. Such comparisons facilitate personnel decisions, such as placements, promotions, salary increases, and training programs. These purposes of performance appraisal are properly referred to as administrative purposes (Belcourt, Sherman, Bohlander, and Snell 2002). From a different perspective, such appraisals can be used as feedback to individuals in order to influence and enhance their subsequent performances. Here, the focus is on developing the employee's skills and abilities to perform the tasks associated with the current job and those that will be required by future, higher-level jobs. Thus, these purposes of performance appraisal are referred to as developmental purposes. The following lists show these differing purposes.

VIEWPOINT

The effect of performance appraisals on organizational performance depends on how they are bundled with other human resource management (HRM) practices.

Even the most sophisticated performance appraisal system, which focuses employees to engage in the "right" behaviors, will have little impact upon firm-level outcomes unless it is accompanied by selection, placement, and training systems which ensure that employees have the capabilities needed to perform those behaviors; reward and compensation systems which ensure that employees are motivated to do what is needed [in order] to further corporate goals; and job design systems which allow employees the opportunity to engage in behaviors that impact firm-level outcomes. Thus, PMSs [performance management systems] should be defined as all the HR [human resource] practices employed by an organization to ensure that employees have the means, the motivation, and the opportunity to improve firm-level performance. (DeNisi and Smith 2014, p. 144)

Administrative Purposes

To give employees feedback so that they know how their performance compares to their own expectations and to the performance of others

To gather data on which to base decisions on pay and promotions

To help communicate the decisions regarding pay and promotion

To aid decisions on employee retention or dismissal

To warn employees about unsatisfactory performance

Developmental Purposes

To help employees improve their performance and further develop their skills

To increase commitment to the organization through discussion of an employee's future career opportunities and plans

To motivate employees by providing recognition and support

To strengthen supervisor–subordinate relationships

To identify individual and organizational problems that require resolution

Cleveland, Murphy, and Williams (1989) provided a more comprehensive classification of the uses of performance appraisal. They conceived of performance appraisal as involving

- between-person evaluation,
- within-person evaluation,
- systems maintenance, and
- documentation.

Figure 13.1 illustrates these four classes and the specific uses of performance appraisal.

As noted earlier, between-person uses of performance appraisal are concerned largely with HRM decisions, such as salary increases, promotions, transfers, and terminations. Within-person uses, on the other hand, focus on developing the individual by identifying strengths and weaknesses and assigning the individual to suitable positions and training programs. These two traditional functions of performance appraisal lead to a more general function of maintaining the organization as a whole. That is, the results of performance appraisal of all employees provide insights into the effectiveness of the human resource system, the developmental and training needs of the whole organization, and

> ### DIVERSITY MANAGEMENT OF HUMAN RESOURCES
>
> When valuing diversity, we must be aware of, acknowledge, and accept the benefits of diversity in an organization (Chelladurai 2014). One way to highlight the value of diversity in management practice is through performance appraisal, which is valuable as both an administrative and a developmental tool. If an organizational value is to provide meaning to personnel, the organization must make a concerted effort to explicitly integrate it into all internal organizational communication (Kerwin, MacLean, and Bell-Laroche 2014a). When managers and leaders directly link the appreciation and accommodation of diversity (as a shared organizational value) into performance appraisals (which serve an administrative purpose), the organization's paid staff and volunteers begin to "live" the values and reap their benefits through increased commitment and performance, thus serving a developmental purpose (Kerwin et al. 2014a, 2014b).

the setting and articulating of organizational goals for employees.

Finally, even as performance appraisals provide the foundation for human resource management decisions, they also provide the justification and documentation for such decisions. As noted in chapters 9 and 11, the HRM practices of an organization are governed by legal requirements. When someone challenges the legality of an HRM decision, the organization can defend itself based on records from a fair and accurate system of performance appraisals. Fairness and accuracy can be enhanced by clearly specifying what should be evaluated, when it should be evaluated, and who should do the evaluation (Schuler and Jackson 1996).

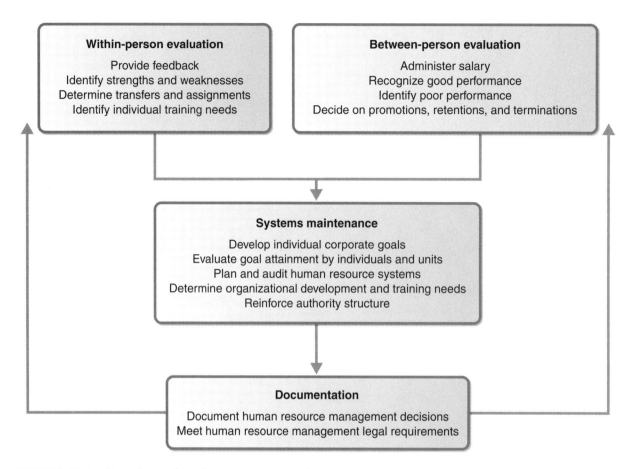

FIGURE 13.1 Functions of performance appraisal.

Performance appraisal involves a formal system of evaluating an employee's performance in terms of specified outcomes and the behaviors required for achieving those outcomes. Performance appraisal can be used to develop an employee's skills and competencies and to make personnel decisions, such as salary increases, bonuses, promotions, and dismissals.

WHAT SHOULD BE EVALUATED

Perceptions of the fairness of performance evaluation depend on several factors. Perhaps the most critical factor involves what is being evaluated, and many of the problems associated with performance appraisal stem from confusion over this matter. Campbell's (1993) theory of performance outlines several domains of performance in an orga-

nizational context. His domains of performance, described in the following sections, are relevant to sport organizations.

Job-Specific Task Performance

Job-specific task performance relates to the content of the job description (see chapter 11), which specifies the tasks that the job holder should complete. To the extent that the job description is specific and detailed, assessment of job-specific task performance would appear to be an easy process. For example, when a fitness club employs a person to recruit customers for the club and its various programs and sets a standard (e.g., 100 customers), the club can easily measure the performance of the employee against that standard. However, the club's interest in retaining those customers makes appraisal problematic because customer retention is relatively more dependent on many other factors, including the performance of fitness consultants and fitness leaders, facility maintenance, and other supportive features. That is, several other individuals are involved in retaining customers.

Two issues are involved here. First, the manager can judge the work done by a fitness consultant (i.e., the human service) not only by the number of customers served but also by the quality of the service provided. In other words, performance in human services (i.e., the work of the fitness consultant and the exercise leader) is harder to measure than quantifiable sales. Therefore, if performance evaluation in these instances is based solely on the criterion of number of clients served, then the evaluation suffers from criterion deficiency (Saal and Knight 1995). By the same token, if performance evaluation includes criteria that are irrelevant to performance (e.g., employee age, gender, or marital status), then it suffers from criterion contamination (Saal and Knight 1995).

The second issue here involves interdependence among tasks. Whenever the performance of one task depends on other tasks, it can be difficult to isolate and assess the performance of one specific job. In other words, when the attainment of an organizational objective depends on collective work, the manager cannot easily identify an individual's performance. Nevertheless, job descriptions do provide a basis for performance evaluation of job-specific task behaviors.

Written and Oral Communication

Many jobs require extensive communication with co-workers, superiors, subordinates, or clients. For instance, a university athletics director must articulate clearly and succinctly the department's mission, goals, and specific processes for diverse audiences, including university officials, students, athletes, coaches, and the media. This communication generally takes the form of oral presentations and interviews, as well as written documents. If the communication is not clear, the director may be misunderstood or misquoted. As another example, an event manager needs to communicate clearly to both paid and volunteer workers regarding all steps and procedures for staging an event. Any ambiguity or vagueness in communication may lead to serious difficulties. Similarly, a fitness leader's instructions to class members must be clear and straightforward. In all of these cases, written and oral communication constitute part of the **performance domain** and need to be evaluated.

Supervision and Leadership

Of course, some jobs also carry supervisory responsibilities; that is, the member may be expected to supervise and provide leadership to selected individuals. For example, a senior employee in a city recreation department may be required to supervise and provide coaching and guidance to selected junior employees. The senior's ability to positively influence the juniors and enhance their performance is critical to the organization. Campbell (1993) contended that the manager of the senior employee should recognize, evaluate, and suitably reward such leadership as part of an individual's performance domain.

Management and Administration

Another domain of performance identified by Campbell (1993) is the responsibility residing in some higher-level jobs to set and state the organizational mission, monitor organizational activities toward the mission, and distribute the budget to various units or programs. This domain of performance and its associated responsibilities are relevant mostly to positions in the upper echelons of an organization (e.g., university athletics director, general manager of a professional sport club, city recreation director, chief executive officer of a national sport governing body).

Non-Job-Specific Task Performance

The non-job-specific domain includes all activities outside of the job-specific domain articulated in a job description. In other words, it relates to the general activities of the work group, unit, or organization. For example, when an employee in the ticketing unit of a university athletics department participates in and contributes to groupwide or organization-wide meetings or committees, that person performs tasks that are critical to the organization and its effectiveness. In fact, committee membership is a significant component of the performance evaluation of university professors. Because these committee and leadership functions are critical to the survival and growth of the university, it is only appropriate that the manager adequately recognize and reward the people involved.

One may question whether membership on university or departmental committees can be considered non-job-specific behaviors insofar as they are officially declared to be part of the performance domain. The point, however, is that a professor is not required to participate in such committees. Because these contributions are not specific to a job, they are not outlined clearly in a job description; however, that does not minimize the importance of one's performance in that domain. Similarly, a fitness instructor's job description may not require specifically that he or she contribute to the club's overall management. Yet the instructor may pass on his or her insights about enhancing the overall performance of the club in meetings or other encounters with senior management. Such contributions constitute non-job-specific performance.

Effort

The familiar idea of getting an "A for effort" implies that the extent to which an individual expends his or her effort in performing a job must be taken into account. As noted earlier, the performance in a job may depend on external factors, which means that performance evaluation should not be restricted to outcomes. Instead, managers must also consider the effort that someone puts into a job as equal in importance to the outcomes of that effort.

For example, a person in charge of securing sponsorships for the athletics department of a small college in an urban center may not garner as many sponsorships as expected despite extraordinary efforts. This result could be a function of more attractive options available to the sponsors, such as major universities or professional teams. Therefore, the employee's strong effort should not be overlooked in performance appraisal. More generally, when an individual puts forth considerable effort consistently, frequently, and even in adverse conditions, that person needs to be evaluated positively in that domain of performance. Recall from chapter 8 that a person's motivation can be inferred from his or her investment of time and effort in the job. More specifically, the person's direction, persistence, and intensity of effort are indicators of his or her level of motivation to perform well. According to Campbell (1993), investments of effort should be included in performance appraisal.

Personal Discipline

Chapter 2 emphasizes that self-care exhibited by volunteers may enable them to better serve clients; that is, they become better volunteers. Therefore, self-care needs to be included in evaluations of a volunteer's contributions to the organization. The same concept extends to paid workers. Campbell (1993) expressed this notion in suggesting that a paid employee's personal discipline (which is similar to self-care) is part of the performance domain.

Consider one example offered by Campbell—an employee's use of drugs. If an employee uses recreational drugs, he or she is unlikely to operate at his or her best; therefore, job-specific task performance is likely to suffer. From a different perspective, by using recreational or performance-enhancing drugs, employees tarnish the image of the organization. To discourage the use of drugs, university athletics departments and even professional sport teams can take several steps. If the concern involves an athlete, the university can quickly alleviate the problem through dismissal of the athlete from the athletic team. However, the problem is much more serious when the images of the department and the university are at stake.

Personal discipline is also a critical aspect of job performance in many other areas. For example, employees' personal appearance when they report for work is a function of their personal discipline. If an employee stays up late at night and regularly reports for work in a disheveled state, his or her appearance affects not only individual performance but also the image of the organization.

Facilitation of Peer and Team Performance

The manager must also consider an individual's domain of performance to include the extent to which that person facilitates the performance of individual peers and of the team or work group. Indeed, Campbell (1993) suggested that serving as a role model for other employees is in itself an aspect of performance. One way to do so is to carry out one's job-specific tasks accurately and promptly as a model for other employees. For example, a playground supervisor in a city recreation department may set an example for other supervisors by doing his or her duties meticulously. The supervisor may also help colleagues and superiors as the need arises and thus facilitate the effectiveness of the total program. Such activities constitute a legitimate area of one's performance domain that is subject to evaluation.

 An employee's domain of performance includes not only job-specific task behaviors but also non-job-specific task behaviors, such as effort, personal discipline, and involvement in and facilitation of peer and work group tasks.

Citizenship Behaviors

In addition to the domains of performance outlined by Campbell (1993), organizational effectiveness is also influenced by another, seldom-noticed form of behavior: prosocial behavior, or organizational citizenship behavior. The latter term is more popular, and Organ (1988) introduced and defined it as "individual behavior that is discretionary, [is] not directly or explicitly recognized by the formal reward system, and . . . in the aggregate promotes the effective functioning of the organization" (p. 4). The operative word is *discretionary*, which means that the behavior is not specified in the job description, not required by other organizational rules, and not expected by others. It encompasses all of the little things that individuals in an organizational context may do of their own volition that contribute indirectly to organizational effectiveness.

For example, a fitness club employee may come to work before the scheduled time in order to "tidy up" the place; the accountant at the club may step up to the reception desk to help the receptionist at a time of heavy demand; an experienced exercise leader may help a novice leader settle into the job. Similarly, a ticketing clerk in an athletics department may spend part of the lunch hour picking up trash in the stadium. These organizational citizenship behaviors contribute to organizational growth and effectiveness.

Podsakoff, Ahearne, and MacKenzie (1997) suggested that "citizenship behaviors may enhance organizational performance because they 'lubricate' the social machinery of the organization, reduce friction, and increase efficiency" (p. 263). As outlined by these authors, the specific benefits of citizenship behaviors include freeing up resources devoted to maintenance functions for more productive uses, enhancing co-workers' performance, coordinating group activities, and making the group and organization a more attractive setting to work in.

Organ (1988) classified the varying kinds of citizenship behaviors into altruism, conscientiousness, sportsmanship, courtesy, civic virtue, peace keeping, and cheerleading. These categories are described in figure 13.2.

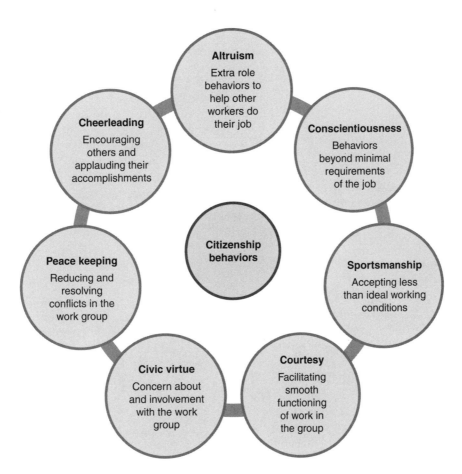

FIGURE 13.2 Categories of citizenship behavior.
Based on Organ 1988.

VIEWPOINT

As noted by Lambert (2000), employee assessments of work–life benefits in an organization are positively related to organizational citizenship behaviors. That is, when employees feel a connection between work and home life, they are more inclined to enhance their own performance and engage in organizational citizenship behaviors. One way to foster positive work–life relationships is to allow employees opportunities to connect their work lives and personal lives through social media. For example, civic virtue can be enhanced if an employee is connected to the organization's Twitter account, follows the organization's posts in their spare time, and retweets those posts as a sign of concern for and engagement with the organization. These behaviors may not receive formal appraisal but they can serve as mechanisms for improving performance through connectedness.

Managers generally acknowledge the importance of organizational citizenship behaviors; it is difficult, however, to integrate such behaviors into the formal performance appraisal process because they are so varied and are not comparable to each other. Thus, citizenship behaviors are not explicitly acknowledged and assessed as a component of task performance. However, evidence suggests that managers do use their perceptions of citizenship behaviors in evaluating the task performance of their subordinates (Podsakoff, MacKenzie, and Hui 1993). That is, managers tend to subjectively use an employee's citizenship behaviors in appraising that person's task performance—a process purported to be objective.

Podsakoff, MacKenzie, and Hui (1993) advanced several reasons that a person's citizenship behaviors influence managers in evaluating task performance. One reason involves the norms of reciprocity or fairness. Insofar as a manager believes that an individual's extra-role behaviors contribute to his or her own performance as well as that of the organization, the manager is likely to evaluate more positively that person's task performance. Managers may also believe that good employees engage in citizenship behaviors in addition to behaviors associated with their work roles.

Yet another reason is that citizenship behaviors stand out because the work-role behaviors are required of every employee. Therefore, perceptions of distinctive behaviors come to the forefront in performance appraisal, and they can influence the process. Furthermore, because citizenship behaviors are based on a person's internal and stable dispositions, such behaviors may be given greater weight than task performance per se. Managers may also believe that task performance and citizenship behaviors are highly correlated.

Some of the reasons that managers use citizenship behaviors in performance appraisal are legitimate and functional; others are inappropriate and dysfunctional. For example, as discussed earlier, it is legitimate to include reciprocity and fairness insofar as these citizenship behaviors contribute to managerial and organizational effectiveness. However, managers' perceptions of citizenship behaviors can be subjective and prone to influences such as favoritism and gender or cultural bias. For example, in sport and recreation, the concept of "sportsmanship" may be linked to employees working extra hours in the evening and on weekends. Although these behaviors may provide excellent examples of citizenship that could be linked to enhanced perceptions of high-quality performance, the ability to engage in such behaviors may be limited for women (who are often the primary caregivers in the family) and ethnic minorities (who may have religious obligations at certain times). In such cases, it would be unfair to link these citizenship factors to performance appraisal.

Citizenship behaviors are engaged in voluntarily by an individual in order to help another employee, a work group, or the organization. These behaviors are not specified as part of the role assigned to the person; therefore, they are seldom monitored. Yet they are critical to organizational health and image. Managers may favorably evaluate an employee's task performance based on his or her citizenship behavior for several reasons, including a sense of reciprocity, a certain conception of what makes for a "good" employee, and the distinctiveness of such behavior.

On the other hand, directly linking citizenship behaviors with task performance must be viewed with caution for three reasons. First, citizenship behaviors may not all relate to increased performance. In their study of work groups in a paper mill, Podsakoff, Ahearne, and MacKenzie (1997) assessed three forms of citizenship behaviors: helping behavior (i.e., altruism), sportsmanship, and civic virtue. Their results showed that only helping behavior and sportsmanship exerted significant effects on group performance; civic virtue had no effect.

Second, as pointed out by Organ, Podsakoff, and MacKenzie (2006) and Podsakoff, Ahearne, and MacKenzie (1997), the effects of citizenship behaviors on performance can be evaluated properly only if managers consider such behaviors of an individual over time or average such behaviors over all individuals in a group. That is, a person's sporadic citizenship behaviors may not have much effect on group performance. Podsakoff and colleagues' finding of a relationship between selected citizenship behaviors and group performance was based on measures of group citizenship behaviors and group performance indexes.

The third issue involves the distinction between citizenship behaviors and political influence tactics (Podsakoff, MacKenzie, and Hui 1993). That is, employees may engage in citizenship behaviors only to influence decision makers. Whereas citizenship behaviors are done for the benefit of others in the organization, or the organization itself, political influence tactics are used for the benefit of the doer. Managers can understand the distinction between the two intentions and are familiar with individuals who have these differing orientations. However, Podsakoff, MacKenzie, and Hui raised a more basic question: Does it matter? They argue that

> if one is interested in the impact of the employee's behavior on organizational effectiveness, it is not clear that the intentions of the employee are as relevant. In this situation, does it really matter why an employee comes to work extra early or stays extra late? As long as the employee is really working, it should enhance the effectiveness of the organization. (p. 33)

Thus, managers must be careful about including an individual's citizenship behaviors in performance appraisal. One solution to the problem is to separate task performance from citizenship behavior and to reward them separately. For instance, if employees A and B perform equally well, they should be given equal performance ratings. If, however, employee A engages in more constructive citizenship behaviors, then he or she must be given an additional reward in some tangible or intangible way. By the same token, if employee C performs at a lower level but exhibits good citizenship, then he or she must be evaluated lower on task performance and rewarded less for task specific performance. The opportunity for citizenship performance ratings and rewards is applicable in the case of employee C. Before implementing this logic, however, managers must inform all employees that citizenship behaviors are important and that they constitute part of the performance appraisal and reward system.

In sum, the performance domain includes all tasks specified in a job description as well as other unspecified activities, including citizenship behaviors as warranted. A comprehensive list of the elements of the performance domain is presented in table 13.1.

Deficiency in and Contamination of Performance Measures

As shown by the foregoing discussion, managers must include in the domain of performance all pertinent activities associated with a job; otherwise, such performance measures will be incomplete and therefore deficient. On the other hand, managers must also ensure that what they include in the measurement scheme does not contain any element that is not part of the job or any element that depends on external factors. If extraneous elements are included, then the performance measures are contaminated (Saal and Knight 1995).

As noted by J. MacLean (2001, p. 46), "a fitness instructor might be evaluated using the following criteria: ability to effectively teach fitness activities; use of voice; talent for encouraging participants; effective management of the class rosters; ability to vary class activities to prevent boredom; and willingness to gear activity closely to advertised content. . . . [However, to] make the fitness instructor responsible for the organization's yearly profit margins would in effect contaminate the criteria for evaluating this specific position." To avoid this pitfall, J. MacLean described a stepwise procedure to ensure that the appropriate criteria are included in a performance appraisal: (a) job assessment, which leads to (b) the creation of a job description, which contributes to (c) the definition of the domain of performance. The development of these steps is outlined in figure 13.3.

TABLE 13.1 Significant Domains of Performance

DOMAIN	EXAMPLES
Job-specific task performance	• Exhibiting written and oral communications skills • Supervising and leading • Managing and administrating by articulating organizational goals, allocating resources, and monitoring goal attainment
Non-job-specific task performance, including group or unit activities	• Maintaining consistent, frequent effort even in adverse conditions • Exhibiting personal discipline, including following rules • Providing support, training, and guidance to facilitate group or unit performance
Citizenship behaviors	• Volunteering to carry out task activities that are not formally part of the job • Persisting with extra enthusiasm or effort when necessary in order to complete tasks • Helping and cooperating with others • Endorsing, supporting, and defending organizational objectives

From Campbell 1993; Organ 1988; Schuler and Jackson 1996.

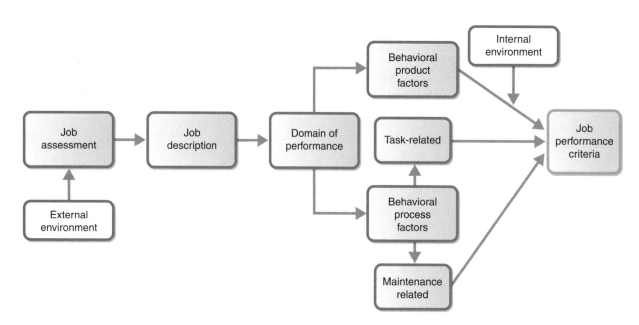

FIGURE 13.3 Comprehensive model for the development of job-specific performance appraisal criteria.
Reprinted, by permission, from J. MacLean, 2001, *Performance appraisal for sport and recreation managers* (Champaign, IL: Human Kinetics), 29.

 When a performance measure does not capture the total domain of performance, it is deficient. On the other hand, if a performance measure subsumes factors that are not related to an individual's performance, it is contaminated.

Outcome-Based Versus Behavior-Based Performance Criteria

J. MacLean's (2001) reference within figure 13.3 discusses behavior-based criteria; in evaluating performance, however, sport and recreation managers must consider the distinction between behavior-based criteria and outcomes-based criteria. As noted earlier, performance appraisal is problematic when the jobs in an organization are interdependent—that is, when the performance (or outcome) of one job is influenced by the performances of other individuals in other jobs.

Consider a student's involvement in group projects for courses. A project may turn out to be excellent because of the first-rate work done by other members of the project team. Similarly, a project may fail due to ineffective and substandard performance by other members. Therefore, if a professor evaluated a given student's personal performance only on the basis of outcome (i.e., the quality of the project), the judgment would not be fair. The same would be true if, as discussed earlier, a fitness club manager based his or her evaluation of a fitness instructor only on the club's membership retention rate. Therefore, researchers generally agree that choosing outcomes as the sole criteria for performance appraisal is not a good strategy (e.g., Saal and Knight 1995; Schuler and Jackson 1996).

The alternate strategy is to base performance evaluation on the behaviors that an employee is supposed to exhibit in order to complete the job; as noted earlier, these behaviors are outlined in the job description. For example, a university expects a public relations person in the athletics department to be courteous to those who seek information, to collate all pertinent and correct information for distribution, to be regularly in contact with media people, and to be available at specified times. When that person engages in these behaviors consistently and effectively, the manager should evaluate that person's behavior as good without reference to the outcomes. The department or the team may get bad publicity in spite of the employee's optimal performance for other reasons (e.g., animosity between the press and the coaches).

In addition, the organization may have adopted the process of management by objectives. In this approach, the manager and the employee jointly set objectives for the employee to attain within a given period (usually one year). This process involves aligning the employee's objectives with the goals of the unit and of the organization; the objectives should also be consistent with the employee's capabilities and past achievements. The central rationale for management by objectives is the idea that setting challenging and achievable objectives is motivational (Saal and Knight 1995). The objectives then serve as the criteria for evaluating the employee at the end of the specified period. Although these objectives are good indicators of the performance domain, they still focus on what outcomes should be attained. Managers need to move beyond this frame of mind in performance appraisal and assess the *behaviors* that are most conducive to the attainment of desired outcomes.

 In assessing a person's performance, it is more useful to focus on the behaviors the person should perform in order to achieve the desired outcomes than it is to focus on the outcomes themselves, which may also be influenced by various other factors.

In a study relevant to the question of what to evaluate, J.C. MacLean and Chelladurai (1995) developed a scheme for performance appraisal of coaches. In this scheme, the domain of coaching performance is defined as all behaviors and tasks associated with coaching. It consists of six dimensions that reflect both the outcomes (products) and the processes associated with coaching; that is, it includes the results, as well as the activities purported to lead to those results. The outcomes may accrue to the team as a whole or to the coach. The process factors consist of direct and indirect behaviors aimed at task achievement as well as behaviors oriented toward sustaining the system by supporting and maintaining the administration and public relations activities. The researchers noted as well that a coach's behaviors should reflect the philosophy and values of the organization.

J. MacLean (2001) highlighted the need to accurately define performance measures by outlining the value of focusing on the behaviors required for a given position. Specifically, she discussed factors related to behavioral product, behavioral process (task-related), and behavioral process (maintenance-related) that are involved in the performance of job positions. She emphasized that no single category can provide a valid measure of an employee's performance and thus each category must be addressed in an evaluation tool. The criteria for performance appraisal by category are outlined in table 13.2.

TABLE 13.2 Example Performance Appraisal Criteria by Categories

	ROLE	CRITERIA
BEHAVIORAL PRODUCT FACTORS	Coach	Win–loss record; number of blue-chip athletes recruited; athlete performance improvement from season to season; coach's invited public appearances; playoff appearances
	Recreational director	Number of participants in programs; average participant satisfaction scores; yearly profit margins; balanced male and female programming
BEHAVIORAL PROCESS FACTORS (TASK-RELATED)	Coach	Ability to communicate with athletes; use of effective game tactics and strategies; scouting of opponents; recruitment of high-quality athletes; effective teaching
	Recreational director	Ability to communicate with athletes; use of effective game tactics and strategies; scouting of opponents; recruitment of high-quality athletes; effective teaching
BEHAVIORAL PROCESS FACTORS (MAINTENANCE-RELATED)	Coach	Compliance with organization's philosophy; effective work with staff members; involvement with professional association; adherence to budget; monitoring of athlete eligibility
	Recreational director	Purchasing of equipment; attendance of conferences and appropriate workshops; adherence to budget; involvement in professional association; coordination of publicity and effective public relations

Reprinted, by permission, from J. MacLean, 2001, *Performance appraisal for sport and recreation managers* (Champaign, IL: Human Kinetics), 27.

The outline developed by J. MacLean (2001) is applicable to positions in sport management. For example, an assistant director of a university recreation department who is in charge of intramural competitions can be evaluated on the basis of several factors, including the following:

- Performance of the unit in terms of number of sports and number of teams served and smooth operation of competitions (i.e., behavioral product factors)

- Recognition by the university newspaper in the form of an article, headline, or tweet and student organizations (i.e., behavioral process factors: maintenance-related)

- Planning and organizing of intramural competitions, where the assistant director is evaluated on effective deployment of personnel, interpersonal skills, and the nature of interactions with subordinates and participants (i.e., behavioral process factors: task-related) during planning and organizing processes.

- Attendance at conferences and seminars to learn more about running the unit effectively (i.e., behavioral process: maintenance-related)

- Adherence to university and department policies and procedures and effective interaction with superiors and colleagues (i.e., behavioral process: task-related)

- Links with similar operations both inside and outside the university (i.e., behavioral process: maintenance-related)

- Promotion of the unit and its activities (i.e., behavioral process: maintenance-related)

The preceding list provided by MacLean (2001) is generally transferable to many other positions in sport management.

Barber and Eckrich (1998) took the approach of identifying evaluation criteria for coaches of specific sports. For example, they put forth the following eight dimensions for NCAA basketball coaches: technical skill development, fundraising skills, program success, public relations, coach–player relationships, administrative skills, role modeling, and support of the student-athlete model. They also identified seven dimensions of evaluation criteria for NCAA cross country coaches; though some of the labels differed, the content of these dimensions closely resembled that of the eight dimensions for basketball coaches. These fifteen dimensions are subsumed by the model proposed by MacLean and Chelladurai (1995).

EVALUATION OF COACHING PERFORMANCE

One of the issues confronting coaches and their employers (or supervisors) is how to properly evaluate coaching performance in the context of educational institutions and sport organizations at the community, regional, and national levels. Mercier (2000) offered the following advice for coaches.

- Regarding what is (or should be) evaluated, the most important issue is to establish with one's employer a set of specific, measurable, realistic goals, including performance goals for the team and the athletes. Such goals may include relationships with parents, community leaders, and members of the media. It is also essential to establish standards of conduct and the means for assessing whether those standards have been met. Coaching competencies should also be evaluated.

- The information used in the evaluation process should relate to the agreed-on performance goals and should come from knowledgeable individuals, including athletes and parents.

- Coaches should avoid certain pitfalls in evaluation, particularly in the interface between the coach and evaluators. These pitfalls include holding the meeting during or just after a competition, lack of sufficient time to prepare for the meeting, last-minute substitutions of evaluators, inclusion of one's own subordinates at the meeting, and lack of data to inform the meeting. Details about the nature and timing of the evaluation should be part of the employment contract.

WHEN TO CONDUCT PERFORMANCE APPRAISAL

The right time to conduct performance appraisal depends on whether the purpose is developmental or administrative. If the purpose is developmental, then the appraisal is most likely to be focused on an individual and therefore can be tailored to suit the individual's needs and experience. For example, a novice employee may need more guidance and coaching; therefore, several appraisals can be carried out over a short period of time. On the other hand, a senior employee who has worked with the organization for a long time may not need such guidance and coaching.

Most often, performance appraisal is carried out for administrative or evaluative purposes to make judgments about salary, merit, bonuses, training, or promotion. In addition, managers can use these data to decide whom to retain and whom to release. Such purposes presuppose that the manager evaluates all employees during the same time period, which the manager has specified in advance. Usually, organizations carry out such performance appraisals each year, at the end of either the fiscal year or the calendar year. Some employees may be evaluated on their anniversary dates.

In some cases, a more elaborate and stringent performance appraisal may be employed after some years have elapsed. Two examples in a university setting are performance evaluation of professors for tenure purposes and evaluation of coaches for extending or discontinuing the contract of their employment. In both cases, evaluation may be conducted each year for the purposes of merit pay or bonus. In addition, the professor must be appraised more rigorously after five to seven years of employment for tenure purposes. The assumption is that it takes that long for a young university professor to carry out research and publish a few papers. Similarly, a coach may need from three to seven years to build a strong team and the traditions associated with it. Therefore, the contract usually

If performance appraisal is focused on employee development, then managers should conduct appraisals as frequently as is appropriate and according to a schedule that meets the developmental needs of the individual. If managers use performance evaluation to make personnel decisions, they should conduct the evaluations at specified intervals (usually annually) using a uniform protocol for all employees.

covers an extended period of time, at the end of which the university rigorously appraises the coach's performance.

WHO SHOULD DO THE APPRAISAL

An equally important consideration in performance appraisal is who should be involved in the process. One basic assumption that managers must make in this regard is that no one person has complete information about an employee's performance. Even employees themselves, though they may have an idea of how well they have done, may not know how that level of performance compares with the performance levels of others. Supervisors, on the other hand, may form a performance judgment based on their observation of several employees but may not fully recognize the reactions of customers to an individual employee. Thus, the quantity and quality of information about the performance of an individual are distributed among several sources. For instance, information about the performance of a fitness instructor may reside in the minds of the supervisors, co-instructors, and even locker room attendants. More important, customers may have the best information about how well the instructor is performing.

As a result, many organizations use all of these sources in evaluating an employee's performance. For example, the performance appraisal of university professors is usually based on student evaluation of teaching (i.e., information from clients), observer evaluation of teaching (i.e., information provided by professional colleagues in the organization), number of publications in reputable journals (i.e., information from professional reviewers of the journals), and the dean's or director's evaluation.

In addition, several scholars (e.g., Fitzsimmons and Fitzsimmons 2011; Lengnick-Hall 1996; Parasuraman, Berry, and Zeithaml 1985) and practicing managers have recently emphasized the need to use customer satisfaction as a significant, if not the sole, indicator of individual or organizational performance. The issue of customer or client satisfaction is elaborated in chapter 16.

To make a performance appraisal effective, managers need to compile comprehensive and accurate information from several sources, including the individual, his or her co-workers and superiors, and clients or customers.

ERRORS IN RATING

Whenever an individual's performance is evaluated, the appraiser or rater should guard against any type of error creeping into the evaluation. Some of the most common errors are addressed in this section.

Distributional Errors

Consider the various professors marking your assignments or examinations. One professor may mark assignments strictly, whereas another may mark them leniently, perhaps due in part to inflationary pressures to give high grades. These pressures, in turn, may be born out of notions of equality or fear of retribution from students or subordinates. A third professor may be neither lenient nor strict but may tend to place all students in the central range of scores. These habits of different raters illustrate errors that involve, respectively, strictness (i.e., stringency in rating all performances low), leniency (i.e., softness in rating all performances high), and central tendency (i.e., reluctance or inability to use either end of the possible score range). Belcourt and colleagues (2002) viewed all three of these errors as **distributional errors**.

The ideal way for professors to rate students is to use a wide range of scores to contrast the better assignments with the poorer assignments. Figure 13.4 contrasts the ideal means of rating with the habits of strictness, leniency, and central tendency. One issue here is that while the professors may vary in their rating tendencies, their appraisal of students relative to each other may not differ much. For example, professor X gives the numerical grades of 81, 83, and 85 to students Jane, John, and June, respectively. Professor Y gives the numerical grades of 89, 91, and 93 to the same students in the same order. Professor Z gives the grades of 86, 87, and 88 to the same students in the same order. The numerical grades given by the three professors do not match, and they reflect the different errors of strictness, leniency, and central tendency (see figure 13.4). However, the relative ranking of the three students is the same in all three cases; therefore, one can say that all of the professors were fair (or conversely unfair) in their evaluations.

The problem arises when an external agent looks at these grades and concludes that, say, June did well in the course that professor Y taught but less well in the course that professor X taught. That conclusion may not reflect reality. Another issue relates to the fact that in the case of each professor, the ratings are lumped together. Thus, it becomes difficult to distinguish between the three students.

360-DEGREE APPROACH TO EVALUATION: FEEDBACK FROM MULTIPLE SOURCES

As the name implies, a 360-degree evaluation enlists feedback from a set of observers who are in the circle or domain of the candidate's operation. For instance, observers providing the feedback in the evaluation of an aerobics instructor might include his or her supervisor and co-instructors, the locker and equipment room attendants, athletic trainers, and, of course, clients. Because these observers perceive the candidate's activities and interactions from different angles, their feedback cumulatively provides a holistic evaluation.

A single individual (e.g., the supervisor) would not be able to perceive or assess all domains of an employee's performance. However, those who work with the employee and those who interact with the employee on a daily basis would be able to make good judgments about how the employee carries out his or her various job duties. Feedback from these several sources provides a fuller and more accurate picture than do the perceptions and judgments of a single individual.

Feedback from various sources also provides a sense of their diverse reactions to the given employee's behaviors and job performance. Consider Bobby Knight, the highly successful (now-retired) college basketball coach. His combative mannerisms and intense reactions during competitions infuriated some observers. But one important source of feedback consists of the players themselves, the direct clients of the coach's services. For the most part, Knight's players perceived and judged him as effective. In fact, several players over the years were very eager to play for him.

A manager who plans to use 360-degree feedback must also be aware of some inherent problems with the approach. For one thing, observers may be reluctant to provide honest feedback for fear that their comments could hurt the employee's career. Instead, they may provide positive but false feedback. Furthermore, observers do not all have the same opportunities to see the employee in action; as a result, feedback provided from some observers may not be based on actual performance.

The 360-degree approach provides the employee with feedback from the supervisor, peers, reporting staff members, co-workers, and customers. From the organization's perspective, the process leads to

- improved feedback from multiple sources;
- identification of personal and organizational performance development needs;
- reduced risk of discrimination based on demographic factors (e.g., race, age, gender);
- improved customer service (when the feedback is from customers); and
- clear assessment of training needs.

In embarking on this process, sport and recreation managers must ensure that the feedback sought focuses on the competencies and job duties identified in the job description. Furthermore, those who are asked to contribute information should be trained in the process and in how to provide constructive feedback. The feedback should focus more on strengths and less on weaknesses in order to motivate employees to improve their performance. Managers should also be aware of the possibility that providers of feedback may inflate or deflate ratings in order to make an employee look good or bad. They should also realize that 360-degree feedback increases the paperwork aspect of evaluation, as well as the associated time and effort.

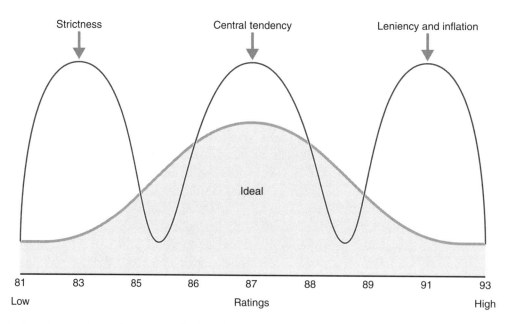

FIGURE 13.4 Comparisons between ideal and erroneous performance ratings.

For instance, the three numerical grades given by each professor would be converted to identical letter grades (e.g., all As, Bs, or Cs, depending on the grading conversion used in the academic system). Thus these practices do not distinguish between good and bad students and therefore are not fair to the students or to the educational system.

In other organizational contexts, similar errors may result in unfair decisions about how to distribute rewards or promotions. For example, two or more administrators in charge of different regions of a city recreation department may succumb to any of these errors (i.e., leniency, strictness, or central tendency) in evaluating their subordinates. Although their evaluations may be consistent in terms of the relative performance of their own employees, the errors will cause a problem in any attempt to use these evaluations as the basis for merit raises or promotions across the entire department. When the director of the department makes final decisions about salary increases or promotions, he or she is faced with evaluations from the different regions that are subject to the three types of errors; therefore, the decisions are unlikely to be fair.

Temporal Errors

Belcourt and colleagues (2002) referred to another set of rating errors as **temporal errors**. These errors include recency error, which is the tendency to rate the annual performance of an employee based on the employee's most recent behavior. For example, a playground supervisor may be evaluated based on his or her performance in the month of November or December, and the rating may be used to reflect his or her performance throughout the year. However, the supervisor's performance in the previous 10 months might not have been as good or as bad as the performance in the last two months.

Another type of temporal error is contrast error, which is the tendency for a rater to compare a student or employee with another person who has just been rated. Professors are relatively likely to succumb to this error. When they are marking a stack of assignments or examinations, they are likely to rate a student based on how they rated another student just beforehand. If the other student was rated poorly, this student looks good by contrast and is likely to receive a better grade than might have been the case otherwise. By the same token, a student may compare poorly with another who was rated earlier and therefore receive a poorer grade than he or she otherwise might have. In other words, in this error, the student's grade for an assignment depends not only on the quality of his or her own work but also on the order in which the professor marks the assignments.

Contrast error can occur just as easily when an athletics director is evaluating several coaches or when a city recreation director is evaluating a number of supervisors for administrative purposes. The director in either case should guard against being influenced by the ratings given to the preceding candidate.

> ## COMPONENTS OF EFFECTIVE PERFORMANCE APPRAISALS
>
> Recognizing the importance of performance appraisal, Ivancevich and Matteson (2002) suggested the following steps to ensure that the evaluation process is carried out effectively. These steps are as relevant to sport organizations as they are to business and industrial firms.
>
> - *Employee participation:* If employees are allowed to participate in the evaluation process, they are likely to be more satisfied with it. To the extent that they are involved in deciding the procedures to be adopted, they also feel a sense of procedural justice as discussed in chapter 9.
>
> - *Specific performance goals:* Employees perform better when sport and recreation managers ensure that the goals are specific rather than general (e.g., 20 season tickets to be sold in a day rather than "sell as many as you can").
>
> - *Training of managers:* Because performance evaluation is a critical component of a manager's job, the manager must be trained in both the substance and the style of performance evaluation.
>
> - *Communication of results:* No matter how well the performance evaluation has been carried out, its potency is lost if the results are not properly communicated to the employee. Soon after completing the evaluation, the manager needs to communicate complete information to the employee and provide the information in a very warm and friendly way. This step is critical in creating a sense of informational justice and interpersonal justice as discussed in chapter 9.
>
> - *Recognizing and reinforcing good performance:* Very often, managers tend to focus on the deficiencies in employee performance and overlook the good aspects. To ensure all employees are able to develop both personally and professionally, it is critical that good performances be recognized and reinforced.
>
> - *Continuous performance appraisal:* Although there are deadlines and specific schedules for formal performance appraisals, sport and recreation managers need to make appraisal a continuous affair carried out throughout the year.

Other Rater Errors

In some cases, good performance in one aspect of the job may be transferred to other aspects of the job. This tendency is referred to as halo error. For example, a school may use a teacher-coach's performance in coaching to evaluate his or her teaching. A university may evaluate a professor's teaching based on his or her reputation for research and publishing. Similarly, a fitness club may use the activity level of instructors during a class to evaluate them on the substance of their instruction. And, as noted earlier, a manager may evaluate employees highly on task performance based on their citizenship behaviors.

In yet another form of error, raters judge employees based on their perceptions of themselves. That is, supervisors may tend to view positively the performance of employees that they perceive to be like themselves in some respects. For example, a supervisor who comes to the office very early in the morning may view all those who come early quite positively. This is not surprising, because people tend to have a "soft spot" for people who are similar to themselves (e.g., went to the same schools, follow the same teams, had a similarly rough time in the past). However, if raters allow these feelings to influence their evaluation of performance, they commit what is referred to as similarity error.

Finally, another form of error in performance evaluation is the use of inappropriate substitutes for performance, such as an individual's level of congeniality or manner of dressing. The receptionist in a tennis club, for example, may be quite polite and courteous to customers and exhibit a great sense of humor when interacting with them. However, although these are desirable qualities in a receptionist, they do not reflect the accuracy with which the receptionist records customers' requests for tennis courts or informs them when and for how long they can use a court.

Managers who carry out performance appraisals should guard against being strict or lenient or placing everyone in the center of the performance range (i.e., making distributional errors). They should also avoid basing their judgments only on a person's recent performances or on how another individual was evaluated earlier (i.e., making temporal errors). Finally, superior performance in one aspect of the job should not be transferred to other areas (i.e., halo effect).

VIEWPOINT

Theoretically, as managers, we should be interested in ends; that is, in getting the job done! However, as the recent turn of unethical behavior in sport has spread around the globe (e.g., FIFA bribing scandals, NCAA student-athlete corruption issues, doping issues in international competitions), we must focus not just on the end result of performance but also on the means for getting there. Specifically, as noted by Werbel and Balkin (2010), "Organizations that use outcome-based performance evaluations are likely to have employees who perceive higher benefits of misconduct and lower perceived costs of misconduct, compared to organizations that use behavior-based performance evaluations" (p. 323). In other words, when evaluation focuses solely on outcome—and as long as expected outcomes are being produced—then the actions that employees take to get to the outcome are never judged. Thus, acceptance of unethical behavior may be implicitly embedded in the organizational culture in the structure and emphasis of the performance appraisal.

Current Performance and Future Potential

Beer (1987) pointed out another problem in performance evaluation as used by managers for making decisions about promotions. An employee may be performing well in the current job because he or she possesses the necessary abilities and experience; however, current performance does not guarantee that that employee will perform well in another job if the new job requires different abilities. For example, an athletic trainer in a university athletics department may be performing extraordinarily well in working with and treating injured athletes. Even so, the university athletic director must be careful when deciding whether to promote the person to the position of supervisor of athletic trainers because the requirements of that job differ from those of the current job. Instead of working with injured athletes, the supervisor works with equally qualified athletic trainers and coordinates their activities. Thus, successful performance as an athletic trainer does not guarantee effective performance as a supervisor.

Beer's (1987) solution to this problem was to separate the evaluation of current performance from the evaluation of potential for future performance. This is, in fact, the practice in many organizational contexts. Better performers at one level of the organization are targeted for training and evaluation for future promotions to the next-higher level. Individuals who do well in the training and in subsequent tests and examinations or other forms of evaluation are chosen for promotions. In sum, a manager should evaluate current performance separately from future potential and should communicate decisions about each type of evaluation to the employee (Beer 1987).

Rater and Ratee Reactions

Personal reactions of the rater and the employee may create two significant problems in performance appraisal (Beer 1987). The first problem involves rater ambivalence and avoidance. Some superiors are uncomfortable with their roles in making decisions that affect subordinates' job or career progress. Thus, they are reluctant to perform a realistic appraisal because they fear the consequences to the ratee. In addition, they are not capable of managing the interpersonally difficult situations associated with performance appraisal. In sum, they are uncertain about their subjective evaluations and aversive regarding the need to let subordinates know where they stand.

The second problem stems from the conflict between the evaluative and developmental objectives of performance appraisal. This conflict places the superior in the position of both judge and helper. Therefore, the subordinate may become defensive about the process, blame circumstances or other people, question the appraisal system, or demean the data sources. These reactions may lead to open

VIEWPOINT

As the famous Peter principle (Peter 1972) has it, "In a hierarchy, every employee tends to rise to his [or her] level of incompetence" (p. 4). Peter went on to explain that "for every job that exists in the world, there is someone, somewhere, who cannot do it. Given sufficient time and enough promotions, he [or she] will eventually arrive at that job and there he [or she] will remain, habitually bungling the job, frustrating his [or her] coworkers, and eroding the efficiency of the organization" (pp. 4-5). Peter employed humor to drive home the point that competence in the current job does not guarantee good performance in a higher position.

INTENTIONAL ERRORS IN PERFORMANCE APPRAISALS

The reasons for errors in performance appraisal can generally be traced to individual differences between raters. That is, one rater may tend to be lenient, whereas another may tend to be strict. These errors are unintentional. However, raters may also commit errors intentionally for political reasons.

Longenecker, Sims, and Gioia (1987) noted that managers may be intentionally lenient in their evaluations for any of several reasons. These reasons include maximizing merit raises for their subordinates, helping an individual who has personal problems, avoiding confrontations with employees, putting up a facade of good performance by the unit, and rewarding an employee who is showing improvement. Longenecker et al. also suggested that supervisors may give quite favorable ratings to an employee whom they dislike in the hope that the organization will promote the person out of the unit. By the same token, managers may intentionally deflate the performance ratings of an employee in order to prod the person to exert more effort, to punish a rebellious employee, to suggest that an employee should leave the organization, or to build a record of poor performance so that an employee can be fired later.

hostility and denials. The worst-case scenario occurs when the superior is ambivalent and the subordinate is defensive and resistant.

According to Beer (1987), one solution to the problem is to uncouple the evaluative and developmental aspects of the appraisal. He suggested instituting two separate processes and using appropriate, but different, performance data for the two purposes. When the purpose is evaluative, outcome data may be more appropriate; that is, the focus is placed on what the employee has done or achieved. When the purpose is developmental, then behavioral data are more appropriate (e.g., specific performance-related behaviors assessed with behavioral rating scales). The emphasis here is on how employees do their work and on the improvements they can make in this regard.

Interpersonal difficulties in performance appraisal may relate to supervisors' lack of confidence in their judgment and reluctance to appraise correctly because of the possible effects on others' careers. Subordinates may become defensive and find fault with the system, the rater, or colleagues because of conflicts between the developmental and administrative objectives of the performance appraisal. Supervisors and subordinates may also be unwilling or unable to manage the difficult interpersonal situation posed by performance appraisal.

VIEWPOINT

When performance has been good, when superiors and subordinates have an open relationship, when promotions and salary increases are abundant, when there is plenty of time for preparation and discussion— in short, whenever it's a pleasure— performance appraisal is easy to do. Most of the time, however, and particularly when it is most needed and most difficult (e.g., when performance is substandard), performance appraisal refuses to run properly. (Beer 1987, p. 286)

ROLE OF THE SPORT OR RECREATION MANAGER

Referring back to the model of motivation outlined in chapter 8, performance appraisals are an essential element in examining how employee effort leads to employee satisfaction. Specifically, the amount of effort put forth by an employee is linked to the employee's performance and therefore to his or her potential to obtain rewards and satisfaction.

Without proper performance appraisals, employees may view the distribution of rewards as inequitable and thus reduce their efforts moving forward. This is particularly relevant in sport and recreation organizations, where increased effort is needed during peak periods. For example, an employee who is involved in course setup (operations) for golf championships throughout a tournament season may receive formal performance appraisals from her direct-report manager after each tournament. These appraisals provide quick snapshots of what she accomplished during tournament setup as well as areas for improvement (with recommendations to aid improvement). The performance appraisal is delivered in hard copy in person, and time is offered to the employee to respond to the appraisal.

The employee's reward is directly tied to the accomplishments addressed in her performance appraisal, and her satisfaction increases. Therefore, her efforts remain strong through the remaining championships in the season. The role of the sport or recreation manager here is threefold: ensure that formal performance appraisals are scheduled (even if they are short due to time constraints), provide written and oral feedback (two-way communication), and ensure that the appraisal is delivered by the appropriate individual (in this example, the direct-report manager).

Case Study

Developing a Performance Appraisal

You have just been hired to serve as special events coordinator for a professional baseball team. You work in the event operations and management department and report to two of the department's directors—one for operations, the other for management. According to your employment contract and job description, you begin your employment with a three-month probation period during which you must prove that you have the "right stuff" to do the job. You decide to ask your director of operations what criteria will be used to judge your performance. The director is quite busy and simply refers you to the "essential functions" in your job description:

- Maintain and manage existing accounts and coordinate on-site events.
- Maintain existing accounts and generate repeat business as well as new sales from each account.
- Conduct on-site client tours of the ballpark.
- Help create and coordinate client sales events.
- Help meet the department's sales goals by generating new sales and developing new business streams and sources.
- Prepare and distribute contracts, reports, event sheets, audiovisual requests, special projects, and related material for department staff as requested.

- Maintain existing database and use it as a tool for generating sales and maintaining events.
- Complete all aspects of event coordination for client events at the ballpark.
- Actively coordinate some facets of events before and during the actual event.
- Provide superior customer service to clients and prospects during events.

Still a little confused, you visit your director of management, who is busy with tour prep. He insists that performance appraisal should not be a problem and that you just need to do a good job. Feeling somewhat confused, you decide to create a memo of what you think your performance appraisal should look like. You figure you can keep

it on file and use it in the future, if you are able to secure a director position of your own, as a tool for making sure everyone is on the same page with regards to the evaluation.

Case Study Tasks

1. Using Ivancevich and Matteson's (2002) steps to ensure an effective performance appraisal, discuss the steps needed to ensure effective performance appraisal for this position within this professional baseball club.

2. Based on the essential functions listed in the description, create a performance evaluation form that you could present to your directors as a means of evaluating your performance at your three-month probation review.

CHAPTER PURSUITS

SUMMARY

This chapter emphasizes the importance of performance appraisal, which serves the administrative purposes of monitoring and evaluating employee performance and making personnel decisions, such as salary increases and promotions. Performance appraisal may also be developmental; this type of appraisal identifies employees' strengths and weaknesses and forms the basis for further coaching, guidance, and training. The performance domain includes not only job-specific task behaviors but also non-job-specific behaviors and citizenship behaviors. In addition, it includes the person's level of effort in carrying out his or her assignments, as well as the person's communication and leadership skills.

Managers need to be cautious about possible distributional errors in performance appraisal (e.g., leniency, strictness, lumping every performance into the central range); they also need to guard against temporal errors (e.g., evaluating an individual's performance based on recent events or in a manner that is biased by comparison with recent evaluation of other candidates).

When performance appraisals are used for developmental purposes, they may be more individualized and conducted more frequently. When

they are used for evaluative purposes, they must be carried out during specified time periods (e.g., quarterly or annually) by means of uniform processes for all employees. Performance evaluation must also be based on comprehensive information drawn from the candidate, co-workers, supervisors, and clients or customers.

KEY TERMS

administrative purpose 243

developmental purpose 243

distributional error 256

performance appraisal 243

performance domain 247

temporal error 258

UNDERSTAND

1. Quite often, universities admit students to graduate programs on the basis of their performance in the last year or two years of their bachelor's degree program. How does this practice relate to the recency error as discussed in the chapter? Do you approve of this practice? Explain.

2. Consider a commercial fitness club and the fitness unit of a university intramural department. Should the process of performance appraisal for fitness instructors differ between these two settings? Explain.

INTERACT

1. Some sport and recreation managers may include participation in committee meetings as a component of job performance for evaluation purposes. How would you categorize this aspect of performance? Discuss the pros and cons of considering it as part of an evaluation.

2. Recall a few firings of professional and university coaches in the last two years. What were the reasons given in each case? Compare the reasons for firing professional coaches with the reasons for firing university coaches.

Reward Systems

After reading this chapter, you will be able to

- explain the purposes of rewards in an organization,
- describe the various types of rewards in an organization,
- explain the various bases or criteria by which rewards can be distributed, and
- understand how various criteria and various rewards can be mixed to create a reward system that addresses individual differences.

As noted in chapter 13, one of the purposes of performance appraisal is administrative—specifically, to facilitate personnel decisions about salary, wages, merit pay, promotion, and similar rewards. Volunteers, of course, work for intrinsic rewards (see chapter 2), and paid workers may also seek and receive intrinsic rewards. At the same time, paid workers, by definition, work for the material resources provided by their jobs. Thus, it is critical to understand the realm of **reward systems** in organizations. Accordingly, this chapter describes the purposes, types, bases, and mixes of rewards. It also highlights some ways in which rewards can be matched with individual preferences and how the work schedule itself can be used as a reward.

Although intrinsic rewards and extrinsic rewards can both be motivational, there is an important distinction between the two. As discussed in chapter 8, intrinsic rewards are largely a function of job content. Organizations and their managers may seek to enhance the intrinsic appeal of a job by following the prescriptions of Hackman and Oldham and of Herzberg (see chapter 10) for redesigning jobs. However, it is individuals themselves who derive and administer intrinsic rewards. To the extent that

intrinsic rewards reside in the job itself and are administered by workers, the organization has less control over them than it has over extrinsic rewards, such as pay and bonuses. Therefore, this chapter focuses, for the most part, on extrinsic rewards.

PURPOSES OF REWARD SYSTEMS

Let us begin with a description of the **purposes of reward systems** in organizations. These purposes have been explained from different perspectives (e.g., Belcourt, Sherman, Bohlander, and Snell 2002; De Cenzo and Robbins 2002; Entrekin and Scott-Ladd 2014; Lawler 1987; Schuler and Jackson 1996), which are collated and described in the following subsections.

Attracting and Retaining Good Employees

Every organization is engaged in competition with other organizations (in the same business or in other businesses) for recruiting and retaining productive employees. For instance, two professional sport organizations may be seeking good candidates for front-office jobs; similarly, two fitness clubs may be in need of a good accountant, or two university athletics departments may need to hire lawyers to direct their compliance units.

The managers in these contexts must remember that the potential candidates are employable in different kinds of organizations. For instance, an accountant may find a lucrative job with a construction company, a law firm, a hospital, or a university. Similarly, a lawyer can find employment at other universities or in other kinds of organizations. Therefore, a sport organization must ensure that its reward structure at least matches the market rate if it wants to recruit and retain good employees. In order to be effective, then, a reward system must be competitive with those of other firms seeking a particular kind of competency and talent, and, ultimately, it must be more attractive to prospective candidates.

Reducing Absenteeism

According to Lawler (1987), organizations can design reward systems to reduce absenteeism by linking bonuses and other perks to levels of attendance. This strategy is particularly useful in compensating for low job content and poor working conditions that cannot be improved. For

example, as explained in chapter 8, some jobs in facility management may be simple and routine and, therefore, may lack motivational properties. Thus, individuals in those jobs are susceptible to absenteeism. The facility manager may attempt to reduce such absenteeism by linking certain rewards to attendance. For example, the manager may set a policy of giving a monetary bonus or extra days of paid leave for perfect or near-perfect attendance.

Motivating Enhanced Performance

Organizational effectiveness is enhanced through employee performance, which, in turn, can be facilitated by an effective reward system. Recall the Porter and Lawler (1968) model of motivation discussed in chapter 8. The model suggests that the linkage between performance and rewards (both intrinsic and extrinsic) strongly influences subsequent performance. According to this model, a reward can motivate performance if the reward is attractive to the individual, the reward is tied to a certain level of performance, and the individual perceives that level of performance to be attainable. In other words, even as organizational rewards can be seen as rewards for past performance, they also influence motivation for future performance. Accordingly, managers must try to make rewards attractive to individuals and offer rewards to employees who achieve realistic levels of performance.

Developing Employee Skills

A reward system can be used to enhance organizational effectiveness if rewards are used to increase employees' skill levels. As noted in chapter 8, performance is a function of effort as well as ability. On the basis of that premise, an organization can design reward systems to reward individuals who develop their skills and in turn contribute to greater productivity and organizational effectiveness. For instance, many school systems in the United States and Canada increase the base salary of their teachers after they have upgraded their training to a higher level. Note that the notion of skill development is not far removed from performance; indeed, performance in a job is in large part reflective of the skill that an individual possesses. Similarly, a promotion is presumably based on a person's having acquired the skills necessary to perform the higher-level job.

VIEWPOINT

Whilst we must reward people to ensure that we can compete effectively in the appropriate employment markets, the way we do [so] should reflect our particular organization. It is the culture and values that define the brand, and rewards should reflect these, not blindly follow the market. So I strongly advocate an approach of "best fit," not "best practice." (Rose 2014, p. 12)

Facilitating Organizational Culture and Strategic Objectives

Yet another way in which reward systems can influence organizational effectiveness is by fostering and maintaining the organizational culture that furthers the specific goals and aims of the organization. Lawler (1987) noted that "reward systems can shape culture precisely because of their important influence on motivation, satisfaction, and membership. The behaviors they evoke become the dominant patterns of behavior in the organization and lead to perceptions of what it stands for, believes in, and values" (p. 258). For example, Lawler suggested that high levels of pay may create a culture of elitism and that member participation in pay decisions may create a culture of participation. The relatively high salaries paid to athletes and coaches in professional sport do project an image of elitism and cultivate that sense among athletes and coaches. In contrast, if a profit-oriented fitness or tennis club engages its

---

DIVERSITY MANAGEMENT OF HUMAN RESOURCES

In Chelladurai's (2014) integrative framework for managing diversity, managers activate deep-level thinking by encouraging their personnel "to express their preferences for specific goals or courses of action, or their perspectives on a problem and solutions for it" (p. 350). Managers can encourage this expression by identifying rewards that are meaningful to volunteers and staff and attaching these rewards to behavior that is linked to appreciation and acknowledgment of the benefits of diversity in an organization. For example, if managers reward diverse opinions and processes during meetings, a culture of diversity (and its benefits) may develop and help the organization (and the individuals in it) reach full potential.

---

employees in pay and bonus decisions, it facilitates a culture of participation and ownership among them.

Defining and Reinforcing Organizational Structure

Similarly, reward systems can define and strengthen the organizational structure that embodies the status hierarchy (i.e., the relative vertical position of each member of the organization, in comparison to one another). As Lawler (1987) noted, a highly differentiated reward system supports relatively rigid bureaucratic behavior and centralized authority and motivates people to seek promotion to higher ranks. In contrast, a more egalitarian reward system is consistent with a more participative management style and helps retain professional specialists and experts in nonmanagement positions.

To extend Lawler's (1987) notions to the sporting context, directors and assistant directors of a university athletics department may be paid very high salaries, whereas lower-level managers and workers may be paid less than the market rate. Such a scheme reinforces a top-down bureaucratic orientation. In contrast, a private sport marketing firm may recruit and hire qualified professional marketers and pay them salaries commensurate with their qualifications, their achievements, and market rates. As Lawler pointed out, this egalitarian approach is consistent with the presence of technical specialists (i.e., sport marketers).

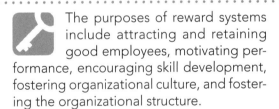

The purposes of reward systems include attracting and retaining good employees, motivating performance, encouraging skill development, fostering organizational culture, and fostering the organizational structure.

TYPES OF REWARDS

The **types of rewards** available in organizations can be described in terms of the following dimensions: intrinsic and extrinsic rewards, financial and nonfinancial rewards, career rewards and social rewards, direct and nondirect rewards, performance-based and membership-based rewards, and work schedules as rewards (De Cenzo and Robbins 2002; Schuler and Jackson 1996). Let us examine each dimension in some detail.

Intrinsic Versus Extrinsic Rewards

The discussion of individual motivation in chapter 8 distinguishes between intrinsic rewards and extrinsic rewards that accrue to individual employees in their task performance. As discussed in chapter 8, the significance of intrinsic motivation in employee performance is emphasized both in Herzberg's (1968) two-factor theory and in Porter and Lawler's (1968) model of motivation. In addition, the proposition that intrinsic rewards in the job itself constitute a potential source of motivation provides the basis for the practice of job enrichment and for the tenets of the job characteristics model. Thus, managers must always be attuned to opportunities for enriching their employees' jobs.

An equally potent source of motivation consists of the extrinsic rewards (e.g., pay, bonuses, promotions) offered by the organization. As noted in chapter 8, the one difficulty with regard to extrinsic rewards is that employees may perceive them as inequitable if the distribution of such rewards is not based on clear, firm, and meaningful criteria—that is, if rewards are not linked properly to performance. The purpose of this section is to outline the basic features of a good extrinsic reward system.

Financial Versus Nonfinancial Rewards

Financial rewards directly enhance the employee's financial well-being; for example, salaries, wages, and bonuses are financial rewards that the recipient can take home and use for any purpose. Nonfinancial rewards, on the other hand, do not increase the financial payoff to the employee: "Instead of making the employee's life better off [of] the job [as financial rewards do], nonfinancial rewards emphasize making life on the job more attractive" (De Cenzo and Robbins 1994, p. 413). This type of reward includes things such as office furnishings, parking spaces, and top-line computers in the office. As these examples show, nonfinancial rewards are motivational in their own right. That is, they not only facilitate task performance but also create a sense of status and prestige and the associated positive feelings. However, although these rewards provide no financial benefit, they do entail some financial cost for the organization.

Career Rewards Versus Social Rewards

From a different perspective, Schuler and Jackson (1996) classified nonmonetary (nonfinancial) rewards into the subcategories of career rewards and social rewards. As the term implies, career rewards are aimed at one's career in terms of job security and career growth. For example, a commercial tennis club might offer job security instead of large salary increases. In another example, universities commonly offer free tuition to their employees if they upgrade their skills and qualifications. In this case, the university does not incur much expense, but the financial and personal benefit to the employees is great.

Social rewards, on the other hand, involve the good feelings that an employee experiences in relation to social comparisons that may result from a title, a private office, or other such status symbol. Think of the significance of a key to the executive lounge—that special, spacious room with access to comfortable work space, relaxation bars, and complimentary food and drink for the exclusive use of executives. Some people consider getting

---

STATUS IN REWARD SYSTEMS

Reward systems reinforce the hierarchical structure of an organization; they may also delineate the critical areas of operation in an organization. For instance, a university athletics department may pay the marketing director more than it pays the heads of other departments in order to reflect the importance placed on the respective functions. In a more familiar example, university athletics departments generally pay the football and basketball coaches more than they pay the coaches of other sports, for the obvious reason that these sports are more popular and capable of generating revenue. At the same time, a university may pay more for, say, the basketball coach than for the football coach if basketball is a key part of that university's history and tradition.

access to the lounge a great privilege and therefore a great reward.

Direct and Indirect Compensation

Schuler and Jackson (1996) also noted that monetary (financial) compensation may be either direct or indirect. Direct compensation takes such forms as basic salary, wages, merit pay, and bonuses. Indirect compensation is divided into public protection, private protection, paid leave, and life cycle benefits (Schuler and Jackson). Law requires organizations to provide public protection compensation, such as contributions toward social security and premiums for unemployment and disability insurance. Private protection relates to the organization's creating or contributing to a worker pension plan, life insurance, or savings. Paid leave involves the organization's allowing its employees to be absent with full pay for the purposes of further training, illness, vacation, and other legitimate reasons. Finally, life cycle benefits are aimed at enhancing the quality of life for employees through such things as child care and elder care programs, extended maternity and paternity leave plans, and park and playground facilities.

 Intrinsic rewards (residing in the job) and extrinsic rewards may be either financial or nonfinancial (e.g., training, titles). Indirect compensation involves public protection (e.g., social security payments), private protection (e.g., contributions to pension and savings programs), or paid leave.

Performance-Based Versus Membership-Based Rewards

Performance-based rewards are linked directly to performance by the individual or the group. The organization evaluates the performances and proffers rewards based on that evaluation. In contrast, the organization allocates membership-based rewards on the basis of an individual's membership in specified groups, including the organization itself. Such rewards typically take the form of increases (e.g., cost-of-living increases) as a percentage of one's salary, seniority-based increases, and education-based increases. The focus is on speci-

fying what membership in which group is critical to the organization and which members belong to which groups.

For instance, several universities have recently allocated relatively more increases to female administrators and coaches in order to correct past inequalities in salary based on gender. In this case, the only criterion for distribution is whether one is a member of the female gender. Similarly, base salaries for directors, assistant directors, and lower-level employees of a city recreation department may be graded progressively higher, and every employee may be entitled to the base salary associated with the cadre of employment to which he or she belongs.

The categorizations offered by De Cenzo and Robbins (2002) overlap considerably with those provided by Schuler and Jackson (1996). Figure 14.1, which combines these categorizations, can help you understand the various forms that rewards can take. A sport manager should be able to identify from the various forms of rewards those that are most relevant and feasible in his or her own context (i.e., the organization and its resources, the types of work done, and the types of employees).

Another classification of benefits has been provided by J.R. Gordon (2002):

- Health protectors (e.g., medical insurance, dental insurance)
- Income protectors (e.g., accidental death insurance, disability insurance, life insurance, pension)
- Income supplements (e.g., bonuses, profit-sharing plan, stock options)
- Time off with pay (e.g., holidays, maternity or paternity leave, sick leave, vacation)
- Other benefits (e.g., professional association or club membership, company vehicle, child care, flexible work arrangement, subsidized meals)

As you may have noticed, most of these benefits overlap the ones listed in figure 14.1.

As pointed out in chapter 2, some incentives that are relevant to paid workers may motivate volunteers as well. For example, young persons may volunteer to work in a sport organization in order to gain experience and skills and thereby enhance their chances of securing a job. This benefit is consistent with the career rewards offered to a paid worker. That is, the sport organization can help by exposing the student volunteer to increasingly complex tasks so that he or she can develop needed competencies. The organization can also motivate

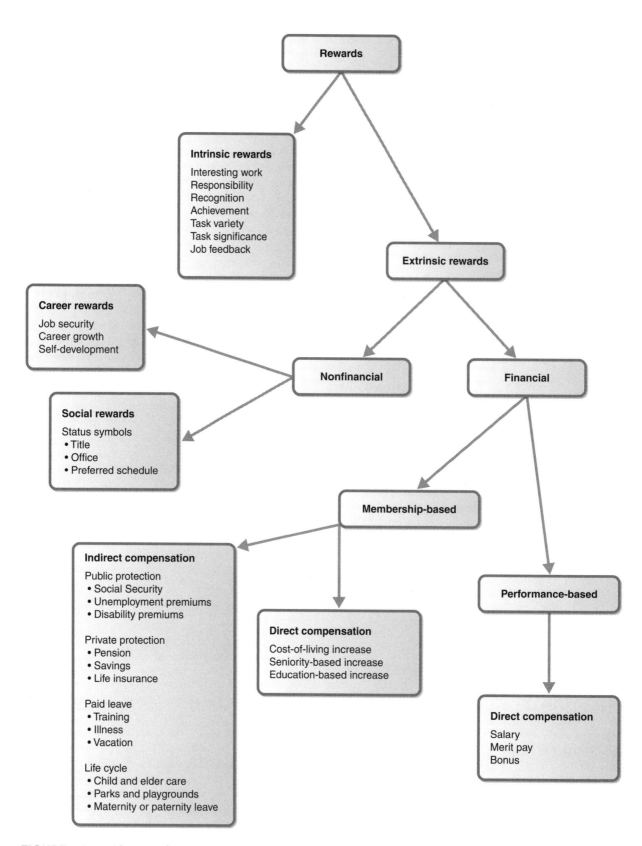

FIGURE 14.1 Classes of organizational rewards.

volunteers through social rewards, such as titles and other status symbols.

In summary, managers should recognize that altruistic motives do not preclude the effects of other incentives. In fact, as long as a sport organization needs the contribution of volunteers, and as long as organizations compete for volunteers, a sport manager must take the necessary steps to offer sufficient tangible and intangible rewards for volunteers.

Work Schedules as Rewards

An organization can use strategies related to work schedules that employees may perceive as rewards and that may not entail additional expenditures by the organization. Here we discuss four of these strategies: shorter work week, staggered daily schedule, flextime, and telecommuting.

REWARDS FOR VOLUNTEER WORKERS

The description of various forms of rewards has more to do with rewards for paid full-time workers than for other types of workers. However, insofar as many sport organizations capitalize on services provided by volunteers, managers need to be concerned with rewards for volunteer workers as well. Obviously, the major form of rewards for volunteers is that of intrinsic rewards. Although these rewards are generalizable to all workers, they are more critical to volunteer workers because monetary rewards are not applicable to them. Intrinsic rewards for volunteers include the satisfaction derived from serving others. As noted in chapter 2, one reason for which volunteers join a sport organization is their altruistic motive to serve others. To the extent that a sport organization's goals are oriented toward serving others, it provides a forum for volunteers to satisfy their altruistic motives.

However, managers cannot be satisfied with this assumption. Because many other organizations also offer opportunities to satisfy altruistic motives, volunteers are likely to choose one organization over another for reasons other than altruism. Thus, a sport manager must also be concerned with creating other incentives for volunteers. For instance, the manager might enrich a volunteer's job by assigning progressively more challenging tasks with increasing responsibilities. If that volunteer desires enriched jobs and is capable of adequately performing them, then the sport manager gains two significant benefits for the organization. First, the organization retains an effective volunteer capable of performing in higher-level jobs. Second, it reduces costs because the volunteer performs more challenging jobs without the cost of salary and benefits.

The emphasis on intrinsic rewards and job enrichment should not minimize the importance of other rewards for volunteers. For instance, as noted earlier, nonfinancial rewards, such as parking spaces, office settings, and office equipment, make life at work more enjoyable and attractive. This fact is just as relevant to volunteers as it is to paid workers. Volunteers devote time and effort on behalf of the organization, and they need not suffer from the lack of a suitable or even pleasant work environment. Thus, sport managers need to make efforts to provide volunteers with a workplace that is comfortable and attractive.

Furthermore, although volunteers may be willing to extend their time and effort to a sport organization, some may not be able to incur any expenses on behalf of the organization. For example, when a volunteer must drive to several locations in a city to carry out assigned tasks (e.g., as a referee in a youth sport league), he or she incurs the cost of transportation. In such a case, reimbursing the volunteer for the expenses is only appropriate.

Shorter Work Week

A sport organization may adopt a scheme in which the traditional five-day work week is shortened to three or four days, during which the employee is expected to put in the same total hours as in a traditional work week. For example, if an employee in the ticketing department worked 8 hours per day for a regular five-day work week, he or she would work a total of 40 hours (8 × 5). In a four-day work week, that employee would work 10 hours per day to reach the same total of 40 hours for the week (10 × 4). In this scheme, the expense to the organization does not change; that is, employees are not paid any more or less than in a standard work week.

Even so, the organization earns the goodwill of employees who are more satisfied with their work schedules and more motivated to perform well. Some studies have shown that shorter work weeks resulted in less absenteeism and fewer requests for time off for personal reasons (Saal and Knight 1995; Schuler and Jackson 1996). From the employees' perspective, the shorter work week offers more leisure time and decreases commuting time.

On the downside, working longer hours each day may mean lower productivity at the end of the day. For example, an exercise leader is likely to be more tired and less effective in the last two hours of work in a four-day work week than in a five-day work week. Furthermore, the scheme may not benefit everybody in the organization. For instance, working mothers and fathers may find that the longer hours each day hinder their child-rearing and child-minding activities. Another problem is that the good feelings about the shorter work week may not last for long as one gets used to the routine. In addition, employees may have reservations about a shorter work week if the employer fixes and dictates the number of days and the number of hours of work. Therefore, sport managers may consider allowing their employees to choose the work week that best suits them.

Staggered Daily Schedule

A staggered daily schedule involves variations in the times that employees report to work and leave work. This approach requires that every worker put in a certain number of hours per day but allows those hours to be staggered. That is, some workers may be allowed to report to work earlier and leave earlier (e.g., one hour earlier), and others may come to work later and leave later. Employees may also be rotated every week (or over any fixed period of time) through the various schedules, thus creating variety. Workers may enjoy changing schedules instead of sticking to a permanent daily schedule. However, it is important for managers to discuss preference for scheduling with employees to determine if they like or dislike variation in scheduling as a source of reward.

Another benefit of the staggered daily schedule is that the manager can tailor it to suit the needs and preferences of individual workers. If possible, the manager may give employees a choice of daily schedule. Reporting early and leaving early may be attractive to some employees, whereas reporting late and leaving late may be attractive to others. This approach, however, creates more work for management because it is necessary to keep track of the schedules for individual workers and monitor their adherence to their chosen schedules.

Flextime

Flextime is a scheme that originated in Germany, where it is called *Gleitzeit*, meaning "gliding time" (French 2003). In this system, the manager expects an individual to work a given number of hours each week but permits the person to choose, within limits, when to work those hours. Usually, the plan includes a given number of core hours (i.e., from four to six hours, such as from 10 a.m. to 4 p.m.) with a flexibility band surrounding the core. In some cases, one can accumulate extra hours and take a day off at the end of the month. One is expected to finish the given jobs, and the scheme emphasizes paying for productivity rather than for attendance.

Some research has shown that this arrangement reduces employee tardiness, decreases absenteeism, reduces job fatigue, and increases loyalty (Saal and Knight 1988). The scheme would be helpful to individuals who manage both career and family roles. On a daily basis, the employee has complete control over scheduling the portion of work hours that fall outside of the specified core hours. Although employees may enjoy having such flexibility in their work schedule, managers must note that they cannot effectively direct their employees outside of the core time. It may even be difficult to evaluate their performances outside of the core time given that managers will have less face-to-face time to observe performance.

Telecommuting

Telecommuting involves working from home and connecting with the office via phone, Skype, or other technology to handle such matters as meetings, conference calls, and budget discussions. This practice is becoming more commonplace as a method to reward employees by providing flexibility in "work space." Such opportunities save organizations money by reducing office space and equipment requirements even as they provide self-motivated, independent employees with the freedom to conduct work in their own space and perhaps on their own schedule (Goodman 2013).

However, the use of telecommuting opportunities as rewards for employees must be handled with caution. Potential risks include distractions, overwork due to the workday's informal structure, and lack of strong organizational culture due to reduced face time between employees (Goodman 2013). Thus, managers must be strategic in how they set up and offer telecommuting opportunities in their reward structure, and they must ensure proper assessment of employees to determine who is a good fit for this type of reward.

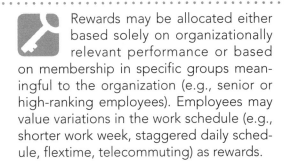

Rewards may be allocated either based solely on organizationally relevant performance or based on membership in specific groups meaningful to the organization (e.g., senior or high-ranking employees). Employees may value variations in the work schedule (e.g., shorter work week, staggered daily schedule, flextime, telecommuting) as rewards.

BASES OF REWARDS

The most critical concern in using rewards is to determine the bases on which rewards are distributed to members of the organization. To inform that determination, this section outlines general themes regarding criteria for deciding who gets what and how much of it. Some of the concepts presented in this section necessarily parallel those discussed earlier because the purposes and types of rewards are intertwined with the **bases of rewards**.

Job as the Base

A traditional approach in distributing rewards is to base them solely on the type of job that a person performs. That is, the manager evaluates the job in relation to other jobs, then uses that evaluation to make decisions about rewards. Thus, a locker room attendant may be paid less than a coach, and a caretaker may be paid less than an exercise specialist at a fitness club. According to Lawler (1987), "This approach is based on the assumption that job worth can be determined, and that the person doing the job is worth only as much to the organization as the job itself is worth" (p. 260). This assumption is valid in most circumstances, and it provides an objective basis for allocating rewards.

The notion of job worth parallels the notion of intrinsic rewards in a job. Generally speaking, jobs of higher worth entail relatively more responsibility, greater autonomy, and greater opportunities for achievement; these characteristics are also key ingredients of job enrichment. As noted in chapter 10, one difficulty faced by a manager when enriching jobs is that workers (and their labor unions) may expect more salary for the work. In the view of these parties, job enrichment increases job worth, and the pay should be commensurate with that worth.

STAGGERED START TIME

One of the difficulties encountered by employees in large urban centers is that of traffic jams during rush hours. The problem is more pronounced, of course, at the beginning of the workday when everybody wants to get to the office and at the end of the office day when everybody is in a hurry to get home. One way to alleviate this problem is to schedule the workday to begin at different times (e.g., 7:30, 8:00, and 8:30 a.m.) and to end correspondingly at different times (e.g., 3:30, 4:00, and 4:30 p.m.). This practice is known as staggered start time (Gottlieb, Kelloway, and Barham 1998; Pierce, Newstrom, Dunham, and Barber 1989). Hypothetically speaking, if all organizations in an urban center had three start times, traffic jams would be cut by 67 percent because at any one time only one-third of the workforce would be driving to work.

Skill as the Base

Another approach is to reward employees on the basis of the skills they possess. The assumption here is that the skills under consideration are those that can be used in the organization. For example, one's skills in gardening may not have much relevance in a fitness and recreation club or in the public relations unit of an athletics department. However, skills related to first aid or accounting may be meaningful in either of these two organizational contexts. The first advantage of a skill-based scheme is to engender in employees the belief that the organization values their personal growth: "This policy can create a climate of concern for personal growth and development and produce a highly talented work force" (Lawler 1987, p. 260). Such feelings, in turn, lead to greater commitment to the organization and increased motivation in job performance.

The organization also benefits by enhancing its human capital. That is, workers become more knowledgeable and capable of handling additional duties. As a result, the organization has a flexible workforce at its disposal to use whenever necessary.

The main negative aspect of a skill-based reward system is that it costs more than a job-based scheme. That is, a job incumbent may acquire more skills than necessary to execute that job effectively. If all job incumbents possess more skills than necessary for their respective jobs, and if the organization implements the skill-based scheme, then the organization will spend more money than if it implements a job-based scheme. Consider our previous example of an exercise leader who acquires accounting skills. Imagine the situation in which all exercise leaders at a fitness club acquire accounting skills and the accountants qualify as exercise leaders. If the club were to adopt a skill-based reward scheme, it would pay for all of these skills even though they would be largely redundant.

Given these concerns, many organizations prefer to base their reward schemes on the jobs themselves. This approach is based on the rationale that different jobs require different skills, which are identified by the organization in the various job descriptions. That is, job-based schemes take into account the skills needed for specific jobs; therefore, they are skill-based schemes. However, if an organization desires a flexible workforce, it should adopt the skill-based scheme, generally speaking. This is particularly true of smaller organizations that can afford only a few employees. If, for example, the fitness club in our previous example employs only one or two exercise leaders, then it may find that paying

those leaders for enhancing their accounting skills is more advantageous than hiring an accountant.

Seniority as the Base

It is a common practice for many organizations, particularly government agencies, to base their reward systems on seniority. In this approach, the organization uses the number of years that a person has been in a job as the basis for salary increases or bonuses. As compared with the reward bases discussed earlier, seniority provides an easily measured and objective base, which is why many organizations adopt this approach. Furthermore, the organization can justify using the approach by linking seniority to job skills and mastery. That is, the organization can expect a person performing a job for a number of years to have mastered the skills associated with that job, thus entitling the person to higher pay than a newcomer would receive.

However, seniority-based reward schemes do not necessarily subsume the advantages of job-based and skill-based schemes in all contexts. Indeed, in recent years, the nature of many jobs has been altered by vast and rapid changes in technology. For instance, an older accountant in a university athletics department may not be familiar with or skilled in the use of computers for accounting purposes. In contrast, a younger person may be more likely to have mastered that aspect of the job and to be more proficient at it than the older accountant. Furthermore, seniority may not even bear on certain kinds of jobs. For instance, being effective as an exercise leader depends largely on mastery of current knowledge, energy, and enthusiasm—attributes that have no association with seniority. Thus, seniority-based reward schemes would not help motivate a young exercise leader; in fact, it would have a negative effect on his or her motivation.

Performance as the Base

Another form of reward scheme bases rewards on employee performance. A simple example is that of piece rate, which is adopted in many manufacturing organizations. In this approach, an employee who produces 110 units gets a bigger reward than does a person who produces 100 units. At first sight, this method seems to provide a reliable, valid, and objective measure for a reward scheme. However, this approach may be viable in some circumstances but unrealistic in others. Consider, for example, an athletic trainer. Although the number of injured clients served is critical, the quality of the service

VIEWPOINT

The decision of whether to relate pay to performance is a crucial one in any organization. It can be a serious error to assume automatically that they should be related. A sound linkage can contribute greatly to organizational effectiveness. But a poor job can be harmful. Specifically, if performance is difficult to measure and/or rewards are difficult to distribute on the basis of performance, a pay-for-performance system can motivate counterproductive behaviors, invite lawsuits charging discrimination, and create a climate of mistrust, low credibility, and managerial incompetence. (Lawler 1987, p. 263)

of junior trainers, facilitate the performance of other trainers, and suggest ways to improve the club's overall operation. As noted in chapter 13, all of these behaviors can be included in performance appraisal.

Given the fundamental notion that organizational effectiveness depends on individual performances, the emphasis on individual performance is legitimate and logical. Accordingly, performance-based reward schemes facilitate individual performances and thus organizational effectiveness. However, as noted in chapter 13, performance appraisal raises two key issues. The first concerns what should constitute performance, as discussed in the previous section. The second issue involves how to measure different aspects of performance. If performance appraisal is deficient or contaminated, then performance-based reward schemes suffer as well. Lawler (1987) summarized the difficulties associated with performance-based schemes: "A true merit pay or promotion system is often more easily aspired to than done. . . . It is difficult to specify what kind of performance is desired and often equally difficult to determine whether that performance has been demonstrated" (pp. 260-261).

Rewards can be distributed on the basis of the relative worth of the jobs themselves, of employees' skills and competencies, of seniority, or of performance.

provided must also be considered. Furthermore, the severity and complications of an injury may prohibit an athletic trainer from attending to and serving many more clients.

As noted in chapter 13, performance in a job may comprise several components in addition to the number of units produced. More specifically, the domains of performance include several non-job-specific aspects, such as citizenship behaviors. For example, the athletic trainer in our ongoing example might contribute to the training and development

Mix of Rewards

An organization can use more than one criterion or base to structure its reward system (i.e., its **mix of rewards**). For example, a university campus recreation department might figure annual salary increases as a given percentage of an employee's salary to provide a cost-of-living increase, as a given dollar amount for the same or similar jobs, and in various amounts as merit increases. Percentage increases to cover the rising cost of living tend to yield higher dollar amounts to senior employees, who usually earn more than do junior employees. On the other hand, awarding an equal number of dollars for all employees irrespective of seniority is a job-based reward; that is, everyone receives the same amount for performing the same or similar jobs. This equal dollar amount translates into a larger percentage increase for junior employees. Merit pay is allotted on the basis of performance as judged through regular performance appraisal.

Thus, the hypothetical reward system in this campus recreation example uses a mixture of job-based, skill-based, seniority-based, and performance-based criteria. Sport managers must consider the flexibility that such a perspective offers in instituting a reward system in their organizations. Instead of trying to choose one best base for rewards, they must look at a mix of bases that are meaningful to their employees and feasible in their organizational contexts.

> Sport managers may employ a mix of bases for distributing rewards. One portion may be based on job category, another portion on cost of living, and another portion on merit.

REWARD SYSTEMS AND MEMBER PREFERENCES

Member preferences constitute another relevant element in the structure of reward systems. The foregoing discussion of various forms of rewards and various bases for distributing them implicitly assumes that the reward system influences all employees in the same way and in the same direction. However, this is not always the case. As noted previously, for example, a shorter work week may not be acceptable to working mothers and fathers.

For another example, consider the case of group-based benefits, such as group insurance and dental care. Group insurance plans and medical schemes are less costly for members than are individually organized plans. Therefore, these organizationally arranged group benefits constitute significant indirect rewards. Yet they may not have the desired effect on all employees. For instance, if an employee's spouse has extensive medical coverage for the whole family from his or her employer, then any coverage received by the employee in his or her own job is redundant. Therefore, it loses its motivating potential. In another example, some educational institutions convert part of the total package of rewards into free tuition to employees' children. This benefit would hold no motivating potential (and potentially be demotivating) for employees who have already paid heavily to educate their children in the past.

Cafeteria-Style Benefits

One recent method of alleviating the problem of varied preferences for type of rewards is referred to as a cafeteria-style benefit program. In this type of scheme, an individual is allowed to choose from among a set of differentially priced perks and benefits for a given total amount. For instance, employees of a sport marketing firm may be allowed to choose from among several benefits (e.g., medical coverage, pension contribution, paid leave, and straight cash) for the total of the bonus allotted in a year (e.g., $1,000).

This approach can satisfy various preferences among employees. Older employees, for instance, may opt for more medical coverage, whereas younger employees may prefer straight cash in order to pay for children's expenses. In each case, however, the total cannot exceed the limit of $1,000. According to Lawler (1987), "The theory is that if individuals are allowed to tailor their own reward packages to fit their particular needs, the organization will get the best value for its money, because it will give people only those things that they desire" (p. 265).

> In designing a reward system, managers must consider the preferences of employees. A cafeteria-style benefit package permits employees to choose the mix of benefits that they like without any additional cost to the organization. Managers can extend similar logic to all forms of rewards.

Lump-Sum Payments

The term *lump-sum payment* is used in conjunction with both bonuses and salary raises. Bonuses are lump-sum payments to employees in recognition of their performance during a specified period (e.g., quarterly, semiannual, or annual bonuses). Unlike salary and merit increases, however, a bonus is not added to one's base salary. Thus a bonus requires that a worker must perform above a certain level each year in order to receive the reward. In contrast, because salary and merit increases are added to one's base salary, the increase given in one year will continue to be given each year even though the worker might not perform at the same level in subsequent years.

Thus sport managers may consider bonuses as an option because they can be tied to organizational performance in each year. For example, a commercial fitness club may offer larger bonuses when it makes huge profits and smaller amounts when its profits are lower. With this approach, the club is not committed to a huge salary account in the coming years because bonuses are not added to base salaries. Tying bonuses to organizational profit levels makes clear that bonuses may not be appropriate for nonprofit organizations.

Lump-sum payments may also be made when salary or merit increases are announced. The traditional practice is to include the increase in the base salary and to distribute the increase over the next 12 months. Thus, a ticket office staffer who receives a $2,400 annual increase will see his or her monthly paycheck increase by $200 for the next 12 months. What if, instead, the athletics department offers to pay the $2,400 as a lump-sum payment at the beginning of the year? What effect would this proposal have? Although the lump-sum payment of $2,400 is the same as the $200 over 12 months, psychologically it looks like a much larger amount. Furthermore, lump-sum payments tend to accentuate the salary or merit increases between high and low performers. For example, a $2,400 increase relative to a $1,200 increase sounds more impressive than a $200 monthly increase relative to a $100 monthly increase.

Apart from the psychological boost offered by lump-sum payments, these payments may also be more attractive to workers because the lump sum can be used as an investment. For example, a young member of the event management office might use the amount as a down payment for a car or house or even as a loan payoff. An employee's view of lump-sum payments is a function of personal habits, orientations, and needs. Some employees are careful in financial matters, whereas some are spendthrifts who cannot hold onto the money they get. Some have an immediate need for a lump-sum amount, whereas others (e.g., a mother or father with a newborn baby) may need a steady income over the next 12 months.

Due to these different uses for the money, a sport organization may leave the choice between a lump-sum payment and a monthly increase to its employees. In fact, an employee may find the resulting good feeling and sense of control to be motivational in itself. Furthermore, the organization achieves the objective of tailoring its reward scheme to individual needs and preferences.

VIEWPOINT

Reward carries strong messages. If you want to see what an organization values, look at what it pays for, not what it says. Words are cheap and it is easy to make statements about what is important in an organization. However, if you say one thing but pay for something quite different, you can guess which message will have the greater effect on what people will actually do. (Rose 2014, p. 15)

ROLE OF THE SPORT OR RECREATION MANAGER

As noted by Rose (2014), sport and recreation managers must determine which rewards are most relevant to staff and volunteers. A manager must avoid making assumptions about what staff and volunteers value in rewards. The manager must also ensure that reward expectations are understood, reward policies are communicated, and feedback is solicited to ensure that personnel view the reward types and distribution as valuable, fair, and equitable.

For example, the director of sales and marketing for a professional cricket team may decide that tickets for an upcoming cricket match make a perfect reward for her sales team members who sell 5 percent more than their quota. However, because most members of her sales team have young families who typically lack the flexibility to attend evening matches, the reward type she has selected (though attractive to some) will not be valued by this particular sales team. Therefore, the reward will be relatively meaningless in terms of its effect on employee satisfaction and effort. This example illustrates the importance of communicating continually with subordinates to identify intrinsic and extrinsic rewards that are valued and thus will have the desired effects.

Case Study

Determining an Appropriate Reward System

You are director of sales for a professional American football team that is heading into the new season with dismal prospects of making the playoffs. The ownership and general manager have highlighted through various media outlets that this will be a rebuilding year, thus implicitly telling fans that there may be more losses than wins during the upcoming season. As the person responsible for both client sales and corporate suite sales, you know that winning teams sell more tickets; thus the task of selling tickets to your home games this year is a tall order.

You realize that you may need to be creative in motivating your sales team to get out there and pound the pavement. You know that, according to the model of motivation, employee effort, performance, and satisfaction can be influenced by the use of rewards. You decide that rewarding your staff for increasing their quantity of sales may be the best option for maintaining the team's in-house fan base this season. Given that performance-based salary increases are not in the budget this year (as directed by the executive suite), you first look to your options for intrinsic rewards and nonfinancial extrinsic rewards. You also review the roster of your sales team in an effort to determine which rewards are appropriate for which positions. The following roles fall under your supervision:

- One senior account executive, who oversees all client relations and ensures that they meet the highest standards
- One senior manager of suite sales and services, who is responsible for client relations in connection to corporate suites and services and for ensuring that all corporate clients' needs are met
- Three corporate sales account executives, who are responsible for increasing sales to corporate clients (both general tickets and suite purchases)
- Three client sales coordinators, who are responsible for increasing both general and group ticket sales

You also recognize that as sales director in such a competitive market for sport jobs, you need to demonstrate initiative by giving the team's top executives a plan for managing the sales team during this rebuilding season. You know that your sales team will need an extra push in order to keep people excited about coming to the stadium. Thus, you must put a plan in place.

Case Study Tasks

1. Reflect on the classes of organizational rewards highlighted in figure 14.1. Choose a reward strategy to motivate the individuals in each role listed in the case study.

2. Construct a memo addressed to the executive suite (i.e., owner, president, and general manager) detailing your awareness of the need to focus on sales during this rebuilding season and the strategies you have chosen to motivate employees by means of rewards. When discussing reward distribution for each role, describe why each classification of reward would be useful for each role.

CHAPTER PURSUITS

SUMMARY

An organization's reward system should be aimed at attracting and retaining good employees, motivating them toward higher performance, developing human capital (i.e., skill and competency development), cultivating and maintaining organizational culture, and strengthening the organizational structure. The reward system must abide by the letter and spirit of all legal requirements. Although rewards can be either intrinsic or extrinsic, this chapter focuses on extrinsic rewards, which can be financial (e.g., salary increase) or nonfinancial (e.g., office furnishings, preferred parking space). Nonfinancial rewards can be oriented either toward the employee's career progress (e.g., training paid for by the organization) or toward one's social status (e.g., title, other status symbols). Indirect compensation can take the form of publicly sanctioned protection of employees (e.g., payment of premiums for social security and unemployment insurance) or of health insurance or organizationally sanctioned pension and savings plans. Rewards can also take the form of varying work schedules, such as a shorter work week or flextime.

Rewards can be distributed on the basis of the job itself, the skills one possesses, one's number of years in service (i.e., seniority), or one's performance. Managers need to be creative in mixing the types and bases of rewards to suit member needs and preferences. Sport managers can conceive of several configurations of types of rewards, bases for those rewards, member choices, and timing of rewards within the boundaries set by legal requirements. Involving members in this process brings forth not only their unique needs and preferences but also their ingenuity in developing an effective reward system for the organization. In addition, the opportunity to participate in designing the reward system serves as a reward in itself by giving employees a sense of ownership over the selected scheme and its fairness.

KEY TERMS

bases of rewards 273

mix of rewards 275

purposes of reward systems 265

reward system 265

types of rewards 267

UNDERSTAND

1. Consider your own experience as a volunteer or paid worker in a sport organization. Describe the organization's reward system and the system's specific components. What were your reactions to each of those components?

2. Review the ways in which an employee's work schedule can be varied as part of a reward system. What kind of schedule would you like when you get a job after graduation? Explain why. Would your preference be the same after, say, 15 years? Why, or why not?

INTERACT

1. What mix of rewards would you like if you worked in (a) a university athletics department, (b) a professional sport club, and (c) a commercial tennis club? For each type of organization, weigh the relative importance of your own preferences and the organizational characteristics in your choice of the rewards.

2. If you were the owner or manager of one of the organizations in the previous question, what system of rewards would you institute? Would it be different from the system you would prefer as a worker? Explain.

CHAPTER

15

Internal Marketing

---LEARNING OBJECTIVES---

After reading this chapter, you will be able to

- define and describe the process of internal marketing,
- explain the process- and people-oriented approaches to internal marketing,
- understand the relevance of marketing principles in internal operations,
- relate internal marketing to human resource management, and
- explain how the production and marketing of services come together to form a seamless operation leading to high-quality services.

Chapter 1 identifies and describes the various forms of services that are relevant to sport management. Chapters 2 through 4 address the three types of human resources associated with those services: volunteers, professionals, and clients. Chapters 5 through 8 delve into individual differences in ability, personality, values, and motivation. And chapters 9 through 14 examine the human resource management practices of organizational justice, job design, staffing and career considerations, leadership, performance appraisal, and reward systems.

These discussions focus on all of the workers in an organization, as well as clients. However, an important distinction needs to be made between the production of an organization's services and the marketing of those services. Consider, for example, some of the significant activities of a typical fitness club. It is heavily engaged in recruiting high-quality instructors and specialists, getting the most advanced equipment, and coordinating the activities of members and the use of equipment with a view to offering clients the best possible services. But all of these efforts are made in vain if there are no clients to buy into the services offered. This is

where marketing comes into play. Marketing the club involves conducting promotional and advertising campaigns to highlight the club's products, setting up membership categories, and signing up customers. Thus, sport management as a field is engaged in both **production and marketing** of sport products.

In marketing efforts, the example of a fitness club is of course dealing with people. But those people (i.e., future customers) are outside of the organization, whereas human resource management (HRM) practices are geared toward people in the organization. Nevertheless, both human resource practices and marketing practices are aimed at influencing people; therefore, some approaches are applicable to both endeavors. On the basis of this perspective, some authors have proposed a functional area labeled **internal marketing** as a management strategy for improving productivity and its quality.

In essence, internal marketing involves applying the principles of external marketing to influence the organization's employees. In other words, "internal marketing is the philosophy of treating employees as customers" and involves "attracting, developing, motivating, and retaining qualified employees through job-products that satisfy their needs" (Berry and Parasuraman 1991, p. 151). As you may realize, the idea of attracting, developing, motivating, and retaining is the focus of the human resource management practices discussed in this book. From this perspective, then, internal marketing is not something new, despite its novel label; it is, however, significant in that it allows us to apply marketing principles to the management of human resources (R.J. Varey and Lewis 1999). Such approaches could help improve human resource practices for the benefit of employees, but internal marketing is also touted for what it can do to improve the quality of the services offered to customers, which in turn can enhance the organization's image in the minds of consumers.

Even the basic idea of viewing employees as customers is not new. Recall the theories of motivation (e.g., Herzberg, Mausner, and Snyderman 1959; Maslow 1943; Porter and Lawler 1968; Vroom 1964; discussed in chapter 8), leadership (e.g., Bass 1985; Chelladurai 1993a; Fiedler 1973; House 1971; discussed in chapter 12), job design (e.g., Hackman and Oldham 1980; discussed in chapter 10), performance appraisal (e.g., Cleveland, Murphy, and Williams 1989; Schuler and Jackson 1996; discussed in chapter 13), and reward systems (e.g., Lawler 1987; discussed in chapter 14). All of these approaches imply giving special treatment to employees, facilitating their accomplishment of work, and making their work experiences pleasant and satisfying. Managerial practices based on these theories are

aimed at developing and retaining good employees. Thus there are considerable overlaps between the two streams of thought. However, as R.J. Varey and Lewis (1999) pointed out, although internal marketing is not new, the active market-oriented approach to managing employees is new. In their view, internal marketing may lead to "mindful management."

As Lings and Greenley (2010) noted,

Internal marketing directed at employees within an organization "aligns and motivates employees with a company's market objectives and encourages employees to perform better and to offer superb service, which ultimately improves customer retention and enhances the success of the company." (p. 321)

Figure 15.1 illustrates the distinctive qualities and the commonality of human resource management and marketing.

 Given that the field of sport and recreation management involves both the production and marketing of sport products, internal marketing is a human resource management strategy to improve quality of production by treating employees like customers. Ultimately, employee outcomes are served through job "products" (e.g., training, orientation, rewards), which are structured to meet the needs of employees.

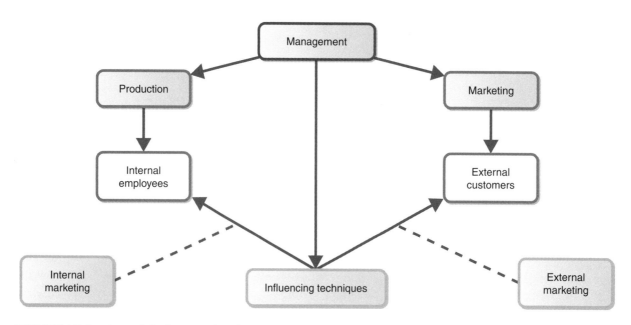

FIGURE 15.1 A model of internal and external marketing.

FORMS OF MARKETING

Before discussing internal marketing specifically, we must understand the forms of marketing that play a role in shaping human resource management practice. Key concerns include the processes of production and marketing and the triangle of marketing, which inform the internal communication strategies of any sport or recreation organization.

Production and Marketing of Products

A useful beginning is to view management as concerned with both the production and the marketing of its products. Because production processes are internal to the organization and marketing processes are oriented toward customers outside of the organization, the units and practices associated with production and marketing have been viewed as distinct and separate operations. From this perspective, the production phase warrants recruitment and hiring of qualified individuals to carry out the production processes. As these individuals enter the organization and become employees, managing them involves motivating them to perform as expected, providing appropriate leadership and supervision, and rewarding them according to either their performance or the employee–organization contract or both. The effectiveness of these practices is reflected in the organization's meeting employee needs and in the employees' satisfaction and commitment to their work and the organization.

The operations in the marketing function are aimed at securing and retaining customers outside of the organization. Emphasis in the past has been placed on the traditional marketing mix, which consists of the "four Ps": product, price, promotion, and place. More recently, marketing scholars have expanded this mix to include seven Ps: the original four, as well as physical evidence, processes, and people. The emphasis on people (i.e., customers) led progressively to the conception of relationship marketing, which is based on the notion that it is cheaper to retain existing customers than to recruit new ones. Thus marketing must be geared toward cultivating a relationship between the customer and the organization and gaining the customer's commitment to the organization and its products. It is only natural to extend this expanded version of the marketing mix to the employees and their activities that produce the product.

Triangle of Marketing

Kotler (1994) conceived of three types of marketing that can be formed into a triangle: external, interactional, and internal (see figure 15.2). External marketing consists of conventional marketing aimed at selling an organization's products to external customers (e.g., selling tickets to hockey games or attracting customers to use golf courses). This function is generally carried out without the participation of those who create the product. For example, those who maintain a golf course do not normally engage in marketing that course.

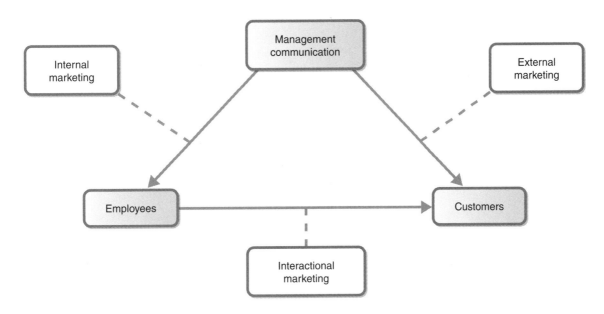

FIGURE 15.2 Kotler's (1994) triadic marketing operations.

MANAGEMENT VERSUS MARKETING

The management, production, and marketing functions of an organization can be compared as follows:

> It is not uncommon for people to distinguish between management and marketing based on the idea that management is concerned with production while marketing is concerned with the exchange of products. This is far from the truth. . . . [T]he concept of management refers to coordination of people, their activities, and limited resources to achieve goals and objectives. A goal of a sport enterprise could be to produce an excellent team and stage exciting sport competitions. Similarly, another goal of the same enterprise would be to sell all the seats in the stadium and secure sponsorships for its programs. The enterprise may set up two units to achieve these objectives. Each unit may consist of several positions hierarchically organized, and these positions would carry out different activities. Further, each unit may be allotted a certain budget. If the units are to achieve their respective objectives, their resources, activities, and people need to be coordinated properly. And that is management. So it is more meaningful to consider management as a process applicable to both production and marketing. (Chelladurai 2005, p. 116)

A related debate addresses the question of whether production or marketing is more important to an organization. Obviously, of course, production and marketing are highly interrelated, and both are critical to an organization. One cannot market something if it is not produced, and there is no point in producing something if it cannot be marketed. Despite this reality, marketing is considered more critical in many types of organizations, and rightly so. Why? We can identify several differences between the two functions that make marketing more critical for an organization.

First, the production function is internal to the organization, whereas marketing is externally oriented. Thus production by an excellent team is carried out within the organization; for example, coaches and facility and event managers are employees of the organization. As for the athletes, they can be employees, students, or members of the organization, depending on whether it is a professional franchise, a scholastic institution, or a sport club. In contrast, marketing is externally oriented in the sense that spectators and sponsors are external to the organization.

This distinction creates a difference in the relative control that the organization can exercise in the production versus the marketing of its products. The people, processes, and resources involved in production are under the organization's control, whereas spectators and sponsors are independent of the organization. Thus, it is easier to manage the production function than it is to manage the marketing function. We can also argue that the technology associated with the production of an excellent team is, relatively speaking, better known and better mastered (e.g., coaching, event management, and facility management) than is the technology associated with marketing (e.g., consumer psychology).

A final distinction derives from the fact that the production function involves the expenditure of resources, whereas the marketing function involves acquisition of resources. In many types of organizations, units that deal with elements in the external environment or secure necessary resources are likely to wield greater power and influence. Therefore, marketing is likely to be accorded greater status than is production in most sport organizations. However, units that produce products that are excellent and sought after by the public, such as the football and basketball programs in Division I universities, are likely to possess clout equal to if not greater than that of marketing.

VIEWPOINT

Barnes, Fox, and Morris (2004) relate internal marketing to relationship marketing as follows:

Whilst Relationship Marketing (RM) recognizes the importance of bringing the external customer into the company, Internal Marketing (IM) emphasizes the equally important need for management to view the company as a market where there exists an internal supply chain of internal suppliers and customers. (p. 595)

More recently, Kanibir and Nart (2012) concluded that

RM represents an approach from a strategic perspective in marketing science, and thus it can be viewed as one of the parts of strategic marketing management with a customer orientation. As competitive behaviors of organizations are in transition owing to changes in demographics and psychographics, and the market environment, exploring the ways of delivering high-level customer value in a sustainable manner is essential for them to remain in

a strong market position over their competitors. (p. 1384)

Their research highlights the need for human resource managers to be acutely aware of how the new technological marketplace influences the internal workplace and how RM can be strategically leveraged to enhance emotional labor and service quality, thereby enhancing customer relations. Specifically, RM can be used to develop strong internal ties between employees and organizations by increasing an individual's emotional attachment to the organization. For example, the presence of social media in the workplace helps individuals develop relationships with co-workers by creating another platform for engagement outside of the office walls. Further, superiors can leverage these relationships as an internal marketing strategy by strategically promoting social media connections and interactions within daily tasks to positively influence employee embeddedness. In this context, employee embeddedness is defined by all of the factors that go into retaining an individual in an organization.

Interactional marketing, in contrast, relates to services (Kotler 1994). As noted earlier, a frontline employee of a service organization is involved in the production of that service. At the same time, the employee also markets the product, both by creating quality in the service and through interpersonal interactions with consumers. The third type of marketing is internal marketing (the substance of this chapter), in which the organization focuses on its own employees (i.e., the internal market).

PROCESS VERSUS PEOPLE ORIENTATION IN INTERNAL MARKETING

Lings (2004) classified approaches to internal marketing into two strands: **process versus people orientation**. The first strand focuses on the processes

involved in delivering a service. In this perspective, every employee is considered an internal customer in the sense that he or she receives some service or support from other employees. The second strand of writings on internal marketing focuses on human resources and their development.

Process-Oriented Internal Marketing

The process-oriented approach to internal marketing stems from the principles of total quality management (TQM). Total quality management focuses on the internal processes that build quality into the final product; it is concerned with continual improvement of product quality (Robbins, Coulter, and Stuart-Kotze 2003). The technique relies heavily on scrutinizing every step in the production process and ensuring that quality is maintained at each step.

For instance, McDonald's ensures quality in its production of French fries and hamburgers by procuring the right raw material, processing that material, distributing the processed food to its franchises, and, finally, setting up a protocol for cooking the processed food. You may be familiar, for example, with the buzzer that goes off in the frying machine to warn the attendant that the fries are properly cooked. The major focus of research on TQM, and in the practice of it, has been placed on the manufacturing sector of tangible products (e.g., French fries and Big Macs in our example). This does not deny the fact that the production of *services* can also be subjected to quality control and enhancement. In fact, in the case of McDonald's, every step in the process just described can be seen as a service to the next step.

In a similar manner, a recreation department in a large university may seek to ensure the quality of its towel services by buying durable and moisture-absorbing towels, procuring appropriate automatic machines to wash and dry the towels, and securing the right types of detergents. The process of getting clean towels to the front desk also involves multiple steps: making sure that soiled towels are not damaged as they are collected and transported to the washing machines, correctly setting the washing and drying machines, using proper doses of detergent for every wash, and transporting the washed towels to clean storage bins. Each step can be subjected to quality analysis.

An extension of this approach to internal marketing would focus on the *people* involved in the foregoing steps—for example, the person who collects the used towels, the person who transports the used towels to the washing machine, the person who oversees the washing and drying machines, the person who collects the washed towels and folds and stores them, and the person who dispenses the towels to customers. Because these persons are sequentially involved in the production of the towel service, each is a supplier of service to the next one in the process, who is deemed a customer at that point. That person then turns into a supplier to the next person in the process, and so on. "The basic premise of this approach to internal marketing is that, by increasing the quality of service transactions with internal customers, organizations can positively influence the quality of service transactions with external customers" (Lings 2004, p. 407). Thus, the principles of marketing can be emphasized at every **employee-to-employee interface**, each of which is in effect a supplier–customer interface.

This view makes eminent sense when we consider that many operations in an organization are sequential and that an employee in this sequence interacts both with the employee in the previous stage and with the employee in the subsequent stage. In the first case, the focal employee is the customer of the previous employee, who supplies whatever the focal employee needs. In the next stage, the focal employee is the supplier of whatever is needed by the next employee (i.e., the customer). Insofar as interactions between employees can be seen as supplier–customer transactions, marketing principles can be applied (Berry 1981).

Recognizing that internal marketing is the process of creating a market wherein the internal customers' wants and needs are met, Lings (2004) identified the following steps to ensure quality of services provided by employees to each other:

1. Creating internal awareness of internal service quality
2. Identifying internal customers and suppliers
3. Identifying the expectations of internal customers
4. Communicating these expectations to suppliers
5. Identifying and implementing behavioral changes to ensure delivery of high-quality service
6. Measuring internal service quality and providing feedback to suppliers

 Sport and recreation managers must engage in external marketing, interactional marketing, and internal marketing to be successful. Specific to this chapter, internal marketing involves process-oriented total quality management which requires (1) continual reflection on internal procedures that improve the quality of products and (2) the development of a service culture.

Human Resource–Oriented Internal Marketing

The second strand of writings on internal marketing centers on human resources. This strand is "grounded in the belief that external marketing

SERVICE CULTURE

In Dunmore's (2002) view, internal marketing is "concerned with the resources and activities occurring within an organization that influence the nature of its culture and competitiveness as a route to achieving its purpose" (p. 23). Noting that service orientation and service attitude are key sources of competitive advantage in providing outstanding customer service, Kelemen and Papsolomou-Doukakis (2004) argued that internal marketing "acts as a culture change programme which aims to transform the individuals along the lines of service quality and customer focus" (p. 122). But what is culture?

Hofstede (1997) defines organizational culture as the collective programming of the human mind to espouse an ideology, a set of beliefs, and shared values. With a view to building a strong culture, organizational members are encouraged by organizational leaders in various ways to share the organizational values, purposes, and processes. In the service industry, there is talk of the **service culture** as "a sense of the intangibles that bring people to share a common vision of the organization and its goals, that ensure the seamlessness of process that equates to service excellence, and that tie the various functions of organizations together in common purpose" (B. Schneider and Bowen 1995, p. 238). Internal marketing can facilitate the cultivation of a culture of marketing orientation and superior customer value.

The strategy of applying internal marketing to effect organizational change is akin to that of social marketing, which is "a social-change management technology involving the design, implementation, and control of programs aimed at increasing the accessibility of a social idea or practice in one or more groups of target adopters" (Kotler and Roberto 1989, p. 24). In our context, internal marketing can be equated with the marketing of a social campaign in which one group (in our case, managers) attempts to persuade others (i.e., employees) to accept the service culture embodied by customer orientation and service quality.

---

success is, in part, contingent on the firm having satisfied and motivated employees and that creating satisfied and motivated employees is the role of internal marketing" (Lings 2004, pp. 407-408). The impetus for this perspective on internal marketing comes from service management and service marketing literature.

One fundamental aspect of service management and service marketing is the realization that the service provider (i.e., contact person) is partly or fully involved in the production of the service and, at the same time, is part of the marketing process. This dual role makes the service provider a critical employee of the enterprise. As Lings (2004) noted, "The attitudes and behaviors of customer-contact employees influence customers' perceptions of the service they receive" (p. 405). As shown in figure 15.3, the service employee (i.e., contact person) serves as a lens through which a customer sees the organization. This lens may provide a clear picture of the organization or distort or refract the image. Given the significance of service providers, we must satisfy their needs just as we do the needs of customers.

 Within internal marketing strategies, a human resource–oriented (people) focus also plays a large role in serving internal stakeholders. Specifically, sport and recreation managers must realize that employees (i.e., service providers) are active members of the production and marketing of services. Thus, employee needs must be served to ensure a quality service is presented to customers. The recognition of diverse needs may also foster a culture that serves diverse clientele.

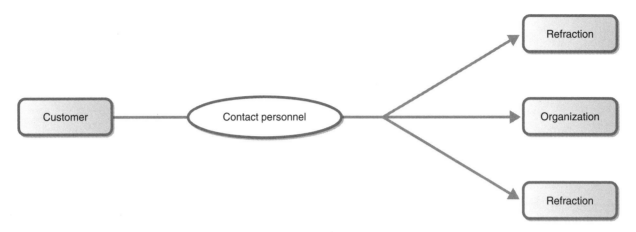

FIGURE 15.3 Organization's image filtered through the lens of contact personnel.
Based on Lings and Brooks 1998.

DIVERSITY MANAGEMENT OF HUMAN RESOURCES

According to Chelladurai's (2014) integrative framework for managing diversity, the realization of benefits from diversity management can exert an effect beyond the organization's walls. Specifically, a service provider who has adopted an awareness, acknowledgment, and acceptance of the value of diversity possesses the capability to positively alter the image of the organization in the eyes of his or her clients. Therefore, if, for example, a fitness instructor for a large fitness chain exemplifies the value of diversity in activating and accommodating diverse clientele, then the club's image in the minds of clientele may also be enhanced.

MARKETING PRINCIPLES IN INTERNAL OPERATIONS

The principles associated with marketing to external customers can be applied to employees, who are in fact "internal customers" (Berry 1981). In this regard, the writings of Parasuraman and associates (e.g., Berry 1981; Parasuraman, Zeithaml, and Berry 1985, 1991; Berry and Parasuraman 1991) emphasize two key factors: (1) dimensions of service quality, known as SERVQUAL dimensions, and (2) gaps in the provision of a service, addressed by **gap theory** (Frost and Kumar 2000).

SERVQUAL Dimensions

Parasuraman and colleagues' (1990) **service quality dimensions** are relevant to the management of internal operations. These dimensions are tangibles, reliability, responsiveness, assurance, and empathy.

The tangibles dimension includes office space, lighting, and other physical attributes of the workplace. Organizations and managers generally try to provide optimal working conditions for their employees; work environments are also subject to government regulations. In terms of services, a more important aspect of tangibles consists of the facilities and equipment offered to customers. For example, when we take our car to an auto repair shop, we may be entertained in a beautifully decorated waiting room equipped with television, magazines, newspapers, and coffee.

Such facilities, amenities, and physical surroundings are referred to as the servicescape (Bitner 1992), and this emphasis on physical surroundings has been extended to sport venues, which have been labeled as the sportscape (Wakefield, Blodgett, and Sloan 1996). The servicescape includes the facilities (e.g., golf course clubhouses),

TECHNOLOGY IN HUMAN RESOURCE MANAGEMENT

There are many creative ways to connect internally with employees. One example of internally communicating with personnel is seen through IBM's Beehive platform. Beehive is a social networking website that has been adopted by IBM and operates behind the company's internal web-based firewall. As with other social networking sites, Beehive supports the "friending" of other people, provides an individual profile page for each user, and incorporates content sharing in the form of photo and list sharing (Geyer et al. 2008). IBM built Beehive to enable sharing between colleagues and has not limited the types of content that can be shared by employees. For example, Beehive allows employees to share content with one another that is either personal or professional in nature.

Given this openness of sharing, DiMicco et al. (2008) conducted a study to find out why people at IBM used the Beehive site. The researchers found that Beehive users identified two work-related motivational factors for using the site: career advancement and the ability to convince colleagues to support ideas and projects. Specifically, "employees use[d] Beehive to present themselves professionally and to network with those they believe[d] . . . [could] assist them in their career goals within IBM. And those looking to promote a project or idea use[d] the site's features to advertise and gather support from other users for their plans" (DiMicco et al., 2008, p. 715). From the perspective of strategic human resource management, managers can use the Beehive platform to foster goal achievement. Specifically, the management of interaction on Beehive helps employees maintain and develop connections within the company and network and advance career goals, which increases employees' social capital and ability to achieve task-related goals.

the surrounding scenery, the quality of playing surfaces (e.g., tennis courts), and the equipment (e.g., treadmills in a fitness club). The most relevant aspect of the servicescape for internal marketing is identified in Bitner's suggestion that it affects employee attitudes and behaviors. That is, employees are more motivated and excited about using an organization's facilities and equipment if those resources are in good shape and allow easy access and ease of maintenance.

The second dimension, reliability, involves the performance of the promised service. For example, if a fitness club advertises that its facilities (including showers and washrooms) are clean, then clients expect them to be, in fact, clean and sanitary. Similarly, employees themselves expect such cleanliness and sanitary conditions in their workplace. In another example, if an organization keeps its promise to pay employees at agreed-upon rates on a weekly, biweekly, or monthly basis, then it maintains its reliability in relation to that service. Similarly, if in the process of recruiting, a sport organization promises to train employees, then it is expected to fulfill that promise.

The third dimension, responsiveness, relates to meeting the needs and preferences of clients. In youth sport, the organizers usually provide two different experiences in the form of competitive leagues and recreational leagues. This is based on the belief that the participants have differential needs and preferences. In addition, the leaders in the two leagues help clients achieve their respective goals with prompt service in terms of teaching and guidance. The same thinking is applied in internal marketing to address the needs and preferences of employees. For example, when volunteers offer to help with youth sports, the organizers should verify their preferences regarding competitive versus recreational leagues and assign them accordingly. As another example, when a worker does not know how to carry out a certain task efficiently, it is the responsibility of the manager to show the worker how the task is performed and to teach the necessary skills.

The fourth dimension, assurance, consists of the courtesy and respect extended to customers in the provision of knowledgeable service. For instance, a client entering a fitness club (or tennis club or clubhouse) expects that he or she will be welcomed with courtesy and respect by the receptionist and reservation clerks. Similarly, if a client signs up for instructional classes, he or she is expected to be knowledgeable about the activity and to be pleasant and patient. Such an approach creates trust and confidence in the organization. In the context of internal marketing, the same approach of courteous and respectful service is expected at every stage of the service supply chain.

Finally, empathy involves giving clients attention that is caring and individualized. Clearly, every client is unique in terms of abilities, skills, and personality. Hence, for example, leaders in youth sport try to spend as much time as possible in attending to individual clients and tailoring instruction and guidance to suit their needs. Similarly, employees in an organization may also be given extended individualized attention by other employees, including supervisors. For example, it is not uncommon for co-workers to make an extra effort to cheer up an employee who has suffered a loss (e.g., divorce, death in the family). In addition, co-workers and supervisors often take the time to help an employee learn new skills or master the operation of new equipment. These gestures (planned or otherwise) contribute to the empathy experienced by the employee.

Gap Theory

In the view of Parasuraman and associates (1985), a service organization may fail to satisfy its customers because of five gaps between what is expected and what is delivered.

1. The first gap lies between what management perceives to be the customer expectations and what the customer actually expects. For instance, a customer in a fitness club may like to be left alone with an exercise bicycle, but the organization may perceive the customer to expect constant supervision and guidance from a fitness expert.

2. The second gap lies between management's perception of customer expectations and management's specifications for satisfying those expectations. In the example just cited, for example, management might assign an unqualified employee to guide the customer.

3. The third gap lies between what was specified by management and what was delivered. This scenario involves a failure to follow specifications on the part of the employee. For instance, a sales clerk might forget to give the credit card back to the customer after a transaction, or a receptionist at a tennis club might forget management's instruction to tell clients that certain courts will be closed for repairs during the next week.

4. The fourth gap lies between what was communicated to the customer and what was delivered. For example, a promise to provide a customer with expert golf instruction might not have been kept.

5. The fifth gap lies between what the customer expected and what the customer perceived the service to be. This final gap is of utmost importance, because the customer's satisfaction and decision about continuing the service are based on how wide this gap is.

Gap Model in Internal Marketing

The extension of the gap model to internal marketing is illustrated in figure 15.4, which shows the frontline employee (i.e., the service employee in contact with the customer) as the internal customer and the support staff (i.e., other employees, supervisors, and managers facilitating the core service) as the suppliers of required services to the frontline employee. Frontline staff hold certain expectations for the kinds of services they should get from the support staff. They also have perceptions of what services they receive and the quality of those services. A gap between the frontline employee's expectations and his or her perceptions (gap 1 in the figure) can result in dissatisfaction and frustration on the part of the employee. Such frustration is likely to translate into poor service to the external customer.

Consider a case in which a fan comes to the stadium with a ticket defaced by rain. The ticket taker does not know how to handle the situation and does not have the authority to decide. Therefore, he or she seeks a supervisor's help. If such help is not forthcoming, the result will

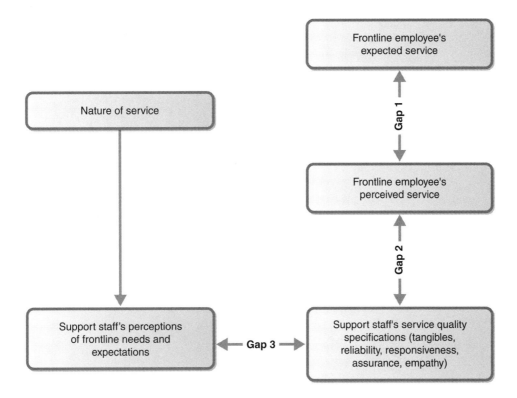

FIGURE 15.4 Gaps in internal service quality sequence.
Based on Frost and Kumar 2000.

be a frustrated employee, a dissatisfied fan, and a host of disgruntled customers waiting in line.

Figure 15.4 also shows a gap (gap 2) between management's specifications for the service from support staff to the frontline employee and the actual service rendered. In the example just mentioned, management might have given specific orders to gate operations supervisors that they should be available to ticket takers at all times throughout the event. If a supervisor does not follow this specification, the result produces gap 2 and poor service for that customer and other customers in the line.

The final gap (gap 3) shown in figure 15.4 lies between management's perceptions of the needs of frontline employees and the specifications designed to meet those needs. In our example, even if management recognizes that frontline employees may face unusual incidents and therefore need immediate access to supervisors to resolve issues, manage-

ment may yet fail to facilitate easy and quick access. One means for creating such access is to provide each frontline employee and supervisor with a walkie-talkie.

 The Gap Model in external marketing can readily be applied to the internal marketing context. Specifically, gaps can exist (1) between expectations and receivables of service employees, where the gap results in dissatisfied employees that ultimately provide lower quality services. Additional gaps exist when there is a disconnect (2) between specifications for a service and the service actually delivered and (3) perceptions of the needs of service employees and the processes designed to meet those needs.

LINE OF VISIBILITY

Even though a customer of a service organization gets to know the frontline service provider, the customer may not be aware of all interactions involving other employees who facilitate (directly or indirectly) the provision of high-quality service. In the earlier example of towel service, for instance, the client is familiar with the person in the cage who hands out the towel but may not know the steps involved in the towel service or the persons in charge of those steps. Lings and Brooks (1998) refer to this familiarity (or lack thereof) as the line of visibility, which is shown in the following figure.

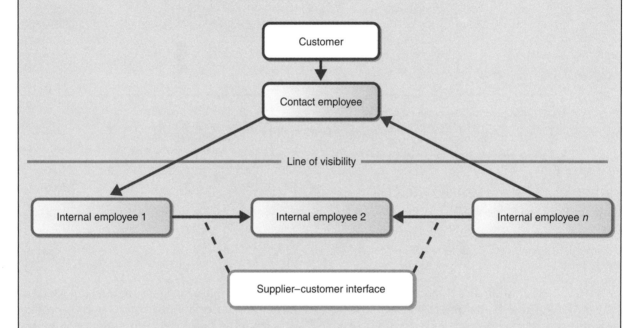

Based on Lings and Brooks 1998.

Lings and Brooks (1998) suggest that supplier–customer interfaces below a given customer's line of visibility can be identified through service blueprinting—that is, representing service processes in flowcharts that depict interrelated activities. In other words, the organizational activities that are visible to the external consumer belong to the domain of external marketing. In contrast, internal marketing focuses on activities that are *not* visible to the external consumer but are essential for delivering high-quality service.

FUNCTIONS OF INTERNAL MARKETING

A manager can use internal marketing as a strategic management practice to fulfill several functions. The following sections outline internal marketing as a tool for change, internal marketing within larger HRM practice, and the distinction between a marketing department and marketing functions in sport and recreation organizations.

Internal Marketing as a Tool for Change

Several authors have suggested that internal marketing can be used as a tool for managing change in an organization (e.g., Ahmed and Rafiq 2002; R. Varey 1995; R.J. Varey and Lewis 1999). To Varey and Lewis, internal marketing is a "goal-oriented social process, and a conceptual system for continually creating strategic organizational change in response to [both] the macro-environment (society) and the micro-environment (the community which constituted the organization)" (pp. 937-938). Similarly, Ahmed and Rafiq define internal marketing as "a planned effort using a market-like approach directed at motivating employees, for implementing and integrating organizational strategies towards customer orientation" (p. 10).

Both of these definitions suggest that employees as customers can be influenced to accept changes in organizational strategies, policies, and structure and to help implement them for the success of the organization. In this view, internal marketing also serves to overcome resistance to organizational change and to coordinate and integrate employees and their activities. This latter function of employee coordination implies considerable interactions between employees in their work processes. To the extent that employees are involved in interdependent work processes, they provide inputs to facilitate each other's work. The interfaces at which such inputs are given and received are analogous to an interface between a service provider and a customer. Accordingly, employees may be encouraged to treat fellow employees as customers of their services.

Such marketing efforts include articulating the vision and mission of the organization and convincing members that they are worthy of such a lofty mission (Rafiq and Ahmed 2000), disseminating all pertinent information, and developing competencies (Arndt 1979). These processes, in fact, reflect the essential arguments of transformational leadership (e.g., Bass 1985; Conger and Kanungo 1987; Yukl 1981), which is aimed at altering the values and goals of members, evoking their higher-order needs, and enhancing their self-esteem. Thus a transformational leader could espouse the value of service or customer orientation. Such efforts can lead to higher aspirations and greater effort on the part of members, thus resulting in performance beyond expectations.

Internal Marketing and Human Resource Management

As you may have realized, some of the steps and principles advocated in internal marketing parallel the human resource management practices advocated in previous chapters of this book. Even so, because the term *marketing* is associated with a unit other than the human resources unit, one might think that internal marketing is a separate set of functions or processes. This is not the case. Advocates of internal marketing readily acknowledge the close links between human resource management and internal marketing (e.g., Dunmore 2002; Joseph

1996; Lings and Greenley 2005). To repeat, Berry and Parasuraman (1991) note that "internal marketing is attracting, developing, motivating, and retaining qualified employees through job-products that satisfy their needs. Internal marketing is the philosophy of treating employees as customers and . . . the strategy of shaping job-products to fit human needs" (p. 151).

The focus here is on employees as customers, and the purpose of internal marketing is to enhance employees' motivation and increase their satisfaction. If we replaced the words "internal marketing" in Berry and Parasuraman's (1991) definition with "human resource management," we would be defining the specialized function of human resource management. Similarly, Lings and Greenley (2005) note that internal marketing is a set of *employee-friendly* managerial behaviors, which is, in essence, the goal of human resource management.

In discussing the relationship between the organization and the employee, Lings and Greenley (2005) brought in the concept of equity of exchange, whereby employees make judgments about their inputs into organizational efforts and what they get from the organization (the essence, respectively, of chapter 9 on organizational justice and of chapters 13 and 14 on performance appraisal and reward systems). In this regard, Joseph (1996) asserted that "internal marketing is the application of marketing, human resource management, and allied theories, techniques, and principles to motivate, mobilize, co-opt, and manage employees at all levels of the organization to continuously improve the way they serve external customers and each other" (p. 55).

Dunmore (2002) noted that internal marketing is grounded in many management disciplines, such as marketing (particularly service marketing theory), customer service, human resource management, corporate strategy, operations management, and quality management. "Therefore internal marketing is not a 'wholly-owned subsidiary' of marketing theory and practice or the exclusive domain of marketers" (p. 7). Rather, internal marketing is aimed at integrating functional strategies across an organization and therefore belongs to everyone in the organization.

Bansal, Mendelson, and Sharma (2001) proposed that the link between internal marketing and external marketing resides in the internal customer's (i.e., the employee's) behaviors, particularly extra-role behaviors directed at external customers. These extra-role behaviors are a function of the internal customer's (employee's) loyalty, job satisfaction, and trust in management. These employee attitudes, in turn, are cultivated by human resource management practices composed of employment security, extensive training, generous rewards, sharing of information, employee empowerment, and reduced status distinction.

The close relationship between internal marketing and human resource management is further illustrated by the five sets of managerial behaviors associated with internal market orientation as identified by Lings and Greenley (2005, 2010). These sets are as follows:

1. *Formal information generation—written:* Managers can use surveys and questionnaires to elicit employees' beliefs about the exchanges between the organization and themselves, as well as their attitudes and values.

2. *Formal information generation—face-to-face:* Managers can use in-person interviews to obtain in-depth information about employees' beliefs and attitudes.

3. *Informal information generation:* Managers can gain great insight into employees' feelings and attitudes through their daily interactions with employees.

4. *Information dissemination and internal communication:* Internal communication is the key to bridging employee attitudes and behaviors with organizational goals. It is a means of communicating organizational goals, strategies, and expectations of employees. Such communication can be either formal (e.g., official announcements, reports) or informal (through everyday interactions with employees).

5. *Responsiveness to the internal market:* Organizations and their managers need to respond to the information gathered. Such responses could include creating jobs to meet the needs of employees; moreover, by "augmenting internal product offerings (jobs) with such things as flexible working hours,

- -

Internal marketing is a fundamental process that goes beyond basic marketing theory and is grounded in customer service, human resource management, corporate strategy, operations management, and quality management. The key to successful internal marketing is integrating numerous functional strategies across the entire organization.

- -

salaries, and other benefits, managers can facilitate internal exchange" (Lings and Greenley 2005, p. 293). Such augmentation could also include elements such as status symbols and desirable job titles.

Marketing Department Versus Marketing Functions

The discussion so far has highlighted the similarities between internal marketing and human resource management. It has also highlighted the fact that in service operations, the frontline service provider is a critical employee who acts both as the producer of a service and as the marketer of that service. In addition, the discussion has implied that every worker in the service chain is a producer and a marketer of support services. All of this points to the fact that the functions of marketing (i.e., influencing people to accept a product, a value, an ideology, a policy, a change) are not confined to the specialized unit known as the marketing department but rather are diffused across multiple units. Of course, there is no doubt that the marketing department is best suited to researching the market, identifying appropriate marketing strategies, planning marketing efforts, and communicating them to the relevant market segments. However, these efforts are facilitated by other units in the organization, their employees, and their activities.

As noted earlier, service providers are involved in interactional marketing (see figure 15.2), and their attitudes and behaviors toward clients influence the public's image of the organization (see figure 15.3). Consider the case in which the marketing unit of a university athletics department is mounting a carefully planned media event for the basketball team. Invitations have gone out to media personnel around the city, meticulous hospitality arrangements have been made, the cooperation of the coaches has been secured, and everything is set to go. Still, the success of the event depends largely on the interactions between the basketball players and the media. At this point, the players are involved in marketing the basketball program.

Similarly, the NFL's efforts to promote itself and the game of football include community programs across the United States. More specifically, the NFL has partnered with the United Way to establish the Hometown Huddle program, in which each team and its personnel participate in a community

A CONTINGENCY VIEW OF INTERNAL MARKETING

As mentioned earlier, considerable overlaps exist between the processes advocated by the literatures on internal marketing and human resource management. In fact, the only significant difference between the two literatures consists of advocacy for treating employees as customers. Although such a perspective is attractive, however, it is not applicable or practical in certain circumstances.

In chapter 1, we made a distinction between consumer service operations and professional service operations. To recap, as compared with professional services, consumer services are characterized by the following features: less information needed to provide the service, tasks that are more routine, shorter duration of interface between supplier and customer, and a simpler and more standard product. In line with these characteristics, the blueprinting of consumer service operations is highly structured, with precise specifications for each step of the service delivery. Consumer service operations also entail a more rigid hierarchy, standard procedures, and strict control.

Thus the need for and the feasibility of internal marketing are considerably less in consumer service operations than in professional service operations. Furthermore, insofar as the task itself is routine and there is no flexibility in operations or decisions about operations, the needs of individual employees do not come into play. Therefore, satisfying their needs (the essence of treating employees as customers) is not a critical condition of quality for that specific service.

In one of the classical studies (Whyte 1949) of restaurant services, the researchers found considerable friction between the waitresses and the cooks in a certain restaurant. The waitresses would take orders from patrons and then vocally transmit the information to the cooks. The male cooks did not relish the women's "ordering" them to do their work. From the researchers' perspective, this male–female role distinction was the crux of the problem. Their solution was for the waitress to write down the order and clip a copy of the order to a revolving board. The cooks would then prepare the written orders as they were received. That is, the interpersonal interaction between the waitress and the cook was eliminated. The ambience in the restaurant was also improved by the elimination of the shouting to transmit orders.

The foregoing limitation of internal marketing is restricted to the employee-to-type of employee supplier–customer relationships. The literature on internal marketing fails to distinguish between the two levels of interfaces—that is, between the management-to-employee and the employee-to-employee levels. With that distinction in mind, internal marketing is relevant even in consumer services operations in the **management-to-employee interface**. That is, it is still meaningful for management to treat the employees in consumer service operations as customers in order to cultivate their service orientation and commitment to the organization.

project. It is a brilliant plan, but its success rests in the players' hands. The success of the initiative depends on their genuine love of their communities, their belief in the selected projects, and their wholehearted involvement in those projects.

The foregoing analysis shows that the boundaries between marketing and production units tend to fade away in service operations and that the functions they perform tend to dovetail into each other. This is what B. Schneider and Bowen

(1995) refer to as **seamless service**: "The goal in designing seamless service is to end up with what has been labeled a 'service logic' that drives the activity of all organizational functions. The term 'logic' stands for the implicit and explicit principles that drive organizational performance" (p. 200). As service logic brings all units into an external focus on customer expectations and needs, it tends to break down the barriers between units and to create a seamless flow of service operations. Efforts to create a seamless enterprise can be aided by internal marketing.

ISSUES IN INTERNAL MARKETING

Managers must recognize the advantages of internal marketing and promote and practice it. At the same time, they should be aware of the problems and pitfalls associated with internal marketing (Lings and Brooks 1998). For instance, involvement in satisfying internal customers may lead to neglect of external customers. Furthermore, internal marketing tends to focus on interactions between employees as suppliers and customers but not on questions about the processes that make those inter-

actions necessary. For example, if a service involves four steps carried out by four different employees, then internal marketing would be justifiably concerned with the interactions in the interfaces between employees. It would not, however, raise the question of whether those four operations could be streamlined into just three or even two operations. Such streamlining might, in fact, be more critical in ensuring quality service than the interactions between the four employees.

The exclusive focus on treating employees as customers may also increase what Lings and Brooks (1998) referred to as sequential pass-off activities, in which the supplier-employees are more concerned with pleasing the customer-employee on interpersonal levels than with the quality of the product being passed on. Such pass-off activities are likely to narrow the vision, create fiefdoms, and foster dominance–subservience relationships between employees.

ROLE OF THE SPORT OR RECREATION MANAGER

To reiterate once more, Berry and Parasuraman (1991) highlighted that "internal marketing is attracting, developing, motivating, and retaining qualified employees through job-products that satisfy their needs" (p. 151). It is the role of the sport or recreation manager to practice internal marketing when recruiting both paid staff and volunteers. Specifically, a manager could ask, How do we attract volunteers to our organization or event? The simple answer is to provide and promote job products and event products that satisfy volunteers' needs.

For example, Kim, Zhang, and Connaughton (2010) found that women were motivated to volunteer because of factors related to their values (humanitarianism or concern for the beneficiary of volunteering) and their desire for increased understanding (gaining knowledge and new skills). Thus, when marketing a volunteer position to women in their sample, Kim et al. suggested that it might be helpful to promote the humanitarian values and learning skills that can be fostered and developed in the volunteer experience. As these findings indicate, a manager must understand the needs of the population of volunteers that he or she is pursuing and create a marketing plan that highlights fulfillment of those needs through the volunteer experience.

Case Study

Creating an Internal Marketing Plan

The chief executive officer of Tennis Australia (TA) has noticed that commitment to facility development has dropped significantly over the last 10 years. The CEO has met with the TA board of directors on several occasions to craft a vision document highlighting TA's commitment to facility development and management over the next 5 to 10 years (Tennis Australia 2015). The mandate of the framework emphasizes the need to align with state and territorial associations across Australia in order to mobilize the plan's action steps. This is a tall task, but one that can greatly benefit the sport of tennis by producing more active players, greater champions, more devoted fans, and healthier communities. In sum, better facilities will enhance the sport environment for current and prospective participants and fans.

Imagine that you are the CEO in this scenario. As mandated by the TA board, you must activate the vision plan by creating action steps for moving forward. You realize that you must market and manage this plan externally to gain buy-in from member associations, individual members, and external stakeholders (e.g., consumers). You also see that the foundation for this buy-in needs to be built within the organization. You go back to your notes on internal marketing and realize that you must look to your executive team first and market this idea effectively to staff.

Here are the members of the executive team (Tennis Australia 2015):

Chief Executive Officer

Most senior corporate administrator; in charge of managing Tennis Australia

Chief Operating Officer

Second in command; responsible for overseeing ongoing business operations (e.g., championship management)

General Manager of Performance

Responsible for managing all athletic performance elements of Tennis Australia (e.g., athlete development)

Commercial Director

Responsible for helping Tennis Australia maintain consistent growth while avoiding obstacles in the sport marketplace

Director of Media and Communications

Holder of direct authority over media relations and community outreach (e.g., public relations)

Director of Events and Facilities

Holder of direct authority over event and facility management; direct report of Chief Operating Officer

Director of Participation

Holder of direct authority over athlete participation in Tennis Australia; direct report of General Manager of Performance

In order to increase service orientation among the executive team and engage Tennis Australia's consumer and membership base, you decide to create an internal marketing plan to promote the organization's Tennis 2020 vision (Tennis Australia 2015).

Case Study Tasks

1. Review the Tennis 2020 vision document found on the Tennis Australia website at www.tennis.com.au/about-tennis-australia/national-strategy.

2. Review Lings and Greenley's (2005) five sets of managerial behaviors associated with the internal marketing orientation, then discuss how you would use internal marketing to connect your executive team to the vision document.

3. Provide details about how you would connect each of the seven executive positions to the vision document.

CHAPTER PURSUITS

SUMMARY

In describing the process of internal marketing, this chapter emphasizes the practice of "treating employees as customers." It also emphasizes the service chain in which each employee acts both as a supplier of service to the next person in the chain and as a customer of the previous person in the chain. These concepts lead to the suggestion that marketing principles can be applied to the interfaces between employees and between the organization and its employees. These two sets of interfaces can be addressed through the five dimensions of service quality. The chapter also covers the ways in which gaps can occur between expectations for service, perceptions of service delivered, and specifications of quality for such service. Service logic can be applied to create a seamless operation (i.e., between various units of the organization) in producing quality service.

KEY TERMS

employee-to-employee interface 286

gap theory 288

internal marketing 281

management-to-employee interface 295

process versus people orientation 285

production and marketing 281

seamless service 296

service culture... 287

service quality dimensions.............................. 288

UNDERSTAND

1. Define internal marketing and explain its relationship to human resource management.
2. Discuss the relevance of internal marketing to the various forms of services produced by sport organizations.

INTERACT

1. Consider the proposition of employee as customer in regard to your own work experiences.
   - In what ways were you treated as a customer? Give specific examples.
   - In what respects were your needs as an employee ignored? Give specific examples.
2. In your own work experiences, how did the treatment of you as a customer affect your job performance?

PART IV

ATTITUDINAL OUTCOMES

Part I of this book describes the human resources available to a sport manager—specifically, volunteers, professional workers, and clients. Part II addresses individual differences between these sets of human resources—that is, individual differences in ability, personality, values, and motivation. Part III outlines some of the critical processes in managing human resources, including organizational justice, job design, staffing and career considerations, leadership, performance appraisal, and reward systems. These managerial processes are undertaken in order to achieve certain critical outcomes. The focus in this text is on human resource–related outcomes rather than on productivity outcomes. Two of these human resource–related outcomes are job satisfaction and commitment, which serve as the focus of part IV of the book.

The outcomes in any organizational context are of two kinds: productivity and member reactions. Productivity involves the extent to which the organization achieves its purpose. For profit-oriented organizations, such productivity often (and more easily than some other outcomes) can be measured by the profit made—specifically, the absolute dollar amount of profit. Alternatively, an organization may be concerned with its rate of return on capital; the issue here is profit as a percentage of capital outlay. When an enterprise makes $100,000 more than a competitor, it might be satisfied with that outcome. However, the $100,000 profit may represent only a 10 percent return

on its capital outlay, whereas the competitor may get a 15 percent return. Similarly, a fitness firm might aim either to make a profit of $10,000 or to get a 15 percent return on its capital outlay. Likewise, a professional sport franchise might focus either on absolute dollar profit or on a rate of return.

A closely related outcome is productivity, or efficiency, which involves maximizing output relative to a given input. Although all organizations are concerned with efficiency, it becomes a singular concern in times of crises. For example, dwindling financial resources have increasingly forced educational institutions to consider efficiency in their operations. To counter the reduction in financial resources, organizations may seek to increase efficiency through downsizing or rightsizing. More specifically, many university athletics departments are currently involved in efficiency drives to make up for the extra demands placed on their resources by Title IX requirements and gender equity movements. Similar concerns with efficiency can cause a fitness club or city recreation department to drop programs that are not in strong demand. They may also reduce their staff, either by firing or through attrition.

Some organizations may also emphasize their share of the market. For instance, General Motors (GM) has been and is the dominant enterprise in the U.S. automobile industry, holding the largest share of that market. Although stiff competition from Ford, Chrysler, and foreign corporations has eroded some of

GM's market share, the corporation cherishes its continuing status as one of the major players in the market. Even universities tend to set as one objective the recruitment of a percentage of the total student population in their respective regions. Similarly, businesses that provide fitness and sport services compete for market share in their geographical areas. And one concern for any professional sport franchises in a large metropolitan area (e.g., New York, Chicago) is to compete with other entertainment agencies for the share of the dollars that local citizens are willing to spend on entertainment.

Another indicator of productivity is the growth of an organization—that is, growth in terms of profit, total revenue, market share, number of employees, number of active members, or number of products or activities offered. The growth concept is equally relevant to nonprofit organizations. For instance, a department of sport management may seek to increase its number of faculty members and the number of courses that it offers. Because size is often equated with status, it is not uncommon for nonprofit organizations to emphasize growth of membership as their primary objective. In sport, many athletics departments tout the number of men's and women's sports they support. Similarly, a city recreation department may emphasize the number of playgrounds and arenas it operates or the number of participants in its programs.

Organizations may also endeavor to become market leaders in terms of the products they produce or their methods of production. For example, nonprofit sport clubs do not make millions in profit; however, they do constantly strive to provide the best programming for participants and are challenged by participants, parents, and other external stakeholders to produce services that are accessible to all. In addition, sporting goods manufacturers compete with each other to introduce new and improved products, such as footwear and protective equipment. Similarly, universities (and departments of sport management) take pride in offering new and more relevant courses or programs.

Because this text focuses primarily on the management of human resources, part IV focuses on human resource–related outcomes.

It is granted that if an organization does not achieve productivity outcomes, then the concern with human resource outcomes may become moot because the organization itself may cease to exist. However, productivity outcomes themselves may depend on human resource–related outcomes. Therefore, it is important to address outcomes as they relate to human resources.

Accordingly, chapter 16 examines the concept of satisfaction. The traditional practice in organizational and industrial psychology has been to focus on the job satisfaction of the organization's paid employees. This text, however, focuses on satisfaction in three groups: paid workers, volunteer workers, and clients. As noted earlier, these three sets of human resources are critical to the success of most sport organizations. Volunteers, by definition, are not concerned with pay or other organizationally sanctioned monetary benefits; therefore, the chapter outlines the meaning and significance of other aspects of their work.

Equally important is the notion of client satisfaction. Modern thrusts in management, such as total quality management, emphasize customer-focused operations that are especially relevant to the context of service. Quality assurance practices, such as keeping the premises and equipment clean, providing quick responses to clients' requests, and establishing a congenial atmosphere, are all aimed at satisfying customers. In the case of sport and recreation, customer-focused operations are even more important because the clients not only consume the services but also help produce them. Thus, this chapter delves into the satisfaction of participants in leisure and athletic services.

Chapter 17 addresses organizational commitment. Strong commitment to the organization on the part of members, such as paid and volunteer workers, as well as clients, provides a clear indication of an organization's effectiveness. Such commitment reflects members' attachment not only to the organization but also to the organization's goals and processes. In other words, organizational commitment may be seen as an endorsement of the management practices described in part III of this book.

Satisfaction

LEARNING OBJECTIVES

After reading this chapter, you will be able to

- define the concept of job satisfaction,
- explain how dissatisfaction stems from a discrepancy between what is expected and what is received,
- describe job satisfaction as a function of need satisfaction,
- describe various facets of satisfaction and their relationships to needs, and
- explain the critical aspects of participant satisfaction in sport and physical activity.

This chapter begins by describing various theories of job satisfaction and their relevance to sport management, then addresses the satisfaction of volunteers as a distinct class of workers. The chapter also discusses client satisfaction. Relating job satisfaction to sport and recreation clients is somewhat unorthodox, because descriptions and discussions of customer or client satisfaction typically relate to a product that a customer or client has purchased or consumed. However, as noted earlier, sport and recreation clients also are involved in the production of services. Therefore, it is only appropriate to consider their satisfaction with the organizational and interpersonal processes used in the production of a service, as well as the quality of the service. With the client in perspective, we then introduce the topics of participant satisfaction, satisfaction with services, leisure satisfaction, and athlete satisfaction. The chapter concludes by considering the **measurement** of satisfaction and describing two of the more popular instruments for measuring job satisfaction.

Researchers have made various attempts to define and describe job satisfaction. As pointed out by Dawis and Lofquist (1984), these definitions agree that **job satisfaction** is in essence "a pleasurable affective condition resulting from one's appraisal of the way in which the experienced job situation meets one's needs, values, and expectations" (p. 72). In a similar vein, Rice, McFarlin, and Bennett (1989) posited that

satisfaction is determined, in part, by the discrepancies resulting from a psychological comparison process involving the appraisal of current job experiences against some personal standards of comparison (e.g., what workers want, feel entitled to, see others getting, have experienced in the past, etc.). (p. 591)

Balzer, Kihm, and colleagues (1997) defined job satisfaction slightly differently as "the feelings a worker has about his or her job or job experiences in relation to previous experiences, current expectations, or available alternatives" (p. 6).

Put simply, job satisfaction consists of attitudes that people have about their jobs. Attitudes, in turn, are "relatively stable affective, or evaluative, dispositions toward a specific person, situation, or other entity" (Saal and Knight 1988, p. 296). An attitude comprises a cognitive component (i.e., a belief about the target entity), an emotional component (i.e., a degree of like or dislike for the target entity), and a behavioral component (i.e., the tendency to act in specific ways toward the target entity).

Job satisfaction is perhaps the most-studied topic in management and industrial psychology. At the same time, these research efforts have been frustrating and futile because they have not yielded a strong relationship between job satisfaction and any other organizationally relevant factor. More precisely, any evidence found of a relationship with other organizationally relevant outcome variables (e.g., performance, absenteeism, turnover) has been weak (Saal and Knight 1995; Schermerhorn, Hunt, and Osborn 1997). This confusing state of affairs may lead some managers to be indifferent to the notion of job satisfaction and more concerned with the "bottom-line" issue of productivity.

One theoretical as well as practical difficulty with the concept of job satisfaction is that it is highly individual in the sense that people react in different ways to the same job situation. Regarding this issue, Ivancevich and Matteson (2002) stated the following:

> Job satisfaction depends on the level of intrinsic and extrinsic outcomes and how the jobholder views those outcomes. These outcomes have different values for different people. For some people, responsible and challenging work may have neutral or even negative value depending upon their education and prior experience with work providing intrinsic outcomes. For other people, such work outcomes may have high positive values. People differ in the importance they attach to job outcomes. Those differences alone would account for different levels of job satisfaction for essentially the same job tasks. (p. 234)

Amid these various viewpoints, the position taken in this book is that of Balzer, Smith, and colleagues (1990), who argued that job satisfaction holds great significance at three levels: humanitarian, economic, and theoretical. At the humanitarian level, most managers are concerned with the welfare of their workers: "Furthermore, since job satisfaction

VIEWPOINT

Given the demanding schedules of sport and recreation managers—for example, working many evenings and weekends—job satisfaction at the humanitarian level can be positively influenced by strategically offering telecommuting opportunities. As noted by Oldham and Da Silva (2015), the power to choose a moderate amount of telecommuting (i.e., two or three days per week) can give employees a sense of autonomy and freedom by having more control over their scheduling and their pace and means of work. This freedom is directly related to an increase in job satisfaction and employee engagement (Oldham and Da Silva).

has been found to be related to life satisfaction and mental and physical health, improved satisfaction has become an important outcome in its own right" (Balzer et al. 1990, p. 6). To emphasize the importance of effectively managing employee satisfaction, Vecchio (2003) stated, "Given that most people must work, and that most people will spend the majority of their adult lives at work, it can be argued that employers have a moral obligation to make the experience personally rewarding (or, at minimum, not painful or dehumanizing)" (p. 266).

At the economic level, management should be interested in job satisfaction because "increased satisfaction with aspects of the job may prove to be a bonus to the organization in many areas, including reduced absenteeism, decreased turnover, and fewer work-related accidents" (Balzer, Smith, et al. 1990, p. 6). Finally, at the theoretical level, the concept of job satisfaction is incorporated into many theories of work motivation and work behavior. Theoretical concerns relate to satisfaction either as a direct cause of increased work performance and cooperation or as a consequence of such behavior leading to organizational rewards.

The lack of a relationship between job satisfaction and other variables associated with productivity may be due to measurement problems. That is, it may be that a strong relationship exists between job satisfaction and productivity but researchers have failed to adequately measure one or both of these concepts and, therefore, have been unable to identify the strong link between them. For instance, Fisher and Locke (1992) pointed out that the problem may reside in measuring job behavior as a single type of act over a limited time by a single method, when in fact job satisfaction is a general attitude. However, "a strong attitude–behavior correlation will . . . occur [only] when there is correspondence between the levels of aggregation represented in the attitude and behavior measures" (Fisher and Locke 1992, p. 166).

Furthermore, as Ostroff (1992) noted, most of the research linking satisfaction and other outcomes was conducted on an individual level. According to Ostroff, "It is likely that a study of satisfaction–performance at the organizational level would show that organizations that have more satisfied employees are more productive and profitable than organizations whose employees are less satisfied" (p. 963). This assertion is made because the satisfaction and performance of individuals makes a large contribution to overall organizational performance. Specific to this call, Wood, Van Veldhoven, Croon, and de Menezes (2012) found that increases in employee job satisfaction were linked to increases in organizational financial performance, labor productivity, and high-quality organizational outputs.

Another concern addresses the fact that other factors may constrain and control one's performance. For example, lackluster performance by other workers who are dissatisfied may counterbalance a significant contribution made to a group task by a satisfied worker. Therefore, unless we find ways to reconcile individual and organizational performance, some of the commonly accepted measures of performance may indeed be invalid.

There is another important reason for the interest in job satisfaction. Description of the services provided in sport and recreation suggests that most clients engage in sport and physical activity for their own enjoyment, fun, and well-being. Given their engagement in the activity, they are partial employees of the sport and recreation enterprise. Therefore, their positive feelings about their involvement, and about the organizational processes facilitating it, provide critical measures of the enterprise's effectiveness.

Finally, when measuring performance in elite sport or in other competitions, measurements that focus only on wins and losses cannot be used to judge participant satisfaction with activities because these contests are zero-sum games. That is, for every winner, there must be a loser. For example, a mere one or two points may decide an NBA game in which the two teams together score more than 200 points, yet one team is declared a winner and the other is labeled a loser. Although the losers may be disappointed with the loss, they may also be fully satisfied with their efforts, their teamwork, their preparatory practice sessions, and the coaching they received. These feelings of satisfaction are important in their own right. Therefore, for all of the reasons cited, job satisfaction should be considered an outcome that is independent of other organizational factors and should be valued for its own sake.

 Job satisfaction is a critical outcome in and of itself from multiple perspectives: economic, humanistic, and moralistic. Because the human resources in sport and recreation include both paid and volunteer workers—and because sport and recreation clients are partial employees—the concept of satisfaction should be extended to all three of these components of the industry's human resources.

THEORIES OF JOB SATISFACTION

Because of the importance attached to job satisfaction by theorists and practitioners alike, researchers have made various attempts to define and describe job satisfaction and to identify its sources (i.e., **facets of satisfaction**). This section deals with a few of the better-known theories.

Herzberg's Two-Factor Theory

As noted in chapter 8, Herzberg and his colleagues found in their study of engineers and accountants that one set of factors was associated with their subjects' satisfaction and another set was associated with their dissatisfaction (Herzberg 1966; Herzberg, Mausner, and Snyderman 1959). According to the researchers' theory, the presence in a job of the first set of factors (termed *motivators*) is directly related to satisfaction, whereas their absence leads to a neutral state. On the other hand, absence of the second set of factors (termed *hygienes*) leads to dissatisfaction, and their presence leads to a neutral state. Because these authors postulated that satisfaction and dissatisfaction are two different continuums affected by two different sets of factors, the theory is called a two-factor, or dual-factor, theory.

The motivator factors relate to the job's content, such as the challenge, achievement, recognition, and autonomy that one experiences in performing one's tasks. These satisfactions are mediated personally and are not controlled by external agents. On the other hand, the hygiene factors relate to the context in which the job is performed and include elements such as company policy and procedures, working conditions, supervision, and interpersonal relations within a work group. These aspects of a job lie largely beyond the individual's control.

Herzberg's two-factor theory has been criticized from several perspectives by various authors (e.g., Evans 1986; Kanfer 1990; King 1970; J. Schneider and Locke 1971; Soliman 1970). The most serious problem is that the theory predicts the same level of satisfaction for all members performing the same or similar jobs (i.e., jobs possessing the same level of motivators and hygiene factors). In other words,

they theory overlooks the fact that people react to their jobs in different ways and that people in the same or similar jobs are satisfied differently with their jobs. Therefore, it is necessary to focus on processes within the individual in order to more fully grasp the concept of satisfaction.

Lawler's Facet Model of Satisfaction

Recall that the Rice et al. (1989) definition of satisfaction included the notion of **discrepancy** arising out of a psychological comparison between what one receives and a standard of comparison. The extent of discrepancy is related to the level of job satisfaction. This idea of discrepancy permeates most other theories of job satisfaction, although the theories differ in specifying the standards of comparison. The following section addresses some of these theories (e.g., needs-based satisfaction theories, Minnesota Model of Job Satisfaction, Locke's

JOB SATISFACTION AND COMPARISON TO OTHERS

Smucker and Kent (2004) investigated differences in job satisfaction between administrators in three segments of the sport industry—professional sport, the fitness realm, and parks and recreation departments. They found that administrators in parks and recreation departments were less satisfied than those in the other two segments in regard to promotional opportunities, co-workers, and overall job. Smucker and Kent suggested that this difference could be attributed to the fact that the parks and recreation departments are more bureaucratized, requiring strict adherence to rules and the authority structure. According to these authors, the lower satisfaction among these personnel could be due to the "strict reliance upon rules and authority" and "could possibly create rigid formal interactions between employees themselves including supervisors" (p. 39). They also found that administrators who did not make comparisons with a referent other (e.g., an individual in a similar position or at the same level of the organizational hierarchy) were less satisfied with promotion than were those who did make such comparisons. This result seems to align with definitions of job satisfaction. If such comparisons show that a given individual is better off than the referent other, then the first individual is likely to be more satisfied. In contrast, when individuals do not compare their experience with another's, their satisfaction is likely to be influenced by their perceived job situation itself.

In Smucker and Kent's (2004) study, respondents who did not have a comparison referent felt that they did not have many promotional opportunities and indicated they would react negatively with this perceived lack of opportunities. In contrast, those who did compare themselves with others felt that the others had the same level of opportunity or even less. Therefore, their reactions to the situation would have been more positive. This study illustrates how comparing oneself with others in the workplace can influence one's satisfaction in either direction.

value-based theory of satisfaction, Smith's facets of job satisfaction) and the standards of comparison they contain.

Lawler (1973) provided a good example of a discrepancy theory of job satisfaction (see figure 16.1) in suggesting that job satisfaction is a function of the extent to which what one receives from a job (box b in the figure) matches what one thinks one should receive from that job (box a). This simple comparison becomes more complex when several other factors come into play to determine one's perceptions, both of what one ought to receive and of what one actually receives. As illustrated in figure 16.1, critical determinants of what one ought to receive include individual skill, experience, and other assets that one brings to the job situation (i.e., perceived personal job inputs), as well as the difficulty and responsibility of the job (i.e., perceived job characteristics). In addition, the person also considers what comparable others bring to the situation and what they get (i.e., perceived inputs and outcomes of referent others). As for the per-

ceived amount received (box b), the actual outcome received is compared with the perceived outcomes of referent others.

For example, an employee in a sport marketing firm will be satisfied if he or she perceives that the rewards (e.g., merit pay) are consistent with the time and effort that he or she put into the job and with his or her performance (e.g., business generated). At the same time, this person would compare his or her rewards (relative to personal job inputs and performance) with the rewards received by comparable others (relative to their job inputs and performance). If the comparison is not favorable, the person will be dissatisfied.

Lawler's approach is based, to some extent, on Adams' (1963) theory of inequity, which is discussed in chapter 8. Such comparisons, as well as judgments about fairness of reward distribution and subsequent satisfaction or dissatisfaction, also relate to the concepts of performance appraisal and distributive justice, which are discussed in chapters 13 and 9, respectively.

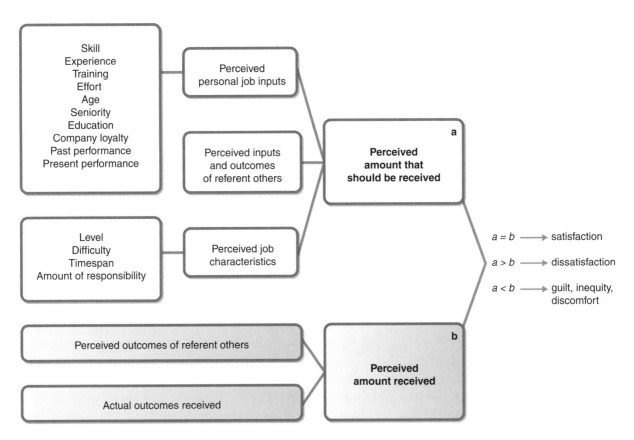

FIGURE 16.1 Lawler's facet model of satisfaction.

Adapted, by permission, from E.E. Lawler, III, 1973, *Motivation in work organizations* (Pacific Grove, CA: Brooks/Cole). Copyright E.E. Lawler.

Need-Based Satisfaction Theories

Some theorists have suggested that job satisfaction is a function of the extent to which one's needs are satisfied in a job (i.e., **need satisfaction**) (D.C. McClelland 1961; Murray 1938). These need theories, discussed in chapter 8, suggest that need deprivation leads to a state of tension and unhappiness. To the extent that a job can fulfill several of the needs that are important to a person, the job can serve as a source of satisfaction for that individual. Accordingly, a person who has a high level of need for achievement may be satisfied with a challenging job, but a person who has a low level of that need may be dissatisfied with the same job. Conversely, two individuals may have different needs that are satisfied by the same job. For example, a fitness instructor may have a high level of need for achievement that can be satisfied by the challenge of helping clients get fit and healthy. Another instructor who has a high level of need for affiliation can satisfy that need through positive task and social interactions with clients.

Minnesota Model of Job Satisfaction

Researchers at the University of Minnesota have been working on the concept of job satisfaction for a long time (Dawis, England, and Lofquist 1964; Dawis and Lofquist 1984). Their approach emphasizes the notion of needs. More specifically, these authors have identified 20 needs relevant to the job context and categorized them into six dimensions. These dimensions and the associated needs are applied to sport and recreation in the sidebar. Measurement of the extent to which these needs are satisfied in a job is carried out through the Minnesota Satisfaction Questionnaire, which is described later in this chapter.

Locke's Value-Based Theory of Satisfaction

From a different perspective, Locke (1976) argued that individuals place more or less value on each of all possible outcomes from their jobs. These outcomes may include, for example, salary, prestige, or desirable working conditions. Some may value

DIVERSITY MANAGEMENT OF HUMAN RESOURCES

The actualization element referred to by Chelladurai (2014) in his integrative framework for managing diversity outlines the potential benefits for an organization whose members value diversity and accept and activate diversity management strategies. From the perspective of employees, McKay and Avery (2015) suggested that creating a climate in which diversity is valued can lead to extensive employee benefits, including increased satisfaction and well-being. These benefits derive from the fact that valuing diversity creates a culture of inclusion in which distinctive people, ideas, and points of view are embraced. Thus, employees are more satisfied with their work environment because they feel valued for their unique contribution to the organization.

salary more than others do (i.e., they want or desire more salary); some may place a higher value on the prestige associated with their jobs. According to Locke, the match between what an individual values (or desires) in a job and what is actually present in that job influences the individual's level of job satisfaction. For example, some students graduating from degree programs in sport management prefer to work in a university athletics department for the sake of prestige and status even though the salary may be lower than in other types of organizations.

Smith's Facets of Job Satisfaction

P.C. Smith and her associates have been researching the topic of job satisfaction for decades (Balzer, Kihm, et al. 1997; P.C. Smith, Kendall, and Hulin 1969). These authors have demonstrated that the essence of job satisfaction can be captured through

APPLYING THE FACETS OF THE MINNESOTA MODEL OF JOB SATISFACTION

- *Comfort dimension:* Rachel is involved in a sport sales job where the sales quotas are comfortable and not stressful to meet. She fills her eight-hour workday and is able to keep busy. She can work independently on a variety of tasks associated with selling the sport product. Rachel is paid relatively well as compared with her colleagues and is satisfied that her office space is clean and healthy. All in all, her sales position provides steady employment.

- *Autonomy dimension:* Rick works as a sport analytics specialist with a professional sport club. His boss allows him to take initiative when creating data management models and to apply his own ideas when addressing player-related factors that may contribute to enhanced on-field performance. Rick can make decisions on his own and present his work to upper management.

- *Altruism dimension:* Omar works in community relations with a semiprofessional sport organization. Omar's work involves providing needed services to the community around the team and allows him the opportunity to give back to other people. He is involved in community projects that feel morally right and give him the opportunity to develop friendships with co-workers and community members.

- *Status dimension:* Phyllis is an intern in an intercollegiate athletics department. The athletics director often publicly recognizes interns for a job well done and highlights the prestige of working in an athletics department on a university campus. In the local community, Phyllis' family members and friends tend to be in awe of her placement in the athletics department. In terms of career implications, Phyllis knows that internships can lead to full-time positions in the department if the intern works hard. In addition, the athletics director is known for allowing senior interns the chance to provide direction for junior interns.

- *Safety dimension:* Emilio is director of human resource management for a national sport governing body. The organization has established comprehensive policies and procedures for human resource management, and Emilio's executive director encourages him to apply them in an equitable manner. Emilio's work environment is predictable and stable. He believes his direct supervisors support him in his decisions about personnel and provided him with appropriate training.

- *Achievement dimension:* Tamara is the marketing manager of a province-level sport association. The organization has adopted an online tracking system that encourages Tamara to track her marketing hits and allows her to see the results of her marketing efforts. She can use these statistics to showcase her marketing abilities to upper management in meetings.

measurement of five facets of a job: work itself, pay, promotions, co-workers, and supervision. The sidebar defines these facets in the context of sport and recreation. The authors also suggested that it is possible to measure one's overall satisfaction with a job. The instrument used to measure both the five facets and overall job satisfaction is known as the Job Descriptive Index, which is described later in this chapter.

Job dissatisfaction stems from a discrepancy between what one perceives to be one's inputs and what one expects to receive in terms of intrinsic or extrinsic rewards. Facets of job satisfaction reflect employee needs or clusters of needs.

FACETS AND EXAMPLES RELATED TO LOWER RATINGS OF SATISFACTION IN THE JOB DESCRIPTIVE INDEX

Pay

As a sport event manager, one would rate satisfaction lower if

- he or she receives less pay than expected,
- he or she perceives the pay received to be less than warranted by the input or effort required by the event responsibilities,
- his or her pay is less than that received by the marketing manager, or
- his or her pay does not meet the financial needs and standards of the economy to which he or she is accustomed.

Promotions

As a sponsorship coordinator, one would rate satisfaction lower if

- the sport organization's promotion policy and administration of that policy are viewed as nonexistent or unfair, or
- promotions to sponsorship manager or director are seen as infrequent, unimportant, or undesired.

People on the Job

As a sport club membership coordinator, one would rate satisfaction lower if

- interactions with co-workers are unfavorable,
- interactions with members or clients are unfavorable, or
- interactions with volunteers are unfavorable.

Job in General

As a sport event manager, one would rate satisfaction lower if

- one does not see the long-term benefit of the event manager position; or
- the pay, promotions, work, supervision, or people involved in the job are viewed as inadequate or dysfunctional.

Supervision

As a sport club membership coordinator, one would rate satisfaction lower if

- the membership director (i.e., the coordinator's direct supervisor) is viewed as lacking knowledge and competence in his or her role, or
- the membership director is unpleasant and rude.

Work

As a sponsorship coordinator, one would rate satisfaction lower if

- one's director did not allow him or her to be creative with proposals,
- sponsorship tasks were invariable and did not use one's knowledge and skills,
- increased tenure is not accompanied by increased autonomy and task complexity, or
- the tasks of the job are not intrinsically challenging.

VIEWPOINT

Job satisfaction and dissatisfaction are multifaceted. Employees tend to experience differing levels of satisfaction between various facets of work, and each facet can exert independent effects on an individual's overall satisfaction with work (Spector 1997). Therefore, a danger exists in examining job satisfaction at an aggregated level because recommendations for "theory and practice tend to be built on overarching frameworks which, by definition, ignore subtleties in how characteristics of work can relate to various facets of satisfaction" (Fila, Paik, Griffeth, and Allen 2014, p. 640). By examining satisfaction as a multifaceted concept, managers can assess which individual job facets (e.g., supervisor, pay, co-workers) require direct management over time.

SATISFACTION WITH VOLUNTEER WORK

The foregoing discussion of job satisfaction is based on theories and research pertaining to paid work. Because our focus is on three types of human resources (i.e., paid workers, volunteer workers, and clients or participants), the discussion now moves beyond the satisfaction theories related to paid work to the unique facets of satisfaction relevant to volunteer workers and clients.

The study of satisfaction in volunteer work has been sparse and sporadic because, until recently, researchers believed that volunteer work was based solely on altruism, implying that volunteers had no expectation of any kind of return. In the absence of such expectations, studying satisfaction in volunteering has no point. However, as seen in chapter 2, individuals also volunteer for various reasons other than altruism. Volunteer work, then, is an exchange of one's time and effort for satisfactions and psychic rewards gained in that work (Gidron 1983). Therefore, volunteer satisfaction needs to be studied and understood. Such an understanding can assist sport managers in recruiting and retaining the volunteers in their organizations.

In any discussion of volunteer satisfaction, the first thing to remember is that volunteerism involves work. That is, as Gidron (1983) wrote,

> It involves a situation where there is a job to be done, the job can utilize one's skills and creativity, one's efforts can bear fruit in the form of results or achievements, and one can be recognized for it. (p. 21)

Thus, volunteer work is quite similar to paid work in some respects; as a result, some of the facets of satisfaction relating to paid work may also be relevant to volunteer work (see the sidebar titled "Facets and Examples Related to Lower Ratings of Satisfaction in the Job Descriptive Index"). For instance, satisfaction with supervision or co-workers should be equally meaningful in paid and volunteer work. Similarly, interactions with clients should offer the same kinds of satisfactions and frustrations for paid and volunteer workers. (Obviously, satisfactions relating to pay, fringe benefits, or promotions are not be relevant to a volunteer worker.) For example, paid and volunteer workers involved in the Special Olympics derive the same kinds of satisfaction in serving their clients and have similar reactions to the supervision that they receive.

At the same time, of course, volunteer work is unique in several respects. Gidron (1983) pointed out that because volunteer work is undertaken freely, one may engage in it or discontinue at will, whereas paid work is necessary for the livelihood of most people. This critical distinction establishes different kinds of relationships (and different forms of compliance) with the organization for paid workers than for volunteer workers. For paid workers in most organizations, the level of pay can be equated with recognition of good work, but this concrete form of recognition is unavailable in the case of volunteer workers. In addition, as Gidron stated, "In many cases volunteer work is an addition to and not a substitute for the major activity in which one engages, such as salaried work, study, or homemaking" (p. 21). Thus a volunteer worker may bring to the situation different needs or expectations than does a paid worker. Fulfillment of those needs and expectations is critical for the involvement of volunteers in sport and recreation organizations.

In his study of volunteer work, Gidron (1983) identified 12 factors that could serve as sources of satisfaction for volunteers (see the sidebar for an example of each factor in the sport volunteer context). More specifically, volunteers and paid workers are equally concerned with the work itself, as well as with task achievement, task convenience, stress

EXAMPLES OF THE FACETS OF JOB SATISFACTION AMONG SPORT VOLUNTEERS

Work Itself

The work of a sport volunteer must be challenging and interesting. The volunteer will be involved in using his or her skills and knowledge and will be given independence when completing tasks.

> **Example:** A volunteer is satisfied when assigned the task of creating a new Twitter feed for an upcoming international event. She is allowed to be creative in the timing and content of tweets, as well as the targets of the messaging.

Task Achievement

Any of the tasks that a volunteer is assigned should allow the volunteer to see the task to completion.

> **Example:** A volunteer is involved in the process of course setup for a golf championship from start to finish.

Task Convenience

The scheduling of volunteers must ensure that the location and hours of work are convenient.

> **Example:** A volunteer who works a 9-to-5 job is given shifts that run from 6 p.m. to 9 p.m. to avoid conflicts with her work schedule.

Stress Factors

Stress and lower satisfaction result when volunteers lack the necessary knowledge and experience to complete the assigned role, lack essential materials, or lack knowledge of job requirements.

> **Example:** A volunteer coach with a local soccer club is not given a job description or orientation and therefore feels like he does not grasp his responsibilities.

Family

Volunteers need support from family members for their volunteer activity.

> **Example:** A young woman volunteers for a national sport event in her community with support from her partner for being involved in the activity and away from home.

---

factors, relationship with supervisor (both instrumental [task-based] and expressive [interpersonal]), and relationship with client. In contrast, some sources of satisfaction are unique to volunteering, including family support, social acceptance through volunteering, peer recognition (as Gidron defines it), and other volunteers. These sources are deemed unique to volunteering in that they involve satisfaction derived from engagement in a leisure-based activity. Gidron also found that the factors contributing most to volunteer satisfaction were the work itself, task achievement, task convenience, and lack of stressors. In his words,

> In order to be satisfied, a volunteer needs, above all, a task in which self-expression is possible—a task which is seen as a challenge, a task where achievements can be seen. . . . The volunteer should not have to waste time getting to work, looking for tools, or arguing with officials about what to do and how to do it. (p. 32)

A note of caution is in order here about work itself. The foregoing conclusion of Gidron (1983) is that managers strive to enrich the job for all volunteers (for more on job enrichment, see chapter 10). As noted earlier, however, not all individuals have the same degree of need for growth in the workplace or possess the necessary skills and traits to be successful in an enriched job. From a different perspective, a volunteer may be involved in a highly enriched job in his or her full-time paid work (e.g., medical doctor, architect, university professor). To

Supervisor (Instrumental)

The volunteer work situation includes a supervisor who outlines clear and concise work responsibilities and helps the volunteer learn new things.

Example: A media relations volunteer has a manager who provides clear instructions about which media outlets to contact and how to do so.

Professionals

The volunteer should feel accepted and appreciated by the professional (paid) workers.

Example: Volunteer chairpersons have a strong working relationship with their paid staff counterparts.

Social Acceptance

The volunteer should be enabled to feel that his or her work is accepted as worthwhile by people inside and outside of the organization.

Example: The executive director of a national sport organization highlights the importance of volunteers.

Client

The volunteer needs to see agreement, cooperation, and appreciation from people such as clients, consumers, and spectators.

Example: A volunteer coach is supported by a cooperative and appreciative group of players and parents.

Recognition

The volunteer needs recognition in the form of social media mentions, events (e.g., appreciation parties), and gifts of sport merchandise.

Example: Volunteers are interviewed by the media as a key component to sport event success, where their impact on the event and community is highlighted.

Supervisor (Expressive)

The volunteer needs to feel as though he or she is encouraged, appreciated, and accepted by supervisors.

Example: A volunteer coordinator provides a "champions breakfast" on the morning of an event to show appreciation for volunteers.

Other Volunteers

Volunteers need an environment that fosters friendship and teamwork among volunteers.

Example: Volunteer coaches from a local football club get together every Friday for coffee.

---

such a volunteer, the need for growth and achievement can be fulfilled through paid work rather than volunteer work. In fact, that kind of volunteer may indeed seek a "mindless" volunteer job.

This view is consistent with the work of Kabanoff and O'Brien (1980), who identified three possible relationships between work and nonwork: the compensatory hypothesis (i.e., nonwork activities compensate for deficiencies in the workplace and vice versa), the generalization or spillover hypothesis (i.e., work and nonwork satisfactions correlate positively or parallel each other), and the segmentation hypothesis (i.e., work and nonwork activities exert independent effects on an individual). By extending the notions of compensation and segmentation, one could suggest that individuals who hold enriched jobs in paid work may be content with routine jobs in their volunteer work and that routine work offers different effects in the paid and volunteer contexts. By the same token, some volunteers may be involved in highly routine paid jobs but possess the skills and inclination to be involved in enriched volunteer jobs. Such volunteers may indeed seek challenging jobs in their volunteer work.

 A job is a job regardless of whether it is done by a paid worker or a volunteer worker. Therefore, some of the same factors in and around a job may affect both paid and volunteer workers. In addition, volunteer workers may bring other needs and expectations to be fulfilled.

PARTICIPANT SATISFACTION

Participant satisfaction is a more complicated issue because participation can take several forms. As noted in chapter 4, people participate for different reasons; therefore, participant services can be classified into different categories—specifically, the pursuit of pleasure, skills, excellence, and health and fitness. Participants in each of these activities have differing orientations, needs, and expectations. Therefore, it is appropriate to consider satisfaction separately for each of these categories. Unfortunately, few researchers have made the effort to understand the dynamics of satisfaction in these contexts. However, the findings from other, similar contexts can be extrapolated to participation in sport and recreation.

Satisfaction With Services

Berry and Parasuraman (1991) suggested that consumers of a service use five dimensions to evaluate that service (see table 16.1).

Berry and Parasuraman's (1991) five dimensions of evaluation can be perceived as sources of satisfaction for the consumers of sport and recreation services. In fact, the descriptions of the five dimensions appear quite germane to some of the services in our field, such as those offered by a commercial fitness club. For instance, overweight and unfit clients must persevere and work hard to alleviate their problems, and their motivation to put forth this effort can be enhanced by a fitness instructor who is empathetic and responsive (two of Berry and Parasuraman's dimensions) to their needs and frustrations. For another example, consider the services provided by athletic trainers. Clients expect these services to be reliable (i.e., the training is dependable and accurate), responsive (i.e., the trainer helps promptly), assured (i.e., the trainer creates trust through knowledge and courtesy), and empathetic (i.e., the trainer provides individualized attention). Of course, the tangibles (i.e., the setting, including facilities and equipment) must also be adequate.

Leisure Satisfaction

The definition and description of satisfaction in the field of leisure also yields concepts that are relevant to sport and recreation. In fact, because most

TABLE 16.1 Dimensions of Service Evaluation

DIMENSION	DESCRIPTION
Reliability	Ability to perform the promised service dependably and accurately
Tangibles	Appearance of physical facilities, equipment, personnel, and communication materials
Responsiveness	Willingness to help customers and provide prompt service
Assurance	Employees' knowledge, courtesy, and ability to inspire trust and confidence
Empathy	Provision of caring, individualized attention to customers

Adapted from Berry and Parasuraman 1991.

participants engage in sport and physical activity as leisure activities, let us begin by defining leisure activities and **leisure satisfaction**.

> Leisure activities (representing participation) were defined as non-obligatory and non-work activities which individuals choose to do in their free time, excluding activities that meet biological needs such as eating and sleeping. Activities can be active or inactive, such as sports, outdoor activities, social activities, or hobbies. (Ragheb and Tate 1993, p. 62)

This broad definition includes all of the activities in which our clients participate; it also subsumes the notion that volunteer work is a leisure activity. Therefore, a discussion of leisure satisfaction carries great implications for sport and recreation managers.

Beard and Ragheb (1980) did pioneering work on leisure satisfaction. They argued that understanding the subjective meanings that people attach to their leisure participation is critical to leisure management; moreover, they argued that such meanings can be captured through the measurement of leisure satisfaction. They defined leisure satisfaction as the positive perceptions or feelings an individual forms, elicits, or gains as a result of engaging in leisure activities and choices. It is the degree to which one is presently content or pleased with his/her general leisure experiences and situations. This positive feeling of contentment results from the satisfaction of felt or unfelt needs of the individual. (p. 22)

Beard and Ragheb (1980) proposed a six-dimensional scheme of leisure satisfaction that was confirmed through statistical procedures in subsequent research. Their six facets of leisure satisfaction are described in table 16.2.

All six of these dimensions or facets of leisure satisfaction are applicable to sport and recreation clients and to volunteer workers; in fact, most, if not all, of them are equally relevant to paid workers as well. In this regard, note the close correspondence between some of the six dimensions of leisure satisfaction and several of the facets of job satisfaction discussed earlier. For instance, the psychological and educational dimensions of leisure satisfaction parallel the facet of satisfaction with work in the **Job**

TABLE 16.2 Dimensions of Leisure Satisfaction

DIMENSION	DESCRIPTION
Psychological	Benefits such as a sense of freedom, enjoyment, involvement, and intellectual challenge
Education and intellectual	Intellectual stimulation and opportunities to learn about oneself and one's surroundings
Social	Rewarding relationships with other people
Relaxation	Relief from stress and strain
Physiological	Physical fitness, health, weight control, and overall well-being
Aesthetic and environmental	Aesthetic rewards derived from pleasing, interesting, beautiful, and generally well-designed activities

Adapted, by permission, J.G. Beard and M.G. Ragheb, 1980, "Measuring leisure satisfaction," *Journal of Leisure Research* 12(1): 20-33.

Descriptive Index of Balzer, Kihm, and colleagues (1997) and the facets of achievement and autonomy in the Minnesota Model of Job Satisfaction. Similarly, the social dimension of leisure satisfaction is similar to the Job Descriptive Index facets of supervision and people on the job. Finally, the aesthetic dimension of leisure satisfaction contains elements included as working conditions in the Minnesota model.

However, the relaxation and physiological dimensions of leisure satisfaction are unique to leisure participation; that is, they do not have corresponding facets in the job satisfaction literature. Obviously, these two dimensions are significant components as far as sport and recreation clients are concerned, and they are germane to volunteer work as well. Indeed, sport and recreation volunteers may engage in sport and recreation activities as a means of relief from the stress and strain of paid work or of household chores.

Note that Berry and Parasuraman's (1991) dimensions of service focus on the processes of delivering a service which include employee behavior and that Beard and Ragheb's (1980) scheme emphasizes the outcomes experienced by clients. One might argue that outcomes are related logically to appropriate processes and, therefore, that emphasis on either the processes or the outcomes yields the same results. However, in reality, processes are not perfectly related to desired outcomes. The matter is further confounded when the outcomes hold meaning only as perceived by clients. Therefore, sport managers need to focus on both the processes and the outcomes that their clients experience.

Athlete Satisfaction

The need to discuss **athlete satisfaction** separately stems from two unique features of athletics (Chelladurai and Riemer 1997). First, athletes are the prime beneficiaries of intercollegiate athletics; that is, intercollegiate athletics exists for student-athletes (Knight Foundation 2001). Interestingly, some people dispute that student-athletes are the prime beneficiaries given that large amounts of revenue from intercollegiate sport ends up with the institution. Second, when intercollegiate athletics is perceived as entertainment, athletes become the prime producers of such entertainment (Chelladurai and Riemer). Furthermore, athletes spend an inordinate amount of time in training relative to the time spent in competition (i.e., time of performance).

CUSTOMER SATISFACTION AND CUSTOMER LOYALTY

Regarding the relationship between customer satisfaction and customer loyalty, Albrecht and Zemke (2002) hold that only those who are "extremely satisfied" are likely to express loyalty to an organization and its products. Those who are merely "satisfied" or "somewhat satisfied" are likely to switch. In Albrecht and Zemke's words,

> If your organization improves its average ratings on a five-point customer satisfaction survey from one to two (unsatisfactory to poor), from two to three (poor to satisfactory), or even from three to four (satisfactory to good), you'll see only negligible or modest corresponding improvements in customer loyalty. But make the leap from four to nearly five on that scale, from ratings of good to excellent, and you see dramatic spikes in measures of expressed loyalty. . . . In other words, someone who rates you a five, or excellent, is, on average, two to six times more loyal than someone who rates you a four. Those who rate you from one to four will be "at risk" any time a competitor makes a better, or perhaps just different, offer, or simply for the novelty of trying someone new. . . . But loyal customers are more than just today's sale. They are tomorrow's and the next month's sale as well. (pp. 79-80)

We can extend the same arguments to services within the purview of sport management (e.g., spectator sport, fitness club services).

For example, a high school basketball team may spend two hours per day for four days in preparation for a Friday game that lasts less than two hours. Therefore, for our purposes, the satisfaction of an athlete regarding what happens during the training sessions is just as important as what happens in the competition itself.

Another unique element of athletics that is relevant was mentioned in connection with the NBA example given earlier: the fact that contests are zero-sum games (i.e., for every winner, there is a loser). For example, two profit-oriented fitness clubs competing with each other might each make a profit and therefore be a "winner," but only one team can be the champion in any given sport league or competition. Therefore, managers of athletics programs need to go beyond mere win–loss records in assessing the effectiveness of their programs. According to Chelladurai and Riemer (1997), "Athlete satisfaction may indeed prove to be the ultimate measure of organizational effectiveness of an athletic program" (p. 135). Thus, the satisfaction of athletes plays a significant role from the perspective of management.

On the basis of this line of reasoning, Chelladurai and Riemer presented a classification of facets of athlete satisfaction, which is shown in table 16.3.

Some of these facets bear resemblance to those identified by other authors in the contexts of leisure and of paid and volunteer work; others are unique to the athletic context (e.g., playing time, strategy selection, loyalty to athletes, and scholarships). At first glance, it may appear that because participation in athletics is voluntary—and because a given sport has the same basic rules and performance requirements both for elite athletes and for recreational participants—the facets of satisfaction should be similar across athletes, recreation participants, and volunteer workers. However, as noted in chapter 4, athletics is a pursuit of excellence with its own bottom-line requirements, particularly the exclusive focus on the job at hand; in every other context, such exclusivity is not imposed. Because of the total involvement of the athlete in both the physical and psychological sense, it is necessary to measure athlete satisfaction from perspectives different from those used in other contexts.

TABLE 16.3 Facets of Athlete Satisfaction

BROAD CATEGORY	SPECIFIC FACET	DESCRIPTION
Performance	Team	Team's performance in competitions
	Individual	Individual's personal performance
Improvement	Team	Extent to which the team improves its performance over time
	Individual	Extent to which one improves one's personal performance over time
Leadership	Practice	Training methods employed, severity of workouts, and orderliness of practice sessions
	Ability use	Extent to which the coach uses the abilities of all athletes efficiently and effectively
	Strategy selection	Appropriateness of the strategies selected by the coach
	Equity in playing time	Amount of time for which an athlete is used in competitions based on ability, talent, or effort
	Equitable rewards	Extent to which the coach rewards and recognizes all athletes equitably
	Loyalty to athletes	Loyalty and support from the coach
	Attitude regarding winning	Positive and balanced attitude toward winning
	Ethics	Extent to which the coach rewards and recognizes all athletes equitably
Teammates	Task	Extent to which teammates contribute to and facilitate one's task learning and performance
	Social	Extent to which interactions within the team are warm, friendly, and cohesive
Support staff	—	Help and assistance received from support staff (e.g., academic counselors, trainers, managers)
Administration	Facilities and equipment	Quality and availability of facilities and equipment for practices and games
	Scholarships	Number and amounts of scholarships awarded to the team
	Budget	Budget allotted to the team relative to other teams (e.g., for travel and uniforms)
Community support	—	Support from the university community, alumni, local public, and media

Based on Chelladurai and Riemer 1997.

 The facets of satisfaction in sport participation generally reflect those in other forms of services and work settings. Because athletes are prime beneficiaries as well as prime producers of entertainment, their satisfaction is both a major responsibility of athletics administrators and a useful evaluative measure for athletics programs.

Coach Satisfaction

In discussing athlete satisfaction, we noted that athletics differs from other work enterprises and, therefore, that athletes are subject to different kinds of experiences than are regular workers. The same thinking applies to coaches. Although coaches are comparable to other managers in many respects, they also face different contingencies in their work. Therefore, it is appropriate to develop coaching-specific measures of satisfaction. With this in mind, Chelladurai and Ogasawara (2003) have identified 11 facets of satisfaction in the job of coaching at the intercollegiate level; these facets are described in table 16.4. Although several of the facets are measured by other scales used in the context of regular employment, some are unique to coaching—for instance, satisfaction with facilities, media and community support, team performance, and athletes' academic progress.

MEASUREMENT OF SATISFACTION

So far, this chapter has focused on identifying and describing various facets of satisfaction relevant to paid workers, volunteer workers, and clients. Although such descriptions are important in their own right, their usefulness is realized fully only when they are validly and reliably measured. Before exploring the various methods of measuring satisfaction, let us discuss the issue of global versus facet satisfaction.

Global Versus Facet Satisfaction

Job satisfaction may be viewed either as a global effect of one's feelings about a job overall or as a collection of feelings about different aspects of a job. Viewing job satisfaction as a global concept may be useful in some respects; however, from a managerial perspective, it is more appropriate to view job satisfaction as comprising satisfactions with different facets of a job. This dominant view has led to the development of several schemes to describe and measure the facets of a job, some of which were described earlier. In this approach, after measuring a worker's satisfaction with different facets of a job, researchers sum or average these scores to derive a measure of overall satisfaction.

This practice has been questioned by W.K. Balzer and her associates (1990). Specifically, as described earlier in the chapter, they argued that although measures of the facets of a job may help managers identify and rectify problems in the job situation, "they do not indicate whether employees are satisfied with their job overall" (p. 8). In other words, a composite index of the sum (or mean) of

TABLE 16.4 Facets of Satisfaction in Coaching

FACET	ITEM
Supervision	Supervisor's decision making, delegation of duties, and handling of employees, including feedback offered
Coaching job	Pride in the significance of coaching, enjoyment of coaching, and sense of accomplishment
Autonomy	Freedom in, and responsibility for, one's own independent work
Facilities	Quality and adequacy of facilities and scheduling
Pay	Pay in relation to work done and to that of similar jobs elsewhere
Team performance	Team's improvement and performance during regular season, championships, and tournaments
Amount of work	Amount of work and administrative duties
Colleagues	Friendship and cooperation among coaches in one's institution
Athletes' academic performance	Academic progress of one's athletes
Job security	Security of one's job
Media and community support	The quality of facilities available for the team

Adapted from Chelladurai and Ogasawara 2003.

the facets fails to represent overall feelings because it does not make clear whether satisfaction in one aspect compensates for dissatisfaction in another; whether such computations give equal weight to each facet, thus denying individual differences in the importance attached to these facets; whether the time frames associated with the facets may be short-term, whereas overall satisfaction is a long-term effect; and whether simply adding the scores on a specified number of facets overlooks other aspects not included in the measurement scheme but important to the worker.

For these reasons, Balzer, Kihm, and colleagues (1997) suggested that one should measure overall satisfaction separately. In fact, their measure of satisfaction contains subscales to measure five facets of a job and a separate scale to measure overall job satisfaction. These tools are described in the following section.

Job Descriptive Index

The Job Descriptive Index is perhaps the most popular scale for measuring job satisfaction (Balzer, Kihm, et al. 1997; P.C. Smith et al. 1969). It measures P.C. Smith's five facets of a job as described earlier (i.e., work itself, pay, promotions, co-workers, and supervision) and the job in general. Definitions of these facets, and a sample item for measuring each one, are provided in the sidebar titled "Facets and Examples Related to Lower Ratings of Satisfaction in the Job Descriptive Index."

The Job Descriptive Index contains 72 items (i.e., words or phrases) that measure the five facets (i.e., 18 for work, 9 for pay, 9 for promotion, 18 for supervision, and 18 for people). The measure of overall job satisfaction contains 18 items. Typically, workers (or research subjects) are asked to indicate whether a given word or phrase about a particular facet describes (or does not describe) that aspect of their job. One responds "Y" for yes if the item describes the facet in question, "N" for no if it does not, and "?" if one cannot decide. Here is an example:

Pay

___ Bad

___ Well paid

___ Less than I deserve

For positively worded items, the scoring scheme allots three points for a "Y" response, zero points for an "N" response, and one point for a "?" response. The scoring is reversed for negatively worded items;

that is, an "N" response to a negatively worded item receives three points, whereas a "Y" response receives zero points. The sum (or mean) of the item scores for each facet is used as the score for that facet. The scores in facets containing only 9 items (i.e., pay and promotion) are then doubled so that they are comparable with scores for the facets containing 18 items.

This section describes some of the studies that have used the Job Descriptive Index (JDI) and job-in-general (JIG) scale. Pastore (1994) employed both the JDI and the JIG scale in her study of satisfaction among NCAA coaches. She found that female coaches expressed greater satisfaction than did male coaches in regard to pay, promotion, supervision, and job in general. In addition, Division III coaches were more satisfied with pay, promotion, and co-workers than were coaches in the other two divisions, and coaches in different sports varied in their satisfaction with specific facets. Robinson, Peterson, Tedrick, and Carpenter (2003) employed the same instruments (i.e., JDI and JIG scale) in their study of NCAA Division III athletics administrators and found that these administrators were generally satisfied with their positions; however, those who were employed as full-time athletics administrators were more satisfied than those who held other administrative positions.

Using the JDI, Snyder (1990) found no gender differences in satisfaction with work, supervision, pay, promotions, and co-workers among full-time and part-time coaches in four-year institutions in California. However, the leader behavior of athletics directors had differential effects on the satisfaction of male and female coaches. Although athletics directors' consideration behavior (i.e., behavior expressing concern for members' well-being and for a warm and friendly group atmosphere) had a significant effect on satisfaction with supervision for both genders, the leaders' structuring behavior (i.e., behavior reflecting a concern for clarity of roles and task performance) affected satisfaction with co-workers only among female coaches. Snyder argued that perceptions that structuring behavior was extended uniformly to all members could have led to the women's increased satisfaction with co-workers.

In a study of the effects of transformational leadership on job satisfaction among employees of Canadian YMCA organizations, M. Wallace and Weese (1995) used the JIG scale of Balzer, Smith, and colleagues (1990) to measure overall satisfaction with the job. They found that transformational leadership did not exert significant effects on employee satisfaction with the job in general. This result was contrary to previous research results and to the authors' expectations. M. Wallace and Weese noted that the lack of a relationship between transformational leadership and employee satisfaction could be a function of YMCA employees being particularly altruistic in their desire to help their clients enrich their lives.

The Minnesota Satisfaction Questionnaire

The Minnesota studies have been quite comprehensive. The researchers (Dawis et al. 1964; Dawis and Lofquist 1984; Weiss, Dawis, England, and Lofquist 1967) have developed a questionnaire to assess the importance attached by individuals to 20 aspects of a job. This scale is known as the Minnesota Importance Questionnaire. Similarly, the authors have developed a scale named the Minnesota Job Description Questionnaire to measure a worker's perception of his or her work situation. Both of these Minnesota measures are used in counseling for work adjustment.

Of more relevance to the present context is the measurement of job satisfaction. The Minnesota Model of Job Satisfaction includes 20 work-related needs (see the sidebar titled "Applying the Facets of the Minnesota Model of Job Satisfaction"). On the basis of this model, the same group of scholars (Dawis et al. 1964; Dawis and Lofquist 1984) developed the **Minnesota Satisfaction Questionnaire**, which contains 100 items measuring 20 aspects of a job that correspond to the 20 work-related needs. The respondent indicates the level of satisfaction with each aspect on a five-point scale, ranging from very dissatisfied to very satisfied. The short form of the Minnesota Satisfaction Questionnaire, which contains 20 items (i.e., one critical item from each of the 20 facets), also measures overall job satisfaction.

One example of research using this questionnaire in our context is that of Koehler (1988). She administered the questionnaire to 23 female and 7 male corporate fitness managers and found that her subjects were least satisfied with advancement and compensation (i.e., the mean was less than 16 on a 25-point scale). Koehler suggested that these lower levels of satisfaction reflected the lack of opportunities available in the recently emergent field of corporate fitness. The finding could also be an artifact of her sample, since most of her subjects were women, who traditionally have been paid less than male counterparts. On the other hand, Koehler

found that the subjects were most satisfied with social service and moral values (i.e., the mean was more than 22 on a 25-point scale). She argued that

at first glance, the results of this study seem consistent with the nature of corporate fitness at this time. First to consider is the value of improved health and fitness for employees within the workplace. With this purpose in mind, it should not be surprising that the factors of social service and moral values would provide a great deal of satisfaction for corporate fitness managers. Moreover, given that the backgrounds of the subjects included such emphases as physical education, recreation, health, nursing, and nutrition, it is understandable that the subjects would have a social-service and moral value orientation. (p. 104)

Job Diagnostic Survey

You may recall the job characteristics model of Hackman and Oldham (1980) described in chapter 10. To measure the variables in their model, the authors developed a scale called the Job Diagnostic Survey. Several of the items measure employee satisfaction with job security, pay, co-workers, and supervision. In addition, some items measure growth satisfaction and general satisfaction. Each facet, along with a representative item, is presented in the accompanying sidebar. In taking the survey, respondents express their satisfaction with the aspect of the job described by each item on a seven-point scale ranging from extremely dissatisfied to extremely satisfied. Although several authors have used the entire Job Diagnostic Survey to test the propositions of the job characteristics model, others have used only the satisfaction component in other research.

In our context, Cleave (1993) studied the effects of job characteristics, as described in Hackman and Oldham's (1980) model, on the job satisfaction of administrators of physical education, recreational sport, and intercollegiate athletics in Canada and Illinois. She used the scales that were developed by Hackman and Oldham and refined by Idaszak and Dragow (1987). She found that job characteristics partially influenced the psychological states that, in turn, enhanced general satisfaction and internal work motivation. In addition, job characteristics exerted a direct positive effect on growth satisfaction.

**SAMPLE ITEMS FROM THE JOB DIAGNOSTIC SURVEY:
THE CASE OF A RECREATION FACILITY MANAGER**

- Job security: I am satisfied with how secure things look for me in my future as the recreation facility manager for this organization.
- Pay: I am satisfied with the degree to which I am fairly paid for the work I do as the recreation facility manager.
- Supervision: I am satisfied with the amount of support and guidance I receive from the board of directors.
- Growth: I am satisfied with the amount of independent thought and action I can exercise in my role as the recreation facility manager.
- General: I am satisfied with the kind of work I do as the recreation facility manager.

Choosing a Measure of Satisfaction

The Job Descriptive Index, the Job Diagnostic Survey, and the Minnesota Satisfaction Questionnaire are just three examples of tools for measuring satisfaction in the workplace. Managers in sport and recreation may use any of these methods or an alternative method. What is more critical is the selection of specific facets or components relevant to the job at hand, to the paid and volunteer workers in the organization, and to the clients of the organization. In this context, the characteristics of a good scheme for measuring job satisfaction outlined by Balzer, Smith, and colleagues (1990) should serve as very useful guidelines for us all. According to these authors, satisfaction measures should

- include the principal aspects of job satisfaction;
- be easy to administer and complete;
- be easy to score and interpret;
- apply to all jobs in all organizations;
- show evidence that they are measuring what they are supposed to measure in a consistent fashion; and
- be useful for identifying problems, choosing solutions, and evaluating changes.

The fourth characteristic is meaningful only if one is interested in studying job satisfaction across different organizations. In contrast, a manager who wants to study satisfaction in one organization in order to identify problem areas would disregard that specific guideline and focus instead on including the aspects that are critical and relevant to his or her own organizational context.

Given the uniqueness of certain organizational contexts or occupational characteristics, one may develop a special satisfaction scale applicable to a given context. For instance, Li (1993) investigated the job satisfaction and performance of coaches in Chinese specialized sport schools wherein talented youngsters were trained and groomed to be elite athletes. To do so, he designed a nine-item scale of job satisfaction applicable to that specific organizational context. He found that his subjects were relatively well satisfied with their jobs (i.e., the mean was higher than four on a seven-point scale). He also found that the leadership provided by the school administrator exerted a significant effect on coaches' job satisfaction but did not affect their performance.

With reference to facets of athlete satisfaction, Riemer and Chelladurai (1998) have developed a scale to measure most of the facets described in table 16.3. The scale is named the Athlete Satisfaction Questionnaire (ASQ) and can be obtained from Dr. Harold Riemer or Dr. Chelladurai. Similarly, Ogasawara and Chelladurai (1998) developed a scale to measure satisfaction among sport coaches and named it the Coach Satisfaction Questionnaire (CSQ). The CSQ is available from Dr. Etsuko Ogasawara or Dr. Chelladurai. These efforts show that sport and recreation managers can develop their own satisfaction scales to suit their own purposes.

ACCESSING THE QUESTIONNAIRES

The measurement instruments described here are copyrighted, which means that researchers must secure permission to use them. Access to the measures may be obtained as follows:

Minnesota Satisfaction Questionnaire

The Minnesota Satisfaction Questionnaire is a copyrighted scale that can be purchased by contacting the publishers at the University of Minnesota in the Department of Psychology as a part of the Vocational Psychology Research unit.

Job Descriptive Index

The Job Descriptive Index is a copyrighted scale that can be purchased by contacting the publishers in the Department of Psychology at Bowling Green State University.

Job Diagnostic Survey

The Job Diagnostic Survey is available to the public, so it may be used without the author's permission (Hackman and Oldham 1980). However, interested individuals may contact the publishers of the book, the Addison-Wesley Publishing Company (an imprint of Pearson), to confirm this or to secure the book itself.

Although several instruments are available for measuring job satisfaction, sport managers should judiciously choose the ones that best suit their organizational context. It is also possible for managers to create their own scales to measure satisfaction with specific aspects of the jobs in their organization.

ROLE OF THE SPORT OR RECREATION MANAGER

Given the growing complexity of the sport industry, we must understand that measures of job satisfaction will differ by context (e.g., professional sport organization versus sport-for-development agency), by job (e.g., program director versus ticket sales manager), by category of worker (e.g., paid staff versus volunteer or intern), and by individual (e.g., Beth versus Rick). Thus it is increasingly relevant for sport and recreation managers to investigate measures of job satisfaction, tailor them to their specific workforce, and continually monitor levels of satisfaction (particularly during times of higher and lower workload).

For example, in regard to Hackman and Oldham's (1980) Job Diagnostic Survey, the facets of satisfaction may change depending on the context in which personnel are operating. For example, during planning and preparation to host a small or medium-sized sporting event, supervision satisfaction might be the most influential facet of satisfaction for interns. Specifically, during the chaotic environment of event preparation, a respectful supervisor who provides information when needed can go a long way toward enhancing the satisfaction of interns who are essentially learning on the job (and typically without pay). After the event is staged and schedules become less frantic, the same interns may link satisfaction to the facet of growth. Thus the manager may find that giving the interns increased autonomy and opportunity to exercise independent thought will enhance their job satisfaction.

Sport and recreation managers must also understand the unique satisfaction factors for individuals in different positions in the organization. For example, a membership sales manager for a local fitness club may experience increased satisfaction when the factors of growth and pay are targeted. However, the program director for the same club may find satisfaction with supervision when he or she is granted autonomy in decision making. Thus, managers should both consider job satisfaction measures that are universal and allow for fluctuations and differences where gaps and peaks of satisfaction can be identified. Furthermore, a performance appraisal (as outlined in chapter 13) should include a measure of satisfaction for the purpose of gaining feedback from personnel regarding their own state of mind.

Case Study

Measuring and Increasing Satisfaction

As the human resource manager for a professional hockey team in Europe, you are responsible for training and developing junior ticket sales staff (a total of 25 individuals). The sales staff is responsible for cold-calling potential new ticket buyers, connecting with current ticket purchasers to increase their commitment to attendance (e.g., repeat purchases), and increasing season ticket package sales. In order to increase employee satisfaction and thus reduce turnover, you decide to administer the Job Diagnostic Survey with your employees to determine the factors and level of satisfaction on your sales team as a whole.

At the start of the work week, you call a short meeting to let the team members know that their opinions matter. Then you promptly hand out the surveys. A sales team member asks several questions and expresses worry that filling out the survey might negatively affect her job security. You understand this concern and makes sure to ease the team members' worries by having each person sign a confidentiality agreement noting that no one's name will be linked to his or her survey responses.

Once you analyze the data, you find that in general your staff members have rated the growth and co-worker factors as quite low. This concerns you, but you quickly realize that you can use your skills in human resource management to address these satisfaction factors and ensure that your sales team is satisfied moving forward.

Case Study Tasks

1. Given your team's low levels of satisfaction on the growth and co-worker factors, what can you do to ensure that your staff members are satisfied? List and describe five management strategies that you could adopt to improve these specific satisfaction factors.

2. Create a step-by-step plan to help management measure employee satisfaction on a semiannual basis moving forward. Your plan should include the specific time of year of measurement (with justification), as well as a discussion of the instruments and techniques that will be used for measurement.

CHAPTER PURSUITS

SUMMARY

Job satisfaction consists of the affective reaction that individuals have to their jobs and their experiences in their jobs. It is multifaceted and involves factors such as salary, security, achievement, and challenge; these various facets of job satisfaction may be related to one's needs and values. The concept of job satisfaction can be extended to volunteers, whose work experiences are quite similar to those of paid workers in many respects. Sport and recreation managers can also conceive of their clients as partial employees of their organizations and can view client satisfaction as most critical to their operations. Accordingly, some of the dimensions of service proposed elsewhere are quite relevant to sport and recreation managers. Similarly, the facets of satisfaction developed in the context of leisure studies are germane to sport and recreation operations because most of these services serve as leisure activities for clients.

KEY TERMS

athlete satisfaction 313

discrepancy 304

facets of satisfaction 303

Job Descriptive Index 313

job satisfaction 301

leisure satisfaction 312

measurement 301

Minnesota Satisfaction Questionnaire 318

need satisfaction 306

UNDERSTAND

1. The rationale for developing specific satisfaction questionnaires for athletes and coaches hinges on the fact that athletics is unique in many respects. Can you extend the argument to other sport management contexts? Select

a specific context (e.g., fitness club instructor), explain its unique features, and identify how they would affect an employee's job satisfaction.

2. Compare the theories of job satisfaction presented in the text. Discuss the significance and applicability of these theories to two specific enterprises in sport management (e.g., fitness clubs, golf courses, city recreation departments, intercollegiate athletics, high school athletics).

INTERACT

1. Consider your own experiences as a participant in sport and physical activity. In thinking about these experiences, recall the service providers, other participants, and the settings of your participation. Which of these experiences was most satisfying? Why? Your answer should touch upon all relevant factors, such as the activity itself, your performance in it, the service provider (e.g., leader, teacher, coach), and other participants (e.g., teammates, opponents).

2. Which of your participation experiences considered in the previous question was least satisfying? What factors contributed to your dissatisfaction? Compare your response with the responses of others in your group.

CHAPTER 17

Commitment

LEARNING OBJECTIVES

After reading this chapter, you will be able to

- define and describe organizational commitment;
- understand the bases or motives underlying organizational commitment;
- distinguish between the affective, continuance, and normative forms of commitment;
- distinguish between the different foci (or targets) of organizational commitment;
- explain the antecedents and consequences of organizational commitment;
- distinguish between organizational commitment, occupational commitment, job satisfaction, and job involvement; and
- explain how an organization's supportiveness and a member's sense of personal importance contribute to organizational commitment.

Chapter 16 addresses satisfaction on the part of professional workers, volunteer workers, and clients (the three forms of human resources). More specifically, it focuses on their reactions to, and sense of satisfaction with, their experiences in their jobs and the associated organizational practices. The level of satisfaction of an organization's human resources is an important outcome variable, particularly for sport and recreation organizations. An equally important outcome variable is referred to as **organizational commitment**. One meaning of the word *commitment* is "the state or an instance of being obligated or emotionally impelled" (Merriam-Webster 2016). Thus, friends commit to each other, athletes commit to the pursuit of excellence, health-seeking individuals commit to a training or dieting regimen, and volunteers commit to a cause. It is this meaning—committing oneself to some-

thing—that applies to the concept of organizational commitment.

Our interest in organizational commitment stems from the fact that unless members of an organization are committed to the organization and to its goals and processes, they are not likely to participate wholeheartedly in organizational activities or to discharge their duties to the best of their abilities. An organization may have all the resources it requires, including human resources, yet fail to reach its potential if its members are not committed to the organization. The organization needs its members to expend their efforts in ways that are meaningful for the organization and to exploit material resources to maximal advantage.

From a different perspective, organizational commitment creates a sense of belonging among members and contributes to their well-being. In the

323

absence of organizational commitment, members operate in an alienating environment that may cause them undue stress and unhappiness. Therefore, organizations and their managers must focus on cultivating organizational commitment for the benefit of both the organization and its members.

> Organizational commitment is a critical outcome variable because it underscores a worker's whole-hearted participation in organizational activities, exertion of his or her efforts, and performance in those activities. The collective commitment of workers contributes to organizational success.

This chapter addresses the key concept of organizational commitment—that is, the extent to which workers in an organization are committed to the organization, its goals and values, and its processes. The chapter begins by defining organizational commitment and describing various forms of such commitment in terms of the bases of commitment (i.e., the reasons or rationale) and the foci of commitment (i.e., the specific targets of attachment). The chapter also describes the antecedents and consequences of organizational commitment and compares organizational commitment with occupational commitment, **job involvement**, and job satisfaction.

Like many other topics in organizational psychology, organizational commitment has been conceptualized and defined in different ways. For instance, Buchanan (1974) defined organizational commitment as "a partisan affective attachment to the goals and values of an organization, to one's role in relation to these goals and values, and to the organization for its own sake, apart from its purely instrumental worth" (p. 533). The emphasis here is on the organization's goals and values and the individual's role in relation to those goals and values. These two elements contribute to the development of a psychological attachment to the organization.

In another definition, Mowday, Porter, and Steers (1982) described organizational commitment as

> the relative strength of an individual's identification with and involvement in a particular organization. Conceptually, it can be categorized by at least three factors: (a) a strong belief in and acceptance of the organization's goals and values; (b) a willingness to exert considerable effort on behalf of the organization; and

(c) a strong desire to maintain membership in the organization. (p. 27)

In expanding the meaning of organizational commitment from a mere attachment to a willingness to work on behalf of the organization and a desire to continue membership in the organization, Mowday et al. (1982) provided a greater impetus to the study of organizational commitment.

These definitions refer to the attitudinal and affective elements of an organization. With the development of a positive attitude toward and liking for the organization and its goals, individuals are likely to continue membership in the organization and to exert effort on its behalf. For example, an employee of a city recreation department may accept the organizational goals and values of providing high-quality recreation opportunities for community members. The employee may also may perceive the department's processes for providing those services to be purposeful and effective. Furthermore, the individual may perceive his or her role in the total operation as quite meaningful. These perceptions and feelings may lead the person to develop a sense of commitment to the organization.

In contrast to this view of organizational commitment, H.S. Becker (1960) suggested that "commitment comes into being when a person, by making a side bet, links extraneous interest with a consistent line of activity" (p. 32). Becker's position was that an individual may get locked into a line of activity (e.g., continuing membership in an organization) because of his or her past investments in an activity or because of the costs associated with discontinuing that activity. According to Becker, side bets can be broadly categorized into the following groups: (a) generalized cultural expectations (i.e., the expectations of important reference groups), (b) self-presentation concerns (i.e., consistency in presenting a public image), (c) impersonal bureaucratic arrangements (i.e., organizational policies relating rewards to long-term employment), (d) individual adjustments to social positions (i.e., confining oneself to one set of skills relevant to a particular organization), and (e) nonwork concerns (i.e., attachment to other factors outside the organization).

In this view, organizational commitment is based on the material cost of withdrawing from an organization and losing the side bets. In the example of the city recreation department employee, the person might evaluate the investments he or she has made in terms of time and effort, friendships, and development of skills specific to that organization that are not transferable to other organizations. The individual might then consider the cost of leaving the organization in terms of the loss of those investments and other accrued advantages, such as pension and benefits. Along with the effort and time needed to move to another organization, the person might evaluate the existing opportunities for such movement. When the perceived benefits and ease of moving to another organization fall short of the "sunken" costs in leaving the present organization, the individual is likely to continue membership in the current organization. In these calculations, the focus is on the individual and his or her courses of action (i.e., continuing or discontinuing membership in the organization) rather than on the organization itself.

Wiener (1982) articulated a third perspective on organizational commitment. In his view, organizational commitment is normative in the sense that individuals tend to be committed to the organization because of their belief that it is the right thing to do. This belief is born out of one's personal values of loyalty and duty. Wiener went on to suggest that organizations must explicitly state their value systems and recruit and hire employees who share that value system, which in turn cultivates their sense of loyalty and duty to the organization. Examples of this type of commitment are seen in the context of military and athletic teams. Soldiers and athletes stick with their teams no matter how adverse the conditions may be.

MULTIDIMENSIONALITY OF ORGANIZATIONAL COMMITMENT

The three contrasting perspectives on organizational commitment that have been described—liking for the organization, cost of leaving the organization, and sense of loyalty and duty—suggest that an individual can commit to the organization for more than one reason. That is, people may be committed to an organization because they like it, they are constrained from leaving by the heavy cost of moving elsewhere, or they believe that being committed is right. As noted by T.E. Becker and colleagues (T.E. Becker 1992; T.E. Becker, Billings, Eveleth, and Gilbert 1996), it is useful to distinguish the *bases* of organizational commitment (i.e., the motives or reasons for it) from the *foci* of commitment (i.e., the individuals, groups, or units an employee is attached to). The following section elaborates on the bases and **foci of commitment**.

VIEWPOINT

When examining the effect of culture on organizational commitment, Meyer, Stanley, et al.'s (2012) meta-analysis suggests that

> organizations operating in multiple countries may find differences in the nature and level of employee commitment. These differences, particularly those involving NC [normative commitment], might be anticipated based on differences in cultural values. This could have important implications for management practice. For example, there is some evidence suggesting that cultural values moderate the effects of HRM practices on commitment (Williamson et al. 2009). The effects of increases in autonomy and pay level were greater for employees holding individualist as opposed to collectivist values. There is also some evidence that cultural values moderate the relations between commitment and its consequences. . . . For example, NC has been found to relate more strongly to turnover intentions and performance in collectivist compared to individualist cultures. Therefore, as noted above, understanding the implications of cultural differences in commitment will require looking beyond mean differences to consider differences in associations with other variables of interest (e.g., HRM practices; leadership style; retention; performance). (p. 242)

Bases of Commitment

In their work on organizational commitment, Meyer and Allen (1997) described organizational commitment in terms of three distinct components:

- Affective commitment
- Continuance commitment
- Normative commitment

In the words of Meyer and Allen,

> Affective commitment refers to the employee's emotional attachment to, identification with, and involvement in the organization. Employees with a strong affective commitment continue employment with the organization because they *want to*. Continuance commitment refers to an awareness of the costs associated with leaving the organization. Employees whose primary link to the organization is based on continuance commitment remain because they *need to*. Finally, normative commitment reflects a feeling of obligation to continue employment. Employees with a high level of normative commitment feel that they *ought to* remain with the organization. (p. 67, emphasis added)

The three components, then, are indeed based on three different reasons for individuals to be committed to the organization. Figure 17.1 illustrates these three components of organizational commitment and their content.

Affective Commitment

Affective commitment, also referred to as identification commitment (O'Reilly and Chatman 1986), reflects "the degree to which an individual is psychologically attached to an employing organization through feelings, such as loyalty, affection, warmth, belongingness, fondness, happiness, pleasure, and so on" (Jaros, Jermier, Koehler, and Sincich 1993, p. 954). That is, the employee approves of and likes the organization and its processes, and the extent of this liking impels him or her to commit to, and work hard on behalf of, the organization. This emotional attachment is facilitated by the supervisor's leadership and the social and task relations in the work group.

Continuance Commitment

Continuance commitment, a derivative of H.S. Becker's (1960) side-bet theory, refers to attachment to an employing organization based on "the degree to which an individual experiences a sense of being locked in place because of the high costs of leaving" (Jaros et al. 1993, p. 953). As noted earlier, continuance commitment is based on cost–benefit analysis of the choice between remaining with the organization and leaving it. O'Reilly and Chatman (1986)

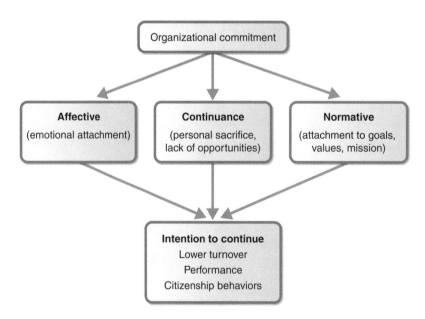

FIGURE 17.1 Components of organizational commitment.

DIVERSITY MANAGEMENT OF HUMAN RESOURCES

"The most important rationale for management of diversity is the optimization of individual potential and the quality of life for all" (Chelladurai 2014, p. 355). The integrative framework for managing diversity includes an important connection between proactive diversity management and positive individual outcomes. For example, an employee may feel more valued by the organization when management cares about his or her development and quality of life. Thus, proactively valuing diversity can create an emotional or affective connection between an employee and the organization in that the organization is viewed as a place where the person can reach her or his potential. This connection may be particularly relevant in the sport and recreation context, where individuals are striving to be the best they can be in a competitive environment. Furthermore, increased commitment is correlated with increased employee performance (T.E. Becker et al. 1996; Mathieu and Zajac 1990), thus making proactive diversity management essential for enhanced outcomes on both the individual and the organizational level.

labeled this component "compliance commitment," and some other authors refer to it as "calculative commitment" (Mathieu and Zajac 1990, p. 172).

The emphasis in this form of commitment is on whether the individual will continue his or her membership in the organization; it does not reflect a person's concern with organizational goals or their achievement. Therefore, even if the person decides to continue with the organization, he or she may not put forth any extra effort for the benefit of the organization but may instead work only up to the minimum expected. In other words, the person may simply comply with the minimal requirements of the organization (hence the term "compliance commitment").

As noted earlier, one factor underlying continuance commitment is the cost of leaving the organization, and the other is the lack of opportunity to move to another organization. These two factors are related but separate and distinct; therefore, it is fruitful to view continuance commitment as consisting of personal sacrifice and lack of alternatives, and this view is supported by evidence (Meyer, Allen, and Gellatly 1990; McGee and Ford 1987). In fact, these two components have been labeled "continuance commitment–low alternatives" and "continuance commitment–high sacrifice" (Meyer and Allen 1997).

For example, a manager in a city recreation department may find that other cities do not have openings and thus may continue to work in the present department. Even if other cities do have

job openings, the manager may decide to continue in the present job because of the sacrifices involved in making a move, such as losing pension benefits, leaving friends and family, and disrupting the education of one's children. The notion of perceived sacrifices is what H.S. Becker (1960) implied in his exposition of side bets, or sunken costs. Recently, Powell and Meyer (2004) reported strong relationships between H.S. Becker's (1960) five classes of side bets and continuance commitment–high sacrifice.

Normative Commitment

The third component of organizational commitment, **normative commitment**,

> is the degree to which an individual is psychologically attached through an internalization of [the organization's] goals, values, and missions. This form of commitment differs from affective commitment because it reflects a sense of duty, an obligation, or calling, to work in the organization, but not necessarily emotional attachment. It differs from continuance commitment because it does not necessarily fluctuate with personal calculation of inducements or sunk costs. (Jaros et al. 1993, p. 955)

For instance, a worker may identify with organizational goals and take it as a duty or obligation to work in that organization and facilitate the achievement of those goals. Thus normative commitment is distinguished from both affective commitment (which reflects an emotional attachment to the organization) and from continuance motivation (which involves calculation of inducements and costs) (Jaros et al. 1993).

Meyer and Allen (1997) suggested that these three components are not mutually exclusive—that all three components may bear on individuals in their decision to continue membership in an organization and to work toward the organization's goals. For instance, the recreation employee in the previous example might continue to work for the department because the organizational environment, including leadership and work group processes, is acceptable (i.e., affective commitment); because the cost of leaving is prohibitive (i.e., continuance commitment); or because he or she holds a conviction about being involved in providing recreation services for the community (i.e., normative commitment).

In summary, the three components of organizational commitment (i.e., affective, continuance, and normative commitment) stem from three different bases: emotional attachment, cost–benefit analysis, and internalization and acceptance of organizational goals, respectively. The natural question now is, Which of these forms of commitment is more critical to the organization?

From an organization's perspective, the most desirable situation is for the employee to be committed to the organization based on pride and desire for membership (i.e., the affective component) and to share a sense of duty and obligation to achieve organizational goals (i.e., the normative compo-

nent). An organization can expect such an employee to remain in and work hard for the organization. In contrast, commitment based only on emotional attachment increases the chances that the employee will remain with the organization but does not guarantee maximal effort toward achieving organizational goals. On the other hand, internalizing organizational goals without emotional attachment leads to the expectation that the worker will do his or her best to achieve organizational goals but does not exclude the possibility that the worker may leave for another organization with similar goals. Regarding continuance commitment, the member may remain with the organization without putting forth best efforts on behalf of the organization. Any extra effort put forth at all would be based only on calculations of personal benefit.

Foci of Commitment

In the discussion of components of organizational commitment, the focus is on an employee's commitment to the organization as a whole, and that focus is reflected in the label "organizational commitment." However, because an organization may have various goals and because it is made up of several units and constituencies, an employee may be committed differentially to these aspects of the organization (T.E. Becker 1992; T.E. Becker et al. 1996; Reichers 1985). For example, a university athletics department includes units such as facility management, event management, marketing, ticketing, and personnel. From another perspective, the department also has different constituencies,

VIEWPOINT

Taken together, considerable evidence across a wide variety of samples and performance indicators suggests that employees with strong affective commitment to the organization will be more valuable than those with weak commitment. Similar, albeit weaker, effects are reported for normative commitment. The picture that emerges from the existing research on continuance commitment, however, is rather disconcerting. As with affective and normative commitment, employees who believe that strong costs are associated with leaving their organization are unlikely to do so. At the same time, however, they are also less likely to make positive contributions to the organization. Indeed, evidence suggests that employees with strong continuance commitment might be poorer performers, engage in fewer citizenship behaviors, and exhibit more dysfunctional behaviors than those with weak continuance commitment (Meyer and Allen 1997, p. 38).

O'REILLY AND CHATMAN'S SCHEME OF ORGANIZATIONAL COMMITMENT

O'Reilly and Chatman (1986) proposed a somewhat different scheme to describe three bases of organizational commitment: compliance, identification, and internalization. According to these authors,

> Compliance occurs when attitudes and behaviors are adopted not because of shared beliefs but simply to gain specific rewards. . . . Identification occurs when an individual accepts influence [in order] to establish or maintain a satisfying relationship; that is, an individual may feel proud to be part of a group, respecting its values and accomplishments without adopting them as his or her own. Internalization occurs when influence is accepted because the induced attitudes and behavior are congruent with one's own values; that is, the values of the individual and the group or organization are the same. (p. 493)

Although O'Reilly and Chatman's (1986) scheme is somewhat similar to that of Meyer and Allen (1991, 1997), there is a significant difference between the compliance commitment in O'Reilly and Chatman's model and the continuance commitment in Meyer and Allen's model. Specifically, continuance commitment refers to an employee's continuing membership in the organization but does not indicate anything about that employee's behavior and performance. In contrast, compliance commitment not only reflects an employee's decision to continue membership in the organization but also suggests that the employee will do whatever it takes to gain his or her personal rewards.

---

such as the athletes themselves, the general student body, alumni, university administrators, the general public, the media, donors, suppliers, and the NCAA. From yet another perspective, the department is characterized by hierarchical levels (e.g., athletics director, assistant directors, and supervisors of various units), as well as work groups within each unit.

An employee of the athletics department may be attached to one or more of these elements to varying degrees. For example, an employee in the ticketing unit may be more committed to that unit and to the supervisor and co-workers in the unit and may be less committed to the unit concerned with facility management. As another example, a coach may be committed, to varying degrees, to the coaching occupation, the university's president and athletics director, other coaches in the department, and the athletes themselves. In contrast, in some cases, an individual's commitment may not extend beyond his or her particular unit at all. For example, an academic counselor may be quite committed to the unit and the athletes it serves but may not extend that commitment to other units or to the athletics department as a whole.

These different foci are not mutually exclusive; that is, a person may be simultaneously attached to the organization's goals, management, workers, clients, and owners. The strength of such attachments, however, may vary across the different targets. Organizational commitment, then, is best viewed as a collection of multiple commitments to various constituencies of the organization (Reichers 1985). Furthermore, taken cumulatively, commitments to all of these foci indicate the person's commitment to the organization as a whole (see figure 17.2).

 A worker may be committed to organizational goals, units, hierarchical levels, co-workers, and clients on one or more of the bases of commitment: affective commitment (i.e., emotional attachment), continuance commitment (i.e., costs of discontinuing membership), and normative commitment (i.e., conviction that one ought to strive to achieve organizational goals).

FIGURE 17.2 Organizational commitment as a collection of commitments.

OCCUPATIONAL COMMITMENT

The conclusion that commitment can be directed toward the organization, its leadership, a work group, co-workers, or organizational goals raises the possibility of such psychological attachment to other entities in the organizational context. Indeed, organizational commitment has been contrasted with what is referred to as occupational commitment (Blau, Paul, and St. John 1993; Meyer and Allen 1997; Vandenberg and Scarpello 1994). Occupational commitment refers to a person's belief in and acceptance of the values of his or her chosen occupation or line of work and to a willingness to maintain membership in that occupation (Vandenberg and Scarpello). That is, employees in a sport organization may be committed differentially to the

VOLUNTEERS' ORGANIZATIONAL COMMITMENT

Although the global concept of organizational commitment is pertinent to both paid and volunteer workers, the three components of organizational commitment (i.e., affective, continuance, and normative) are likely to carry different implications for volunteer and paid workers. As covered in chapter 2, an individual may volunteer for altruistic reasons, and his or her choice of one organization over another may be a function of the extent to which the organizational processes and work group characteristics are congruent with that individual's needs and preferences. Thus, a volunteer's continued participation in a particular organization may reflect both normative commitment born out of altruistic motives and affective commitment born out of liking for the organizational process and interpersonal interactions.

The implication for sport managers is that although one can expect a volunteer to carry out the assigned tasks adequately based on normative commitment (i.e., altruistic reasons), one can expect greater motivation and performance if affective commitment is also cultivated. Sport managers should also note that a volunteer's normative commitment could be extended to other organizations with similar goals. That is, the volunteer might switch allegiance to another organization if he or she does not develop an affective commitment to the present organization.

In other words, continuance commitment may be less relevant to volunteer workers than to paid workers because no monetary sacrifice is involved. However, a volunteer may consider his or her costs, in terms of efforts expended on behalf of the organization and the status and prestige gained in an organization, as sunken costs. For example, a volunteer member of a national sport governing body might be reluctant to leave that organization for another, similar one. This volunteer may see sunken costs in the time and effort that he or she has spent building up the organization, the recognition that he or she receives from followers of the sport, and the network that he or she has built. Concern with these costs moderates any thought of leaving the organization.

PROFILES OF ORGANIZATIONAL COMMITMENT

We have identified various bases or components of organizational commitment, as well as the various foci, or targets, of such commitment. These distinctions provide the basis for the grid presented in table 17.1. The table illustrates the differing profiles of two employees, Jane and John, in the same work unit (e.g., the marketing unit of a university athletics department), according to their bases and foci of commitment. Jane and John are shown to differ in the extent to which they are committed to various foci and also in the bases of their commitments. Specifically, Jane is more committed to co-workers than John is, whereas John is more committed to the supervisor than Jane is. The two are committed equally, however, to the work unit, although their bases of commitment differ—Jane's is normative, whereas John's is affective. Such differences can also be found in commitment to other aspects of the department.

Jane and John are placed in different cells of this grid to illustrate only the possibility that Jane (or John) may have a higher level of one or more aspects of organizational commitment than the other does. The placement does not show the absolute strength of commitment in any one cell. For example, even though Jane is shown as having a higher level of affective commitment to the organization than John does, her level in this form of commitment may be lower than that of other members. The level could also be lower than that of her commitment to other aspects.

TABLE 17.1 Grid of Bases and Foci of Commitment

| FOCI | BASES | | |
	AFFECTIVE (EMOTIONAL ATTACHMENT)	CONTINUANCE (COST–BENEFIT ANALYSIS)	NORMATIVE (ACCEPTANCE OF ORGANIZATIONAL GOALS)
Organization	Jane	John	
Management			
Supervisor	John		
Work unit	John		Jane
Co-workers			Jane

organization and to their occupation. As suggested in chapter 3, professionals are characterized by a sense of loyalty to their profession. Such loyalty is independent of one's commitment to the employing organizations. This view can be extended to all occupations. For example, a marketing specialist and an athletic trainer in an athletics department may be committed as much to their respective occupations as they are to the department itself.

Conceivably, occupational commitment and organizational commitment can even contradict each other. As Vandenberg and Scarpello (1994) noted, the occupational value system may posit that values such as collegial control, self-control, autonomy, and loyalty to clients are juxtaposed against organizational value systems of organizational or managerial control, discipline, and loyalty to the organization. Vandenberg and Scarpello also pointed out that the occupational values system is learned over a period of time, before entry into any given organization, whereas the organizational value system is learned only after entry into an organization. Given these contradictory value systems, managers can expect that as occupational commitment increases, organizational commitment decreases, and vice versa.

It is also possible for an individual's commitment to the occupation to be congruent with his or her commitment to the organization. Consider, for example, a private sport marketing firm that employs three marketing professionals. The firm may allow its employees considerable independence, autonomy, and initiative to identify and implement profitable projects. If so, then an employee's activities are constrained by relatively few rules and procedures. Such an approach is consistent with the entrepreneurial nature of the firm. In this case, the values and goals of the marketing occupation and those of the firm are likely to be congruent; therefore, an individual's commitments to these two entities may not be in conflict.

In contrast, if the same marketing professional works in a university athletics department, he or she may find that adherence to occupational values is at odds with organizational values and processes. More specifically, the university department's greater emphasis on educational values and bureaucratic rules and regulations are, to some extent, inconsistent with the occupational values of marketing. Thus, in this case, the possibility of conflict exists between organizational and occupational commitment.

DEVELOPMENT AND EFFECTS OF ORGANIZATIONAL COMMITMENT

So far, the chapter has described organizational commitment from the perspectives of the motives behind one's psychological attachment to an organization (i.e., bases of commitment) and the targets of such attachment (i.e., foci of commitment). In addition to understanding the meaning of commitment in its various manifestations, it is necessary to gain insight into the development of organizational commitment and its effects on other organizationally relevant factors. The following sections deal with these issues as **antecedents and consequences of organizational commitment**.

VIEWPOINT

According to Griffeth, Horn, and Gaertner (2000), whether a volunteer stays or leaves a volunteer position with an organization depends largely on the person's level of commitment. Thus, we must understand the conditions in which volunteers commit to an organization or role. Bang, Ross, and Reio (2012) suggested that volunteer motivation connects directly to an individual's values and that the volunteer's commitment is affected by how well those values are served. In their study of 214 volunteers with nonprofit sport organizations in the United States, these authors concluded that allowing volunteers an opportunity to express positive emotions during a volunteer experience can increase the likelihood of the volunteer committing to the organization for a longer period of time.

Antecedents of Organizational Commitment

Researchers have made several attempts to relate commitment to specific variables at the personal, work-group, and organizational levels. For example, an analysis of previous studies (Mathieu and Zajac 1990) showed a positive relationship between organizational commitment and personal characteristics of age and perceived competence; job characteristics of skill variety, challenge, and job scope; and leader characteristics of initiating structure, consideration, communication, and participative leadership. In contrast, organizational commitment was related negatively to perceived role ambiguity, role conflict, and role overload.

Although most of these relationships were moderate, organizational commitment was correlated more strongly with perceived personal competence, job challenge, job scope, leader communication, and participative leadership. The key point for management is that these more strongly correlated variables (all but personal competence) fall within management's sphere of control. That is, management can manipulate them to facilitate the development of organizational commitment. For example, job scope can be enhanced to include greater skill variety and challenge (job design and job enrichment are covered in chapter 10). Similarly, a manager can consciously modify his or her leadership to be more communicative and participative (an in-depth review of leadership is provided in chapter 12). In sum, organizations can provide an environment well suited for individuals to grow and develop their competence.

Meyer and Allen (1997) derived two significant themes underlying several research studies that showed a relationship between organizational commitment and several antecedent factors. In their view, good work experiences of employees give the impression that "the organization is supportive of its employees, treats them fairly, and enhances their sense of personal importance and competence by appearing to value their contributions to the organization" (p. 46). The two themes embedded in this statement are (a) **supportiveness and fairness** from the organization's perspective and (b) **personal importance and competence** from the individual's perspective.

Although supportiveness and fairness should always be reflected in the general policies and procedures of an organization, they should also be demonstrated in the manager's face-to-face and day-to-day interactions with subordinates. As discussed in chapter 12, managers need to clarify a worker's role and how it relates to organizational goals and processes, provide the necessary coaching and guidance to enhance the employee's competence, and impress on the worker the significance of his or her contributions. In doing so, the manager is likely to demonstrate supportiveness while enhancing the employee's sense of personal importance and competence. Recalling the discussion of organizational justice in chapter 9, we know that perceived fairness is critical for the development of organizational commitment; therefore, procedural, distributive, and interactional justice must be maintained if workers are to develop organizational commitment.

Kent and Sullivan (2003) found that high scores on the four dimensions of self-efficacy (Feltz, Chase, Moritz, and Sullivan 1999) were significantly correlated with Meyer and Allen's (1997) affective and normative dimensions of organizational commitment. We could interpret this finding to mean that those who feel competent in their jobs are likely to be more committed to their organization. In other words, one's self-efficacy is an antecedent of organizational commitment. Therefore, organizational practices (e.g., creating person–task fit, training employees) should be focused on cultivating a sense of task-specific self-efficacy in employees.

Embeddedness and Organizational Commitment

Mitchell, Holtom, Lee, and Erez (2001) introduced the notion of embeddedness, which represents a collection of links that tie an employee to an organization. Job embeddedness is "like a net or a web in which an individual can become stuck" (p. 1104). As the links can vary in myriad ways, individuals can be embedded in different ways. Job embeddedness can be described in terms of (a) the number of links an individual has to other people or activities, (b) the extent of fit between the individual and the job and community, and (c) the ease of breaking the links.

For example, a sport manager might find that her children enjoy going to local schools and are receiving a very good education. Because she does not want to uproot her children from such a comfortable environment, she may not wish to apply

TECHNOLOGY IN HUMAN RESOURCE MANAGEMENT

Allen and Shanock (2013) noted that the way in which an employee is socialized into an organization can significantly increase the individual's perceived organizational support, thus strengthening his or her embeddedness and affective commitment. More generally, it has become increasingly relevant for managers to think critically about effective ways to socialize employees into an organization. As noted by DiMicco et al. (2008) social networking platforms (e.g., Beehive, discussed in chapter 15) provide employees with opportunities to connect with colleagues in new and meaningful ways, both in and out of the physical office space. These platforms provide an innovative way for employees to share work and life information (at their discretion), thus providing a mechanism to socialize new and current employees while increasing employee embeddedness and commitment.

for positions elsewhere. This sense of embedded-ness has nothing to do with her experiences in her organization, but it may exert a strong influence in her commitment to the organization. Organizational commitment can also be affected by other attachments to the community or to the climate. In another example, a coach might become imbedded in an organization due to the facets of satisfaction and the two types of commitment (organizational and occupational).

Consequences of Organizational Commitment

The most critical outcomes that researchers have studied as consequences of commitment are performance and **turnover**. By definition, committed workers stay with the organization (thus reducing turnover) and work toward attaining organizational goals (i.e., delivering good performance). From a practical perspective, sport managers need to be concerned with both outcomes; that is, their interest lies in retaining good performers.

Performance

Unfortunately, the relationship between organizational commitment and performance is not strong. This low commitment–performance relationship can be attributed to several factors, such as the variation in abilities of individuals, the resources made available to individuals, and the degree to which the task is dependent on other people or tasks. Furthermore, as Mathieu and Zajac (1990) noted, the commitment–performance relationship may also be either strengthened or weakened by organizational policies themselves:

> The relationship between organizational commitment and performance is likely to be moderated by such factors as pay policies. One would expect that calculated commitment [i.e., continuance commitment] would exhibit high positive correlation with performance in instances where pay is tied closely to performance (e.g., piece-rate system), and less so where there is little connection (e.g., straight salary systems). Alternately, attitudinal commitment [affective commitment] could be expected to correlate more positively with performance when role expectations are

clearly defined than when they are ambiguous. (p. 185)

T.E. Becker and colleagues (1996) raised another issue affecting the commitment–performance relationship. As discussed earlier, an employee may be committed differentially to different foci, such as work group, supervisor, and organization. In this scenario, the work group and the supervisor are closer to the employee than the wider organization is in terms of task and social interactions:

> It seems to us that norms regarding in-role behaviors are often established by such local foci as supervisors and work groups. If so, their commitment to local foci should lead to an acceptance of performance norms. . . . We suspect that, for most employees, local foci are psychologically more proximal than are global foci [e.g., organizational commitment]. . . . Further, because of their proximity and regular interaction with employees, local foci are probably more effective than global foci in monitoring, rewarding, and influencing employee behaviors. Proximity and regular interactions also make it easier for employees to seek and receive feedback on actions consistent with the values and goals of local foci. (T.E. Becker et al. 1996, p. 467)

This comment points to the pivotal role of the work group and the supervisor in cultivating organizational commitment in an individual employee. That is, the group norms are reflected in the extent to which the work group and the supervisor share the organizational goals and values and work toward achieving them—when examining shared goals and values, a high degree of organizational commitment characterizes the work group itself. Specifically, to the extent that the employee is committed to the work group or the supervisor, he or she is more likely to abide by the group norms and, in turn, exhibit organizational commitment.

Turnover

As compared with the commitment–performance relationship, the relationships of organizational commitment to intention to leave and to actual turnover are stronger. This is a critical finding because turnover can be costly to an organization in terms of recruiting new candidates and training

VIEWPOINT

With regard to the low correlation between organizational commitment and outcomes of interest, Meyer and Allen (1997) pointed out that even small changes in employee performance attributed to organizational commitment may greatly influence an organization's bottom line. Performance is a function of many factors, including an individual's ability and experience, the resources available to the individual, and the individual's motivation. A manager can expect commitment to enhance an employee's motivation, which is fundamental to increased performance. At the same time, task design may control and constrain performance, as is the case in an assembly line. Performance may also differ according to the foci of commitment. However, small increments in organizationally relevant outcomes as a function of different foci of commitment would make an organization competitive.

CORRELATES OF ORGANIZATIONAL COMMITMENT

One of the difficulties that both researchers and practitioners face is that organizational commitment is closely related to several other work attitudes. The two work attitudes more closely related to organizational commitment are job satisfaction and job involvement. Although the relationships between these work attitudes are strong, the attitudes are distinct enough to be considered separately, particularly because they are critical to organizational success.

Organizational Commitment and Job Satisfaction

As discussed by Meyer and Allen (1997), research permits the conclusion that organizational commitment is distinguishable from job satisfaction. Mowday et al. (1982) distinguished commitment from satisfaction in stating that commitment is a global affective response to the whole organization and that job satisfaction is an immediate and limited reaction to job experiences. Conceivably, an individual may be attached to the organization because his or her values are consistent with the goals of the organization or because of the status of the organization. However, the specific job that the individual performs may not be satisfying to the extent that it does not meet individual needs and desires. Thus, organizational commitment is more global, encompassing all the attributes of the organization, whereas job satisfaction is confined to one's job.

Mowday et al. (1982) also noted two other distinctions between organizational commitment and job satisfaction. First, organizational commitment takes time to develop, whereas job satisfaction is often an immediate reaction to the job. This distinction exists probably because the individual is exposed to the job on a daily basis and because exposure to organizational processes and practices geared toward achieving the organization's goals takes time to affect the individual. Consider, for example, the distribution of organizational rewards, such as salary increases. The process is normally an annual

them. In addition, high employee turnover may tarnish the organization's image sufficiently to trigger the perception that the organization is a bad place to work. Thus, sport managers must be concerned with organizational commitment as a critical outcome variable in itself despite the fact that it is not correlated strongly with performance.

Workers who perceived having personal competence and experiencing good job scope and leadership scored higher than others on organizational commitment. This finding matters because lower organizational commitment leads to higher intention to leave and to higher actual turnover, which is a costly proposition for the organization.

one, and the evaluation of the equitability of distribution of rewards is rather subjective. Therefore, any judgments that an individual makes about the reward system are likely to result from experiences over a period of time. Thus, cultivation of organizational commitment takes time.

The other attribute marking a contrast between organizational commitment and job satisfaction is the variability of the feelings. Although organizational commitment takes more time to develop, it is less variable in the sense that individuals do not easily change their liking for and allegiance to the organization. In contrast, job satisfaction can change rapidly with any changes in job attributes. For example, an individual in an athletics department who is dissatisfied with his or her job at the moment may become satisfied if the job is altered to include some challenge and autonomy.

As compared with job satisfaction, organizational commitment is more global, takes more time to develop, and is less variable. Job satisfaction is an immediate reaction to job experiences that varies with changes in the job situation.

Organizational Commitment and Job Involvement

Blau (1986) and Blau and Boal (1987, 1989) highlighted the distinction between job involvement and organizational commitment. They defined job involvement as "the extent to which an individual identifies psychologically with his/her job," whereas organizational commitment is "the extent to which an employee identifies with the nature and goals of a particular organization and wishes to maintain membership in that organization" (Blau and Boal 1989, p. 116). Thus, "job involvement and organizational commitment represent two related but distinct types of work-related attitudes because of their different referents" (Blau 1986, p. 578). The referents are, of course, the job and the organization, respectively. To some, the job is an important source of their self-image, so they do care about the job and tend to identify psychologically with it.

Blau and Boal (1987) also suggested that a job may satisfy one's intrinsic growth needs while the organization may offer social and other extrinsic rewards. This idea that the job and the organization

may satisfy different sets of needs is the essence of Herzberg's (1968) two-factor theory, discussed in chapter 8, and of Hackman and Oldham's (1980) job characteristics model, described in chapter 10. In another difference, job involvement implies that individuals who are highly involved with their job spend their time and effort on tasks associated with the job; in contrast, individuals who have a high level of organizational commitment help to facilitate group maintenance and goal accomplishment. Thus, both job involvement and organizational commitment are functional; more important, they are not antithetical to each other.

Although both job involvement and organizational commitment are desirable from the perspective of the organization, individuals may differ in the relative emphasis they place on these two psychological attachments. That is, a person can have a high level of both job involvement and organizational commitment, a low level of both, or a high level of one and a low level of the other. Blau and Boal (1987) categorized people in an organization into four classes based on high and low combinations of job involvement and organizational commitment (see figure 17.3).

Individuals in the first class, who are referred to as institutionalized stars, have a high level of both job involvement and organizational commitment. These individuals make ideal employees. However, although the organization benefits from such individuals, it also suffers great costs when they leave the organization—in having to replace them, incurring immediate productivity losses, and experiencing disruption of communication flow. People in the second class, referred to as lone wolves, are involved in the job but are not as committed to the organization or its goals as are the institutionalized stars. Because lone wolves are not attached to the organization, they are likely to move on to another organization if it provides better task-related opportunities.

Individuals in the third class, referred to as corporate citizens, do not see their work as personally important but are attached to the organization and its goals. Blau and Boal (1987) suggested that corporate citizens are not as valuable as institutionalized stars or even lone wolves. Yet their role in the organization is significant to the extent that they contribute to work-group cohesiveness and inter-unit cooperation. The fourth category consists of individuals, labeled "apathetics," who have a low level of both job involvement and organizational commitment. To them, the work is not important personally, and the organization and its goals are

Organizational commitment

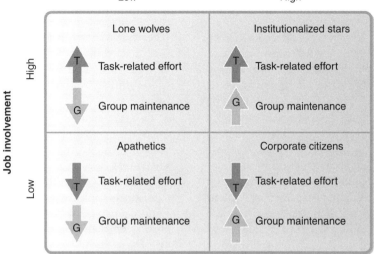

FIGURE 17.3   Interaction of organizational commitment and job involvement.
Adapted from Blau and Boal 1987.

not appealing. They tend to exert the minimal effort and therefore "represent the least valued members to an organization" (Blau and Boal 1987, p. 296). Departure of any member falling into this final category may benefit the organization in the sense that somebody who belongs in any of the other three functional categories can replace the employee who left.

Scholars in sport management have investigated commitment in sport organizations. One study examined differences in organizational and occupational commitment among NCAA Division I coaches, NCAA Division III coaches, and Japanese coaches (Chelladurai and Ogasawara 2003). No significant difference was found between Division I and Division III coaches in either organizational commitment or occupational commitment. However, the American coaches were significantly higher than the Japanese coaches in occupational commitment, whereas Japanese coaches expressed higher levels of organizational commitment than did American coaches.

The authors (Chelladurai and Ogasawara 2003) suggested that this difference might be related to cultural differences between the Americans and the Japanese. Given that lifetime employment and loyalty to the employing organization are pervasive in Japanese culture, it was not surprising that Japanese coaches expressed higher levels of organizational commitment. Even so, both American and Japanese

VIEWPOINT

Although organizational commitment may facilitate retention of employees and increase their efforts, this commitment can also have a downside. As Avanzi, Zaniboni, Balducci, and Fraccaroli (2014) noted,

Indeed, employees strongly identified with and committed to their organizations become more willing to devote effort to achieving organizational goals, but this may subject them to numerous stressors, and in the long term, they may suffer exhaustion. (p. 455)

This pitfall may be particularly problematic in sport organizations where employees have been found to have higher levels of employee identification due to their level of sport fandom, which in turn leads to relatively high levels of commitment (Swanson and Kent 2015).

coaches were more committed to the occupation than to the organization (the study measured organizational and occupational commitment as unidimensional constructs).

Other research has measured the four dimensions of commitment—affective, calculative–high cost, calculative–low alternatives, and normative commitment—of NCAA Division I and Division III coaches (B.A. Turner and Chelladurai 2005). The ratings of all four commitment dimensions were unaffected by a coach's division, gender, and marital status. However, high scores on each of these dimensions were negatively correlated with intention to leave. Similarly, those who were committed to the occupation in the affective, normative, and continuance–low alternatives dimensions were less likely to leave the occupation. This study also found that the extent of commitment to the organization was significantly correlated with both perceived and actual performance.

Job involvement differs from organizational commitment because the foci of attachment are the job and the organization, respectively. In addition, job involvement is based on intrinsic rewards, whereas organizational commitment is fostered by extrinsic rewards. On the basis of the relative strengths of job involvement and organizational commitment, employees can be categorized as institutional stars, lone wolves, corporate citizens, or apathetics.

ROLE OF THE SPORT OR RECREATION MANAGER

From an organizational perspective, the most desirable situation is one in which an employee is committed to the organization based on pride and desire for membership (i.e., the affective component) and shares a sense of duty and obligation to achieve organizational goals (i.e., the normative component). In this chapter, we have noted that one of the antecedents to commitment is embeddedness, which, in this case, refers to an individual's dependence on his or her environment (i.e., work setting).

In a study by Odio, Wells, and Kerwin (2014), student employees in an intercollegiate athletics department were surveyed regarding how they were oriented into their roles and how embedded they became in their intern role and department. The results demonstrated that student supervisors and administrators (but not the orientation process or co-workers) influenced how the employees felt they were transitioned into the organization, which in turn predicted their levels of affective commitment. Furthermore, and to the point, the relationship between affective commitment and student supervisors and administrators was influenced significantly by the closeness of an employee's identification with and connection to the organization.

Commitment in the case of student employees is variable. Given that most student employees are motivated by utilitarian factors (e.g., gaining experience for career success, earning money to sustain one's personal life), continuance commitment (rather than affective commitment) may be high for student employees who are weighing the cost versus the benefit of their employment. Given that embeddedness can be a key to enhancing commitment (Odio et al. 2014), how do we use these findings to enhance the affective commitment of our student employees?

Leaders (e.g., student supervisors and administrators) in sport and recreation organizations should be mindful of the role that they play in how employees form their identity with an organization. For example, for student employees, these leaders may be the first (and only) touch point to the organization itself. Thus, the leaders play a key role in introducing the organization to the employee. The results presented by Odio et al. (2014) showed that the orientation process did not improve socialization, which suggests that the process missed an opportunity to help student employees feel as though they are embedded in "something special."

To convert continuance commitment into affective and normative commitment, leaders must communicate a message that is meaningful to their employees. As a sport and recreation manager in this situation, you would want to link orientation and training to values that may resonate with employees—particularly, student employees. Chapter 7 discusses the types of values that employees may hold, as well as ways to align those values with an organization's values. In these ways, both the orientation process and subsequent leader interaction should be used as tools to socialize individuals for the purpose of fostering a higher level of affective commitment.

Overall, in order to improve commitment in an organization, sport and recreation managers should develop engaging orientation programs that give employees the opportunity to connect with superiors and co-workers across time. Specifically, staging orientation events that continue through an employee's first several months with the organization (rather than simply just a day or two) can help an employee feel embedded, promote the development of organizational identity (i.e., employees feeling that the organization is part of who they are), and increase the likelihood of organizational commitment.

Case Study

Increasing Commitment Through Engagement

As managing director of customer service for a fitness club in Philadelphia, you are responsible for hiring and training new customer service representatives (CSRs), and you have been told by the head office that you need to reduce CSR turnover at your club. To fulfill this directive, you want to ensure that you choose the appropriate human resource management strategy. Therefore, you do some research, and, after reviewing a number of academic journal articles, you come across an article by Lubinsky, Doherty, and Kerwin (2011) outlining the positive effect of corporate philanthropy on employee commitment. Corporate philanthropy (CP) involves the "giving of corporate resources to address non–business community issues that also benefit the firm's strategic position" (Saiia et al. 2003, p.170). As you read the article, you discover that when fitness clubs engage in CP in their community, employees develop a higher level of affective commitment. In order to meet the mandate of the head office, you do some legwork to find out which community issues are most relevant to your CSR team; you then set up a plan to get your team involved in a meaningful way.

Case Study Tasks

1. Search for community-based projects and nonprofit organizations in Philadelphia that may be of interest. Pick three projects or organizations, and discuss why they may be relevant to employees at the fitness club.

2. Discuss the steps that you should take to actively engage the CSR team with the project or organization in an effort to increase commitment.

CHAPTER PURSUITS

SUMMARY

This chapter defines and describes organizational commitment from a global perspective. It also describes the specific components of affective, continuance, and normative commitment as involving, respectively, emotional attachment, calculations of the cost of leaving the organization, and sense of duty. The chapter also notes that commitment may be targeted toward the organization as a whole or toward top management, supervisors, a work group, co-workers, clients, or other such constituencies of the organization. Thus, the multidimensionality of organizational commitment is derived from both the bases and the foci of commitment.

Managers can facilitate the development of organizational commitment through organizational practices that provide support to members, create a sense of fairness among members, enhance members' competence, and foster feelings of personal importance among members. Organizational commitment is related, albeit weakly, to performance. However, even small increments in performance can be significant in gaining a competitive edge for the organization. A stronger relationship exists between organizational commitment and turnover. Because turnover is costly in terms of replacing and training newcomers, managers need to be concerned with developing organizational commitment among their members.

The chapter also outlines the relationships between organizational commitment, occupational commitment, job satisfaction, and job involvement. Organizational commitment and occupational commitment (i.e., identification with the values of the occupation) may be incongruent in some organizational contexts and congruent in other contexts. Job satisfaction involves an immediate reaction to job experiences and is variable as the job situation changes. Organizational commitment involves a global attitude that takes time to develop and is stable over time. Finally, although job involvement contributes to high-quality performance, the ideal worker has a high level of both job involvement and organizational commitment. The least desirable worker is one who has a low level of both attributes.

KEY TERMS

affective commitment... 326

antecedents and consequences
    of organizational commitment...................... 332

continuance commitment............................... 326

foci of commitment 325

job involvement... 324

normative commitment 327

organizational commitment............................ 323

personal importance and competence 333

supportiveness and fairness 333

turnover.. 334

UNDERSTAND

1. Describe the three components of organizational commitment. Discuss the relevance of these components to fans' attachment to intercollegiate teams.

2. Referring again to fans of intercollegiate teams, identify the targets of their attachment. Explain the relative significance of these targets.

INTERACT

1. Considering your own experience with a sport or recreation organization, identify a person to whom, or a unit to which, you were committed. Describe your relationship with that person or unit. Explain the reasons or motives behind your commitment to that person or unit.

2. How did the commitment you described in answering question 1 affect your performance or satisfaction? Explain.

CONCLUSION

The Future of Human Resource Management in Sport and Recreation— Guiding Themes

╭─────────────── **LEARNING OBJECTIVES** ───────────────╮

After reading this chapter, you will be able to

- understand the general themes that should guide human resource practices in sport and recreation,
- relate these themes to the content of the book's chapters,
- describe the concept of person–organization fit, and
- describe the role of technology when adopting human resource management practices in sport and recreation.

╰───╯

This conclusion gathers the major principles of the managerial practices described in the book, including the influence of technology, into general themes that serve as the foundation of, and provide guidance for, effective management of human resources. In other words, these themes should drive and underlie all managerial practices. The themes highlight human resource management (HRM) practices from both humanistic perspectives and the perspective of performance imperatives. Before discussing the themes, however this section reiterates the significance of human resource management itself. As noted earlier, HRM should focus on the financial imperatives of business enterprises. After all, all innovations in running an organization depend largely on the people who implement the organization's policies and procedures. Hence, any attention to human resource management should yield greater returns through greater productivity of the workers and their commitment to the organization.

In addition to the increasing sophistication of both employees and consumers (i.e., technology provides greater opportunities for communication, engagement, and connectedness), their perceptions of what constitutes good human resource management practices and their expectations for such practices have been heightened. At the same time, management attention to human resources has been refocused by the cumulative effects of modern

worker–client awareness, alertness, influence, and altered values based on how heavily the sport and recreation industry has been affected by the digital revolution. Furthermore, because sport and recreation organizations are agencies of society at large and are sustained by society, they and their managers bear responsibility for catering to the welfare of their workers and enhancing their quality of life. After all, almost all adults in a society work in an organization. Thus, management of human resources merits extreme care not only from the economic, efficiency, and quality perspectives but also from the perspective of social responsibility.

Technological innovations grow by the minute, and human resource management practices must follow suit. In particular, the use of **social media platforms** to enhance human resource management practice has increased exponentially over the last decade (Benson, Morgan, and Filippaios 2014; Leftheriotis and Giannakos 2014). The increasing use of social media platforms such as LinkedIn and Twitter implies that human resource managers must understand the potential of these tools as mechanisms for managing employee behavioral patterns (Benson et al. 2014). For example, LinkedIn has become a recruitment and selection tool as human resource managers use it to help post job advertisements and filter candidates onto short lists for interviewing.

Technological advances may be most apparent in service organizations. As noted in the chapter 1, human resources gain greater significance in service organizations because their products are intangible rather than tangible, because customer involvement is necessary for the production of services, and because the consumption of services occurs simultaneously with their production (S.E. Jackson and Schuler 1992; B. Schneider and Bowen 1992). This link between production and service is strengthened by technology and the increasing importance of social media, which increase the opportunities for connecting with customers (DiMicco et al. 2008; Skeels and Grudin 2009). Specifically, social media serve as a mechanism for connecting with consumers "on the fly" to ensure that feedback is received and managed.

These developments, including the possibility of instantaneous connection with consumers via technology, cast service providers (i.e., frontline workers) in a different and more significant role than that of workers in conventional organizations. As noted by B. Schneider and Bowen (1992, 1995), frequent contacts of service providers with both clients and the organization make them both a part of the organization and a part of the consumers' world.

In this way, service employees serve as **boundary spanners** who provide the vital link between the organization and its critical markets.

This view of service providers as boundary spanners has led to the suggestion that a service firm should be viewed as an inverted triangle (see figure C.1). The frontline workers are at the top, and all other units (including management) are viewed as support units (J.A. Fitzsimmons and Fitzsimmons 2001; Grönroos 1990; B. Schneider, Wheeler, and Cox 1992). For example, the core service provided by a tennis professional is facilitated by support services from other units, such as facility and equipment maintenance, reception, and accounting. Management coordinates the activities of all of these units and creates an environment that enhances the quality of the service provided by the service professional. The idea of the inverted triangle is presented here simply to provide a contrast with the traditional bureaucratic hierarchy, in which management sits at the top and issues orders to those below, including the service providers.

The role of service providers as boundary spanners is much more pronounced in the case of human services, which are unique because their inputs are human beings. The input is variable, of course, in terms of factors such as age, gender, and fitness level; therefore, the processes of human services cannot be fully standardized. Although a client's expectations may be legitimate, only **professional** experts can decide on the service to be provided.

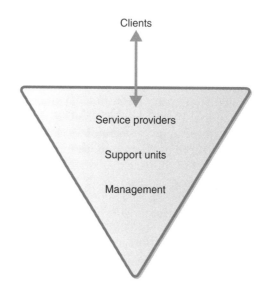

FIGURE C.1 Service providers as boundary spanners.

Finally, sport and recreation clients who serve as the input get involved actively in the process (J. Williamson 1991), and this fact is more and more evident in the two-way communication that marks the age of the digital industry.

This last factor—active involvement of sport and recreation clients in the production of **participant services**—is problematic in two ways. First, the client's active involvement may hinder the employee's activities and judgment; second, the client may not comply with the expert's directions (Hasenfeld 1983). These two issues are accentuated in the sport and recreation context because the production of some services requires clients to engage in quite agonistic and prolonged activities. For instance, the provision of fitness- and health-oriented services depends on the extent to which the client adheres to the service provider's guidance and participates in vigorous activities. Similarly, the pursuit of excellence in sport requires the client to undergo strenuous practice sessions and forego other, more pleasurable activities.

These unique characteristics of human services in sport and recreation highlight the significance of human resource management in ensuring that service providers are both professionally competent and skilled at social interaction. More specifically, a service provider must be proficient in communicating with clients and recognizing the power of online communication (e.g., Facebook). For example, a trainer can now provide motivation to a client beyond the gym walls by posting a motivational quotation or healthy living recipe on the client's Facebook page. This type of interaction cultivates a stronger connection to clients (one not bound by time or place) that was unavailable to sport and recreation managers just a decade ago.

THEME 1: PRODUCTS

Chapter 1 discusses the notion that every organization or industry exists to exchange one or more products with its environment and that the production and marketing of such products define the industry and the organizations in it. Accordingly, chapter 1 presents the classes of services produced by sport and recreation organizations and outlines the differences between them. The three broad categories of sport and recreation products and services are **egalitarian sport**, **elite sport**, and **entertainment sport**. Egalitarian sport products and services include

- consumer pleasure and consumer health services (i.e., scheduling facilities and equipment and organizing and conducting tournaments) for clients who may engage in the activity for pleasure or health reasons, and
- human sustenance and human curative services (e.g., organizing and conducting exercise and fitness programs) to sustain the client's present status or cure a deficiency in fitness, health, or physical appearance.

The type of product or service that a sport or recreation organization offers to the public affects the human resource management practices in which the organization's managers engage. For example, the ways in which we hire employees, train them, and orient them toward customer service differs for managers in consumer services operations as compared with those in human services operations. Thus, a sport organization must define its own business (i.e., its products and services) before instituting specific HRM programs.

THEME 2: PEOPLE

Another consideration in instituting HRM practices is to understand the types of people or human resources available to a sport organization. Generally, three forms of human resources are involved in the production and marketing of sport services: volunteer workers, paid professional workers, and clients. From the perspective of **strategic management**, these three forms of human resources constitute an organization's internal and external markets. The attributes of these three forms of human resources are addressed in chapters 2, 3, and 4, which are summarized here.

Volunteers

As noted in chapter 2, the nearly 8 billion hours of volunteer work contributed annually in sport and recreation point to the financial importance of volunteers in this sector. In addition to this economic value, volunteers bring credibility and legitimacy to an organization, objectivity and open-mindedness in evaluating organizational activities, creativity in designing organizational activities and processes, and an avenue for connecting with the community. Sport and recreation managers must be cognizant of these benefits and make every effort to recruit and retain volunteers.

One specific area to which managers should be attuned is that of the incentives that motivate volunteers. Knoke and Prensky (1984) presented three broad categories of incentives: utilitarian, affective, and normative. Utilitarian incentives may take the form of extending one's household work of child-rearing and child-minding functions or enhancing one's abilities, expertise, and experience through volunteer work. Affective incentives reflect one's desire for interpersonal relations, a sense of belonging to a group, and the prestige and status associated with such membership. Finally, normative incentives reflect one's sense of doing what is right and what is good for the community, which may be embedded in organizational goals and programs. In order to make the best use of available volunteers, sport and recreation managers need to gain insight into what incentives are critical for those volunteers and how organizational activities can provide these incentives.

Professionals

Chapter 3 provides an elaborate description of what a profession is and how an occupation attains professional status. Sport managers must recognize that professionally oriented individuals are likely to prefer considerable autonomy in their jobs; in addition, they are likely to be influenced by the principles and guidelines established by external professional associates. These professional orientations can become points of friction between an organization (including its managers) and a professionally oriented worker. Therefore, an astute manager balances these individual orientations and organizational requirements. Managers must also be aware of tensions between professional and personal life. Specifically, the boundaries between these two areas of life have been blurred by the increasing prevalence of information technology, which can thereby contribute to stress and burnout among professional employees.

From a different perspective, it is *not* critical that workers in the sport and recreation field (including managers) be considered as professionals per se. That is, striving to be professional is more important than striving to be a profession. Being professional emphasizes the application of technical skills based on advanced education and training by competent personnel who follow codes of conduct or ethics and who are committed to their calling and to serving the public.

Professionalism and Volunteerism

Although conflicts may occur between volunteer and professional workers in an organization, they are likely to be transitory. Fundamentally, both groups are impelled by the desire to learn and know, to act or do something effectively, and to serve and help others. Thus, sport and recreation managers need to minimize the differences between the two sets of workers and highlight the underlying core values that motivate both groups.

Clients

The third set of human resources consists of clients themselves; their attributes, and the reasons for including them as a set of human resources, are addressed in chapter 4. The significance of clients as a set of human resources hinges on two factors. First, the only sustainable evaluation of services is based on client perceptions of a service provider's performance (Zeithaml, Parasuraman, and Berry 1990). Second, as noted earlier, sport and physical activity services require active physical exertion by the client or customer (Chelladurai 1992); therefore, securing clients' compliance is necessary to ensure the production of services. Thus, clients constitute a significant set of human resources in the context of sport and recreation.

The classification of sport products or services is based partly on the motives of clients. Therefore, HRM practices directed toward clients must consider client motives for participation—that is, the pursuit of pleasure, the pursuit of skill, the pursuit of excellence, and the pursuit of health or fitness—which provide a basis for human resource management practice (Chelladurai 1992). For example, if a client is motivated by the pursuit of pleasure, that client may participate in physical activity because he or she enjoys the kinesthetic sensations experienced during physical activity or the competition involved in certain activities (e.g., a game of squash). Only during participation can the person enjoy the pleasures that he or she seeks. To serve this motive, then, employees must be trained to understand how to enable pleasure in participation.

The desire to acquire physical skills during activity may be an inevitable motive for engaging with sport and recreation products and services. In fact, developing physical skill may be the driving force for consumer participation in a physical activity. That is, individuals may focus on perfecting their skills through continued vigorous physical activity. Others may participate in vigorous physical activity for the primary purpose of reaping the health-related benefits (e.g., fitness, stress reduction, relaxation) that accrue as a consequence of participation. Whatever the motive, employees must be trained and given performance evaluations that reflect the ability to meet these consumer needs.

While these motives are distinct from each other, the activity (e.g., weight training) chosen to satisfy any one of them may also satisfy other motives. From the HRM perspective, however, we must determine the *primary* purpose for participation in a physical activity in order to smoothly coordinate its development and implementation. Furthermore, service providers (i.e., paid and volunteer workers) must be even more attuned to client motives than are the managers themselves, thus highlighting the strategic human resource management function of communicating with clients through social networking technology (e.g., Facebook, LinkedIn, Twitter).

Here, a note of caution is in order. The view of clients as partial employees of the organization is restricted only to participant services. That is, clients or customers in **spectator services** and **sponsorship services** do not participate in the production of the service, so they do not constitute our human resources.

THEME 3: PURPOSES OF HUMAN RESOURCE MANAGEMENT

The chapters in part II of the book detail individual differences in ability, personality, values, and motivation. The chapters in part III address organizational justice, job design, staffing and career considerations, leadership, performance appraisal, and reward systems. Collectively, these elements underscore the **purposes of human resource management**. This section explicates the purposes of human resource management from two perspectives—that of the organization and that of its members.

Organizational Perspective

When human resource management is viewed from the perspective of the organization, it needs to accomplish two important functions: the technical and the control aspects of the organization (S.E. Jack-

son and Schuler 1992). The concern in the technical perspective is to ensure that a person in a given job possesses the right skills to effectively perform that job. Accordingly, emphasis is placed on hiring people with the right technical skills, training them further in those skills, appraising their performance, and compensating them on the basis of skill-related performance (S.E. Jackson and Schuler). Because the delivery of consumer services requires simple skills, the processes of hiring and training these employees are also simple and straightforward. It is also relatively easy to replace such employees (e.g., caretakers, locker room attendants).

Human services, however, require that employees be well educated and highly trained in their specialties in order to be able to process the information flow and make optimal decisions. Furthermore, replacing human services employees (e.g., tennis professional, exercise physiologist) is difficult. Therefore, managers must be creative and innovative when recruiting, selecting, and hiring these employees.

The control aspect (labeled as citizenship in this book) addresses the predictability and reliability of social interactions to ensure behavior in accordance with organizationally approved norms and values. That is, the desired ends are social performance and job performance. In sum, the organization should design human resource management to develop both technical and citizenship skills and behaviors.

With regard to training employees to engage in effective service encounters, Humphrey and Ashforth (1994) provide a useful scheme that outlines two types of knowledge structures: script structure and categorical knowledge structure.

1. A script structure addresses a service worker's expectation for a series of coherently organized events in a successful service encounter, as well as alternative courses of action available for every event. Developing script knowledge requires training employees in both the technical skills needed to provide the service (e.g., techniques and strategies of coaching) and the various stages of providing that service (e.g., progressive training regimen during practice sessions).

2. A categorical knowledge structure addresses an understanding of different types of clients with specific needs, wants, and personal characteristics. Such knowledge generates client prototypes for which specific programs are developed.

Essentially, developing categorical knowledge helps employees understand who their customers are, whereas developing script knowledge helps employees understand the various service options available to meet variable customer needs (Humphrey and Ashforth 1994). As noted in chapter 11, in the sport and recreation context, training based on categorical knowledge outlines the distinction between various classes of customers (e.g., youth, women, elderly persons) and provides valuable information about their motives for participation (e.g., pleasure, excellence, health).

Member Perspective

B. Schneider and Bowen (1992, 1993) suggested that human resource management should be designed to foster two kinds of climates in an organization: employee well-being and service. Fostering a climate for employee well-being involves redesigning jobs to create more challenge and autonomy, ensuring the safety and security of employees, reducing their stress, and having superiors treat them warmly and considerately. The essential thrust of the argument is that "the culture employees experience will be the culture customers experience" (B. Schneider and Bowen 1995, p. 240). This is a form of osmosis, wherein the effects of human resource management practices filter through to clients. B. Schneider and Bowen (1992) noted that a climate of employee well-being is a necessary precondition for, but does not presuppose, a service climate.

Burnout among personnel has been identified as a major problem in a variety of organizational settings (Aiken, Clarke, Sloane, Sochalski, and Silbner 2002; Apker and Ray 2003; Maslach 2003; McManus, Winder, and Gordon 2002). Burnout is likely to result in absenteeism, reduced quality of job performance, and higher organizational costs (Aiken et al. 2002; Maslach 2003). Boyd, Lewin, and Sager (2009) estimated that in the United States alone such outcomes cost organizations up to $300 billion annually. One of the main reasons for employee burnout is the blurring of the line between work and family life resulting from the uptake of technology. As noted in chapter 3, Kossek and Lautsch (2012) highlight the fact that employees preferences for segmenting or integrating their work and life roles have been overrun by the demands of 24-7 access enabled by technological innovation.

In addition to enriched jobs, the climate for service entails promoting creativity and quality in service. In fact, B. Schneider, Wheeler, and Cox

(1992) called it the climate of passion for service. Along similar lines, Grönroos (1990) proposed that "[human resource management] practices should be geared to foster a service culture where there is an appreciation for good service . . . [and which] is considered a natural way of life at work" (p. 244). Employee perceptions of passion for service within the organization result in greater responsiveness to customer opinion, efficient procedures for delivering services, and greater emphasis on service to external customers. In addition, passion for service is reflected in the HRM practices of hiring, performance feedback, internal equity of compensation, and training. In summary, human resource management practices need to foster both a climate for employee well-being and a passion for service; in the sport and recreation context, the climate for service necessarily subsumes the welfare of the clients.

Person–Organization Fit

As made clear by the foregoing discussion of creating and maintaining both employee-oriented and service-oriented climates (B. Schneider and Bowen 1992)—as well as concern with technical and control aspects (S.E. Jackson and Schuler 1992)—"the focus of HRM practices must be the organization, rather than the job. . . . Entry, training, and reward issues need to be reconceptualized so they address the organizational imperative of service" (B. Schneider and Bowen 1992, p. 8). In other words, the focus must be on addressing HRM practices aimed not at the traditional person–job fit but at **person–organization fit**.

Thus, managers have a twofold responsibility: recruit employees with the requisite personality and ability to (a) participate in and promote the organizational climate for positive customer service and (b) effectively perform the tasks of a particular job. Moreover, as outlined in figure C.2, in order to develop person–organization fit, managers must focus on two streams of fit. First, managers must train and develop employees to enhance the fit between one's knowledge, skills, and abilities and the task demands. Second, managers must focus on the fit between overall personality (i.e., traits, interests, and values) and the climate of the organization. In other words, the person must fit both the content and the context of the job.

The training programs of human resource management should focus on "developing a holistic view of the service organization; developing skills concerning how various tasks are to be performed;

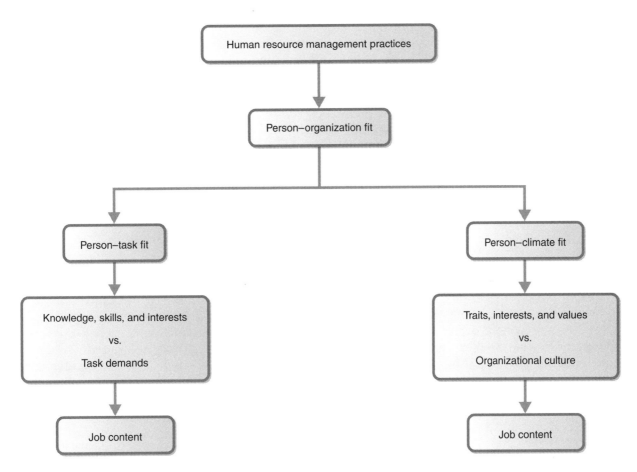

FIGURE C.2   Components of person–organization fit.

and developing communication and service skills" (Grönroos 1990, p. 253). Similarly, B. Schneider and Bowen (1992) divided the content of training into technical job skills, interpersonal or customer relationship skills, and cultural values and norms.

Once the organization has recruited and trained workers (i.e., both volunteer and paid workers), the next major task in human resource management is to institute structural and procedural mechanisms to motivate the employees. In this context, two emergent approaches or concepts are present—empowerment and organizational justice.

THEME 4: EMPOWERMENT

There is a growing realization among scholars and practitioners that current organizational and managerial practices tend to underestimate and underuti-

lize the skills of employees. In fact, only 5 percent to 10 percent of employees' abilities are tapped for organizational purposes (Ivancevich and Matteson 2002). Several chapters in the book have outlined ways and means of identifying and using employees' talents and abilities, and all such guidelines are encompassed by one overarching process—that of **empowerment**. Dictionary meanings for the word *empower* include the following: "to give power or authority to," "to authorize," "to give ability to," and "to enable." (Merriam-Webster 2016).

The two components of empowerment—possessing authority or power and the ability to exercise it—are derived from organizational processes that include the following:

- Designing jobs to ensure that individuals enjoy challenge, responsibility, and autonomy
- Sharing power throughout the organization so that individuals are able to exercise appropriate authority in doing their jobs

- Sharing information about the organization, its units, and its performance so that individuals can make intelligent and effective decisions in carrying out their assignments
- Sharing knowledge to perform various tasks of the organization and to enhance the expertise and information base of members
- Sharing rewards based on organizational and individual performance (B. Schneider and Bowen 1995)

The process of empowerment results in some demands. For one thing, empowerment strategy implies that managers must let go of their authority and control and adjust to a new environment of empowerment. Other basic assumptions include the notion that the members of an organization are willing and able to take on more authority and make good decisions and that they possess the ability to execute those decisions. Furthermore, empowerment can be too expensive for low-cost, high-volume operations. Despite these limitations, the process of empowerment may prove to be beneficial and, at times, necessary. The best approach is to consider empowerment as a philosophy of management and to try to progressively institute the processes of empowerment.

A manager can best begin the process of empowerment with the content of a job. For example, a sport marketing director might give employees autonomy in selecting would-be sponsors and determining how to present their case to them. This step is similar to job enrichment as discussed in chapter 10. Allowing such discretion empowers marketing employees by giving them the authority or power to decide on courses of action. Despite this

move, an employee still may not be empowered fully because the empowerment initiative may not be supported by the goals of the organization, its organizational structure, the process of performance appraisal, or the organization's reward systems. To the extent that these contextual factors inhibit empowerment, they must be modified to enhance employee empowerment. Because these factors span the whole organization, changing them takes considerable time and effort (Ford and Fottler 1995).

What may prove to be problematic for sport managers is the distinction between management practices toward empowerment (e.g., sharing of power and information) and the psychological empowerment that members actually feel. The notion of empowerment loses all its potency if members do not *feel* empowered. A member's feeling of being empowered is referred to as psychological empowerment, which is "a motivational construct manifested in four cognitions: meaning, competence, self-determination, and impact. Together, these four cognitions reflect an active, rather than a passive, orientation to the work role" (Spreitzer 1995, p. 1444). These four cognitions, described in table C.1, combine additively and lead to intrinsic task motivation.

Even though empowerment is quite meaningful, managers must be cognizant of three constraints on the process. First, some members may not possess the ability needed to manage an empowered job. For example, they may not be able to analyze a problem correctly and arrive at an appropriate solution. In such a case, empowerment may prove to be counterproductive. From a different perspective, some members may not be inclined toward empowered jobs. They may prefer a simplified and specialized

TABLE C.1 Dimensions of Psychological Empowerment

DIMENSION	DESCRIPTION
Meaning	Meaning involves the value of a work goal. It is a fit between the requirements of a work role and beliefs, values, and behaviors.
Competence	Competence involves an individual's belief in his or her capability to perform activities with skill. The focus is on efficacy in a specific work role (not global efficacy).
Self-determination	Self-determination involves an individual's sense of having choice in initiating and regulating actions. It reflects autonomy in the initiation and continuation of work behaviors and processes.
Impact	Impact involves the degree to which an individual can influence strategic, administrative, or operating outcomes at work.

Adapted from Spreitzer 1995.

job in which they merely follow routines. Finally, some operations in an organization may involve a high volume of service encounters of little duration and substance—for example, the towel service in a large fitness club or university recreation department. These high-volume, low-cost operations do not permit empowerment to a large extent.

THEME 5: REWARD SYSTEMS

Chapter 14 presents a detailed discussion of reward systems. One concern with a reward system is whether it serves the purpose for which the manager created it in the first place. In this regard, S. Kerr (1975, 1995) cautioned against a persistent folly of most reward systems. In his view, conventional reward systems tend to reward noncritical behaviors and merely hope for more critical behaviors. For example, most businesses and government agencies reward their employees for regular attendance or punish them for absence and tardiness. A city recreation department, for instance, may reward its employees for reporting as scheduled for work and special assignments. The department then hopes that the employees in attendance will carry out their assignments adequately. In sport, a manager or coach may emphasize teamwork but reward star performers more than other team members. S. Kerr (1995) suggested that this folly of rewarding A and hoping for B persists because managers

- are fascinated with objective criteria, such as attendance or the number of points scored in a game;
- overemphasize highly visible behaviors; and
- emphasize morality or equality rather than efficiency.

In addition, because services are intangible, the associated critical employee behaviors cannot be assessed easily. Therefore, managers may take the easy way out and reward employees on the basis of attendance or number of clients served. This issue is accentuated in the case of human services. From a different perspective, reward systems in service operations may fail if they rely solely on monetary rewards that can satisfy only the need for security (B. Schneider and Bowen 1995). Sport and recreation managers must understand the dynamics of intrinsic rewards inherent in delivering a service and must foster such rewards because they satisfy the need for achievement and self-esteem.

THEME 6: ORGANIZATIONAL JUSTICE

Chapter 9 outlines the concept of organizational justice as an emerging area of concern in human resource management. A manager's responsibility to uphold organizational justice is particularly critical in the areas of personnel and budgetary decisions, policies and procedures associated with those decisions, and management's and leadership's treatment of workers in dispensing the decisions. These domains are referred to, respectively, by the following terms:

- Distributive justice (which involves outcomes for individuals or groups)
- Procedural justice (which involves the procedures used to reach decisions)
- Interactional justice (which involves the manner in which a decision is communicated to individuals)

The chosen principle for distribution of resources (i.e., equity, equality, or need) should be consistent with organizational values and purposes. In a solidarity-oriented organization, the principle of equality may be more relevant; in a productivity-oriented organization, the principle of equity may be more appropriate.

Procedural justice can be maintained if managers

- consistently apply procedures over time and across individuals,
- suppress personal and built-in biases,
- represent the concerns of all parties,
- conform to community standards of ethics and morality,
- allow for correction of any wrong decisions, and
- make all procedures public before acting on them.

Finally, interactional justice is based largely on how managers and supervisors interact with their subordinates. Positive supervisor–subordinate interactions are of course important in general, and they are even more critical when managers need to announce personnel or budgetary decisions to concerned parties. Even if the decisions and associated processes were fair, perceptions of fairness are reduced if the recipients believe that the communication of the decisions was not straightforward or that the interaction was not warm. This is particularly relevant in our digitally inflected industry. As sport and recreation managers now operate with increased transparency, decisions and decision processes are more readily available to the public and thus open to scrutiny, both internally and externally. As a result, managers must be aware of messages communicated electronically and exchanged via social media outlets in order to ensure perceptions of justice remain high among personnel.

THEME 7: PSYCHOLOGICAL CONTRACT

The relationship between an employee and the organization is defined and described in various chapters. For instance, when a fitness club advertises for a position, the call for applications indicates what the organization is willing to offer (e.g., pay, benefits, flexibility in work hours) in return for the contributions of the would-be employee in terms of ability, expertise, and effort. These mutual exchanges are further clarified during the recruiting and hiring stages. When an individual joins the organization, the organization and the individual make a written formal agreement, which is constituted by documents such as a job description, employment contract, policies about salary scales, and procedures for merit assessment and promotion.

Another critical aspect of employment is the psychological contract—that is, the implicit set of expectations agreed to by the organization and its members. This contract is defined as "an unwritten agreement between the individual and [the] organization which specifies what each expects to give to and receive from the other. While some aspects of an employment relationship, such as pay, may be explicitly stated, many others are not. These implicit agreements which may focus on exchanges involving satisfaction, challenging work, fair treatment, loyalty, and opportunity to be creative may take precedence over written agreements" (Ivancevich and Matteson 2002, p. 169). The elements of the psychological contract include those of the formal contract as well as additional informal and implied elements, such as the privileges and obligations of both the person and the organization.

Public and Real Psychological Contract

Tosi and Mero (2003) refer to two boundaries of the psychological contract: public and real. The public boundary is known to external others (e.g., superiors and colleagues) and tends to consist of the minimal set of activities defined by the formal contract. For example, the psychological contract of a youth soccer coach is defined by the public boundary of the team's practice and game schedule. The coach may also expect, for example, that he or she will undertake such activities between 4 p.m. and 10 p.m. on weekdays.

However, the real boundary of the coach's psychological contract—that is, its true limit—is defined by the organizational expectations associated with the coaching position. For example, the general manager of the club may expect the coach to conduct extra training sessions and register the team for travel tournaments on additional weekdays and on weekends. The expectation from the general manager is that coach will give his or her best effort, as well as additional time. Meanwhile, the coach has his or her own expectations of how the general manager will reciprocate in terms of extra remuneration (e.g., mileage coverage, benefits, privileges).

For another example, consider a fitness club that is downsizing its operations and does not renew the services of an aerobics instructor. Although such action is legally permissible and legitimate from a business perspective, the aerobics instructor may still feel disappointed that the club did not live up to the tacit understanding that it would not let go of its good employees.

Most often, such psychological expectations relate to one's needs, values, and attitudes. For instance, an individual who joins an intercollegiate athletics department expects that the department will do everything to safeguard the health and welfare of the athletes (which reflects a personal value) and of employees (which reflects a personal need for security).

Individual Contributions and Organizational Inducements

From a different perspective, the psychological contract consists of a combination of employee contributions and organizational incentives (Schermerhorn, Hunt, and Osborn 1997). That is, it can exist and be meaningful only if the employee's contributions hold meaning for the organization and if the incentives offered by the organization hold meaning for the employee. To summarize, in order to be effective in developing satisfaction and commitment, the exchange of met expectations between employee and organization must be balanced and equal.

Given that the tangible incentives associated with employees are not relevant to volunteer workers, the notion of a psychological contract requires further reflection for managers in organizations that use volunteers. Specifically, these managers must recognize that the psychological contract includes elements such as

- providing an individual with the opportunity to express his or her altruistic and helping tendencies through specified activities of the organization, and
- providing an individual the opportunity to engage in activities in which his or her valued abilities can be used.

To review, chapter 2 presents the utilitarian, affective, and normative incentives that motivate volunteers. An organization that critically assesses and addresses these incentives in its personnel policies for recruiting and retaining volunteers will be more effective in meeting the expectations of its psychological contract with individual volunteers. When volunteer expectations are not understood (or worse, go unmet), the volunteer's commitment to the organization and maximal effort cannot be ensured.

THEME 8: PSYCHOLOGICAL CLIMATE

Although almost everyone recognizes and promotes the importance of managing human resources for organizational performance, little effort has been made to explain how HRM might lead to organizational performance. Recently, Bowen and Ostroff (2004) have introduced the concept of HRM system strength to define a strong organizational or psychological climate, which in turn promotes a common understanding among employees of what

behaviors are appropriate and what behaviors will be rewarded. In the view of these authors, HRM practices cultivate and promote a psychological climate that "is an experiential-based perception of what people 'see' and report happening to them as they make sense of their environment" (p. 205). In the process, employees get a sense of what activities they should carry out, how, and under what management practices. They also get a sense of the behaviors expected of them that are supported and rewarded by management. "Organizational [psychological] climate is a shared perception of what the organization is like in terms of practices, policies, procedures, routines, and rewards" (Bowen and Ostroff, p. 205).

Carless (2004) noted that psychological climate involves a worker's judgment of the extent to which the work environment contributes to his or her sense of well-being. Thus it involves one's *perception* of the environment rather than the environment per se. In Carless' view, a positive psychological climate is characterized by

- role clarity—the degree to which work expectations and responsibilities are clearly defined;
- supportive leadership—the extent to which supervisors support their staff members;
- participative decision making—the degree to which employees are involved in decision making about workplace issues;
- professional interaction—the quality of communication and support between employees;
- appraisal and recognition—the extent to which feedback and acknowledgment are given;
- professional growth—the extent to which skill development is encouraged and supported; and
- goal congruence—the degree of congruence between individual goals and those of the organization.

Bowen and Ostroff (2004) argue that human resource practices should be driven by strategic goals and should be integrated so as to link human capital to organizational performance. The linkages between the organization's strategic goals, human resource practices, psychological climate, employee reactions, and goal achievement are illustrated in figure C.3.

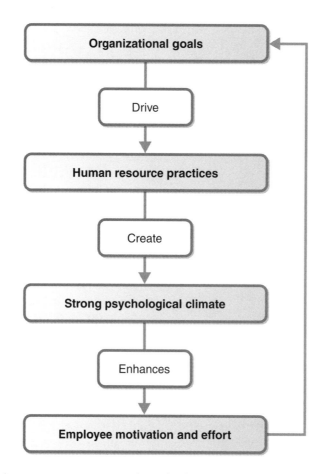

FIGURE C.3 Linkages between organizational goals, human resource practices, strong psychological climate, employee motivation and effort, and attainment of goals.

THEME 9: NAVIGATING TECHNOLOGY WHEN MANAGING HUMAN RESOURCES

The psychological climate of a sport or recreation organization is influenced by the technology adopted by that organization. More specifically, the type and frequency of an organization's technology use (e.g., social media) are correlated with the organization's strategic goals, human resource practices, psychological climate, employee reactions, and goal achievement. For example, a state or provincial sport organization may set a strategic goal to increase its volunteer pool for hosting its next event. The ability of employees to craft and deliver the needed marketing message to potential volunteers is influenced heavily by the type of technology adopted for the messaging.

Managers must first identify which types of technology (e.g., social media platform) their personnel are comfortable using, then determine which technology provides comfort or ease of access for the community (i.e., potential volunteers). Goal achievement is negatively influenced if employee comfort with one platform (e.g., Facebook) does not match the platform comfort of the target group. Therefore, as emphasized by Skeels and Grudin (2009), in order to strategically manage technological platform use, managers should gather information about the type and frequency of use by both internal and external stakeholders.

DIVERSITY MANAGEMENT OF HUMAN RESOURCES

 Technology use in HRM practice can be informed by Chelladurai's (2014) discussion of the influence of time:

As group members become familiar with each other, they may also become more disposed to developing and understanding an appreciation for different perspectives (Pelled et al. 1999). By the same token, individuals may cultivate the ability to frame and state their views in juxtaposition with others' perspectives. Thus, members may develop a shared understanding of the task and its requirements, as well as of the processes involved in solving problems. (p. 353)

In our digital age of technology, we can often engage individuals instantaneously. However, as human resource managers, we must actively recognize that when we engage someone, we may not necessarily be developing an appreciation and understanding of his or her unique perspective. For example, when we use technology as an efficient tool for reaching a large audience to strategically recruit human resources, we must actively recognize the time it takes to get to know an individual and appreciate that face-to-face interaction should not be lost when we adopt technological processes and platforms.

As noted in chapter 7, technology (e.g., social media) can be used as a strategic communication tool to manage and promote an organization's brand and increase employee commitment. Specifically, when developing processes for training and performance appraisal, managers should review an organization's mission and values and ensure that these features foster positive growth and appeal to both internal and external stakeholders. Technology and communication strategies can then be leveraged to link employees and consumers to the buzzwords, mission, and values associated with the organization.

In this way, the concept of psychological climate becomes increasingly relevant. Both managers and employees can start conversations through forums such as Facebook, Twitter, and Snapchat that provide a foundation for leveraging positive psychological climate and presenting positive organizational attributes to build the organization's brand. Thus, in the global sport and recreation industry, technology inevitably plays a large role in recruiting, training, developing, and retaining employees, volunteers, and clients. Therefore, sport and recreation managers must understand the technology available to them, the social media outlets commonly used by employees and stakeholders, and the strategic application of technology to HRM practice.

CHAPTER PURSUITS

SUMMARY

In conclusion, human resource management as a component of strategic management must be tailored to be consistent with the type of business that a sport organization undertakes and the types of human resources at its disposal. Effective human resource management rests on a foundation provided by several key themes. These themes describe the purposes of human resource management from the perspective of the organization and that of the individual, stress the need to create a fit between person and organization, describe the notion of empowerment, and describe the three forms of organizational justice (distributive, procedural, and interactional).

Finally, navigating the use of technology in HRM practices has become an inevitable reality for sport and recreation managers. In order to strategically manage the social media platforms at their disposal, human resource managers must reflect on their type of organization, its goals, its products, the technologies associated with those products, and the markets it serves. These themes are powerful tools that sport and recreation managers can use in enhancing human capital and securing member commitment and productivity through the 21st century and beyond.

KEY TERMS

boundary spanners.. 342

egalitarian sport.. 343

elite sport 343

entertainment sport.. 343

empowerment.. 347

participant services.. 343

person–organization fit.................................... 346

professional 342

purposes of human resource management..... 345

social media platforms 342

spectator services.. 345

sponsorship services.. 345

strategic management...................................... 343

worker–client awareness................................. 342

UNDERSTAND

1. Based on your own experiences, what aspects of human resource management are addressed adequately in sport and recreation management? What aspects are not carried out well?

2. This chapter discusses the role of technology in human resource management. List the social media platforms that are relevant in the sport and recreation industry. What experience have you had with these platforms on a personal level? On a professional level?

INTERACT

1. What experience have you had with the empowerment approach to human resource management? What are your reactions to that experience?

2. Discuss a scenario in which the use of LinkedIn would be appropriate to improve human resource management practice in a sport or recreation organization. Link your scenario to a specific human resource management practice from this textbook.

3. Discuss a scenario in which the use of Twitter would be appropriate to improve human resource management practice in a sport or recreation organization. Link your scenario to a specific human resource management practice from this textbook.

Appendix

This appendix contains the Code of Ethics of the North American Society for Sport Management (NASSM; accepted June 1992). The NASSM Code of Ethics has been developed to ensure that the scholars and practitioners who are NASSM members are committed to a high level of ethical practice and service. This code is directed toward high quality management practice that contribute to a body of knowledge in sport, exercise, and related expressive activities in the lives of all people.

CANONS OR PRINCIPLES

The following canons or principles, arranged according to category or dimension, shall be considered by the sport manager in the performance of professional duties:

Category I: The Professional's Conduct as a Sport Manager

A. *Individual welfare:* The sport manager should hold paramount the safety, health, and welfare of the individual in the performance of professional duties.

B. *Service where competent:* The sport manager should perform services only in his or her areas of competence.

C. *Public statements:* The sport manager should issue public statements in an objective and truthful manner, and shall make every effort to explain where statements are personal opinions.

D. *Solicitation of employment:* The sport manager should seek employment only where a need for service exists.

E. *Propriety:* The sport manager should maintain high standards of personal conduct in the capacity or identity of the physical and health educator.

F. *Competence and professional development:* The sport manager should strive to become and remain proficient in professional practice and the performance of professional functions.

G. *Integrity:* The sport manager should act in accordance with the highest standards of professional integrity.

Category II: The Professional's Ethical Obligations to Students and Clients

H. *Primacy of students' and clients' interests:* The sport manager's primary responsibility is to students and clients.

I. *Service as agent or trustee:* The sport manager, when acting in professional matters for an employer or a student or client, should be a faithful agent or trustee.

J. *Rights and prerogatives of clients:* The sport manager should, in considering the nature of the relationship with the student or client, make every effort to foster maximum self-determination on the part of the student or client.

K. *Confidentiality and privacy:* The sport manager should respect the privacy of students and clients and hold in confidence all information obtained in the course of professional service.

L. *Fees:* When setting fees for service in private or commercial settings, the sport manager should ensure that such fees are fair, reasonable, considerate, and commensurate with the service performed and with due respect to students' or clients' ability to pay.

Category III: The Professional's Ethical Responsibility to Employers or Employing Organizations

M. *Commitments to employers or employing organizations:* The sport manager should adhere to any and all commitments made to the employing organization. The relationship should be characterized by fairness, nonmaleficence, and truthfulness.

Category IV: The Professional's Ethical Responsibility to Colleagues and Peers and to the Profession

N. *Respect, fairness, and courtesy:* The sport manager should treat colleagues with respect, courtesy, fairness, and good faith.

O. *Dealing with colleagues' students or clients:* The sport manager has the responsibility to relate to the students and clients of colleagues with full professional consideration.

P. *Maintaining the integrity of the profession:* The sport manager should uphold and advance the values and ethical standards, the knowledge, and the mission of the profession.

Q. *Development of knowledge:* The sport manager should take responsibility for identifying, developing, and fully utilizing established knowledge for professional practice.

R. *Approach to scholarship and research:* When engaged in study or research, the sport manager should be guided by the accepted conventions of scholarly inquiry.

Category V: The Professional's Ethical Responsibility to Society

S. *Promoting the general welfare:* The sport manager should promote the general welfare of society.

T. *Community service:* The sport manager should regard as primary his or her professional service to others. He or she should assist the profession in making information and services relating to desirable physical activity and health practices available to the general public.

U. *Reporting code infractions:* The sport manager has an ethical responsibility to society in that minor and major infractions by colleagues should be reported to the appropriate committee of the professional society (when and where such a mechanism exists).

References

Adams, J.S. (1963). Toward an understanding of inequity. *Journal of Abnormal Social Psychology, 67*, 422-436.

Adams, J.S. (1965). Inequity in social exchange. In L. Berkowitz (Ed.), *Advances in experimental social psychology* (Vol. 2, pp. 267-299). Santa Monica, CA: Goodyear.

Adams, J.S. (1977). Inequity in social exchange. In B.M. Staw (Ed.), *Psychological foundations of organizational behavior*. Santa Monica, CA: Goodyear.

Adkins, B., and Caldwell, D. (2004). Firm or subgroup culture: Where does fitting in matter most? *Journal of Organizational Behavior, 25*, 969-979.

Adkins, C.L., Ravlin, E.C., and Meglino, B.M. (1996). Value congruence between coworkers and its relationship to outcomes. *Group and Organization Management, 21*, 439-462.

Adler, N.J. (2002). *International dimensions of organizational behavior* (4th ed.). Cincinnati: South-Western.

Adorno, T., Frenkel-Brunswick, E., Levinson, D., and Sanford, R.N. (1950). *The authoritarian personality*. New York: Harper & Row.

Ahmed, P.K., and Rafiq, M. (2002). *Internal marketing: Tools and concepts for customer-focused management*. Oxford: Butterworth-Heinemann.

Aiken, L.H., Clarke, S.P., Sloane, D.M., Sochalski, J., and Silber, J.H. (2002). Hospital nurse staffing and patient mortality, nurse burnout, and job dissatisfaction. *Journal of the American Medication Association, 288*(16), 1987-1993.

Akehurst, G. (2009). User-generated content: The use of blogs for tourism organisations and tourism consumers. *Service Business, 3*(1), 51-61.

Albrecht, K., and Zemke, R. (2002). *Service America in the new economy*. New York: McGraw-Hill.

Allen, D.G., and Shanock, L.R. (2013). Perceived organizational support and embeddedness as key mechanisms connecting socialization tactics to commitment and turnover among new employees. *Journal of Organizational Behavior, 34*(3), 350-369.

Allport, G.W. (1937). *Personality*. New York: Holt, Rinehart & Winston.

Allport, G.W., and Odbert, H.S. (1936). Trait names: A psychological study. *Psychological Monographs*, No. 47.

American Medical Association. (2015). *Wikipedia*. https://en.wikipedia.org/wiki/American_Medical_Association.

Amis, J., and Slack, T. (1996). The size-structure relationship in voluntary sport organizations. *Journal of Sport Management, 10*, 76-86.

Apker, J., and Ray, E.B. (2003). Stress and social support in health care organizations. In T.L. Thompson, A.M. Dorsey, K.I. Miller, and R. Parrott (Eds.), *Handbook of health communication* (pp. 347-368). Mahwah, NJ: Erlbaum.

Archer, W., and Davidson, J. (2008). Graduate employability: What do employers think and want? Council for Industry and Higher Education. http://aces.shu.ac.uk/support/staff/employability/resources/CIHE%20-%200802Grademployability.pdf.

Arndt, J. (1979). Toward a concept of domesticated markets. *Journal of Marketing, 43*, 69-75.

Arnold, J.A., Arad, S., Rhoades, J.A., and Drasgow, F. (2000). The Empowering Leadership Questionnaire: The construction and validation of new scale for measuring leader behaviors. *Journal of Organizational Behavior, 21*, 249-269.

Asimov, N. (2016, February 10). Cal considers sports budget cuts, layoffs to close big deficit. *SF Gate*. www.sfgate.com/education/article/UC-Berkeley-looking-at-sports-cuts-layoffs-to-6819196.php.

Atchley, R.C. (1989). A continuity theory of normal aging. *The Gerontologist, 29*(2), 183-190.

Auld, C.J. (1997). *Professionalisation of Australian sport administration: The effects on organisational decision making: Full report*. Australian Sports Commission.

Auld, C.J., and Godbey, G. (1998). Influence in Canadian national sport organizations: Perceptions of professional and volunteers. *Journal of Sport Management, 12*(1), 20-38.

Australian Bureau of Statistics. (2010). Volunteer work, Australia. www.abs.gov.au/Ausstats/abs%40.nsf/e8ae5488b598839cca25682000131612/124e5675ad3aed8cca256a71000019c5!OpenDocument.

Avanzi, L., Zaniboni, S., Balducci, C., and Fraccaroli, F. (2014). The relation between overcommitment and burnout: Does it depend on employee job satisfaction?. *Anxiety, Stress, & Coping, 27*(4), 455-465.

Ayer, S. 2009. Corporate giving Canada: The latest data, trends, and implications. *Imagine Canada.* http://www.imaginecanada.ca/sites/default/files/www/en/partnershipforum/ayer_en_june2011.pdf

Bach, S., and Edwards, M.R. (2013). *Managing human resources* (5th ed.). Chichester, UK: Wiley.

Backman, S.J., and Crompton, J.L. (1991). The usefulness of selected variables for predicting activity loyalty. *Leisure Sciences, 13*, 205-220.

Ball, D.W. (1973). Ascription and position: A comparative analysis of "stacking" in professional football. *Canadian Review of Sociology and Anthropology, 10* (2), 97-113.

Balzer, W.K., Kihm, J.A., Smith, P.C., Irwin, J.L., Bachiochi, P.D., Robie, C., et al. (1997). *Users' manual for the Job Descriptive Index (JDI; 1997 revision) and the Job In General scales.* Bowling Green, OH: Bowling Green State University.

Balzer, W.K., Smith, P.C., Kravitz, D.A., Lovell, S.E., Paul, K.B., Reilly, B.A., and Reilly, C.E. (1990). *Users' manual for the Job Descriptive Index and the Job In General scales.* Bowling Green, OH: Bowling Green State University.

Bandura, A. (1986). *Social foundations of thought and action: A social cognitive theory.* Englewood Cliffs, NJ: Prentice Hall.

Bandura, A. (1997). *Self-efficacy: The exercise of control.* New York: Freeman.

Bang, H., Ross, S., and Reio, T.G., Jr. (2012). From motivation to organizational commitment of volunteers in non-profit sport organizations: The role of job satisfaction. *Journal of Management Development, 32*(1), 96-112.

Bansal, H.S., Mendelson, M.B., and Sharma, B. (2001). The impact of internal marketing activities on external marketing outcomes. *Journal of Quality Management, 6*, 61-76.

Barber, H., and Eckrich, J. (1998). Methods and criteria employed in the evaluation of intercollegiate coaches. *Journal of Sport Management, 12*, 301-322.

Barker, R. (2010). No, management is not a profession. *Harvard Business Review, 88*(7-8), 52-60.

Barnes, B.R., Fox, M.T., and Morris, D.S. (2004). Exploring the linkage between internal marketing and service quality: A case study of a consulting organization. *Total Quality Management, 15*(5-6), 593-601.

Barney, J. (1986). Organizational culture: Can it be a source of sustained competitive advantage? *Academy of Management Review, 11*, 656-665.

Barney, J. (1991). Firm resources and sustained competitive advantage. *Journal of Management, 17*(1), 99-120.

Barney, J. (1995). Looking inside for competitive advantage. *Academy of Management Executive, 9*(4), 49-61.

Barrick, M.R., and Mount, M.K. (1991). The big five personality dimensions and job performance: A meta-analysis. *Personnel Psychology, 44*, 1-26.

Barsade, S.G., Brief, A.P., and Spataro, S.E. (2003). The affective revolution in organizational behavior: The emergence of a paradigm. In J. Greenberg (Ed.), *Organizational behavior: The state of the science* (2nd ed., pp. 3-52). Mahwah, NJ: Erlbaum.

Bass, B.M. (1985). *Leadership and performance beyond expectations.* New York: Free Press.

Bass, B.M. (1990, Winter). From transactional to transformational leadership: Learning to share the vision. *Organizational Dynamics*, 19-31.

Batson, C.D. (1991). *The altruism question: Toward a social-psychological answer.* Hillsdale, NJ: Erlbaum.

Bauer, H.H., Stokburger-Sauer, N.E., and Exler, S. (2008). Brand image and fan loyalty in professional team sport: A refined model and empirical assessment. *Journal of Sport Management, 22*(2), 205.

Bauer, T.N., Truxillo, D.M., Sanchez, R.J., Craig, J.M., Ferrara, P., and Campion, M.A. (2001). Applicant reactions to selection: Development of the Selection Procedural Justice Scale (SPJS). *Personnel Psychology, 54*(2), 387-419.

Baydoun, R., Rose, D., and Emperado, T. (2001). Measuring customer service orientation: An examination of the validity of the Customer Service Profile. *Journal of Business and Psychology, 15*(4), 605-620.

Beamish, R. (1985). Sport executives and voluntary associations: A review of the literature and introduction to some theoretical issues. *Sociology of Sport Journal, 2*, 218-232.

Beard, J.G., and Ragheb, M.G. (1980). Measuring leisure satisfaction. *Journal of Leisure Research, 12*(1), 20-33.

Becker, B., and Gerhart, B. (1996). The impact of human resource management on organizational performance: Progress and prospects. *Academy of Management Journal, 39*(4): 779-801.

Becker, H.S. (1960). Notes on the concept of commitment. *American Journal of Sociology, 66*, 32-42.

Becker, T.E. (1992). Foci and bases of commitment: Are they distinctions worth making? *Academy of Management Journal, 35*, 232-244.

Becker, T.E., Billings, R.S., Eveleth, D.M., and Gilbert, N.L. (1996). Foci and bases of employee commitment: Implications for job performance. *Academy of Management Journal, 30*, 464-482.

Beer, M. (1987). Performance appraisal. In J.W. Lorsch (Ed.), *Handbook of organizational behavior* (pp. 286-290). Englewood Cliffs, NJ: Prentice Hall.

Beer, M., and Spector, B. (1985). *Readings in human resource management*. Simon and Schuster.

Belcourt, M., Sherman, A.W., Bohlander, G.W., and Snell, S.A. (2002). *Managing human resources* (3rd Canadian ed.). Scarborough, ON: Nelson Thomson Learning.

Bennis, W. (1997). *Organizing genius: The secrets of creative collaboration*. Reading, MA: Addison-Wesley.

Benson, V., Morgan, S., and Filippaios, F. (2014). Social career management: Social media and employability skills gap. *Computers in Human Behavior, 30*, 519-525.

Berry, L.L. (1981). The employee as customer. *Journal of Retail Banking, 3*, 25-28.

Berry, L.L., and Parasuraman, A. (1991). *Marketing services: Competing through quality*. New York: Free Press.

Bies, R.J., and Shapiro, D.L. (1987). Interactional fairness judgements: The influence of causal accounts. *Social Justice Research, 1*, 199-218.

Bitner, M.J. (1990). Evaluating service encounters: The effects of physical surroundings and employee responses. *Journal of Marketing, 54*, 69-82.

Bitner, M.J. (1992). Servicescapes: The impact of physical surroundings on customers and employees. *Journal of Marketing, 56*, 57-71.

Blau, G.J. (1986). Job involvement and organizational commitment as interactive predictors of tardiness and absenteeism. *Journal of Management, 12*, 577-584.

Blau, G.J., and Boal, K. (1989). Using job involvement and organizational commitment interactively to predict turnover. *Journal of Management, 15*, 115-127.

Blau, G.J., and Boal, K.B. (1987). Conceptualizing how job involvement and organizational commitment affect turnover and absenteeism. *Academy of Management Review, 12*, 288-300.

Blau, G.J., Paul, A., and St. John, N. (1993). On developing a general index of work commitment. *Journal of Vocational Behavior, 42*, 298-314.

Blau, G.J., and Ryan, J. (1997). On measuring work ethic: A neglected work commitment facet. *Journal of Vocational Behavior, 51*, 435-448.

Bloodworth, A., McNamee, M., and Bailey, R. (2012). Sport, physical activity, and well-being: An objectivist account. *Sport, Education, and Society, 17*(4), 497-514.

Bodtker, A.M., and Jameson, J.K. (2001). Emotion in conflict formation and its transformation: Application to organizational conflict management. *International Journal of Conflict Management, 12*(3), 259-275.

Boone, T. (2012). ABC of professionalism and vision. *Professionalization of Exercise Physiology, 15*(4), 1-13.

Bowen, D.E., and Ostroff, C. (2004). Understanding HRM-firm performance linkages: The role of the "strength" of the HRM system. *Academy of Management Review, 29*(2), 203-221.

Bower, G.G., and Hums, M.A. (2014). Examining the mentoring relationships of women working in intercollegiate athletic administration. *Mentoring & Tutoring: Partnership in Learning, 22*(1), 4-19.

Boyd, N.G., Lewin, J.E., and Sager, J.K. (2009). A model of stress and coping and their influence on individual and organizational outcomes. *Journal of Vocational Behavior, 75*(2), 197-211.

Brewster, C., Mayne, L., and Tregaskis, O. (1997). Flexible workings in Europe. *Journal of World Business, 32*(2), 133-151.

Brown, M.A. (1976). Values—A necessary but neglected ingredient of motivation on the job. *Academy of Management Review, 1*(4), 15-23.

Buchanan, B. (1974). Building organizational commitment: The socialization of managers in work organizations. *Administrative Science Quarterly, 19,* 533-546.

Buchmueller, T.C. (1999). Fringe benefits and the demand for part-time workers. *Applied Economics, 31,* 551-563.

Buckworth, J., and Dishman, R.K. (2007). Exercise adherence. In G. Tenenbaum and R.C. Eklund (Eds.), *Handbook of sport psychology* (3rd ed., pp. 509-536). New York: Wiley.

Burke, R.J. (1984). Mentors in organizations. *Group and Organizational Studies, 9,* 253-272.

Burton, L., and Welty Peachey, J. (2014). Ethical leadership in intercollegiate sport: Challenges, opportunities, future directions. *Journal of Intercollegiate Sport, 7*(1), 1-10.

Bush, G.W. (2003). President's radio address on December 20, 2003. www.whitehouse.gov/news/releases/2003/12/20031220.html.

Buskirk, R.H. (1974). *Modern management and Machiavelli.* New York: New American Library.

Byon, K.K., Zhang, J.J., and Baker, T.A. (2013). Impact of core and peripheral service quality in consumption behavior of professional team sport spectators as mediated by perceived value. *European Sport Management Quarterly, 13*(2), 232-263.

Campbell, J.P. (1993). A theory of performance. In N. Schmitt, W.C. Borman, and associates (Eds.), *Personnel selection in organizations* (pp. 35-70). San Francisco: Jossey-Bass.

Campion, M.A., and Thayer, P.W. (1985). Development and field evaluation of an interdisciplinary measure of job design. *Journal of Applied Psychology, 70*(1), 29-43.

Cappelli, P. (1995). Rethinking employment. *British Journal of Industrial Relations, 33,* 563-602.

Cappelli, P., and Keller, J.R. (2013). Classifying work in the new economy. *Academy of Management Review, 38*(4), 575-596.

Carless, S.A. (2004). Does psychological empowerment mediate the relationship between psychological climate and job satisfaction? *Journal of Business and Psychology, 18*(4), 405-425.

Carron, A.V., and Chelladurai, P. (1981). Cohesiveness as a factor in sport performance. *International Review of Sport Sociology, 2*(16), 21-41.

Carter, N. (1983). Collaboration and combat in networking. In M.S. Moyer (Ed.), *Managing voluntary organizations: Proceedings of a conference* (pp. 63-76). Toronto: York University, Faculty of Administrative Studies.

Castellano, W.G. (2014). *Practices for engaging the 21st century workforce.* Upper Saddle River, NJ: Pearson.

Cattell, R.B. (1957). *Personality and motivation, structure, and measurement.* Yonkers-on-Hudson, NY: World Book.

Caughron, J.J., Mumford, M.D., and Fleishman, E.A. (2012). The Fleishman Job Analysis Survey: Development, validation, and applications. In M.A. Wilson, W. Bennett, S.G. Gibson, and G.M. Alliger (Eds.). *The handbook of work analysis: Methods, systems, applications, and science of work measurement in organizations* (pp. 231-246). New York: Routledge.

Certo, S.C. (1992). *Modern management: Quality, ethics, and the global environment* (5th ed.). Boston: Allyn & Bacon.

Chandler, J. (2015, April 15). Volunteer trends. National Council of Nonprofits. www.councilofnonprofits.org/thought-leadership/volunteer-trends.

Chang, K., and Chelladurai, P. (2003). Comparison of part-time workers and full-time workers: Commitment and citizenship behaviors in Korean sport organizations. *Journal of Sport Management, 17,* 394-416.

Chatman, J.A. (1989). Improving interactional organizational research: A model of person-organization fit. *Academy of Management Review, 14,* 333-349.

Chatman, J.A. (1991). Matching people and organizations: Selection and socialization in public accounting firms. *Administrative Science Quarterly, 36,* 459-484.

Chelladurai, P. (1978). *A contingency model of leadership in athletics.* Unpublished doctoral dissertation, University of Waterloo, Waterloo, ON.

Chelladurai, P. (1981). The coach as motivator and chameleon of leadership styles. *Science Periodical on Research and Technology in Sport.* Ottawa, Canada: Coaching Association of Canada.

Chelladurai, P. (1985). *Sport management: Macro perspectives.* London, ON: Sports Dynamics.

Chelladurai, P. (1987). The design of sport governing bodies: A Parsonian perspective. In T. Slack and C.R. Hinings (Eds.), *The organization and administration of sport* (pp. 37-57). London, ON: Sports Dynamics.

Chelladurai, P. (1992). A classification of sport and physical activity services: Implications for sport management. *Journal of Sport Management, 6,* 38-51.

Chelladurai, P. (1993a). Leadership. In R.N. Singer, M. Murphey, and L.K. Tennant (Eds.), *Handbook of research on sport psychology* (pp. 647-671). New York: Macmillan.

Chelladurai, P. (1993b). Styles of decision making in coaching. In J.M. Williams (Ed.), *Applied sport psychology: Personal growth to peak performance* (2nd ed., pp. 99-109). Palo Alto, CA: Mayfield.

Chelladurai, P. (1995a, September). *Human resource management in sport and recreation.* Keynote address presented at the Third European Congress on Sport Management, Budapest, Hungary.

Chelladurai, P. (1995b). Total quality management in sport industry. *Journal of Japan Society of Sports Industry, 5*(1), 23-39.

Chelladurai, P. (1996, October). Quality in sport services. Paper presented at the plenary session of the Fourth European Congress on Sport Management, Montpelier, France.

Chelladurai, P. (2005). *Managing organizations for sport and physical activity: A systems perspective.* Scottsdale, AZ: Holcomb Hathaway Publishers.

Chelladurai, P. (2012). Leadership and manifestations of sport. In S. Murphy (Ed.). *The Handbook of Sport and Performance Psychology* (pp. 328-342). New York: Oxford University Press.

Chelladurai, P. (2014). *Managing organizations for sport and physical activity: A systems perspective* (4th ed.). Scottsdale, AZ: Holcomb Hathaway Publishers.

Chelladurai, P. (2015). *Corporate social responsibility and discretionary social initiatives in sport: A position paper.* Unpublished manuscript, Troy University, Alabama.

Chelladurai, P., and Arnott, M. (1985). Decision styles in coaching: Preferences of basketball players. *Research Quarterly for Exercise and Sport, 56,* 15-24.

Chelladurai, P., and Carron, A.V. (1977). A reanalysis of formal structure in sport. *Canadian Journal of Applied Sport Sciences, 2,* 9-14.

Chelladurai, P., and Carron, A.V. (1982, May). Individual and task differences, and preferred leadership. Paper presented at the annual conference of the North American Society for the Psychology of Sport and Physical Activity, College Park, MD.

Chelladurai, P., and Haggerty, T.R. (1978). A normative model of decision styles in coaching. *Athletic Administrator, 13,* 6-9.

Chelladurai, P., Haggerty, T.R., and Baxter, P.R. (1989). Decision style choices of university basketball coaches and players. *Journal of Sport and Exercise Psychology, 11,* 201-215.

Chelladurai, P., and Kuga, D.J. (1996). Teaching and coaching group and task differences. *Quest, 48,* 470-485.

Chelladurai, P., Kuga, D.J., and O'Bryant, C.P. (1999). Individual differences, perceived task characteristics and preferences for teaching and coaching. *Research Quarterly for Exercise and Sport, 70*(2), 179-189.

Chelladurai, P., and Ogasawara, E. (2003). Satisfaction and commitment of American and Japanese collegiate coaches. *Journal of Sport Management, 17,* 62-73.

Chelladurai, P., and Quek, C.B. (1995). Decision style choices of high school basketball coaches: The effects of situational and coach characteristics. *Journal of Sport Behavior, 17,* 276-293.

Chelladurai, P., and Riemer, H.A. (1997). A classification of facets of athlete satisfaction. *Journal of Sport Management, 11,* 133-159.

Chelladurai, P., and Saleh, S.D. (1980). Dimensions of leader behavior in sports: Development of a leadership scale. *Journal of Sport Psychology, 2,* 34-45.

Chelladurai, P., and Turner, B. (2006). Styles of decision making in coaching. In J.M. Williams (Ed.), *Applied sport psychology: Personal growth to peak performance* (5th ed., pp. 140-154). Boston: McGraw-Hill.

Chen, C.C., and Hooijberg, R. (2000). Ambiguity intolerance and support for valuing-diversity interventions. *Journal of Applied Social Psychology, 30*(11), 2392-2408.

Chen, L. (2004). Membership incentives: Factors affecting individuals' decisions about participation in athletics-related professional associations. *Journal of Sport Management, 18,* 111-131.

Chesley, N. (2014). Information and communication technology use, work intensification, and employee strain and distress. *Work, Employment, and Society, 30,* 1-22.

Cho, Y. (2009). Unfolding sporting nationalism in South Korean media representations of the 1968, 1984, and 2000 Olympics. *Media Culture & Society, 31*(3), 347-364.

Christie, R., and Geis, F. (1970). *Studies in Machiavellianism.* New York: Academic Press.

Cialdini, R.B., Schaller, M., Houlihan, D., Arps, K., Fultz, J., and Beamna, A.L. (1987). Empathy-based helping: Is it selflessly or selfishly motivated? *Journal of Personality and Social Psychology, 52,* 749-758.

Clary, E.G., Snyder, M., Ridge, R.D., Copelande, J., Stukas, A.A., Haugen, J., et al. (1998). Understanding and assessing the motivations of volunteers: A functional approach. *Journal of Personality and Social Psychology, 74,* 1516-1530.

Cleave, S. (1993). A test of the job characteristics model with administrative positions in physical education and sport. *Journal of Sport Management, 7,* 228-242.

Cleveland, J.N., Murphy, K.R., and Williams, R.E. (1989). Multiple uses of performance appraisal: Prevalence and correlates. *Journal of Applied Psychology, 74,* 130-135.

Clinton, W.J. (1997). Remarks at the Opening Ceremony of the Presidents' Summit for

America's Future in Philadelphia, April 28, 1997.

Retrieved from: https://www.gpo.gov/fdsys/pkg/PPP-1997-book1/pdf/PPP-1997-book1-doc-pg505.pdf

Coaching permits. (2016). Ohio Department of Education. http://education.ohio.gov/Topics/Teaching/Educator-Licensure/Audiences/Coaching-Permits.

Colquitt, J.A. (2001). On the dimensionality of organizational justice: A construct validation of a measure. *Journal of Applied Psychology, 86,* 386-400.

Colquitt, J.A., and Greenberg, J. (2003). Organizational justice: A fair assessment of the state of the literature. In J. Greenberg (Ed.), *Organizational behavior: The state of the science* (2nd ed., pp. 165-210). Mahwah, NJ: Erlbaum.

Colquitt, J.A., Greenberg, J., and Zapata-Phelan, C.P. (2005). What is organizational justice? A historical overview. In J. Greenberg and J.A. Colquitt (Eds.), *Handbook of organizational justice* (pp. 3-36). Mahwah, NJ: Erlbaum.

Clinton urges service stints. (1997, April 29). *Columbus Dispatch,* p. A1.

Colyer, S. (2000). Organizational culture in selected Western Australian sport organizations. *Journal of Sport Management, 14*(4), 321-341.

Conger, J.A., and Kanungo, R.N. (1987). Toward a behavioral theory of charismatic leadership in organizational settings. *Academy of Management Review, 12,* 637-647.

Conger, J.A., and Kanungo, R.N. (1998). *Charismatic leadership in organizations.* Thousand Oaks, CA: Sage.

Connor, P.E., and Becker, B.W. (1975). Values and the organization: Suggestions for research. *Academy of Management Journal, 18*(3), 550-561.

Corporation for National and Community Service. (2013). Research brief: Volunteering in America research highlights. http://2013.volunteeringinamerica.gov/research.cfm.

Correll, S.J., Kelly, E.L., O'Connor, L.T., and Williams, J.C. (2014). Redesigning, redefining work. *Work and Occupations, 41*(1), 3-17.

Cousquer, G.O., and Beames, S. (2013). Professionalism in mountain tourism and the claims to professional status of the International Mountain Leader. *Journal of Sport and Tourism, 18*(3), 185-215.

Cronin, M. (1999). *Sport and nationalism in Ireland: Gaelic games, soccer, and Irish identity since 1884.* Dublin: Four Courts Press.

Cunningham, G.B. (2008). Creating and sustaining gender diversity in sport organizations. *Sex Roles, 58*(1-2), 136-145.

Cuskelly, G. (2004). Volunteer retention in community sport organisations. *European Sport Management Quarterly, 4,* 59-76.

Cuskelly, G., Hoye, R., and Auld, C. (2006). *Working with volunteers in sport: Theory and practice.* New York: Routledge.

Cuskelly, G., McIntyre, M., and Boag, A. (1998). A longitudinal study of the development of organizational commitment amongst volunteer sport administrators. *Journal of Sport Management, 12*(3), 181-202.

Cuskelly, G., and O'Brien, W. (2013). Changing roles: Applying continuity theory to understanding the transition from playing to volunteering in community sport. *European Sport Management Quarterly, 13*(1), 54-75.

Daft, R.L. (2015). *The leadership experience* (6th ed.). Stamford, CT: Cengage Learning.

Dawis, R.V., England, G.W., and Lofquist, L.H. (1964). A psychological theory of work adjustment.

In *Minnesota studies in vocational rehabilitation* (Vol. 15). Minneapolis: University of Minnesota Industrial Relations Center, Work Adjustment Project.

Dawis, R.V., and Lofquist, L.H. (1984). *A psychological theory of work adjustment: An individual-differences model and its applications.* Minneapolis: University of Minnesota Press.

De Cenzo, D.A., and Robbins, S.P. (1994). *Human resource management: Concepts and practices.* New York: Wiley.

De Cenzo, D.A., and Robbins, S.P. (2002). *Human resource management* (7th ed.). New York: Wiley.

Deci, E.L., and Ryan, R.M. (1985). *Intinsic motivation and self-determination in human behavior.* New York: Plenum Press.

DeNisi, A., and Smith, C.E. (2014). Performance appraisal, performance management, and firm-level performance: A review, a proposed model, and new directions for future research. *The Academy of Management Annals, 8*(1), 127-179.

DePratto, B. (2014, December 2). Special report: The impact of volunteerism and charitable giving. TD Economics. www.td.com/document/PDF/economics/special/CharityVolunteering.pdf.

DeSensi, J.T. (1995). Understanding multiculturalism and valuing diversity: A theoretical perspective. *Quest, 47,* 34-43.

Deutsch, M. (1975). Equity, equality, and need: What determines which value will be used as the basis of distributive justice? *Journal of Social Issues, 31*(3), 137-149.

DeVaro,, J., Li, R., and Brookshire, D. (2007). Analysing the job characteristics model: New support from a cross-section of establishments. *International Journal of Human Resource Management, 18*(6), 986-1003.

DiMicco, J., Millen, D.R., Geyer, W., Dugan, C., Brownholtz, B., and Muller, M. (2008, November). Motivations for social networking at work. *Proceedings of the 2008 ACM Conference on Computer-Supported Cooperative Work* (pp. 711-720). Association for Computing Machinery.

Doherty, A., and Hoye, R. (2011). Role ambiguity and volunteer board member performance in non-profit sport organizations. *Nonprofit Management and Leadership, 22*(1), 107-128.

Doherty, A.J. (1997). The effect of leader characteristics on the perceived transformational/transactional leadership and impact of interuniversity athletic administrators. *Journal of Sport Management, 11,* 275-285.

Doherty, A.J., and Carron, A.V. (2003). Cohesion in volunteer sport executive committees. *Journal of Sport Management, 17*(20), 116-141.

Doherty, A.J., and Danylchuk, K.E. (1996). Transformational and transactional leadership in interuniversity athletic management. *Journal of Sport Management, 10,* 292-309.

Doherty, A., Patterson, M., and Van Bussel, M. (2004). What do we expect? An examination of perceived committee norms in non-profit sport organisations. *Sport Management Review, 7*(2), 109-132.

Dolan, S., Garcia, S., and Richley, B. (2006). *Managing by values: A corporate guide to living, being alive, and making a living in the 21st century.* New York: Palgrave Macmillan.

Dovidio, J.F. (1995). With a little help from my friends. In G.G. Brannigan and M.R. Merrens (Eds.), *The social psychologists: Research adventures* (pp. 98-113). New York: McGraw-Hill.

Drucker, P.F. (1992). *Managing for the future: The 1990s and beyond.* New York: Truman Talley Books/Dutton.

Dubrin, A.J. (2002). *The winning edge: How to motivate, influence, and manage your company's human resources.* Cincinnati: South-Western.

Dunmore, M. (2002). *Inside-out marketing: How to create an internal marketing strategy.* London: Kogan Page.

Eagly, A.H., and Carli, L.L. (2007). *Through the labyrinth: The truth about how women become leaders.* Harvard Business Press.

Eitzen, D.S., and Sage, G.H. (1986). *Sociology of North American sport* (3rd ed.). Dubuque, IA: Brown.

Ellis, S.J., and Noyes, K.H. (1990). *By the people: A history of Americans as volunteers.* San Francisco: Jossey-Bass.

Entrekin, L., and Scott-Ladd, B.D. (2014). *Human resource management and change.* London: Routledge.

Epstein, C.F., Seron, C., Oglensky, B., and Saute, R. (2014). *The part-time paradox: Time norms, professional life, family, and gender.* London: Routledge.

Etzioni, A. (1969). The semi-professions and their organization. New York: Macmillan.

Etzioni, A. (1973). The third sector and domestic missions. *Public Administration Review, 33,* 314-327.

Evans, M.G. (1986). Organizational behavior: The central role of motivation. *Journal of Management, 12*, 203-222.

Everhart, C.B., and Chelladurai, P. (1998). Gender differences in preferences for coaching as an occupation: The role of self-efficacy, valence, and perceived barriers. *Research Quarterly for Exercise and Sport, 69*(2), 188-200.

Fagenson, E.A. (1989). The mentor advantage: Perceived career/job experiences of proteges versus non-proteges. *Journal of Organizational Behavior, 10*, 309-320.

Farrell, J.M., Johnston, M.E., and Twynam, G.D. (1998). Volunteer motivation, satisfaction, and management at an elite sporting competition. *Journal of Sport Management, 12*(4), 288-300.

Feltz, D.L., Chase, M.A., Moritz, S.E., and Sullivan, P.J. (1999). Development of the multidimensional coaching efficacy scale. *Journal of Educational Psychology, 91*, 765-776.

Fiedler, F.E. (1954). Assumed similarity measures as predictors of team effectiveness. *Journal of Abnormal and Social Psychology, 49*, 381-388.

Fiedler, F.E. (1967). *A theory of leadership effectiveness.* New York: McGraw-Hill.

Fiedler, F.E. (1973). Personality and situational determinants of leader behavior. In E.A. Fleishman and J.G. Hunt (Eds.), *Current developments in the study of leadership* (pp. 41-60). Carbondale: Southern Illinois University Press.

Fielding, L.W., Pitts, B.G., and Miller, L.K. (1991). Defining quality: Should educators in sport management programs be concerned with accreditation? *Journal of Sport Management, 5*, 1-17.

Fiely, D. (2006). For Ohio Stadium ushers, game day is pay enough. *Columbus Dispatch.* (2006, September 23). pp.A1, A4.

Fila, M.J., Paik, L.S., Griffeth, R.W., and Allen, D. (2014). Disaggregating job satisfaction: Effects of perceived demands, control, and support. *Journal of Business and Psychology, 29*(4), 639-649.

Fisher, C.D., and Locke, E.A. (1992). The new look in job satisfaction research and theory. In C.J. Cranny, P.C. Smith, and E.F. Stone (Eds.), *Job satisfaction: How people feel about their jobs and how it affects their performance* (pp. 165-194). New York: Lexington Books.

Fitt, L.W., and Newton, D.A. (1981). When the mentor is a man and the protege a woman. *Harvard Business Review, 59*(2), 56-60.

Fitzsimmons, J., and Fitzsimmons, M. (2011). *Service management: Operations, strategy, and information technology* (7th ed.). Boston: McGraw-Hill.

Fitzsimmons, J.A., and Fitzsimmons, M.J. (2001). *Service management: Operations, strategy, and information technology* (4th ed.). New York: McGraw-Hill.

Flashman, R., and Quick, S. (1985). Altruism is not dead: A specific analysis of volunteer motivation. In L.F. Moore (Ed.), *Motivating volunteers: How the rewards of unpaid work can meet people's needs.* Vancouver, BC: Vancouver Volunteer Center.

Fleishman, E.A. (1992). *Fleishman job analysis survey.* Bethesda, MD: Management Research Institute.

Florida State University Campus Recreation. (2015). Kiteboard. http://campusrec.fsu.edu/sports/clubs/kiteboard.

Florida State University Campus Recreation. (2015). Our mission & values. http://campusrec.fsu.edu/our-mission-values.

Florida State University Campus Recreation. (2015). Sport clubs. http://campusrec.fsu.edu/sports/clubs.

Folger, R. (1987). Distributive and procedural justice in the work place. *Social Justice Research, 3*, 141-183.

Folger, R., and Cropanzano, R. (2001). Fairness theory: Justice as accountability. In J. Greenberg and R. Cropanzano (Eds.), *Advances in organizational justice* (pp. 89-118). Stanford, CA: Stanford University Press.

Folger, R., and Greenberg, J. (1985). Procedural justice: An interpretive analysis of personnel systems. In K.M. Rowland and G.R. Ferris (Eds.), *Research in personnel and human resource management* (Vol. 3, pp. 141-183). Greenwich, CT: JAI Press.

Ford, R.C., and Fottler, M.D. (1995). Empowerment: A matter of degree. *Academy of Management Executive, 9*, 21-31.

Forsyth, P., and Danisiewicz, T.J. (1985). Toward a theory of professionalism. *Work and Occupations, 12*(1), 59-76.

French, W.L. (2003). *Human resources management* (5th ed.). Boston: Houghton Mifflin.

Friedson, E. (1973). Professions and the occupational principle. In E. Friedson (Ed.), *Professions and their prospects* (pp. 19-38). Beverly Hills, CA: Sage.

Frost, F.A., and Kumar, M. (2000). INTSERQUAL—an internal adaptation of the GAP model in a large service organization. *Journal of Services Marketing, 14*(5), 358-377.

Gaskill, L.R. (1991). Same-sex and cross-sex mentoring of female proteges: A comparative analysis. *Career Development Quarterly, 40*, 48-63.

Gelfand, M.J., Kuhn, K.M., and Radhakrishnan, P. (1996). The effect of value differences on social interaction processes and job outcomes: Implications for managing diversity. In M.N. Ruderman, M.W. Hughes-James, and S.E. Jackson (Eds.), *Selected research on work team diversity* (pp. 53-71). Washington, DC: American Psychological Association.

Geyer, W., Dugan, C., DiMicco, J.M., Millen, D.R., Brownholtz, B. and Muller, M. (2008). Use and reuse of shared lists as a social content type. *Proceedings of the 2008 Computer–Human Interactions Conference* (p. 1545). New York: ACM Press.

Giannakos, M.N., Chorianopoulos, K., Giotopoulos, K., and Vlamos, P. (2013). Using Facebook out of habit. *Behaviour & Information Technology, 32*(6), 594-602.

Gibson, H., Willming, C., and Holdnak, A. (2002). "We're Gators . . . not just Gator fans": Serious leisure and University of Florida football. *Journal of Leisure Research, 34*(4), 397-425.

Gidron, B. (1983). Sources of job satisfaction among service volunteers. *Journal of Voluntary Action Research, 12*, 20-35.

Gilbert, L.A., and Rossman, K.M. (1992). Gender and the mentoring process for women: Implications for professional development. *Professional Psychology: Research and Practice, 23*(3), 233-238.

Gill, D.L., Gross, J.B., and Huddleston, S. (1983). Participation motives in youth sports. *International Journal of Sport Psychology, 14*, 1-14.

Gilliland, S.W. (1993). The perceived fairness of selection systems: An organizational justice perspective. *Academy of Management Review, 18*, 694-734.

Godin, B. (2006). Knowledge-based economy: Conceptual framework or buzzword? *Journal of Technology Transfer, 31*, 17-30.

Goetsch, D.L., and Davis, S.B. (1997). *Introduction to total quality: Quality management for production, processing, and services* (2nd ed.). Upper Saddle River, NJ: Prentice Hall.

Goldberg, L.R. (1990). An alternative description of personality: The big-five factor structure. *Journal of Personality and Social Psychology, 59*, 1216-1229.

Goldthwait, J.T. (1996). *Values: What they are and how we know them*. Amherst, NY: Prometheus Books.

Goode, W.J. (1969). The theoretical limits of professionalization. In A. Etzioni (Ed.), *The semi-professions and their organization* (pp. 266-313). New York: Free Press.

Goodman, E. (2013). Telecommuting: Is it right for you and your business? The dos, don'ts, perks, and drawbacks to a controversial issue in the changing office landscape. *Journal of Property Management, 78*(4), 16-21.

Gordon, C.W., and Babchuk, N. (1959). A typology of volunteer organizations. *American Sociological Review, 24*, 22-29.

Gordon, J.R. (2002). *Organizational behavior: A diagnostic approach* (7th ed.). Upper Saddle River, NJ: Prentice Hall.

Gordon, L.V. (1970). Measurement of bureaucratic orientation. *Personnel Psychology, 23*, 1-11.

Gornick, J.C., and Jacobs, J.A. (1996). A cross-national analysis of the wages of part-time workers: Evidence from the United States, the United Kingdom, Canada, and Australia. *Work Employment and Society, 10*, 1-27.

Gosden, E. (2015, April 10). David Cameron: 15 million workers to get three days' paid volunteering leave each year. *The Telegraph*. www.telegraph.co.uk/news/general-election-2015/11526478/David-Cameron-15-million-workers-to-get-three-days-paid-volunteering-leave-each-year.html.

Gottlieb, B.H., Kelloway, E.K., and Barham, E.J. (1998). *Flexible work arrangements: Managing the work-family boundary*. Chichester, England: Wiley.

Gough, H.G. (1969). *California Psychological Inventory* (rev. ed.). Palo Alto, CA: Consulting Psychologists Press.

Gough, H.G. (1984). A managerial potential scale for the California Psychological Inventory. *Journal of Applied Psychology, 69*, 233-240.

Government of Canada. (1992). *Sport: The way ahead*. The report of the Minister's Task Force on Federal Sport Policy (H93-104/1992E). Ottawa, ON: Government of Canada, Fitness and Amateur Sport.

Graves, C.W. (1970). Levels of existence: An open system theory of values. *Journal of Humanistic Psychology, 10*(2), 131-155.

Greenberg, J. (1987). A taxonomy of organizational justice theories. *Academy of Management Review, 12*, 9-22.

Greenberg, J. (1990). Organizational justice: Yesterday, today, and tomorrow. *Journal of Management, 16*, 399-432.

Greenberg, J. (1993). The social side of fairness: Interpersonal and informational classes of organization justice. In R. Cropanzano (Ed.), *Justice in the workplace: Approaching fairness in human resource management* (pp. 79-103). Hillsdale, NJ: Erlbaum.

Greenberg, J., and Colquitt, J.A. (Eds.). (2013). *Handbook of organizational justice*. New York: Psychological Press.

Greenleaf, R.K. (1977). *Servant leadership: A journey into the nature of legitimate power and greatness*. New York: Paulist Press.

Greer, D.L., and Stewart, M.J. (1989). Children's attitude toward play: An investigation of their context specificity and relationship to organized sport experiences. *Journal of Sport and Exercise Psychology, 11*, 336-342.

Griffeth, R.W., Horn, P.W., and Gaertner, S. (2000). Meta-analysis of antecedents and correlates of employee turnover: Update, moderator tests, and research implications for the next millennium. *Journal of Management, 26*(3), 463-488.

Grönroos, C. (1990). *Services marketing and management*. Lexington, MA: Lexington Books.

Grönroos, C. (2007). *Service management and marketing* (3rd ed.). Chichester, UK: Wiley.

Guilford, J.P. (1967). *The nature of human intelligence*. New York: McGraw-Hill.

Hackman, J.R., and Lawler, E.E. (1971). Employee reactions to job characteristics. *Journal of Applied Psychology Monograph, 55*, 259-286.

Hackman, J.R., and Oldham, G.R. (1976). Motivation through the design of work: Test of a theory. *Organizational Behavior and Human Performance, 16*, 250-279.

Hackman, J.R., and Oldham, G.R. (1980). *Work design*. Reading, MA: Addison-Wesley.

Hackman, J.R., Oldham, G., Janson, R., and Purdy, K. (1975). A new strategy for job enrichment. *California Management Review, 17*(4), 57-71.

Hall, D.T. (1976). *Careers in organizations*. Pacific Palisades, CA: Goodyear.

Halpin, A.W., and Winer, B.J. (1957). A factorial study of the leader behavior description. In R.M. Stogdill and A.E. Coons (Eds.), *Leader behavior: Its description and measurement*. Columbus: Ohio State University.

Hamm, S., MacLean, J., Kikulis, L., and Thibault, L. (2008). Value congruence in a Canadian nonprofit sport organisation: A case study. *Sport Management Review, 11*(2), 123-147.

Hamm-Kerwin, S., and Doherty, A. (2010). Intragroup conflict in nonprofit sport boards. *Journal of Sport Management, 24*(3), 245-271.

Hamm-Kerwin, S., Misener, K., and Doherty, A. (2009). Getting in the game: An investigation of volunteering in sport among older adults. *Leisure/Loisir, 33*(2), 659-685.

Hancock, M.G., and Hums, M.A. (2015). A "leaky pipeline"?: Factors affecting the career development of senior-level female administrators in NCAA Division I athletic departments. *Sport Management Review, 19*, 198-210.

Hansen, H., and Gauthier, R. (1989). Factors affecting attendance at professional sport events. *Journal of Sport Management, 3*, 15-32.

Harman, A., and Doherty, A. (2014). The psychological contract of volunteer youth sport coaches. *Journal of Sport Management, 28*(6), 687-699.

Hasenfeld, Y. (1983). *Human service organizations*. Englewood Cliffs, NJ: Prentice Hall.

Hasenfeld, Y., and English, R.A. (1974). Human service organizations: A conceptual overview. In Y. Hasenfeld and R.A. English (Eds.), *Human service organizations: A book of readings* (pp. 1-23). Ann Arbor: University of Michigan Press.

Hathaway, S.R., and McKinley, J.C. (1967). *Minnesota Multiphasic Personality Inventory* (rev. ed.). New York: Psychological Corporation.

Haug, M. (1975). The deprofessionalization of everyone? *Sociological Focus, 8*, 197-213.

Hay, R., and Gray, E. (1974). Social responsibilities of business managers. *Academy of Management Journal, 17*, 135-143.

Heiligers, P.J.M., and Hingstman, L. (2000). Career preferences and the work-family balance in medicine: Gender differences among medical specialists. *Social Science and Medicine, 50*, 1235-1246.

Henderson, K.A. (1981). Motivations and perceptions of volunteerism as a leisure activity. *Journal of Leisure Research, 13*(3), 208-218.

Henderson, K.A. (1985). Issues and trends in volunteerism. *Journal of Physical Education, Recreation and Dance, 56*(1), 30-32.

Hendry, L.B. (1968). The assessment of personality traits in the coach-swimmer relationship and a preliminary examination of the "father-figure" stereotype. *Research Quarterly, 39*, 543-551.

Hendry, L.B. (1969). A personality study of highly successful and "ideal" swimming coaches. *Research Quarterly, 40*, 299-305.

Heneman, H.G., Schwab, D.P., Fossum, J.A., and Dyer, L.D. (1983). *Personnel/human resource management*. Homewood, IL: Irwin.

Herzberg, F. (1966). *Work and the nature of man*. Cleveland: World.

Herzberg, F. (1968). One more time: How do you motivate people? *Harvard Business Review, 46*, 53-62.

Herzberg, F. (1974). The wise old Turk. *Harvard Business Review, 52*(5), 70-80.

Herzberg, F. (1987 September-October). One more time: How do you motivate people? *Harvard Business Review* (Exhibit I).

Herzberg, F., Mausner, B., and Snyderman, B.B. (1959). *The motivation to work*. New York: Wiley.

Higgins, M.C., and Kram, K.E. (2001). Reconceptualizing mentoring at work: A development network perspective. *Academy of Management Review, 26*, 264-288.

Hill, S.E., Bahniuk, M.H., and Dobos, J. (1989). The impact of mentoring and collegial support on faculty success: An analysis of support behavior, information adequacy, and communication apprehension. *Communication Education, 38*(1), 15-33.

Hilliard, S. (1990). Smashing the glass ceiling. *Black Enterprise, 21*(1), 99-108.

Hinings, C.R., and Slack, T. (1987). The dynamics of quadrennial plan implementation in national sport organizations. In T. Slack and C.R. Hinings (Eds.), *The organization and administration of sport* (pp. 127-151). London, ON: Sports Dynamics.

Hitt, M.A., Black, J.S., and Porter, L.W. (2005). *Management*. Upper Saddle River, NJ: Pearson Prentice Hall.

Hockey Canada (2015a). *Who is Hockey Canada?* Retrieved from http://www.hockeycanada.ca/en-ca/Corporate/About/Basics/Mandate-Mission.aspx

Hockey Canada (2015b). *Governance Organizational Structure*. Retrieved from http://www.hockeycanada.ca/en-ca/Corporate/About/Basics/Structure

Hofstede, G. (1997). Organization culture. In M. Warner (Ed.), *Concise international encyclopedia of business and management* (pp. 540-558). London: International Thompson Business Press.

Hogan, J., Hogan, R., and Busch, C.M. (1984). How to measure service orientation. *Journal of Applied Psychology, 69*, 167-173.

Holbeche, L. (2005). *The high performance organization: Creating dynamic stability and sustainable success*. Oxford: Elsevier Butterworth-Heinemann.

Hood, J.N. (2003). The relationship of leadership style and CEO values to ethical practices in organizations. *Journal of Business Ethics, 43*, 263-273.

House, R.J. (1971). A path-goal theory of leader effectiveness. *Administrative Science Quarterly, 16*, 321-338.

House, R.J., and Dessler, G. (1974). The path-goal theory of leadership: Some post hoc and a priori tests. In J.G. Hunt and L.L. Larson (Eds.), *Contingency approaches to leadership*. Carbondale: Southern Illinois University Press.

House, R.J., and Mitchell, T.R. (1974). Path-goal theory of leadership. *Journal of Contemporary Business, 3*, 81-97.

House, R.J., and Podsakoff, P.M. (1994). Leadership effectiveness: Past perspectives and future directions for research. In J. Greenberg (Ed.), *Organizational behavior: The state of the science*. Hillsdale, NJ: Erlbaum.

Hovland, C., Janis, I., and Kelley, H. (1953). *Communication and persuasion*. New Haven, CT: Yale University Press.

Howard, D.R., and Crompton, J.L. (1995). *Financing sport*. Morgantown, WV: Fitness Information Technology.

Hoy, W.K., and Miskel, C.G. (2005). *Educational administration: Theory, research, and practice* (7th ed.). New York: Random House.

Hughes, C.L., and Flowers, V.S. (1975). Toward existentialism in management. *Conference Board Record, 12*, 60-64.

Humphrey, R.H., and Ashforth, B.E. (1994). Cognitive scripts and prototypes in service encounters. *Advances in Services Marketing and Management, 3*, 175-199.

Hums, M.A., and Chelladurai, P. (1994a). Distributive justice in intercollegiate athletics: Development of an instrument. *Journal of Sport Management, 8*, 190-199.

Hums, M.A., and Chelladurai, P. (1994b). Distributive justice in intercollegiate athletics: The views of NCAA coaches and administrators. *Journal of Sport Management, 8*, 200-217.

Hunt, D., and Michael, C. (1983). Mentorship: A career training and development tool. *Academy of Management Review, 8*, 475-480.

Idaszak, J.R., and Drasgow, F. (1987). A revision of the Job Diagnostic Survey: Elimination of a measurement artifact. *Journal of Applied Psychology, 72*, 69-74.

Ilsley, P.J. (1990). *Enhancing the volunteer experience: New insights on strengthening volunteer participation, learning, and commitment*. San Francisco: Jossey-Bass.

Independent Sector. (2015). The value of volunteer time. www.independentsector.org/volunteer_time.

Inglis, S. (1997). Roles of board in amateur sport organizations. *Journal of Sport Management, 11*, 160-176.

Institute for Volunteering Research. (2015). What do volunteers do? www.ivr.org.uk/ivr-volunteering-stats/178-what-do-volunteers-do.

International Basketball Federation (FIBA). (2015). *FIBA 2014-2019 strategy*. http://www.fiba.com/en/Module/c9dad82f-01af-45e0-bb85-ee4cf50235b4/4cf008b4-618b-48c9-b163-68bdd69eaf8b

Ivancevich, J.M., Konopaske, R., and Matteson, M.T. (2011). *Organizational behavior and management* (9th ed.). New York: McGraw-Hill Irwin.

Ivancevich, J.M., and Matteson, M.T. (2002). *Organizational behavior and management* (6th ed.). Boston: McGraw-Hill/Irwin.

Jackson, B., Dimmock, J.A., Gucciardi, D.F., and Grove, J.R. (2011). Personality traits and relationship perceptions in coach–athlete dyads: Do opposites really attract?. *Psychology of Sport and Exercise, 12*(3), 222-230.

Jackson, D.N. (1984). *Personality Research Form Manual*. Port Huron, MI: Sigma Assessment Systems.

Jackson, J.A. (1970). Professions and professionalization: Editorial introduction. In J.A. Jackson (Ed.), *Professions and professionalization* (pp. 3-15). Cambridge: Cambridge University Press.

Jackson, S.E., and Schuler, R.S. (1992). Human resource management practices in service-based organizations: A role theory perspective. *Advances in Services Marketing and Management, 1*, 123-157.

James, K., Chen, D., and Cropanzano, R. (1996). Culture and leadership among Taiwanese and U.S. workers: Do values influence leadership ideals? In M.N. Ruderman, M.W. Hughes-James, and S.E. Jackson (Eds.), *Selected research on work team diversity* (pp. 33-52). Washington, DC: American Psychological Association.

Jamieson, L.M. (1987). Competency-based approaches to sport management. *Journal of Sport Management, 1*, 48-56.

Jaros, S.J., Jermier, J.M., Koehler, J.W., and Sincich, T. (1993). Effects of continuance, affective, and moral commitment on the withdrawal process: An evaluation of eight structural equation models. *Academy of Management Journal, 36*, 951-995.

Jehn, K.A., Northcraft, G.B., and Neale, M.A. (1999). Why differences make a difference: A field study of diversity, conflict, and performance in workgroups. *Administrative Science Quarterly, 44*, 741-763.

Jennings, E.E. (1967). *The mobile manager: A study of the new generation of top executives*. Unpublished doctoral dissertation, University of Michigan.

Jordan, J.S., Gillentine, J.A., and Hunt, B.P. (2004). The influence of fairness: The application of organizational justice in a team sport setting. *International Sports Journal, 8*, 139-149.

Joseph, W.B. (1996). Internal marketing builds service quality. *Journal of Health Care Marketing, 16*(1), 54-64.

Jung, D.I., and Avolio, B.J. (2000). Opening the black box: An experimental investigation of the mediating effects of trust and value congruence on transformational and transactional leadership. *Journal of Organizational Behavior, 21*, 949-964.

Jurkus, A.F. (1978). Professionalism in management. In L.R. Bittel and M.A. Bittel (Eds.), *Encyclopedia of professional management* (pp. 983-985). New York: McGraw-Hill.

Kabanoff, B., and O'Brien, G.E. (1980). Work and leisure: A task attributes analysis. *Journal of Applied Psychology, 65*, 596-609.

Kanfer, R.L. (1990). Motivation theory and industrial/organizational psychology. In D.M. Dunnette (Ed.), *Handbook of industrial and organizational psychology* (pp. 75-170). Palo Alto, CA: Consulting Psychologists Press.

Kanibir, H., and Nart, S. (2012). The effects of internal relationship marketing on superior customer relations as competitive performance: Evidence from healthcare industry. *Procedia - Social and Behavioral Sciences, 58*, 1378-1385.

Kanter, R.M. (1977). *Men and women of the corporation.* New York: Basic Books.

Katz, D., Maccoby, N., Gurin, G., and Floor, L. (1951). *Productivity, supervision, and morale among railroad workers.* Ann Arbor: University of Michigan.

Katz, D., Maccoby, N., and Morse, N. (1950). *Productivity, supervision, and morale in an office situation.* Ann Arbor: University of Michigan.

Katz, R.L. (1972). Skills of an effective administrator. *Harvard Business Review, 52*, 90-102.

Kaynak, E., Salman, G.G., and Tatoglu, E. (2008). An integrative framework linking brand associations and brand loyalty in professional sports. *Journal of Brand Management, 15*(5), 336-357.

Kelemen, M., and Papsolomou-Doukakis, I. (2004). Can culture be changed? A study of internal marketing. *Services Industries Journal, 24*(5), 121-135.

Kent, A., and Sullivan, P.J. (2003). Coaching efficacy as a predictor of university coaches' commitment. *International Sports Journal, 7*(1), 78-87.

Kerr, G.A., and Stirling, A.E. (2015). Professionalization of coaches to reduce emotionally harmful coaching practices: Lessons learned from the education sector. *International Journal of Coaching Science, 9*(1), 21-35.

Kerr, S. (1975). On the folly of rewarding A, while hoping for B. *Academy of Management Journal, 18*, 769-783.

Kerr, S. (1995). On the folly of rewarding A, while hoping for B. *Academy of Management Executive, 9*, 7-14.

Kerr, S., and Jermier, J.M. (1978). Substitutes for leadership: Their meaning and measurement. *Organizational Behavior and Human Performance, 22*, 375-403.

Kerwin, S. (2015). Understanding conflict in sport and entertainment organizations. *Sport and Entertainment Review, 1*(3), 75-82.

Kerwin, S., Doherty, A., and Harman, A. (2011). ïIt's not conflict, it's differences of opinionî: An in-depth examination of conflict in nonprofit boards. *Small Group Research, 42*, 562-594.

Kerwin, S., Jordan, J., and Turner, B. (2015). Organizational justice and conflict: Do perceptions of fairness influence disagreement? *Sport Management Review, 18*, 384-395.

Kerwin, S., MacLean, J., and Bell-Laroche, D. (2014a). The value of managing by values. *Journal of Applied Sport Management, 6*(4), 27-50.

Kerwin, S., MacLean, J., and Bell-Laroche, D. (2014b). The mediating influence of management by values in nonprofit sport organizations. *Journal of Sport Management, 28*(6), 646-656.

Kerwin, S., Warner, S., Walker, M., and Stevens, J. (2015). Exploring sense of community among small-scale sport event volunteers. *European Sport Management Quarterly, 15*(1), 77-92.

Kikulis, L.M. (2000). Continuity and change in governance and decision making in national sport organizations: Institutional explanations. *Journal of Sport Management, 14*(4), 293-320.

Killian, R.A. (1976). *Human resource management.* New York: AMACOM Press.

Kim, M., Zhang, J., and Connaughton, D. (2010). Comparison of volunteer motivations in different youth sport organizations. *European Sport Management Quarterly, 10*, 343-365.

King, N. (1970). Clarification and evaluation of the two-factor theory of job satisfaction. *Psychological Bulletin, 74*, 18-31.

Klemp, G.O., Jr., and McClelland, D.C. (1986). What characterizes intelligent functioning among senior managers? In R.J. Sternberg and R.K. Wagner (Eds.), *Practical intelligence: Nature and origins of competence in the everyday world* (pp. 31-50). New York: Cambridge University Press.

Knight Foundation. (2001). *A call to action: Reconnecting college sports and higher education.* Miami, FL: John S. and James L. Knight Foundation.

Knoke, D. (1986). Associations and interest groups. *Annual Review of Sociology, 12,* 1-21.

Knoke, D. (2001). *Changing organizations: Business networks in the new political economy.* Boulder, CO: Westview Press.

Knoke, D., and Prensky, D. (1984). What relevance do organization theories have for voluntary associations? *Social Science Quarterly, 65*(1), 3-20.

Knoppers, A. (2015). Assessing the sociology of sport: On critical sport sociology and sport management. *International Review for the Sociology of Sport, 50*(4-5), 496-501.

Koehler, L.S. (1988). Job satisfaction and corporate fitness managers: An organizational behavior approach to sport management. *Journal of Sport Management, 2,* 100-105.

Kossek, E.E., and Lautsch, B.A. (2012). Work–family boundary management styles in organizations: A cross-level model. *Organizational Psychology Review, 2*(2), 152-171.

Kotler, P. (1994). *Marketing management.* Englewood Cliffs, NJ: Prentice Hall.

Kotler, P., and Roberto, E.L. (1989). *Social marketing: Strategies for changing public behavior.* New York: Free Press.

Kouri, M.K. (1990). *Volunteerism and older adults.* Santa Barbara, CA: ABC-CLIO.

Kram, K.E. (1980). *Mentoring process at work: Developmental relationships in managerial careers.* Unpublished doctoral dissertation, Yale University.

Kram, K.E. (1983). Phases of the mentor relationship. *Academy of Management Journal, 26,* 608-625.

Kram, K.E. (1985). *Mentoring at work.* Glenview, IL: Scott, Foresman.

Kram, K.E. (1988). *Mentoring at work: Developmental relationships in organizational life.* Lanham, MD: University Press of America.

Lambert, S.J. (2000). Added benefits: The link between work–life benefits and organizational citizenship behavior. *Academy of management Journal, 43*(5), 801-815.

Landy, F.J., and Becker, W.S. (1987). Motivation theory reconsidered. In L.L. Cummings and B.M. Staw (Eds.), *Research in organizational behavior* (Vol. 9, pp. 1-38). Greenwich, CT: JAI Press.

Lapchick, R.E. (1991, Summer). Professional sports: The racial report card. *Center for the Study of Sport and Society Digest, 2*(1), 4-8.

Lawler, E.E., III. (1973). *Motivation in work organizations.* Pacific Grove, CA: Brooks/Cole.

Lawler, E.E., III. (1987). The design of effective reward systems. In J.W. Lorsch (Ed.), *Handbook of organizational behavior* (pp. 255-271). Englewood Cliffs, NJ: Prentice Hall.

Lawrence, P.R., and Lorsch, J.W. (1967). *Organization and environment: Managing differentiation and integration.* Campridge, MA: Harvard University Press.

Lawson, H.A. (1979). Paths toward professionalization. *Quest, 31*(2), 231-243.

Leading social networks worldwide as of April 2016, ranked by number of active users (in millions). (2016). *Statista.* www.statista.com/statistics/272014/global-social-networks-ranked-by-number-of-users.

Lee, D.R. (1996). Why is flexible employment increasing? *Journal of Labor Research, 17*(4), 543-553.

Leftheriotis, I., and Giannakos, M.N. (2014). Using social media for work: Losing your time or improving your work? *Computers in Human Behavior, 31,* 134-142.

Legge, K. (1995). HRM: Rhetoric, reality and hidden agendas. In J. Storey (Ed.), *Human resource management* (pp. 33-59). London: Routledge.

Lengnick-Hall, C.A. (1995). The patient as the pivot point for quality in health care delivery. *Hospital and Health Services Administration, 38*(3), 45-56.

Lengnick-Hall, C.A. (1996). Customer contributions to quality: A different view of the customer-oriented firm. *Academy of Management Review, 21,* 791-824.

Leonardi, P.M., Treem, J.W., and Jackson, M.H. (2010). The connectivity paradox: Using technology to both decrease and increase perceptions of distance in distributed work arrangements. *Journal of Applied Communication Research, 38*(1), 85-105.

Leventhal, G.S. (1980). What should be done with equity theory? New approaches to the study of fairness in social relationships. In K.J. Gergen, M.S. Greenberg, and R.H. Willis (Eds.), *Social exchange: Advances in theory and research* (pp. 27-55). New York: Plenum Press.

Levinson, D.J. (1978). *The seasons of a man's life.* New York: Knopf.

Levitt, T. (1973). *The third sector: New tactics for a responsive society.* New York: AMACOM Press.

Lewin, K. (1935). *A dynamic theory of personality.* New York: McGraw-Hill.

Li, M. (1993). Job satisfaction and performance of coaches of the spare-time sports schools in China. *Journal of Sport Management, 7,* 132-140.

Lings, I.N. (2004). Internal market orientation: Construct and consequences. *Journal of Business Research, 57,* 405-413.

Lings, I.N., and Brooks, R.F. (1998). Implementing and measuring the effectiveness of internal marketing. *Journal of Marketing Management, 14,* 325-351.

Lings, I.N., and Greenley, G.E. (2005). Measuring internal market orientation. *Journal of Service Research, 7*(3), 290-305.

Lings, I.N., and Greenley, G.E. (2010). Internal market orientation and market-oriented behaviours. *Journal of Service Management, 21*(3), 321-343.

Livnat, Y. (2003). Benevolence and justice. *The Journal of Value Inquiry, 37*(4), 507-515.

Local Government Management Board. (1993). Managing tomorrow. In *Panel of Inquiry report* (p. 8). London: Local Government Management Board.

Locke, E.A. (1976). The nature and causes of job satisfaction. In M.M. Dunnette (Ed.), *Handbook of industrial and organizational psychology.* Chicago: Rand McNally.

Locke, E.A. (1997). Prime movers: The traits of great business leaders. In C.L. Cooper and S.E. Jackson (Eds.), *Creating tomorrow's organizations: A handbook for future research in organizational behavior* (pp. 75-96). Chichester, England: Wiley.

Locke, E.A. (2003). Good definitions: The epistemological foundation of scientific progress. In J. Grennberg (Ed.), *Organizational behavior: The state of the science* (2nd ed., pp. 415-444). Mahwah, NJ: Erlbaum.

London, M. (1991). Career development. In K.N. Wexley (Ed.), *Developing human resources* (pp. 5.152-5.184). Washington, DC: Bureau of National Affairs.

Longenecker, C.O., Sims, H.P., and Gioia, D.A. (1987). Behind the mask: The politics of employee appraisal. *Academy of Management Executive, 1,* 183-193.

Lorsch, J.W., and Morse, J.J. (1974). *Organizations and their members: A contingency approach.* New York: Harper & Row.

Lovelock, C., and Gummesson, E. (2004). Whither services marketing? In search of new paradigm and fresh perspectives. *Journal of Service Research, 7*(1), 20-41.

Lovelock, C.H. (2001). *Services marketing: People, technology, strategy* (4th ed., p. 2). Upper Saddle River, NJ: Prentice Hall.

Loy, J.H., and McElvogue, J.F. (1970). Racial segregation in American sport. *International Review of Sport Sociology, 5,* 5-24.

Lubinsky, M., Doherty, A., and Kerwin, S. (2011). Coroporate philanthropy toward the community and organisational commitment in the fitness sector. *International Journal of Sport Management and Marketing, 10*(1/2), 1-20.

Luthans, F. (2010). *Organizational behavior* (12th ed.). New York: McGraw-Hill.

Luthans, F., and Avolio, B.J. (2003). Authentic leadership development. In K.S. Cameron, J.E. Dutton, and R.E. Quinn (Eds.), *Positive organizational scholarship* (pp. 241-258). San Francisco: Berrett-Koehler.

Machievellianism. (1976). *Merriam-Webster's Dictionary of the English Language* (2nd ed.). Cleveland: Collins-World.

MacLean, J. (2001). *Performance appraisal for sport and recreation managers.* Champaign, IL: Human Kinetics.

MacLean, J.C., and Chelladurai, P. (1995). Dimensions of coaching performance: Development of a scale. *Journal of Sport Management, 9,* 194-207.

Maddi, S.R. (2001). *Personality theories: A comparative analysis* (6th ed.). Homewood, IL: Dorsey Press.

Maehr, M.L., and Braskamp, L.A. (1986). *The motivation factor: A theory of personal investment.* Lexington, MA: Lexington Books.

Mahony, D.F., Hums, M.A., and Riemer, H.A. (2002). Distributive justice in intercollegiate athletics: Perceptions of athletic directors and athletic board chairs. *Journal of Sport Management, 16*, 331-356.

Mahony, D.F., and Pastore, D. (1998). Distributive justice: An examination of participation opportunities, revenues, and expenses at NCAA institutions. *Journal of Sport and Social Issues, 22*(2), 127-152.

Malloy, D.C., and Agarwal, J. (2001). Differential association and role-set configuration: The impact of significant others upon the perception of ethical climate in a sport organization. *Journal of Sport Management, 15*(3), 195-218.

Manchester United legend Sir Alex Ferguson gives his blueprint for success. (2013). *The Guardian.* www.theguardian.com/football/2013/sep/10/alex-ferguson-manchester-united-blueprint.

Martin, C.L. (1990). The employee/customer interface: An empirical investigation of employee behaviors and customer perceptions. *Journal of Sport Management, 4*, 1-20.

Martin, L.A., and Fraser, S.L. (2002). Customer service orientation in managerial and non-managerial employees: An exploratory study. *Journal of Business and Psychology, 16*(3), 477-484.

Maslach, C. (2003). *Burnout: The cost of caring.* Cambridge, MA: Malor.

Maslow, A.H. (1943). A theory of human motivation. *Psychological Review, 50*, 370-396.

Mason, D.E. (1984). *Voluntary nonprofit enterprise management.* New York: Plenum Press.

Mathieu, J.E., and Zajac, D.M. (1990). A review and meta-analysis of the antecedents, correlates, and consequences of organizational commitment. *Psychological Bulletin, 108*, 171-194.

Matthews, G., Zeidner, M., and Roberts, R.D. (2002). *Emotional intelligence: Science and myth.* Cambridge, MA: MIT Press.

Mayer, J.D., and Salovey P. (1997). What is emotional intelligence? In P. Salovey and D. Sluyter (Eds.), *Emotional development and emotional intelligence: Implications for educators.* (pp. 3-31). New York: Basic Books.

McClelland, D. (1996). Foreword. In N. Boulter, M. Dalziel, and J. Hill (Eds.), *People and competencies: The route to competitive advantage* (2nd ed., pp. 15-19). London: Kogan Page.

McClelland, D.C. (1961). *The achieving society.* New York: Van Nostrand.

McClelland, D.C. (1975). *Power: The inner experience.* New York: Irvington.

McClelland, D.C., and Burnham, D.H. (1976). Power is the great motivator. *Harvard Business Review, 54*, 100-110.

McClelland, D.C., and Winter, D.G. (1969). *Motivating economic achievement.* New York: Free Press.

McCrae, R.R., and Costa, P.T. (1987). Validation of the five-factor model of personality across instruments and observers. *Journal of Personality and Social Psychology, 52*, 81-90.

McGee, G.W., and Ford, R.C. (1987). Two (or more?) dimensions of organizational commitment: Reexamination of the affective and continuance commitment scales. *Journal of Applied Psychology, 72*, 638-642.

McKay, P.F., and Avery, D.R. (2015). Diversity climate in organizations: Current wisdom and domains of uncertainty. *Research in Personnel and Human Resources Management, 33*, 191-233.

McManus, I.C., Winder, B.C., and Gordon, D. (2002). The causal links between stress and burnout in a longitudinal study of UK doctors. *The Lancet, 359*(9323), 2089-2090.

McPherson, B.D. (1975). Past, present and future perspectives for research in sport sociology. *International Review of Sport Sociology, 10*(1), 55-72.

McPherson, J.M., and Smith-Lovin, L. (1986). Sex segregation in voluntary organizations. *American Sociological Review, 51*, 61-79.

McShane, S.L. and Von Glinow, M. (2010). *Organizational behavior* (5th ed.). Burr Ridge, IL: McGraw-Hill.

Megginson, D., and Clutterbuck, D. (2005). *Techniques for coaching and mentoring.* Oxford: Elsevier Butterworth-Heinemann.

Meglino, B.M., Ravlin, E.C., and Adkins, C.L. (1989). A work values approach to corporate culture: A field test of the value congruence process and its relationship to individual outcomes. *Journal of Applied Psychology, 74*, 424-432.

Meglino, B.M., Ravlin, E.C., and Adkins, C.L. (1992). The measurement of work value congruence: A field study comparison. *Journal of Management, 18*, 33-43.

Meindl, J.R. (1989). Managing to be fair: An exploration of values, motives, and leadership. *Administrative Science Quarterly, 34*, 252-276.

Mercier, R. (2000). Being professional about your employment. *Canadian Journal for Women in Coaching Online, 1*(1). www.coach.ca/women/e/journal/sep2000/print.htm.

Merriam-Webster. (2016). Simple definition of commitment. https://www.merriam-webster.com/dictionary/commitment

Merton, R.K. (1982). *Social research and the practicing professions.* Cambridge, MA: ABT Books.

Meyer, J.P., and Allen, N.J. (1991). A three-component conceptualization of organizational commitment. *Human Resource Management Review, I*, 61-89.

Meyer, J.P., and Allen, N.J. (1997). *Commitment in the workplace: Theory, research, and application.* Thousand Oaks, CA: Sage.

Meyer, J.P., Allen, N.J., and Gellatly, I.R. (1990). Affective and continuance commitment to the organization: Evaluation of measures and analysis of concurrent and time-lagged relations. *Journal of Applied Psychology, 75*, 710-720.

Meyer, J.P., Stanley, D.J., Jackson, T.A., McInnis, K.J., Maltin, E.R., and Sheppard, L. (2012). Affective, normative, and continuance commitment levels across cultures: A meta-analysis. *Journal of Vocational Behavior, 80*(2), 225-245.

Milano, M., and Chelladurai, P. (2011). Gross domestic sport product: The size of the sport industry in the United States. *Journal of Sport Management, 25*(1), 24-35.

Miller, H.B. (1982). Altruism, volunteers and sociology. In J.D. Harman (Ed.), *Volunteerism in the eighties.* Washington, DC: University Press of America.

Miller, H.E., and Terborg, J.R. (1979). Job attitudes of part-time and full-time employees. *Journal of Applied Psychology, 64*(4), 380-386.

Mills, P.K., and Margulies, N. (1980). Toward a core typology of service organizations. *Academy of Management Review, 5*, 255-265.

Mills, P.K., and Morris, J.H. (1986). Clients as "partial" employees of service organizations: Role development in client participation. *Academy of Management Review, 11*(4), 726-735.

Mischel, W. (1973). Toward a cognitive social learning reconceptualization of personality. *Psychological Review, 80*, 252-283.

Misener, K., Doherty, A., and Hamm-Kerwin, S. (2010). Learning from the experiences of older adult volunteers in sport: A serious leisure perspective. *Journal of Leisure Research, 42*(2), 267-289.

Mitchell, T.R., Holtom, B.C., Lee, T.W., and Erez, M. (2001). Why people stay: Using job embeddedness to predict voluntary turnover. *Academy of Management Journal, 44*, 1102-1121.

Mitchelson, B., and Slack, T. (1983). *The volunteer sport administrator.* Ottawa, ON: Canadian Association for Health, Physical Education, and Recreation.

Mondy, R.W., and Noe, R.M. (1993). *Human resource management* (5th ed.). Boston: Allyn & Bacon.

Morford, W.R. (1972). Toward a profession, not a craft. *Quest, 18*, 88-93.

Morrison, I. (1986). A new era for volunteerism: An overview. In *A new era for volunteerism.* Proceedings of a conference, Toronto, June 1-3, 1986. Toronto: United Way of Greater Toronto.

Morrow, P.C., and Goetz, J.F. (1988). Professionalism as a form of work commitment. *Journal of Vocational Behavior, 32*, 92-111.

Morse, J.J. (1976). Person-task congruence and individual adjustment and development. *Human Relations, 28*, 841-861.

Morse, J.J., and Young, D.F. (1973). Personality development and task choices: A systems view. *Human Relations, 26*(3), 307-324.

Mount, M.K., and Barrick, M.R. (1995). The big-five personality dimensions: Implications for research and practice in human resources management. In *Research in personnel and human resource management* (Vol. 13, pp. 153-200). Greenwich, CT: JAI Press.

Mowday, R.T., Porter, L.W., and Steers, R.M. (1982). *Employee-organization linkages: The psychology of commitment, absenteeism, and turnover.* New York: Academic Press.

Moyer, M.S. (1985). Voluntary action research: A view from Canada. *Journal of Voluntary Action Research, 14*(2-3), 15-16.

Mullin, B.J., Hardy, S., and Sutton, W.A. (2000). *Sport marketing* (2nd ed.). Champaign, IL: Human Kinetics.

Murray, H.A. (1938). *Explorations in personality*. New York: Oxford University Press.

Murrell, A.J., and Dietz, B. (1992). Fan support of sport teams: The effect of a common group identity. *Journal of Sport and Exercise Psychology, 14*, 28-39.

Myers, I. (1987). *Introduction to type: A description of the theory and application for the Myers-Briggs Type Indicator*. Palo Alto, CA: Consulting Psychologists Press.

Nadler, D.A., Hackman, J.R., and Lawler, E.E., III. (1979). *Managing organizational behavior*. Boston: Little, Brown.

NASSM (2016). *Purpose and history*. Retrieved from http://www.nassm.org/NASSM/Purpose

Newby, T.J., and Heide, A. (1992). The value of mentoring. *Performance Improvement Quarterly, 5*(4), 2-15.

Niehoff, B.P., and Moorman, R.H. (1993). Justice as a mediator of the relationship between methods of monitoring and organizational citizenship behavior. *Academy of Management Journal, 36*, 527-556.

Nieva, V.F., and Gutek, B.A. (1981). *Women and work*. New York: Praeger.

Noe, R.A. (1988). Women and mentoring: A review and research agenda. *Academy of Management Review, 13*, 65-78.

Odio, M. A., Wells, J., and Kerwin, S. (2014). Full-time student, part-time employee: Capturing the effects of socialization influences on affective commitment for student employees. *Event Management, 18*(3), 325-336.

Odiorne, G. S. (1984). *Strategic management of human resources*. Jossey-Bass.

Ogasawara, E., and Chelladurai, P. (1998, May). Gender differences in job satisfaction and commitment among NCAA coaches. Paper presented at the annual conference of the North American Society for Sport Management, Buffalo, NY.

Ogilvie, B.C., and Tutko, T.A. (1966). *Problem athletes and how to handle them*. London: Pelham Books.

Oldham, G.R., and Da Silva, N. (2015). The impact of digital technology on the generation and implementation of creative ideas in the workplace. *Computers in Human Behavior, 42*, 5-11.

O'Reilly, C.A., and Chatman, J. (1986). Organizational commitment and psychological attachment: The effects of compliance, identification, and inter-nalization of prosocial behavior. *Journal of Applied Psychology, 71*, 492-499.

Organ, D.W. (1988). *Organizational citizenship behavior: The good soldier syndrome*. Lexington, MA: Lexington Books.

Organ, D.W., Podsakoff, P.M., and MacKenzie, S.B. (2006). *Organizational citizenship behavior: Its nature, antecedents, and consequences* (p.186). Thousand Oaks, CA: Sage.

Organization for Economic Cooperation and Development (OECD). (2013a). *OECD data: Part-time employment rate*. https://data.oecd.org/emp/part-time-employment-rate.htm.

Organization for Economic Cooperation and Development (OECD). (2013b). *OECD factbook*. www.oecd-ilibrary.org/economics/oecd-factbook-2015-2016_factbook-2015-en.

Osborn, R.N., and Hunt, J.G. (1975). An adaptive-reactive theory of leadership: The role of macro variables in leadership research. In J.G. Hunt and L.L. Larson (Eds.), *Leadership frontiers*. Kent, OH: Kent State University.

Osborn, L.A., and Stein, C.H. (2016). Mental health care providers' views of their work with consumers and their reports of recovery-orientation, job satisfaction, and personal growth. *Community Mental Health Journal, 52*, 757-766.

Ostroff, C. (1992). The relationship between satisfaction, attitudes, and performance: An organizational level analysis. *Journal of Applied Psychology, 77*, 963-974.

Palisi, B.J., and Jacobson, P.E. (1977). Dominant status and involvement in types of instrumental and expressive voluntary associations. *Journal of Voluntary Action Research, 6*, 80-88.

Parasuraman, A., Zeithaml, V.L., and Berry, L.L. (1985). A conceptual model of service quality and its implications for future research. *Journal of Marketing, 49*, 41-50.

Parasuraman, A., Zeithaml, V.A., and Berry, L.L. (1990). Perceived service quality as a customer-based performance measure: An empirical examination of organizational barriers using an extended service quality model. *Human Resource Management, 30*(3), 335-364.

Parasuraman, A., Zeithaml, V.A., and Berry, L.L. (1991). Refinement and reassessment of the SERVQUAL scale. *Journal of Retailing, 67*, 420-450.

Parsons, F. (1909). *Choosing a vocation*. Boston: Houghton Mifflin.

Pastore, D.L. (1994). Job satisfaction and female college coaches. *Physical Educator, 50*(4), 216-221.

Pastore, D.L. (2003). A different lens to view mentoring in sport management. *Journal of Sport Management, 17*, 1-12.

Pelled, L.H., Eisenhardt, K.M., and Xin, K.R. (1999). Exploring the black box: An analysis of work group diversity, conflict, and performance. *Administrative Science Quarterly, 44*(1), 1-28.

Perlini, A.H., and Halverson, T.R. (2006). Emotional intelligence in the National Hockey League. *Canadian Journal of Behavioural Science, 38*(2), 109-119.

Peter, L.J. (1972). *The Peter prescription: How to make things go right*. New York: Bantam Books.

Peters, R. (1987). *Practical intelligence: Working smarter in business and everyday life*. New York: Harper & Row.

Pettinger, R. (1997). *Introduction to management* (2nd ed.). London: Macmillan.

Phillips, J.S. (1984). The accuracy of leadership ratings: A cognitive Leader Expertise in Sport categorization perspective. *Organizational Behavior and Human Performance, 33*, 125-138.

Phillips, M. (1982). Motivation and expectation in successful volunteerism. *Journal of Voluntary Action Research, 11*(2), 118-125.

Pierce, J.L., Newstrom, J.W., Dunham, R.B., and Barber, A.E. (1989). *Alternative work schedules*. Boston: Allyn & Bacon.

Pincus, C.S., and Hermann-Keeling, E. (1982). Self-help systems and the professional as volunteer: Threat or solution? *Journal of Voluntary Action Research, 11*(2-3), 85-96.

Pinder, C.C. (1984). *Work motivation*. Glenview, IL: Scott, Foresman.

Pinder, C.C. (2008). *Work motivation in organizational behavior (2nd ed.)*. New York: Psychology Press.

Pitts, M.K. (1998). Demand for part-time workers in the U.S. economy: Why is the distribution across industries uneven? *Social Science Research, 27* (2), 87-108.

Podsakoff, P.M., Ahearne, M., and MacKenzie, S.B. (1997). Organizational citizenship behavior and the quality and quantity of work group performance. *Journal of Applied Psychology, 82*, 262-270.

Podsakoff, P.M., MacKenzie, S.B., and Hui, C. (1993). Organizational citizenship behaviors and managerial evaluation of employee performance: A review and suggestions for future research. In G.R. Ferris (Ed.), *Research in personnel and human resource management* (Vol. 11, pp. 1-40). Greenwich, CT: JAI Press.

Porter, L.W., and Lawler, E.E. (1968). *Managerial attitudes and performance*. Homewood, IL: Irwin.

Poulton, E.C. (1957). On prediction in skilled movement. *Psychological Bulletin, 54*, 467-478.

Powell, D.M., and Meyer, J.P. (2004). Side-bet theory and the three-component model of organizational commitment. *Journal of Vocational Behavior, 65*(1), 157-177.

Price, J., Farrington, N., and Hall, L. (2013). Changing the game? The impact of Twitter on relationships between football clubs, supporters, and the sports media. *Soccer & Society, 14*(4), 446-461.

Price, M.E., and Van Vugt, M. (2015). The service-for-prestige theory of leader–follower relations: A review of evolutionary psychology and anthropology literatures. In S.M. Colarelli and R.D. Arvey (Eds.), *The biological foundations of organizational behavior* (pp. 169-201). Chicago: The University of Chicago Press.

Prime Minister's Office. (2012). David Cameron thanks Olympics volunteers. www.gov.uk/government/news/david-cameron-thanks-olympics-volunteers.

Qualman, E. (2011, August 16). Social network users statistics. *Socialnomics*. www.socialnomics.net/2011/08/16/social-network-users-statistics/.

Qualman, E. (2012, June 6). 10 new 2012 social media stats—Wow! *Socialnomics*. www.socialnomics.net/2012/06/06/10-new-2012-social-media-stats-wow/.

Raelin, J.A. (1987). The professional as the executive's ethical aide-de-camp. *Academy of Management Executive, 1*(3), 171-182.

Rafferty, A.E., and Griffin, M.A. (2004). Dimensions of transformational leadership: Conceptual and empirical extensions. *Leadership Quarterly, 15*, 329-354.

Rafiq, M., and Ahmed, P.K. (2000). Advances in the internal marketing concept: Definition, synthesis and extension. *Journal of Services Marketing, 14*(6), 449-462.

Ragheb, M.G., and Tate, R.L. (1993). A behavioral model of leisure participation, based on leisure attitude, motivation and satisfaction. *Leisure Studies, 12*, 61-70.

Ragins, B.R. (1989). Barriers to mentoring: The female manager's dilemma. *Human Relations, 42*(1), 1-22.

Ragins, B.R., and Cotton, J.L. (1991). Easier said than done: Gender differences in perceived barriers to gaining a mentor. *Academy of Management Journal, 34*, 939-951.

Rawls, J. (1999). *A theory of justice* (rev. ed.). Cambridge, MA: Harvard University Press.

Rees, W.D. (1996). *The skills of management* (4th ed.). London: International Thomson Business Press.

Reichers, A.E. (1985). A review and reconceptualization of organizational commitment. *Academy of Management Review, 10*, 465-476.

Reis, H.T. (1986). The multidimensionality of justice. In R. Folger (Ed.), *The sense of injustice* (pp. 25-61). New York: Plenum Press.

Rice, R.W., McFarlin, D.B., and Bennett, D.E. (1989). Standards of comparison and job satisfaction. *Journal of Applied Psychology, 74*, 591-598.

Richard, O.C., and Kirby, S.L. (1999). Organizational justice and the justification of work force diversity programs. *Journal of Business and Psychology, 14*(1), 109-118.

Riemer, H.A., and Chelladurai, P. (1998). Development of Athlete Satisfaction Questionnaire (ASQ). *Journal of Sport and Exercise Psychology, 20*, 127-156.

Riley, S., and Wrench, D. (1985). Mentoring among women lawyers. *Journal of Applied Social Psychology, 15*, 374-386.

Robbins, S.P. (1997). *Essentials of organizational behavior* (5th ed.). Upper Saddle River, NJ: Prentice Hall.

Robbins, S.P. (2000). *Managing today!* (2nd ed.). Upper Saddle River, NJ: Prentice Hall.

Robbins, S.P., Coulter, M., Leach, E., and Kilfoil, M. (2012). *Management* (10th ed.). New York: McGraw-Hill Irwin.

Robbins, S.P., Coulter, M., and Stuart-Kotze, R. (2003). *Management* (7th ed.). Toronto: Prentice Hall.

Robbins, S.P., and Judge, T.A. (2010). *Essentials of organizational behavior* (10th ed.). Upper Saddle River, NJ: Prentice Hall.

Robinson, M.J., Peterson, M., Tedrick, T., and Carpenter, J.R. (2003, Summer). Job satisfaction of NCAA Division III athletic administrators. *International Sports Journal*, 46-57.

Rodell, J.B. (2013). Finding meaning through volunteering: Why do employees volunteer, and what does it mean for their jobs? *Academy of Management Journal, 56*(5), 1274-1294.

Rogers, J.K. (1995). Just a temp: Experience and structure of alienation in temporary clerical employment. *Work and Occupations, 22*, 137-166.

Rokeach, M. (1973). *The nature of human values.* New York: Free Press.

Rose, M. (2014). *Reward management.* London: Kogan Page.

Ross, C.E., and Wright, M.P. (1998). Women's work, men's work, and the sense of control. *Work and Occupations, 25*, 333-355.

Ross, S.D., Russell, K.C., and Bang, H. (2008). An empirical assessment of spectator-based brand equity. *Journal of Sport Management, 22*(3), 322.

Rothstein, M.G., and Goffin, R.D. (2006). The use of personality measures in personnel selection: What does current research support? *Human Resource Management Review, 16*(2), 155-180.

Rotter, J. (1966). Generalized expectancies for internal vs. external control of reinforcement. *Psychological Monographs, 80*(1) (Whole No. 609).

Russell, R.F., and Stone, A.G. (2002). A review of servant leadership attributes: Developing a practical model. *Leadership & Organization Development Journal, 23*(3), 145-157.

Rynes, S.L., Gerhart, B., and Minetter, K.A. (2004). The importance of pay in employee motivation: Discrepancies between what people say and what they do. *Human Resource Management, 43*(4), 381-394.

Saal, F.E., and Knight, P.A. (1988). *Industrial/organizational psychology: Science and practice.* Pacific Grove, CA: Brooks/Cole.

Saal, F.E., and Knight, P.A. (1995). *Industrial/organizational psychology: Science and practice* (2nd ed.). Pacific Grove, CA: Brooks/Cole.

Sagawa, S., and Segal, E. (2000). *Common interest, common good: Creating value through business and social sector partnerships*. Boston: Harvard Business School Press.

Saiia, D.H., Carroll, A.B., and Buchholtz, A.K. (2003) Philanthropy as strategy: When corporate charity "begins at home." *Business & Society*, 42(2), 169–201.

Salovey, P., and Mayer J.D. (1990). Emotional intelligence. *Imagination, Cognition, and Intelligence, 9*, 185-211.

Sanchez, J.I., and Fraser, S.L. (1996). *Customer Service Skills Inventory (CSSI): Research and interpretation manual*. New York: McGraw-Hill/London House.

Sasser, W.E., Olsen, R.P., and Wyckoff, D.D. (1978). *Management of service operations*. Rockleigh, NJ: Allyn & Bacon.

Scandura, T.A., and Ragins, B.R. (1993). The effects of sex and gender role orientation on mentorship in male-dominated occupations. *Journal of Vocational Behavior, 43*, 251-265.

Schein, E.H. (1978). *Career dynamics*. Reading, MA: Addison-Wesley.

Schermerhorn, J. R., Hunt, J. G., and Osborn, R. N. (1991). *Managing organizational behavior*. (4th ed.). New York: Wiley.

Schermerhorn Jr, J. R., Hunt, J. G., and Osborn, R. N. (1997). Organizational Behavior, New York: John Wiley & Sons. Inc. http://www. hr-guide. com.

Schermerhorn, J.R., Hunt, J.G., and Osborn, R.N. (2011). *Organizational behavior* (9th ed.). New York: Wiley.

Schlesinger, T., Egli, B., and Nagel, S. (2013). "Continue or terminate?" Determinants of long-term volunteering in sports clubs. *European Sport Management Quarterly*, 13(1), 32-53.

Schmenner, R.W. (1995). *Service operations management*. Englewood Cliffs, NJ: Prentice Hall.

Schneider, B., and Bowen, D.E. (1992). Personnel/human resource management in the service sector. *Research in Personnel and Human Resources Management, 10*, 1-30.

Schneider, B., and Bowen, D.E. (1993). The service organization: Human resources management is crucial. *Organizational Dynamics, 21*(4), 39-52.

Schneider, B., and Bowen, D.E. (1995). *Winning the service game*. Boston: Harvard Business School Press.

Schneider, B., Wheeler, J.K., and Cox, J.F. (1992). A passion for service: Using content analysis to explicate service climate themes. *Journal of Applied Psychology, 77*, 705-716.

Schneider, J., and Locke, E.A. (1971). A critique of Herzberg's classification system and a suggested revision. *Organizational Behavior and Human Performance, 12*, 441-458.

Schuler, R.S., and Jackson, S.E. (1996). *Human resource management: Positioning for the 21st century* (6th ed.). Minneapolis: West.

Schutz, R.W., Smoll, F.L., Carre, F.A., and Mosher, R.E. (1985). Inventories and norms for children's attitudes toward physical activity. *Research Quarterly for Exercise and Sport, 56*, 256-265.

Schwartz, S.H. (1992). Universals in the content and structure of values. In M. Zanna (Ed.), *Advances in experimental social psychology* (Vol. 25, pp. 1-65). New York: Academic Press.

Shamir, B., and Eilam, G. 2005. "What's your story?": A life-stories approach to authentic leadership development. *Leadership Quarterly*, 16, 395-417.

Shapiro, G.L., and Farrow, D.L. (1988). Mentors and others in career development. In S. Rose and L. Larwood (Eds.), *Women's careers: Pathways and pitfalls*. New York: Praeger.

Sheldon, W.H. (1954). *Atlas of men: A guide to somatotyping the adult male at all ages*. New York: Harper & Row.

Shin, S.J., Kim, T.Y., Lee, J.Y., and Bian, L. (2012). Cognitive team diversity and individual team member creativity: A cross-level interaction. *Academy of Management Journal, 55*(1), 197-212.

Sills, D.L. (1972). Voluntary associations: Sociological aspects. In D.L. Sills (Ed.), *International encyclopedia of the social sciences* (Vol. 16). New York: Cromwell, Collier-Macmillan.

Simons, R. (2011). *Human resource management: Issues, challenges, and opportunities*. Oakville, ON: Apple Academic Press.

Sinclair, R.R., Martin, J.E., and Michel, R.P. (1999). Full-time and part-time subgroup differences in job attitudes and demographic characteristics. *Journal of Vocational Behavior, 55*, 337-357.

Singer, M.R. (1987). *Intercultural communication: A perceptual approach*. Englewood Cliffs, NJ: Prentice Hall.

Siomkos, G.J., Rao, S.S., and Narayanan, S. (2001). The influence of positive and negative affectivity on attitude change toward organizations. *Journal of Business and Psychology, 16*(1), 151-161.

Skeels, M.M., and Grudin, J. (2009, May). When social networks cross boundaries: A case study of workplace use of Facebook and LinkedIn. *Proceedings of the ACM 2009 International Conference on Supporting Group Work* (pp. 95-104). Association for Computing Machinery.

Skirstad, B., and Hanstad, D.V. (2013). Gender matters in sport event volunteering. *Managing Leisure, 18*(4), 316-330.

Slack, T.S. (1985). The bureaucratization of a voluntary sport organization. *International Review for the Sociology of Sport, 20*(3), 145-165.

Smith, D.H. (1981). Altruism, volunteers, and volunteerism. *Journal of Voluntary Action Research, 10*(1), 21-36.

Smith, S. (1986). Technology and its impact on the voluntary sector. In *A new era for volunteerism*. Proceedings of a conference, Toronto, June 1-3, 1986 (pp. 82-89). Toronto: United Way of Greater Toronto.

Smith Maguire, J. (2001). Fit and flexible: The fitness industry, personal trainers and emotional service labor. *Sociology of Sport Journal, 18,* 379-402.

Smith, P.C., Kendall, L.M., and Hulin, C.C. (1969). *The measurement of satisfaction in work and retirement.* Chicago: Rand McNally.

Smucker, M.K., and Kent, A. (2004). The influence of referent selection on pay, promotion, supervision, work, and co-worker satisfaction across three distinct sport industry segments. *International Sports Journal, 8*(1), 27-43.

Snyder, C.J. (1990). The effects of leader behavior and organizational climate on intercollegiate coaches' job satisfaction. *Journal of Sport Management, 4,* 59-70.

Soliman, H.M. (1970). Motivation-hygiene theory of job attitudes. *Journal of Applied Psychology, 55,* 452-461.

Sonnenfeld, J.A., and Peiperl, M.A. (1988). Staffing policy as a strategic response: A typology of career systems. *Academy of Management Review, 13,* 588-600.

Spector, P.E. (1997). *Job satisfaction: Application, assessment, causes, and consequences.* Beverly Hills, CA: Sage.

Sport Law and Strategy Group. (2015). Vision, mission, values. www.sportlaw.ca/about-us/vision-mission-values/.

Spreitzer, G.M. (1995). Psychological empowerment in the workplace: Dimensions, measurement, and validation. *Academy of Management Journal, 38,* 1442-1465.

Sproull, L.S. (1984). Beliefs in organizations. In P.C. Nystrom and W.H. Starbuck (Eds.), *Handbook of organizational design: Vol. 2. Remodeling organizations and their environments* (pp. 203-224). New York: Oxford University Press.

Starc, G. (2005). Two sides of the same coin: Skiing and football in the Slovenian nation-building process. *Kinesiologia Slovenica, 11*(2), 64-88.

Stebbins, R. (1982). Serious leisure: A conceptual statement. *Pacific Sociological Review, 25,* 251-272.

Stebbins, R.A. (2001). Serious leisure. *Society, 38*(4), 53-57.

Stebbins, R.A. (2015). Career (serious leisure) volunteering. In *Leisure and the Motive to Volunteer: Theories of Serious, Casual, and Project-Based Leisure* (pp. 23-34). London: Palgrave Macmillan.

Steckel, R., and Simons, R. (1992). *Doing best by doing good.* New York: Penguin Books.

Steffy, B.D., and Jones, J.W. (1990). Differences between full-time and part-time employees in perceived role strain and work satisfaction. *Journal of Organizational Behavior, 11,* 321-329.

Stephens, W.N. (1991). *Altruists and volunteers: Life histories.* Walla Walla, WA: MBA.

Stewart, R. (1982). The relevance of some studies of managerial work and behavior to leadership research. In J.G. Hunt, U. Sekaran, and C. Schriesheim (Eds.), *Leadership: Beyond establishment views* (pp. 11-30). Carbondale: Southern Illinois University Press.

Stogdill, R.M. (1963). *Manual for the Leader Behavior Description Questionnaire—form XII.* Columbus: Ohio State University.

Stone, A.G., Russell, R.F., and Patterson, K. (2004). Transformational versus servant leadership: A difference in leader focus. *Leadership & Organization Development Journal, 25*(4), 349-361.

Stone, E.F., and Gueutal, H.G. (1985). An empirical derivation of the dimensions along which characteristics of jobs are perceived. *Academy of Management Journal, 28,* 376-396.

Storey, J. (2007). *Human resource management: A critical text.* Cengage Learning EMEA.

Sullivan, P.J., and Kent, A. (2003). The relationship between coaching efficacy and leadership style among university coaches. *Journal of Applied Sport Psychology, 15*(1), 1-11.

Sullivan, W. (1997). *Entrepreneur Magazine: Human resources for small businesses.* New York: Wiley.

Swanson, S., and Kent, A. (2014). The complexity of leading in sport: Examining the role of domain expertise in assessing leader credibility and prototypicality. *Journal of Sport Management, 28,* 81-93.

Swanson, S., and Kent, A. (2015). Fandom in the workplace: Multi-target identification in professional team sports. *Journal of Sport Management, 29*(4), 461-477.

Taylor, J.C., and Bowers, D.G. (1972). *Survey of organizations: A machine-scored standardized questionnaire instrument.* Ann Arbor: University of Michigan, Institute for Social Research.

Taylor, T., Doherty, A., and McGraw, P. (2008). *Managing people in sport organizations: A strategic human resource management perspective.* New York: Routledge.

Tedrick, T., and Henderson, K. (1989). *Volunteers in leisure.* Reston, VA: American Alliance for Health, Physical Education, Recreation and Dance.

Tennis Australia. (2015). National Strategy. www.tennis.com.au/about-tennis-australia/national-strategy.

Tett, R.P., Guterman, H.A., Bleier, A., and Murphy, P.J. (2000). Development and content validation of a "hyperdimensional" taxonomy of managerial competence. *Human Performance, 13*(3), 205-251.

Thibault, L. (2009). Globalization of sport: An inconvenient truth. *Journal of sport management, 23,* 1-20.

Thibault, L., Slack, T., and Hinings, B. (1991). Professionalism, structures and systems: The impact of professional staff on voluntary sport organizations. *International Review for Sociology of Sport, 26*(2), 83-97.

Thibaut, J., and Walker, L. (1975). *Procedural justice: A psychological analysis.* Hillsdale, NJ: Erlbaum.

Thompson, J.D. (1967). *Organizations in action.* New York: McGraw-Hill.

Todd, S., and Kent, A. (2009). A social identity perspective on the job attitudes of employees in sport. *Management Decision, 47,* 173-190.

Tomlinson, A., and Young, C. (Eds.). (2006). *National identity and global sports: Culture, politics, and spectacle in the Olympics and the football World Cup.* Albany, NY: State University of New York Press.

Topic, M.D., and Coakley, J. (2010). Complicating the relationship between sport and national identity: The case of post-socialist Slovenia. *Sociology of Sport Journal, 27*(4), 371-389.

Toren, N. (1975). Deprofessionalization and its sources. *Sociology of Work and Occupations, 2,* 323-337.

Törnblom, K.Y., and Jonsson, D.S. (1985). Subrules of the equality and contribution principles: Their perceived fairness in distribution and retribution. *Social Psychology Quarterly, 48,* 249-261.

Törnblom, K.Y., and Jonsson, D.S. (1987). Distribution vs. retribution: The perceived justice of the contribution and equality principles for cooperative and competitive relationships. *Acta Sociologica, 30,* 25-52.

Tosi, H.L., and Mero, N.P. (2003). *The fundamentals of organizational behavior: What managers need to know.* Malden, MA: Blackwell.

Tosi, H.L., Mero, N.P., and Rizzo, J.R. (2000). *Managing organizational behavior* (4th ed.). Malden, MA: Blackwell Business.

Trail, G.T. (1997). *Intercollegiate athletics: Organizational goals, processes, and personal values.* Unpublished doctoral dissertation, Ohio State University.

Turner, A.N., and Lawrence, P.R. (1965). *Industrial jobs and the worker: An investigation of response to task attributes.* Boston: Harvard Graduate School of Business Administration.

Turner, B.A., and Chelladurai, P. (2005). Organizational and occupational commitment, intention to leave and perceived performance of intercollegiate coaches. *Journal of Sport Management, 19,* 193-211.

Tyler, T.R., and Bies, R.J. (1990). Beyond formal procedures: The interpersonal context of procedural justice. In J.S. Carroll (Ed.), *Applied social psychology and organizational settings* (pp. 77-88). Hillsdale, NJ: Erlbaum.

Ulrich, D. (1997). *Human resource champions: The next agenda for adding value and delivering results.* Boston: Harvard Business School Press.

United States Golf Association. (2015). Volunteer job descriptions. http://2016uswomensopen.com/descriptions.php.

U.S. Department of Labor, Bureau of Labor Statistics. (2016, February 25). *Volunteering in the United States* [Press release]. www.bls.gov/news.release/pdf/volun.pdf.

US Lacrosse. (2013). We are US Lacrosse. www.uslacrosse.org/about-us-lacrosse.aspx.

US Soccer. (2015). About Us. www.ussoccer.com/about/about-us-soccer.

Uzzi, B., and Barsness, Z.I. (1998). Contingent employment in British establishments: Organizational determinants of the use of fixed term hires and part-time workers. *Social Forces, 76*, 967-1005.

Vaillancourt, F., and Payette, M. (1986). The supply of volunteer work: The case of Canada. *Journal of Voluntary Action Research, 15*(4), 45-56.

Vallerand, R.J. (2007). Intrinsic and extrinsic motivation in sport and physical activity. In G. Tenenbaum and R.C. Eklund (Eds.), *Handbook of sport psychology* (3rd ed., pp. 59-83). New York: Wiley.

Vandenberg, R.J., and Scarpello, V. (1994). A longitudinal assessment of the determinant relationship between employee commitments to the occupation and organization. *Journal of Organizational Behavior, 15*, 535-547.

van der Roest, J.W., Vermeulen, J., and van Bottenburg, M. (2015). Creating sport consumers in Dutch sport policy. *International Journal of Sport Policy and Politics, 7*(1), 105-121.

Van de Ven, A.H., and Delbecq, A.L. (1974). A task contingent model of work-unit structure. *Administrative Science Quarterly, 19*, 183-198.

Van Dyne, L., and Ang, S. (1998). Organizational, citizenship behavior of contingent workers in Singapore. *Academy of Management Journal, 41*, 692-703.

Van Rooy, D.L., and Viswesvaran, C. (2004). Emotional intelligence: A meta-analytic investigation of predictive validity and nomological net. *Journal of Vocational Behavior, 65*(1), 71-95.

Varey, R. (1995). A model of internal marketing for building and sustaining competitive service advantage. *Journal of Marketing Management, 11*, 45-52.

Varey, R.J., and Lewis, B.R. (1999). A broadened conception of internal marketing. *European Journal of Marketing, 33*(9), 926-944.

Vecchio, R.P. (2003). *Organizational behavior: Core concepts* (5th ed.). Mason, OH: Thomas/South-Western.

Volunteering England [now National Council for Voluntary Organisations]. (2015). www.volunteering.org.uk/aboutus.

Vroom, V.H. (1964). *Work and motivation.* New York: Wiley.

Vroom, V.H., and Jago, A.G. (1978). On the validity of the Vroom-Yetton model. *Journal of Applied Psychology, 63*, 151-162.

Vroom, V.H., and Jago, A.G. (1988). *The new leadership: Managing participation in organizations.* Englewood Cliffs, NJ: Prentice Hall.

Vroom, V.H., and Yetton, R.N. (1973). *Leadership and decision-making.* Pittsburgh: University of Pittsburgh Press.

Wakefield, K.L., Blodgett, J.G., and Sloan, H.J. (1996). Measurement and management of the sportscape. *Journal of Sport Management, 10*, 15-31.

Wallace, L., Wilson, J., and Miloch, K. (2011). Sporting Facebook: A content analysis of NCAA organizational sport pages and Big 12 conference athletic department pages. *International Journal of Sport Communication, 4*(4), 422-444.

Wallace, M., and Weese, W.J. (1995). Leadership, organizational culture, and job satisfaction in Canadian YMCA organizations. *Journal of Sport Management, 9*, 182-193.

Wann, D.L., and Branscombe, N.R. (1993). Sports fans: Measuring degree of identification with their team. *International Journal of Sport Psychology, 24*, 1-17.

Warriner, C.K., and Prather, J.E. (1965). Four types of voluntary associations. *Sociological Inquiry, 35*, 138-148.

Wasserman Media Group. (2016). About Wasserman. http://www.teamwass.com/about

Watson, D. (2000). *Mood and temperament.* New York: Guilford.

Watson, D., and Clark, L.A. (1984). Negative affectivity: The disposition to experience aversive emotional states. *Psychological Bulletin, 96*, 465-490.

Watson, D., Clark, L.A., and Tellegen, A. (1988). Development and validation of brief measures of positive and negative affect: The PANAS scale. *Journal of Personality and Social Psychology, 54*, 1063-1070.

Weaver, M.A., and Chelladurai, P. (1999). A mentoring model for management in sport and physical education. *Quest, 51,* 24-38.

Weaver, M.A., and Chelladurai, P. (2002). Mentoring in intercollegiate athletic administration. *Journal of Sport Management, 16,* 96-116.

Weber, L. (2015, April 14). Today's personality tests raise the bar for job seekers. *The Wall Street Journal.* www.wsj.com/articles/a-personality-test-could -stand-in-the-way-of-your-next-job-1429065001.

Weber, M. (1947). *The theory of social and economic organization* (A.M. Henderson and T. Parsons, Trans.). New York: Oxford University Press (original work published 1922).

Weber, M. (1958). *The Protestant ethic and the spirit of capitalism.* (T. Parsons, Trans.). New York: Scribner (original work published 1904-1905).

Weese, W.J. (1995). Leadership and organizational culture: An investigation of Big Ten and Mid-American Conference campus recreation administrators. *Journal of Sport Management, 9,* 119-134.

Weese, W.J. (1996). Do leadership and organizational culture really matter? *Journal of Sport Management, 10,* 197-206.

Weiss, D.J., Dawis, R.V., England, G.W., and Lofquist, L.H. (1967). *Manual for the Minnesota Satisfaction Questionnaire.* In *Minnesota studies on vocational rehabilitation* (Vol. 22). Minneapolis: University of Minnesota Industrial Relations Center, Work Adjustment Project.

Welty Peachey, J., Bruening, J., Lyras, A., Cohen, A., and Cunningham, G.B. (2015). Examining social capital development among volunteers of a multinational sport-for-development event. *Journal of Sport Management, 29*(1), 27-41.

Welty Peachey, J., Damon, Z.J., Zhou, Y., and Burton, L.J. (2015). Forty years of leadership research in sport management: A review, synthesis, and conceptual framework. *Journal of Sport Management, 29*(5), 570-587.

Werbel, J., and Balkin, D.B. (2010). Are human resource practices linked to employee misconduct?: A rational choice perspective. *Human Resource Management Review, 20*(4), 317-326.

Werther, W.B., Davis, K., Schwind, H.F., Das, H., and Miner, F.C. (1985). *Canadian personnel management and human resources* (2nd ed.). Toronto: McGraw-Hill Ryerson.

Whyte, W.F. (1949). The social structure of the restaurant. *American Journal of Sociology, 54*(4), 302-310.

Wicks, B.E., and Crompton, J.L. (1987). An analysis of the relationship between equity choice preferences, service type and decision making groups in a U.S. city. *Journal of Leisure Research, 19,* 189-204.

Wicks, B.E., and Crompton, J.L. (1990). Predicting the equity preferences of park and recreation department employees and residents of Austin, Texas. *Journal of Leisure Research, 22,* 18-35.

Wiener, Y. (1982). Commitment in organizations. A normative view. *Academy of Management Review, 7*(3), 418-429.

Wiener, Y. (1988). Forms of value systems: A focus on organizational effectiveness and cultural change and maintenance. *Academy of Management Review, 13,* 534-545.

Wiersma, L.D., and Sherman, C.P. (2005). Volunteer youth sport coaches' perspectives of coaching education/certification and parental codes of conduct. *Research Quarterly for Exercise and Sport, 76*(3), 324-338.

Wilensky, H.L. (1964). The professionalization of everyone? *American Journal of Sociology, 70,* 137-158.

Williamson, I.O., Burnett, M.F., and Bartol, K.M. (2009). The interactive effect of collectivism and organizational rewards on affective organizational commitment. *Cross Cultural Management: An International Journal, 16,* 28–43.

Williamson, J. (1991). Providing quality care. *Human Services Management, 87*(1), 18-27.

Wolensky, R.P. (1980). Toward a broader conception of volunteerism in disasters. *Journal of Voluntary Action Research, 8,* 43-50.

Women's Sports Foundation. (2013). Sandra Vivas: Chair of the board of trustees. www.womens sportsfoundation.org/en/home/media-center-2/ wsf-leadership/sandra-vivas.

Wood, S., Van Veldhoven, M., Croon, M., and de Menezes, L.M. (2012). Enriched job design, high involvement management, and organizational performance: The mediating roles of job satisfaction and well-being. *Human Relations, 65*(4), 419-445.

Wynne, B.E., and Hunsaker, P.L. (1975). A human information-processing approach to the study of leadership. In J.G. Hunt and L.L. Larson (Eds.), *Leadership frontiers*. Kent, OH: Kent State University.

Yammarino, F. (2013). Leadership: Past, present, and future. *Journal of Leadership & Organizational Studies, 20,* 149-155.

Yukl, G.A. (1981). *Leadership in organizations*. Englewood Cliffs, NJ: Prentice Hall.

Yukl, G.A. (2002). *Leadership in organizations* (5th ed.). Upper Saddle River, NJ: Prentice Hall.

Yukl, G.A., and Van Fleet, D.D. (1992). Theory and research on leadership in organizations. In M.D. Dunnette and L.M. Hough (Eds.), *Handbook of industrial and organizational psychology* (2nd ed., pp. 147-197). Chicago: Rand McNally.

Yusko, K.P., and Bellenger, B.L. (2012). Considering generational differences in assessing work values: A unifying approach. In W.I. Saucer and R.R. Sims (Eds.), *Managing human resources for the millennial generation* (pp. 183-200). Charlotte, NC: Information Age.

Zeigler, E.F. (1989). Proposed creed and code of professional ethics for the North American Society for Sport Management. *Journal of Sport Management, 3,* 2-4.

Zeithaml, V.A., Parasuraman, A., and Berry, L.L. (1990). *Delivering quality service: Balancing customer perceptions and expectations*. New York: Free Press.

Zey, M.G. (1984). *The mentor connection*. Homewood, IL: Dow Jones-Irwin.

Zey, M.G. (1985). Mentor programs: Making the right moves. *Personnel Journal, 64*(2), 53-57.

Index

Note: The italicized *f* and *t* following page numbers refer to figures and tables, respectively.

A

abilities. *See also* competencies
  cognitive 78, 79-81, 80*t*
  defined 78
  emotional intelligence 82-85, 85*t*
  as individual-difference variable 222-223
  inherent (potential) vs. current 78, 79
  issues in study of 78-79
  leader behavior and 228
  performance and 78, 128-129
absenteeism reduction 266, 272
accommodation, in diversity management 6
achievement 141
activation, in diversity management 6
actualization outcome 67, 130
Adams, J.S. 137-138
adjustive function of values 115
administrative purpose 243, 244-245
affective commitment 326, 328
affective incentives 35, 344
Albrecht, K. 64
Allen, N.J. 326-328
altruism, in volunteers 36-38, 38*f*
ambiguity tolerance 99, 100
American values 121
apathetics 336-337
aptitude. *See* abilities
Ashforth, B.E. 345-346
ASQ (Athlete Satisfaction Questionnaire) 319
associations, defined 29
assurance (SERVQUAL) 289-290, 312*t*
athlete satisfaction 313-314, 315*t*
Athlete Satisfaction Questionnaire (ASQ) 319
athletic trainers 50
attitudes
  defined 302
  individualism 98-99, 100
  toward authority 98, 225
  values and 108-109, 109*f*

attitudinal outcomes. *See* job satisfaction; organizational commitment
attributional confidence 118
authentic leadership 235
authoritarian personality 96-97, 98
authority, attitude toward 98, 225
autocratic decision making 236, 237
autonomy
  personal responsibility and 176
  professional status and 49-50
  as task attribute 170-171

B

Bandura, A. 133-134
Bauer, T.N. 197
Becker, H.S. 324-325
beliefs 108, 109*f*
benevolence 157
Big Five personality domains 93, 95*f*, 96
biological factors in job design 181-182, 181*t*
body of knowledge 44, 52-53
body type and temperament 92
bonuses 277
boundary spanners 342, 342*f*
Braskamp, L.A. 139-142
Brooks, R.F. 292
bureaucracy (term) 97
bureaucratic orientation 97-98, 97*f*
Burnham, D.H. 228
burnout 51, 344, 346
business perspective of justice 148

C

calculative commitment 327
Campion, M.A. 180-183
campus recruiting 195
career anchors 206-207, 207*t*
career orientation 206, 207
career rewards 268
careers
  in changing workplace 209
  defined 206
  individual 206-208, 207*t*
  mentoring in 210-214

organizational systems 208-210, 208*f*
  stages of 207-208
Carless, S.A. 351
categorical knowledge structures 203, 345-346
causal beliefs 108
central tendency 256-258, 258*f*
charismatic leadership 233-234
Chatman, J. 329
choice, in procedural justice 159
citizenship behaviors 248-251, 249*f*
clients and customers
  as human resources 16-17, 61, 64, 344
  input-throughput-output roles 62, 62*f*
  interactions with 102, 168, 178, 180
  "listening" to 64
  loyalty of 314
  managers' role in motivation of 69, 69*f*
  motive-based programming for 67, 68*t*
  motives for participation 65-69, 65*t*, 344-345
  participation in service production 17, 61, 63-65
  physical exertion of 63
  satisfaction of 312-313, 312*t*, 313*t*
coaches
  evaluation of 255
  satisfaction in 316, 316*t*
  vs. teachers 179
coaching efficacy 134, 134*t*
Coach Satisfaction Questionnaire (CSQ) 319
coactively dependent tasks 183
code of ethics 44
cognitive abilities 78, 79-81, 80*t*
collectivism, values of 113
comfort, as job design outcome 181, 181*t*
communication
  with authority 168
  evaluation of 247

communication *(continued)*
  internal 289
  values and 118
community sanction 44
compensation, as reward 269
compensation hypothesis 34
compensatory justice 161
competence values 111
competencies. *See also* abilities
  defined 78
    managerial 80-81, 81t, 82f, 84, 85-87, 86-87t
    organizational commitment and 333
    professional status and 52, 54
complexity
  cognitive 225
  as job attribute 180
  in professionalization 47-48
compliance commitment 327, 329
conflict resolution 115
congruence hypothesis 34
consideration behavior 219
consumer health services 12
consumer pleasure services 12
consumer services 10, 11t, 47
content theories of motivation 126-127
contingent workers 194
continuance commitment 326-327, 328, 329
continuing motivation 139
contrast error 258
coordination of tasks 174, 183-185, 185f, 186
corporate citizens 336
CSQ (Coach Satisfaction Questionnaire) 319
cultural influences
  on organizational commitment 325, 337
  on personality 90-91
current capacity 78, 79
customers. *See* clients and customers
cutbacks, and justice principles 155

D
Danisiewicz, T.J. 46-47
Dawis, R.V. 318
decision control 158
decision making
  as cognitive process 236
    decision styles 237, 237f, 239
    problem attributes and 238-239, 238t
    as social process (participative) 236-237
    values in 115
decruitment 203
deprofessionalization 50
developmental humanism 4
developmental purpose 243, 244-245
direct compensation 269
direction, in motivation 139
discrepancy theories 304-307, 305f
discrimination
  in hiring 198
  strategic position and 174
distributional errors 256-258
distributive justice 149f, 161f
  among athletic teams 154-156
  applying principles of 152-154
  in community recreation 156-158
  in cutbacks 155
  principles of 150-152, 150t, 349
  sample case for evaluating 156f
diversity management
  actualization in 67, 130
  ambiguity tolerance and 99
  framework for 6
  in hiring process 198
  individual outcomes and 327
  job satisfaction and 306
  management by values in 118
  organization's image and 288
  perceptions of justice and 154
  performance appraisals in 245
  rewards and 267
  skills and abilities in 81
  task attributes and 225
  training in 55
  in volunteers 28
Drucker, P.F. 218
Dungy, Tony 234
duty (value) 119

E
efficiency, as job design outcome 181, 181t. *See also* productivity
  effort
    evaluation of 248
    in motivation 127
effort–reward probability 128
egalitarian sport 12, 13f, 343
ego-defensive function of values 115

elite sport 12-14, 13f, 343
embeddedness 333-334, 338-339
emotional intelligence 82-85, 85t
empathy (SERVQUAL) 290, 312t
employee benefits
  cafeteria-style 276
  as rewards 269, 270f
employee–client interface 9-11
employee-oriented leadership 219
employee referral 195
employees. *See also* performance appraisals; staffing
  attitudes toward 221
  as costs vs. capital 4
  as customers 282, 293, 295
  empowerment of 347-349, 348t
  knowledge structures for 345-346
  organizational climate for 346
  values of 118-120, 119f
  volunteering by 33-34
employee-to-employee interface 286
employee turnover 334-335
empowering leadership 234, 234t
empowerment 347-349, 348t
entertainment sport 13f, 14, 343
environmental influences
  on abilities 78
  on personality 90-91
equality principle 150t, 151-152, 153
equity principle
  in distributive justice 150-151, 150t
  vs. equality 153
  in inequity theory of motivation 137-138, 138f
  of rewards 130-131
essentiality of occupations 46-47, 52
ethics
  in justice concept 148
  NASSM's 45, 355-356
  regulative code of 44
event sponsors 68
excellence, as motive 66
exclusivity of occupations 47, 52
expectancy 132f, 133
experienced meaningfulness 175-176
expertise, unique 168
expressive organizations 29f, 30
external marketing 283, 283f
external regulation 63
extrinsic motivation 63

extrinsic rewards 127, 129-130, 131*f*, 268

F

Facebook. *See* social media
facets of job satisfaction 306-308
fairness. *See also* organizational justice
    organizational commitment and 333
    organizational justice and 147-148, 157
false claims, in hiring process 198-199, 202*f*
feedback loops. *See also* job feedback
    in motivation theory 131-132
    in multidimensional leadership 222*f*, 229
Fiedler, F.E. 226-227
financial rewards 135, 268
firing employees 203
Fleishman Job Analysis Survey 79
flextime 272
Forsyth, P. 46-47
Frey, Kevin 232

G

gap theory 290-291, 291*f*
gender differences
    in job satisfaction 317
    in mentoring 213
generality of ability 79
genetic influences 90
goals
    of staffing 190
    values and 116
goods, vs. services 7-8
government regulations for staffing 199*t*
Greenley, G.E. 294
group members
    leader behavior and 222-223, 225
    rewards and 276
Gueutal, H.G. 180
Gummesson, E. 8

H

Hackman, J.R. 174-180
Hall, D.T. 207-208
halo error 259
health-related motives 66
heritability 78
Herzberg, F.
    on job enrichment 167-168, 167*f*

two-factor theory 136, 137*f*, 303-304
heterogeneity, of services 7-8
hiring process 196-198, 200-201*t*, 202*f*, 204
House, R.J. 224
household production 35
HRM. *See* human resource management
Hughes, Cameron 172-173
human capital 4, 35
human curative services 12, 47
human resource management (HRM)
    defined 4
    imperatives of 1-2, 5
    internal marketing and 293-294
    models of 4, 17-18, 18*f*
    products produced and 343
    purposes of 345-347
    significance of 3-5, 7, 341-343
    volunteers and 39
human resources. *See also*
        professional workers;
        volunteers
    clients and customers as 16-17, 61, 64, 344
    as costs vs. capital 4
    importance of 1
    paid professional workers 15-16, 16*t*
    spectators as 68
    volunteers 15-16, 16*t*
human services 11-12, 47
human sustenance services 12
Humphrey, R.H. 345-346

I

Ideal Palace (*Le Palais Idéal*) 169
identification commitment 326, 329
identified regulation 63
image building 48, 53
independent tasks 182
indirect compensation 269
individual differences. *See also*
        abilities; motivation;
        personality; values
    person–task fit and 145
    preferred leader behavior and 225
    task attributes and 179-180
    variables in 73-75, 222
individualism
    attitude toward 98-99, 100
    values of 113

inequity theory of motivation 137-138, 138*f*. *See also* equity principle
informational justice 160, 161
informative incentives 49
inherent (potential) capacity 78, 79
initiating structure 219
injury risk 173
institutionalized stars 336
instrumentality 132*f*, 133
instrumental–productive organizations 29-30, 29*f*
instrumental values 110-112
intangibility, of services 7
integrated regulation 63
intelligence, in leaders 219
intensity, in motivation 139
interaction, in jobs 171-172
interactional justice 149*f*, 159-161, 161*f*, 349-350
interactional marketing 283*f*, 285
interactively dependent 183
interdependence
    diversity management and 184
    job design and 182-183, 185, 185*f*
    in performance appraisals 247, 253
interindividual differences 74
internalization commitment 329
internal marketing
    defined 281-282, 292-293
    external marketing and 282*f*
    functions of 292-296
    gap theory in 290-291, 291*f*
    issues in 296
    line of visibility in 292
    in marketing triangle 283-285, 283*f*
    process- vs. people-oriented 285-287
    production and marketing in 281, 283
    SERVQUAL dimensions in 288-290
internships 172-173
interpersonal justice 160, 161
intraindividual differences 74
intrinsic motivation 63
intrinsic rewards 127, 129, 131*f*, 265, 268
introjected regulation 63
Ivancevich, J.M. 259

J

Jackson, D.N. 93, 94-95*t*

Jackson, Phil 234
job analysis 79, 191-192, 191*t*
job-based rewards 273, 274
job descriptions 192-193, 193*f*, 198
Job Descriptive Index 313, 317-318, 320
job design
    Campion and Thayer's approach 180-183, 181*t*
    defined 165
    employee motivation and 174-177, 175*f*
    strategies of 165-169
    task attributes in 169-173
    task coordination in 183-185
    task dependence in 182-183
    task variability in 185-186
    volunteers and 180
Job Diagnostic Survey 318-319, 320
job embeddedness 333-334, 338-339
job enlargement 166-167
job enrichment
    characteristics of 167-169, 167*f*
    implementing task attributes for 177-179, 178*f*
job feedback
    in enriched jobs 167, 178-179
    motivation and 176-177
    as task attribute 171
job interview questions 200-201*t*
job involvement, and organizational commitment 336-338, 337*f*
job rotation 166
job satisfaction
    comparison to others and 304
    defined 301-302
    diversity management and 306
    Herzberg's two-factor theory 303-304
    as job design outcome 181, 181*t*
    Lawler's facet model 304-305, 305*f*
    Locke's value-based theory 306
    measuring 316-320
    Minnesota Model 306, 307
    in multidimensional leadership 228-229
    need-based theories 306
    organizational commitment and 335-336
    relation to other variables 302-303
    rewards and 130
    Smith's facets of 306-308

    in volunteers 309-311
job simplification 166
job specification 192
justice. *See* organizational justice

K
KBE (knowledge-based economy) 4
Kent, A. 304
Knight, Bobby 257
knowledge-based economy (KBE) 4
knowledge of results 176-177
knowledge structures 201-203, 345-346
Kotler, P. 283-285

L
Lawler, E.E., III
    facet model of satisfaction 304-305, 305*f*
    motivation model 127-132, 127*f*
leadership
    authentic 235
    benevolence and justice in 157
    charismatic 233-234
    decision making and 235-239
    defined 217-218
    empowering 234, 234*t*
    evaluation of 247
    Fiedler's contingency model 226-227
    House's path-goal theory 224
    intelligence and 219
    leader behavior 218-221, 220*t*
    McClelland theory of managerial motivation 228
    multidimensional model of 221-229, 222*f*, 232*f*
    physical appearance and 93, 219
    qualities of 83
    role in sport 223
    servant 234-235
    substitutes for 230
    transactional 229-231, 231*t*
    transformational 229-234, 231*t*, 232*f*, 317-318
    values and 118
    in volunteers 21
learning opportunities 168
legal considerations
    in hiring 199-200*t*
    perspective on justice 148
    in reward systems 275
Legge, K. 4
leisure satisfaction 312-313, 313*t*

leniency error 256-258, 258*f*
life satisfaction 141-142
line of visibility 292
Lings, I.N. 292, 294
Locke, E.A. 126, 306
locus of control 99, 100, 100*t*
lone wolves 336
Lopiano, Donna 233, 234
Lovelock, C. 8
loyalty
    of customers 314
    as value 119
lump-sum payments 277

M
Machiavelli, Niccolò 102
Machiavellianism 102-103, 103*f*
MacLean, J. 251, 253-254
macro variables 221-222
Maehr, M.L. 139-142
management
    vs. marketing 284
    McClelland theory of motivation 228
    professional status of 51-52
    values of 118-119, 119*f*
management by objectives 253
management by values (MBV) 116, 118
management-to-employee interface 295
managerial competencies 80-81, 81*t*, 82*f*, 84, 85-87, 86-87*t*
managerial potential 104-105
Managing for the Future (Drucker) 218
Margulies, N. 10-11
marketing. *See also* internal marketing
    departments vs. functions 294-296
    forms of 283-285
    vs. management 284
Maslow, A.H. 134-136
Maslow's need hierarchy 134-136, 135*f*
mass (egalitarian) sport 12, 13*f*, 343
Matteson, M.T. 259
MBV (management by values) 116, 118
McClelland, D.C. 228
meaningfulness of job 175-176
mechanistic factors in job design 181-182, 181*t*

membership-based rewards 269-271

mentors and mentoring
    defined 210
    functions of 210-211, 211*t*
    mentor-protégé relationships 212-214
    model of 211*f*
    outcomes of 211-212
    peer mentoring 214
Meyer, J.P. 325, 326-328
Mills, P.K. 10-11
mimic professions 50
Minnesota model of job satisfaction 306, 307, 313
Minnesota Satisfaction Questionnaire 318, 320
moral values 111
motivation
    Adams' inequity theory and 137-138, 138*f*
    Bandura's self-efficacy theory 133-134
    client participation motives 65-69, 65*t*, 344-345
    content theories of 126-127
    defined 125-126
    Hackman, Oldham job characteristic model of 174-177, 175*f*, 179-180
    Herzberg's two-factor theory 136, 137*f*
    in internship 172-173
    issues in study of 131
    in job design 181-182, 181*t*
    Maslow's need hierarchy and 134-135, 135*f*
    McClelland theory of managerial 228
    as personal investment 139-142, 140*f*
    Porter and Lawler's model 127-132, 127*f*
    process theories of 126-127
    rewards and 128, 129-132, 131*f*, 266
    role of sport manager in 69, 69*f*
    traits of 126
    values in 115
    Vroom's expectancy theory 132-133, 132*f*
motivational properties, of tasks 174-177
multidimensional leadership model 222*f*

    actual leader behavior in 225-228
    consequences of 228-229
    preferred leader behavior in 223-225
    required leader behavior in 221-223
    transformational leadership and 232-233, 232*f*
mutual adjustments 184

N

NASSM ethics 45, 335-336
National Volunteer Week 23
natural work units 178
need-based satisfaction theories 126-127, 306
need principle 150*t*, 152
negative affect 99-101
normative beliefs 108
normative commitment 325, 327-328
normative incentives 35-36, 344
norms 109-110
North American Society for Sport Management (NASSM) ethics 45, 355-356

O

Obamacare 275
occupational commitment 330-332
occupational identity 206
occupations. *See* professions and occupations
Oldham, G.R. 174-180
optional interaction 172
O'Reilly, C.A. 329
organizational change 292-293
organizational commitment
    antecedents of 332-333
    bases of 326-328, 326*f*
    consequences of 334-335
    defined 324
    downside of 337
    embeddedness and 333-334, 338-339
    foci of 328-329, 330*f*
    job involvement and 336-338, 337*f*
    job satisfaction and 335-336
    vs. occupational 330-332
    O'Reilly and Chatman's scheme of 329
    perspectives on 324-325
    profiles of 331, 331*t*

    in student employees 338-339
    in volunteers 330, 332
organizational culture or climate
    employee well-being and service in 346
    psychological climate 351-352, 352*f*
    reward systems and 266, 267
    service culture 287
organizational justice 149*f*, 161*f*
    distributive 149-158
    interactional 159-161
    managing perceptions of 161-162
    perspectives and importance of 148
    procedural 158-159, 162, 197
    summary of 349-350
organizational structure 267, 268
organizational values 116-121

P

paid professional workers. *See* professional workers
participant services 67, 343
participant (egalitarian) sport 12, 13*f*, 343
participative decision making 236-237
part-time employees 194
pass-off activities 296
Patient Protection and Affordable Care Act 275
pay. *See* financial rewards
peer mentoring 214
Peiperl, M.A. 208-210
perceptual-motor factors in job design 181-182, 181*t*
performance
    abilities and 78, 128-129
    expectations of 128
    motivation and 139-140
    in multidimensional leadership 228-229
    organizational commitment and 334, 335
    rewards and 266, 269-271, 274-275
performance appraisals
    citizenship behaviors in 248-251, 249*f*
    criterion deficiency or contamination 247, 251
    current vs. potential performance in 259

performance appraisals (*continued*)
defined 244
effective 259
firm-level outcomes of 244
job-specific tasks in 246-247, 252f
non-job-specific tasks in 247-251
outcome- vs. behavior-based 253-254, 254t, 260
procedural justice and 162
purposes of 243-245, 246f
rating errors in 256-260, 261
reactions to 260-261
steps in developing 251, 252f
task interdependence and 247, 253
360-degree approach 257
when to conduct 255-256
who should conduct 256
performance domains 247-251, 252t
perishability, of services 7
persistence, in motivation 139
personal accountability 168
personal discipline 248
personal growth 141
personal importance 333
personal investment 140f
behavioral indicators of 139-141
outcomes of 141-142
personality
actual leader behavior and 226-228
Big Five domains 93, 95f, 96
conflicts due to 105
defined 89-90
determinants of 90-92
preferred leader behavior and 225
traits germane to HRM 96-105
trait theories 93-96
as trait vs. state 91
type theories 92
Personality Research Form (Jackson) 93, 94-95t
personality tests 96
personal responsibility 176
personal (self-centered) values 111-112
person–occupation fit 206
person–organization fit 190, 205, 346-347, 347f
person–task fit 73-74, 145
Peter, L.J. 261
Peter principle 261
phenomenological beliefs 108
physical demands of job 180

planning, as coordination method 184
pleasure-seeking motives 66
policy volunteers 21
political influence 251
Porter, L.W. 127-132
positive affect 99-101, 102
practical intelligence 85
preferred leader behavior 223-225
proactively-reactively dependent 183
problem-solving styles 103-104, 104t
procedural justice 149f, 158-159, 161f, 162, 197, 349
process control 158, 159
process theories of motivation 126-127
Procrustean approach 166
production-oriented leadership 219
productivity
indicators of 299-300
as value 153
professional associations 49
professional authority 44, 53
professionalism
characteristics of 53-54
in sport management 51-54, 58
values of 55-56, 56f
professional services 9-10, 11t
professional status
autonomy and 49-50
competencies and 52, 54
rewards and 267, 268
of sport management 51-54, 58
vs. sport service type 47
training and 44, 51
professional workers
professional orientation of 344
as volunteers 56
vs. volunteers 15-16, 16t, 55-57, 344
professions and occupations
autonomy and status of 49-50
defined 44-45
deprofessionalization of 50-51
vs. professionalism 344
professionalization process 46-48, 46f
profitability 1, 5
prosocial (citizenship) behavior 248-251, 249f
protégés 210-214
psychological climate 351-352, 352f

psychological contract 204-205, 350-351
psychological states 175-177, 175f
purposive incentives 49

Q
quality 61

R
racial discrimination 174
recency error 258
recreation (term) 14-15
recreation management. *See* sport and recreation management
recruiting
process of 195-196
rewards and 265-266
of volunteers 39, 196
regulative code of ethics 44
relationship marketing 283, 285
reliability
as job design outcome 181-182, 181t
as SERVQUAL dimension 289, 312t
rentals, as services 8-9
required interaction 171-172
required leader behavior 221-223
resource-based perspective 3
resource control 168
resource distribution 149
responsiveness (SERVQUAL) 289, 312t
retributive justice 154
rewards
bases of 273-275
equity of 130-131
job satisfaction and 130
meeting objectives of 349
member preferences and 276-277
mix of 275-276
motivation and 128, 129-132, 131f, 266
purposes of 265-267
types of 127, 129-130, 267-273, 270f
for volunteers 269-271
Rokeach, M.
beliefs, values, and attitudes 108-110, 109f
functions of values 113-115
terminal and instrumental values 110-112
role modeling, as performance domain 248

role perception 129

S

safety of workers 181-182

Samaranch, Juan Antonio 233

satisfaction. *See* job satisfaction

Schein, E.H. 206-207

Schwartz, S.H. 113

script knowledge structures 201-203, 345

seamless service 296

Selection Procedural Justice Scale (SPJS) 197

self-actualization function of values 115

self-centered (personal) values 111-112

self-efficacy, and organizational commitment 333

self-efficacy theory of motivation 133-134, 134*t*

semiprofessions 50

seniority-based rewards 274

seniors, as volunteers 196

serious leisure 31

servant leadership 234-235

Service America in the New Economy (Albrecht and Zemke) 64

service culture 287

service employees
    as customer lens 287, 288*f*
    serving the public 180
    training 202

service orientation 101-102, 102*t*

service providers, as boundary spanners 342, 342*f*

service quality dimensions 288-290, 312*t*

services
    categories of 8
    characteristics of 7-9, 9*f*
    defined 7
    vs. goods 7-9
    human 11-12
    professional vs. consumer 9-11, 11*t*
    sport and recreation 12-15, 13*f*
    transfer of ownership framework 8-9, 9*f*
    types and relationships 13*f*

servicescape 288-289

service volunteers 21

sexual connotations, in mentoring 213

Sheldon, W.H. 92

side-bet theory 324-325

similarity error 259

Simons, R. 7

simultaneity, of services 8

situational characteristics, and leader behavior 221-222, 224

situational cues, and personality 91, 92

skill and skill development
    as client motive 66
    employee rewards and 266, 274

skill variety 170

Smith, P.C. 306-308

Smucker, M.K. 304

social cognitive theory (Bandura) 133-134

social influences 91

social learning theory (Bandura) 133-134

social marketing 287

social media
    for brand association management 117
    for client communication 62, 343, 345
    effects on HRM 342
    for employee communication 136
    job design and 181
    organizational commitment and 333
    process control and 158
    as recruiting tool 195
    in relationship marketing 285
    use statistics 16
    for volunteer management 36
    work–life relationships and 250

social responsibility 2, 5

social rewards 268

social values 111-112

solidarity, as value 153

solidary incentives 49

Sonnenfeld, J.A. 208-210

specificity of ability 79

spectators, as human resources 68

spectator services 345

SPJS (Selection Procedural Justice Scale) 197

sponsorship services 345

sport
    societal functions of 65
    term 14-15

sport and recreation management
    competencies required in 85-87

professional status of 51-54, 58

sport sociology and 53

sport and recreation services 12-15, 13*f*

sportscape 288-289

sport sociology 53

stacking 174

staffing
    decruitment 203
    government regulations 199*t*
    hiring process 196-198, 200-201*t*, 202*f*, 204
    needs assessment 191
    person–organization fit in 346-347, 347*f*
    psychological contract 204-205, 350-351
    purpose and focus of 190-195
    recruiting 39, 195-196, 265-266
    training 201-203

staggered work schedules 272, 273

standardization, as coordination method 183

standards, values as 113-115

Stanley, D.J. 325

status. *See* professional status

Stern, David 233

Stone, E.F. 180

strategic management 5, 343

strategic position 172-173

strictness error 256-258, 258*f*

substitute for performance error 259

supervision, evaluation of 247

supportiveness, and organizational commitment 333

T

tangibles (SERVQUAL) 288, 312*t*

task attributes
    described 169-173
    diversity management and 225
    implementing for job enrichment 177-179, 178*f*
    individual differences and 179-180
    job meaningfulness and 175-176
    personal responsibility and 176

tasks
    combining for job enrichment 177-178
    coordination of 174, 183-185, 185*f*, 186
    dependence of 182-183, 184, 185, 185*f*, 225, 247, 253

tasks *(continued)*
  effects on distributive justice 153-154
  identity of 171
  motivational properties of 174-177
  significance of 170-171
  variability of 170, 185-186
teaching, vs. coaching 179
technology. *See also* social media
  choosing types of 352
  effects on employees 51, 170, 183, 346
  effects on HRM 342-343, 353
  for internal communication 289
  job candidate abilities in 84
telecommuting 272-273, 302
temporal errors 258
terminal values 110-112
terminations 203
Thayer, P.W. 180-183
tokenism 213
total quality management (TQM) 61, 285-286
training
  in diversity management 55
  process of 201-203
  professional status and 44, 51
transactional leadership 229-231, 231*t*
transfer of ownership 8-9, 9*f*
transformational leadership
  charismatic leadership and 233-234
  dimensions of 231-232, 231*t*
  job satisfaction and 317-318
  multidimensional model and 232-233, 232*f*
  vs. servant 234-235
  vs. transactional 229-231, 231*t*
turnover 334-335

U
U.S. National Volunteer Week 23
utilitarian incentives 34-35, 49, 344
utilitarian instrumentalism 4

V
valances 133, 133*f*
value-based theory of satisfaction 306
values
  attitudes and 108-109, 109*f*
  beliefs and 108, 109*f*
  conflicts and incongruities in 118-119, 119*f*
  congruence in 107-108, 116, 119-120
  defined 107, 108
  development of 122
  discrepancies in 111
  functions of 113-115
  hierarchy of 112, 113*f*
  as HRM imperative 1, 5
  management by values 116, 118
  national 121-122
  norms and 109-110
  in organizations 116-121, 153
  of professionalism 55-56, 56*f*
  sources of 110
  terminal vs. instrumental 110-112
  types of 112-113, 114*f*
value system 108, 112
vertical loading (job enrichment) 167-168, 167*f*, 178
Vivas, Sandra "Sandy" 233
voice, in procedural justice 159
voluntary organizations
  accessibility to 30-32
  classification of 29-30, 29*f*
  defined 29
  members vs. workers in 30
  professionalization of 57, 58
  status in 32
Volunteer Functions Inventory 35-36
volunteers
  altruism and 36-38, 38*f*
  corporate employees as 33-34
  defined 15, 36
  demographics of 32, 33*t*
  diversity in 28
  economic value of 25-28, 343
  former athletes as 33
  history of 22
  job design and 180
  job fit in 205
  job satisfaction in 309-311
  motives of 34-36, 344
  need for 22-25
  Ohio State football ushers 25
  older 196
  at Olympic Games 24
  organizational commitment in 330, 332
  as partial clients 39
  professional 56
  vs. professionals 15-16, 16*t*, 55-57, 344
  psychological contract with 205
  recruitment and management of 39, 196
  research on 26-27
  rewards for 269-271
  serious-leisure 31
  social benefits of 28, 343
  U.S. National Volunteer Week 23
  values of 55-56, 56*f*
  workers vs. members 30
Vroom, V.H. 132-133

W
women. *See* gender differences
worker–client awareness 342
work ethic 121
work schedules
  in enriched jobs 168
  job satisfaction and 302
  as rewards 271-273
work week, shortened 272

Y
Yukl, G.A. 220

Z
Zemke, R. 64

About the Authors

Photo courtesy of Troy University.

Packianathan Chelladurai, PhD, is a distinguished professor in the School of Hospitality, Sport, and Tourism Management at Troy University in Troy, Alabama. Widely recognized as a leader in the field of sport management, Chelladurai has taught human resource management in sport and recreation for the past 40 years in both Canada and the United States. He is the author of six books, including *Sport Management: Macro Perspectives*, which was the first book to apply organizational theory to sport management. He has also written more than 115 journal articles and 39 book chapters. His writings on leadership and decision making are particularly well known; perhaps best known are his *Multidimensional Model of Leadership* and the *Leadership Scale for Sports (LSS)*, which has been translated into more than 15 languages. In 1991, he served as editor of the *Journal of Sport Management*. He is a founding member of the North American Society for Sport Management (NASSM) and the European Association of Sport Management (EASM). He is a long-standing member of the prestigious National Academy of Kinesiology.

Chelladurai received an MASc and a PhD in management science from the University of Waterloo. In 1990, the American Academy of Kinesiology and Physical Education elected him as a corresponding fellow of the academy. In 1991, he was the first recipient of NASSM's most prestigious honor, the Earle F. Zeigler Award. In 2005, the European Association of Sport Management bestowed on him its first-ever Award of Merit for Distinguished Services to Sport Management Education. In 2015, the EASM named its most prestigious award after Dr. Chelladurai. He was the recipient of that award in that year.

Photo courtesy of Brock University.

Shannon Kerwin, PhD, is an assistant professor in the department of sport management at Brock University. Her research relates to how personal and organizational values align in order to enhance important organizational outcomes.

Kerwin is a member of the North American Society for Sport Management (NASSM) and Academy of Management. She received the NASSM Research Fellow award for research in sport management in 2015 and received the Chancellors Chair of Teaching Excellence award from Brock University for assessing leadership development among students in 2016. She has coauthored chapters in three sport management textbooks and has over 30 articles in academic journals. Kerwin enjoys reading, running, and playing with her two children.